BISMARCK

AND THE DEVELOPMENT OF GERMANY

VOLUME II

The Period of Consolidation, 1871–1880

OTTO VON BISMARCK, JULY 3, 1871. (ALFRED FUNKE, *DAS BISMARCK-BUCH DES DEUTSCHEN VOLKES*,
W. BOBACH & CO., LEIPZIG, 1921, VOL. 2, P. 17.)

BISMARCK

AND THE DEVELOPMENT OF GERMANY

VOLUME II

The Period of Consolidation, 1871–1880

Otto Pflanze

PRINCETON UNIVERSITY PRESS

PRINCETON, NEW JERSEY

✠

Bismarck and the Development of Germany

VOL. 1: THE PERIOD OF UNIFICATION, 1815–1871

VOL. 2: THE PERIOD OF CONSOLIDATION, 1871–1880

VOL. 3: THE PERIOD OF FORTIFICATION, 1880–1898

✠ ✠ ✠

Library of Congress Cataloging-in-Publication Data
(Revised for volume 2)

Pflanze, Otto.
Bismarck and the development of Germany.
Previously published in 1963 in one volume.
Contents: v. 1. The period of unification, 1815–1871
—v. 2. The period of consolidation, 1871–1880.
1. Bismarck, Otto, Fürst von, 1815–1898. 2. Germany
—History—1815–1866. 3. Germany—History—1866–1871.
4. Germany—History—1871–1918. I. Title.
DD218.P44   1990   943'.07   89–11004
ISBN 0-691-05587-4 (v. 1)
ISBN 0-691-05588-2 (v. 2 : alk. paper)

This book has been composed in Linotron Goudy

Princeton University Press books are printed
on acid-free paper, and meet the guidelines for
permanence and durability of the Committee on
Production Guidelines for Book Longevity
of the Council on Library Resources

Printed in the United States of America by
Princeton University Press, Princeton, New Jersey

1   3   5   7   9   10   8   6   4   2

For

HERTHA HABERLANDER PFLANZE

✠

✦ CONTENTS ✦

BOOK FOUR: *The Change of Front Completed, 1879–1880*

✤ ABBREVIATIONS ✤
Used in the Footnotes

AWB   Heinrich von Poschinger ed., *Aktenstücke zur Wirtschaftspolitik des Fürsten Bismarcks* (2 vols., Berlin, 1890).

BA   Bundesarchiv der Bundesrepublik Deutschlands (Koblenz).

BFA   Bismarck Family Archive (Friedrichsruh).

BGB   *Bundes-Gesetzblatt des Norddeutschen Bundes* (1867–1871).

BP   Heinrich von Poschinger, ed., *Fürst Bismarck und die Parlamentarier* (2d ed., 3 vols., Breslau, 1894–1896).

BR   Horst Kohl, ed., *Die politischen Reden des Fürsten Bismarck* (14 vols., Stuttgart, 1892–1905).

DDF   Ministère des Affaires Étrangères, *Documents diplomatiques français, 1871–1914*, 1re Série (1871–1900, 16 vols., Paris, 1929–1959).

DZA   Das Zentralarchiv der Deutschen Demokratischen Republik (Potsdam and Merseburg).

GP   Johannes Lepsius, Albrecht Mendelssohn Bartholdy, and Friedrich Thimme, eds., *Die grosse Politik der europäischen Kabinette 1871–1914* (39 vols., Berlin, 1922–1927).

GSA   Geheimes Staatsarchiv der Stiftung Preussischer Kulturbesitz (Berlin-Dahlem).

GSP   *Gesetzsammlung für die königlich preussischen Staaten* (Berlin, 1851ff.).

GW   Herman von Petersdorff and others, eds., *Bismarck: Die gesammelten Werke* (15 vols., Berlin, 1923–1933).

HW   Julius Heyderhoff and Paul Wentzcke, eds., *Deutscher Liberalismus im Zeitalter Bismarcks. Eine politische Briefsammlung* (2 vols., Bonn, 1925–1927).

RGB   *Reichsgesetzblatt* (1871 ff.)

SBHA   *Stenographische Berichte über die Verhandlungen des Landtages: Haus der Abgeordneten.*

SBHH   *Stenographische Berichte über die Verhandlugen des Landtages: Herrenhaus.*

SBR   *Stenographische Berichte über die Verhandlungen des Reichstages.*

SEG   Heinrich Schulthess, ed., *Europäischer Geschichtskalender* (81 vols., Nördlingen and München, 1860–1940).

✤ INTRODUCTION ✤
To Volumes Two and Three

ON JUNE 16, 1871, the German Kaiser, preceded by Bismarck, Roon, and Moltke, entered the city of Berlin on horseback in triumph at the head of forty thousand troops newly returned from France. George Bancroft, the American minister, described the scene. "The *via triumphalis* was about three miles long, through streets as wide and in some places thrice as wide as Broadway." Cannon captured from the French were parked in close order on both sides of the route, which was also lined by "flag-staffs garlanded and festooned with oak-leaves and evergreens." At intervals stood three huge statues made of linen covered with gypsum and stuffed with straw: at the start a "gigantic image, representing the city of Berlin"; at midpoint "a colossal victory, having on her right hand and left statues of Strassburg and Metz"; at the end "a Germania receiving back into her arms Alsace and Lorraine." More than one million people crowded the sidewalks under a brilliant sun and, when night came, every house and building in Berlin was illuminated. At the opera a glittering company of royalty, nobility, and generals viewed two pageants specially composed for the occasion. "The first represented Justice as having done its work in the late war, and now introducing Peace attended by all the Seasons and all the Arts. The second showed Barbarossa spellbound in his cave, dreaming on till the empire should be restored, and seeing in his visions what the spectators saw in *tableaux vivants*, the epoch-making incidents of German history, from the crusades and early humble fortunes of the younger branch of the Hohenzollerns, to the moment when its chief was upborne at Versailles as emperor by the arms of the princes of Germany." Germany, Bancroft concluded, enjoyed a "feeling of security such as it never had before."[1]

While Germany reveled in the euphoria of triumph, the rest of Europe shuddered. Three stunning victories within six years had elevated Prussia, whose qualifications for great power status had been questioned before 1866, to a leading position among European nations. Two great powers had been humbled by the superior discipline of its soldiers, the competence of its generals, and brilliance of its political leadership. Geographical size and position, rapidly growing industrial and financial strength, larger population, and the size and capacity of its army made the new German Reich the most formidable

---

[1] George Bancroft to Hamilton Fish, June 20, 1871. 42d Cong., 2d sess., House of Representatives, *Papers Relating to the Foreign Relations of the United States* (Washington, 1871), pp. 397–399.

power on the continent. Bismarck, whose chance of survival had been widely discounted in 1862, was now the dominant figure in German and European politics. Naturally questions arose. What new goals would the "man of blood and iron" now pursue? What new conquests might be necessary to satiate a people steeped in the history and legends of medieval empire? What Germanic people or German-speaking minority would be the next target of the German quest for national unity?

Contrary to these expectations, German unification did not introduce a new era of conquest and bloodshed in Europe. Instead, it was the prelude to a period of international order that lasted, despite many crises, more than forty years. After 1871 Bismarck, whose direction of German foreign policy went almost unchallenged for nearly half that time, became an arbiter of peace rather than war. In his view Germany was externally a satiated state whose interests in foreign policy were now best served by the preservation of the European balance of power as reconstructed in the wars of Italian and German unification. From 1871 to 1890 his foreign policy was the defensive shield behind which the German nation coped with the problems of internal unification. No word and no task was more often in Bismarck's expressed thoughts during these decades than that of "consolidation" (Konsolidierung). During the 1880s as the problems—and failures—mounted, the word changed, significantly, to "fortification" (Befestigung).

The problems of national unity were regional, cultural, and social in character. In 1871 it was by no means certain that the states and dynasties of the German Reich, after decades and centuries of independence, would fully accept their new status as member states of a federal union. This was true even of Prussia, whose ministers and officials were inclined to view the emerging imperial government either as an enemy of Prussian interests or as an extension of Prussian power and authority. In all of the great wars fought on the European continent since the Reformation one or more German states had collaborated with outside powers against their German neighbors. Bismarck could not assume that the conception of self-interest that dictated such combinations would now disappear. The exclusion of Austria from Germany, furthermore, had upset the equilibrium between the Catholic and Protestant churches and populations. Catholics now found themselves a minority in a largely Protestant country headed by a Protestant dynasty. Political unity under these terms raised again the old question of Germany's religious division.

These issues were closely linked to the additional problem of Germany's ethnic minorities. The German Reich of 1871 had a population in excess of 41 million, of whom well over 3 million were non-Germans, judged on the basis of language. Of these minorities by far the largest was Prussia's Poles, followed by Danes, Frenchmen, Lithuanians, Wends, and Czechs. In addition, more than one million German-speaking Alsatians thought of themselves as Frenchmen. All of these minorities except the Danes were of Cath-

VICTORY PARADE IN BERLIN, JUNE 16, 1871. THE LINE OF MARCH PASSED THROUGH THE BRANDENBURG GATE, WHERE KAISER WILHELM I, SURROUNDED BY HIS GENERALS (BISMARCK INCLUDED), PAUSED IN THE PARISER PLATZ TO RECEIVE A LAUREL WREATH PRESENTED BY WHITE-CLAD MAIDS OF HONOR, FOLLOWING THE AGE-OLD TRADITION OF ADVENTUS. THE SMUDGED IMAGES ARE MOVING HORSEMEN THAT THE WET PLATE PROCESS COULD NOT FIX. (BILDARCHIV PREUSSISCHER KULTURBESITZ.)

BEYOND THE PARISER PLATZ LIES THE AVENUE UNTER DEN LINDEN, DECORATED ON THIS OCCASION WITH A HUGE VELARIUM SUSPENDED BETWEEN TWO VICTORY COLUMNS. PAINTED BY ANTON VON WERNER, THE ALLEGORICAL SCENE REPRESENTED "BATTLE AND VICTORY." TO THE LEFT AND RIGHT BEYOND ARE ROWS OF CAPTURED FRENCH CANNON. (BILDARCHIV PREUSSISCHER KULTURBESITZ.)

THE PUBLIC CELEBRATED ALONG THE LINE OF MARCH. DRAWING BY KNUT EKWALL. (BILDARCHIV PREUSSISCHER KULTURBESITZ.)

THE PARADE ENDED IN THE LUSTGARTEN, WHERE AN EQUESTRIAN STATUE OF KING FRIEDRICH WILHELM III WAS UNVEILED BEFORE ASSEMBLED TROOPS. (BILDARCHIV PREUSSISCHER KULTURBESITZ.)

olic faith, and in the Polish case Catholicism and national identity were closely linked. Their involuntary incorporation into the "German nation" inevitably increased the sense of divergent national identity among the subject peoples. Here too the danger existed that a combination of foreign and domestic foes might endanger the frontiers and unity of the German Reich.

These problems of lateral (that is, regional and ethnic) unity were accompanied and soon overshadowed by problems of vertical (that is, social) cohesion. Germany's national unification occurred in a period of unparalleled economic growth marked by both industrial and agrarian expansion. The internal consolidation of the German Reich, begun in prosperity (1871–1873), had to continue during a severe depression (1873–1879), an economic earthquake whose aftershocks continued to the end of Bismarck's chancellorship. The critical social and political question of the era of industrialization was whether the old Prussian establishment (crown, cabinet, bureaucracy, Protestant church, officer corps, and gentry) would both accept and integrate into the traditional order the new elites produced by commercial and industrial expansion and by the rapid growth of finance capitalism. In view of the Russian experience in the same era, another significant issue was whether the traditional order would be able to appease and integrate the new intelligentsia (the academically trained elite of scholars, journalists, lawyers, jurists, and civil servants) whose dissidence had found expression since the 1830s in philosophical radicalism, liberal politics, and socialist agitation. Would the new elites of *Bildung und Besitz* find a place within the old order or would they turn against it, as had seemed possible during the revolution of 1848 and the constitutional conflict of 1862–1866?

This book is the middle volume of a trilogy, all three of which deal primarily with the role of Otto von Bismarck in the development of these related problems.[2] In the previous volume it was shown how in successive stages the Prussian establishment, both consciously and unconsciously, faced the task of their resolution. In this volume and its sequel we shall see that the final burst of economic expansion that paralleled, and the depression that followed, Germany's political unification raised to an acute level the problem of social consolidation, that is, the task of integrating the steadily growing stratum of factory and mine workers into a national consensus. Could an expanded Prussian-German establishment prevent or overcome the alienation of urban labor and thereby limit the growth of a socialist doctrine that attacked its institutions, system of property rights, and class privileges? Of the many tasks of national consolidation that the Bismarck government undertook, this proved to be the most critical.

---

[2] The author's acknowledgments and an account of the genesis of the entire work are to be found in the prefaces to volume one. The introduction to the same volume contains a statement of the "Bismarck problem" as it has developed since 1945 and a "discourse on method" that are relevant to all three volumes.

We shall see that the deep current in what Bismarck called the "stream of time"—that is, economic development, demographic redistribution, and financial concentration—provided the most effective means of consolidation during his chancellorship. Another deep current that contributed to it was the growth of German national sentiment. After centuries of internal division and external weakness the Germans had achieved a new status in Europe and in the world. Military might, material progress, and cultural and scientific achievement gave to most Germans a sense of national pride that tended to dissolve particularistic sentiments and interests (except among ethnic minorities, where the opposite occurred). These material and moral deep currents (the term "deep structure" popularized by the *Annales* school is too static) had an immanent force that tended to solidify the German union independently of governmental action. The crucial question of the Second Reich was whether Bismarck's policies and actions would contribute to that stabilization on the upper levels of the stream, where conflicting currents and eddies provided some latitude for intervention and control. Would his vision and skill suffice to provide the sluices and channels that would direct the flow? Could the most powerful statesman of the age reconcile or overcome the divisions between the German majority and ethnic minorities, between Catholics and Protestants, between the old agrarian and new industrial elites, and between those elites and urban labor? Could the unifier of the German states unite the German people?

These are the chief problems and themes with which the trilogy is concerned. They have determined in large part its shape and the distribution of historical material it contains. Readers will note that the proportionate space allocated to foreign policy in the last two volumes is considerably less than in the first. This distribution was determined by the themes of consolidation and fortification. Until 1871 Bismarck's foreign policy had a creative, thereafter a protective role in German development. The acts of unification created the crucible within which the process of internal integration could proceed. Thereafter the task of Bismarck's foreign policy was to shelter that process against outside intervention. This is not to diminish Bismarck's continuing impact on international politics but merely to assert that the most enduring consequences of his statesmanship for German development after 1871 were in the field of domestic affairs.

Bismarck's skepticism concerning the capacity of statesmen to control, much less determine the destiny of peoples, was not entirely justified. The tenacity with which he clung to power to the end shows that he too was aware that it mattered whose hand was on the switches and valves in Berlin. From this it follows that his personality and character are important for an understanding of German history in this period. Important also was the ebb and flow of Bismarck's mental and physical health, to which increasing attention is given in these two volumes. We shall see that there was a close relationship at times between his political behavior and the state of his mind and body. For a fuller statement of the author's views on the role of personality in history, the interrelationships between economics, society, and politics, and the systems character of parliamentary and international politics, see the introduction to the second edition of the previous volume.

BOOK ONE

The Reich of Iron
and Blood

Recent historical developments in Germany press toward the centralization of forces and political arrangements, and their natural and unavoidable consequence must be the gradual absorption [by the Reich] of its member states. In my opinion all that can be done is to impede and delay this development until the public has turned away from the pursuit of special, particularistic interests toward the complete union of Germany into a single state. Back of the unceasing pressure of the unifying political parties is a driving element that converts ideal goals into practical necessities. It is the powerful development of material interests, of industrial activity, of commerce and trade. To slow the progress of things in some degree and make the transition less painful for those whom it affects requires a constant, exhausting struggle.

—*Oswald von Nostitz-Wallwitz, Saxon envoy*
at Berlin, in 1873

✠

CHAPTER ONE

Consolidation and Cleavage

RUSSIA must do for the whole of Germany what it has done for itself. Once it made the conquered forget the conquest in the regions won from Poland, France, and Saxony, elevating the inhabitants of these regions to a feeling of unity and equality [with the rest of Prussia]. Now it must erase the distinction between victor and vanquished, which no people can tolerate indefinitely, replacing the consciousness of belonging to separate states and peoples [*Stämme*] with a proud and happy loyalty to a German commonwealth headed by the King of Prussia."[1] By these means Bismarck expected in 1867 to solve the formidable problem of integrating and consolidating united Germany. The population of the North German Confederation, later of the German Reich, was to be welded together primarily through the activity of government and by the dynastic loyalty that such activity, reinforced by time and shared experience, would create. In this way the Hohenzollern had succeeded over two centuries (1640–1840) in building a sense of statehood and Prussianism among the disparate peoples of East Prussia, Pomerania, Brandenburg, Silesia, Westphalia, and the Rhineland. To the end of his life Bismarck clung to the belief that dynastic loyalty was the backbone of German nationalism.[2]

Certainly the imperial tradition, the "nationalization" of Prussian-Hohenzollern history, and the personal charisma of Bismarck and Wilhelm I expedited the psychological integration of the German Reich. Their role in forging a sense of German nationhood was probably as important—and as unmeasurable—as the achievements in German cultural life in the age of Goethe, Schiller, Kant, and Hegel. Yet there were other, material forces that contributed to that end—forces of which Bismarck was aware, but to which he paid little attention in his memoirs. In 1869 he spoke of trade and commerce as "the most fruitful root" from which consolidation (*Zusammenwachsen*) of the North German Confederation could be expected.[3] In this he was

---

[1] Bismarck to Crown Prince Friedrich Wilhelm, Apr. 2, 1867. *GW*, VI, 255.

[2] See the revealing chapter "Dynastien und Stämme" in his memoirs *GW*, XV, 197–203.

[3] This remark was made in a cabinet meeting of Mar. 14, 1869, which discussed whether to situate the Superior Court of Commerce of the North German Confederation in Leipzig or Berlin. Bismarck favored Leipzig, arguing that to locate the court in Saxony would conciliate its citizens and help "consolidate the entire confederation." This prospect outweighed the disadvantage of separating the nation's highest court from the principal seat of government. *DZA* Merseburg, Rep. 90a, B, III, 2b, Nr. 6, vol. 81.

wiser than he knew. Within the frontiers of the empire the German sense of nationhood was consolidated by the continuing growth of industry, the increase and redistribution of population, the new technology of transportation and communication, the steady expansion of German capitalism and of interlocking relationships between giant banks and industrial enterprises. What Bismarck's diplomatic talents and the striking power of the Prussian army created was chiefly consolidated by the activities of German businessmen and laborers.

At the same time the social transformation wrought by industrialization also produced new fissures in German society that the Bismarck regime could not close. The German nation-state became divided internally by conflicting social interests and their matching ideologies, producing fears as well as anticipations of the civil conflict that finally erupted after 1918. But in other respects economic growth tended to consolidate the national union, to bind the nation together with new sinews of self-interest and psychological cohesion. Their cumulative effect was to reduce the significance of internal political boundaries and to build a sense of nationhood that transcended, though it did not extinguish, the particularistic sentiments of an earlier epoch. It is not too much to say that within one decade this economic consolidation made irreversible by any ordinary means what had been decided in 1866–1871. What had been accomplished by political acumen and military prowess could no longer be undone—except by political stupidity and military catastrophe. Growing social and ideological divisions coupled with increasing economic and national consolidation—such was the paradox of Germany's Second Reich.

Germany Enters the Industrial Age

After three decades of acceleration German industrialization reached a momentum during the period of unification that was maintained thereafter despite temporary setbacks. The construction of railways, the main propulsive force during the period of acceleration, reached a grand climax in the early 1870s, by which time the major lines had been built. Although the building of local lines remained important in the German economy until the end of the century, other sectors now assumed the primary burden of sustaining the growth achieved. By 1870 German textile manufacturers had made the transition from hand to mechanical spinning. The acquisition of Alsace-Lorraine, furthermore, doubled the number of spindles operating in Germany. While slower in development, mechanical weaving surged ahead in the 1860s and 1870s. The armament, machine, and machine tool industries reached a level equal to and even superior to the products of foreign competitors (except in farm machinery where the United States was preeminent). During the 1880s public utilities—gas, water, sewers, and streetcars—played a major role in the construction industry. The same period saw a great expansion in German shipbuilding. By the end of the century two new industries—chemicals and electrical equipment—had appeared in which Germany excelled in both innovation and production. These several expanding industries perpetuated the growth previously derived chiefly from railway construction.[4]

Despite temporary reverses, German heavy industry set new production records, decade after decade. Coal and pig iron were joined by steel at mid-century, as the invention of new furnaces (by Bessemer in 1856, Siemens-Martin in 1866, and Gilchrist Thomas in 1878) opened the way to its mass production. Because it removed phosphorous from iron ore, the last of these processes was particularly important for Germany, which was scantily endowed with nonphosphorous ores. Although familiar, the advancing statistics (in millions of tons) are still worth pondering.

	1870	1880	1890	1900
Coal	34	59.1	89.3	146.8
Pig iron	1.4	2.7	4.6	8.5
Steel	0.3	0.7	2.3	6.7

By Bismarck's death in 1898 Germany had surpassed France and Belgium to become the continent's leading industrial power. By 1914 it had also surpassed Britain and was, after the United States, the second industrial nation of the world.[5]

Despite massive emigration (4,875,300 between 1840 and 1900), Germany also surpassed France to become in Bismarck's time the most populous country in Europe except for Russia. A new wave of fecundity (following that which climaxed in the 1830s) arrived in the 1860s with a steep increase in the annual birth rate that tapered off in the 1870s as new methods of birth control were introduced. Thereafter the birthrate fell, but so did the deathrate. Improved nourishment, sanitation, and medical services increased the average life span. Total population attained 40,059,000 in 1871, 45,234,000 in 1880, 49,428,000 in 1890, and 56,367,000 in 1900. Naturally industrialization produced great changes in the occupations and distribution of this population. Whereas 51 percent of the working force was still employed in agriculture, forestry, and fisheries during the 1860s, as against 28 percent in industrial pursuits, the figures were 38 percent against 37 percent in 1900.[6] Between

[4] Joseph A. Schumpeter, *Business Cycles* (New York, 1939), I, 351ff.

[5] A.J.P. Taylor, *The Struggle for Mastery in Europe, 1848–1918* (Oxford, 1954), pp. xxix–xxx. Taylor's statistics have been corrected from the following sources: Arthur Spiethoff, *Die wirtschaftlichen Wechsellagen: Aufschwung, Krise, Stockung* (Tübingen, 1955), II, tab. 20; *Statistisches Handbuch für das deutsche Reich* (Berlin, 1907), I, 252, 259.

[6] Walther Hoffmann, *Das Wachstum der deutschen Wirtschaft seit der Mitte des 19. Jahrhunderts* (Berlin, 1965), pp. 35, 172–173; John Knodel, *The Decline of Fertility in Germany, 1871–1939* (Princeton, 1974), pp. 246–262; Gerd Hohorst, Jürgen Kocka, and Gerhard A. Ritter, *Sozialge-*

1871 and 1910 the population of rural areas (parishes with less than 2,000 inhabitants) sank from 63.9 percent to 29.9 percent, while that of the big cities (over 100,000 inhabitants) rose from 4.8 percent to 21.3 percent.[7] The rural population remained fairly stable in total numbers (about 26,000,000) as the towns absorbed almost all of the increase. Berlin had 826,341 inhabitants in 1870, 1,578,794 in 1890, and 1,888,848 by 1900. Its nearest competitor, the seaport of Hamburg, grew from 239,107 to 705,738 during these three decades. What industrialization meant to the Ruhr region can be judged by the expansion of Essen from 51,513 to 118,862 and Düsseldorf from 69,365 to 213,711 persons in the same period.[8]

The tensions in German society were heightened by the vagaries of the business cycle. The wave of prosperity and expansion in world capitalism that began in the 1840s mounted, with brief interruptions in 1858–1861 and 1866–1868, to a grand climax in 1873. During the early years of the Kulturkampf, of Bismarck's collaboration with the liberals, and of his quarrel with ultraconservatives, Germany was absorbed in a business boom of extraordinary proportions. For example, pig iron consumption rose from 1,374,000 tons (35.8 kilograms per capita) in 1869 to 2,954,000 tons (71.5 kilograms per capita) in 1873, while its price increased from 66.2 to 145.5 marks per ton. Wholesale prices for industrial products generally escalated by 40 percent. The entire capitalist system experienced this trend and these fluctuations, but the final ascent of 1871–1873 was particularly steep in Germany. Several factors were responsible: the removal in 1870 of restrictions on formation of joint-stock companies; the general optimism engendered by the long rise in output during preceding decades, the exhilaration following victory over France and fulfillment of national unity; and the inflationary effect of the 5 billion francs paid by the French as a war indemnity, part of which was used to liquidate the debts of the federal states. Optimism, speculation, and fraud were rampant as millions of citizens from scullery maids to titled aristocrats gambled in securities. The first sign of danger, a crash on the Vienna bourse on May 9, 1873, went unheeded in Germany. In October the overburdened house of paper came tumbling down.[9]

The crash of 1873 introduced a new epoch in German and world capital-

schichtliches Arbeitsbuch II: Materialien zur Statistik des Kaiserreichs, 1870–1914 (2d ed., 1978), p. 26; Antje Kraus, ed., Quellen zur Bevölkerungsstatistik Deutschlands, 1815–1875 (Boppard, 1980), pp. 338–339.

[7] Wolfgang Köllmann, "Grundzüge der Bevölkergungsgeschichte Deutschlands im 19. und 20. Jahrhundert," Studium Generale, 12 (1959), p. 389.

[8] Statistiches Handbuch, I, 38; Köllmann, "Grundzüge der Bevölkerungsgeschichte," pp. 388–389.

[9] Spiethoff, Die wirtschaftlichen Wechsellagen, II, tab. 2, 13, 25; Alfred Jacobs and Hans Richter, Die Grosshandelspreise in Deutschland von 1792 bis 1934. Sonderhefte des Instituts für Konjunkturforschung, vol. 37 (Berlin, 1935), pp. 34–45; Heinrich Bechtel, Wirtschaftsgeschichte Deutschlands im 19. und 20. Jahrhundert (Munich, 1956), III, 182–188.

ism, the exact nature of which is still in dispute. Following the business cycle theories of Nikolay Kondratieff, Joseph Schumpeter, and Arthur Spiethoff it has been popular to dub the period 1873 to 1896 that of the "great depression," a downward "long wave" in economic development that followed and preceded upward waves of approximately the same duration.[10] Further research has shown, however, that the downward "trend period" of 1873–1896 cannot be verified empirically. Although prices fluctuated on a lower plane, industrial output grew steadily after 1879, as German entrepreneurs constantly consolidated, rationalized, and modernized the processes of production. Real wages soon surpassed the peak of 1873–1875 and continued to ascend until 1900. From 1873 to 1893 the number of employed persons grew by 28 percent, the net domestic product (at standard prices) by 58 percent, an expansion that compares favorably with the 36 and 68 percent achieved in the next twenty years.[11] Though the long waves are now disputed, no authority questions that the period 1873–1894 was marked by repeated fluctuations of short duration. We shall see that the brevity of the upswings and longevity of the downswings during 1879–1894 bred a mood of insecurity and pessimism among businessmen that spread out into the society at large.[12]

The agrarian sector of the German economy was in even deeper trouble. During the late 1870s the golden age of German agriculture, which began in the 1830s, commenced to fade. For three decades population growth, urban development, the Zollverein, railway transport, and flourishing exports had produced high prices and profits, particularly for the big landowners in the east. Production expanded steadily as new acreage was put to the plow and the Thaer technique of crop rotation delivered increased yields. By 1865, however, most of the arable land was under cultivation, and the Thaer system had attained optimum benefits. There followed a period of relative stagnation in production that lasted until after 1890, when chemical fertilizers became common. In animal production alone significant increases were achieved in these years, and this was made possible only by importing fodder. Before the 1860s agrarian production had increased at a more rapid rate than did population, creating surpluses that trans-Elbian producers sold in foreign markets. But after 1870 the relationship of food supply to population reversed, creating a problem of food supply that required imports; Germany had more mouths than its farmers could feed.[13]

---

[10] See particularly Hans Rosenberg, *Grosse Depression und Bismarckzeit* (Berlin, 1967) and Hans-Ulrich Wehler, *Bismarck und der Imperialismus* (Cologne, 1969).

[11] For a current summary of the state of the discussion on the "great depression" thesis see Karl Erich Born, *Wirtschafts- und Sozialgeschichte des deutschen Kaiserreiches (1867/71–1914)* (Stuttgart, 1985), pp. 107–119. On wage levels see Gerhard Bry, *Wages in Germany, 1871–1945* (Princeton, 1960), pp. 51–79.

[12] See vol. 3, ch. 1.

[13] Graf H. W. Finck von Finckenstein, *Die Entwicklung der Landwirtschaft in Preussen und*

We shall see that this problem was solved by massive imports of foreign grain and other foodstuffs from Russia, North America, and the Argentine.[14] What was beneficial to the urban masses spelled disaster for German agriculture. The flood of grain produced by American farmers on cheap, virgin soil and transported at low cost by railway and steamship depressed prices in European grain markets during the 1870s. The German market was sheltered for a time, but it too began to feel the effects of new competition in the following decade. Stagnating production, high costs, and declining prices produced an agrarian crisis in Germany of serious proportions.

Bismarck unified Germany in a period of general prosperity in agriculture and industry. During most of the rest of his chancellorship he was compelled to govern in a period of economic difficulty in both areas. It was a period, furthermore, that saw a fundamental redistribution of financial and social power in Germany. Falling prices compelled heavy industrialists to cut costs by expanding their facilities and increasing production. Through mergers and takeovers large firms absorbed the smaller. Heavy industry and big banking established their dominance over light industry and mercantile interests. The relative weight of industrial and agrarian capital shifted steadily in favor of the former. Factory labor continued to expand in numbers and prosperity relative to artisan labor. Again the question arose: could the old Prussian-German establishment adjust to the new facts of economic and social life? Could it assimilate the new entrepreneurial elite of heavy industry and high finance and could it prevent the alienation of industrial labor?

During Bismarck's chancellorship Germany made enormous strides in that process of transformation that historians have come to call "modernization." The sheer weight of economic, technological, and population growth contributed in powerful ways to the consolidation of the union he had created by political and military means. Older cleavages of the kind that the Germans called "particularism"—those based on regional peculiarities, historical traditions, dynastic loyalties, and religious affiliation—tended to diminish without disappearing. They were superseded in importance by newer or deepened cleavages of an economic and social nature—based on occupation, interest groups, social status, and class identification. The attack on political Catholicism during the 1870s (the Kulturkampf) is evidence of the lingering existence of the older divisions in German society; the assault on social democracy after 1878 (the antisocialist statute) and the shift from free trade to protectionism (tariff act of 1879) testify to the new. The older cleavages had

---

Deutschland 1800–1930 (Würzburg, 1960), pp. 98–108; Eberhard Bittermann, Die landwirtschaftliche Produktion in Deutschland, 1800–1950 (Halle-Saale, 1956), pp. 13ff., 24; Walther G. Hoffmann, "The Take-Off in Germany," in W. W. Rostow, ed., The Economics of Take-Off into Sustained Growth (London, 1964), pp. 101–102.

[14] See pp. 283–285.

threatened the achievement and perpetuation of German unity; the newer ones jeopardized the stability of the social-political order.

Demographic Consolidation

As long as water remained the chief mode of transport, Germany had no natural center of commerce and population comparable to London or Paris. In contrast to the river systems of Britain and France, those of central Europe tended to divert rather than concentrate the life of the people. The Danube turned Austrian Germans toward the Slavic regions in the southeast; the Rhine linked southwestern Germany to the low countries; the Weser, Elbe, Oder, and Vistula oriented the northern population toward the Baltic and North Seas. Mountainous areas between the river systems made it difficult to connect their upper basins through canals, whose construction was further hampered by political disunion. Germany did not inherit a system of Roman roads such as were the birthright of England and France. Not until the 1840s did it begin to overcome this handicap by constructing gravel or "metalled" roads. Although 30,000 kilometers of such roads were built by 1857, their immediate value was to expand the trading radius of the cities; they did not provide a national system of communication. The long-distance transport of heavy goods such as coal, iron, and grain was prohibitively expensive.[15]

The construction of railways solved the problem of transport dramatically within two generations. The length of German lines in kilometers reached 14,776 in 1865, 29,970 in 1875, 37,571 in 1885, and 46,500 in 1895.[16] Almost from the moment of its invention shrewd observers foresaw the potential of the railway for knitting together the German nation. Goethe's remark to Eckermann in 1828 is often cited: "I have no fear that Germany will not become united; our good roads and future railroads will do their part."[17] During the 1830s Friedrich List urged construction of a nationwide rail network as the "Siamese twin" of the Zollverein; together, he predicted, they would unite the German people into a great, wealthy, cultured, and powerful nation.[18] Looking backward during the 1880s, Heinrich von Treitschke judged that the railway was a mixed blessing. On the one hand, the conquest of space had produced a new appreciation of material values and an unprecedented drive for gain and pleasure; by throwing the social classes together, mass trans-

[15] Karl Lamprecht, *Deutsche Geschichte der jüngsten Vergangenheit und Gegenwart* (Berlin, 1912), I, 123ff.

[16] Hauptverwaltung der deutschen Reichsbahn, *Konjunkturschwankungen im Reichsbahnverkehr* Sonderhefte des Instituts für Konjunkturforschung, vol. 38 (Berlin, 1936), p. 7.

[17] Johann Peter Eckermann, *Gespräche mit Goethe in den letzten Jahren seines Lebens* (Basel, 1945), II, p. 656.

[18] Erwin Beckerath and Otto Stühler, eds., *Friedrich List: Schriften, Reden, Briefe* (Berlin, 1929–1935), III (1), 347. See also III (2), and VII, 65–68.

port had obscured social distinctions and superficially enlarged the horizon and knowledge of the average man. On the other hand, the railway had also closed the gap in Germany between intellectual greatness and economic poverty and had built a material foundation for the growing political power of the nation. When Germany could be crossed at its narrowest point in three hours, the common man became conscious of the "whole lying vileness" of the German small states; "he began to comprehend what it meant to be a great nation." Borders lost their significance and prejudices declined, once the Germans had "the good fortune to know each other."[19]

To what degree the new age of transport actually had the psychological effect before 1870 that Goethe and List prophesied and Treitschke presumed is difficult to say. Travel and personal contact can sometimes heighten more than diminish local patriotism and awareness of cultural differences. In all probability the railway made its greatest contribution to cultural fusion within Germany by making feasible the mass migration and resettlement of millions of people. Before unification legal and political barriers restricted this movement. After 1867 they were leveled by a series of legislative acts, the most important of which were the statutes of 1867 on freedom of migration (*Freizügigkeit*) and of 1870 on poor relief (*Indigenat*). The former established the right of citizens to migrate, settle, obtain property, and enter business in all parts of the North German Confederation; the latter granted the right of poor relief to migrants, although limiting it to those over twenty-four years of age who had resided for two years in the district where aid was sought. As amended by the Reichstag, the latter statute made confederate rather than state citizenship the criterion for claiming welfare aid, a provision that seriously breached the federal character of the union. Other laws that significantly eased migration were the abolition of compulsory passports (1867), prohibition of marriage on the basis of residence, income, poverty, occupation, and Jewish faith (1868), imprisonment for debt (1868), restrictions on incorporation (1870), and double taxation (1870).[20] These statutes were among the important fruits of Bismarck's collaboration with the National Liberal party, which valued their integrative effect. Almost every exercise of its legislative power, for that matter, brought the central government into direct contact with the citizens, heightening its impact upon their daily lives.

The constitution of 1867 and a citizenship statute (1870) established dual citizenship. Confederate citizenship depended on the gain or loss of state citizenship, a fact that made the latter ostensibly more important. Yet state citizenship steadily lost significance under a statute of 1870 that made citizenship

---

[19] Heinrich von Treitschke, *Deutsche Geschichte im neunzehnten Jahrhundert* (Leipzig, 1927), IV, 585.

[20] BGB (1867), 33–39, 55–58; (1868), 149–151, 237–238; (1870), 119–120, 360–373, 375–386.

a matter of residence, descent, and application.[21] "A German professor," wrote Heinrich Triepel, "who is much in demand and often 'called' can with ease gradually acquire eight or more state citizenships, of which eventually most are completely devoid of importance to him. His sons inherit them all in the cradle and, unless they should happen to study jurisprudence, they do not know how wealthy they are in 'fatherlands'. . . . In a few generations all of this will be still much more obscure and confused. State citizenship is being swallowed up by Reich citizenship."[22]

Cheap and swift transport by railway, the removal of legal barriers, and the promise of a better livelihood led millions of Germans to migrate. By 1907 28,982,807 of Germany's total population (60,378,235) were no longer living in the communities of their birth; of these migrants 20,041,373 were born in the same province or state in which they resided, while 8,941,433 were born outside it. Considering the probable number of persons who had migrated and died before 1907, it is estimated that between 22 and 24 million persons had moved from one region to another since 1860. The growing industrial centers drew most of their migrants from the surrounding region; the larger the city the wider the hinterland from which they came. But many also came from distant regions. The most striking instance was the east-to-west current that began in the 1860s and mounted with each decade. After the last arable lands had been plowed around 1865 and agrarian difficulties began in the 1870s, the farms and latifundia of eastern Prussia could no longer absorb the growing work force produced by Germany's most fecund birthrate. The "flight from the land" (East and West Prussia, Silesia, Posen, and Pomerania) began, first to Berlin and after 1880 to the Ruhr. (Many had a still more distant goal— the open prairies and growing cities of the American Midwest.) According to the census of 1907, 95 percent of the migrants from the northeast to the Ruhr city of Gelsenkirchen were peasants who became wage laborers. But not all migrants were low on the social scale. Some were public employees whose place of work was prescribed by the state, while others were entrepreneurs drawn to the big cities by opportunities for their capital and talent. The same census shows that 70 percent of the small group of migrants to Munich from the northeast were bourgeois. Of the sixteen important industrialists who were presidents of the Elberfeld-Barmen chamber of commerce between 1831 and 1917, more than half were first (6) or second (4) generation migrants— this in a city noted for its continuity of economic development and its pronounced sense of tradition.[23]

---

[21] BGB (1870), 355–360.

[22] Heinrich Triepel, *Unitarismus und Föderalismus im deutschen Reiche* (Tübingen, 1907), p. 58; Paul Laband, "Die geschichtliche Entwicklung der Reichsverfassung seit der Reichsgründung," *Jahrbuch des öffentlichen Rechts*, 1 (1907), pp. 12–14.

[23] Köllmann, "Grundzüge der Bevölkerungsgeschichte," pp. 386–388; Karl Erich Born, "Der soziale und wirtschaftliche Strukturwandel Deutschlands am Ende des 19. Jahrhunderts," in Hans

· Internal migrations increased the disparity in population between the agrarian east and industrial west. By 1910 the Rhine province, Westphalia, and Saxony had more inhabitants than did the entire Reich in 1871. The highest population density was reached in the Rhine province, where 67 percent of the population lived in urban areas (more than half in large cities) in contrast to East Prussia's 27 percent. During these four decades the population of Westphalia increased by more than 600 percent, the Rhine province by 247 percent, Saxony by 237 percent, Baden by 261 percent, East Prussia by 155 percent.[24] Out of the reshuffling and restructuring of German society there emerged in the great centers of population a sense of regional identification based on real and imagined characteristics of dialect, mores, and temperament that distinguished them from other Germans. *"Berliner"* and *"Hamburger"* came to connote in the popular mind peoples as distinct in speech and character traits as Saxons, Swabians, or Badenese. The new urban-industrial region in the west became a giant crucible that fused those arriving from the east with the native population to produce, according to Wilhelm Brepohl, a new German *Volksstamm*, the *Ruhrvolk* of Rhineland-Westphalia, in which the east German dominated biologically, the west German culturally.[25] The arrival in significant numbers of Polish peasants (30,000 by 1890, 300,000 by 1910), on the other hand, created an ethnic minority that the western cities could not soon assimilate.[26]

Financial Consolidation

The growth in industrial output and steadily thickening network of transport and communication were accompanied by an expansion and concentration of German business enterprise. While it inhibited, German political disunity had never blocked the migration of capital between states and regions in Germany. The growth of the joint-stock company and of new investment opportunities during 1850–1870 greatly increased the flow. In contrast to the

Ulrich Wehler, ed., *Moderne deutsche Sozialgeschichte. Neue wissenschaftliche Bibliothek*, vol. 10 (Cologne, 1966), pp. 271–272; and Klaus Bade, "Transnationale Migration und Arbeitsmarkt im Kaiserreich: Vom Agrarstaat mit starker Industrie zum Industriestaat mit starker agrarischer Basis," in Toni Pierenkemper and Richard Tilly, eds., *Historische Arbeitsmarktforschung* (Göttingen, 1982), pp. 182–211.

[24] Wolfgang Köllmann, "The Process of Urbanization in Germany at the Height of the Industrialization Period," *Journal of Contemporary History*, 4 (1969), pp. 62–65.

[25] Wilhelm Brepohl, *Der Aufbau des Ruhrvolkes im Zuge der Ost-West Wanderung* (Recklinghausen, 1948), pp. 28–30, 152ff. See also Wolfgang Köllmann, "Binnenwanderung und Bevölkerungsstrukturen der Ruhrgebietsgrossstädte im Jahre 1907," *Soziale Welt*, 19 (1958), pp. 219–233, and *Bevölkerungsgeschichte Deutschlands. Studien zur Bevölkerungsgeschichte Deutschlands* (Göttingen, 1974), p. 39.

[26] Hans Ulrich Wehler, "Die Polen im Ruhrgebiet bis 1918," *Moderne deutsche Sozialgeschichte. Neue wissenschaftliche Bibliothek*, vol. 10 (Cologne, 1966), pp. 437ff.

United States, the doctrine of laissez-faire was never applied in Germany against monopolies and the concentration of economic power. Here its goals were lower tariffs and reduced government paternalism, not the guarantee of competition and protection of small producers. By actively engaging in company promotion, moreover, the German corporate banks furthered the amalgamation of banking and industrial capital and hence the accumulation of economic power in the hands of a relatively small number of firms and individuals. The center of this new, interlocking financial structure was Berlin, which became the financial as well as political capital of united Germany. Its basic axis was on Prussian soil extending from Berlin westward to the Ruhr and eastward to Upper Silesia. This became the armature around which the business life of Germany revolved.[27]

The expansion and concentration were made possible by the joint-stock, or corporate, form of business enterprise. As in other countries, this proved to be the only form of business organization capable of accumulating the enormous supplies of capital needed for German industrialization during the middle decades. As has been shown, the Prussian state had earlier (through its power to charter and supervise corporate enterprises) severely restricted use of the joint-stock company in industry and nearly prohibited its use in banking.[28] Even so, 397 joint-stock companies capitalized at 3,043,000,000 marks were founded in Prussia between 1826 and June 1870. An early fruit of liberal collaboration with Bismarck was the statute of June 11, 1870, which abolished controls on incorporation. The result was a rush to incorporate (928 firms capitalized at 2,781,000,000 marks during 1871–1873) and, after the crash of 1873, to amalgamate and consolidate. The *Gründerjahre* saw the final victory of the corporate over the partnership and single-ownership forms of business organization.[29]

The virtual prohibition of corporate banks in Prussia before 1870 favored private banking houses, particularly in Berlin, Cologne, and Frankfurt. But it also contributed to the growth of a few joint-stock or commandite banks founded during the period of the German "takeoff," namely, the *Schaafhausen'scher Bankverein* at Cologne (1848), *Disconto-Gesellschaft* at Berlin (1851), *Darmstädter Bank* (1853), *Berliner Handelsgesellschaft* (1856), and *Mitteldeutscher Kreditverein* at Meiningen (1856). The fact that the *Disconto-Gesellschaft* and *Berliner Handelsgesellschaft* had to be organized on a commandite basis (composed of active partners with unlimited liability and inactive partners with limited liability) did not prevent their growth. Under David and Adolf

---

[27] See particularly Helmut Böhme, *Deutschlands Weg zur Grossmacht: Studien zum Verhältnis von Wirtschaft und Staat während der Reichsgründungszeit 1848–1881* (Cologne, 1966), pp. 333ff.

[28] See vol. 1, pp. 107–114.

[29] J. Riesser, *The German Great Banks and their Concentration in Connection with the Economic Development of Germany* (Washington, 1911), p. 38; Helmut Gebhard, *Die Berliner Börse von den Anfängen bis zum Jahre 1896* (Berlin, 1928), p. 30.

Hansemann the *Disconto-Gesellschaft* became Germany's strongest bank. During the 1860s it led the "Prussian consortium," a syndicate of corporate and private banks that did a profitable business in floating Prussian state loans, beginning with the mobilization loan of 1859. The consortium extended its operations to the financing of industry and was of "decisive importance" for the further development of banking credit in Prussia and Germany. "Henceforth the Prussian consortium not only regulated and directed the traffic in state and local government securities but also established the financial and bank-technical foundation for the later industrial growth of Germany, for its capital exports and thereby for its world economic position."[30]

Capital and management for the new corporate and commandite banks were originally supplied by private banking houses. Yet the private banks were increasingly overshadowed after 1870 by the giants to which their investments had given life. Their clientele, mostly aristocratic, was limited and likewise their capital resources. They were unable to supply the massive outlay of capital needed for industrial expansion during 1871–1872 or to absorb the shocks of the decline that followed. The largest and best connected (for example, Schickler, Bleichröder, Warschauer, Mendelssohn, Oppenheim, and Rothschild-Frankfurt) survived and continued to prosper. But they were compelled to limit their major flotations to government loans and leave the more risky business of company promotion to the great corporate banks. As the bankers of princes and ministers and as the underwriters of government bond issues they maintained close connections with the ruling establishment and came to be among its principal supporters and beneficiaries.[31]

Both the boom and bust of the 1870s furthered the growth and dominance of a few great corporate banks. During the *Gründerjahre* the *Disconto-Gesellschaft* and some other banks established subsidiaries with numerous branches throughout the country. The *Provinzial-Discontogesellschaft*, for example, opened offices in Hanover, Bernburg, Strassburg, Hamburg, Duisburg, Braunschweig, Hameln, Ludwigshafen, and Halle. The subsidiaries did not survive the depression and their liquidation in the late 1870s interrupted the first attempt to create nationwide banking networks. During these years, nevertheless, the larger banks extended their business radius and clientele by absorbing many of the new corporate banks created by the boom. Two new major banks, the *Deutsche Bank* at Berlin (1870) and *Dresdner Bank* (1872), whose managements avoided speculative excesses during the boom, were particularly active in taking over distressed enterprises. By various devices—branches, agencies, affiliates, corporate and commandite subsidiaries—the larger banks (except for the *Berliner Handelsgesellschaft*, whose operations re-

[30] Manfred Pohl, *Konzentration im deutschen Bankwesen, 1848–1980* (Frankfurt a. M., 1982), pp. 31–96; Böhme, *Deutschlands Weg*, pp. 219–221.

[31] Böhme, *Deutschlands Weg*, pp. 351–353.

mained centralized) expanded their influence during the 1880s. Already out-classed in capital resources, the private banks and smaller corporate banks were now surpassed in breadth and depth of organizational structure, in the variety of services they could offer, and hence in the capacity to develop new business.[32]

Its position at the center of government and at the hub of the German railway system assured that Berlin would also become a center of industry and finance. After the 1840s it became important for machine manufacture (Julius Freund and Franz Egells) and locomotives (August Borsig), later for electrical equipment (Werner Siemens and Johann Halske) and chemicals (Ernst Schering and Samuel Kunheim). The concentration of so many industrial and mercantile enterprises, businessmen, and wage earners naturally pre-sented excellent opportunities for banks. But Berlin was also the seat of many Prussian and imperial offices significant for public finance, including the semipublic Prussian Bank, Prussia's principal bank of issue, and the Prussian *Seehandlung* through which government funds were channeled into private undertakings of public interest. During the period of accelerated industriali-zation the Prussian Bank commenced (some say in 1857, others 1866) to as-sume central banking functions as the principal depository of government funds and the lender of last resort to other banks.[33]

The foundations of what has been called the Ruhr-Berlin-Upper Silesia financial axis were laid in the prosperous years 1850–1856 when Berlin's major banks (*Disconto-Gesellschaft*, *Berliner Handelsgesellschaft*, and *S. Bleich-röder*) financed railway enterprises connecting the capital with the rapidly developing industrial areas in the east and west. Until 1870, however, scar-city of capital prevented all but the *Disconto-Gesellschaft* from extending its engagements significantly in the Ruhr. Hence the financial organization of heavy industry remained largely local. But this changed dramatically in the boom years 1871–1873. Leading entrepreneurs of the Ruhr and Silesia (for example, Friedrich Grillo, William Mulvaney, Count Guido Henckel von Donnersmarck) turned to Berlin for the funding of the mergers, reorganiza-tions, expansions, and new enterprises that marked those busy years. Most of the 174 corporations (capitalized at 613,000,000 thalers) founded in the Ger-man iron and coal industry during 1871–1874 were financed in Berlin. Indus-trial securities overtook railway shares as major objects of investment and

---

[32] Paul Wallich, *Die Konzentration im deutschen Bankwesen. Münchener volkswirtschaftliche Studien*, vol. 74 (Stuttgart, 1905), pp. 16ff., 24, 34ff.; Riesser, *German Great Banks*, pp. 635ff.; Böhme, *Deutschlands Weg*, pp. 341ff.

[33] Richard Tilly, *Financial Institutions and Industrialization in the Rhineland, 1815–1870* (Madison, 1966), p. 45; Riesser, *German Great Banks*, pp. 653ff; Paul Hirschfeld, *Berlins Gross-Industrie* (3 vols., Berlin, 1897–1901); H. Rachel and Paul Wallich, *Berliner Grosskaufleute und Kapitalisten* (2d ed., Berlin, 1967); Hartmut Kaelble, *Berliner Unternehmer während der frühen Industriali-sierung* (Berlin, 1972).

speculation on the Berlin bourse and even threatened the hitherto leading role of Prussian state bonds.[34]

The war of 1866 and its consequences brought Berlin capitalists a long step closer to financial hegemony over southern Germany. The political and financial eclipse of Frankfurt occurred almost simultaneously. In the past the large private banks of Frankfurt, principally the Rothschilds, had been the chief suppliers of credit to south German governments. Since 1860 Rothschild had also possessed an official monopoly of the flotation of Prussian bonds in the south. But the business recession of 1866 followed by the threat of war produced a financial crisis in Germany that made it impossible for Rothschild to continue this function. Hence the Prussian government turned for war credits to the Prussian consortium. But the Frankfurt bankers were also unable to underwrite the war loans of south German governments, compelling them to resort to local banks and to the sale of government-owned railway shares at a poor price. The crisis sharply revealed the limited reserves of the south German money market. "After 1866 southern Germany began to cover its financial needs directly in Berlin."[35]

The Frankfurt bourse suffered a similar fate. At mid-century, when the sale of government securities was still the chief business of stock exchanges, the Frankfurt exchange was the most important in Germany. By the 1860s, however, railway shares had become the lifeblood of the securities business, and most were launched on the Berlin bourse, as were the increasing number of industrial securities in the 1870s. By century's end the corporate stocks listed on the Berlin exchange numbered 698, compared with Frankfurt's 301, Dresden's 133, Hamburg's 125, and Leipzig's 93. After 1870 the Frankfurt bourse was badly outdistanced by its Berlin counterpart, which became one of the leading stock exchanges of the world.[36]

To many southerners this new financial dependency upon Berlin was objectionable—as distasteful as the commercial dependency created by the Zollverein and the political and military dependency resulting from the war of 1866. In order to escape it, their governments strove in the years 1866–1870 to build up their own banking institutions. Yet these new firms were weak and their efforts to create new money by questionable financial practices added to the inflation of the boom years after 1870. Nor did Hamburg, Germany's principal port, succeed in establishing its supremacy in international banking. When a group of Hamburg bankers founded an *Internationale Bank* in 1870, Berlin financiers reacted immediately by establishing the *Deutsche Bank* (a symptomatic title) with branches in Hamburg, Bremen, London, Shanghai,

[34] Böhme, *Deutschlands Weg*, pp. 191ff.

[35] *Ibid.*, pp. 213–216; Pohl, *Konzentration*, pp. 99–100.

[36] Werner Sombart, *Die deutsche Volkswirtschaft im neunzehnten Jahrhundert* (2d ed., Berlin, 1909), pp. 210–212; Hans and Manfred Pohl, *Deutsche Bankengeschichte* (Frankfurt a. M., 1982), II, 149–153, 232–235.

and Yokohama. Although compelled to expand its domestic operations with the decline in foreign trade after 1873, the *Deutsche Bank* commanded the field of international payments and credits to exports. The magnetic attraction of the Berlin money market is shown by the migration of the *Darmstädter Bank* to the Prussian capital after 1871. The management of the *Dresdner Bank*, originally established to nourish the growth of Saxon industry, decided in 1876 over vigorous protests by Saxon stockholders to erect a branch office in Berlin, which became after 1881 its center of operations. Even the *Schaaf-hausen'scher Bankverein*, whose business had remained largely concentrated in the Ruhr, moved its headquarters from Cologne to Berlin after 1891. Failure to migrate to Berlin cost the *Mitteldeutscher Kreditverein*, on the other hand, its position as one of Germany's six leading banks.[37]

The capstone of the German banking system was the *Reichsbank* established by law in 1875 as a semipublic bank of issue that absorbed the Prussian Bank. While technically not a joint-stock bank, the *Reichsbank* was legally a corporation. Its capital of 120,000,000 marks was supplied by private investors; its management, by state officials under Bismarck's authority as the Reich chancellor. At the time of the *Reichsbank*'s founding, thirty-two German banks had the right to issue paper money; their banknotes were worth 130,000,000 marks as against the *Reichsbank*'s 250,000,000 marks. By the end of 1876, fourteen had surrendered the privilege; by 1900, all but seven. Their note circulation was 175,000,000 marks in contrast to the *Reichsbank*'s 1,138,000,000 marks. Branches of the *Reichsbank* were established throughout the country, numbering 330 by 1900. Although not engaged in company promotion, the *Reichsbank* cultivated other aspects of banking business, including deposits, "giro" accounts, Lombard loans, and discounting of bills. Most importantly, it assumed central banking functions for all Germany, being the final source of credit for other banks and controlling through its discount rate the general cost of credit and the flow of gold to and from foreign countries.[38] With the *Reichsbank*, furthermore, Germany took the final step in creating a unified currency. Earlier statutes had prepared the way by establishing the mark as the basic currency unit (1871) and restricting its convertibility to gold (1873). When France, the United States, and other countries followed suit, gold became an international standard, with considerable benefits for the expansion of world trade. These reforms were among the most important fruits of Bismarck's collaboration with the national liberals. Germany had achieved a single currency and an interdependent banking system

37 Böhme, *Deutschlands Weg*, pp. 322ff.; Wallich, *Konzentration*, pp. 52ff., 348ff.; Riesser, *German Great Banks*, p. 654; Pohl and Pohl, *Deutsche Bankengeschichte*, II, 236–242; Pohl, *Konzentration*, pp. 109–112.
38 Riesser, *German Great Banks*, pp. 141ff.; Sombart, *Deutsche Volkswirtschaft*, pp. 186–187, 192; Pohl and Pohl, *Deutsche Bankengeschichte*, II, 243–257; Pohl, *Konzentration*, pp. 103–107.

embracing the entire country, a major gain for the consolidation of the Reich and a basic guarantee of its continued unity.[39]

A unique feature of the German banking system, one that favored concentration of capital and economic power, was the active participation of the great corporate banks in the founding and expansion of industrial enterprises. From their inception the *Schaafhausen'scher Bankverein, Darmstädter Bank, Disconto-Gesellschaft,* and *Berliner Handelsgesellschaft* were designed for this function. While this practice was to be found among major banks everywhere, German banks carried it to an extreme by making company promotion their principal business. In this they resembled the French *Crédit Mobilier* rather than their British and American counterparts. They specialized in long-term loans, both secured and unsecured, and in underwriting capital issues for industrial and commercial enterprises. Frequently they held in their portfolios, either for investment or speculation, large blocks of stocks and bonds that gave them an important and even decisive voice in the management of the firms involved. But the reverse was also true—firms to which long-term loans were made or in which the banks had large investments were often represented on the directorates of the banks. "The interrelations between banks and industries fostered the process of concentration in both fields. In the course of its rapid growth, industry shifted its weight more and more from the smaller and medium-sized companies to those firms which by their nature required huge capital investments, such as the heavy industries, the electrical industries, and shipbuilding. It became increasingly necessary that large, efficient, and rich banks exist to shoulder the task of industrial financing. Thus industrial concentration became a powerful incentive to banking concentration."[40] The result was a degree of interdependence between banking and industrial capital, between big banks and big industries, unknown elsewhere in the capitalist world.

By the late 1870s the basic structure of German capitalism with its system of interlocking financial relationships, and its concentration of industrial and financial power along the line Rhine-Berlin-Silesia, had already been established. The German federal union had been welded together by material

---

[39] Gustav Stolper, Karl Häuser, and Knut Borchardt, *The German Economy 1870 to the Present* (New York, 1967), pp. 18–19.

[40] Stolper et al., *German Economy,* p. 28; Riesser, *German Great Banks,* pp. 336ff., 653ff.; Otto Jeidels, *Das Verhältnis der deutschen Grossbanken zur Industrie* (Munich, 1905), pp. 99ff.; Pohl, *Deutsche Bankengeschichte,* II, 258–295; Pohl and Pohl, *Konzentration,* pp. 88ff. Interlocking relationships between banking and industrial capital were not always harmonious, and some large, closely held firms (for example, Krupp, Hoesch, Thyssen) avoided the embrace of the banks in order to preserve their autonomy. Wilfried Feldenkirchen, "Das Wachstum der Eisen- und Stahlindustrie des Ruhrgebiets (1879–1914)," in Hermann Kellenbenz, ed., *Wachstumssch-wankungen. Beiträge zur Wirtschaftsgeschichte,* vol. 13 (Stuttgart, 1981), pp. 215–222, and Helmut Böhme, "Bankenkonzentration und Schwerindustrie," in Hans-Ulrich Wehler, ed., *Sozial-geschichte Heute* (Göttingen, 1974).

bonds that only the most violent political or military events could sever. The particularism of state and region gave way to social and ideological frictions as the main source of divisiveness in German society.

Social Cleavage

The relocation of millions of people produced major problems of assimilation. For those with capital or special talents the personal adjustment was probably minor; for peasants and village artisans it is presumed to have been more difficult. Yet the transition from hoe and plow to machine and mine face may have been less "traumatic" than the romanticizers of peasant life assumed.[41] Most migrants were independent cottagers rather than hired hands on the latifundia of the gentry.[42] They chose to swap the precarious existence of the small farmer or village artisan for the more secure livelihood of an unskilled mine or factory worker. What drew them to the city was the prospect of a higher living standard: better pay, shorter hours, less exertion, and more independence, including the chance to found a family at a younger age. Furthermore, the city offered the workingman far more diversion, the chance for a more exciting life than was to be had in the isolated hamlets beyond the Elbe. Not all ended in factories or underground in the coal seams; for every worker in industry another was required to supply the many auxiliary services of urban life.[43]

Like those who emigrated across the ocean, many who took the road to Berlin and the Ruhr hoped to find there the chance to ascend to a higher rung on the social ladder, an opportunity denied them and their children in the rigidly stratified society of the east. Bismarck himself endorsed this dream, asserting to the Reichstag that a peasant who went west might become a Krupp or Borsig, whereas in the east he had no prospect of becoming a big

[41] Without much empirical evidence concerning the actual life of rural immigrants to the industrial towns, historians tend to presume that it was traumatic: "Industry provided work, but nothing more. It judged the immigrant neither by origin nor family, but only by his ability to fit into the economic process. Outside his place of work he was almost always left to himself as one individual in the mass of individuals, while the rural or small-town world had embraced and ordered him in all aspects of his life." Wilhelm Brepohl, *Industrievolk im Wandel von der agraren zur industriellen Daseinsform* (Tübingen, 1957), pp. 160–161. See also Wolfgang Köllmann, "Industrialisierung, Binnenwanderung und 'Soziale Frage,' " *Vierteljahrschrift für Wirtschafts- und Sozialgeschichte*, 46 (1959), p. 61, and *Bevölkerungsgeschichte Deutschlands*, p. 39. James H. Jackson has shown that these impressionistic observations have little basis in fact insofar as the average migrant's experience is concerned. "Family Life and Urbanization in the Ruhr Valley, 1843–1890" (dissertation, University of Minnesota, 1979).

[42] Köllmann, "Grundzüge zur Bevölkerungsgeschichte," p. 388; Eberhard Franke, *Das Ruhrgebiet und Ostpreussen* (Marburg, 1934), pp. 29ff.

[43] Köllmann, "Industrialisierung, Binnenwanderung und 'Soziale Frage,' " p. 48, and "Process of Urbanization," pp. 70ff.

HOUSING IN INDUSTRIAL BERLIN: THE HOHENZOLLERN PALACE, DESIGNED BY ANDREAS SCHLÜTER AND
COMPLETED IN 1698. (LANDESBILDSTELLE BERLIN.)

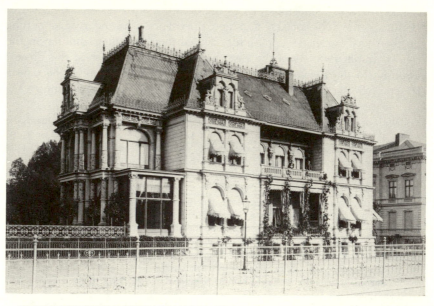

HOUSING IN INDUSTRIAL BERLIN: VILLA MONPLAISIR IN THE RAUCHSTRASSE, IN 1885. (BILDARCHIV
PREUSSISCHER KULTURBESITZ.)

HOUSING IN INDUSTRIAL BERLIN: MIDDLE CLASS APARTMENTS (SECOND AND THIRD FLOORS) IN THE PETRISTRASSE, ABOUT 1885. (BILDARCHIV PREUSSISCHER KULTURBESITZ.)

HOUSING IN INDUSTRIAL BERLIN: ARTISAN QUARTERS IN THE MÖCKERNSTRASSE. (BILDARCHIV PREUSSISCHER KULTURBESITZ.)

HOUSING IN INDUSTRIAL BERLIN: WORKERS' QUARTERS AT AM KRÖGEL 19, IN 1897. (BILDARCHIV PREUSSISCHER KULTURBESITZ.)

HOUSING IN INDUSTRIAL BERLIN: HUTS OF THE HOMELESS ON THE OUTSKIRTS OF THE CITY IN 1872. ETCHING BY GEORG KOCH. (BILDARCHIV PREUSSISCHER KULTURBESITZ.)

property owner.[44] But the historical record shows that the open frontier, free or cheap land, and young towns of the American West offered to the Pomeranian or Mecklenburg peasant and village artisan a greater opportunity for *embourgeoisement*—not only for themselves but also for their children and grandchildren—than was to be found in the mines and mills of the Ruhr and the factories of Berlin and other proliferating cities of western and southern Germany. In both countries the emerging entrepreneurial elite of the lower over-stratum (*Oberschicht*) of society was primarily recruited from the middle-stratum (*Mittelschicht*); in Germany the percentage that came from the under-stratum (*Unterschicht*), a small minority in the United States, was miniscule. With few exceptions (notably Silesian aristocrats) Germany's entrepreneurs came from its lower and upper middle-stratum, particularly merchants, small industrialists, and higher officials (in both business and government). According to one estimate, nearly 45 percent stemmed from the intelligentsia (*Bildungsbürgertum*) of the middle-stratum, an educated elite prepared by training and experience to take advantage of the opportunities industrialization offered. Among those composing the under-stratum artisans had some chance (a little better than 15 percent) for social ascent; mine and factory workers, almost none (0.5 percent).[45]

A major reason for Germany's social immobility in the midst of economic change was the continuing influence of social structures and attitudes inherited from earlier centuries. Industrialization changed and weakened but did not liquidate the German estate (*ständische*) mentality. It inhibited, with some exceptions, the old landowning nobility (*Adelsstand*) from becoming bankers or industrialists and created a new entrepreneurial elite (*Bürgertum*), many of whom yearned for ennoblement. Proliferation of the middle-stratum created a greatly enlarged and more diversified middle estate (*Mittelstand*); in the under-stratum a growing body of mine and factory workers (*Arbeiterstand*) stood beside the older peasant estate (*Bauernstand*), with which it shared a common origin but few common interests. The persistence of the estate tradition in Germany from the age of absolutism to the mid-twentieth century—despite the major changes in demographic, economic, and social structures that attended the German industrial revolution—is an extraordinary phenomenon, which in its degree demarcates the German experience from that

---

[44] To the Reichstag on Aug. 3, 1879. *BR*, VII, 406–409.

[45] Wilhelm Stahl, *Der Elitekreislauf in der Unternehmerschaft* (Zurich, 1973); Hartmut Kaelble, "Sozialer Aufstieg in den USA und Deutschland, 1900–1960," in Hartmut Kaelble, ed., *Geschichte der sozialen Mobilität seit der industriellen Revolution. Neue wissenschaftliche Bibliothek*, vol. 101 (Königstein, 1978), pp. 109–125 (see also the essays by Frederick Marquardt and David Crew in the same publication); Jürgen Kocka, *Unternehmer in der deutschen Industrialisierung* (Göttingen, 1975), pp. 42–54, and *Lohnarbeit und Klassenbildung. Arbeiter und Arbeiterbewegung in Deutschland 1800–1875* (Bonn, 1983); Helmut Zwahr, *Zur Konstituierung des Proletariats als Klasse: Strukturuntersuchungen über das Leipziger Proletariat während der industriellen Revolution* (Berlin, 1978).

of other western European countries. Such was the force of tradition that social attitudes placing a greater value on social origin and status than on talent and performance persisted through unconscious and sometimes conscious (both are evident in Bismarck) adaptation to changing material circumstances.[46]

Population growth, urban development, internal migration, transition from an agrarian to an industrial society, continuing transformation of the social structure within the estate tradition—all produced an evident need for new loyalties and systems of belief. Uprooted from his native soil with its traditions, familial ties, and fixed social relationships, the individual naturally groped for ideological convictions capable of supplying a new sense of security and destiny. Some migratory groups of the upper *Mittelstand*—businessmen whose affairs took them to distant cities, students who matriculated at remote universities, professors who repeatedly responded to calls from other universities, state officials who were transferred from one region to another—often became avid German nationalists. But the migrating east-Elbian peasant or artisan, who had once gotten his *Weltanschauung* from the village pastor and his politics from the local landlord and *Landrat*, tended as a proletarian to find his new value system in socialism. Nationalism and socialism provided Germans with new spiritual bonds to replace those dissolved by economic and social change. In this way the uprooted solved their "identity crises."[47]

The experience of the Anglo-Saxon world shows that it was by no means inevitable that the working class in industrialized societies should have been won to Marxian socialism in the nineteenth century. To determine why the German experience was different is an acute problem in German social history. One line of investigation has focused on peculiarities in German religious and intellectual development that explain why neither the Protestant church nor the "religion of German idealism" developed an interest in social amelioration. German idealism has often been called the religion of the German intelligentsia. Because of its rejection of natural law, its doctrine of obedience to positive law, its view of the state as separate from civil society and as embodying higher values, and its dedication to aesthetic individualism, German idealism did not develop "a meaningful social ethic," only a "pluralistic ethic in terms of individual development." While other possibilities had

[46] Jürgen Kocka, "Stand-Klasse-Organisation: Strukturen socialer Ungleichheit in Deutschland vom späten 18. bis zum frühen 20. Jahrhundert im Aufriss," in Hans-Ulrich Wehler, ed., *Klassen in der europäischen Sozialgeschichte* (Göttingen, 1979), pp. 137–165; Hartmut Kaelble, *Soziale Mobilität und Chancengleichheit im 19. und 20. Jahrhundert* (Göttingen, 1983), pp. 230–235. For an illuminating discussion of the historical usage of *Bürgertum* and *Mittelstand*, see Schulamit Volkov, *The Rise of Popular Antimodernism in Germany: The Urban Master Artisans, 1873–1896* (Princeton, 1978), pp. 123–146.

[47] Brepohl, *Industrievolk*, pp. 160–161. On the appeal of nationalism and the psychological need it fulfilled for societies in social change see particularly Boyd C. Shafer, *Faces of Nationalism: New Realities and Old Myths* (New York, 1972), pp. 220ff.

been evident in its early history and in the pietistic movement of the eighteenth and nineteenth centuries, the Lutheran church had become identified with authoritarian rule and with older occupational groups in German society—nobility, peasantry, and artisans. In accordance with their tradition Lutheran pastors spoke of faith but not of concrete problems of economic survival and social justice. Lutheranism no longer had relevance for urban workers, who ceased to attend services and left their children unbaptized.[48]

By contrast, the Catholic church retained its appeal for a wide spectrum of German society in the nineteenth century. Catholic intellectuals gave up the attempt to harmonize Catholic doctrine with German idealism, resigned themselves to remaining outside the mainstream of German intellectual life, and cultivated all the more Catholicism's international character and connections. While allied with conservatives and even reactionary forces, the Catholic church never surrendered its claim to sit in judgment over the social and political policies of secular states.[49] Hence it was in a better position than German Protestantism to cope with the social effects of industrialization. In southern and western Germany the Catholic church was able to construct and consolidate a broadly based social and political alliance ranging from aristocrats to peasants and proletarians. Its success prevented the German working class from developing a united front. Socialism flourished chiefly in Protestant Germany.[50]

While the character of German idealism and Lutheran Protestantism presented barriers to social understanding and action, it was still not inescapable that the formerly Protestant segment of German labor would turn to socialism in search of new values and a new explanation of its situation and destiny. Earlier it has been shown that important liberal and conservative leaders understood the political importance of winning and holding the allegiance of the urban worker. Since the 1840s the pietistic Lutheran minister Johann Wichern had sought not only the moral regeneration of the poor, but also their social improvement; yet charity remained the primary social function of the Inner Mission he founded. The attempts of the conservative Victor Aimé Huber to found housing, consumption, and savings bank cooperatives did not thrive. While more successful, the cooperatives established by the left-liberal Hermann Schulze-Delitzsch were limited in scope, and many proletarians

[48] Hajo Holborn, "German Idealism in the Light of Social History," in *Germany and Europe: Historical Essays by Hajo Holborn* (Garden City, N.Y., 1970), pp. 1–32. See also Fritz Fischer, "Der deutsche Protestantismus und die Politik im 19. Jahrhundert," *Historische Zeitschrift*, 171 (1951), pp. 503–518.

[49] Holborn, "German Idealism," pp. 27–28.

[50] For the contrasting positions of German Lutheranism and Catholicism on the issue of social amelioration see: William O. Shanahan, *German Protestants Face the Social Question*. Vol. 1: *The Conservative Phase, 1815–1871* (Notre Dame, 1954); Emil Ritter, *Die katholisch-soziale Bewegung im 19. Jahrhundert und der Volksverein* (Cologne, 1954); and Ernst Troeltsch, *The Social Teaching of the Christian Churches* (2 vols., New York, 1960).

soon outgrew the educational societies (*Arbeiterbildungsvereine*) that patronizing liberals established for their cultural improvement. In view of the failure or limited success of private efforts at social reform, it seemed evident to both Hermann Wagener, the conservative journalist and Prussian official, and to the followers of the deceased Ferdinand Lassalle, the democrat who turned socialist, that only the state could supply the initiative and resources for social reform.[51] It will be seen that this too was the conclusion of many "academic socialists" (*Kathedersozialisten*) of the 1870s and, belatedly, of Bismarck himself.[52]

The Critical Decade in German Social Relations: 1866–1875

The progress of industrialization during the third quarter of the nineteenth century did not produce a general transformation of German society. The transformed regions were those with major deposits of coal and iron ore, cities favorably situated on old waterways and new railway networks, and towns endowed with commercial and banking capital or good governmental connections. And yet in 1871 almost 64 percent of Germany's population still lived in villages of fewer than two thousand inhabitants.[53] Growth was regionalized and uneven; likewise, its social effects. The bottom stratum of German society did not yet contain a proletarian class of industrial wage earners conscious of a common identity and a common cause. (Not until after 1900—some think even later—did the mass "working class" of Marx's vision materialize.)[54] In the mining towns, larger cities, and industrializing regions, nevertheless, were growing pockets of wage earners who were at varying stages in the evolution of proletarian class-consciousness. What happened within those pockets during the last four decades of the nineteenth century was extremely important for the future of German social relations. In them were initially hundreds, eventually thousands, of laborers who reached, albeit at uneven tempo, the conviction that their future lay in self-help rather than in further reliance upon the state for protection, existing political parties for representation, and the men of "education and property" (*Bildung und Besitz*) in the upper level of the German *Mittelstand* for leadership.

In retrospect, the critical period in the growth of working class alienation

---

[51] See vol. 1, pp. 226–233.

[52] See pp. 285–290 and vol. 3, ch. 6.

[53] Wolfram Fischer, Jochen Krengel, and Jutta Wietog, *Sozialgeschichtliches Arbeitsbuch I: Materialien zur Statistik des Deutschen Bundes, 1815–1870* (Munich, 1982), pp. 37–38; Hohorst et al., *Sozialgeschichtliches Arbeitsbuch II*, pp. 42–52.

[54] Vernon Lidtke, "Burghers, Workers and Problems of Class Relationships 1870 to 1914: Germany in Comparative Perspective," in Jürgen Kocka, ed., *Arbeiter und Bürger im 19. Jahrhundert: Varianten ihres Verhältnisses im europäischen Vergleich. Schriften des Historischen Kollegs* (Munich, 1986), pp. 28–52; Kocka, *Lohnarbeit und Klassenbildung*, particularly pp. 201–203.

in Germany was that of 1866–1875. What the government, political parties, and employers did or did not offer in these years was decisive in determining whether labor would be satisfied with its place in the German social order. In the north German constitution of 1867 labor received the secret ballot in national elections; during the years 1865–1869 it gained a limited right to organize and strike.[55] Whether urban labor would use the ballot to express hostility toward the system appears to have depended upon whether it would succeed in establishing labor unions and striking for the achievement of concrete, visible economic and social gains.

Although often circumvented, anticombination laws had existed for at least two decades in the statute books of most German states. In Prussia both employers and employees had been forbidden the right to organize in the industry code (*Gewerbeordnung*) of 1845 and subsequent ordinances of 1849 and 1851. Saxony's repeal of the anticombination law in 1861 led to increasing criticism of the prohibition in Prussia. Liberal deputies (Julius Faucher and Schulze-Delitzsch) and some industrialists (including Borsig, Freund, Siemens, Halske) argued for the right to organize on various grounds: since employers' "combinations" were less visible and never prosecuted, workers were justified in regarding the prohibition as discriminatory and oppressive; the prohibition was an unjustifiable and harmful interference by government in the economic process, leading workers to believe that their wages were held down and general welfare inhibited by the state and not the natural law of the marketplace; since labor was a commodity, its value could only be determined by the law of supply and demand in a free market.[56] Prussian officials in industrial regions shared these convictions, as did Bismarck himself. Like them, Bismarck did not expect repeal to increase greatly the number of labor unions or work stoppages. Strikes were expensive and unions would require time to accumulate funds. Workers would consider the issues and measure their chances for success with care. Caution would prevail.[57]

These views, derived from the writings of Frédéric Bastiat and John Stuart Mill, were propagated by leaders of the Progressive party during the Prussian constitutional conflict. The perennial attempts (beginning in 1862) of Faucher, Schulze-Delitzsch, and others to gain parliamentary approval of a bill legalizing labor unions (with some restrictions) popularized the issue and

---

[55] BGB (1869), 245–282.

[56] See Wolfgang Ritscher, *Koalitionen und Koalitionsrecht in Deutschland bis zur Reichsgewerbeordnung* (Stuttgart, 1917), pp. 203–268; Hermann Müller, *Geschichte der deutschen Gewerkschaften bis zum Jahre 1878* (Berlin, 1918), pp. 33–41; Ulrich Engelhardt, "Gewerkschaftliche Interessenvertretung als Menschenrecht: Anstösse und Entwicklung der Koalitionsrechtsforderung in der preussisch-deutschen Arbeiterbewegung 1862/63–1865," in Ulrich Engelhardt, Volker Sellin, and Horst Stuke, eds., *Soziale Bewegung und politische Verfassung* (Stuttgart, 1976), pp. 538–598.

[57] Bismarck to Itzenplitz, Jan. 26, 1865. Hans Rothfels, *Bismarck: Deutscher Staat* (2d ed., Munich, 1965), pp. 317–319.

educated labor as to its significance. By 1864–1865 conservatives (Hermann Wagener, Moritz von Blanckenburg), socialists (Wilhelm Liebknecht, Ferdinand Lassalle), and Catholics (Bishop Ketteler, August Reichensperger) were contesting the progressives' monopoly of the cause. The competition for worker support in the constitutional struggle between crown and parliament aroused the participation of the workers themselves; in assemblies and petitions they called for the unrestricted right to organize. This demand exceeded the intentions even of the progressives. In February 1865 the Bismarck government seized control of the issue by sending Minister of Commerce Count Heinrich von Itzenplitz to inform the Chamber of Deputies that, although the cabinet accepted the need to legalize unions, abolition of anticombination laws could only take place as part of a general reform of the industry code of 1845, a reform that would require preparatory consultations and enquiries within and outside the government. One year later, the government introduced a bill that would have permitted worker coalitions for industrial, agricultural, and household workers. But the war of 1866 interrupted the deliberations and, furthermore, altered the balance of social and political forces in Prussia and northern Germany. Although it granted the right to organize and strike, the industry code of the North German Confederation (1869) kept important restrictions: open shop, freedom to cancel union membership, criminal penalties for coercion of nonstrikers, and no corporate legal status for unions.[58]

After Itzenplitz's declaration of 1865 the Prussian government ceased to enforce anticombination laws, which adept labor leaders had in any case learned to circumvent. During the 1860s workers in some trades (printers and tobacco workers led) had revived the abortive movement of 1848–1849 for the creation of local, regional, and finally national occupational associations (Berufsvereine). This popular movement paralleled the phenomenal growth of bourgeois "voluntary associations" in the same decade. Socialist and social-liberal "worker politicians" founded labor organizations, basins with which to catch the current. In 1868–1869 were founded the Lassallean Allgemeiner deutscher Arbeiterschaftsverband (Johann Baptist von Schweizer), the Marxist-oriented Deutsche Gewerksgenossenschaften (August Bebel and Wilhelm Liebknecht), and the progressive Verband der deutschen Gewerkvereine (Max Hirsch and Franz Duncker).[59] At issue in the competition between these or-

[58] DZA Merseburg, Rep. 120, BB, I, 1, Nr. 12, Vols. 1–3; SBHA (1865), I, 119–202; Heinrich Volkmann, Die Arbeiterfrage im preussischen Abgeordnetenhaus, 1848–1869 (Berlin, 1968), pp. 142–197.

[59] Ulrich Engelhardt, "Nur vereinigt sind wir stark": Die Anfänge der deutschen Gewerkschaftsbewegung, 1862–63 bis 1869–70 (2 vols., Stuttgart, 1977); Willy Albrecht, Fachverein-Berufsgewerkschaft-Zentralverband: Organisationsprobleme der deutschen Gewerkschaften 1870–1890 (Bonn, 1982), pp. 41–104. The Lassallean union was soon renamed Allgemeiner Deutscher Arbeiterunterstützungsverband.

ganizations was whether German workers would be integrated into bourgeois society (the objective of the Hirsch–Duncker movement) or alienated from it (the objective of the socialist movements). Could the Prussian-German establishment, broadened in these years to include the entrepreneurial elite and German intelligentsia, be widened further to include the industrial working class? Or would German workers conclude from bitter experience that the Marxian concept of the "class struggle" was not mere theory but also a concrete reality with which they had to cope in daily life?

The dramatic events in foreign affairs that led to German unification in 1870–1871 have overshadowed and tended to obscure parallel events in German economic and social history that were no less important. The climactic acceleration in German economic development that occurred in 1869–1873 has already been described. Less well known is the fact that the *Gründerjahre* was accompanied by a wave of strikes and work stoppages that far exceeded in frequency, breadth, and seriousness those of any previous period in nineteenth-century Germany. The number and duration of such interruptions increased in tempo with the boom. Of 805 strikes between 1864 and 1873, 222 occurred in 1873 alone. A wide variety of industries was affected, including mining, smelting, machinery, textiles, building, and the artisan trades. Some strikes involved only a few individuals; others, hundreds and even thousands. No less than twenty-one thousand miners went on strike in the Ruhr region in 1872.[60]

For laborers, as for businessmen, the *Gründerjahre* appeared to present unparalleled opportunities for material gain. The rapid acceleration of business activity in the years 1869 to 1873 produced a labor shortage, a sharp increase in labor's real earnings, and a determination by workers to seek a greater share in the prosperity their labor produced.[61] The most frequent demands of the strikers were for pay increases, ranging from 10 to 60 percent (usually 25 percent), and a reduction of the working day from eleven and twelve to ten hours

[60] Walter Steglich, "Eine Streiktabelle für Deutschland, 1864 bis 1880," *Jahrbuch für Wirtschaftsgeschichte*, 1960/II, pp. 235–283. A recent count gives higher figures for 1872 (352) and 1873 (283). Klaus Tenfelde and Heinrich Volkmann, eds., *Streik: Zur Geschichte des Arbeitskampfes in Deutschland während der Industrialisierung* (Munich, 1981), p. 294. For a contemporary effort to assess the extent of the walkouts see *Amtliche Mitteilungen des Deutschen Handelstages, Die Arbeitseinstellungen in Deutschland* (Berlin, 1873). On the Ruhr strikes see Klaus Tenfelde, *Sozialgeschichte der Bergarbeiterschaft an der Ruhr im 19. Jahrhundert* (Bonn–Bad Godesberg, 1977), pp. 436–486. The files of the Prussian Ministry of Commerce show how broad the spectrum of worker discontent became in the late 1860s. DZA Merseburg, Rep. 120, BB, VII, 1, Nos. 1, 2, 3.

[61] For the most recent calculations see Ashok V. Desai, *Real Wages in Germany 1871–1913* (Oxford, 1968), p. 34. Desai estimates that real wages rose in mining nearly 50 percent; in machine manufacture over 30 percent; in building, printing, and iron and steel manufacture around 20 percent; and in textile enterprises nearly 10 percent. See also Bry, *Wages in Germany*, pp. 54, 71.

(and restoration of the eight-hour day in mines). But there were other demands, including union recognition, guarantees for collective bargaining, reinstatement of fired labor leaders, control over work supervisors and employment practices, abolition of fines, and "better and more humane treatment." Most strikes were local and spontaneous. Some small strikes were successful, but the largest—the miners' strikes at Schweidnitz (Waldenburg) in 1869 and in Silesia and the Ruhr region in 1872—were failures. Actual violence was minimal, despite many threats and some actions against nonstrikers and strikebreakers.[62]

Many work stoppages were nipped in the bud by employers, who either threatened to discharge or actually discharged workers (particularly "agitators") making "unacceptable demands." In other cases, according to a German Commercial Association report, the strikers soon returned to work after being "enlightened about their interests" by employers. Where these tactics did not work, employers imported workers "in order to avoid any negotiations with the strikers and any concessions." To the same end production was shifted to other plants; "a very effective measure proved to be the substitution of machine for handicraft production." In the major strikes at Waldenburg, Essen, and elsewhere employers collaborated by refusing any concessions, instituting lockouts, blacklisting discharged employees, identifying and exchanging information on strike leaders, and by providing mutual help in filling the most pressing orders. In general, the employers also had the assistance of the government, which on occasion sent the police, gendarmes, and soldiers to protect property and overawe the workers.[63]

Although they contributed to the unrest in some cases, labor union agitators did not cause the "strike fever" of 1869–1873. The union movement was too young and inexperienced for such a task. For Marxists, moreover, trade unionism had as yet little appeal; their orientation was toward the disruption of, not accommodation to, the capitalistic system. The real issue was not who caused but who would benefit from the strikes. Waldenburg's workers (9,000 of the 10,000 miners in the area), for example, requested leadership from Max Hirsch and yet struck against his advice. Their main demand was for union representation. To Hirsch union recognition and collective bargaining meant abandonment of "employer absolutism" and recognition of "equality of status [Gleichberechtigung] for employees." Would owners, he asked, permit labor "to stand next to them" or only "under them?" Employers adamantly refused to deal with the union; and Hirsch's search for adequate financial support as far away as England proved fruitless.[64] The collapse of the Waldenburg strike had

---

[62] Handelstag, *Arbeitseinstellungen*, pp. 51–53.

[63] *Ibid.*, passim.

[64] Ulrich Engelhardt, "Zur Verhaltensanalyse eines sozialen Konflikts, dargestellt am Waldenburger Streik von 1869," in Otto Neulch, ed., *Soziale Innovation und sozialer Konflikt* (Göttingen, 1977), pp. 69–94, and Engelhardt, *"Nur vereinigt sind wir stark,"* pp. 1070–1206.

disastrous consequences for the Hirsch–Dunker unions. At the time the strike began, the union could already claim 268 affiliated local unions (*Ortsvereine*) with about 30,000 members. By the end of 1870 the membership had fallen (the war also had a depressing influence) to 6,000, recovering in 1874 to 357 locals with 22,000 members. The depression of 1873–1879, which ought to have promoted union membership, actually reduced the Hirsch–Dunker unions to 16,500 members (365 local unions).[65] Although the movement grew in later decades, the possibility that it would ever represent the whole or even the largest segment of German labor was gone.

The failures of 1869–1873 may have been decisive in convincing German labor that neither the government nor the major political parties could be expected to protect workers in the economic struggle. Earlier it was shown that state paternalism, which had once shielded mine workers from excessive exploitation, ended with the mining law of 1861.[66] One of the objectives of miners in 1869–1873 was to restore the eight-hour shift they had possessed under the old law. Many workers still clung, with diminishing faith, to the tradition that the king, ministers, and officials stood above the economic struggle, ready to intervene in behalf of the weak. But in 1869–1873 the government's response was to order out the troops and police and, as will be shown, prosecute and incarcerate those who claimed to represent politically the interests of proletarians.[67] What Liebknecht said of the Waldenburg strike can be said of the strike movement of 1869–1873 in general. "The government's attitude is making the workers into democrats; the employers' attitude is making them into socialists."[68]

---

[65] *Handwörterbuch der Staatswissenschaft* (2d ed., Jena, 1900), IV, 649; but see also the statistics in Albrecht, *Fachverein-Berufsgewerkschaft-Zentralverband*, p. 529. For Albrecht's account of the effect of the Waldenburg strike and the war of 1870–1871 on the liberal trade unions see *ibid.*, pp. 89–95, 261–280.

[66] See vol. 1, pp. 288–289.

[67] See pp. 285–310.

[68] Quoted in Engelhardt, "*Nur vereinigt sind wir stark*," p. 1100.

CHAPTER TWO

Bismarck's Character

The Rewards of Statesmanship

"THE GERMAN nation is sick of principles and doctrines, of literary greatness and of theoretical existence. What it wants is power, power, power! And whoever gives it power, to him it will give honor, more honor than he can imagine."[1] This prophecy by Julius Fröbel, written in 1859, was more than fulfilled. From a grateful ruler Bismarck received a steady stream of titles, medals, and gifts. In 1865 he was awarded the title "count" (*Graf*) and in 1871 that of "prince" (*Fürst*) carrying the predicate "serene highness" (*Durchlaucht*). The *Landwehr* officer with but one year's service in the army was promoted up the ranks to colonel general of the cavalry (with the rank of field marshal) and made honorary commander of the Magdeburg Cuirassiers. Other rewards were a hereditary seat in the Prussian House of Lords and appointment as hereditary grandmaster of the Pomeranian hunt. Naturally he received all the medals and decorations the Kaiser could bestow, including the successive classes of the Iron Cross, Red Eagle, and Black Eagle and climaxed by the treasured *Pour le Mérite*, ordinarily granted only for exceptional valor in combat.

The generosity of the monarch was matched by that of the public. Honorary degrees came from faculties of the universities of Halle, Göttingen, Erlangen, Tübingen, Giessen, and Jena; honorary citizenships from Berlin, Hamburg, Lübeck, Bremen, Stuttgart, Dortmund, Essen, Dresden, and dozens of other cities. His name was to be found throughout the land: on streets, squares, plazas, buildings, bridges, tunnels, obelisks, towers, ships, fortifications, a town (formerly Braubauerschaft), a mountain peak, an iron foundry, a dye (dark brown), a vodka, a rose, a jelly doughnut, and a pickled herring. In the far Pacific a sea, a mountain, and an archipelago received his name; in southeast Africa, a mountain and a palm tree (*Bismarckia nobilis*); on the Dakota plains, a city (founded by a railway company eager to attract German investors). Painters, sculptors, and photographers competed to reproduce his image. His birthdays brought a flood of telegrams, letters, eulogies, poems, and personal gifts. Nationwide celebrations were held on his seventieth birthday (1885) and the twenty-fifth anniversary of his appointment as minister (1887).[2] Not all of his admirers were Germans. On July 4, 1875, he was pre-

---

[1] Quoted in Theodore Hamerow, *The Social Foundations of German Unification, 1858–1871* (Princeton, 1972), p. 11.

[2] The sources for these many honors are too numerous to cite individually. They can be found in the works edited by Horst Kohl: *Fürst Bismarck: Regesten zu einer wissenschaflichen Biographie*

sented with a walking stick carved out of a beam from which had once hung the Liberty Bell in Philadelphia.[3]

The recipient of these many honors was not always pleased. During his years in the diplomatic service he had grown contemptuous of statesmen who coveted titles, ribbons, medals, and other such "Byzantine" pomp and circumstances. "What is the good of that to me?" he snapped on being told of his promotion to lieutenant general on January 18, 1871 (the day of the Kaiser proclamation at Versailles and of one of his most bitter conflicts with Wilhelm I). He had enough "gewgaws," he said, on receiving the first class of the Iron Cross; he felt ashamed to wear it as long as so many who had been in combat, like his own sons, went unrewarded.[4] Neither Bismarck nor his wife was flattered by their elevation to the dignity of count and countess. As scions of two of the oldest aristocratic families in the Altmark and Pomerania, they had no need of an additional title. "It was contrary to my desires," Bismarck complained in 1876, "that his majesty made me a prince. Earlier I was a rich count, now I am a poor prince." After 1890 he refused to use the title "Duke of Lauenburg" awarded to him on retirement by Wilhelm II.[5]

The gifts he did appreciate were material. In 1867 he received 400,000 thalers from Wilhelm with which to purchase the entailed estate at Varzin in Pomerania. In 1871 Wilhelm presented to him the Sachsenwald in the duchy of Lauenburg, a huge domain valued at 1,000,000 thalers (3,000,000 marks). From the association of German Railways he received in 1871 a private rail-

des ersten Reichskanzlers (2 vols., Leipzig, 1891–1892); Anhang zu den Gedanken und Erinnerungen von Otto Fürst von Bismarck (2 vols., Stuttgart, 1901); and Bismarck-Jahrbuch (6 vols., Leipzig, 1894–1899). See also numerous letters in GW, XIV (part two) and the works edited by Heinrich von Poschinger: BP and Bismarck-Portefeuille (5 vols., Stuttgart, 1889–1900). In 1903 someone listed 165 German memorials to Bismarck (statues, columns, towers, etc.) and did not claim to have found them all. The memorials to Bismarck exceeded by far those to Kaiser Wilhelm I, particularly in Bavaria and Catholic Germany. Thomas Nipperdey, "Nationalidee und Nationaldenkmal in Deutschland im 19. Jahrhundert," Historische Zeitschrift, 206 (1968), pp. 577–582.

[3] Kohl, ed., Bismarck-Regesten, II, 112. Visitors to the German exhibit at the Philadelphia World Exposition in 1876 found German goods "cheap and bad," but also chauvinistic: "Germans and Prussians advancing in battalions, the Emperor, the princes, Bismarck, Moltke, and Roon who meet us in all ends and corners, whether painted, embroidered, printed, lithographed, or woven, whether in procelain, bronze, zinc, iron, or pottery." Article in the Hamburgische Correspondenz, July 6, 1876, quoted in Ivo Lambi, Free Trade and Protection in Germany 1868–1879. Vierteljahrschrift für Sozial- und Wirtschaftsgeschichte, 44 (Wiesbaden, 1963), p. 74.

[4] Moritz Busch, Bismarck: Some Secret Pages of His History (London, 1898), I, 359, and Tagebuchblätter (Leipzig, 1899), I, 391–393, 571, 577; II, 108. After his anger at Wilhelm had cooled Bismarck apparently did take some pride in the Iron Cross, first class. It was the decoration he most frequently wore. GW, VII, 462; VIII, 23. By 1878 he had received every decoration Wilhelm could appropriately bestow. A new one had to be invented to celebrate the chancellor's achievement at the Congress of Berlin. Freiherr Lucius von Ballhausen, Bismarck-Erinnerungen (Stuttgart, 1920), p. 147; Kohl, ed., Anhang, I, 280–281.

[5] Kohl, ed., Anhang, I, 215–216; Lucius, Bismarck-Erinnerungen, p. 93; Robert von Keudell, Fürst und Fürstin Bismarck Erinnerungen aus den Jahren 1846 bis 1872 (Berlin, 1901), p. 224.

way car emblazoned (to his distress) with the princely coat of arms.[6] To honor his seventieth birthday a committee, headed by the Duke of Ratibor, president of the Prussian House of Lords, raised a princely sum in excess of 2,300,000 marks. The appeal for contributions was dubbed "Otto pence" (an allusion to the pope's "Peter's pence") and its unspecified purpose was presumed to be charity. To the surprise of some contributors, a majority on the committee then voted to commit 1,150,000 marks of the sum (fortified by an additional 350,000 marks raised from German bankers) for the purchase of Schönhausen II, an estate that the Bismarck family had been forced to sell early in the century. Bismarck appears to have accepted this decision without compunction. With the remaining half of the fund, he established the "Schönhausen Foundation," devoted to the support of needy students in training to become teachers in the nation's higher schools and widows and orphans of deceased teachers in those institutions. But he also arranged privately with Bleichröder to devote a small part of the trust to poor relief at Schönhausen, where the foundation was to be situated, and to invest some of the capital in mortgages with which to refinance debts on his estates.[7]

While he appreciated its political value, Bismarck did not deliberately cultivate personal popularity while he was in office. (We shall see that this was less true of his retirement years.) "He bore nothing more easily than the feeling of being the most hated man in Germany during the constitutional conflict," wrote Christoph von Tiedemann, by no means a Bismarck idolater. "That after the Austrian war the waves of enthusiasm in public opinion raised him high above his fellow men also left him cold. He cared nothing for popularity."[8] A grand seigneur of the old tradition, he regarded himself not as a public servant, but as a "vassal" (Lehnsmann) of the king or, at most, servant of the state. He disliked political huckstering and contact with crowds. During nearly three decades as minister-president and chancellor he gave almost no public speeches outside parliament, preferring to manipulate public opinion through the newspaper press. By the late 1860s artists, cartoonists, and photographers had made his image familiar to millions, and he could not appear in public without attracting attention. He regretted the loss of anonymity, complaining to Lucius about spontaneous ovations to which he was compelled to respond with smiling face on his travels. At his favorite spa, Bad Kissingen in Bavaria, he felt like a "fossil" on display. "I have ceased to be an individual," he once remarked. "Whenever I appear, they stare at me as though I were an event. No sooner do I step into the street than I hear behind me clattering footsteps of hundreds of people who pursue me."[9]

[6] GW, VIII, 9–10; Lucius, Bismarck-Erinnerungen, p. 20.

[7] Fritz Stern, Gold and Iron: Bismarck, Bleichröder, and the Building of the German Empire (New York, 1977), pp. 300–301.

[8] Christoph von Tiedemann, Sechs Jahre Chef der Reichskanzlei unter dem Fürsten Bismarck (2d ed., Leipzig, 1910), p. 479.

[9] Lucius, Bismarck-Erinnerungen, p. 114; BP, I, 258; GW, VIII, 504; BR, XI, 167.

As the years advanced this distaste for contact with the public grew. In Berlin he nearly ceased in the 1880s to attend social functions outside his own home, including those at court. His contacts with the king and crown prince were limited to private audiences and exchanges of messages.[10] Yet he maintained that his door was open to any minister or deputy who wished to speak with him. While parliament was in session, he held weekly dinners and soirées (later changed to luncheons) at which he was a genial host. He disliked cities and retreated for months to his estates at Varzin and Friedrichsruh. How much healthier he would have been, he was fond of saying, if only he had remained a rural Junker. He regarded Berlin as ugly and unhealthy, maintaining that every house had a bad smell and that shortly "the place would become utterly intolerable. . . . I have always longed to get away from large cities and the stink of civilization." On long rides and walks through the woods and meadows of his estates he renewed his contact with nature and reflected on the policies he was to pursue. "I have always made my most important decisions," he told a physician, Eduard Cohen, "alone, in the forest."[11]

Bismarck's Taste

Bismarck's dislike of pomp and circumstance was also evident in his various dwellings. In 1862 he moved into the narrow two-story building at Wilhelmstrasse 76 that housed the Foreign Ministry. Constructed at the beginning of the eighteenth century as a private home, it was, inside and out, the "least pretentious building in the Wilhelmstrasse." Bismarck often made fun of its plainness, but instigated no changes. On the first floor were the offices and cubicles of the counselors and clerks of the foreign office, and on the second were the minister's office, reception rooms, and private quarters of the Bismarck family. In the rear was an extensive private garden shaded by old trees, where the chancellor frequently walked. Visitors were astonished at the simplicity of their reception. No portier in dress uniform with "Cerberus demeanor" guarded the portals. "One must ring just as one does at the homes of ordinary mortals." In the antechamber were no lackeys in gold and silver livery of the kind favored by diplomats and ministers. Bismarck received his visitors in a plain, sparsely furnished office of medium size dominated by a large mahogany desk. "No provincial prefect in France would have been satisfied with such modest surroundings." In 1878 the Bismarcks moved into the adjacent Palais Radziwill at Wilhelmstrasse 77, a somewhat grander residence. Purchased by the government in 1874 at a cost of 2,000,000 thalers, the Radziwill mansion contained stately rooms and salons more suitable for official entertainment than No. 76, which was retained for office space. To

---

[10] GW, VIII, 517.
[11] Busch, *Tagebuchblätter*, III, 165; GW, VII, 212, and VIII, 513.

THE WILHELMSTRASSE. FROM RIGHT TO LEFT: THE FOREIGN OFFICE (NO. 75) AND CHANCELLERY (NO. 76). AT THE EXTREME LEFT IS THE PALAIS RADZIWILL (NO. 77), WHICH BECAME THE CHANCELLOR'S RESIDENCE IN 1878. (BILDARCHIV PREUSSISCHER KULTURBESITZ.)

SCHLOSS FRIEDRICHSRUH IN THE SACHSENWALD NEAR HAMBURG, FRONT VIEW. (ARTHUR REHBEIN, *BISMARCK IM SACHSENWALD*, BUCHVERLAG DER GESELLSCHAFT ZUR VERBREITUNG KLASSISCHER KUNST G.M.B.H., BERLIN, 1925.)

the Baroness von Spitzemberg the new quarters, redecorated and refurnished by the Bismarcks, looked expensive, but "right ordinary and often tasteless."[12]

The impression created by Bismarck's country homes was similar to that of Wilhelmstrasse 76. "Internally as well as externally, there is no pretension, no love of luxury about the residence of the chancellor and his family," Moritz Busch wrote of Varzin, "though it is at the same time pleasant and comfortable throughout. It is the house of a prosperous country gentleman rather than the chateau of a prince. Almost all floors, it is true, are inlaid, but the ceilings of the smaller rooms are simply whitewashed. There are no luxurious carpets, draperies, artistic carvings, or clocks of great value." The residence at Friedrichsruh was even less impressive. Originally an inn frequented by vacationing burghers from Hamburg, it was purchased in 1879 and converted into a home by Bismarck after he received the surrounding Sachsenwald. To this "simple building of bourgeois appearance" constructed in the Swiss cottage style generally favored for railway stations he added two large wings in 1883. The result was "a large irregular structure without style, but roomy and well furnished." Close by was a railway station on the main line to Berlin, at which the citizens of nearby Hamburg debouched for weekend *Spaziergänge*, hopeful of getting a glimpse of the famous resident. For privacy Bismarck was compelled to construct a high brick wall along the railway and intersecting road. Day and night the trains puffed by the chancellor's dwelling and the whistling and rattling of the locomotives disturbed the quiet of the compound. It was a commodious, but not stately, mansion of the kind expected of a man of Bismarck's wealth and status.[13]

To Count Philipp zu Eulenburg the *Schloss* at Friedrichsruh revealed something important about its owner and his family—the Bismarcks lacked sense of beauty or *Gemütlichkeit*. "The complete tastelessness of the exterior is even exceeded by the room furnishings inside. The extraordinarily large upholstered furniture is covered with bright cretonne. Some interesting old family pictures in gold frames, many photographs in black frames, watercolors, fancy clocks, and strange allegorical pictures—the gifts of enthusiastic Americans— stand out, garish and ugly on walls papered in white. The carpets laid in all rooms have shrieking colors, like the bright yellow cretonne [of the furniture] on which are printed bright flowers and Arabesques. I have never seen American country homes, but perhaps Friedrichsruh makes an impression similar to them. It bears the stamp of utility with an inclination toward comfort, but it defies every taste."[14] Eulenburg's vision was somewhat jaundiced, but even

---

[12] Busch, *Tagebuchblätter*, II, 177–219; BP, I, 25, 133–136; Rudolf Vierhaus, ed., *Das Tagebuch der Baronin Spitzemberg* (Göttingen, 1961), pp. 171–172; Lucius, *Bismarck-Erinnerungen*, p. 53.

[13] Busch, *Tagebuchblätter*, II, 457–477, 500ff.; Lucius, *Bismarck-Erinnerungen*, pp. 76–77; GW, VIII, 578–579.

[14] Philipp zu Eulenburg-Hertefeld, *Aus 50 Jahren* (Berlin, 1923), pp. 203–204.

the Baroness von Spitzemberg, an intimate friend of the Bismarcks and their frequent guest, spoke of Bismarck's "lack of a sense of beauty in itself and in his surroundings."[15] His dwellings became cluttered with art objects, most of which were busts and portraits of ancestors, members of the family, kings of Prussia, foreign statesmen (including photographs of Ulysses S. Grant and George Bancroft), and historical paintings such as Anton Werner's depictions of the Kaiser proclamation at Versailles and of the Congress of Vienna (both gifts of the Kaiser). After listening to Bismarck describe his only visit to Italy (1847), an Italian visitor remarked, "The artistic side of our country appears to have made no impression on him."[16] Only once did Bismarck come near the principal art gallery in Berlin, stopping at the entrance to get out of the rain. German scholars and writers, nurtured on the concept of the *Kulturstaat*, were distressed that the founder and chancellor of the German Reich did nothing to promote the arts and sciences.[17]

Yet Bismarck was not uncultured in other respects. His letters and dispatches show that he was a master of the German language. His literary talent would have enabled him, if circumstances had required it, to become a highly effective journalist and feuilletonist. Many of his letters to family and friends are masterpieces of epistolary art—alternately witty, tender, ironic, pungent, reflecting his quickly shifting moods. Throughout his career he fought against the malaise that affects every bureaucracy—the tendency toward official jargon, pomposity of phrase, contradiction in content. His state papers are notable for their clear, unadorned style; often lengthy, they are seldom verbose. He avoided *Fremdwörter* and insisted on German in preference to Latin script.[18]

His native literary talent was nurtured by constant reading. The Baroness von Spitzemberg usually found on his desk a work by Schiller, a volume of lyric poetry, or a light novel (*Schmöker*) that he read for relaxation. His parliamentary speeches, which were extemporaneous in execution, contain frequent quotations, usually from Goethe, Schiller, and Shakespeare, but occasionally from Gellert, Scheffel, Uhland, Friedrich Kind, Horace, and Thomas Moore. The baroness reported that he acquired the works of Chamisso, Uhland, Heine, and Rückert for each of his residences. "When I get very exasperated and exhausted, I read preferably these German lyricists; that revives me." Among the classic authors Schiller remained his favorite "as a person-

[15] *GW*, VIII, 598.

[16] Edmund Mayor, secretary to Francesco Crispi, Oct. 2, 1887. *GW*, VIII, 583.

[17] Otto Graf zu Stolberg-Wernigerode, "Unbekannte Gespräche mit Bismarck," *Süddeutsche Monatshefte*, 27 (1929–1930), pp. 312–313; Heinrich and Julius Hart, "Offener Brief an den Fürsten Bismarck," in *Kritische Waffengänge* (Leipzig, 1882), pp. 1–8 (the author thanks Susan C. Miller for this reference).

[18] Herbert von Bismarck, ed., *Fürst Bismarcks Briefe an seine Braut und Gattin* (2d ed., Stuttgart, 1906).

ality." "He regards Goethe," Cohen reported, "to be a genuine bureaucrat, prouder of his ministerial dignity than of his poetic talent." He knew Faust, Part I, intimately; Part II he considered "incomprehensible and therefore unenjoyable."[19] On occasion his guests were surprised at how well read Bismarck appeared to be in contemporary belles-lettres. One evening during the war against France he discussed with his dinner companions Friedrich von Spielhagen's *Problematische Naturen*, Gustav Freytag's *Soll und Haben*, and Fritz Reuter's *Ut de Franzosentid* und *Ut mine Stromtid*. House guests in 1880 found him acquainted with feuilletonist Paul Lindau's monthly *Nord und Süd* and the recently published memoirs of Louis Schneider, reader to Friedrich Wilhelm IV and Wilhelm I, and of Karoline Bauer, a leading actress. He also read foreign authors. George Eliot, he admired, having read *Adam Bede*, but he did not care for Victor Hugo. Turgenev, he remarked in 1882, was "the most gifted of all living authors."[20]

During the imperial age Berlin became one of the great centers for the performing arts. But Bismarck was not seen in its theaters, concert halls, and opera houses. Dislike of public attention was not the only reason. The necessity of paying for a ticket and being confined to a seat, he said, robbed him of all enjoyment—"music should be given as freely as love." At home he listened to piano and vocal music (Mozart, Schubert, Löwe) performed by his wife and Robert von Keudell. But Johanna's duties as mother and housewife gave her less time to play, and, after Keudell left Bismarck's service in 1872, the occasional musicales in the Bismarck household ceased. Bismarck complained that the melodies echoed in his head for hours and robbed him of sleep. Richard Wagner he found distasteful both as a composer and as a person (they met once at a dinner) and for an interesting reason: "Wagner demanded admiration all the time. He always wanted to be number one, but I was too busy for that."[21]

Philosophy still left Bismarck cold. Schopenhauer was the philosopher most in vogue during the second half of the century, and naturally the new school of philosophic pessimism came up for discussion in the Bismarck household. The prince listened, puffing on his pipe, but was not inspired to read. When asked whether he had met Schopenhauer during their mutual

[19] Spitzemberg, *Tagebuch*, pp. 212, 239; GW, VIII, 384, 394, 504; Poschinger, ed., *Bismarck-Portefeuille*, IV, 98.

[20] Busch, *Tagebuchblätter*, II, 28; GW, VIII, 392, 421, 447, 457, 505; Tiedemann, *Sechs Jahre*, p. 62. In 1876 Christoph von Tiedemann found in Bismarck's study at Varzin works by Spielhagen, Luise Mühlbach (a prolific writer of historical novels), and Count Putlitz (a counselor of Crown Prince Friedrich Wilhelm who wrote one-act comedies). Tiedemann, *Sechs Jahre*, p. 62.

[21] Keudell, *Bismarck*, pp. 61–68; Poschinger, ed., *Bismarck-Portefeuille*, IV, 98; "Bismarcks Persönlichkeit: Ungedruckte persönliche Erinnerungen," *Süddeutsche Monatshefte*, 19 (1921), pp. 110, 120. The editor of *Süddeutsche Monatshefte* did not reveal the name of the author of this memoir, and I have not been successful in identifying him. The document, however, has the ring of authenticity.

years in Frankfurt am Main, he replied (1884), "He had no need of me, nor I of him. I have never had time or cause to concern myself with philosophy. When I was at the university, Schopenhauer was not yet known. I know nothing of his system." After the concept of the primacy of will over intellect had been explained to him, he replied, "That may be right. At least I have often noticed that my will had decided before my thoughts were finished."[22]

The most significant developments in German intellectual life during the middle decades of the century were in the fields of historical writing and scientific theory rather than in literature and philosophy. Bent on diversion rather than information, the chancellor appears to have read less history than in earlier years. In a discussion of French literature in 1884 (in which he spoke of an early interest in the romantic poet Pierre de Béranger), he judged that Hippolyte Taine was superior to "the majority of recent German historians. . . . There are two sorts of historians: one kind makes the waters of the past clear so that one can see to the bottom; the other makes the water muddy. To the first belongs Taine, to the second [Heinrich von] Sybel."[23] How much he read of Ranke is difficult to determine, but he possessed and evidently read parts of *Die römischen Päpste* (seventh edition, published in 1878), *Die englische Geschichte*, and *Die Weltgeschichte* ("*Der alte Ranke ist doch ein Esel*"). The two men knew each other for more than forty years, and on Ranke's death in 1886 Bismarck wrote of him with affection and respect (nurtured by the coincidence of their political views).[24] Heinrich von Treitschke he valued as a publicist and staunch supporter of his policies after 1866, but ultimately as a historian as well. Of the five volumes of Treitschke's *Geschichte Deutschlands im neunzehnten Jahrhundert*, he found the last covering the period 1840–1848, to be "masterfully written." Bismarck even found some time for the *Römische Geschichte* of Theodor Mommsen, the only major German scholar to oppose him openly after 1871. In 1880 he read at least some of Johannes Janssen's *Geschichte des deutschen Volkes seit dem Ausgang des Mittelalters*. "It is quite interesting to read about the age of the Reformation as described by an opponent of it. Furthermore, the work is very well written. Naturally Luther appears here in a very different light." No more than in earlier years did he read systematically; he leafed the pages until some passage caught his attention, moving on when his interest lagged.[25]

The widespread popular interest in scientific theory characteristic of the second half of the century seems to have affected Bismarck minimally. Busch chanced to record in 1888 that Darwin was held in "high esteem by the

---

[22] Tiedemann, *Sechs Jahre*, pp. 14–15; GW, VIII, 504; Lucius, *Bismarck-Erinnerungen*, p. 137.
[23] GW, VIII, 504.
[24] GW, VIII, 498; XIV, 593, 853, 934, 969; Maria Fehling, *Bismarcks Geschichtskenntnis* (Stuttgart, 1922), pp. 74–79, 96–99.
[25] GW, VIII, 383. Fehling, *Geschichtskenntnis*, pp. 79–80.

chief,"[26] but it is not clear whether Bismarck read any of the works of Darwin or of Darwin's numerous popularizers. More than likely he merely heard the theory of evolution discussed. Certainly Darwin's influence may be seen in Bismarck's theorizing about the value and inevitability of struggle among the species. If he read Ludwig Büchner's *Kraft und Stoff*, the popular work from which the reading public gained its knowledge of the new developments in physics, he never wrote or (so far as the record shows) spoke of it. Nor did the technological developments of the century seem to interest him greatly, although he did consent to demonstrations of the telephone at Varzin in 1877 and Edison's phonograph ("a very clever instrument") at Friedrichsruh in 1889.[27] The growth of science and technology and their application in the industrial revolution were rapidly transforming Bismarck's world, but his intellectual interests remained largely those of an educated aristocrat of the old regime.

Appearance and Manner

In his memoirs Lucius von Ballhausen described Bismarck as he appeared in the Prussian Chamber of Deputies in 1863 at the height of the constitutional conflict. "At that time he still wore civilian dress; his bushy mustache was still red-blonde like his hair, which he still had, although it was even then sparse. His tall, broad-shouldered figure at the ministers' bench appeared powerful and impressive. There was something provocative about the nonchalance of his bearing, gestures, and way of speaking. He held his right hand in the pocket of his brightly colored trousers, and his manner reminded me strongly of the 'crowing seconds' at Heidelberg student duels. In speaking he already at that time appeared to search for words in long drawn-out sentences and always found the most effective ones, giving quick, striking responses. The impression he made on me was Junker-like, yet highly forceful, like an old corps student—particularly the way in which, with seeming good humor, he pumped malice into his agitated opponents." As the years advanced, the hairline receded to an outer gray-white fringe; the mustache gave way for a time in the early 1880s to a luxuriant full beard. His carriage remained erect and his gait military, despite increasing age and weight; nor did time change the irregular speech pattern, the rapier-like stroke, the mixture of humor and acerbity, the arrogance and condescension.[28]

After attaining the rank of major general in 1866 Bismarck always wore the white uniform of the cuirassiers while in Berlin—not always correctly to

[26] Busch, *Tagebuchblätter*, III, 259.

[27] Tiedemann, *Sechs Jahre*, p. 217; GW, VIII, 664–665.

[28] Lucius, *Bismarck-Erinnerungen*, pp. 1–2. For other descriptions of Bismarck see GW, VII, 163, 231, 236–237, 309, 380; VIII, 23–24, 192–193, 258, 264–265, 539; and BP, I, 141; II, 283–284.

Moltke's amusement. He valued the promotion, so he told Tiedemann, because the closed neck of the general's uniform freed him from the daily struggle with starched collars; to Keudell he explained that the high collar protected his throat and prevented colds. But the garment had other uses. Wilhelm was a soldier at heart, and Bismarck liked to stress that he was just a royal officer doing his duty in the service of the king.[29] The uniform, moreover, projected a more formidable image before his colleagues and parliamentary deputies. At any rate Bismarck did not wear it at Varzin, Friedrichsruh, Bad Kissingen, or Bad Gastein. There his customary attire was a long black coat, white neckerchief, and an enormous wide-brimmed felt hat. His forester at Friedrichsruh described him as he appeared in the woods one day in November 1883: "Slick raincoat, high boots, hunting cap with large bill, spectacles, officer's white gloves, long cane, accompanied by his dog Tyras—picturesque!" Only once, according to Tiedemann, did he ever attempt to wear formal civilian attire—with grotesque results: double breasted morning coat, "antediluvian" stand-up collar (popularly known as *Vatermörder*), and an enormous cylinder hat. His wife was dismayed.[30]

Those who saw Bismarck never forgot the massive head with its arched forehead and energetic chin, bushy eyebrows, drooping mustache, and large protruding eyes. Undoubtedly the eyes were his dominant feature. They mirrored his swiftly changing moods, alternately stern and forbidding, smiling and lively. Visitors meeting him for the first time were impressed by his courtesy and congeniality, but felt uncomfortable under the searching gaze. "The prince surveyed me with a glance that seemed to bore right through my head," was a typical reaction. The smile that played on his lips was genial, yet easily transformed by a slight shift of the mouth into one of devastating irony.[31] When well, his physique and manner exuded vigor, strength, and self-confidence. The effect of his bulldog appearance was heightened by the mastiffs (Sultan and Flora, later Tyras and Rebecca) that accompanied him on his walks in the country and stood guard at his office in the Wilhelmstrasse. On occasion Tyras, who was particularly savage, terrified servants, visitors (Gorchakov!), and even Johanna.[32]

---

[29] GW, VII, 177, 288, 309; Tiedemann, *Sechs Jahre*, pp. 480–481; Keudell, *Bismarck*, p. 386; Lucius, *Bismarck-Erinnerungen*, p. 4; Kohl, ed., *Anhang*, I, 233–234; BP, I, 26–27.

[30] GW, VIII, 489; Tiedemann, *Sechs Jahre*, p. 481. Bismarck was evidently sensitive about his shortsightedness. He did not wear spectacles in public (at most a lorgnette) and was never photographed or painted wearing them. "In Friedrichsruh," he quipped, "I always wear spectacles, for everything I see interests me; in Berlin, I never wear them because nothing there interests me." GW, VIII, 449. For the lorgnette see BP, I, 141.

[31] GW, VII, 163, 231; VIII, 23, 644; Ernst Feder, ed., *Bismarcks grosses Spiel: Die geheimen Tagebücher Ludwig Bambergers* (Frankfurt, 1933), p. 298.

[32] GW, VIII, 26, 627; BP, I, 144, 203–204; Arthur von Brauer, *Im Dienste Bismarcks* (Berlin, 1936), p. 99; Tiedemann, *Sechs Jahre*, p. 416; Busch, *Secret Pages*, II, 181, 252. The death of Sultan in 1877, after a severe punishment from Bismarck's hand, was a personal tragedy for

BISMARCK WITH TYRAS AND REBECCA, RETURNING FROM A WALK IN THE FOREST AT FRIEDRICHSRUH.

Bismarck's portraits and photographs were many, and the line-drawings derived either from them or from life and published in scores of newspapers and
magazines made his image well known to millions. His image stared from the
walls of innumerable homes, along with those of the Kaiser and Moltke (not
only in Germany, but also as far off as the author's ancestral home in Tennes-
see). In those depictions the public saw the same massive head and piercing
eyes that impressed his visitors but none of the humor and geniality they reported. The expression frozen by camera and brush is invariably unsmiling,
forceful, and autocratic—the blood and iron Bismarck. "There is no good
picture of me," Bismarck once complained. "Actually I have a dreamy, sentimental nature."[33] But what the pictures portray is what the photographers
and artists saw. If dreamy and sentimental, he did not project it.

Most of Bismarck's guests found him a fascinating conversationalist. "If the
point does not lie in the words, it lies in the tone. *That* one has to hear and
to have heard. What he says is full of shadings, colors, allusions, innuendoes,
and refinements that one cannot recapitulate. The voice, demeanor, well-
calculated pauses—all have the effect of giving emphasis to the thought he
wishes to express. One moment he strikes a jolly tone, the next moment he
becomes serious or acts so at least."[34] This description by an Italian who visited Bismarck only once is matched by one from Baroness von Spitzemberg
who saw him often. "I only wish I could write down what all my forceful friend
revealed in all kinds of little remarks, jokes, and sudden insights—momen-
tarily very serious, even melancholic, then harsh and vital, then mild again,
amiable, wise, and tolerant of mankind's weaknesses, if not of men themselves. The apparent contradictions in this powerful personality have an intense magic that always captivates anew."[35] On social occasions Bismarck
loved to relate details about his experiences at crucial moments in his career,
such as the revolution of 1848, his clashes with the Austrian envoys at Frankfurt, his interview with Wilhelm at the time of his appointment in 1862, the
military and diplomatic campaigns of 1866 and 1870–1871. Strangers were
often astonished at how casually he seemed to speak about seemingly sensitive
political matters, particularly about his relationship to the king and royal family. Many guests found him a "jovial" and considerate host full of entertaining

---

Bismarck, one that seems to have affected him more deeply than any other personal loss of his
adult life. Tiedemann, *Sechs Jahre*, pp. 211–212. When Tyras died in 1889, Bismarck did not
have the heart to tell his wife, leading her to believe that the animal was in the care of a veteri-
nary hospital. GW, XIV, 992–994. To Bismarck's distress Wilhelm II presented him with a woe-
ful substitute for Tyras: "a caricature of a dog, with a huge head, watery eyes, lean body, small
chest, completely without pedigree, not at all comparable to the elegant Rebecca." But Bismarck
resisted the temptation to have the animal put away; "he is so fond of me and has such good,
faithful eyes." Dec. 5, 1889. Spitzemberg, *Tagebuch*, p. 265.

[33] Lucius, *Bismarck-Erinnerungen*, p. 56.
[34] GW, VIII, 591.
[35] Spitzemberg, *Tagebuch*, p. 238.

stories. Some were less entranced, noting that he tended to turn the conversation into a monologue and that his stories usually centered on his own achievements and the follies of others.[36]

In writing his memoirs, Christoph von Tiedemann also found it difficult to describe the very complicated character of the man with whom he was closely associated for six years. "He was certainly a man poured from a single mold and yet the most astonishing contradictions fought each other in him." Even the sycophantic Moritz Busch was compelled to admit that at times, when looking back on his achievements, Bismarck seemed to feel like "God the father on the seventh day. . . . But he also has softer moments—moments of apparent dissatisfaction with his achievements and his fate." One such moment came on a Sunday in October 1877 when he reflected, "But for me three great wars would not have taken place, eighty thousand men would not have been killed and would not now be mourned by parents, brothers, sisters, and widows." "Faust complains about having two souls in his breast," Bismarck once said to Keudell, "but I harbor a whole crowd of them, and they quarrel. It is like being in a republic. . . . I tell most of what they say, but there are whole provinces into which I will never let another person look."[37]

Subordinates and Colleagues

No more than the artists and photographers did Bismarck's subordinates see much of the sentimental side he claimed for himself. "All of us had the impression when he took office," wrote Immanuel Hegel, "that he regarded us with mistrustful eyes, speculating whether we had been bought or were otherwise under someone else's influence. Once he became convinced that we who worked in the cabinet's secretariat were all honest people and good Prussians, we enjoyed his confidence. Still, we were all just instruments for his will; there was no room for a pleasant relationship." When Robert von Keudell, a personal friend, entered Bismarck's service in 1863, Johanna warned him that he must learn to distinguish between minister and friend. "They are two quite different people." Count Friedrich zu Eulenburg, Prussian minister of interior, admonished Keudell, "Your position with Bismarck will be very difficult; you can be sure of that. He is a forceful man and suffers no contra-

---

[36] For two examples of his candor with strangers see: GW, VII, 232–237 (interview with Karl Schurz), and Lucius, Bismarck-Erinnerungen, pp. 7–9. After a parliamentary dinner, Jan. 26, 1873, Ludwig Bamberger wrote in his diary: "Although he had delivered two long speeches in the Landtag, he talked from 5:15 until 8:30 P.M. without pause. He listens only to himself and will not be diverted from the thread of the thoughts he spins out. He weaves into his fabric whatever suits him and lets the rest fall to the floor." Bamberger, Bismarcks grosses Spiel, p. 298. See also BP, I, 16–17.

[37] Tiedemann, Sechs Jahre, p. 480; Busch, Tagebuchblätter, II, 468; Keudell, Bismarck, pp. 220–221.

diction. He reduces those who have anything to do with him to obedience—
resist him however much one will." "I was at that time forty years old," Keudell wrote, "and had long been accustomed to draft official documents with
hardly any corrections by my superiors; but now I was reduced again to the
position of a pupil whose drafts seldom remained unchanged." "Whenever I
entered to deliver an oral report," related Immanuel Hegel, "I gathered all of
my wits firmly together, in order to be equal to anything unexpected. A relaxed, self-satisfied air was not appropriate with him, for one was in that case
in danger of being bypassed or run over."[38]

Bismarck's subordinates soon learned that he would accept neither advice
nor criticism—only information. "He always strove to learn, readily accepted
factual information, and remained open to the daily impressions gained from
commerce with others, from business, and from the press; but, if anyone
sought to give him advice, he was critical or negative." Friedrich Eulenburg
advised Tiedemann never to voice an immediate objection, even when aware
that an instruction could not be carried out; otherwise Bismarck would find
"crushing reasons" for his position and "no power on earth" would be able to
move him. Only later, when the counselor could claim to have made an attempt, would Bismarck listen to and possibly accept the objection.[39] Seldom
was there a word of commendation, even after an assistant had worked
through the night and executed a difficult task. Minor transgressions produced terrifying outbursts of anger, particularly in periods of political tension
or ill health. "I am still not clear," wrote Philipp Eulenburg, "how the same
person could sometimes hold himself so masterfully in check and yet become
at other times on scant provocation so unrestrained." Others had the impression that Bismarck, when angry, never really lost his self-control. "It's useful
for the entire mechanism if I get angry at times," he said. "It puts stronger
steam into the engine."[40]

Men of independent mind found it difficult or impossible to submit to the
kind of self-effacement Bismarck demanded of assistants. Kurd von Schlözer,
whose brilliance Bismarck finally appreciated during their association in St.
Petersburg, refused his overtures in 1862, preferring minor foreign posts to a
subaltern status at Wilhelmstrasse 76 ("I can't sell myself, hide and hair. I am
not the type to be a slave."). Hermann von Thile, who became Bismarck's
principal subordinate in the Foreign Office, found his situation increasingly
difficult. A conservative diplomat of the old school, he objected to the "im-

[38] Immanuel Hegel, *Erinnerungen aus meinem Leben* (Berlin, 1891), pp. 21–22; Keudell, *Bismarck*, pp. 127–129.

[39] Keudell, *Bismarck*, pp. 130, 254–255; Tiedemann, *Sechs Jahre*, p. 41.

[40] Eulenburg, *Aus 50 Jahren*, p. 66; GW, VII, 197; "Bismarcks Persönlichkeit," p. 114. When
no suspicion of personal animus was possible, Bismarck was capable of surprising restraint. In
1867 Keudell accidentally closed a train door on Bismarck's finger, causing a bloody and painful
wound. The chancellor did not utter an unfriendly word. Keudell, *Bismarck*, pp. 378–379.

morality" of his chief's policy in 1866. The minister listened quietly and then "came on like a lion," bitterly reproaching Thile for apostasy. In 1872 Thile again incurred Bismarck's wrath by opposing the Kulturkampf and the chancellor found an opportunity to force his resignation. Although Thile lived until 1889, Bismarck never saw him again and at his death gave no sign of caring. "Never regret and never forgive," was the motto he seemed to live by. Even his most assiduous amanuensis, Heinrich Abeken, to whom Bismarck was the "instrument of God," admitted that his chief was "sometimes very difficult to get on with." After serving Bismarck for six years, Tiedemann resigned fearing loss of self-identity. When Hohenlohe entered the foreign service as ambassador to Paris, Bleichröder warned him that the chancellor "has no consideration and squeezes people like lemons."[41] One could "live with this powerful personality," another observer concluded, "only by becoming either his opponent or his tool."[42]

Yet his subordinates felt the "demonic attraction" of the man and believed they were working for a genius. To Tiedemann Bismarck's various powers seemed uniquely "balanced" and "harmonious"—"capacity for comprehension, ability to make combinations, memory and decisiveness." "He arrived with wonderful sureness at the heart of the matter, however complicated and involved the problem. At first glance he knew how to distinguish between what was essential and what was unessential. . . . As soon as a presentation had been made, he gave his answer without pausing a moment to collect his thoughts. Never have I seen him uncertain in making a decision; he knew immediately what he wanted."[43] Basic decisions on policy, in contrast to the routine transaction of business, were not always reached with such rapidity. Behind the swift dictations that the chancellor gave to Bucher, Tiedemann, Abeken, and others often lay hours of reflection and ripening decision.

Bismarck's colleagues in the Prussian cabinet also suffered from his vulcanic temperament. Under the Prussian collegial system cabinet ministers were theoretically not the inferiors, but the peers of the minister-president. His success in molding the king to his will and his role as chancellor enabled Bismarck to establish an ascendancy over his colleagues. Yet he continued to fume at the "unusable old people" whom he inherited as ministers in 1862 and whom he could not "send away" because Wilhelm liked familiar faces.[44] They resisted

[41] Kurd von Schlözer, *Petersburger Briefe, 1857–1862* (Stuttgart, 1921), pp. 122–126, 261; Johann Sass, "Hermann von Thile und Bismarck," *Preussische Jahrbücher,* 217 (1929), pp. 257ff.; Heinrich Abeken, *Ein schlichtes Leben in bewegter Zeit* (Berlin, 1898), p. 423; Tiedemann, *Sechs Jahre,* 51, 436–437; Friedrich Curtius, ed., *Memoirs of Prince Chlodwig of Hohenlohe-Schillingsfuerst* (New York, 1906), II, 110.

[42] Johannes Versmann, mayor of Hamburg, Oct. 3, 1889. Quoted in Helmut Washausen, *Hamburg und die Kolonialpolitik des deutschen Reiches 1880 bis 1890* (Hamburg, 1968), p. 130.

[43] Tiedemann, *Sechs Jahre,* pp. 126, 485–486; Lucius, *Bismarck-Erinnerungen,* p. 137.

[44] GW, VII, 263.

his attempts to interfere in the affairs of their ministries and on occasion still opposed him on matters of policy in cabinet meetings. Bismarck rejoiced to see them go, one by one, often through his own conniving: Bodelschwingh in 1866, Lippe in 1867, Heydt in 1869, Mühler in 1872, Selchow and Itzenplitz in 1873. There were frictions even in his relationship to Roon, ending only with the latter's retirement in November 1873. Of the original members of his cabinet only Friedrich Eulenburg managed to survive until 1878—by outmaneuvering the chancellor at a critical moment in 1872.

The new ministers and imperial officials—Delbrück, Camphausen, Leonhardt, Falk, Achenbach, Friedenthal—were amenable to Bismarck's "liberal course" in domestic affairs before 1875. His change of front during 1876–1880 produced repeated cabinet crises that ended their careers. The tenure of some of their successors—Hofmann, Hobrecht, Bitter, Stolberg, and Botho Eulenburg—was short. Not until after 1881 was Bismarck's control over the Prussian cabinet secure. In Lucius, Boetticher, Puttkamer, Gossler, Scholz, Maybach, and Friedberg he found ministers both responsive to his will and sympathetic to his more conservative course.

By his own admission Bismarck's capacity for recognizing the achievements of colleagues was limited.[45] His instinct was to command rather than collaborate; hence he detested the Prussian collegial system that obligated him to listen to the views of others. "Whenever I want a spoonful of soup, I have to ask eight asses for permission." At cabinet meetings he was generally polite, but afterward couldn't resist making fun of the ministers, mocking the protruding lower lip of one and carefully clipped beard of another.[46] Ministers and officials who proved to be effective instruments for the execution of his policies were given some freedom of action. Delbrück, Falk, Boetticher, Maybach, and Stephan are cases in point. But when his policy shifted, he expected colleagues and subordinates to follow, regardless of their convictions. Why Delbrück resigned rather than accept the demolition of much of what he had worked a decade to achieve Bismarck professed never to understand.

[45] "I have only a limited capacity to admire other people," Bismarck wrote to Leopold von Gerlach in 1857. "My shortcoming is that my eye is sharper for weaknesses than strengths." *GW*, XIV, 464. In 1870, for example, Bismarck could not bring himself to thank Rudolf Delbrück personally for the privy counselor's formidable achievements in negotiating with the Reichstag, Bundesrat, and lesser states for German unification. He avoided the task by asking his wife to convey his commendation to Delbrück! *Ibid.*, p. 800. In later years he did manage to write letters thanking ministers Maybach and Boetticher. *Ibid.*, p. 946, and Brauer, *Im Dienste Bismarcks*, pp. 191–192. In 1884 Lothar Bucher complained, "I have worked under him now for twenty years, and he has only once (during the constitutional conflict) told me that something I wrote (a newspaper article) was good; and yet I believe I have written many better ones." Heinrich von Poschinger, "Aus den Denkwürdigkeiten von Heinrich von Kusserow," *Deutsche Revue*, 33 (1908), p. 26.

[46] Tiedemann, *Sechs Jahre*, p. 494; *BP*, II, 52.

That he could not extract regressive and protectionist tax bills from a laissez-faire minister of finance like Camphausen irritated and angered him.[47]

Bismarck developed the technique of easing or ejecting a minister from office into a fine art; harsh criticisms in personal letters, attacks in the public press, open disavowals in parliament, and even the threat of his own resignation. Not every tree fell immediately to his axe. Officials with good connections at court were hard to dispose of. Despite the chancellor's dissatisfaction, Albrecht von Stosch survived as chief of the admiralty from 1872 to 1883. To be rid of Harry von Arnim, German ambassador to France, Bismarck had to go to extraordinary lengths, eventually hounding him into exile to avoid prison. In the foreign service Bismarck was even less prone to accept opposition or contrary advice than in other branches of the government. "Like soldiers," he said, "my ambassadors must wheel and turn on command."[48] "I have lived through difficult times," he once complained, "because I have had no one with whom I could consult."[49] But clearly this was a circumstance of Bismarck's own making.

"He subjected the accomplishments of his ministerial colleagues to a criticism that often lacked objectivity," wrote Tiedemann. "In the case of greater political actions, he was accustomed to attribute the successes to himself, while attributing every failure to the appropriate minister." *Nunquam retrorsum* was his motto. "His self-esteem was, like that of Frederick the Great and Napoleon, coupled with a strong dose of cynicism and this led him, not infrequently, to underestimate friends and foes. He saw in friends only tools for his plans—chessmen whom he could shove this way and that way on the chessboard of his policies and whom he could sacrifice when the game demanded it. In enemies he saw only rascals and dumbbells. He could only use friends who completely identified themselves with him. He regarded them with mistrust the moment they permitted themselves to have a different opinion or to adopt a position contrary to his expectations. I have never found that he did full justice to an opponent. For that he was too impassioned, too impetuous, too belligerent. In this respect, as in many others, he was like Luther. Every attack, even the smallest, aroused him to counterattack, and he was always ready to repay a needle prick with a sword thrust."[50]

Not long after escaping Kullmann's bullet at Bad Kissingen in 1874 Bismarck wrote to the Kaiser: "Anger and hatred are bad advisers in politics, and I pray to God for humility and reconciliation."[51] This was an observation he

---

[47] BR, VIII, 272ff., and IX, 196; GW, VII, 373, and VIII, 250, 395.

[48] BP, II, 210; Busch, *Tagebuchblätter*, I, 237, and II, 405–407; BR, V, 339.

[49] To Eduard Cohen, July 5, 1883. GW, VIII, 474–475.

[50] Tiedemann, *Sechs Jahre*, pp. 495–496. He liked to remind his colleagues of his power, noted Stosch, but whenever anything went wrong he put the blame on them. Ulrich von Stosch, ed., *Denkwürdigkeiten des Generals und Admirals Albrecht von Stosch* (2d ed., Stuttgart, 1904), p. 121.

[51] GW, XIV, 861; Busch, *Tagebuchblätter*, I, 202–203.

often made, and the religious sentiment was undoubtedly genuine. Yet he had difficulty following his own advice. "It is a notable aspect of Bismarck's character," wrote Lucius von Ballhausen, "that he harbors so intensively thoughts of revenge or retribution for injustices he has suffered or believes he has suffered. In his sickly excitability he perceives much as unjust that the other party does not so intend at all."[52] Once on listening to a stanza from Goethe

> Selig wer sich vor der Welt
> Ohne Hass verschliesst,
> Einen Freund am Busen hält
> und mit dem geniesst.

he exclaimed, "What! Without hatred? What a tailor's soul he must have!"[53]

Bismarck's Health

One of the causes of the chancellor's choler was persistent bad health. During the constitutional conflict and the Danish War he fluctuated between periods of intense activity, when his energies seemed inexhaustible, and periods of near incapacitation, when he complained of headaches, neuralgia, and discomfort in his left leg. Keudell, his secretary in this period, was "never without concern about his health."[54] After 1865 the intervals of ill health increased in frequency and duration, reaching a climax in 1882–1883. He often doubted whether he would be able to continue in office and repeatedly tendered his resignation on grounds of ill health coupled with political discontent. His afflictions did compel him to surrender the office of Prussian minister-president in 1872–1873 and to contemplate the same step in 1884.

Two of his physical problems stemmed from injuries. Always an indifferent horseman—observers noted that he did not conform to the movements of the horse—he was in his early years a reckless one. Three of the many falls he experienced resulted in bad concussions, and one in 1868 broke three ribs.[55] Only one of these accidents left a lasting injury, caused more by medical maltreatment than by the fall itself. While hunting in Sweden in 1857, he suffered a fall that left him with a painful leg. As noted earlier, the mustard plaster applied by an incompetent doctor at St. Petersburg in 1859 destroyed a vein and nearly cost him the leg itself. In the following year complications—thrombosis, embolism, and pneumonia—endangered his life.[56] Periodically thereafter he suffered an inflammation and swelling in the left leg and foot that forced him to walk with a cane or confined him to bed and sofa. In

---

[52] Lucius, *Bismarck-Erinnerungen*, p. 129.
[53] Busch, *Secret Pages*, II, 320.
[54] Keudell, *Bismarck*, p. 194.
[55] Busch, *Secret Pages*, I, 221–222.
[56] See vol. 1, pp. 139–141.

1874 a would-be assassin shot him in the right hand, leaving it numb and weak. After that he was compelled to dictate many personal letters that he would have preferred to write by hand.[57]

In addition, Bismarck was afflicted increasingly by attacks of neuralgia, rheumatism, and gout (bringing severe pains to his hip, face, and leg), and by migraine headaches, varicose veins, and bouts of grippe, jaundice, shingles, and hemorrhoids. His most persistent ailments, other than the bad leg, were digestive disorders accompanied by severe stomachaches, cramps, and vomiting. Another frequent curse in later years was facial neuralgia (tic douloureux or trigeminal neuralgia), a piercing pain that came and went at intervals and for which there was no lasting remedy. During the 1870s Bismarck was often afraid of a stroke and in 1880 he believed that he had actually suffered one. We shall see that in 1882–1883 both he and his doctors believed that he had but a few months to live.[58]

While Bismarck had real physical ailments, it is apparent that his health problem was also psychological. His collected works, particularly his recorded conversations, are so studded with complaints about the state of his health as to suggest hypochondria. People who were often in his company during the 1870s and 1880s confirm it. "He was very sensitive to bodily pain and discomfort," reads one account, "from which he suffered severely, even to the point of tears. He complained a lot, at times in an exaggerated way. At such times he had a need for sympathy and loving treatment from those around him and grew bitter if he did not receive that in sufficient measure. Often he let himself be diverted by friendly words, jokes, and expressions of sympathy; then he forgot about his complaints. He had a very peculiar attitude toward medicine and doctors. He was very conscious of everything that affected his body, had himself regularly weighed and measured, always had a house physician who visited him every day and for a long period actually had to put him to bed. He had a lively interest in medicines and, if anyone had a headache, gladly gave him a powder. His chief ailment was a stubborn sleeplessness that was treated for a time with opium, later with paraldehyde, also with baths and wet cloths [Wickeln]."[59]

At a parliamentary soirée in May 1872 Bismarck described to his guests what happened on a typical sleepless night. "I can't sleep at all, regardless of what I try. I read then, get out of bed again, walk about in my quarters, smoke—nothing helps. It is often seven o'clock in the morning before I fall fast asleep. Then I often sleep until two o'clock in the afternoon. I know that my nerves are at fault—I left them at Versailles. The shameful part of it is that, when I can't sleep, I recall all the vexations I have had—and in in-

[57] Lucius, Bismarck-Erinnerungen, p. 44; Tiedemann, Sechs Jahre, p. 489.

[58] See vol. 3, ch. 4.

[59] "Bismarcks Persönlichkeit," pp. 114–115. Also Hugo Graf Lerchenfeld-Koefering, Erinnerungen und Denkwürdigkeiten, 1843 bis 1925 (Berlin, 1935), pp. 241–242.

creased measure—never anything pleasant. I find excellent replies to utterances that have annoyed me. This wakes me up all the more, and I don't come to a peaceful sleep."[60] Among the vexations that kept him awake, he confessed to Lucius in 1876, was the memory of injustices suffered at the hands of those rapier-wielding teachers at the Plamann Anstalt who "hated the sons of noblemen." "Then I get downright hot about that and dream in my half-sleep about how to defend myself."[61]

Hypochondria and insomnia were accompanied by gluttony. Those who could afford it probably ate more in the nineteenth century than is common today; yet even contemporaries were astounded by what they observed at the Bismarck family table. "The first time I dined at the Bismarcks [1875]," wrote Tiedemann, "he complained about not having any appetite. Then I watched with growing astonishment as he devoured a three-man serving of every course. He preferred heavy and indigestible foods, and the princess supported this inclination. If he suffered from an upset stomach at Varzin or Friedrichsruh, she had nothing more pressing to do than to telegraph the restaurant Borchardt in Berlin for a shipment of *pâté de foie gras* of the larger size. When this was presented at table on the following day, the prince would open a large breach in it with the first stroke. As it was passed around the table he followed it with jealous glances, the consequence being that everyone present remembered the saying, 'Modesty is a virtue.' " "When the dish came back to him, its volume only slightly diminished, he devoured all that remained. No wonder that after such culinary excesses gastric disturbances were the order of the day."[62]

In 1880 Tiedemann described an average menu at Friedrichsruh. Lunch consisted of "roast beef or beef steak with potatoes, cold roast venison, fieldfare, fried pudding, etc.," dinner of "six heavy courses plus dessert."[63] The final meal ("tea") came at midnight just before retiring, and obviously had something to do with the host's insomnia. During the 1850s and 1860s Bismarck was a chain smoker of cigars from morning to night. Early in 1879 he switched to a pipe, complaining that cigars didn't taste good any more. His lifetime consumption of cigars, he boasted, was "not more than 100,000," and of champagne 10,000 bottles. "During my diplomatic period I not infrequently drank two bottles of champagne at midday."[64] Bismarck was proud of his reputation as a drinker, claiming that in his youth he had been able to

[60] Quoted in Heinrich E. Brockhaus, *Stunden mit Bismarck, 1871–1878* (Leipzig, 1929), pp. 53–54.

[61] Lucius, *Bismarck-Erinnerungen,* p. 85.

[62] Tiedemann, *Sechs Jahre,* p. 484; see also Lucius, *Bismarck-Erinnerungen,* pp. 53–54; Moritz von Blanckenburg's comment to Albrecht von Roon in BP, II, 67–68; and Hans Leuss, *Wilhelm Freiherr von Hammerstein* (Berlin, 1905), pp. 43–44.

[63] Tiedemann, *Sechs Jahre,* p. 417.

[64] Bismarck to Rudolf Ihering, Mar. 28, 1885, in GW, VIII, 516.

down six bottles of wine without getting drunk or sick. According to one report, he normally drank wine with every meal (including breakfast—along with milk and lemon water), beer or sparkling wine during his afternoon ride, and beer during the evening.[65] The Bavarian envoy in Berlin, Count Hugo von Lerchenfeld-Koefering, recalled in his memoirs an evening when Bismarck, after having consumed "several liters of Bock beer" during a soirée, invited him to remain after other guests had left to drink alternately Jamaica rum and champagne, which were topped off at 2:00 A.M. with port. The host became animated and talkative, but appeared otherwise unaffected.[66]

What impressed Bismarck's guests alarmed his doctors. At age thirty-two he weighed 200 pounds (182 *Pfund*), which, since he was tall (six feet, four inches) and heavy set, was presumably his normal weight. At sixty-four he weighed 272 pounds (247 *Pfund*).[67] Naturally his physicians were well aware that his obesity and consumption of tobacco and alcohol had much to do with his other health problems. For years Bismarck was attended by a Berlin physician, Heinrich Struck, who feared as early as 1872 that his patient was headed for a complete breakdown. But Struck was unable to establish any control over the chancellor's habits, and in 1882 finally gave up in exasperation. While he had constant need for them, Bismarck professed to have little faith in physicians, their diagnoses, and their prescriptions. They were "dolts" who "made elephants out of gnats"; the reverse of what they advised was usually correct. Doctors, on the other hand, found him a poor patient. He demanded that they restore his health without changing his life-style. One who treated him in 1856 described him as "hysterical as a woman [*Frauenzimmer*]."[68]

[65] Busch, *Tagebuchblätter*, I, 381, 580; GW, VIII, 498; "Bismarcks Persönlichkeit," p. 121; Poschinger, ed., *Bismarck-Portefeuille*, IV, 95.

[66] Lerchenfeld-Koefering, *Erinnerungen*, pp. 242–243.

[67] Georg Schmidt, *Schönhausen und die Familie von Bismarck* (2d ed., Berlin, 1898), p. 5; Ernst Schweninger, *Dem Andenken Bismarcks* (Leipzig, 1899), p. 25. According to another source, Bismarck's weight (in lbs.) varied as follows:

Year	Weight	Year	Weight
1874	227	1881	255
1875	241	1883	222
1876	253	1885	225
1877	253	1886	227
1878	267	1887	227
1879	272	1888	227
1880	261	1890	227

Augustin Cabanès, "La Médecine Anecdotique: Bismarckiana," *La Chronique Medicale*, 5 (1898), p. 534.

[68] GW, VII, 264–265 and VIII, 22, 286, 389. Struck complained of the "peculiarities" of his patient, who treated himself but blamed the doctor for the result, barring the physician from his

In 1883, however, a young (age 33) Bavarian doctor succeeded where his predecessors had failed. Ernst Schweninger reduced Bismarck's consumption of wine and tobacco, insisted on sensible hours and proper exercise, and introduced a low-fat diet chiefly of fish, including herring, of which the patient became particularly fond. For the next fifteen years he attended Bismarck almost daily and undoubtedly prolonged his life. Both Struck and Schweninger profited from their relationship with Bismarck. The former was appointed head of the *Reichsgesundheitsamt*; the latter, professor of medicine at Berlin—over the protests of the medical faculty. In addition, Schweninger became a prominent society doctor, although never highly regarded by the medical profession.[69]

From the psychoanalytic standpoint Bismarck's relationship to his physicians is revealing. Unable to do without them, he was unwilling to submit his body to their regulation and control. Why he submitted finally to Schweninger presents a problem. We shall see that Schweninger arrived at a propitious moment, for in 1883 Bismarck was thought to have cancer and had been warned that his time was short. Schweninger succeeded because he had an instinctive feel for the psychological needs of his patient. Years later he confided to a historian what occurred on the crucial evening in June 1883 when he won the prince's confidence. "Bismarck was on the verge of a physical collapse. He believed that he had already had a stroke and suffered from severe headaches and complete sleeplessness. No treatment had done him any good. He mistrusted all doctors. A relative, [he said] had taken his life because of a similar disorder; 'That will also be my fate.' 'Tonight, your highness,' said the doctor, 'you will sleep,' 'We shall wait and see,' Bismarck replied skeptically. Schweninger wrapped him in a damp body roll [*Leibwickel*] and gave him some drops of valerian, telling him, however, that it was not a sleeping potion. Then the doctor sat in the easy chair next to his bed and took one of Bismarck's hands in his own, 'like a mother with a restless child,' until the chancellor fell asleep. When he awakened in the morning, the doctor still sat at his side and Bismarck could not believe that it was day and that

---

home (not unusual, according to Struck) during an attack of jaundice in the spring of 1870. Heinrich Struck to an unknown physician, Apr. 18, 1870. GSA, Berlin-Dahlem.

[69] Schweninger had been dismissed from the medical faculty at Munich on a morals charge ("stuprum in a churchyard under blooming lilacs"). On Bismarck's intervention he was "rehabilitated" by the Reich government and appointed to the Berlin medical faculty by the Prussian *Kultusminister* Gustav von Gossler. Schweninger's presence in Berlin was regarded as "in the interest of the Reich" because of his success in treating the chancellor. Lucius, *Bismarck-Erinnerungen*, p. 301. Schweninger regarded medicine as an art rather than a science and was skeptical of the results of medical research, which explains his difficulties with professional colleagues. See his *Der Arzt* in Martin Buber, ed., *Die Gesellschaft: Sammlung sozial-psychologischer Monographien*, vol. 7 (Frankfurt a. M., 1906). On his professional reputation see Sigmund Freud, *The Origins of Psychoanalysis, Letters to Wilhelm Fliess: Drafts and Notes, 1887–1902* (New York, 1954), p. 245.

he had actually slept the entire night. 'From that moment he trusted me.' "[70] Schweninger, it seems, became a surrogate parent. Whatever he lacked as a physician he made up as a practical psychiatrist who knew instinctively what the patient required. He resided for long periods in the Bismarck household, carefully monitoring what the prince ate, drank, and smoked, how he exercised, and when he retired at night. Putting the iron chancellor to bed evidently became a nightly routine. Once when the doctor was away, the prince remarked at bedtime to his daughter, Marie, "I long very much for Schweninger." While Bismarck often complained of the physician's "tyranny," he submitted to it. "I treated the other doctors," he joked, "but Schweninger treated me."[71]

A Diagnosis

In psychoanalytic theory gluttony, hypochondria, and insomnia have been regarded as symptoms of a depressed condition stemming from trauma suffered in early childhood that have been reawakened by some adverse event in the life of the adult.[72] Earlier it was shown that the most important personalities in Bismarck's early life—an affable but ineffectual father, a domineering yet distant and self-absorbed mother, and harsh and unsympathetic teachers— did not satisfy his emotional needs. To survive psychologically in an unempathic environment he was compelled to rely on his own innate physical and intellectual gifts. He did not achieve psychological independence gradually— by first relying on others and then emancipating himself from that dependence, step by step—but by a comparatively short transition. As a consequence, his sense of autonomy was both intense and vulnerable. It required buttressing both within (through self-control, personal achievement, and self-esteem) and without (through religious faith, a responsive home environment, and personal dominance).[73]

[70] Karl Alexander von Müller, *Mars und Venus: Erinnerungen, 1914–1919* (Stuttgart 1954), p. 79. The use of *Wickeln* (a layer of damp cloth covered by a dry outer layer) is a form of therapy still practiced by some physicians in Germany. It is believed capable of curing a variety of ailments. Schweninger employed it against insomnia, but its actual function may have been to suggest the womb. Valerian is derived from an herb and has tranquilizing properties. Müller, a professional historian, was in the habit of making notes of his conversations with celebrities and used the notes in writing his memoirs. Unfortunately these notes were inaccessible to me. Letter from Alexander von Müller to the author, Feb. 2, 1971.

[71] Ernst Schweninger, "Blätter aus meiner Erinnerung," in Arthur von Brauer, Erich Marcks, and Karl Alexander von Müller, eds., *Erinnerungen an Bismarck* (Stuttgart, 1915), pp. 203, 221.

[72] Hilde Bruch, "Psychopathology of Hunger and Appetite," in Sandor Rado and George E. Daniels, eds., *Changing Concepts of Psychoanalytic Medicine* (New York, 1956), p. 186; Sandor Rado, "Psychodynamics of Depression from the Etiologic Point of View," *Psychosomatic Medicine*, 13 (1951), pp. 51–55; Gregory Rochlin, "The Dread of Abandonment," *Psychoanalytic Study of the Child*, 15 (1960), pp. 451–470.

[73] See vol. 1, pp. 33–38. In this and following passages the author has benefited from the

Bismarck himself identified one source of the trauma that influenced the formation of his character. An aide, Friedrich von Holstein, wrote in his diary in January 1884: "The chief's uncharitable way of judging people and his inability to attach himself to other human beings were partly inherited from his mother, partly fostered by her. A pleasure-loving woman, she sent him when he was six or seven to a boarding school, of whose severity he often speaks. He has brought his wife to such a pitch of bitterness against his mother by telling these stories that Princess Bismarck often speaks of her with characteristic lack of restraint." Recently Johanna had remarked, "I hope the worthless creature is now being suitably tortured for it." An uncomprehending guest asked, "Whom do you mean, Princess?" "His mother," Johanna responded. "*Whose* mother?" "Bismarck's mother." The silence that followed was broken by the chancellor, "Yes, my pessimism can be traced back to my mother and the training she gave me as a child."[74] Appropriately this conversation occurred at dinner. Through gluttony the adult Bismarck compensated for the emotional starvation he experienced as a child.

In contrast to constant complaints about his mother and teachers, Bismarck reminisced rarely about the failure of his father to give him a proper upbringing. Yet we have seen that the father, who was socially inept and dominated by his wife, did not provide the young Otto with the strong, idealizable image that he required for the solution of his oedipal problem. This may have been the reason why Bismarck as a young man abandoned his intellectual flirtation with republicanism and identified himself so strongly with the aristocracy as an estate, despite his often expressed contempt for Prussian aristocrats as individuals. In the idealized social caste of the Junkers, with its long tradition of leadership in the army and government and its ethic of service and sacrifice, he evidently found the strength and authority that his father lacked. This view would explain not only Bismarck's choice of a career and his compulsiveness in pursuing it, but also the pathology of his adult conduct.

While his physicians attributed the "bankruptcy" of his nervous system to overwork, irregular hours, and improper diet, Bismarck himself attributed it

---

advice of Thomas Kohut and from the works of Heinz Kohut, "Thoughts on Narcissism and Narcissistic Rage," in *The Psychoanalytic Study of the Child*, 27 (1972), pp. 360–400, and *The Restoration of the Self* (New York, 1977).

[74] Norman Rich and M. H. Fisher, eds. *The Holstein Papers: The Memoirs, Diaries, and Correspondence of Friedrich von Holstein, 1837–1909* (4 vols., Cambridge, Eng., 1955–1963), II, 64. Another frequent visitor in the Bismarck household wrote, "The prince himself complained about his appetite, which he, as he once said to me, had inherited from his mother, who was a heavy eater." Lerchenfeld-Koefering, *Erinnerungen und Denkwürdigkeiten*, p. 242. Among his many complaints about life at the Plamann Anstalt was that the pupils "ate little and poorly." *GW*, VII, 465, and VIII, 207. Another pupil remembered the fare as plain but adequate. Ernst Krigar, *Kleine Mittheilungen aus der Jugendzeit des Fürsten Bismarck in der Plamannschen Pensions-Anstalt* (Berlin, 1873), pp. 20–21.

LUISE WILHELMINE VON BISMARCK IN 1823, WHEN SHE WAS 33 AND OTTO WAS 8. PAINTING BY
F. FRÉGÉVIZE. (ARCHIV FÜR KUNST UND GESCHICHTE, BERLIN.)

to political opposition. The first critical illness of his life, that of 1859–1860, had physical causes (an injured leg, pneumonia, and rheumatic fever). But its severity stemmed from years of frustration—the unwillingness of his superiors in Berlin to adopt the aggressive stance he advocated against Austria, his exile in St. Petersburg by the new-era government, and the decision of that government to seek a fiscal reform (liquidation of exemptions from the real estate tax previously enjoyed by noble estates, including Schönhausen and Kniephof) with which he strongly disagreed. The real cause of his nearly fatal illness was, in Bismarck's words, "an explosion of all the anger I accumulated during eight years in Frankfurt." Alexander von Below, his host during that difficult winter, agreed. The greatest danger to Bismarck's health, he wrote to Blanckenburg, was his profession. Bismarck had been accustomed for too long to concentrate his energies on "extreme thoughts and feelings." The cure was simple: "Love thine enemies!" This was the best "door" through which to release "the mounting pressures from the darkness of his sick body and the best medicine against the amazing visions and thoughts [Vorstellungen] that threaten to draw him into death."[75]

The foes that aroused in Bismarck this self-destructive anger were domestic rather than foreign. In the scramble of European politics he expected the great powers to further their own interests; this was the natural law of the European political system. Hence in 1866 and 1870 Bismarck rallied to endure the hardship and fatigue of military campaigns. His assistants marveled at the "well nigh superhuman" working capacity he displayed during the summer and fall of 1870. "C'est la guerre," he explained. "All at once I have nerves like wire."[76] The relapses suffered after both wars he blamed on conflicts with the king, generals, ministers, and political parties. What injured Bismarck most, however, was growing opposition from members of his own social class. Many Junker conservatives openly broke with his government on the Kulturkampf and other issues in 1872. Their alienation cost Bismarck many personal friends, Duz-Brüder, with whom he had been on intimate terms most of his life. They accused him of betraying his social class, of harming its interests and those of the monarchy, of violating the divine order and falling away from God. To Bismarck it was incomprehensible that conservatives would refuse to support the king's government on any major issue of policy. To deny support was like desertion on the battlefield; active opposition was treachery. The most savage attacks made upon Bismarck came from conservatives rather than democrats, socialists, or Catholics. Led by the Kreuzzeitung itself, they questioned not only his policies, but his ethics and his honesty.[77]

[75] Alexander von Below-Hohendorf to Moritz von Blanckenburg, Dec. 7, 1859. [Hans Goldschmidt, ed.], "Neue Briefe von und über Bismarck, Deutsche Allgemeine Zeitung (July 9, 1937), Vol. 76, Nr. 312–313, Beiblatt.

[76] Busch, Tagebuchblätter, I, 63, 268–269; GW, XIV, 780.

[77] In his diary (Apr. 1884) Friedrich von Holstein recorded Bismarck's own explanation of the difference between foreign and domestic foes: "In diplomatic affairs I fully recognize people's right to contradict me and resist my plans. The bear has a right to defend itself against me. It is quite a different thing if the bear (that is, a foreign power) bites me or if my dog bites me." Rich and Fisher, eds., Holstein Papers, II, 113.

Once before Bismarck had felt deserted and betrayed by conservatives with whom he had so often "eaten from the same bowl." In 1860 he complained that the conservative press did not defend him against attacks by liberal newspapers. "One ought not to rely on men," he remarked bitterly. "I am thankful for every impulse that draws me within myself."[78] In December 1870 he wrote to his wife from Versailles, "To be a minister too long and to be successful with God's help is to feel distinctly the cold tide of disfavor and hate rising higher and higher right up to the heart. One gains no new friends; the old ones die or back off in disaffection. Furthermore, the cold descends from above—that is the natural history of all rulers, even the best. Yet every favorable inclination requires reciprocity if it is to last. In short, I am freezing emotionally [geistig], and I long for your company and to be with you in the solitude of the country."[79] During the 1870s he withdrew into the circle of his family, spending many months of the year far from Berlin on distant estates at Varzin in Pomerania and Friedrichsruh near Hamburg. When in Berlin he seldom appeared at court, which he believed dominated by enemies, or in public, except for parliament and for the dinners and soirées at which he entertained members of parliament. His alienation from members of his own social caste was compounded by fear of assassination. During the 1870s the number of groups capable of producing an assassin grew steadily—ultraconservatives, ultramontane Catholics, Poles, socialists, and anarchists. After Kullmann's attempt on his life in 1874, Bismarck kept a loaded pistol on his office desk; in public he carried it "or at least a knife" in his pocket. Two policemen in civilian dress followed him at a discrete distance and patrolled his quarters at night.[80]

At his own hearth this beleaguered man found the sense of security and dominance that he no longer felt while among his fellow Junkers and his countrymen. Johanna von Puttkamer was a plain, pious, somewhat retiring person who contrasted sharply with other women whom Bismarck courted or admired. Laura Russell, Isabella Loraine-Smith, Marie von Thadden, and Katharina Orlov are all described, like his mother, as beautiful and spirited. (Of Otilie von Puttkamer we have no known description.) Yet his letters to Johanna before and after marriage in 1847 reveal a genuine emotional attachment; the earliest have the cathartic quality of a rueful sinner confessing the details of his misspent youth in the expectation of absolution. Three children were born in fast succession: Herbert in 1848, Wilhelm ("Bill") in 1849, Marie in 1852. He required of his wife what he had missed as a child in his own home—a maternal figure with warmth, simplicity, and dependence, without social aspirations or pretensions. At the beginning of his diplomatic career in

[78] Bismarck to Alexander von Below-Hohendorf, Aug. 22, 1860. GW, XIV, 561–562.
[79] GW, XIV, 800.
[80] Brockhaus, Stunden, pp. 116–117; Eulenburg, Aus 50 Jahren, pp. 132–133.

ISABELLA LORAINE-SMITH IN THE 1830S.
(COURTESY OF ALLAN PALMER.)

MARIE VON THADDEN-TRIEGLAFF, WIFE OF
MORITZ VON BLANCKENBURG, ABOUT 1842.
(BILDARCHIV PREUSSISCHER KULTURBESITZ.)

PRINCESS KATHARINA ORLOV, WIFE OF RUSSIAN DIPLOMAT PRINCE ALEXIS ORLOV. DATE UNKNOWN.
(FÜRST NIKOLAI ORLOFF, *BISMARCK UND DIE FÜRSTIN ORLOFF*, BECK'SCHE BUCHHANDLUNG, MÜNCHEN,
1936.)

JOHANNA VON BISMARCK IN 1855. (FÜRST HERBERT VON BISMARCK, ED., *FÜRST BISMARCKS BRIEFE AN SEINE BRAUT UND GATTIN*, J. G. COTTA'SCHE BUCHHANDLUNG NACHFOLGER G.M.B.H., STUTTGART, 1900.)

1851 he stated his needs eloquently in a letter designed to reassure her about the new life ahead. "I did not marry you in order to have a society wife for others, but in order to love you in God and according to the requirements of my own heart, to have a place in this alien world that no barren wind can cool, a place warmed by my own fireplace, to which I can draw near while it storms and freezes outside. And I want to tend my own fire and lay on wood, blow the flames, and protect it and shelter it against all that is evil and foreign."[81]

A search in marriage for the kind of nurture provided by a mother is a common phenomenon. Bismarck's problem was complicated by the unconscious need to replace both the mother that was (educated, libidinally desirable, and socially accomplished), whom he sought in various relationships, and the mother that was not (warm, loving, protective, with strong maternal instincts), whom he found in Johanna. One cannot say that he was entirely satisfied with his choice. This daughter of a Pomeranian Junker family was a country maiden of limited experience who knew little of the high society in which her husband aspired to make his career. "No one believes," he once said, "how difficult it was for me to make out of Fräulein von Puttkamer a Frau von Bismarck; I fully succeeded only after the deaths of her parents."[82] Many of his early letters to her testify to this effort, which, despite his claim, was never fully successful.[83] Beautiful, stylish, and sophisticated women continued to attract him. Although the encounters were platonic, one was not without cost. In 1865 he chanced to meet an acquaintance, Pauline Lucca, a celebrated opera singer, outside their hotel in Bad Ischl (Austria) and accompanied her at her invitation to a photographer's studio, where she had an appointment. On a whim they sat for a joint portrait, two copies of which he sent to Johanna. But the "joke" turned sour when the photographer began selling unauthorized prints to the public. Scandal threatened, and steps had to be taken to compel him to destroy the plate and remaining prints.[84]

Johanna's chief interest in life was family and household—her husband and children, their health, nourishment, careers, and general welfare. In 1887, her oldest son Herbert explained to his brother-in-law, Count Kuno zu Rantzau, the dynamics of the Bismarck household. Johanna was, he said, "composed only of a sense of duty and self-denial." She had deluded herself into thinking that she was born to serve husband and children. Even though she

---

[81] Bismarck to Johanna von Bismarck, May 14, 1851. GW, XIV, 211–212. See also his letter of Aug. 21, 1865. Ibid., 703–704.

[82] Quoted without source in Arnold Oskar Meyer, Bismarck: Der Mensch und der Staatsmann (Stuttgart, 1949), p. 86. See also Ernst Engelberg, Bismarck: Urpreusse und Reichsgründer (Berlin, 1985), pp. 367–372.

[83] Bismarck, ed., Briefe an Braut und Gattin, pp. 7ff.

[84] GW, XIV, 704, 709; Paul Liman, Bismarck in Geschichte, Karikatur und Anekdote (Stuttgart, 1915), pp. 97–98.

BISMARCK AND PAULINE LUCCA AT BAD ISCHL, AUGUST 22, 1865. (BILDARCHIV PREUSSISCHER KULTURBESITZ.)

enjoyed the theater, Johanna was reluctant to attend lest she neglect a family duty or be absent when Otto needed to talk to her. To him she never admitted any need of her own, even when he thought to inquire. Continuing self-sacrifice was a compulsion, and every lapse in fulfilling its demands left her with a sense of guilt. In earlier years she always had a "dame de compagnie," as well as nannies and governesses, to share the burden of running the household; but now, although old and weak, she bore it all without assistance—household accounts, correspondence with providers, supervision of servants, and the like. "Service" to her husband remained her only concern, and yet this too now had its adverse side. Even the smallest mishap in the household sufficed to arouse her to the point of unnecessarily involving her husband. For him the consequence was a sleepless night and passing health problem. "Papa is himself exhausted and in need of rest; he has too much on his mind to

WITH FAMILY AND FRIENDS ON THE ISLAND OF RÜGEN IN THE FALL OF 1866. FRONT ROW, LEFT TO RIGHT: PRINCESS WANDA VON PUTBUS, BISMARCK, HIS DAUGHTER MARIE; BACK ROW, LEFT TO RIGHT, COUNT ARCHAMBAUD-TALLEYRAND, PRINCE WILHELM VON PUTBUS, JOHANNA, COUNT MORITZ VON LOTTUM, FRAU VON ROMBERG. (ULLSTEIN BILDERDIENST.)

converse for hours on end with Mama on the usual subjects—Berlin gossip, Pomeranian relatives, old Frankfurt, etc.—as Mama does with her lady friends."[85]

Bismarck's likes and dislikes, his judgments and hatreds, became hers. When her beloved *Ottochen* waxed bitter over someone's conduct, she outdid him in vehemence, assuming the burden of his anger until he fell silent.[86] Sons Herbert and Wilhelm and son-in-law Rantzau became his closest assistants, attending to his personal needs as well as to affairs of state. Yet an intimate friend and frequent guest found him, "despite all love," not very interested in the personal lives of his family. "There is in him a peculiar aloofness [*Fürsichsein*] amid wife and children."[87]

While dominant in his own household, Bismarck feared that other men, like his father, did not control theirs. His collected writings and conversations display an almost paranoid suspicion of feminine intrigues directed against himself and his policies by the wives of statesmen, diplomats, ministers, and monarchs. In 1881 he bitterly opposed the marriage of his oldest son, Herbert, then thirty-two, to Princess Elisabeth von Carolath chiefly on the grounds that she was related to Baron Walther von Loë and Count Alexander von Schleinitz, whom the chancellor regarded as enemies in league with Empress Augusta, with whom he had feuded since 1848. Augusta he hated and feared to the end, making her the villainess of the memoirs he composed in retirement.[88]

Seen from the psychoanalytic standpoint, Bismarck's behavior in the 1870s shows that the emotional cost of his break with old friends and fellow Junkers was considerable. Their rejection of him reactivated trauma suffered long ago, exacerbated his health problems, and led him to seek at hearth and dining table the narcissistic supplies that his injured self required. Yet he did not abandon the political arena to his foes. His response combined regression with heightened narcissism. Within the refuge of the family, where his omnipotence was unquestioned, he forged the thunderbolts with which to strike down obstructions to his power and policies in the political world. But even here, surrounded by adoring people and constantly accompanied by a faithful and protective dog, his need for love and acceptance was unsatiated. Hence he ate and drank and demanded sympathy by complaining about his health. Bismarck was composed of more blood than iron.

Bismarck had a remarkable talent for converting handicaps into assets. He repeatedly exploited his bad health and nerves in order to gain his will over the king, fellow ministers, and even the Reichstag. At moments of crisis he often asserted that the frictions of political life were no longer endurable and that he, if opposed, would be compelled to resign, depart for Varzin or Friedrichsruh, and leave the country to its fate. So great was his ascendancy in German government and political life after 1870 that this tactic often

---

[87] Spitzemberg, *Tagebuch*, p. 218.

[88] For the origin of the enmity between Bismarck and Augusta see vol. 1, pp. 57 (fn.), 175. Other examples of Bismarck's paranoia on feminine intrigue can be found in: GW, VIb, 137, 139; VII, 151, 195, 197–198, 214, 692; VIII, 692; IX, 126; XV, 135–137; Busch, *Tagebuchblätter*, I, 439ff.; II, 303–304, 412–423; Tiedemann, *Sechs Jahre*, pp. 27, 214–215, 249–250; Lucius, *Bismarck-Erinnerungen*, pp. 28, 31, 91, 101, 110; HW, II, 38–39. See also Louis L. Snyder, "Political Implications of Herbert von Bismarck's Marital Affairs, 1881, 1892," *Journal of Modern History*, 36 (1964), pp. 155–169.

worked. Even severe critics of his domestic policy were convinced of his indispensability in foreign affairs. Objections were overcome, policies adopted,
ministers dismissed, counselors transferred, even parliamentary decisions reversed because the chancellor said his health demanded it. On the other
hand, Bismarck's frequent irritability exacerbated his relationships with colleagues, subordinates, and parliamentary deputies. Those hour-long noctur-
nal debates in which the pacing insomniac conjured up his opponents, rebut-
ted their opinions, and supplied them with malignant motives were hardly
erased from his consciousness by the rising sun and slumber of exhaustion.
They left him bitter and sharp-tongued, cost him the services of able subordinates and colleagues, and imparted a harsh tone to German parliamentary
life that was one of his more unfortunate legacies.

Bismarck's physical and mental state compelled him to spend long periods
each year on his estates. Varzin was ten hours (eight by rail and two by road)
and Friedrichsruh four hours by train from Berlin. While he was there, the
telegraph key chattered and couriers came and went. The chancellor liked to
believe that he could govern as easily from Friedrichsruh as from Berlin. Yet
his lengthy absences from the nerve center of the German government complicated further the very involved bureaucratic relationships, deprived ministers and counselors of the opportunity for quick communication and exchange of information, and often produced misunderstandings as to his
policies and intentions. Even while in Berlin Bismarck's ailments compelled
him at times to curtail radically his contact with high officials; for long periods
he communicated with them only through adjutants. Jangled nerves and
physical weakness often forced him to suspend work or to limit his working
day to two hours. During some years he seldom appeared in parliament to
defend his policies, giving rise to ironical remarks about the "mythical chancellor." His condition, furthermore, was the source of frequent, unsettling
rumors, such as the story that the morphine prescribed by Struck and Schweninger against pain and sleeplessness had made him a drug addict.[89] For nearly
twenty years his political allies feared and his foes hoped for his retirement.
Yet year after year, through crisis after crisis, he clung tenaciously to power
because he could not do otherwise. "He wants to remain at any cost," wrote
Roon in January 1870, "for the present and in the future, because he feels
that the structure he has begun will collapse as soon as he takes his hand
away—making him a laughingstock to the world."[90]

[89] GW, VIII, 709. Hermann Hofmann, *Fürst Bismarck, 1890–1898* (Stuttgart, 1913), I, 261–
262; Müller, *Mars und Venus*, pp. 80–81.

[90] Albrecht von Roon to Moritz von Blanckenburg, Jan. 16, 1870. Waldemar von Roon,
Denkwürdigkeiten aus dem Leben des General-Feldmarschalls Kriegsministers Grafen von Roon (4th
ed., Breslau, 1897), III, 159.

CHAPTER THREE

Wealth and Social Perspective

T O A LATER German chancellor, Prince Bernhard von Bülow, it was one of the great paradoxes of history that Bismarck—"the statesman who as no other had been a product of the German countryside, the squire of Schönhausen, and the dike reeve of the district of Jerichow, the man of whom his wife could say, long after he had become imperial chancellor, that a cabbage interested him more than all his policies"—had been the "instrument of industrialization. As the proverb says: 'What he weaves no weaver knows.' "[1] If one accepts Bismarck's image of himself, that of a simple country squire driven by an inexorable sense of duty to serve the state in an urban environment he hated, his career does appear paradoxical. But the image is inaccurate. More of his early years were spent in Berlin than in the countryside; he grew up a city boy, although not by choice. He became a rich man, but more through gifts and investments in stocks and bonds than through farming. While most of his wealth was invested in estates and rural industries, he was no stranger to the world of capitalism. Nor was he unaware of the progress of social change and what it implied for the stability of the old social and political order.

The interests of agriculture and landowners remained his primary concern; yet he responded to the needs of industrial capitalism and consciously promoted the social amalgamation of the Prussian nobility and upper bourgeoisie. He was also aware that his regime, if it were to endure, could not be based exclusively upon a coalition of propertied elites, but must also serve the interests of the small farmer, rural laborer, artisan, and factory worker. Yet his vision failed him when it came to practical policies to be followed in building the broader consensus of social groups and interests at which he aimed, a consensus intended to overcome the deep fissures in German society and to perpetuate the regime he had constructed. His failure stemmed from the limitations of his own experience and the perspective he derived from that experience, from his narcissistic quest for personal power, and from his incomprehension of the limits of coercion and of materialism in overcoming moral convictions.

[1] Bernhard von Bülow, *Memoirs* (4 vols., Boston, 1931), I, 66.

Bismarck's Fortune

In 1838 Bismarck left government service in part because of his low opinion of its financial prospects. He foresaw that he would be at least forty years of age before he could marry and establish a household, by which time he expected to be "dried out from the dust of the files, a hypochondriac, ill in breast and limbs from sitting." "I hold that the possession of a large fortune is indispensable, if one is to find any pleasure in the service of the state. Only then can I be in a position to appear publicly with the luster I regard as appropriate and, furthermore, be able to surrender easily all the advantages that the office affords as soon as my official duties come into conflict with my convictions or my taste."[2] Ultimately Bismarck did acquire a fortune that gave him the independence he deemed necessary. It was, nevertheless, his career in government that led to wealth, rather than the reverse. But for his services to the state and the connections that it brought he would never have been more than a fairly well-to-do country squire.

In 1887 Bismarck estimated his net worth at about 12,000,000 marks, asserting that in good years when timber prices were high, this capital netted him as much as 300,000 marks, in poor years nothing at all.[3] These estimates made to a journalist (not to the tax collector) appear to have been remarkably close to the actual figures. In comparison with his private income, Bismarck's annual salary as chancellor (54,000 marks) was small; he received no income from his other offices in the Prussian government. His expenses were also heavy, varying annually by his own estimate from 150,000 to 180,000 marks.[4] There were years when he spent far more than he made. In 1884 Bismarck's gross income reached 408,426 marks, his expenses 526,692 marks, leaving a deficit of 118,266 marks. That year his household expenses alone reached 119,500 marks.[5] Higher income and increasing capital permitted debts and deficits on a grander scale. His wealth enabled Bismarck to give some realism

---

[2] GW, XIV, 16.

[3] Moritz Busch, *Tagebuchblätter* (Leipzig, 1899), II, 220. In estimating his net worth Bismarck apparently forgot 1,000,000 marks that he owed in mortgages to Bleichröder! His financial affairs had become so complicated that it is difficult to be sure, even with fairly good sources, of his net worth and annual income. Although we know how much was invested in all of his estates—except Schönhausen I, which he inherited—it is difficult to know their actual resale value at any one time. Schönhausen II cost 1,500,000 marks; Varzin and adjacent properties, 300,000 marks. Friedrichsruh was worth an estimated 3,000,000 marks when acquired. During 1887–1889 his annual net income from the estates averaged 265,400 marks. By 1890 he possessed a portfolio of securities worth about 1,200,000 marks, which at an estimated 4 percent would have yielded 48,000 marks. Hence a private income of 300,000 marks (excluding salary) appears about right. See Fritz Stern, *Gold and Iron: Bismarck, Bleichröder, and the Building of the German Empire* (New York, 1977), pp. 280–303, particularly pp. 291 and 299.

[4] Busch, *Tagebuchblätter*, II, 595; see also the estimate he gave to Eduard Cohen on May 12, 1882, GW, VIII, 448, where the same figure is incorrectly given in marks rather than thalers.

[5] Stern, *Gold and Iron*, p. 298.

to his frequent threats of resignation in the 1870s and 1880s. The ways in which it was acquired and invested are important, furthermore, for an understanding of the perspective from which he viewed the problems of political economy.

Bismarck's father, Ferdinand von Bismarck, owned four estates located in Brandenburg (Schönhausen) and Pomerania (Kniephof, Külz, Jarchelin), all of which were heavily mortgaged. From 1821 to 1839 Ferdinand was an absentee landlord, residing in Berlin, living off rents paid by the leaseholders of these properties. It was a period of depressed prices and low rents in agriculture, and Berlin was fairly expensive. By his gambling, traveling, and high living, furthermore, Otto had incurred debts so "enormous" that he concealed them from his family. Hence he concurred in the family decision to leave Berlin. Otto and brother Bernhard took over the management of the Pomeranian properties in 1838, while Ferdinand assumed that of Schönhausen after his wife's death in 1839. On the father's death in 1845, the sons divided the inheritance. Otto received the two tax-free knight's estates (*Rittergüter*) of Schönhausen and Kniephof and, as compensation, assumed one-half of the real estate tax on the nonnoble estates of Külz and Jarchelin taken by Bernhard.

Bismarck's "flight" to the country did not end his financial problems. Kniephof, valued at 80,000 to 90,000 thalers, still had an indebtedness of about 38,000 thalers in 1847, while the burden on Schönhausen, valued at about 90,000 thalers, was 60,000 thalers.[6] Even if no new debts had been contracted, Bismarck would have needed most of his life to free his property from this encumbrance. Kniephof, too distant to be administered from Schönhausen, was leased in 1847. In November 1848 the master of Schönhausen contemplated selling the property "in order to put an end to all of my financial embarrassment with one blow." But apparently he succeeded in raising from a friend the 3,500 thalers needed to pay off a pressing creditor. This gave him time to negotiate another bank loan and to lease the estate (except for house and garden) in the following year. Evidently the lessees of Kniephof and Schönhausen knew how to make them pay, but not the owner.[7] Together the two estates yielded about 7,300 thalers annually, of which 4,000 went to the

[6] See Charlotte Sempell, "Unbekannte Briefstellen Bismarcks," *Historische Zeitschrift*, 207 (1968), p. 613; Bismarck to Moritz von Blanckenburg, Feb. 12, 1860, in [Hans Goldschmidt, ed.], "Neue Briefe von und über Bismarck," *Deutsche Allgemeine Zeitung* (July 9, 1937), Vol. 76, Nr. 312–313, Beiblatt. The estimated debt on Kniephof presumes that Bismarck went through with his intention to use funds acquired through sale of the inventory to reduce the mortgage of 45,000 thalers by 6,000 to 8,000 thalers. The estimate of Schönhausen's value is by Ulrich Küntzel, *Die Finanzen grosser Männer* (Vienna, 1964), p. 477.

[7] Bismarck to Albert von Below, Nov. 1, 1848. [Hans Goldschmidt, ed.], "Neue Briefe von und über Bismarck," *Deutsche Allgemeine Zeitung* (July 4, 1937), vol. 76, Nr. 304–305, p. 1, 1. Beiblatt. In 1858 Bismarck still owed 2,000 thalers to Pomeranian friends. Johanna von Bismarck to Moritz von Blanckenburg, late December 1885. *Ibid.*

GUTSHAUS AT KNIEPHOF IN POMERANIA. DRAWING BY BERNHARD VON BISMARCK. (ALFRED FUNKE, *DAS BISMARCK-BUCH DES DEUTSCHEN VOLKES*, W. BOBACH & CO., LEIPZIG, 1921, VOL. 1, P. 99.)

SCHLOSS SCHÖNHAUSEN ON THE ELBE, BISMARCK'S BIRTHPLACE. DRAWING BY CHRISTIAN WILHELM ALLERS IN 1893. (CHRISTIAN WILHELM ALLERS AND HANS KRAEMER, *UNSER BISMARCK*, UNION DEUTSCHE VERLAGSGESELLSCHAFT, STUTTGART, 1898.)

bankers, leaving Bismarck, now married and starting a family, with a modest income of about 3,300 thalers.[8] Election to the lower chamber qualified him for a per diem allowance of one thaler while parliament was in session. Yet he was soon compelled, in order to make ends meet, to rent even the house and garden at Schönhausen, where he had intended to spend his summers.[9]

As Prussian envoy to the Frankfurt Diet after 1851 Bismarck had an annual salary of 18,000 thalers. His new station, however, was expensive. In October 1855 he wrote to his brother that the entertainment (*dieser Saus and Braus*) expected of him in Frankfurt made it difficult to stay within his income. The transfer to Russia in 1859 brought an increase in salary to 33,000 thalers, but the cost of moving (10,000 thalers) was high; St. Petersburg was much more expensive than Frankfurt; and his tenure in the post (two years) was short.[10] Near bankruptcy, religious conversion, and marriage, however, had sobered Bismarck. His days of profligacy were over; he was determined to save and accumulate. According to the letter of 1855, he applied the lease money from his estates to the amortization of their mortgages. By selling *Rentenbriefe* (that is, bonds issued by a state *Rentenbank* created under a statute of 1850 to liquidate peasant obligations remaining from the abolition of serfdom) he apparently acquired capital with which to start investing on the bourse.[11]

At Frankfurt Bismarck acquired the financial services of Baron Meyer Carl von Rothschild and through him those of the Rothschild banking houses in Vienna, London, and Paris—the shrewdest and best informed investment counselors in Europe. The Frankfurt Rothschilds continued to manage the bulk of Bismarck's invested capital until 1867 when the end of the constitutional conflict made it safe for him to transfer his account to the Berlin banking house of Gerson Bleichröder. A correspondent of the Rothschilds in the Prussian capital, Bleichröder first became involved with Bismarck in 1859, when the latter needed a Berlin banker to receive and disburse his salary as ambassador to St. Petersburg and later to Paris. The Jewish banker continued to perform his function after Bismarck returned to Berlin as Prussian minister-president in 1862. While the financial services of the Rothschilds and Bleichröder were available to anyone of means, these private bankers were doubly conscious of the wisdom of looking after the interests of anyone with political status. With the proper alchemy political connections could easily be converted into gold. Even before he took full charge of Bismarck's account in 1866–1867 Bleichröder had begun to give his special client investment

[8] Sempell, "Briefstellen," p. 613; GW, XIV, 121.

[9] GW, XIV, 127, 165.

[10] GW, XIV, 502, 512, 520, 545.

[11] Busch, *Tagebuchblätter*, III, 74. Such conversions were common among contemporary landowners and played a role in financing industrialization. Harald Winkel, "Höhe und Verwendung der im Rahmen der Grundlastenablösung bei Standes- und Grundherren angefallenen Ablösungskapitalien," in Wolfram Fischer, ed., *Beiträge zu Wirtschaftswachstum und Wirtschaftsstruktur im 16. und 19. Jahrhundert. Schriften des Vereins für Socialpolitik*, Neue Folge, 63 (1961), pp. 83–99.

advice and to offer him stock options on railway and banking shares floated by the Bleichröder firm. By mid-1867 Bismarck had accumulated nearly 200,000 thalers (600,000 marks) in liquid assets.[12]

While Bismarck had become well-to-do by 1866, the dotations of 1867 and 1871 made him rich. The 400,000 thalers he received in 1867 was granted with the condition that it be spent to purchase an entailed estate. Since this did not cover the cost of Varzin, Bleichröder advanced additional funds (without interest!), which Bismarck repaid through the sale of securities.[13] On acquiring Varzin (14,200 acres with seven villages), he began to lust after adjoining properties. "Every evening," he told visitors in 1868, "I develop a passion to annex these estates; in the morning I can look at them calmly."[14] In the end desire overcame him. By 1874 the total investment at Varzin had reached 20,000 acres worth about 700,000 thalers (2,100,000 marks), part of which was raised through the sale of Kniephof to a nephew. Originally the Sachsenwald comprised 16,875 acres valued at 1,000,000 thalers (3,000,000 marks), normally yielding about 34,000 thalers (102,000 marks) annually. In order to establish a residence there he paid an additional 255,000 marks for the inn and park at Friedrichsruh in 1879. As at Varzin he could not resist further purchases, which eventually brought the total to 20,400 acres. "When a neighbor's property wedges itself into mine," he told Busch, "and I see a fine clump of trees on it that are going to be cut down, I must buy that piece of ground."[15]

This compulsive buying sometimes caused the great annexationist to pay too much for what he got and to accumulate new debts that burdened his income despite mortgages of nearly 1,000,000 marks provided by the faithful Bleichröder at low rates of interest and amortization. Two additional properties came to him without personal expense. In 1871 his wife inherited the *Rittergut* of Reinfeld in Pomerania, and in 1885, as mentioned earlier, a public subscription (supplemented by a gift of 350,000 marks from a group of bankers) enabled him to purchase Schönhausen II at a cost of 1,500,000 marks. With Schönhausen I the Brandenburg property now totalled nearly 5,000 acres.[16]

---

[12] Stern, *Gold and Iron*, pp. 96ff.

[13] GW, XIV, 725, 731–732; Stern, *Gold and Iron*, p. 101.

[14] GW, VIII, 264–265.

[15] Busch, *Tagebuchblätter*, II, 369, 490; III, 220; GW, XIV, 727, 729; Ernst Westphal, *Bismarck als Gutsherr: Erinnerungen seines Varziner Oberförsters* (Leipzig, 1922), p. 12; Stern, *Gold and Iron*, pp. 281, 290. In 1878–1882 the mansion at Friedrichsruh was valued for insurance purposes at 100,800 marks, its contents at 51,555 marks. After the expansion of 1882–1883 the building's value was increased to 132,000 marks and its contents to 60,000 marks. Other buildings on the Sachsenwald estate (*Fideicommissherrschaft Schwarzenbek*) were valued at 552,248 marks on the insurer's books. Lange to Bismarck, Dec. 25, 1882. *Bleichröder Archive*, Kress Library of Business and Economics, Harvard, Box IV.

[16] Alfred Vagts, "Bismarck's Fortune," *Central European History*, 1 (1967), pp. 210–211; Stern,

SCHLOSS VARZIN IN POMERANIA. (BILDARCHIV PREUSSISCHER KULTURBESITZ.)

SCHLOSS FRIEDRICHSRUH NEAR HAMBURG, FRONT VIEW.

By far the smallest of his major possessions, Schönhausen lay on the east bank of the river Elbe in Brandenburg's Altmark; most of it was bottom land and its rich alluvial soil was best suited for grain crops. In the 1870s Bismarck preferred to reside at Varzin. Located on hilly moraine left by the glaciers, Varzin's soil was sandy and marshy, suitable only for timber and potatoes. As an income-producer Varzin was for many years a disappointment. "In my financial affairs I have no luck, perhaps no skill," Bismarck wrote to his brother in July 1871. "At any rate I do not have enough time to concern myself about them. My situation was good before I received the first dotation. Since then Varzin consumes everything." The previous owner had felled far more trees than he planted, and reforestation was expensive.[17] The Varzin books were further unbalanced by an employee who embezzled more than 30,000 marks before committing suicide in 1877.[18] His disappointment over Varzin was one reason why Bismarck chose Friedrichsruh as his principal country residence in that year.[19]

To Bismarck's irritation the public gained a false impression of his income. By July 1871 he was receiving several dozen letters daily requesting "at least 20,000 thalers in loans." During the 1860s he had often responded to requests for help, sending Keudell with as much as twenty-five thalers to succor needy persons. But now *Bettelbriefe* were returned to the senders. The "handsome revenue" he expected to receive from the Sachsenwald would be gratifying, he wrote, if only he wasn't expected to live like a "prince." In view of his actual circumstances, the new title was a "swindle." Perhaps his oldest son Herbert, if he lived long enough and were more clever, could extract a princely income from the former domain.[20]

Since agriculture alone did not suffice to make his estates pay, Bismarck attacked his financial problem by becoming a petty rural industrialist—an activity that added a new dimension to his economic experience. Like other Pomeranian estate owners, he found it profitable to dispose of his potato crop as alcohol rather than food. By 1884 he possessed at Varzin two distilleries with an annual capacity of 179,604 liters.[21] The Wipper River that flowed

---

Gold and Iron, pp. 291, 301. For descriptions of the Bismarck estates see Georg Schmidt, *Schönhausen und die Familie von Bismarck* (2d ed., Berlin, 1898) and *Das Geschlecht von Bismarck* (Berlin, 1908), pp. 364–366, 382–383.

[17] GW, XIV, 821; Busch, *Tagebuchblätter*, I, 467–468.

[18] Westphal, *Bismarck als Gutsherr*, pp. 96–100; Christoph von Tiedemann, *Sechs Jahre Chef der Reichskanzlei unter dem Fürsten Bismarck* (2d ed., Leipzig, 1910), p. 216, gives the figure of 20,000 marks.

[19] Busch, *Tagebuchblätter*, II, 457, 479–80. Johanna also found Varzin remote and lonely. Rudolf Vierhaus, ed., *Das Tagebuch der Baronin Spitzemberg* (Göttingen, 1960), 209.

[20] Busch, *Tagebuchblätter*, II, 368–369; GW, XIV, 821; Robert von Keudell, *Fürst und Fürstin Bismarck: Erinnerungen aus den Jahren 1846 bis 1872* (Berlin, 1901), p. 129.

[21] GW, XIV, 981. Not four distilleries as reported by Vagts or six as reported by George W. F. Hallgarten. See Vagts, "Bismarck's Fortune," pp. 207, 215.

across that estate provided water power for three factories that converted wood pulp into paper. Constructed at Bismarck's expense in 1868–1869, 1870–1873, and 1875–1876, the plants were leased to the brothers Moritz and Georg Behrend, businessmen at nearby Köslin, who contracted to buy their wood from the Varzin forests at a fixed price. During the late 1870s and 1880s this enterprise was intermittently in difficulty. The brothers quarreled, boilers burst, a plant burned down, a flood came, and insolvency threatened. Yet Bismarck disregarded Bleichröder's advice to abandon the Behrends and even lent them money to keep the plants in operation. He had a good reason. By the 1880s these Jewish businessmen paid 78,018 (ultimately 87,105) marks yearly for the privilege of manufacturing pulp in Bismarck's mills; they had become his chief source of income at Varzin.[22]

Friedrichsruh also had industries. At Düneberg on the Elbe Bismarck leased to *Köln-Rottweiler Pulverfabriken* a site for construction of a plant to manufacture explosives—with the proviso that fuel be purchased from the Sachsenwald. Initially the lease brought the prince 10,900 marks annually, later nearly twice that amount. Whether this firm had government contracts is unknown; if so, there is as yet no evidence that Bismarck intervened to secure them. At Schönau, another Sachsenwald property, he constructed and leased another distillery in 1886. In comparison with Varzin, the Sachsenwald had easily accessible timber markets—in Hamburg, England, and the Ruhr. Be-

DIE HAMMERMÜHLE, A BISMARCK PAPER MILL AT VARZIN. DRAWING BY CHRISTIAN WILHELM ALLERS.
(CHRISTIAN WILHELM ALLERS AND HANS KRAEMER, *UNSER BISMARCK*, UNION DEUTSCHE
VERLAGSGESELLSCHAFT, STUTTGART, 1898.)

[22] Stern, *Gold and Iron*, pp. 293–295; Westphal, *Bismarck als Gutsherr*, pp. 48–55, 109.

ginning in 1878 Bismarck's best customer in the Ruhr was Friedrich Vohwinkel, a wholesaler at Gelsenkirchen, who supplied pit props to coal mines. In
turn, Vohwinkel's best customer was the Hibernia corporation, one of the
largest industrial enterprises in Germany. As a member of Hibernia's board of
directors, Bleichröder was in a position to influence its purchasing contracts.
Prompted at the appropriate time by Head Forester Peter Lange, Bismarck's
manager at Friedrichsruh, the banker intervened to make sure that Hibernia
renewed its contracts with Vohwinkel—at a good price in a falling market.
By 1886, Vohwinkel, who always paid on time and never made difficulties (so
Lange reminded Bleichröder), had paid "a full million" for Sachsenwald timber. That Bismarck began in 1879 to take more interest in the financial condition of heavy industry in the Ruhr was not unconnected with his own business operations.[23] An even more direct relationship between his business
interests and governmental policies can be seen in his reaction in 1882–1883
to the attempt of a prospering insurance company to increase the premiums
on buildings located on his Sachsenwald property: he seriously proposed to
nationalize all incorporated fire and hail insurers and moved the Ministry of
Justice to prosecute charges of insurance fraud. Nor were the terms under
which Bismarck advocated in 1886 a state liquor monopoly (higher prices for
raw alcohol distilled by landowners) unconnected with his own investments.[24]

Critics accused Bismarck of administering the Reich like an east-Elbian
estate.[25] While this was unfair, it is certainly true that his pursuit of a private
fortune shows the same personal drive to acquire, consolidate, and control
that he exhibited in public affairs. Recent research has shown that his personal involvement in the management of his securities portfolio was greater
than had been assumed. Bleichröder advised, but Bismarck disposed.[26] The
same is true of the handling of his landed property. He demanded from his
administrators detailed reports on such matters as the extent of acreage tilled,
crops sown, fertilizer used, timber planted and cut, the costs incurred and
prices gained. "A landed property about which I do not know anything holds
no interest for me, and the yield from a share of stock is higher than from real
estate."[27] If the yield was higher, the risk was greater and personal interest
less.

The tree-lover of Varzin and Friedrichsruh followed with keen interest all

[23] Busch, *Tagebuchblätter*, II, 457; Stern, *Gold and Iron*, pp. 296–298. Lange to Bleichröder,
Aug. 21, 1886. *Bleichröder Archive*, Box IV.

[24] Otto Pflanze, " 'Sammlungspolitik' 1875–1886: Kritische Bemerkungen zu einem Modell,"
in Otto Pflanze, ed., *Innenpolitische Probleme des Bismarck-Reiches* (Munich, 1983), pp. 169–175,
182–183.

[25] Küntzel, *Finanzen*, p. 496.

[26] See Stern, *Gold and Iron*, especially chaps. 5 and 12.

[27] Vagts, "Bismarck's Fortune," pp. 213–214.

that went on in his forests from the nursery to the sawmill. His long daily walks and rides had as their aim not only exercise and relaxation, but also the close supervision of the work of his employees. With the help of a forestry expert, John Booth, he experimented, not always successfully, with imported varieties of deciduous trees from Japan and America, particularly Douglas firs.[28] His choice of trees reveals his basic conservatism in most business affairs, "Pine can on occasion bring you a nice piece of money," he once remarked, "but it is apt to undergo great changes, and I prefer deciduous forests. The latter may be compared to Prussian Consols, pine forests to speculative stock." His greatest love were the *Schonungen*, stands of trees that were never to be cut. "I love the big trees; they are ancestors."[29]

According to one observer, Bismarck was not a good manager despite his attention to detail. Although parsimonious, he was the victim of waste and theft. The Bismarck household was "impractical and awkward," unequal to the demands made on it by his position and hospitality. The master resisted innovations, insisting that everything remain as it had been. He was dubious of technical progress, including the introduction of water pipes and electric lights. In building he had "little skill." Advised that a chimney design was defective, he built it anyhow—and was not particularly aroused over the resulting fire. Preparations for his frequent travels were usually delayed and disorganized, to the distress of his aides and servants. He was hardly aware of the inefficiency that surrounded him and took umbrage when anyone tried to bring it to his attention.[30]

Conflicts of Interest

"I am in a position," Bismarck wrote to the Prussian minister of commerce in 1877, "to observe the effect of our legislative and administrative labors because I belong to the governed, not merely to the governing and law-making class, and can personally feel the effects of faulty legislation." In Bismarck's terminology to be among the "governed" was to be a property owner; yet he despised absentee landlords and "coupon-clippers" who let others manage their wealth. The "governed" were active property owners, particularly agrarian and industrial entrepreneurs. "I am the only minister who concerns himself with his estates and knows the faults of our laws and all their chicanery," he complained in 1880. "Most ministers are people of the feather, not

---

[28] See Heinrich von Poschinger, ed., *Persönliche Erinnerungen an den Fürsten Bismarck von John Booth* (Hamburg, 1899); Hermann Lange, *Erinnerungen an den Sachsenwald* (Halle, 1909); and Westphal, *Bismarck als Gutsherr*.

[29] Vagts, "Bismarck's Fortune," p. 210; GW, VIII, 168, 581.

[30] "Bismarcks Persönlichkeit," *Süddeutsche Monatshefte*, 19 (1921), p. 120. GW, VIII, 352, 380.

leather."[31] His low opinion of the bureaucracy and of legislatures stemmed from the conviction that most officials and politicians had no experience in practical affairs. Hence he often intervened on every level of the governmental structure both to set things right and to prevent "too much governing."

Some of these interventions directly affected Bismarck's private affairs. In 1869 Itzenplitz irritated him by refusing to discipline petty officials in Brandenburg who, in executing a public work, dug a ditch across a Schönhausen meadow before asking for permission, which he admittedly was willing to grant. By 1886 he had more clout, intervening at the Ministry of War to prevent the quartering of troops at Schönhausen during military maneuvers.[32] His worst feuds, however, were with Pomeranian officials over his interests at Varzin. In 1869–1870 he complained successfully to the ministers of trade and agriculture over the conduct of the district governor von Götze in Köslin, who had defended the rights of lumbermen, who wished to continue using the Wipper for rafting, against Bismarck and the Behrends, who wished to dam it for water power. A few years later he got the Ministry of Education to restore a school subsidy, whose withdrawal would have increased the taxes on Misdow, one of his properties adjacent to Varzin.[33] When the royal factory inspector for Pomerania ordered the Behrends to correct conditions dangerous to their workers in the pulp mills on the Wipper, his diligence earned him an interview with the mighty German chancellor at Varzin. His superior, Minister of Commerce Achenbach, received a memorandum in which Bismarck questioned the new system of factory inspection as an unnecessary irritant to factory owners, whose consequences were certain to be felt in the next election.[34]

There are stories of similar interventions with local authorities in Lauenburg, the location of the Sachsenwald and Friedrichsruh. Acquired from Denmark in 1864 and purchased from Austria at Gastein in 1865, the duchy of Lauenburg was governed as a separate entity until its incorporation into Prussia as a county in 1876. Bismarck was its minister and for this service received a salary of 4,000 thalers yearly until he took legal possession of the Sachsenwald in 1872. During the period 1872–1876 he is alleged to have paid no property tax (assessed at 1,500 marks annually). According to another story,

---

[31] GW, VIb, 120–122, 218–219; VIc, 340–342.

[32] GW, VIb, 191–194, 309–310; AWB, I, 142–146.

[33] GW, VIc, 150. Erich Förster, *Adalbert Falk* (Gotha, 1927), pp. 626–627.

[34] DZA Merseburg, Rep. 120, III, BB, VII, 4, Nr. 1, Vol. 2, pp. 84–87; AWB I, 258–266. In the imperial archives at Potsdam is a cryptic reference to yet another intervention by Bismarck in behalf of Bernhard Behrend. The Prussian Minister of Finance Bitter reported that in response to Bismarck's inquiry he had suspended an order of provincial tax authorities at Stettin that apparently concerned the stamp tax liability of the Bernhard Behrend Company. Bitter to Bismarck, Aug. 28, 1879. DZA Potsdam, Reichskanzlei, 2082, p. 14.

he later intervened at the Ministry of Interior to force the local *Landrat* to abandon a tax surcharge needed to balance the county budget. On another occasion he is said to have opposed an increase in the tax rate to be used to hire a second teacher for an overcrowded school ("It is not necessary that the children learn more"). He is also said to have coerced the county government (Did the town of Mölln want to lose its garrison?) into presenting him with an island in an adjacent lake worth 5,000 marks and a public building in the Sachsenwald worth 40,000 marks. Roads chiefly beneficial to the prince's logging operations were said to have been constructed at public expense.[35] Whatever the cause, the Bismarcks were not very popular in the region; in 1878 Herbert stood for a Reichstag seat from Lauenburg and was defeated.

In his struggle with local authorities, Bismarck had weapons not accessible to the ordinary citizen. In 1881 he gleefully related to the Reichstag that, because he possessed the "latch to legislation," he had gotten Varzin transferred from the county of Schlawe, dominated by ultraconservative opponents, to that of Rummelsberg, whose officials were "more tolerant" toward his interests.[36] At the other end of the political spectrum Bismarck quarreled with the city government of Berlin, dominated by progressives, over its assessment of horse and rent taxes. In order to limit the latter, he introduced a bill in the Reichstag that restricted the assessed rental value of rent-free dwellings provided for Reich officials to 10 percent of their salaries. Although the Reichstag raised the figure to 15 percent, Bismarck was still able to save 115 marks yearly, a petty sum for a man of his means.[37]

Bismarck's biggest struggle against taxes, however, was with the income tax commission. Higher incomes in Prussia were taxed under a "classified income tax" assessed by a local commission elected either by the county diet or city council. The tax—3 percent of the assessed income—was hardly onerous.

---

[35] Helmut von Gerlach, *Meine Erlebnisse in der preussischen Verwaltung* (Berlin, 1919), pp. 41ff., and *Von Rechts nach Links* (Zurich, 1937), pp. 78ff. Gerlach was a distant relative of Leopold and Ludwig von Gerlach. His stories about Bismarck are mostly unverified and may be distorted or exaggerated. There is evidence, however, that Bismarck sought to punish the town of Mölln by withdrawing its garrison, ostensibly on political not financial grounds. See GW, VIc, 274. That such stories were rife in the neighborhood is evident in Ernst Feder, ed., *Bismarcks grosses Spiel: Die geheimen Tagebücher Ludwig Bambergers* (Frankfurt, 1933), pp. 335–336.

[36] BR, VIII, 368–369.

[37] BR, VIII, 353ff.; IX, 43ff.; Küntzel, *Finanzen*, p. 501. Heretofore the rental had been assessed by estimating what rental the dwelling would bring if privately owned and rented. Bismarck claimed that his political enemies (progressives controlled the city of Berlin) on the board of assessment had not only placed the figure too high, but had also overestimated the amount of space occupied by the Bismarck family in the chancellery. He objected to the horse tax assessment (three and a half marks) because he owned no horses in Berlin, the assessing official having estimated the number of horses by the number of stalls. Forckenbeck, mayor of Berlin, replied that Bismarck had failed to object to the estimate in the alloted time. His critics found it astounding that the chancellor of Germany should take up the time of the Reichstag with such petty matters.

Self-assessment did not yet exist, and the commission had no authority to requisition private financial records. It had to estimate the taxpayer's probable income in view of his real property and, in Bismarck's case, his government salary. Since 1865 Bismarck had been placed in the eighteenth bracket (24,000 to 32,000 thalers); in December 1870, while he was in France, the commission elevated him to the nineteenth (from 32,000 to 40,000 thalers). In March 1871 Johanna filed a "remonstrance," and Bismarck followed it up belatedly in July, protesting that even the eighteenth bracket was unjust. In October the commission relented and left the chancellor in the eighteenth bracket, evidently accepting Bismarck's estimate of his total income at 24,500 thalers (73,500 marks). A tax "reform" of 1873 introduced no change in the assessment procedure, but narrowed the brackets and extended them beyond the previous upper limit (thirty). In 1876–1877 the commission elevated Bismarck to bracket thirty-one (204,000 to 240,000 marks) with a tax bill of 6,120 marks. There he remained until 1890, after fighting off another challenge from the commission in 1880. Since he viewed all direct taxation as unsound, Bismarck had little compunction about cheating on his income tax.[38]

Bismarck's documented interventions are generally couched in terms of principle and the public interest. He wrote of the necessity of protecting property rights, of the dangers of abusing taxpayers who were also voters, using his own case merely to illustrate intolerable errors on the part of the bureaucracy that alienated the public. He explained the gerrymandering of Varzin and his insistence on a national rent-tax law as a justifiable defense against punitive actions by political foes, who wanted him to "atone in my private life for my sins as a minister."[39] Certainly Bismarck had the same right of redress possessed by every citizen in a *Rechtsstaat*. Yet he was no ordinary citizen, as his colleagues and subordinates were well aware. His critics may be pardoned for failing to see the distinction, so clear in Bismarck's own mind, between his roles as governor and governed. What to Bismarck was a defense of principle or an assertion of personal rights appeared to others, like Helmut von Gerlach, to be a misuse of public office for personal gain. As the novelist Theodor Fontane saw it, these traits revealed a petty side to the prince's character that cost him public favor in the 1880s. "This mixture of superman and artful

---

[38] Stern, *Gold and Iron*, pp. 282–283.

[39] *BR*, VIII, 369. In 1880 he complained to a visitor in Friedrichsruh about a proposal to build a railway line (to Altona) through the Sachsenwald, claiming that this would require his mansion to be torn down. If he intervened to advocate another direction for the line, he would be accused of costing the state money for his own convenience. If he let his property be expropriated, on the other hand, he would be accused of wanting a new mansion at public expense. *GW*, VIII, 380–381. Whether he actually intervened at the Reich railway office, as his wife urged, is unrecorded. The mansion stood until bombed in 1945.

dodger [*Schlauberger*], of state-founder and horse-tax evader . . . , of hero and howler, . . . doesn't permit me to have a pure, bright admiration for him."[40]

By the standards of his age, nevertheless, Bismarck's conception of what was honorable in a royal official and of what is today called "conflict of interest" was relatively high. In the recent past it had been common for statesmen (Metternich being a prominent example) to accept retainers from foreign governments. In private Bismarck accused two of his predecessors, Otto von Manteuffel and Alexander von Schleinitz, of being in the pay of Vienna and asserted that he had indignantly refused a bribe offered by an Austrian agent in 1859.[41] Yet his strong feelings on this score did not prevent him from corrupting others through the Guelph fund, particularly the public press whose venality he so often denounced. By Bismarck's time the greatest danger of corruption for ministers and officials was to be found on the bourse rather than in foreign chancelleries. In February 1854 Bismarck gave Meyer Carl von Rothschild advance news, gained by Foreign Office telegram, of the start of the Crimean War; yet he refused (without indignation) the banker's offer to speculate on credit ("Excellency won't risk anything").[42] He did sell securities in 1857 in the expectation, based on official information, that Prussia would attack Switzerland over the issue of Neuchâtel. But peace prevailed and the securities prospered.[43]

At dinner one day in early December 1870 Bismarck denied "the possibility of turning to much account the always limited knowledge that one may have of approaching political events. Such events only affect the bourse afterwards, and the day when that is going to happen cannot be foreseen."[44] Could he really have forgotten so soon that on Sunday, July 10, 1870, he had informed Bleichröder, in reply to the latter's inquiry, that it might be a "good idea" to unload the railway shares in the Bismarck portfolio and that on July 11 rumors of impending war had sent the Berlin stock exchange into sharp decline?[45] And did he not remember that on September 5, after news of Sedan had sent

[40] Küntzel, *Finanzen*, p. 503.

[41] Busch, *Tagebuchblätter*, II, 456. In 1876 Lucius recorded another version of what is evidently the same story, giving the name as "Lewinson (?)," instead of "Löwenstein," the amount as 30,000 thalers instead of 20,000 "or more," and the year as 1862 instead of 1859. In both accounts Bismarck requested that the offer be put in writing and was refused. Freiherr Lucius von Ballhausen, *Bismarck-Erinnerungen* (Stuttgart, 1920), p. 93. In 1866 Bismarck refused a partnership in a shipping enterprise—on curious grounds: "As to the acquisition of a shipping share, I would be quite ready to accept your proposal if I were not convinced on principle that I must decline all participation in mercantile and similar business." Vagts, "Bismarck's Fortune," p. 209.

[42] GW, XIV, 343.

[43] Busch, *Tagebuchblätter*, I, 451–452.

[44] Ibid., I, 467.

[45] Stern, *Gold and Iron*, pp. 128–129. Stern's evidence shows that Bismarck made no effort to correct Bleichröder's assumption that war was not imminent, and his instruction on the sale of the railway stock, dictated to Johanna, was couched in such a way as not to alarm the banker unduly.

the market skyward, he had instructed Bleichröder to sell "whatever you deem correct," knowing that peace, contrary to popular expectations, was still a long way off?[46]

In later years he boasted that he had been wise enough to sell his Russian bonds in 1874, when he heard that Count Peter Shuvalov, "the smartest man" in St. Petersburg, was being sent as ambassador to London. He anticipated "follies" on the part of the Russian government in Balkan affairs. But this was more "poetic hindsight" than foresight, for the Russo-Turkish War was still three years away. Bismarck's liquidation of his Austrian and Russian bonds in 1873–1874 appears to have been based more on general market conditions than on political predictions.[47] After twenty years of investing in foreign government bonds, however, he now decided against it on principle; "such things disturb the vision of a foreign minister and ought not to be."[48] Except for a brief and unsuccessful foray into Russian bonds in 1885, he appears to have carried out his resolve until 1889. "I want to interest myself in my own country and not in foreign securities," he told the Reichstag in May 1889.[49] But shortly thereafter he began to exchange his German government bonds for Egyptian and Mexican bonds. On March 8 and 13, as the final crisis in his relationship to Wilhelm II mounted, he liquidated the rest of his holdings in favor of more Egyptian securities. Did he speculate on his own dismissal? At any rate the Berlin bourse, which had declined for some months, plunged briefly on news of his departure, while the Egyptian bonds grew in value.[50]

All of these financial operations have one thing in common: they were defensive, aimed at the preservation of capital rather than its increase. Had he been challenged, Bismarck would certainly have maintained that there was nothing unethical about them. What he found reprehensible can be seen in his criticism of Manteuffel who used the foreign service to gain fast information on movements of foreign stock markets. Even more blameworthy was the deliberate manipulation of political events in order to influence the price of securities, a practice of which he accused Gramont in 1870.[51] One of the reasons for his anger at Harry von Arnim was the belief that the diplomat had delayed carrying out an instruction in Paris because of the beneficial effect it would have on the bourse, where he was speculating à baisse.[52]

The most questionable transaction in which Bismarck and Bleichröder engaged never became public knowledge. In 1875 Bismarck launched a major

[46] Ibid., p. 143.
[47] Tiedemann, Sechs Jahre, p. 197; Stern, Gold and Iron, pp. 286–288.
[48] GW, VIII, 383.
[49] BR, XII, 639.
[50] Stern, Gold and Iron, pp. 288–289.
[51] Busch, Tagebuchblätter, I, 467; II, 484.
[52] George O. Kent, Arnim and Bismarck (Oxford, 1968), pp. 83–84, 112, 116, 124, 181.

project for the nationalization of the Reich's railways, the details of which will be discussed in a later chapter. Although the proposal failed in the Reichstag, Prussia did convert all of its railways to public ownership. The intention to nationalize the railways was public knowledge, for the matter was debated at great length in the Prussian Landtag, Bundesrat, and Reichstag. To purchase depressed railway shares in the expectation that the price would rise before nationalization was a course open to every investor with the necessary capital. Still such purchases tended to stop the downward trend of railway stocks on the bourse and ultimately to drive up the price. Hence it was ethically dubious for the chancellor of the German Reich, who had advance knowledge of the order in which the lines were likely to be purchased, to invest more than half of his liquid capital in those railways, buying and selling shares valued at more than a million marks over eight years, before most of the major lines were finally in the hands of the government.

Bleichröder, who played an important role in overcoming bureaucratic obstacles to nationalization, also invested heavily in the same railway companies as did his famous client. To Albert Maybach, Prussian minister of public works, who was charged with the execution of the nationalization policy, speculation of this sort by insiders and well connected outsiders was morally outrageous. In 1879, during the Landtag debate on the first nationalization bill, Maybach denounced the bourse as a "poison tree" casting a fateful shadow on the life of the nation. Was the chancellor of the German Reich one of the poisoners? In percentage terms his capital gains were modest but sure—2 to 10 percent over a few months. He may well have rationalized the purchases on the grounds that by voting his shares for nationalization he was performing a public service. But in all probability he was not troubled by the problem.[53]

"Bismarck," wrote Fritz Stern, "would have felt that to ignore the intelligence his position brought him would be tantamount to self-injury. The idea that power should be resolutely unprofitable, that public and private interests might be incompatible because the latter might corrupt the former, did not occur to Bismarck or to other nineteenth-century giants. Power, they knew, brought pain and tribulation as well as exhilaration and possible fame; it certainly should command deference and loyalty, and if these proved profitable, *tant mieux*. Profit was no threat to their integrity nor impoverishment an acceptable reward for service to king and country."[54]

Diplomacy was not the only channel through which a statesman or official could exploit the bourse for private gain. Many officials, lords, and deputies participated in the wild speculation of the *Gründerjahre* (1870–1873), and some used their bureaucratic and political influence to profit from railway con-

[53] Stern, *Gold and Iron*, pp. 208–217.
[54] Ibid., p. 105.

cessions and the licensing of joint-stock companies. In Reichstag speeches in
January and February 1873 Eduard Lasker brought the scandal to public attention, months before the crash proved that many of these ventures were dubious. The consequence was that several accused officials were compelled to
resign, including notably Hermann Wagener. During the following years rumors spread that the dimensions of the scandal were even greater than Lasker
had shown; eventually they surfaced in articles published by Franz Perrot in
the *Kreuzzeitung* (the "era articles" of June 1875), pamphlets written by Otto
von Diest-Daber (September–November 1876), articles in the weekly *Die
deutsche Reichsglocke* (October 1876), and the writings of Rudolph Meyer
(1876–1877).[55]

From evidence recently made available in the Bleichröder papers, it appears that Bismarck did not participate in the speculative orgy of the *Gründerjahre*. Under Bleichröder's guidance he preferred conservative purchases
whose resale turned a modest but persistent profit. The most serious accusation leveled against him by the scandalmongers of the late 1870s was that a
consortium of bankers, including Bleichröder, had rewarded him for his help
in chartering the *Preussische Central-Boden-Credit-Aktiengesellschaft* founded
in 1870 by granting him a stock option (1,000,000 thalers worth of shares)
that produced a windfall profit of 83,000 thalers. There followed a series of
sensational trials for libel (January and February 1877), which ended in judgments against Diest-Daber, Meyer, and two editors of *Reichsglocke*, all of
whom were sentenced to several months in prison. In addition, Diest-Daber,
a prominent Junker, was dismissed from the officer corps.[56]

Although the principal accusation was untrue, these trials did make public
for the first time important details about Bismarck's financial dealings and his
relationship to Gerson Bleichröder. Later in this chapter it will be shown that
the chancellor did promote the founding of *Boden-Credit*, whose charter gave
it a privileged position among German mortgage banks. Modeled on the *Crédit foncier de France*, the bank was established to supply credit to agrarian
landowners. While funded by private capital, its president was appointed and
its directors were confirmed by the Prussian government. Undoubtedly there
was need for such an enterprise, for the absorption of German capital in industrial enterprises during the 1860s had limited the credit available in agriculture. Its needs could not be met by provincial state banks (*Landschaften*)
and private mortgage banks. Not subject to the same legal restrictions, *Boden-
Credit* could issue loans more speedily and on better terms than ordinary banks
engaged in the same business.

Since he was both Bismarck's personal banker and a member of the bankers'

[55] See Gordon R. Mork, "The Prussian Railway Scandal of 1873: Economics and Politics in
the German Empire," *European Studies Review*, 1 (1971), pp. 35ff.

[56] Siegfried von Kardorff, *Wilhelm von Kardorff: Ein nationaler Parlamentarier im Zeitalter Bismarcks und Wilhelms II., 1828–1907* (Berlin, 1936), pp. 89–110.

consortium financing *Boden-Credit*, Bleichröder was called upon to testify during the libel action against Diest-Daber. The banker swore that the charges were false. "More than fifteen years ago when Prince Bismarck became a Prussian minister, he commissioned me to conduct all of his financial affairs. My task was to take care of all income and expenditures for him, to buy and sell securities and properties. I was instructed by the prince in all purchases of securities to direct my attention less toward profits than toward basic security. How little time Prince Bismarck found to care for his private affairs can be shown by the fact that he asked me some time ago whether he then owned or ever had owned *Preussische Central-Boden-Credit* shares. To be certain I ordered my chief bookkeeper to investigate immediately and was able to report to his serene highness that he did possess *Boden-Credit* bonds, but not shares."[57] While the mortgage bonds that Bismarck held in the amount of 400,000 thalers were an income-bearing, not a speculative investment, their purchase did represent a kind of "cut in" arrangement by which financiers rewarded favored customers.[58] Although not guilty of the charges made against him, Bismarck can be criticized for a "conflict of interest" that now, although perhaps not then, would be regarded as ethically dubious.

Support for "Traditional" Social Groups

As shown earlier, Bismarck's economic views were until 1851 the conventional ones appropriate to his background and financial interests. He was opposed to free enterprise, backed guilds, condemned property taxes, favored indirect taxes and low tariffs, distrusted joint-stock enterprises, and was generally anti-industrial and anticapitalistic. During his years in the bustling commercial and financial center at Frankfurt, he came to appreciate the political gains Prussia could make by favoring the interests of industrial capitalism. The renewal of the Zollverein in 1853 without Austria's inclusion was proof that those interests could be harnessed by Prussia. The constitutional conflict of 1862–1866 awakened Bismarck to the political potential of the urban workingman. Yet the actual course followed by the Prussian government during those years was not hostile to the interests of German capitalism and may have contributed to the turnabout of *Mittelstand* attitudes in 1866–1867.[59]

Bismarck's adoption of a national policy required the positive cooperation of business interests over a period of years for the purpose of consolidating the union. The flood of legislation that passed through the Reichstag and Bundesrat after 1867 not only furthered that consolidation but also realized goals

[57] Quoted in Kardorff, *Kardorff*, p. 107.
[58] Stern, *Gold and Iron*, pp. 505–508; Vagts, "Bismarck's Fortune," pp. 220–224.
[59] See vol. 1, pp. 230–233.

that German businessmen had sought for decades: freedom of migration and settlement (1867); uniform weights and measures (1868); a common commercial code and a supreme court to interpret it (1869); an industrial code guaranteeing free enterprise (1869); uniform system of coinage based on the mark (1871); and a central bank of issue, the *Reichsbank* (1875). For German financiers the most important statute of all was that abolishing government control over the establishment of joint-stock companies (1870). Henceforth the founders of a corporation needed only to register the company with a government agency in order to establish it as a juridical person. The long struggle against government restrictions on use of the joint-stock company in industry and banking had ended. These many statutes, particularly the latter, represented the final "breakthrough" of industrial capitalism in Germany, a major victory for entrepreneurs in banking and industry.

The economic legislation of 1867–1875 was primarily the work of Rudolf Delbrück (now chief of the chancellor's office) and of Prussian ministers and counselors—in collaboration with the liberal parties of the Reichstag. Yet the course they steered for nearly a decade followed logically from Bismarck's decision of 1866 and from the policy of internal consolidation that was his chief concern during this epoch. To conservative critics it appeared that the Bismarck government had abandoned the interests of agrarian landowners in favor of industrial capitalism. The Junker in the Wilhelmstrasse seemed to have betrayed the interests of his own caste. This was untrue. Bismarck intervened repeatedly in the operations of the government during these years to promote the interests of "traditional social classes," that is, the artisans, small businessmen, and estate owners—particularly the latter.

The onset of war in June 1866 came during a business recession. News of impending hostilities induced a sharp drop on the bourse, a shrinkage in capital available for credit and investment, and a liquidity crisis among small and large business enterprises. The Prussian government met the problem by lifting the legal limits on interest rates and, as in 1848, by creating loan offices (*Darlehnskassen*) to extend credit to business enterprises in Berlin and other major cities. On June 11, the day on which war became irrevocable, Bismarck took time out from pressing diplomatic business to dictate an opinion (*Votum*) for the Prussian cabinet in which he complained that the measures taken had largely benefited merchants and big industrialists, but not those interests usually hardest hit by such crises: the landowners, small manufacturers, and artisans. Landowners, he declared, were particularly vulnerable to the demands of creditors and to foreclosures. Yet agriculture was the "most important and essential industry" in Prussia, not only because it employed more workers than any other, but also because "the landowners' capacity for achievement is always decisive for the staying power of a state." For the current crisis he proposed measures to ease mortgage payments and suspend imprisonment for debt. For the future he called for new means to counterbalance the power of "big capital over small" and to protect landowners and small businessmen from the "unbridled and arbitrary power" of the finance companies. Other messages sent to individual ministers at this time had a similar purpose: (1) he endorsed the request of a bank, Schuster and Company, for financial support from the treasury on the grounds that its clients were chiefly artisans and small manufacturers; (2) he supported the petition of the Prussian Artisans Association for an end to certain exemptions to the industrial code granted in 1865 to local manufacturers for the training of apprentices outside the guild; and (3) he proposed that the city of Berlin employ "breadless workers" on street projects, if they were permanent residents, and, if not, order them to move to rural areas where a labor shortage was imminent.[60]

Although Prussia's stunning military victory solved the immediate financial crisis, the depression lingered on. In 1867 it was deepened by a bad harvest that drove up grain prices and produced widespread suffering in the eastern regions of the monarchy (particularly the districts of Königsberg and Gumbinnen). Bismarck was sharply critical of the seeming inability of the ministries of interior and commerce either to alleviate the distress or even to collect adequate information on its extent. He was especially concerned over the paucity of information on the part played by the Königsberg grain exchange in the crisis, a lack that revealed a more serious defect: namely, that the state did not possess the organs to keep it in touch with "real life." The Prussian bureaucratic organism, he complained to Eulenburg and Itzenplitz, had been designed to meet the needs of a "state subsisting on agriculture." But recent developments had transformed the "basic character of the state" (significantly, he wrote of "state" rather than "society") and brought into being new structures for which there were no corresponding regulatory or information-gathering agencies within the government. The grain and stock exchanges had grown "without limitation or supervision" and in ways that were dangerous to the "solidity of our industry" and the economy in general. He proposed to Itzenplitz a new government agency to monitor operations of the bourse, advising on new forms of taxation and on ways to curb "unfruitful speculation," particularly in foreign securities. In addition, he suggested that the government follow the British example by creating a suitable organ to gather information on the "condition of the working classes, agrarian as well as industrial, including the small artisan." Itzenplitz rejected all but the latter suggestion, maintaining that attempts to regulate the bourse, tax its operations, and curb speculation would do more harm than good.[61]

From reports supplied by the Ministry of Finance Bismarck concluded (January 1868) that the plight of smaller artisans in the eastern towns was worst and proposed that services of the loan offices created in 1866 be extended to

[60] AWB, I, 85–93.
[61] GW, VIa, 194–196, 208, 215–216, 229–230; AWB, I, 104–114.

include them, "so they can help themselves out of the present calamity." But the "bigger landowners" were also in difficulty and he expected that their adversity would soon take on "greater dimensions." Credits extended by the government provided a palliative, but were subject to abuses that Bismarck was quick to associate with his political foes. What the chancellor wanted was a lasting solution to the credit problems of estate owners. While at Varzin in August 1868 he seized upon a plan conceived by Ernst Senfft von Pilsach, who proposed to lease his estates and sugar mill to a consortium of Rhenish financiers. Bismarck hoped that other landowners would follow the same course, thereby gaining the freedom "to make possible their desirable participation in the political affairs of the country." Only in the west could the capital be found to "take over larger leases." He hoped to set in motion a "stream of prosperous and intelligent leaseholders from the Rhine province to Pomerania and other eastern regions," which would increase land values and promote general prosperity in the area. But Rhenish financiers showed no interest in such projects. Rather than deal directly with the vagaries of crops, weather, and harvests, they preferred to risk their capital indirectly in mortgages issued by a giant bank on the pattern of the *Crédit foncier de France.*[62]

Naturally Bismarck was conscious of the political value of showing his fellow landowners that the government, despite its green light to industrial capitalism, did not neglect their financial interests. Yet his efforts to create mortgage banks for agrarian landowners predated his difficulties with the conservatives in the Prussian Landtag. In March 1863 he had urged his colleagues to consider the respective merits of two major projects for mortgage banks put forward by rival consortiums of bankers and wealthy nobility. But the legal guidelines they established (June 1863) permitted only small institutions that soon proved to be unviable. Bismarck included mortgage law among the legislative powers granted the North German Confederation, and one of his first acts after the constitution went into effect was to initiate in the Bundesrat an inquiry about the advisability of erecting a central mortgage bank under the auspices of the confederation. The committee charged with the inquiry concluded that neither a state bank nor a state-supported private bank was desirable. And nothing came of the proposal (March 1868) for a large confederate mortgage bank based on the common liability of the borrowers (urban and rural), a device intended, according to the prospectus, to "solder the regions of the confederation together as in fire."[63]

Finally in October 1868 Baron Abraham von Oppenheim, a Cologne banker, presented a practicable plan and the promise of adequate financing. He proposed a corporate mortgage bank to be capitalized by French financiers

[62] *AWB*, I, 108–109, 118–120; *GW*, VIa, 405–406.
[63] Heinrich von Poschinger, "Fürst Bismarck und das Bankwesen," *Schmollers Jahrbuch*, 34 (1910), pp. 542–545; *AWB*, I, 113–114, 116–117.

in cooperation with a Prussian consortium consisting of Bleichröder, Oppenheim, Rothschild, and the *Disconto-Gesellschaft*. Through Bismarck's intercession the king himself received Oppenheim, showing his interest in the project and thereby putting pressure on reluctant cabinet members to approve the exceptional features of the plan. A group of wealthy landowners led by the governor-general of Posen, Count Königsmarck, submitted a rival proposal, but financing did not materialize. Eventually the Prussian cabinet yielded to Bismarck's coercive tactics. Thus arose the *Preussische Central-Boden-Credit-Aktiengesellschaft*—a corporate bank, established under Bismarck's auspices, capitalized by bourgeois financiers, intended primarily to serve rural landowners, and equipped with privileges that no similar institution could match.[64]

Amalgamating Elites

Bismarck's economic and social policy in the period after 1867 proceeded on two levels: that of the Prussian and German governments, which, in collaboration with the Reichstag majority, opened the way for the final triumph of industrial capitalism in Germany; and that of Bismarck's own intercessions in economic affairs, which were mostly in the interest of artisans and landowners, particularly the latter.[65] The two levels were interconnected. During the 1840s and 1850s agrarian exports from the eastern regions had provided foreign exchange that stimulated industrial growth. In the late 1860s the capital generated by the German "takeoff" came, through Bismarck's mediation, to the rescue of the eastern estate owners. The victory of Oppenheim's project over Königsmarck's would seem to demonstrate that Prussian agriculture, even in its most prosperous period, could not produce sufficient capital to generate a mortgage bank capable of seeing landowners through the agrarian depressions of the future. Those bourgeois (and Jewish) bankers and financiers of industry, whose services in financing the state debt were already indispensable to Prussia and other German governments, had now shown their value to a gentry that had always regarded them with condescension.

Bismarck's persistent efforts in behalf of the material interests of the Prussian gentry at a time when many were becoming politically alienated reflect his basic conviction, expressed at intervals throughout his career, that the agrarian landowning class was the backbone of the state. In his personal relations, to be sure, he never discriminated, from all reports, between noblemen and bourgeois; he was in fact generally contemptuous of those whom he

---

[64] GW, VIa, 506–507; VIb, 28–29; Poschinger, "Fürst Bismarck und das Bankwesen," 544–547.

[65] Another matter in which he expressed repeated interest was promotion of the fishing industry, particularly oysters, in the North Sea and the sale of fresh fish in Berlin. AWB, I, 118, 127–218, 130.

suspected of demanding privilege by virtue of status rather than performance. During the war of 1870–1871 he often expressed his outrage at those German princes who cluttered up the German headquarters and made claims upon his time without contributing to the war effort. In his choice of ministers and subordinates the emphasis was less upon birth than upon talent, experience, and capacity for subordination. The latter requirement may have inclined him to seek bourgeois replacements for those aristocratic ministers of whose incompetence and independence he so often complained in the 1860s. At any rate Bodelschwingh, Selchow, Itzenplitz, Mühler, and Lippe were all replaced by commoners: Heydt, Camphausen, Hobrecht, Friedenthal, Achenbach, Falk, and Leonhardt. Even the "reactionary cabinet" of the 1880s was manned mostly by commoners: Bitter, Scholz, Boetticher, Gossler, Lucius, Maybach, and Friedberg. Only Puttkamer and Botho Eulenburg belonged to the old aristocracy. Two cabinet members—Friedenthal and Friedberg—were of Jewish origin. Bismarck's social bias favored the gentry as a class, not as individuals. It arose from the values and prejudices of the paternalistic tradition, with which he identified himself, and from the primary form in which his own personal wealth was invested.

Bismarck's involvement with banks and bourses, bonds and shares, in managing his own fortune gave him a better appreciation of the achievements of Prussian financiers and entrepreneurs and of their worth to the Prussian-German establishment. This appreciation can be seen in a previously unknown memorandum of February 1868, in which Bismarck advised the king to give an audience to three bourgeois benefactors who wished to found a "North German Welfare Association." He argued that the proposal had a "social and political importance" that transcended the objection that the new association would duplicate the services of existing organizations patronized by the nobility. The proposal was, he said, the "*first* attempt" of the "*bourgeois* element" to develop, without excluding aristocratic participation, an "*independent*" strength in the area of charitable activity. Traditionally the Hohenzollern monarchy had favored "certain social classes"; now the time had come to encourage the bourgeois and noble estates to cooperate in Christian activities like the *Johanniter-Orden*, hitherto a noble preserve. To rebuff the petitioners would alienate "wide and influential circles." These circles offered the monarchy a social and political support (*Hilfsmittel*) equal to and "in numbers" actually superior to that provided by the nobility. "Human nature, with which we have to reckon on all sides, is the same in all social classes."[66]

In opposing the Reichstag's demand for emolument, Bismarck maintained that membership in parliament must be limited to the "busy classes," by which he meant landowners and businessmen sufficiently wealthy to spend several months of the year on government business without reimbursement.

---

[66] GSA Berlin-Dahlem. H. A., Rep. 51, Nr. 10. The italics are Bismarck's.

"Busy" was meant to exclude capitalists living off invested wealth without managerial functions, but not absentee landowners living off the rent from leased estates![67] His effort to involve wealthy bourgeois politically also influenced his plans for the reform of county government and the Prussian House of Lords. The draft of a new *Kreisordnung* presented by Eulenburg's Ministry of the Interior in September 1869 called for a county diet (*Kreisrat*) chosen by three electoral bodies composed of big landowners, rural communes, and towns. Bismarck advocated a fourth to consist of the biggest taxpayers. This would have strengthened the gentry in those counties where they predominated, but would at the same time have given representation to residents whose wealth, though not derived from landed estates, gave them "prominent social importance." Both groups could be depended upon to support "order and conservation."[68]

Increasing difficulties with the conservative gentry led Bismarck in the winter of 1872–1873 to the opinion that reform of the Prussian House of Lords was even more pressing than that of county government. As established by King Friedrich Wilhelm IV in 1855, the House of Lords was dominated overwhelmingly by landowning noblemen, many of whom had hereditary seats. Prussia lacked, Bismarck believed, "a born, influential, big-landowning aristocracy in the English sense, among whom the king is the first peer." To function effectively, he believed, the upper chamber ought to be able to speak for the "entire propertied class." It should represent "all people of property, among whom I also count the millionaires." No distinction ought to be made, furthermore, between bourgeois and noble landowners in determining the gentry's representation, for bourgeois owners of estates "have become Junkers themselves within a short time and joined the nobility." In addition to "an electoral curia of millionaires" he proposed that mayors of the larger cities and provincial governors ought to belong to the chamber.[69] The House of Lords, in other words, should mirror an enlarged Prussian establishment: aristocrats, generals, gentry, state officials—and capitalists.

To this end Bismarck also approved the blending of the dominant elites through intermarriage and ennoblement. "A little fresh blood will do your family tree some good," the son of Wilhelmine Mencken advised an aristocratic general who was reluctant to permit his son to marry into a prosperous bourgeois family.[70] In 1883 he objected to attempts by the Prussian heraldry office to preserve the exclusive character of the noble estate. The result, he warned Wilhelm, would be to "heighten the contrast between members of the aristocracy and those bourgeois circles that, in terms of education and social position, stand on the same level with noblemen and that, like the

[67] BR, VI, 98; AWB, I, 118–119.
[68] GW, VIb, 142–143.
[69] GW, VIII, 54; Lucius, *Bismarck-Erinnerungen*, pp. 25–26.
[70] GW, VIII, 475–476.

latter, supply the state with officers and higher officials. The strict exclusive-
ness of the German nobility in earlier times is what produced that hatred of
the aristocracy that was especially strong before the last great war and during
the conflict over military reform and that is today more in evidence and more
sharply expressed than it was ten years ago. The prestige of the English nobility is owed to its accessibility to those not born into it. The circumstances
that our nobility is much more numerous and poorer only speaks for the necessity of making it more accessible. A poor, numerous nobility invites bourgeois envy more than a rich one and sharpens the irritation of those whose
requests for entry into this large estate are rejected. The factor of modest
wealth, which the Office of Heraldry uses for rejecting requests [for ennoble-
ment], has another side that speaks for acceptance rather than rejection. A
nobility of limited means is the nursery school for your majesty's officer corps.
To increase the number of young people who are largely compelled to choose
the officer corps as their profession is an advantage for the army. As Frederick
the Great complained in his time, the sons of rich noblemen go 'through the
army like a sieve'; that is, they retire young. By contrast the sons of poor
noblemen serve until pensioned."[71] In 1888 Bismarck repeated his advice to
Friedrich III: "It is in the interest of the nobility to assimilate those individuals whose wealth is in some degree permanently established."[72]

During the quarter century that followed the revolution of 1848 Bismarck
ceased to believe that big landowners and big businessmen, agrarianism and
industrialism, were natural enemies. He came to the conclusion that men of
means—whether of agrarian, commercial, industrial, or banking wealth—
had a common cause in preserving the fabric of society and government. They
were "the governed" whose mutual interest in "order and conservation"
should be institutionalized in the House of Lords and county diets and be
realized politically by the collaboration of conservative and moderate liberal
parties in the Reichstag and Chamber of Deputies in support of the government. To that end he sought to reduce conflicts of interest between agrarian
and industrial capital and to promote the fusion of their social elites. While
the interests of landowners remained his primary concern, he promoted the
expansion of the economic and social foundation of the Prussian-German establishment to include the new men of property.

[71] GW, VIc, 280–281; see also Lucius, *Bismarck-Erinnerungen*, p. 373.
[72] GW, VIc, 389.

❖❖❖

Nationalism and National Policy

SINCE 1863 Bismarck had steadily mastered the idiom of national patriotism in speeches, diplomatic dispatches, and other writings. After 1866 he rewrote his personal history, depicting himself as a German patriot whose aim as a statesman had always been to unify Germany.[1] Yet it would be wrong to conclude that his later expressions of German national sentiment were purely tactical. The utterances were too frequent and made in situations too varied to be explained away as political cant. He too was warmed by the fire he helped to kindle. The problem is not whether Bismarck was moved in these later years by German national sentiment, but by what kind. Did he conceive the German nation as an ethnic and cultural entity, formed and animated by a *Volksgeist*? Or was the German nation for him an entity shaped by the state and associated with its social and political institutions? Was the German Reich a "nation-state" or "state-nation"?[2]

As used here, these terms identify two conflicting traditions in Germany.

[1] On Bismarck's national sentiment in earlier years see vol. 1, pp. 18–23 and 67–70. His conscious adoption of German nationalistic language is evident in many documents of 1863–1866. In the draft of a diplomatic dispatch of May 21, 1863, on the Schleswig-Holstein question, for example, he inserted an inflammatory denunciation of "the system for the domination and exploitation of Germans by Danes." Historische Reichskommission, *Die auswärtige Politik Preussens, 1858–1871* (Berlin, 1932–1939), V, no. 82. For other examples see *Auswärtige Politik Preussens,* IV, nos. 340, 590; V, no. 106; Heinrich Ritter von Srbik, *Quellen zur deutschen Politik Oesterreichs, 1859–1866* (Oldenburg, 1934–1938), IV, no. 1609; GW, IV, 90, 130, 132, 449; VII, 98–99; X, 196; BR, II, 170, 243, 368. Striking evidence of his newly acquired mastery of the idiom of nationalism can be seen in his revision of the draft of Wilhelm's proclamation to the German people in 1866. GW, V, 551–552.

[2] The analysis undertaken here does not aim at a typology of nationalisms as such—although it clearly has implications for that subject—but of German nationalism in the nineteenth century. Underlying the analysis is a general assumption: that nations are not natural (or biological) but historical and psychological phenomena. A nation is constituted when its inhabitants come to believe in its existence. The form it takes is historically determined, that is, shaped by historical experiences (both cultural and political) and by popular conceptions of those experiences, whether derived from folk memories and mythologies or from the works of the historians, philosophers, and literati who touch on and interpret those experiences. After a long hiatus, the study of nationalism has undergone a resurgence of late in Germany. See Heinrich August Winkler, ed., *Nationalism: Neue wissenschaftliche Bibliothek* (Königstein/Taunus, 1978), and *Nationalismus in der Welt von heute: Geschichte und Gesellschaft*, Sonderheft 8 (Göttingen, 1982); Otto Büsch and James J. Sheehan, eds., *Die Rolle der Nation in der deutschen Geschichte und Gegenwart. Einzelveröffentlichungen der Historischen Kommission zu Berlin*, vol. 50 (Berlin, 1985).

In the tradition of Herder, on the one hand, the nation is a spiritual force creating the unique forms of cultural life that characterize and differentiate peoples. After 1869 this tradition received a fresh impulse in the writings of Richard Böckh. Böckh condemned the suppression of alien languages for political purposes as a "despiritualization of the population" and a "crime against the spiritual order of peoples"; the task of civilization was to promote the spiritual development of every ethnic nation. In the tradition of Hegel, on the other hand, the state is the vessel of the *Weltgeist* and as such a divine creation embodying morality—a conception that gave to the state a status never before attributed to it in western political thought. Hegel himself never invested the state with the power to produce ethnic homogeneity, but the Hegelian tradition assumed new forms as Germany passed from the age of the restoration to that of national unification. Divested of its metaphysical trappings, the state remained a *Machtstaat* in the era of *Realpolitik*. Earlier regarded as the product of spirit, the state was now assumed to have the moral authority to enforce conformity of spirit. In *System der Staatslehre* published in 1857 Constantin Rössler declared, "The ruling nationality has the right to denationalize by force when this can be carried out and when required for self-preservation. It can also grant the enclaved alien peoples [*Stämme*] a national development insofar as this is not accompanied by political danger."[3]

The traditions of Herder (nation-state) and Hegel (state-nation) were both alive in modified forms during the Bismarck period, but the German experience conformed more to the latter than the former. Although some German historians have been prone to identify the Hegelian tradition exclusively with liberalism,[4] this is manifestly a distortion. It is true that liberals proved to be intolerant of ethnic minorities in the German revolutions of 1848, but an archconservative, Leopold von Gerlach, penned these lines in 1853: "The task of a state is to increase the dominant part of its population and to diminish the subordinate part. Germanize the Poles, protestantize the Roman Catholics."[5] Heinrich von Treitschke detected two competing forces in history: "the tendency of every state to amalgamate its population in speech and manners into one single mold"; and the impulse felt by every vigorous nationality to construct a state of its own.[6] No sooner had the Hohenzollern monarchy achieved the latter for Germany than it undertook the former. Rightly

---

[3] Theodor Schieder, *Das deutsche Kaiserreich von 1871 als Nationalstaat. Wissenschaftliche Abhandlungen der Arbeitsgemeinschaft für Forschung des Landes Nordrhein-Westfalen,* vol. 20 (Cologne and Opladen, 1961), pp. 26–31; Richard Böckh, *Der deutschen Volkszahl und Sprachgebiet in den europäischen Staaten: Eine statistische Untersuchung* (Berlin, 1869), pp. 1–18; Constantin Rössler, *System der Staatslehre* (Leipzig, 1857), p. 539.

[4] For example, Schieder, *Kaiserreich als Nationalstaat,* p. 24, and Hans Rothfels, *Bismarck: Der Osten und das Reich* (Stuttgart, 1960), pp. 112–113.

[5] Leopold von Gerlach, *Denkwürdigkeiten* (Berlin, 1891–1892), II, 24.

[6] Heinrich von Treitschke, *Politics* (New York, 1916), I, 272.

or wrongly, ethnic differences were believed to be a source of political instability. What the Russians attempted through Russification and Hungarians through Magyarization, the Bismarck government sought to achieve through Germanization. Religious strife in the seventeenth and eighteenth centuries gave birth to the principle of *cuius regio, eius religio*; national strife in the nineteenth century to that of *cuius regio, eius natio*.

Nationalism as a Tactical Weapon

Bismarck was not given to abstractions and did not speak or write with the precision expected of a historian, philosopher, or social scientist when using the terms "nation" or "national." Yet one can ascertain from the context in which he repeatedly used these terms how he conceived them. When the occasion demanded, he spoke the idiom of German idealism. In December 1870, for example, he told the Austrians that the movement for German unification was "a development stemming from the history and spirit of the German people" and hence beyond his control.[7] But such utterances were infrequent. More often Bismarck referred to the nation as closely associated with the state. Hence he still spoke on occasion of the "Prussian nation," "Prussian nationality," and even "north German nationality."[8] The German nation had concrete existence for him only when united under a sovereign state. During 1866–1867 he is said to have often remarked, "My highest ambition is to make the Germans into a nation."[9] The "establishment of the German nationality" is how he sometimes described his life's work.[10] By the "German nation," a term that Bismarck used after 1871, he meant the German Reich, not the German-speaking people of Europe.

"I was born a Junker, but my policy was not that of the Junkers," Bismarck told Moritz Busch in 1881. "I am above all a royalist, then a Prussian and a German. I will defend my king and the monarchy against revolution, both overt and covert, and I will establish and leave behind me a strong and healthy Germany."[11] He was able to make the transition from Prussian to German patriotism in the 1860s because the German union he brought about preserved the essential values he treasured in Prussian society and government.[12]

The Germans, Bismarck often lamented, had a poorly developed national consciousness in comparison with other peoples. They venerated foreign cultures and institutions and emulated other nations at the cost of their own. As

[7] *GW*, VIb, 631.

[8] *GW*, V, 539; VIb, 249–250; XIII, 149; *BR*, IV, 7–8.

[9] *GW*, VII, 18.

[10] *GW*, XI, 118; XII, 551; XIII, 349.

[11] Moritz Busch, *Tagebuchblätter* (Leipzig, 1899), III, 57.

[12] *GW*, XV, 199–203.

emigrants they were quick to shed their ethnic identity and as subjects of
foreign rulers all too ready to establish new loyalties. "The inclination to become enthusiastic for alien nationalities and national aspirations—including
those that can only be realized at the cost of one's own country is a political
disease whose geographical spread is unfortunately limited to Germany."[13] An
invading army, he predicted in the late 1860s, would not meet the kind of
determined resistance in Germany that could perhaps be expected in every
other closed (*geschlossen*) European nation. "Undoubtedly there is . . . something in our national character that resists the unification of Germany."[14]
German attachments tended to be particularistic—to dynasty, *Stamm*, region,
party, and faction rather than to the nation as a whole. These peculiarities
explained why Alsace-Lorraine could have been absorbed into France during
the preceding two centuries, why Germany had lost its unity in the Middle
Ages, and why its reunification had taken so long. But they also explained
the vigor of party politics in the Reichstag and the unwillingness of its majority at times to accept Bismarck's conception of what was good for the country.[15]

Bismarck hoped that the national patriotism generated on the battlefield
in two wars fought for the goal of national unity would overcome these defects
in Germany's "national character." The force of national sentiment, earlier
so useful for the external expansion of Prussia, had now to be capped and
turned inward to solidify the structure he had created. From 1867 onward it
was a principal means by which he sought to reconcile the populations of the
states annexed by Prussia and to integrate the remaining states, their governments and peoples, into the federal system of the North German Confederation and the German Reich. By word and deed he sought to convey the impression that the new Germany was not merely an extension of the Prussian
Machtstaat, to which the citizenry owed mere formal obedience, but also an
organic national state requiring their patriotic allegiance.

This tactic, largely successful in one direction, created new problems in
another. The stress placed on the national character of the German Reich did
help to overcome particularistic loyalties, but it also served to estrange further
those ethnic minorities that lived within the empire's borders. The ethnic
conception that helped to reconcile Hanoverians, Saxons, Bavarians, Swabians, and other German *Stämme* to the rule of Berlin could only heighten
the sense of alienation felt by Poles, Danes, and Frenchmen who demanded
for themselves the same right of ethnic self-determination claimed by Germans. Bismarck's tactical use of German nationalism as a moral reinforcement for a Reich created by Prussian power politics frustrated the political

---

[13] *BR*, II, 123; also I, 30–31, 160–161, and IX, 398.
[14] *BR*, IV, 130; also III, 163.
[15] *BR*, II, 356; V, 74ff.; VII, 126–127.

"SEDAN DAY," THE ANNIVERSARY OF GERMANY'S VICTORY AND NAPOLEON'S CAPITULATION
(SEPTEMBER 2, 1870), BECAME A NATIONAL HOLIDAY, CELEBRATED BY PARADES, ORATIONS, AND
DEDICATIONS. IN 1873 THE VICTORY COLUMN WAS DEDICATED IN THE KÖNIGSPLATZ (ABOVE), AND IN
1895 (THE TWENTY-FIFTH SEDAN DAY) THE BRANDENBURG GATE RECEIVED EXTRA ATTENTION (BELOW).
(BILDARCHIV PREUSSISCHER KULTURBESITZ.)

assimilation of the empire's ethnic minorities and thereby endangered the security of its frontiers. The only practical escape from this dilemma appeared to be their Germanization. Greater ethnic homogeneity, it seemed, was a precondition for the final consolidation of the German Reich.

The Annexed Population of 1866

By annexing the principalities of Hanover, Hesse-Kassel, Nassau, Schleswig-Holstein and the city of Frankfurt, Prussia added 4,300,000 inhabitants to its previous population of 19,501,723.[16] Earlier it was shown that Bismarck preferred complete to partial annexation in the belief that the rulers of the principalities, if left any fragment of their former territories, would become the focus of irredentist movements hazardous to the integration of the annexed territories into Prussia. In view of the later behavior of the Guelph dynasty of Hanover, this may have been a realistic decision. Yet the liquidation of so many thrones and sovereignties increased the resentment of many of the annexed, who now began to describe themselves as "must-Prussians."

As was to be expected, the difficulties encountered were roughly proportionate to the size of the population incorporated. In Nassau (population: 468,311) the problem was minimal. Assured of his property and income (treaty of September 18, 1867), Duke Adolf released his officials and soldiers from their oaths of allegiance. While he did not formally renounce the throne, the duke made no attempt to reassert his sovereignty and in 1890 found compensation for his loss when he succeeded to the throne of the grand duchy of Luxemburg. The citizens of Frankfurt (population: 90,800) were resentful, but helpless. The liquidation of military rule and cancellation of a huge "war indemnity" (imposed despite the fact that the city had not declared war) eased the transition. Hesse-Kassel (population: 763,200) was a more difficult problem. Captured early in the fighting and imprisoned at Stettin, the Elector Friedrich Wilhelm refused to settle with his conquerors. Although he signed a treaty (September 17, 1867) similar to that imposed on the Duke of Nassau, he reasserted his sovereignty in 1868 and suffered impoundment of his properties and income. Before the deposed elector's death in 1875, however, his heir had already come to terms with the Prussian government, recognizing the annexation as irrevocable. Persistent misgovernment before 1866 had in any case made the dynasty unpopular among Hessians; the German national and pro-Prussian movement was strong in the electorate as a consequence. Yet some inhabitants objected to the "hardness, discipline, and sobriety of the east German style," and aristocratic conservatives were reluctant to part with rights that the dynasty had sheltered; Lutherans feared the

---

[16] Population statistics used in this chapter are from Wolfgang Köllmann, ed., *Quellen zur Bevölkerungs-, Sozial- und Wirtschaftsstatistik Deutschlands, 1815–1875* (Boppard am Rhein, 1980).

loss of religious autonomy. Nevertheless, the opposition of the die-hard minority, if vocal, was relatively ineffective.[17]

The inhabitants of Schleswig-Holstein (population: 1,028,600) were divided between a "Prussian party" favoring annexation and an "Augustenburg party" opposing it. The latter had the support of a large majority of voters, including progressives and national liberals. They were disappointed when the National Liberal party in the Reichstag decided that the claims of Prince Friedrich of Augustenburg, while legitimate, must give way before "the eternal right of the future of the German people." Prince Friedrich reserved his claims, but took no action, recognizing that Prussia's victory over Austria had ended his last hope. Before dying in 1880 he had the consolation of seeing his daughter affianced to Prince Wilhelm of Prussia. His would-be subjects were less easily appeased. Two generations of Schleswig-Holsteiners had fought for independence; resentments against Denmark now became resentments against Prussia. The problem was exacerbated by the heavy-handedness of the Prussian bureaucracy, which imposed Prussian laws and taxes with little regard for native traditions and interests, in part against Bismarck's wishes. During the 1870s the region's farmers protested by voting for social democratic candidates to the Reichstag. Schleswig-Holstein became, after Saxony, the second most important stronghold of the social democrats in Germany. Its inhabitants were little reconciled by Wilhelm's declaration that "Germany alone has profited from what Prussia has gained." In 1888 the provincial governor admitted sadly that in twenty years little had been achieved for the "spiritual and political union of the province to Prussia."[18]

The most difficult problem of assimilation was Hanover (population: 1,933,800). A devout believer in divine right, King Georg V of the Guelph dynasty, Germany's oldest, steadfastly refused to accept his fate. From exile in Austria this proud and stubborn descendant of Henry the Lion denounced annexation as "criminal and detestable robbery" and a "flagrant violation" of international law. While releasing his officials and officers from their oath of allegiance, he refused to surrender the possibility of ultimate restoration and conspired to hasten the day of his return. He hoped for diplomatic support from relatives among Europe's leading dynasties, particularly Britain. But he also relied on popular support from those segments of Hanoverian society which out of sentiment or self-interest hoped for a restoration: the nobility, dependent primarily on the Hanoverian state for political power and income

---

[17] Ernst Rudolf Huber, *Deutsche Verfassungsgeschichte seit 1789* (Stuttgart, 1963–1978), III, 591–596.

[18] Oswald Hauser, *Preussische Staatsräson und nationaler Gedanke* (Neumünster, 1960), pp. 26–33, and *Staatliche Einheit und regionale Vielfalt in Preussen* (Neumünster, 1967), pp. 29–30, 109. Werner Franz, "Einführung und erste Jahre der preussischen Verwaltung in Schleswig-Holstein," *Zeitschrift für die schleswig-holsteinische Geschichte*, 83 (1959), pp. 179–180, 203, 226, 236–242; Huber, *Verfassungsgeschichte*, III, 593–594.

(noble estates constituted only 6.5 percent of all land in Lower Saxony); officials and army officers, whose careers were jeopardized by annexation; residents of the capital city who had profited from a free-spending court; peasants and artisans, whose interests had been favored by the anti-industrial policies of the old regime; men of military age who dreaded the longer and more vigorous Prussian military service; Lutherans, who feared incorporation into the Prussian Evangelical church; and Catholics, who objected to national unity under a Protestant dynasty.

Yet the irreconcilable "Guelphs" were opposed by a majority of Hanoverians who did accept Prussian annexation: members of the business and professional classes whose interests were served by national unity; liberals, who detested the autocratic ways of King Georg; and German patriots, whose enthusiasm for national unity outweighed dread of "Prussianization." Many urban workers—politically uncommitted, impoverished by the disruption caused by mobilization and war, and suspicious of their pro-annexationist employers—were initially anti-Prussian, but they had no attachment to the Guelph dynasty and no interest in the preservation of particularism in itself. In the first national election held in Hanover (February 1867) 144,188 voters cast their ballots for pro-annexation candidates, 129,885 for Guelph particularists. From 1871 to 1890 four to eleven Guelph deputies sat in the German Reichstag; the Guelph particularists generally commanded about 30 percent of the Hanoverian electorate.[19]

From the outset Bismarck recognized that Hanover would be "hard to swallow"; its annexation was a "risk" that had to be taken.[20] The size of the opposition appeared formidable, particularly when coupled with overt acts of resistance. In April and May 1867 the Luxemburg crisis raised the prospect of war with France and infused the Guelph movement with fresh hope. Several hundred men, mostly ex-soldiers in the Hanoverian army, crossed the border into the Netherlands and Switzerland to form a "Guelph legion." Equipped with American passports, they migrated in January 1868 to France, where they were quartered for a time in Alsace. Financed by King Georg, they remained in France for more than two years, despite Bismarck's remonstrances to the French government. Georg estimated their strength at approximately 800 men, Bismarck at 1,400.[21]

By chance the Hanoverian problem created for Bismarck a welcome source of income independent of parliamentary control that was highly useful in ma-

---

[19] Ernst Pitz, "Deutschland und Hannover im Jahre 1866," *Niedersächsisches Jahrbuch für Landesgeschichte*, 38 (1966), pp. 86–158; Werner Leffler, *Ursachen und Anfänge der deutsch-hannoverschen (welfischen) Bewegung* (Wismar, 1932), pp. 23–43; Stewart A. Stehlin, *Bismarck and the Guelph Problem* (The Hague, 1973), pp. 98–100, 122, 166ff.; Günther Franz, *Die politischen Wahlen in Niedersachsen, 1867–1949* (Bremen-Horn, 1953), pp. 18, 80.

[20] GW, VII, 147.

[21] Stehlin, *Guelph Problem*, pp. 67ff.; GW, VI, 404–407.

nipulating public opinion at home and abroad throughout the rest of his career. In November 1866 he impounded all funds and properties of the Guelph
dynasty and then opened negotiations with the monarch in Vienna through
a former Hanoverian minister, Ludwig Windthorst, future leader of the German Center party. For the return of 19 million thalers in public funds that
Georg had shipped to Britain before the outbreak of hostilities Bismarck offered the income from 16 million thalers invested in Prussian state bonds and
other securities and the income from certain Guelph properties (the domains
of Calenberg), which were to remain under Prussian administration pending
Georg's formal abdication.[22] While he had no intention of abdicating, Georg
agreed to this settlement, and Bismarck gained its approval by the Prussian
Landtag after considerable difficulty. On the day of final passage (February 18,
1868), however, the king celebrated his silver wedding anniversary in Hietzing, a suburb of Vienna, with a public toast calling upon God to restore his
throne and Hanover's independence.[23] Within a few days fresh reports of the
activities of the Guelph legion and of Georg's connections with it arrived in
Berlin. Bismarck reacted by sequestering Georg's property once more under
the emergency clause of the Prussian constitution, declaring that the income
would be used to counteract Guelph subversion. This action, which was approved by the Prussian Landtag in February 1869, gave birth to the famous
"Guelph fund" (dubbed "reptile fund" by liberal critics).[24]

Prussian espionage, financed by the fund, soon penetrated the Guelphs so
thoroughly that Bismarck boasted he could find out, if he wished, what Georg
ate for breakfast every morning.[25] In February 1870 the drying up of his financial resources compelled the king to disband the legion, only five months
before the war against France. Napoleon's defeat settled the fate of the
Guelph movement, but it did not end the determination of the Guelph family
to recover the lost crown. On Georg's death in 1878 his heir, Ernst August,
reasserted his claims to Hanover; in 1884 he also claimed the succession to
Brunswick on the death of the reigning duke. Not until 1892, after Bismarck
was gone and a new Kaiser sat on the German throne, did Ernst August, by
committing himself never to engage in hostile action against the Reich, secure the release of the property and income promised in 1868. For more than
two decades the obstinacy of the Guelph family and the compliance of the
Prussian Landtag permitted Bismarck to draw upon a secret fund (whose annual income came to more than a million marks), uncontrolled by parliament
or any other government agency. The use he made of the fund extended far

[22] GW, VIa, 30–33, 65–68.

[23] GW, VIa, 131–133; SEG (1868), pp. 50–51. For a description of the court at Hietzing see
SEG (1878), pp. 98–99.

[24] GW, VIa, 235–246, 290, 389–390; XIV, 747; BR, IV, 99ff.; Stehlin, Guelph Problem, pp.
50–59.

[25] Leffler, Ursachen und Anfänge, p. 33.

beyond the annexed regions and the Guelph problem. With it he built up an espionage network, bought up journalists and newspapers, subsidized public projects, assisted colleagues in financial distress, rewarded "friends of the state," bribed the King of Bavaria and the equerry to accept national unity, and eased the conclusion of the Kulturkampf by pensioning bishops and bribing a cardinal.[26]

Negotiations with former rulers were a matter of foreign policy and hence under Bismarck's direct control. For implementation of government policy in all other matters (such as civil and military administration, the judiciary, finance, church affairs) he was dependent upon the cooperation of his colleagues in the Prussian cabinet, particularly Count Eulenburg, minister of interior. At the first sign of resistance in Hanover in late July 1866 Bismarck secured the appointment of a military governor, General Konstantin von Voigts-Rhetz, who was instructed to make inhabitants "feel" the Prussian occupation, thereby encouraging Prussia's friends and frightening its enemies. "Every act of real resistance must be suppressed and punished without leniency." *"Wo nicht Liebe sein will, Furcht sein muss."* Anti-Prussian newspapers were censored or suppressed; recruiters for the Guelph legion were arrested, tried, and imprisoned. Bismarck urged that towns and regions where acts of resistance occurred be fined; indignities suffered by the occupation troops should be severely punished; recalcitrant policemen, officials, and judges should be "purged"; Hanoverian officials should be transferred to Prussia and Prussian officials to Hanover.[27] Yet Bismarck was dissatisfied with the results. In May 1867 he warned Eulenburg that he did not intend to "assume the

[26] Stehlin, *Guelph Problem,* 95, 198–211; Hans Philippi, "Zur Geschichte des Welfenfonds," *Niedersächisches Jahrbuch für Landesgeschichte,* 31 (1959), pp. 190–254; Robert Nöll von der Nahme, *Bismarcks Reptilienfonds* (Mainz, 1968). Although the annual accounts were regularly destroyed, some details concerning the size of the Guelph fund and expenditures from it have been uncovered. The yield, usually about 1,000,000 marks, reached 1,275,000 in at least one year (1878). Gross income in that year was 1,919,000 marks, but administrative costs were 644,000 marks. Finance Minister Hobrecht *Votum,* July 2, 1878, DZA Potsdam, Reichskanzlei, 413, pp. 10–16; also Hobrecht to Bismarck, Dec. 30, 1878. DZA Potsdam, Reichskanzlei, 1400, pp. 1–2, 19, 104ff. Of the net income 77 percent usually went to the Prussian Foreign Office, where it was at Bismarck's disposal, and 23 percent to the Prussian Ministry of the Interior. DZA Potsdam, Reichskanzlei, 1401, pp. 10–10v, 127–129, 142–146. Gerson Bleichröder was the financial agent for investing the funds and for many disbursements. Fritz Stern, *Gold and Iron: Bismarck, Bleichröder, and the Building of the German Empire* (New York, 1977), pp. 110, 132–133, 204–205, 222–223, 263, 266–272, 454 (fn.). For other details about expenditures from the Guelph fund see Dieter Brosius, "Welfenfonds und Presse im Dienste der preussischen Politik in Hannover nach 1866," *Niedersächsisches Jahrbuch für Landesgeschichte,* 36 (1964), pp. 172–206, and Eberhard Naujoks, "Eine Abrechnung über den Welfenfonds (1. April–31. Dezember 1869)," *Publizistik* (Jan.–Mar. 1969), pp. 16–29.

[27] Ludwig Hahn, *Zwei Jahre preussisch-deutscher Politik, 1866–1867* (Berlin, 1868), pp. 373–384; Robert von Keudell, *Fürst und Fürstin Bismarck: Erinnerungen aus den Jahren 1846 bis 1872* (Berlin, 1901), p. 333; GW, VI, 172–173, 200, 236–237, 252–253, 282–283; Stehlin, *Guelph Problem,* pp. 158ff.

responsibility before his majesty for the continuance of the present situation." He complained of "passive resistance" and threatened to disavow all responsibility before the Landtag and Reichstag. Eulenburg, he declared, had tried too hard to spare the Hanoverian nobility or "feudal party"; he ought to have proceeded "much more radically" in Hanover, like Austria had in Bohemia after her triumph in 1620 at the Battle of White Mountain.[28]

In other respects, however, Bismarck believed that his colleagues proceeded much too fast and "too sharply" in integrating Hanover into Prussia. In August 1866 he opposed "Prussianization" of Hanover. Except for introduction of Prussia's military system, "uniformity was to be avoided," and the "individuality" of Hanover respected; Germany had to be shown that "Prussia has the capacity to absorb, without liquidating, all German individualities." To this end he promised that Prussia would carry out the incorporation in consultation with prominent citizens of the new provinces.[29] Yet Eulenburg, Count Lippe (minister of justice), and von der Heydt (minister of finance) were opposed to such consultations, and it was not until June 1867 that Bismarck forced the Prussian cabinet to accept his point of view. A few days later, after Bismarck had departed for rest and recuperation at Varzin, the ministers reversed themselves. They succeeded in getting the approval of Wilhelm, who was unaware of Bismarck's objections, to a flood of unifying ordinances: the introduction of Prussian codes of criminal law and procedure; the subordination of the judiciary to a superior court of appeals in Berlin; introduction of the Prussian stamp tax; abolition of state lotteries in Hanover, Osnabrück, and Frankfurt; the establishment of administrative control by the Prussian state treasury over the capital wealth (chiefly domain funds and treasury surpluses) of the annexed lands. These measures, particularly the latter, shocked and angered even the pro-Prussian and German-national segment of the annexed population. Rudolf von Bennigsen and Count Münster, leaders of the National Liberal and Free Conservative parties, uttered sharp protests.[30]

Back of the dispute between Bismarck and his colleagues was a greater issue. Eulenburg, Lippe, and Heydt wished to perpetuate the centralized, bureaucratic machinery of the Prussian state, while Bismarck favored greater local autonomy through the extension of "self-administration." By preserving the "individuality" of the annexed state, he hoped to establish a pattern for later reorganization of provincial and local government in the rest of Prussia. Once again Wilhelm's trust enabled Bismarck to get the upper hand. Breaking off his vacation in Varzin, Bismarck met the king at Bad Ems, and, when they

[28] GW, VI, 394–395; VII, 225; XIV, 731–732.

[29] GW, VIa, 11; XIV, 733.

[30] GW, VIa, 11–14, 29–30. Hermann Oncken, *Rudolf von Bennigsen* (Stuttgart, 1910), II, 85ff.; Hans Herzfeld, *Johannes Miquel* (Detmold, 1938), I, 132–149; and Pitz, "Deutschland und Hannover," pp. 153–154.

parted, the rumor spread that the dismissals of Eulenburg and Lippe were imminent, but only Lippe resigned. Some financial measures were reversed and consultations were held with *Vertrauensmänner* from all of the annexed lands.[31] In September 1867, as the "transitional year" provided for in the statute of annexation came to a close, Bismarck pushed through the appointment of his own candidate, Count Otto zu Stolberg-Wernigerode, for the position of *Oberpräsident* of the province of Hanover. Stolberg was young (thirty years old) and, as the owner of estates in Hanover, not alien to the region. He was more acceptable to the natives than the kind of "old Prussian" administrator whom Eulenburg preferred. Furthermore, he was Bismarck's man. The chancellor communicated with him directly, over the heads of Heydt and Eulenburg, although he was technically Eulenburg's subordinate.[32]

Stolberg governed as Bismarck directed. In conformity with the wishes of the *Vertrauensmänner*, a provincial diet was established for the former kingdom of Hanover. At its first session the diet passed unanimously a motion introduced by Rudolf von Bennigsen calling for transfer of administrative control over the Hanoverian domain fund (amounting to approximately 16 million thalers) from the Prussian treasury to the new provincial government. Bismarck, who had instructed Stolberg to treat the proposal benevolently, now insisted over the objections of Heydt that the Prussian cabinet present the diet's proposal to the Prussian Landtag in the form of a bill. His purpose was not only to appease Hanoverians, whose taxes had increased 20 percent after annexation, but to establish by law a precedent for greater provincial self-administration throughout Prussia.[33] During 1868 this bill aroused considerable heat in the Prussian House of Lords and Chamber of Deputies. Conservatives were angered by the government's generosity toward the defeated, and they resented the prospect that Hanover, through the possession of its own "provincial fund," would have a better financial status than the old provinces of Prussia. Ultimately the bill passed the Chamber of Deputies by a close vote (197 to 192) over the combined opposition of conservatives and progressives. Even this slim majority had to be purchased by inclusion of an amendment that replaced the fund with an annual grant of five hundred thou-

---

[31] Horst Kohl, ed., *Bismarck-Jahrbuch* (Leipzig, 1898), V, 189–192; GW, VIa, 11–14, 52, 385–386; VII, 215; Horst Kohl, ed., *Anhang zu den Gedanken und Erinnerungen von Otto Fürst von Bismarck* (Stuttgart, 1901), II, 411–417; Heinrich von Poschinger, ed., *Bismarck-Portefeuille* (Stuttgart, 1898–1900), I, 6–7; Heinrich Heffter, *Die deutsche Selbstverwaltung im 19. Jahrhundert* (Stuttgart, 1950), pp. 477–479.

[32] GW, VIa, 48–49, 109–110, 139–140, 212–213. For an account of the integration of Hanover into the structure of the Prussian state see Werner Frauendienst, "Die Assimilierung Hannovers durch Preussen nach 1866," *Niedersächsisches Jahrbuch für Landesgeschichte*, 15 (1950), pp. 310–344. Nothing was added by Heide Barmeyer, "Annektion und Assimilation: Zwei Phasen preussischer Staatsbildung, dargestellt am Beispiel Hannovers nach 1866," *Niedersächsisches Jahrbuch für Landesgeschichte*, 45 (1973), pp. 303–336.

[33] GW, VIa, 59–60, 353–355, 385–386.

sand thalers from the Prussian treasury, an amount nearly equivalent to its income.[34]

For many years Bismarck followed closely the developments in Hanover and the other annexed regions and often intervened in their administration.[35] His treatment of the annexed states illustrates again his use of the classic technique of the iron hand in velvet glove. Prussia's new subjects, he maintained, could best be assimilated by stressing that their independence had been sacrificed for German national unity rather than for Prussian aggrandizement. In two private instructions of February 1870 to Stolberg he described the essence of his assimilation policy. "The decisive factor which the governmental press will have to stress in its efforts to conquer particularistic attitudes lies in the German and not in the Prussian nationality. By the latter expression we Prussians are accustomed to represent the former [!], but it is not the ideal under which we shall succeed in making acceptable to our new countrymen the position that we attained in 1866." The journalists of the subsidized press, he directed, should stress the common lower Saxon tribal background of the Brandenburg and Hanoverian peoples, their joint struggle for the Lutheran religion in the Thirty Years War, and their comradeship in arms during the Seven Years War. In particular, the emphasis must be on their common German nationality and their "common national tasks and interests."[36]

Bismarck did not rely on German nationalism alone to bind Prussia's new subjects to Berlin. Under his prodding the Prussian government promoted economic growth in the annexed areas, particularly through railway construction. Money from the Guelph fund flowed into a host of material and cultural projects: new facilities at the seashore resort of Norderney, road construction, a new church for Hildesheim, four new teaching positions at the University of Göttingen, subsidies for schools and museums.[37] While this largesse probably had an effect, diehard Guelph particularists remained a problem. During the early stages of the war of 1870–1871 Bismarck worried that the French might land on the North Sea coast and foment rebellion in Hanover.[38] In the election of 1878 the Guelph party scored an unexpected success, increasing its Reichstag representation from four to ten deputies. During the runoff election of that year riots (described by a resident as "American conditions")

---

[34] SBHA (1867–1868), III, 1361–1473; GSP (1868), pp. 223–224.

[35] DZA Potsdam, Reichskanzlei, 1400–1401.

[36] GW, VIb, 249–250; Poschinger, ed., Bismarck-Portefeuille, I, 16–17. In 1869 Bismarck protested the destruction of a monument to the Hanoverian army that fought the Prussians at Langensalza and ordered its reconstruction on the same spot, to be paid for out of the Guelph fund. GW, VIb, 171–173; XIV, 772–773; Kohl, ed., Bismarck-Jahrbuch, IV, 92–94.

[37] Poschinger, ed., Bismarck-Portefeuille, I, 5–6, 10–12; GW, VIa, 20; Philippi, "Welfenfonds," pp. 231–236; Stehlin, Guelph Problem, p. 177; Brosius, "Welfenfonds und Presse," pp. 175.

[38] GW, VIb, 392–393, 405–407, 411–412, 414–416, 430; see also GW, VIb, 330; Busch, Tagebuchblätter, I, 44.

broke out in the Elbe port of Harburg. Again Bismarck sought repressive measures, including martial law.[39] In 1880 Wilhelm also concluded that the government had been too tolerant of Guelph agitation, which he believed to be
on the increase.[40] In the election of 1887 Guelph popularity at the polls
reached a peak under the Reich at 113,000 votes. To the end of the empire,
long after the generation of 1866 was gone and Bismarck as well, the Guelphs
remained a small but persistent thorn in the empire's flesh.

The "Polish Problem"

Of the Prussian population of 18,491,220 in 1861, 14 percent was non-German. The Polish minority, numbering 2,265,042, was by far the largest, followed by 139,428 Lithuanians, 83,443 Wends, and 59,850 Czechs. In the
province of Posen the Poles were a majority, constituting 55 percent of the
provincial population; but they were also strong in the province of West Prussia (32 percent) and in the district of Oppeln (59 percent) in Upper Silesia.[41]
Initially leadership of the Polish national movement was in the hands of Polish gentry and clergy; Prussian officals, including Bismarck, continued to regard these groups as the main source of the "Polish problem" long after this
was no longer true.[42] Prussia's abolition of manorialism, encouragement of
free enterprise, construction of roads and railways, and improvement in public education speeded the growth of a new Polish middle class and intelligentsia that joined and eventually superseded the clergy and gentry in promoting
the cause of Polish nationalism. During the 1850s and 1860s Polish voters
sent as many as twenty-six representatives to the Prussian Chamber of Deputies. In 1867 they elected eleven deputies to the Reichstag. Between 1871
and 1890 the Polish caucus in the Reichstag held from thirteen to eighteen
seats.[43] In both chambers the Poles were a persistently dissident group and
enthusiastic participants in antigovernment coalitions.

Before 1870 Prussian policy toward its Polish minority had fluctuated between toleration and repression. Four times the Poles rose against alien rule:
1830–1831, 1846, 1848, and 1863. Although Russia was the chief target of
these insurrections, Prussia felt threatened. In the 1830s Eduard von Flottwell, governor-general of Posen, inaugurated a policy of Germanization. By
spreading "the elements of German life in their material and spiritual rela-

[39] DZA Potsdam, Reichskanzlei, 1400, pp. 5–6, 8, 13–14v, 48ff.; GW, VIc, 119.

[40] DZA Potsdam, Reichskanzlei, 1400, pp. 146–163v; 1401, pp. 47–47v, also pp. 24–29, 34,
44–44v, 75–75v; GW, VIc, 120–121.

[41] Böckh, Volkszahl und Sprachgebiet, pp. 232–241.

[42] BR, X, 310; XI, 442–443, 465; GW, VIc, 329 (fn.); Freiherr Lucius von Ballhausen, Bismarck-Erinnerungen (Stuttgart, 1920), p. 392.

[43] Bernhard Vogel, Dieter Nohlen, and Rainer-Olaf Schultze, Wahlen in Deutschland: Theorie-
Geschichte-Dokumente, 1848–1970 (Berlin, 1971), pp. 268–291.

tionships" through the Polish masses, he hoped to achieve "the complete union of both nationalities." Flottwell's program was ended by Friedrich Wilhelm IV on his succession to the throne in 1840. But the rebellions at the end of the decade liquidated the king's policy of toleration.[44] Eugen von Puttkamer, governor-general of Posen in the 1850s, strove to keep the Poles "in the subordinate position that is their due." They were enemies who could not be reconciled, but whose extermination would be inhuman and impossible— "at least it would take generations."[45] His successor, Carl von Horn, governor-general from 1862 to 1869, began by declaring that Prussia would respect the language, religion, and mores of the Poles, although they would have to learn German as a second tongue. After the rebellion of Russia's Poles in 1863 he changed his tone. "The province will be Germanized in the sense that it will become predominately German and that the Poles who dwell there— even if they keep their nationality and language, as have the Lithuanians and Masurians in East Prussia—do not think any more about rebellion and separation."[46] But Horn was handicapped in his attempt to resurrect Flottwell's policies by Bismarck's need in 1866–1870 to remain on good terms with the Catholic church in order not to alienate south German Catholics. When Horn came into conflict with Archbishop Ledóchowski of Posen-Gnesen, he was removed from his post.[47]

Horn's departure did not mean that Bismarck was insensitive to the "Polish problem." A few months later he complained to the king—an extraordinary step—about the ineffectiveness of the assimilation policies of his colleagues, Minister of Interior Eulenburg and *Kultusminister* Mühler. On the basis of police reports, he charged that the Polish tongue was making inroads on the German, because elementary schools in Polish-speaking regions had failed to offer the instruction in German mandated by a Prussian ordinance of November 1865. The ordinance had foundered on the resistance of Polish clergymen acting as school inspectors.[48] This document signals the beginning of what

[44] See Eduard Flottwell's famous memorandum written on the conclusion in 1841 of his service as governor of Posen: *Denkschrift: Die Verwaltung der Provinz Posen von Dezember 1830 bis zum Beginn des Jahres 1841 betreffend* (Berlin, 1897). On Flottwell's career and policies see Manfred Laubert, *Eduard Flottwell: Ein Abriss seines Lebens* (Berlin, 1919) and *Die preussische Polenpolitik von 1772–1914* (3d ed., 1944), pp. 66–102.

[45] Laubert, *Polenpolitik*, pp. 119–120.

[46] *Ibid.*, pp. 124–128.

[47] *Ibid.*, pp. 131–132.

[48] Bismarck to Eulenburg and Mühler, Mar. 15, 1870. DZA Merseburg, Rep. 2.2.1, Nr. 15006, Vol. 2, pp. 154–155. The minister steadfastly defended his administration against Bismarck's charges. Mühler to Wilhelm I, Apr. 8, 1870. *Ibid.*, pp. 148–153v. In response the king stressed that Polish children must receive adequate instruction in German, so that all could participate in the cultural development of the Prussian people and enjoy progress in all areas of "work and commerce." Resistance must be decisively overcome. *Ibid.*, pp. 163–164. As he prepared for another assault on the Polish problem in the 1880s, Bismarck apparently wondered where he had

eventually became the Kulturkampf against the Catholic church. Polish conduct during the war of 1870–1871 reinforced Bismarck's sense of urgency concerning the problem of assimilation. From the provincial government of Posen came alarming reports of Polish disaffection: open partisanship for France;
the incitement of Polish army reservists to desert; hostile demonstrations at
German victory celebrations; widespread anger at the Versailles proclamation
establishing the "German Empire"; and evidence of a subversive organization.
"No one who is acquainted with the conditions here can doubt that the hearts
of the Polish population are on the whole dedicated to the cause of France in
the war that has broken out." Several battalions of Silesian militia and a reserve regiment of the regular army had to be quartered in the province to
preserve order.[49]

In cabinet meetings on October 13 and November 1, 1871, Bismarck insisted that the time had come to counterattack. "From the Russian border to
the Adriatic Sea we are confronted with Slavic propaganda combined with
that of ultramontanes and reactionaries, and it is necessary openly to defend
our national interests and our language against such hostile activities. . . .
Everywhere in Europe Slavs and Latins [Romanen], in alliance with ultramontanism, seek to preserve crudity and ignorance and fight Germanism, which
endeavors to spread enlightenment. . . . For a long time it has been observed
that in Polish-Catholic regions of the monarchy the Germanizing task of the
elementary schools is pushed into the background, instruction in German is
neglected, and at the same time the area where Polish is spoken grows."[50]
Hounded by Bismarck, Kultusminister Mühler drafted what became the school
inspection act of March 11, 1872, which made explicit the government's
power to appoint and dismiss school inspectors.[51] The targets of this statute
were eighty-six archpriests who supervised the priests functioning as school
inspectors in 2,481 Catholic schools in Posen, Upper Silesia, and West Prussia. The government's purpose was to replace these unpaid officials with
twenty-five to thirty new, full-time, salaried professional school inspectors.[52]
With the passage of this statute the Kulturkampf (see chapter seven) began
in earnest. After unification had been completed Bismarck no longer had to
be gingerly in handling Catholic interests, either in Posen or in Germany.

gotten his statistical information in 1870. Tiedemann to Rottenburg, Mar. 22, 1883. DZA Potsdam, Reichskanzlei, 659, Vol. 1, p. 215.
   [49] Adelheid Constabel, ed., Die Vorgeschichte des Kulturkampfes (Berlin, 1956), pp. 19–21;
Zeitungsbericht, Aug. 16, 1870, DZA Merseburg, Rep. 2.2.1., Nr. 16148 (1870–1879), pp. 14–
15.
   [50] Constabel, ed., Vorgeschichte des Kulturkampfes, pp. 127–128, 136–141.
   [51] GSP (1872), p. 183. Bismarck was deeply involved in the drafting of the statute. DZA
Merseburg, Rep. 76, VII, neu Sekt. 1, Theil II, Nr. 1, Vol. 1, pp. 44–48.
   [52] Mühler to Camphausen and Bismarck, Oct. 28, 1871. DZA Merseburg, Rep. 76, VII, neu
Sekt. 1, Theil II, Nr. 1, Vol. 1, 27–31.

The Kulturkampf had many roots, but the tap root, was, as Bismarck always insisted,[53] the Polish problem.

Although Adalbert Falk, who replaced Mühler as *Kultusminister* in January 1872, made effective use of his power under the new statute, Bismarck was still dissatisfied with the government's effort to stem the tide of Polonization. In February 1872 he addressed a harsh letter to Minister of Interior Eulenburg, deploring the minister's "passivity with regard to Polish conditions. . . . I have the feeling that the ground under us in our Polish provinces, if not obviously crumbling at the moment, has been so undermined that it can collapse as soon as a Polish-Catholic-Austrian policy develops in foreign affairs." Should the minister and his subordinates fail to become "more active and independent" in devising "preventive measures," someone would have to resign—either Eulenburg or himself.[54] Six weeks later, Eulenburg, in explaining to the Prussian Chamber of Deputies why Posen was to be excepted from a new statute granting provincial self-administration, said bluntly, "We must work to the end that the Poles become, first, Prussian and, then, German, but Prussian and German they must become."[55]

During 1872–1873 a series of royal rescripts began the Germanization of the schools in the eastern region. While these orders varied according to regional differences, the basic instruction was everywhere the same: henceforth German was to be the language of instruction in elementary schools in all subjects except religion. In Silesia and Prussia religion could be taught to Polish and Lithuanian children in their mother tongues on the lower level (first two years), but German was obligatory on the two higher levels (three years each) except where "help" was needed to communicate. The rescript for Posen, which came straight from the king, permitted religious instruction in the Polish tongue on the upper levels as well, but only until the pupils could comprehend German. Polish remained a subject of instruction for Polish children: in Posen, five hours weekly on the lower level, three hours weekly on the middle and upper levels (even this could be abolished in "suitable situations" on order of the district government); in Prussia, only on the upper level; in Silesia, on the upper level only on special permission by the

---

[53] For examples see *BR*, X, 294; XI, 433; *BP*, I, 210–211; II, 185; *GW*, VIc, 236–240, 266–268.

[54] *GW*, XIV, 827. Bismarck's alarm was fueled by reports from secret agents. One report enclosed a letter purported to have been written from Zurich by a "well-known agent" of the "Polish National Government" to the editor of a Polish newspaper in Posen, stating that the time for armed insurrection was at hand for the Poles in collaboration with dissident Catholics and socialists. The "Catholic party" would at the "decisive moment" offer the German imperial crown to the Habsburg Kaiser. Bismarck sent the document to Eulenburg with the comment that the content, while "fantastic," deserved "attention." Constabel, ed. *Vorgeschichte des Kulturkampfes*, pp. 179–180. For other indications of Bismarck's alarm see Busch, *Tagebuchblätter*, II, 225, 289–290, 307–308, 327, 361–362.

[55] *SBHA* (1871–1872), III, 1485.

authorities. Schools whose pupils were 25 percent German speaking were to be considered "pure German"; in such cases no alien tongues would be used.[56]

Although issued by the provincial governments, these rescripts were discussed and approved by the cabinet, including Bismarck. The king approved the order on Posen only after the cabinet had quieted his doubts about its pedagogical difficulties.[57] Actually these bureaucratic decisions showed little regard for the pedagogical problems involved in teaching pupils who knew no German and lacked the desire or talent—or both—for learning it. The incentive of the teachers was spurred by a grant from the king's disposition fund of 5,000 thalers to be distributed among teachers who had "vigorously and successfully" promoted the German language among their pupils.[58] Where methods were concerned, teachers received only minimal help from the authorities (summer courses given at teacher training institutes in 1874). They were advised to "attack the matter freely and freshly" by speaking German in the classroom from the first day.[59] Polish citizens complained that their children were no longer learning the basic skills of reading, writing, and arithmetic, but their petitions to the Landtag were coldly dismissed with the advice that "a German education is identical with education as such."[60]

Simultaneously with the attack on the Polish language in the schools the government moved forward with a proposal for its abolition in the state administration, the judiciary, and public affairs in general. In 1870, Count Königsmarck, governor-general of Posen, had justified the policy. If Posen was to be "amalgamated with the rest of the monarchy," he wrote, some way had to be found to breach the "isolation" of the Polish masses from German culture. On a lower cultural and economic plane than the Germans, they were in danger of being "completely dispossessed and extirpated." By accepting German culture, on the other hand, they had the prospect of "regenerating themselves and fusing their individuality [*Eigenart*] with that of the Germans." The aim, Königsmarck claimed, was not "suppression of the Polish nationality," but its "greatest possible reconciliation" with the German. If German were made the only language of justice and government throughout the Prussian monarchy, the Poles and Danes would feel the "compulsion" to

---

[56] Karl Schneider and Eduard von Bremen, *Das Volksschulwesen im preussischen Staate* (Berlin, 1886–1887), III, 473–483.

[57] Falk to Wilhelm I, March 31 and Oct. 21, 1873. DZA Merseburg, Rep. 2.2.1., Nr. 15006, Bd. 2, pp. 178–179, 193–196v, 210–218. The active involvement of Bismarck and the king in shaping the language policy in Catholic seminaries of the Polish region can be seen in *ibid.*, pp. 164–172.

[58] Eulenburg and Falk to Wilhelm I, Aug. 17, 1872. DZA Merseburg, Rep. 2.2.1., Nr. 15006, Bd. 2, pp. 175–176. Also DZA Merseburg, Rep. 76, VII, neu. Sekt. 1, Theil II, Nr. 1, Bd. 1, pp. 44–48. King to Eulenburg and Falk, Aug. 21, 1872. *Ibid.*, pp. 177.

[59] Rudolf Korth, *Die preussische Schulpolitik und die polnischen Schulstreiks* (Würzburg, 1963), pp. 40–63.

[60] SBHA (1876), Anlagen, III, 1546.

learn it.[61] Drafted in 1872, the language of government act (*Geschäftssprach-engesetz*) was delayed until 1876 by discussions within the Prussian government and by parliamentary procedure.[62] The statute made German the language to be used for official business by all Prussian officials, agencies, and political bodies. For a maximum of twenty years (permission granted at five-year intervals) minority tongues might be used "in addition to German" in the oral proceedings and minutes of school boards, county diets, village councils and assemblies, and local courts.[63] The measure was justified, the cabinet explained to the king, because German had been taught for fifty years; "the use of the Polish tongue in house and family, at work and while socializing, in church and at religious services, in the press and literature would be completely undisturbed."[64]

Bismarck's Views on "Germanization"

Historians eager to protect Bismarck's reputation assumed that the concept of "Germanization" was so alien to his thoughts that he could never have used that term.[65] But documents already in print when this Bismarck orthodoxy flourished contradict this view. Two examples from the early period of his presidency show the close connection in his mind between material bonds, national sentiment, and political loyalty. In January 1865 he supported a proposal conceived by Gerson Bleichröder for a land bank in Posen on the grounds that the plan "promised to be of great importance for the gradual Germanization of the grand duchy of Posen, which is for political reasons so desirable." In 1866 he pressed for construction of new rail links with Posen as the quickest and surest way to impregnate "German culture and with it German sentiment."[66] Numerous unpublished documents in the German and

[61] Schieder, *Kaiserreich als Nationalstaat*, pp. 98–108.

[62] Bismarck and the king were closely involved in the drafting and revision of this statute during 1872–1876. DZA Merseburg, Rep. 2.2.1., Nr. 15006, Bd. 2, pp. 173–174, 197–199, 222–223, 240–243; and cabinet meetings of May 23 and 27, 1875, DZA Merseburg, Rep. 90a, B, III, 2b, Nr. 6, Vol. 87.

[63] GSP (1876), pp. 389–392. For the exceptions see the ordinance of Aug. 28, 1876 (*Ibid.*, 393–394) and cabinet to king, Aug. 9, 1876 and Aug. 15, 1878. DZA Merseburg, Rep. 2.2.1., Nr. 15006, Vol. 2, pp. 240–245v. The Gerichtsverfassungsgesetz of Jan. 27, 1877 made German the only language of justice. RGB (1877), p. 74 (paragraph 186).

[64] Cabinet to king, Aug. 9, 1876. DZA Merseburg, Rep. 2.2.1., Nr. 15006, Vol. 2, pp. 240–243v.

[65] See particularly Rothfels, *Bismarck: Der Osten und das Reich*, pp. 68ff. For many years Rothfels's views, first published in *Bismarck und der Osten* (Leipzig, 1934) and *Ostraum, Preussentum und Reichsgedanke* (Leipzig, 1935), were the commonly accepted interpretation of Bismarck's views on the Polish question and German nationalism. See Walther Bussmann, *Das Zeitalter Bismarcks*, in Leo Just ed., *Handbuch der deutschen Geschichte*, vol. 3/II (Konstanz, 1956), p. 247.

[66] Bismarck to Bodelschwingh, Jan. 29, 1865. GW, V, 69–70, and to Bodelschwingh, Eulenburg, and Itzenplitz, Jan. 20, 1866. AWB, I, 74. For other instances, also long in print, in which

Prussian archives, furthermore, show that the word "Germanization" was fairly common in Bismarck's thoughts. For more than twenty years he was the driving force behind the effort to Germanize the Poles.

The actual problem is not whether he used the term, but what he meant by it. Germanization in the form of closer economic ties did not necessarily mean ethnic assimilation. The survival of the East Prussian Masurians and Lithuanians showed that the impregnation of German culture and German sentiment need not deprive minorities of their native tongues.[67] That Bismarck used the terms "Germanization" and "re-Germanization" with regard to the Alsatians reinforces the point; it was their loyalty he needed, not their language, which was already German. As a young man, moreover, Bismarck had gone to the trouble of studying Polish, perhaps intrigued by the Polish peasants (*Kaschuben*) whom he encountered in Pomerania. In 1870 he could still muster enough of the language to attempt conversation with wounded Polish soldiers. He attempted to persuade Crown Prince Friedrich Wilhelm to learn Polish and to have it taught to the future Wilhelm II, asserting that the Great Elector had spoken Polish, as had his successors before Frederick the Great. But the heir to the throne refused, expressing distaste for both people and language ("They must learn German").[68]

To patriotic Poles inclusion in a united Germany was a shocking contradiction. "We find ourselves in a peculiar situation during the proceedings in this chamber," one of their spokesmen told the Reichstag, "when words resound in our ears about the German past, about German mores and customs, about the welfare of the German people. Not that we begrudge the German people their welfare or want to impede their future. But what for you may be a common bond—this past, these mores and customs, this future—is for us more an element of separation vis-à-vis yourselves." Bismarck had once spoken, he continued, of the "right of a nation to exist, to breathe, and to unite." The "divine and inalienable right" that Germans demanded for themselves they should grant to others.[69] To such an argument Bismarck had a standard reply. "The gentlemen belong to no other state and to no other people than to

---

Bismarck used the word "Germanized" see: *GW*, VIc, 329 (fn.); *AWB*, I, 340–341; Lucius, *Bismarck-Erinnerungen*, p. 338. How Rothfels, who knew the published Bismarck sources well, could have overlooked these passages is mystifying. He knew of only two instances recorded in 1863 and 1876 in which Bismarck was reputed to have used the word "Germanization," but he dismissed the first as "unbelievable"; the second, as "isolated." See his *Bismarck: Der Osten, und das Reich*, pp. 80–81 (fn.). As the references in this chapter show, the word and the purpose were commonplace in the deliberations of the Prussian cabinet and ministries (Bismarck included), particularly during the 1880s.

[67] See Walther Hubatsch, *Masuren und Preussisch-Litthauen in der Nationalitätenpolitik Preussens 1870–1920* (Marburg, 1966).

[68] Busch, *Tagebuchblätter*, I, 466, 554–555.

[69] *SBR* (1870), I, 74 (Feb. 24, 1870); see also *SBR* (1867), I, 83–85 (Sept. 24, 1867), and *SBR* (1871), First Session, I, 72 (Apr. 1, 1871), and II, 833 (May 20, 1871).

Prussia, to which I also belong." He denied that Polish deputies had any mandate to speak for the Polish-speaking population of Prussia. "Your countrymen [*Landsleute*] fought with the same courage and with the same devotion to the cause that united us here as did the inhabitants of every other part of Prussia. The countrymen, whom you represent here, are just as thankful for the blessings of Prussian culture as are the inhabitants of Silesia and other provinces."[70]

To attain his objectives simultaneously with Germans and Poles, Bismarck had to talk out of both sides of his mouth. To the former he spoke of German nationalism; to the latter, of Prussian patriotism. Before 1866 it had been possible to see Prussia as a state-nation transcending ethnic differences. Now the claim was incongruous. From the moment in April 1866 when he launched Prussia on a course leading to the creation of a German nation-state, there was no longer any force to Bismarck's contention that the king of Prussia had the same claim on the loyalty of his Polish as on that of his German subjects. If assimilation of the Poles was attainable at all, it could only be through Germanization in the full ethnic sense of the term. The state-nation had to be converted into a nation-state.

Bismarck always contended that his Polish policy was entirely defensive. For ten years, he wrote in 1872, the Poles had made progress in their effort to "undermine the foundations of the Prussian state." "We do not wish to extirpate Polish culture [*Polenthum*]; we wish instead to defend German culture [*Deutschthum*] from being extirpated." Whole villages in Posen, West Prussia, and Upper Silesia, he maintained, had become Polonized, families with German names no longer spoke the tongue of their ancestors.[71] Prussia's task was to deprive Polish peasants and workers of pastoral and aristocratic leadership and, by teaching them German, open their minds to the aims and policies of the government. The announced purpose of the Bismarck government was to introduce ethnic minorities to the "language of state" in order to make them "members of the state," while permitting them to retain their mother tongues.[72] What to Bismarck and to other ministers and officials was a justifiable policy of German self-preservation was to the Poles a drastic threat to their cultural heritage and ethnic identity.[73] In politics the difference between

[70] *SBR* (1871), First Session, I, 98 (Apr. 1, 1871); GW, XI, 147–148. See also the similar reply by the Reichstag deputy Count Renard: "I want to note, in response to Deputy Motty, that the province of Posen contains no Polish citizens, only citizens of the Prussian state." *Verhandlungen des konstituirenden Reichstages* (1867), p. 58. On Apr. 18, 1872, Bismarck responded to protests from Poles at Gostyn as follows: "All of his subjects, whether Polish or German speaking, are equally close to the heart of the king." GW, XIV, 830–831.

[71] GW, XIV, 827; BR, XII, 103–104.

[72] GW, VIc, 241–242, 328–329 (fn.); BR, X, 294; XI, 124–130, 440–447, 465; XII, 103–104.

[73] See particularly the defense of the Polish cause by Ludwig von Jazdzewski in the great debate of Jan. 15–16, 1886. *SBR* (1885–1886), II, 526–536.

offense and defense is often unclear. In this case what was defensive for Germans was offensive to Poles.

The Danish Problem

The annexation of Schleswig-Holstein in 1866 produced another problem of assimilation. Of the 401,925 inhabitants of Schleswig in 1864, 142,940 (36 percent) spoke Danish. Under the treaty of 1864 Danes had the option of choosing Danish citizenship. Those who exercised the option could emigrate with their property to Denmark or remain resident with their property in Schleswig. Not until the wars of 1866 and 1870 did this choice become popular, chiefly among young men subject to military service. Despite their anti-German sentiments, most Danes elected to remain in the homeland where their families had lived for generations. For half a century the Danish minority, seconded by the government and newspaper press of Denmark, protested German rule. The electoral districts were designed to favor German candidates; yet Danish voters managed regularly to elect one protest deputy (two in 1881) to the German Reichstag. Although two Danes were elected to the Prussian Landtag in 1866, they refused to swear allegiance to the Prussian constitution (on the grounds that the oath would recognize the annexation) and were not seated; in 1882 an elected candidate finally accepted the oath—out of practicality, not conviction.[74]

The problem of the Danish minority was exacerbated by the failure of negotiations that might have led to the partition of Schleswig. At the London conference during the war of 1864 the two sides failed to agree on a line of partition and, when the war ended, the Danes were compelled to cede the entire duchy. In article 5 of the Treaty of Prague (1866) Prussia agreed to part with the northern districts of Schleswig, if the inhabitants "show their desire to be united with Denmark in a free vote." During 1867–1868 negotiations between Berlin and Copenhagen foundered on disagreements over the configuration of the frontier and guarantees to be accorded the minorities remaining in mixed regions. A decade later, in the negotiations that led to the Congress of Berlin and the Dual Alliance of 1879 Bismarck gained Austria's consent to void article 5. Since Prussia's commitment had been to Austria, not Denmark, this ended the matter as far as the Wilhelmstrasse was concerned.[75]

---

[74] Böckh, *Volkszahl und Sprachgebiet,* 220–221; Vogel et al., *Wahlen in Deutschland,* pp. 290–291; Otto Brandt, *Geschichte Schleswig-Holsteins* (4th ed., Kiel, 1949), p. 201; and Troels Fink, *Geschichte des schleswigschen Grenzlandes* (Copenhagen, 1958), pp. 157ff.

[75] The diplomatic side of the North Schleswig story has been thoroughly documented: Walter Platzhoff, Kurt Rheindorf, and Johannes Tiedje, eds., *Bismarck und die nordschleswigsche Frage, 1864–1879: Die diplomatischen Akten des auswärtigen Amtes zur Geschichte des Artikels V des Prager Friedens* (Berlin, 1925); Fritz Hahnsen, ed., *Ursprung und Geschichte des Artikels V des Prager Friedens: Die deutschen Akten zur Frage der Teilung Schleswigs, 1863–1879* (2 vols., Breslau, 1929);

Historians have disagreed on whether Bismarck sincerely desired a better ethnic frontier in northern Schleswig. Those who grant him sincerity are uncertain when and why he changed his mind.[76] But there seems to be no reason to doubt that the Danish government, if it had not seriously overestimated its prospects, could have gained at the London conference the same frontier it acquired at Versailles in 1919.[77] In view of the Polish experience Bismarck "held that rule over alien nationalities was scarcely desirable."[78] Once the Danes were defeated, however, he concluded that military considerations must override the ethnic factor in establishing the line of partition. As later in the case of Metz, he accepted the contention of Wilhelm and his generals that Flensburg, Düppel, and Alsen must remain in Prussian hands. But he also desired to establish the new border so far north that no significant German enclave would be left under Danish rule. Since this meant the inclusion of Danish districts in Germany, the Prussian commitment at Prague to hold a plebiscite cannot be taken at full value. Yet the Danes might still have gained a significant rectification of the frontier in the negotiations of 1867–1868 if they could have accepted the border offered and minority guarantees demanded by Berlin.

Bismarck often contended that the surrender of northern Schleswig was made impossible by the resistance of the king, the military, and German public opinion.[79] What he meant was that, in the absence of any compelling reason provided by European politics, there was no need to force a confrontation over the issue with Wilhelm and his generals or to affront German public opinion by ceding what the Danes demanded. No line of partition

and Aage Friis, *Den danske Regering og Nordschlesvigs genforening med Danmark* (4 vols., Copenhagen, 1921–1939), *Det Nordslesvigske Spørgsmaal 1864–1879* (5 vols., 1921–1946), and *L'Europe, Le Danemark et le Slesvig du Nord, 1864–1879* (4 vols., Copenhagen, 1939–1959).

[76] Aage Friis, "Die Aufhebung des Artikels V des Prager Friedens," *Historische Zeitschrift*, 125 (1921–1922), pp. 45–62; Walter Platzhoff, "Bismarck und die nordschleswigsche Frage von 1864 bis 1879," in Platzhoff et al., *Nordschleswigsche Frage*, pp. 3–55, and "Die deutsche Aktenpublikation über den Artikel V des Prager Friedens," *Archiv für Politik und Geschichte*, 4 (1925), pp. 50–57, and 5 (1926), pp. 661–675. See also the debate between Scharff and Winckler: Alexander Scharff, "Deutsche Ordnungsgedanken zum volklichen Leben in Nordschleswig vor 1914," in *Flensburger Tage 1954* (Flensburg, 1955), pp. 53–71 and "Das Volkstums- und Grenzproblem in historischer Sicht," in *Zur Grenzfrage Schleswigs: Vier historische-politische Vorträge* (Kiel, 1954), pp. 19–35; Martin Winckler, "Die Aufhebung des Artikels V des Prager Friedens und Bismarcks Weg zum Zweibund," *Historische Zeitschraft*, 179 (1955), pp. 471–509; "Die Zielsetzung in Bismarcks Nordschleswig-Politik und die schleswigsche Grenzfrage," *Die Welt als Geschichte*, 16 (1956), pp. 211–217, and "Noch einmal: Zur Zielsetzung in Bismarcks Nordschleswig-Politik," *Die Welt als Geschichte*, 17 (1957), pp. 203–210.

[77] Alexander Scharff, "Bismarcks Plan einer Volksbefragung im Herzogtum Schleswig 1864," in *Schleswig-Holstein in der deutschen und nord-europäischen Geschichte* (Stuttgart, 1969), pp. 236–250; Lawrence Steefel, *The Schleswig-Holstein Question* (Cambridge, Mass., 1932), p. 242.

[78] *Auswärtige Politik Preussens*, IX, 913.

[79] Platzhoff, "Bismarck und die nordschleswigsche Frage," pp. 13ff.; *Origines Diplomatiques*, VII, 56; *GW*, V, 266–270, VI, 276, 293, XIV, 852.

acceptable from the military point of view, furthermore, would have ended the ethnic problem; many Danes and Germans would have been left on the wrong side of the frontier. Still, as long as war with France loomed and a revanchist party lowered in Vienna, Bismarck kept open the question of a border rectification. The victory over France ended simultaneously the threat that Napoleon might intervene in behalf of Danish irredentism and that Denmark might ally with a German foe. The prospect of a border rectification no longer served any purpose in Germany's foreign relations. Article 5 was now just an embarrassment, a weak point in the armor of German foreign policy, to be removed at the earliest opportunity. In 1878–1879 Bismarck found his chance.

In the beginning the provincial government of Schleswig-Holstein under the governor Baron von Scheel-Plessen followed, on Bismarck's instructions, a mild policy toward the Danish population. Local administrators who would have preferred a hard line were frequently overruled. More than a thousand young men who opted for Denmark in order to avoid military service were permitted to return under the Convention of Apenrade of January 1872. By 1881, 25,000 Danish citizens were resident in northern Schleswig, in contrast to 4,575 in 1867.[80] Under Prussian regulations of 1864 the affected residents of each school district could decide by majority vote whether German should be the language of instruction in the elementary schools. "A predominant majority bordering on unanimity" could choose three to six hours of instruction weekly in the German language. In early 1870 the Kultusministerium proposed that German be introduced as the sole language of instruction beyond the second or third year in the elementary schools and that Danish be restricted to instruction in religion—"as in the Polish districts of West Prussia and Posen." Bismarck doubted "the necessity of going so far so soon." He advised his colleagues "to be satisfied for now to declare the German language an obligatory subject of instruction, to which about six hours per week must be devoted. In this form the measure would appear to be unquestionably the result of a natural concern for the welfare [of the pupils], distant from the question of Germanization. Later we can go further."[81] The ministers accepted Bismarck's judgment, which was incorporated in an instruction to the provincial government issued on August 26, 1871.[82]

Historians have wondered why the minutes of the cabinet meeting of May

[80] GW, V, 242, 282; Hauser, Preussische Staatsräson, pp. 43–47.

[81] Cabinet meeting of May 30, 1870. DZA Merseburg, Rep. 77, Titel 50, Nr. 84, Vol. 1.

[82] Zeitungsbericht, July 20, 1870, and ministerial order of Aug. 17, 1871. DZA Merseburg, Rep. 77, Titel 50, Nr. 84, Vol. 1. The order is in Hauser, Preussische Staatsräson, pp. 192–193. Perhaps because war intervened, there was a delay in the execution of the decision of May 30, 1870. On May 16, 1871, Bismarck demanded "that the introduction of the German language in the schools of North Schleswig be expedited" in accordance with the cabinet's decision of the previous year. Poschinger, ed., Bismarck-Portefeuille, I, 22.

30, 1870, stand alone in the files of the Prussian cabinet and imperial chancellery as evidence of Bismarck's intentions with regard to the Danish minority. Silence has even been construed as proof of his detachment. Prussian officials, not Bismarck, are seen as the authors of the policy of Germanization that began in northern Schleswig during the late 1870s.[83] But Prussian policy toward the Danish minority cannot be studied apart from Prussian policy toward the Polish and Lithuanian minorities and German imperial policy toward the French minority. Bismarck, the Prussian cabinet, and imperial government had a single policy toward linguistic minorities. That Prussian ministers (including Bismarck) spoke primarily of Posen, West Prussia, and Upper Silesia in formulating and executing that policy was because those regions contained millions who spoke an alien tongue; Schleswig, only thousands.

The successive steps in the government's attack on the "Danish question" were either identical with or parallel to those taken on the "Polish question." The school inspection act of 1872 gave the state the power to end the role of Danish clergymen in the schools. Although the language of government act of 1876 made German the only official language for government business, exceptions were permitted, including several counties inhabited by Danes in North Schleswig. In 1881 this exception was cancelled, five years ahead of its cancellation in French-, Polish-, and Lithuanian-speaking regions.[84] On the grounds that the language of government act of 1876 made necessary an increased knowledge of German, the Schleswig district government in March 1878 was authorized by Berlin (against the better judgment of provincial Governor Scheel-Plessen and county counselors of the four most affected districts) to make obligatory the teaching of German on all levels of all elementary schools in North Schleswig—three hours weekly on the lower level, seven hours on the upper levels. The use of German as the language of instruction was required for two hours weekly on the middle and upper levels. German could be made the sole language of instruction by action of the governor or by the majority vote of affected parents.[85]

Alsace-Lorraine

Through the annexation of Alsace-Lorraine in 1871 the German Reich (population: 41,028,150) acquired a region of 5,605 square miles inhabited by 1,549,600 people grouped in three districts: Upper Alsace (459,600), Lower

[83] See particularly Scharff, "Deutsche Ordungsgedanken," pp. 58–59; Winckler, "Zielsetzung," pp. 54–62; and "Noch einmal," pp. 204ff.

[84] Cabinet to king, Sept. 29, 1881. DZA Merseburg, Rep. 2.2.1., Nr. 15006, Vol. 2, p. 258.

[85] Hauser, Preussische Staatsräson, pp. 71–80, 199–201; also Oswald Hauser, "Zum Problem der Nationalisierung Preussens," Historische Zeitschrift, 202 (1966), pp. 529–541, and Schneider and Bremen, Volksschulwesen, III, 483–494.

Alsace (600,400), and Lorraine (489,400). Of the inhabitants of the two Alsatian districts about 50,000 spoke French. In Lorraine about 135,000 spoke French. Town dwellers tended to be bilingual; Metz and its environs, however, were almost solidly French. Whether French- or German-speaking, the inhabitants of all three districts were opposed to annexation. After two centuries of French rule, the German-speaking population could no longer identify with their ethnic brethren across the border. Participation in the events of the French Revolution and Napoleonic era, particularly in its economic and social reforms, had established new bonds with France that tended to transcend without erasing ethnic differences. During the industrial revolution of the nineteenth century the economy of the region had become intimately linked with the French economy as a whole. Yet there were lingering ethnic and political tensions between Alsace-Lorraine and the rest of France that the German government might have been able to exploit in its effort to assimilate the population.[86]

In Germany there were no illusions about the loyalties of the annexed people—only about the speed with which the German-speaking inhabitants could be assimilated. The Reichstag debate on the annexation bill in May–June 1871 mirrored the variety of motives and expectations with which Bismarck and members of the Reichstag viewed annexation and the problem of assimilation. As before, Bismarck based the case for annexation on the requirements of military security. For three hundred years, he contended, almost every generation of Germans had been compelled to "draw the sword against France." When victorious, the Germans had been prevented by their allies from gaining a defensible frontier. The lack of it had prevented south German governments from pursuing their real interests in times of crisis with France. Without Strassburg, the "sally port" of the French, the south would never feel secure in a united Germany. Speakers for the liberal parties justified annexation upon historical and ethnic grounds, as well as on the requirements of defense. At the extremes were Wilhelm Löwe, who stressed the latter motive to the exclusion of the former, and Franz Wigard, of whom the reverse was true. Typical of the ethnic arguments were the assertions of Eduard Lasker and Max Duncker that the inhabitants were "for the most part our nationality," and "flesh of our flesh and blood of our blood." Only among splinter groups on the extreme left of the chamber (Leopold Sonnemann and August Bebel) was there any conviction that military security and ethnic character were inadequate grounds for denying to the annexed people the right of self-determination. To reject the existence of a "collective will" and the right of

[86] On the general history of Alsace-Lorraine see Karl Stählin, *Geschichte Elsass-Lothringens* (Munich, 1920); Martin Spahn, *Elsass-Lothringen* (Berlin, 1919); and Coleman Phillipson, *Alsace-Lorraine* (New York, 1918), and Dan P. Silverman, *Reluctant Union: Alsace Lorraine and Imperial Germany, 1871–1918* (University Park, 1972).

"collective action by the nation," argued Schulze-Delitzsch, was to attack the "very heart of nationality."

While rejecting history and ethnicity as grounds for annexation, Bismarck believed that the "basically German [*urdeutsch*]" character of the inhabitants would ease their assimilation. That they had been won by the French was in itself evidence that they possessed "in high degree" those Germanic qualities that distinguished Germans from Frenchmen. Their "industry and love of order" had made them a "kind of aristocracy in France." Their "greater ability" and "greater reliability" had given them a place in French military and public service far out of proportion to their actual number. That they identified themselves with France was proof of their "German character," for it was a peculiarity of the Germans that every *Stamm* wished to establish its superiority over its nearest neighbor. Backed by the "glitter" of Paris and the "unified greatness" of France, the Alsatians and Lorrainers had been able to look down on their fellow Germans. Whatever the cause, their antipathy for Germany was a fact, "and it is our duty to overcome it with patience." If sometimes more clumsy than the French, German statesmen were accustomed "to govern with greater benevolence and humaneness." This superiority of the "German nature" would soon seduce "the German hearts of the Alsatians." "I believe therefore that we shall succeed through German patience and German benevolence in winning our countrymen there—perhaps in less time than is now expected."[87]

The ambivalence on which the German effort to assimilate Alsace-Lorraine ultimately foundered was already evident in this debate. The inhabitants were informed that their incorporation in Germany was an act of *Realpolitik*, that they were wanted not for their own sake, but for the terrain on which they lived; yet they were also assured that the Germans had come as liberators, that annexation was but the final stage in the liberation of the German *Volksgeist* from the bondage of French culture. They were told both that they were "German" and that they must be "Germanized" (Treitschke: "The work of Germanization will succeed and must succeed. . . . The voice of the blood will speak again in Alsace"). They were denied equality of status within the new empire because they were anti-German; lacking equality, they were all the more inclined to disloyalty.[88]

Soon after the German armies had moved into northern France, the region to be annexed was separated administratively from the rest of France and placed under a governor-general, Count Bismarck-Bohlen, the chancellor's cousin. The decree creating this office was signed by Wilhelm as king of Prussia and commander-in-chief of the German forces. Bismarck-Bohlen thought

[87] *SBR* (1871), First Session, I, 517–521; II, 813–936, 995–1015. In 1879 he still spoke of this conviction. *BR*, VII, 422–423. The term "Alsatians" was often used by Germans as shorthand for "Alsatians and Lorrainers."

[88] *SBR* (1871), II, 814–818.

that "his main task should be to alleviate the misery caused by the war, and to render the Alsatians well disposed toward the future masters of the country." But the chancellor disagreed, and, while the war lasted, Alsace-Lorraine received no better treatment than the rest of occupied France.[89] The annexation statute (June 9, 1871) ended military rule, but introduced a "dictatorship" lasting until January 1, 1873 (later extended one year). During this period the Kaiser exercised the executive power, acting through the chancellor and a governor-general in Strassburg (now Eduard von Möller). The only restriction placed on the Kaiser's power was the provision that legislation required the agreement of the Bundesrat and that loans and financial guarantees burdening the Reich had to be approved by the Reichstag.[90] Nor did the dictatorship end on January 1, 1874. The executive power remained as before in the hands of Kaiser, chancellor, and governor-general. The Reichstag, enlarged by fifteen members elected from the Reichsland, now shared legislative power with the Bundesrat, which had no representation from the Reichsland. But the Kaiser retained the power to rule by decree pending approval by the Reichstag.[91] The Reichsland was an anomaly in the government of the Reich—a unitary province in a federal state. Alsatians called it "Germany's first colony." Not until 1911 did the Reichsland receive a constitution and a degree of autonomy nearly equivalent to that of the empire's federal states.

The first target of the protest movement of Alsace-Lorraine was the French government, not the German. In February 1871 the seventeen delegates from Alsace and Lorraine to the French National Assembly at Bordeaux protested the assembly's acceptance of Germany's peace terms. Three years later the fifteen deputies elected to the Reichstag demanded, on their first appearance in that body, a plebiscite to ascertain the wishes of the population. Their spokesman—an Alsatian named Teutsch (!), whose request to speak in French was denied—was frequently interrupted by hooting and laughter. The discourtesy, widely reported in the European press, "aroused the impression that Germany was contemptuous of the feelings of its new subjects and stamped their representatives as martyrs of their convictions."[92] "We shall rely on God! We shall rely on the decision of Europe" was Teutsch's final cry. But it was soon evident that the Alsatians could not even rely on each other. The bishop of Strassburg, Andreas Raess, who had signed the plebiscite demand, now disavowed it. "Alsatians and Lorrainers of my faith," he declared, "are not at all inclined to question the validity of a treaty signed by two great powers."[93]

[89] Bertram Winterhalter, "Die Behandlung der französischen Zivilbevölkerung durch die deutschen Truppen im Kriege 1870/71" (dissertation, Freiburg, 1952), pp. 186ff. See also Busch, *Tagebuchblätter*, II, 10.

[90] RGB (1871), pp. 212–213; (1872), pp. 208–209.

[91] RGB (1873), pp. 161–163.

[92] SBR (1874), I, 99–102; III, no. 30.

[93] SBR (1874), I, 102.

The deputies and their constituents divided into three political groups: "protesters," "autonomists," and Catholic clericals. The protesters were uncompromisingly opposed to German rule under all circumstances; the autonomists, although no less opposed to annexation, hoped through collaboration to attain for the Reichsland the status of a German federal state. While protesters and clericals dominated the election of 1874, the autonomists were victorious in 1877; the clericals strove primarily to protect Catholic interests, particularly in Lower Alsace.[94] On arriving in Berlin the autonomists established contact with Bismarck and the National Liberal party. "We come before you," declared their leader August Schneegans, "as German representatives of a German territory."[95]

Bismarck was not opposed in the beginning to the idea of federal autonomy for Alsace-Lorraine. In the annexation debate of 1871 he had contended that the particularistic attitudes that Alsatians had harbored "in typical German fashion" during two centuries of French rule were a foundation upon which the new regime could build. "The more the residents of Alsace feel themselves to be Alsatians, the more they will discard their Frenchness." Once they had fully identified themselves as Alsatians, they would "logically" conceive of themselves as Germans.[96] As a means to that end Bismarck encouraged the Reichsland deputies in 1877 to seek support in the Reichstag for an autonomous Reichsland. Yet he opposed as too far-reaching the program that Schneegans presented in 1878, under which the Reichsland would have been linked to the Reich only by "personal union" under the Kaiser, on the pattern of Luxemburg and the Netherlands. He was alarmed, furthermore, by Schneegans's contention that historically Alsace-Lorraine had always mediated between the two great peoples (*Kulturvölker*) of Europe, transmitting the best of each culture to the other. Both the proposal and the argument made in its defense smacked of neutralization, and a neutralized Alsace-Lorraine, Bismarck believed, would inevitably side with France in any future crisis.[97]

Out of the collaboration between Bismarck, the autonomists, and national liberals came a series of statutes culminating in the act of July 4, 1879, which created a territorial assembly (*Landesausschuss*) chosen indirectly and invested with power to initiate bills. The Kaiser's executive authority was delegated to a governor (*Statthalter*) assisted by a "ministry for Alsace-Lorraine"—in reality a miniature cabinet headed by a legally "responsible" state-secretary and situated in Strassburg. (The imperial office for Alsace-Lorraine at Berlin was dissolved.) This statute, under which the Reichsland was governed until 1911, stopped short of autonomy. Under it all laws passed in Strassburg had to be approved by the Bundesrat (in which the Reichsland now had represen-

[94] Silverman, *Reluctant Union*, pp. 112–114.
[95] BP, II, 248–250, 256.
[96] BR, V, 56–57, 74ff.
[97] BR, VII, 410ff; SBR (1878), I, 395–398; (1879), 556–566; BP, I, 125, 128, 134–235; GW, VIc, 103–106; VIII, 192–194.

tation, but no votes) and by the Kaiser, who also appointed the governor and high officials of the ministry. Bundesrat and Reichstag, furthermore, retained the power to legislate for the territory. The laws they passed took precedence over bills passed by the territorial assembly. The Kaiser, furthermore, kept his power to rule by decree while the Reichstag was not in session.[98]

The limited self-government achieved under this statute did not satisfy the autonomists, not to speak of the protesters. They might have been happier had Bismarck succeeded with his proposal that Crown Prince Friedrich Wilhelm assume the governorship, establish his residence in Strassburg, and play an active role in its government. The territory would then have become the Dauphiné or Wales of the Hohenzollern monarchy. But the plan collapsed in 1878 when the crown prince had to substitute for the Kaiser while the latter recovered from wounds suffered in an attempted assassination.[99] Instead Bismarck chose as governor in succession two prominent figures: Edwin von Manteuffel (1879–1885) and Prince Chlodwig zu Hohenlohe-Schillingsfürst (1885–1894). Even if the Reichsland had received a surrogate monarch in the person of Friedrich Wilhelm, it would have still lacked one of the principal attributes of a federal state—voting membership in the Bundesrat. This Bismarck opposed in the belief that, since the Reichsland delegates would inevitably vote with Prussia in the chamber, it would be unacceptable to the other federal states.[100] The disappointment of the autonomists was keen. They refused to accept posts in the Reichsland administration and, under the influence of Léon-Michel Gambetta, became reconciled to the protesters. Only Schneegans remained loyal to the program of collaboration. Completely isolated by the apostasy of his followers, he retired from politics, accepting a post in the Prussian consular service.[101]

Meanwhile, the task of assimilation was pursued in other ways, one of which was the encouragement of mass emigration in order to rid the territory of its disaffected population.[102] An "option clause" of the Treaty of Frankfurt granted inhabitants the right to emigrate to France. By October 1, 1872, 538,568 persons (one-third of the total population) had declared their intent to do so. Of these 378,777 were already living as émigrés in France and chose to stay there. A disproportionately large number of the 159,791 *Optanten* then resident in Alsace-Lorraine lived in regions that were most solidly German-speaking (91,962 in Upper Alsace, 39,190 in Lower Alsace), while the smallest number (28,639) lived in Lorraine. Yet only 50,148 actually emigrated, of whom 21,739 came from Lorraine. Here the solidly French-speak-

---

[98] *SBR* (1879), pp. 556–671, 1616–1639, 1737–1775; *RGB* (1879), pp. 165–169; *BP*, I, 161–172; II, 261–264, 318, 322–323.

[99] *BP*, I, 161; *GW*, VIII, 256.

[100] *BR*, VII, 419–420.

[101] Stählin, *Elsass-Lothringen*, pp. 226–227.

[102] *GW*, VIc, 22–24.

ing regions were the greatest losers, especially the city and county of Metz. The *Optanten* of 1871–1873 were followed by a steady stream of emigrants in later years. About 300,000 of the 480,000 emigrants from Alsace-Lorraine between 1870 and 1914 settled in France, where they kept alive the cause of recovery and revenge. They were drawn from all classes and occupations. Emigration was difficult for people of property, but relatively easy for artisans, laborers, and professional people. Many were young men eager to evade conscription into the German army. The emigrants were replaced by migrants from "old Germany," some of whom were carpetbagger types. Between 1871 and 1910 the number of "old Germans" residing in Alsace-Lorraine rose from 78,687 to 295,436. Often they met hostility from the natives and returned the same.[103]

Capital also migrated. For the Alsatian textile industry—the most flourishing industry of the region—annexation was particularly disruptive. Manufacturers were cut off from normal markets, spinners and weavers from dyers and printers. Their entry into the German Zollverein, on the other hand, spread panic among German textile manufacturers, whose plants were outmoded in contrast to the Alsatian. The transition was eased by a German-French tariff agreement that held the French border open for Alsatian textiles until 1873. Still, many Alsatian textile manufacturers either abandoned Alsace altogether or at least shifted the center of their operations to branches in France. Their departure depressed the textile machinery and chemical industries. Lorraine iron manufacturers faced the same problem, and here too there was some loss of capital as industrialists shifted their operations to ore fields on the other side of the border. Capital for development of the Lorraine deposits (after the Gilchrist Thomas process made possible the smelting of phosphorous ores) came from "old German" and foreign sources. Initially Lorraine ore was shipped to mills in Rhineland-Westphalia for processing, a natural division of labor. Rhenish and Westphalian iron makers agitated for a Moselle canal for readier and cheaper transport of the ore. But the agitation died in the 1890s when Lorraine industrialists built their own smelters; the partners had become competitors.

Another opportunity for closer economic links between the Reichsland and the rest of Germany came in the 1880s, when Bismarck proposed a state monopoly on the processing and sale of tobacco. The monopoly would have expanded the state-owned tobacco factory in Strassburg (one of the fiscal fruits of annexation) and provided a growing market for local tobacco growers. But Bismarck's project was defeated. Throughout its history the Reichsland was never fully integrated into the German economy. Material ties that

[103] A. Gerardot, *Die Optionsfrage in Elsass-Lothringen* (Strassburg, 1913); Heinz Kloss, "Die Auswanderung aus dem Elsass und aus dem deutschsprachigen Lothringen nach Frankreich," in Paul Wentzcke, ed., *Schicksalswege am Oberrhein* (Heidelberg, 1952), pp. 250–297; Silverman, *Reluctant Union*, pp. 68–73; Stählin, *Elsass-Lothringen*, pp. 214–219.

would have reinforced Germanization were not as strong as they might have been.[104]

As used by Bismarck, the terms "Germanization" and "re-Germanization" had a cultural as well as a political import.[105] Since its conquest by France under Louis XIV, the linguistic map of Alsace-Lorraine appears to have changed little. Attempts by Napoleon III in the 1860s to "Frenchify" the German-speaking population through the schools made little headway. But that did not deter Bismarck from instituting the same policy in reverse after 1871. On April 14, 1871, the teaching of French was prohibited in the lower grades of elementary schools. In October 1872 the prohibition was extended to the upper grades, except where for commercial reasons fluent French was needed; here up to four hours of instruction weekly were permitted. On January 4, 1874, elementary schools were ordered to use German as the language of instruction. Again there were exceptions: classes in which all pupils were French-speaking and mixed classes for which the government made the decision. Schools in French-speaking and mixed districts were required to give five hours of instruction in German weekly and were permitted three to six hours of instruction in French. In the secondary schools French was permitted as the language of instruction wherever all students were French-speaking. Where this was not the case French was used only in courses on the French language and literature. Initially French instruction was permitted in the *Gymnasia* from four to six hours weekly, German instruction for only three. New regulations in 1878 cut French instruction to three and in 1883 to two hours weekly. Until 1888 teachers of science and mathematics were permitted to instruct in French, as long as they taught the German equivalents of technical terms. Students taking science examinations could respond in either French or German. Compositions could be composed in either language, stylistic requirements being less stringent for French-speaking students writing in German. In French-speaking regions normal schools for the education of teachers continued to instruct in French unless directed otherwise by the government. Teaching examinations were normally in German, but exceptions were made for French-speaking candidates.[106]

A restored University of Strassburg was intended to be a major instrument for the cultural penetration of the Reichsland. Founded in 1621, the university had been one of Germany's finest at the end of the eighteenth century. Here Goethe had studied and first met Herder. But in 1793 the revolutionary government had reduced the university to a mere academy for the training of Lutheran pastors. In April 1872 the university was refounded as the *Kaiser*

---

[104] Silverman, *Reluctant Union*, pp. 165–176.

[105] For examples see *GW*, VIc, 320–321; XIV, 961; *BP*, I, 245.

[106] Silverman, *Reluctant Union*, pp. 74–77. That Bismarck was the guiding force in fashioning language policy in the schools can be seen in the minutes of the cabinet meeting in which the matter was first discussed (Mar. 25, 1871). *DZA* Merseburg, Rep. 90a, B, III, 2b, Nr. 6, Vol. 83.

Wilhelm Universität. But the faculty was predominantly Protestant; until 1903 no Catholic theological faculty was provided; and the students came largely from "old Germany." The policy of Germanization was evident in many other areas of public life. German became the language of all official documents, of administration within the bureaucracy, of deliberation in the territorial assembly, and of the courts (unless litigants or witnesses knew only French). The names of streets, highways, and railway stations were Germanized.[107]

As in Hanover Bismarck applied in the Reichsland the classic technique of the iron hand in velvet glove. In his instructions to *Oberpräsident* Möller during the early seventies he directed that collaborators were to be well treated, antipathy was to be met with patience, active opposition with firmness. The "ringleaders" of anti-German agitation were to be expelled, conspirators were to be tried for high treason. Relations between the natives and the French government and French organizations were to be severed, the Reichsland sealed off from French influence. Jesuit schools were to be closed; clerical teachers who were "poisonous in their effect on the German spirit" were to be dismissed. Yet every effort was to be made to avoid the impression that the Reichsland was being "Prussianized." Native officials were to be employed wherever possible. Lesser officials imported from Prussia were to be sternly chastised for discourtesy and high-handedness in dealing with the public; "the French endure injustice better than rudeness." Before important decisions were made by the administration the population was to be consulted through their elected representatives. Treasury surpluses were to be expended in the Reichsland, not transferred to Berlin, lest the impression grow that Alsace-Lorraine was being exploited like a colonial possession.[108]

Bismarck was "pleasantly surprised" by Möller's success in gaining the confidence of the "pro-German" element, but annoyed by the independence the official showed in reporting directly to the Kaiser.[109] As governor, Manteuffel had constitutionally the independence that Möller had usurped, and Bismarck withdrew for a time from active participation in Reichsland affairs. He hoped that Manteuffel's prestige as a field marshal, former chief of the Prussian military cabinet, former governor of Schleswig, military governor of occupied France during 1871–1873, and commander of the 15th Army Corps in Alsace-Lorraine, would impress the natives. Manteuffel governed somewhat in the manner of a petty potentate. On certain days of the week he opened his door to the lowliest citizens, listening to their grievances and accepting their petitions. But his primary effort was devoted to winning the upper class of wealthy businessmen, big landowners, and high churchmen whom he lavishly entertained. Subordinates, who resented his autocratic ways, claimed

---

[107] Silverman, *Reluctant Union*, pp. 81–82. On the expected benefit of the restoration of the university see *SBR* (1871), First Session, I, 895–911.

[108] *GW*, VIc, 20–22; *DZA* Potsdam, Reichskanzleramt, 1452, pp. 153–153v.

[109] Kohl, ed., *Anhang*, I, 267; *GW*, VIc, 90–91, 121.

that the ordinary citizen found that the best channel for the solution of his problems was through these pro-French notables, rather than through government officials. Being Francophile seemed to have its rewards.[110]

Bismarck was critical of Manteuffel's efforts. Germany's future, he believed, lay with the farmers and the inhabitants of the small towns, where only the German dialect was spoken. Here was to be found the unspoiled "German kernel" which would sprout, once the superficial "varnish" (for once his metaphors got out of control) of French culture had been stripped away, into a flourishing "German oak." This was the social stratum whose material interests ought to be nurtured by tax and fiscal reforms. "The obstacle to re-Germanization is to be found among the upper classes of the population, those who have connections with Paris and with French officials and will cling to them as long as they live." This educated upper class of "Parisians" would have to die off before the large towns could be assimilated. "The next generation will become German; the farmers always have been." Bismarck believed that in time the population would come to appreciate the virtues of Prussia's system of communal self-administration, which replaced the unitary and centralized administrative structure of France. But he also expected good results from the long-term effects of universal military conscription and officer training, the German system of public elementary schools, and "the greater stability of German in comparison with French conditions."[111]

[110] Stählin, *Elsass-Lothringen*, pp. 227–238.
[111] GW, VIc, 167–171, 260 (headnote), 289–290, 321; XIV, 924, 961; BR, VII, 421–423; IX, 242–243; BP, I, 245.

BOOK TWO

A Time for "Liberalism,"

1871–1875

There are times when one must govern with liberal policies
and times when one must govern dictatorially. Everything changes;
here nothing is eternal. I require that the structure of the German
Reich and the unity of the German nation stand firm and storm fast.
This must not be just a temporary fieldwork protected on only
a few sides. I have devoted my entire political career
from the very beginning to its creation
and consolidation. . . .

—*Bismarck in 1881.*

✠

━┿━

An Improvised Executive

THE CONSTITUTION of the North German Confederation did not provide for a central executive body. And yet one quickly developed after 1867—the Chancellor's Office (*Bundes-*, then *Reichskanzleramt*)—under Bismarck's direct authority. The functions of that body made the chancellorship, originally described as a minor post, the most powerful and prestigious political office in Germany. By his control over the chancellor's office and its successor, the Imperial Chancellery (*Reichskanzlei*), and over other imperial agencies, Bismarck soon overshadowed his colleagues in the Prussian cabinet. His personal ascendancy both in the Reich and in the Prussian governments ultimately led critics to speak of a "Bismarck dictatorship." Whatever its constitutional implications, this development aided the consolidation of the German Reich. Like the emperorship, the chancellorship became a national office and its incumbent the dominant figure in national politics. The existence of an imperial executive and, in some areas, of an imperial administration transcending Prussia and the other state governments gave to the empire a sharper profile in the German public mind.

The chancellorship and its subordinate agencies never ceased to bear signs of the improvisation that marked their origin. Earlier it was shown that the vagueness of the constitution on the subject of the Reich executive may have been a political gambit on Bismarck's part, that from the outset he may have intended ultimately to assume the position of chancellor and convert it into an important post. Yet he did not have a clear idea in the beginning what the future contours of the position would be, how large an administrative staff it would have, how that staff would be organized, what function it would assume, and above all how it would relate to the Bundesrat and the Prussian cabinet and administration. These uncertainties were by no means liquidated by the decisions Bismarck and Rudolf Delbrück made during the early months and years. On the contrary, they persisted until the end of the Reich itself, for they constituted problems of structure and coordination that were an inevitable outgrowth of the system Bismarck devised and the circumstances of its creation. The German Reich never developed a rationalized state administration clearly delineating the lines of responsibility and the relationships of power. Yet the structure, despite its contradictions and lack of verisimilitude (or was it because of them?) did provide Bismarck with a vehicle for the satisfaction of his power drive. The cost to Germany was considerable, for the system was so closely tailored to his personality and needs that no one after him was able to make it work with the same degree of effectiveness. Even he, furthermore, was dissatisfied with his creation and tinkered continually with it in the hope of rectifying the inadequacies he perceived.

Birth of the Reichskanzleramt

As amended by the constituent Reichstag, article 17 of the north German constitution made the chancellor "responsible" by virtue of his countersignature for decrees and ordinances issued by the confederate presidency. Bismarck did not reject the so-called "Bennigsen Amendment" that produced this result, although he resolutely opposed and defeated every other amendment that would have fundamentally altered the power relationships in his original constitutional draft—giving reason for the surmise that he secretly approved of it.[1] Soon after final adoption of the constitution he obtained from the Prussian cabinet a unanimous declaration that, "as the constitution now reads, only the Prussian Minister-President can be chancellor of the confederation."[2] Armed with this declaration, Bismarck defined the position and its relationship to the Prussian cabinet in a manner suitable to his own ends. The chancellor, he told the ministers in a *Votum* of June 18, 1867, was "the only responsible minister of the confederation" and was to head "the entire administration of the confederation." The chancellor himself would handle the most important affairs, the less important being delegated to a deputy (*Stellvertreter*), who must possess the "complete confidence" of the chancellor. In addition, the chancellor must have full control over all other confederate officials. It was "self-understood," he continued, that the chancellor would not (in fact, could not) undertake anything important without prior agreement by the Prussian cabinet, but this was an "internal matter of the Prussian cabinet" that could not be established in any formal way. Prussian ministers were not to be appointed to the Bundesrat; instead Prussia's delegates to that body would be "high officials" below ministerial rank, who would take their instructions from Bismarck alone.[3]

Bismarck had begun to shape the position that would enable him to dominate the Reich and Prussian administrations in the years to come. In July

---

[1] See vol. 1, p. 359, and Otto Becker, *Bismarcks Ringen um Deutschlands Gestaltung* (Heidelberg, 1958), pp. 371–398. For a contrary view see Rudolf Morsey, *Die oberste Reichsverwaltung unter Bismarck, 1867–1890* (Münster, 1957), pp. 25–28. Morsey conceded that Becker's viewpoint had "much probability for it," but he was still inclined to reject it on the grounds that in later years Bismarck never admitted having had an ulterior purpose but always attributed his assumption of the chancellorship to the necessity produced by the Bennigsen amendment. And yet the point was a sensitive one, and in many similar instances (for example, his promotion of the Hohenzollern candidature of 1870) Bismarck never confessed in later years to ulterior purposes whose existence can now be documented.

[2] Cabinet meeting of May 29, 1867. DZA Merseburg, Rep. 90a, B, III, 2b, Nr. 6, Vol. 79.

[3] GW, VI, 413–415.

1867 he explained to Karl von Savigny why the diplomat could not be offered the chancellorship as originally promised. "Through the responsibility clause the chancellor has become to a degree—if not legally, yet actually—the superior of the Prussian cabinet. . . . You are too well acquainted with constitutional law not to realize that the chancellor thereby receives the power of final decision in the affairs of the Prussian ministries of trade, war, and naval affairs, of the more important parts of the Finance Ministry, and, if the confederate constitution develops correctly, the Ministry of Foreign Affairs. . . . He receives this authority due to the circumstance that he influences the Reichstag by granting or withholding his countersignature. Because of this amendment therefore the chancellor must be simultaneously president of the Prussian cabinet if the new machine is to function at all."[4]

In later years the significance of the responsibility clause was the subject of endless debate among constitutional lawyers. Like the similar clause in the Prussian constitution, the responsibility of the chancellor was never defined; nor was any judicial procedure ever established by which he could be impeached for acts contrary to the law. At least one writer thought that as a consequence the clause had no legal standing; others thought only a "moral responsibility" was involved; still another interpretation held that the provision had a legal character, but, being *lex imperfecta*, was unenforceable.[5] Yet there was general agreement that the Bennigsen Amendment of itself led to the creation of a Reich executive. Hermann Oncken came closer to the probable truth when he wrote, "The constitutional doctrine was able to have this creative importance for the Reich constitution because it coincided with Bismarck's need for power and his political sense. The effect of the doctrine did not reach any further than both held necessary."[6] If indeed it compelled Bismarck to assume the chancellorship, the responsibility clause did not require that the Imperial Chancellor's Office reach the dimensions of power and function that it ultimately did.

During the summer of 1867, nevertheless, Bismarck still thought of the confederate administration in rather modest terms. In his *Votum* of June 18 he proposed that "confederate officialdom" be organized into eight divisions. Through a "central division" the chancellor would coordinate the activities of the other seven divisions, which corresponded to the seven committees of the Bundesrat (military affairs, maritime affairs, customs and taxation, trade and commerce, railways, post and telegraph, justice, and accountancy). The central division was to consist of "at least three members" and a number of assistants; for the other divisions two members and one or more assistants

---

[4] *GW*, VI, 423.

[5] See Otto Pflanze, "Juridical and Political Responsibility in Nineteenth-Century Germany," in Leonard Krieger and Fritz Stern, eds., *The Responsibility of Power: Historical Essays in Honor of Hajo Holborn* (New York, 1967), pp. 162–182.

[6] Hermann Oncken, *Rudolf von Bennigsen* (Stuttgart, 1910), II, 56.

would suffice. The divisions and committees were to be linked, in that high Prussian officers and officials appointed to the Bundesrat to chair its committees, as provided in the constitution, would also function as members of the corresponding divisions.[7]

In the same document Bismarck also proposed the creation of a "vice-chancellorship" to be offered to Savigny. He anticipated correctly that the proud Savigny would reject any such inferior status and had, according to Keudell, already begun to search for another candidate, preferably one of bourgeois origin versed in matters of trade and tariff policy.[8] No one fitted that description better than Rudolf Delbrück, the able *Ministerialdirektor* in the Prussian Ministry of Commerce who for many years had been instrumental in the shaping of Prussian policy in the Zollverein. Writing from Varzin on July 19, Bismarck instructed Thile to discuss the post with Delbrück. "I could expect energetic assistance from him. I am not particular whether he performs his duties more in the confederation or in the Ministry of Commerce, placing the accent here or there. It does not matter whether he assumes the formal title of vice-chancellor or represents me *de facto* and alternates in this capacity with someone from [the ministries] of war, finance, foreign affairs, etc., according to the subject matter concerned. I am ready to yield to his wishes in this regard and would like very much to hear what he thinks about it." Two days later, he wrote that he preferred that the title "vice-chancellor" not be used "for the time being."[9]

These documents show that Bismarck, though firm in the opinion that there must be a central administrative organ under his personal control as chancellor, was undecided in July 1867 concerning what form that organ would take and to what degree its personnel were to be independent of the Prussian bureaucracy. In his reply on July 24 Delbrück went straight to the point. There were, he declared, two alternatives: either Prussian ministers should assume the administrative tasks of the confederation, acting under Bismarck's responsibility, or the entire administration should be placed under the direct control of the chancellor. To Delbrück the latter choice was the "only permissible one." In creating a new institution without precedents to follow, confusion could only be avoided if one person were invested with authority over the bureaucratic machinery. Reviewing the wording of the constitution as "objectively" as possible, Delbrück pointed out that the powers of the chancellor as "minister of the Presidency" were extensive. First of all, he was the "actual administrative head" of the postal and telegraph systems, the

---

[7] *GW*, VI, 414–415.

[8] *GW*, XIV, 728–730; VI, 421–422; VII, 196–197; Horst Kohl, ed., *Anhang zu den Gedanken und Erinnerungen von Otto Fürst von Bismarck* (Stuttgart, 1901), 11, 409–410.

[9] *GW*, XIV, 732–733. The context shows that he had become rather alarmed by Savigny's conception of the powers that should go with the title of vice-chancellor—particularly, the right of access to the Kaiser.

consular service, and confederate financial affairs. Secondly, he was charged with "continuing, organized control" over the administration of the customs and other confederate taxes. Finally, the chancellor must "oversee" the execution of confederate laws by state governments, although in this case no permanent administrative body was required. He was willing, Delbrück declared, to accept the role of chancellor's "deputy" in organizing the confederate executive only if the "horizon" of its affairs was to be as wide as indicated. "An agency without administration is also without power!" The responsibilities of such an office, moreover, were incompatible with his existing duties in the Prussian Ministry of Commerce. He was not willing to surrender his "at present modest post" for "one perhaps more prominent, but powerless."[10]

Evidently Delbrück's memorandum crystallized Bismarck's thought about the character of the future *Reichskanzleramt*. While Delbrück had climbed the bureaucratic ladder step by step during twenty-five years of service, Bismarck was an outsider who had reached the top through parliament and the foreign service. As minister-president and foreign minister he had never been charged with the routine administration of a government ministry dealing with internal affairs. Hence Delbrück's advice that the administration of the confederation had to be separate from that of Prussia and the Bundesrat carried considerable weight. Furthermore, it must now have become clear to Bismarck that the power he wished to wield as chancellor would never be his unless he constructed the central administration according to Delbrück's design.

On August 10, 1867, Bismarck officially proposed the creation of a confederate chancellor's office (*Bundeskanzleramt*), "an organ in which the different administrative branches come together and find their focal point." This document, which Delbrück composed, listed again the various administrative and supervisory functions under the constitution, but added another of which there was no mention in the basic law. The chancellor's office was "to prepare with the cooperation of the departments concerned those matters that are to be brought before the Bundesrat and the Reichstag by Prussia, as leader and member of the North German Confederation."[11] This was the first mention of those "presidential bills" that in the future were to alter considerably the relationship between the chancellor's office and the Bundesrat and Prussian cabinet.

With the official establishment on August 12, 1867, of the *Bundeskanzleramt* there came into being an organ that was to be of fundamental importance for the consolidation of the German Reich and for shifting the constitutional balance away from the federal and decentralistic toward the unitary and cen-

---

[10] Rudolf von Delbrück, *Lebenserinnerungen, 1817–1867* (Berlin, 1905), II, 400–401.
[11] GW, VI, 15–16.

tralistic side. Through it Germany was to acquire a national executive distinct from the Bundesrat and the Prussian cabinet. The substitution of Delbrück, the professional administrator and economic expert, for Savigny, the diplomat, was indicative of the coming transition in the character of the chancellorship. What originally had been presented as a diplomatic post reminiscent of Frankfurt and the German confederation had become an executive position at the head of an administrative body. Bismarck had acquired a new instrument of power with which to fulfill that burning ambition of earlier years, the desire to "dispose over the whole."[12]

Evolution of the Reich Executive

In the beginning Delbrück appeared ideal for the execution of Bismarck's objective.[13] Being bourgeois, he lacked the status-consciousness that made it impossible for Savigny to occupy a subordinate post. An experienced and effective administrator, one of the finest products of the Prussian bureaucracy, he was without social or political ambition. There was little danger that he would try to usurp the power of his superior. In 1862 he had refused the opportunity to become minister of commerce, preferring the anonymity and greater longevity of the privy counselor to the political and often perishable role of a cabinet minister. From this subordinate position, nevertheless, he had been the principal architect of the free-trade economic policy and of the aggressive policy in the Zollverein that finally defeated the Austrian plan for a central European economic union. In 1865 he refused ennoblement, accepting it only after his retirement in 1876. His economic liberalism enabled him to work effectively with the parliamentary majority in the Reichstag after 1867. Yet his tact in handling the federated governments enabled him to be equally effective within the Bundesrat, over which he presided as Bismarck's deputy. Where Delbrück was in charge the bureaucratic machine functioned. Bismarck spoke of him in 1870 as "the only man . . . fully conversant with all the aspects of his office."[14] Yet he was unable to tell even Delbrück to his face how he felt about this achievement. "You know that my capacity for recognition is not very great," he wrote to Johanna in November 1870, asking her to relay to Delbrück his admiration for the energy and success with which the counselor carried out his duties.[15] This praise was not earned without cost.

[12] See vol. 1, p. 349.

[13] On Delbrück see Morsey, *Reichsverwaltung*, pp. 40ff., and Eberhard von Vietsch, *Die politische Bedeutung des Reichskanzleramts für den inneren Ausbau des Reiches 1867 bis 1880* (Leipzig, 1936).

[14] Hermann Oncken, *Grossherzog Friedrich I. von Baden und die deutsche Politik von 1854 bis 1871* (Berlin–Leipzig, 1927), II, 235.

[15] GW, XIV, 800. At the time he charged Johanna with this duty Bismarck and Delbrück were actually together in Versailles!

RUDOLF DELBRÜCK. (BILDARCHIV PREUSSISCHER KULTURBESITZ.)

Delbrück's effectiveness in interpreting and executing Bismarck's will and in submerging his own personality caused him to be called "vice-Bismarck," a sobriquet whose intent was not always kindly.

Because of the vagueness of the constitution and of Bismarck's own views much depended in the beginning upon Delbrück's conception of the chancellor's office and the steps he took to implement it. The decision to submit "presidential bills" meant that the office had to be staffed with officials able to draft laws. Every statute passed by the Reichstag and Bundesrat added to the supervisory functions of the chancellor's office, since the chancellor was charged with the duty of overseeing their administration by the states. The function of direct administration was also destined to grow, for the administrative chores of a modern state could not be performed entirely by state governments. The needs of an industrializing, increasingly complex society forced a steady expansion in the functions of the central government. Inevitably the growth of the imperial administration produced new problems in internal organization and constitutional relationships that strained the monocratic system of ministerial responsibility that was the basis for Bismarck's personal authority. For the time being Delbrück met these problems in ways that were sympathetic to Bismarck's purposes. As the chancellor's deputy he strove to retain full control over the growing functions and divisions of the office he headed. But he also sought to preserve harmony between the central administration and the Prussian cabinet, particularly in the fields of finance and military affairs.

The growth of the chancellor's office after 1867 can be seen in the proliferation of its subordinate divisions. In December of that year it acquired, as provided in the constitution, direct administration over the postal and telegraph systems, which became divisions I and II. In 1871 these divisions extended their authority over the southern states (except for certain "reserved rights" in Bavaria and Württemberg) and in 1872 over Alsace-Lorraine. The purchase of the Thurn and Taxis postal system in 1867 had made the mails a state monopoly. In Heinrich Stephan division I found an able and energetic administrator who aimed to make the presence of the Reich felt throughout Germany through the erection of post offices even in remote villages. In 1871 division III was formed to govern the Reichsland of Alsace-Lorraine. With the annexation of Alsace-Lorraine and the decision to administer it as an imperial territory the chancellor's office gained the power of direct administration over 1,550,000 people.[16] Bismarck saw in this task "a most natural means for creating a closer relationship between north and south."[17] By adding a new dimension to the chancellor's office it also contributed to the growth of centralism. Even after the introduction of the Reich constitution at the beginning of 1874 the chancellor's office continued to exercise executive authority over the Reichsland, including control over its railways, which had become imperial property.

In addition to the three numbered divisions the chancellor's office possessed a "central division" that handled such matters as consular affairs, customs, indirect taxes, accountancy, judicial affairs, the drafting of presidential bills, and the supervisory function over the state governments. The drafting and passage of imperial law codes and creation of a national judiciary led to the creation of division IV for judicial affairs in 1875. Economic legislation, moreover, resulted in the addition to the central division of a number of subagencies; for example, the imperial treasury, war treasury, statistical office, bureau of standards, and bureaus dealing with emigration and shipping.

By 1871 the functions of the chancellor's office had come to represent, as Bismarck expressed it, "approximately those of a combined ministry for commerce and finance."[18] Throughout this development Delbrück clung steadfastly to his original recipe: that of strict centralization under his own authority as president of the office and deputy to the chancellor, playing the "Taikun" to Bismarck's "Mikado."[19] It was evident, however, that some executive functions had to be conducted in bureaus separate from and parallel

[16] See Morsey, Reichsverwaltung.

[17] To Crown Prince Albert of Saxony, Aug. 21, 1870. GW, XIV, 320.

[18] Hans Goldschmidt, Das Reich und Preussen im Kampf um die Führung von Bismarck bis 1918 (Berlin, 1931), p. 158.

[19] Kohl, ed., Anhang, II, 434–436.

to the chancellor's office. The first of these was that of foreign affairs. Initially the foreign relations of the North German Confederation were conducted by the Prussian Ministry of Foreign Affairs, whose envoys were accredited to foreign governments as representatives of the confederation. (Consular and foreign commercial relations were administered by the central division of the Chancellor's Office.) That the diplomatic organ of the central government belonged to a member state was an anomaly, but Bismarck wished to give the member states, including Prussia, time to readjust to their new situation. In 1868–1869 Prussia's financial crisis and pressure from the Chamber of Deputies expedited a change.[20] After January 1, 1870, the Prussian Ministry of Foreign Affairs was transferred to the confederate budget and renamed the Confederate Office of Foreign Affairs. Amid the jubilation of victory in 1871 the word "Reich" was substituted for "confederation" in the titles of both the chancellor's office and the foreign office. Only the Bundesrat retained its old designation, emphasizing its federal character. After August 1871 all imperial agencies and officials were henceforth designated as "imperial" (*Kaiserlich*). These symbolic changes gave to the unitary tendency of these years yet another forward thrust.[21]

The foreign office was Bismarck's personal instrument and this fact, plus the nature and secrecy of its tasks, gave that agency a separate status within the central administration. One of the changes of 1871 in the constitution created a Bundesrat "committee on foreign affairs" chaired by the Bavarian delegate. Although this committee met a few times in 1871, it was, as Delbrück remarked, a "stillborn child." Its only function was to receive communications from the chancellor on foreign affairs. But even this privilege was diminished by the fact that there was another, more important channel for such communications. The Reich Foreign Office also functioned as the Prussian Ministry of Foreign Affairs, controlling Prussia's envoys at the German capitals who maintained contact with the German federal governments. Although the governments of Bavaria and Württemberg continued to maintain legations in foreign countries under their "reserved rights," their envoys no longer had political functions. In this way the facade of sovereignty in foreign relations was maintained for the two southern states, while the building itself was occupied by Bismarck and the Reich Foreign Office.[22]

The second bureau established parallel to the chancellor's office was the Imperial Admiralty (1872). Constitutionally the confederate navy was a national force, in contrast to the army, which was a federal force composed of state contingents. Yet the navy was commanded by the king of Prussia and the command and administrative functions were originally performed by the

---

[20] BR, III, 368ff.; IV, 67ff., 352ff.
[21] Morsey, *Reichsverwaltung*, pp. 63ff.; GW, VIb, 195–197; VIc, 1–2.
[22] Morsey, *Reichsverwaltung*, pp. 104ff.

Prussian naval ministry. Whether naval officials were to be regarded as Prussian or confederate was left undetermined until 1869, when the question of their tax liability forced the issue. To the great distress of Roon, a majority in the Prussian cabinet voted to regard them henceforth as confederate officials. Roon had been unable to follow Bismarck in his migration from Prussian to German nationalism. Now his "Prussian sense of duty" impelled him to resign if Bismarck would not help him influence the king to reverse the cabinet decision. The change in title, he contended, was tantamount to a mediatization of the king of Prussia. Bismarck replied that it was of no consequence under what form the king ruled in Germany, as long as he did so in fact. The inhabitants of Oldenburg, Mecklenburg, and the Hanseatic cities who were liable to naval service would find it easier to serve in a German rather than a Prussian navy. The former they would serve voluntarily, the latter only under duress. "If we could have immediately substituted the term 'German' or even 'north German' for 'Prussian' in 1866, we would now be twenty years ahead. . . . I hope to God that the time will come when our sons will regard it as an honor to serve the sons of the king in a royal German fleet and in a royal German army."[23] By appealing to Roon's sense of fealty to the king and the house of Hohenzollern, Bismarck succeeded in overcoming his scruples.

Nevertheless, the position of the navy remained anomalous. While a confederate force, it was commanded by the king of Prussia acting through the naval high command (Oberkommando der Marine), which was a Prussian agency. The confederate officials who administered it under the chancellor's responsibility actually labored in the Prussian naval ministry headed by Roon, who was not a Reich official. In 1871 the confusion was compounded when Wilhelm became commander-in-chief of the navy as German Kaiser rather than Prussian king and Roon recombined the command and administrative functions by taking charge of the Oberkommando and reintegrating it into the Prussian naval ministry, from which it had been separated in 1861. An imperial decree of January 1, 1872, cleared away this bureaucratic confusion by transforming the Prussian naval ministry into the Imperial Admiralty.[24] The first "chief" of that body was General Albrecht von Stosch, who had distinguished himself as an organizer in the war of 1870. There was no longer any doubt that the navy, its command and its administration, were imperial rather than Prussian. Yet another ambivalence remained that was to be the source of difficulty in years ahead. For his command functions the chief of the admiralty was responsible only to the Kaiser, for his administration he acted under the responsibility of the German chancellor. The two functions were

---

[23] Waldemar von Roon, Denkwürdigkeiten aus dem Leben des General-Feldmarschalls Kriegsministers Grafen von Roon (4th ed., Breslau, 1897), III, 117–127; GW, VIb, 133–136; XIV, 755.

[24] It was not until 1874, however, that Bismarck succeeded in getting the title "royal navy" expunged from all documents dealing with naval personnel. See Morsey, Reichsverwaltung, pp. 127ff.

difficult to separate. Furthermore, the chief of the admiralty was also made a minister without portfolio in the Prussian cabinet, where he was the collegial equal of the minister-president. In 1871 Bismarck was willing to concede to Stosch a measure of autonomy in his conduct of the administrative function. But Stosch was an independent soul, unwilling "to dance to Bismarck's pipe." In the end this attitude, complicated by the ambiguity in his relationship to the chancellor, led to his downfall.[25]

The Reich and Prussia

The origins of the *Reichskanzleramt*—its quarters, personnel, and finance— were almost entirely Prussian. Originally the office was housed at Wilhelm-strasse 74 in rooms made available by the Prussian *Staatsministerium*. As in the case of Delbrück, its leading officials were transferred from the Prussian to the confederate service. A credit of twenty thousand thalers from the Prussian treasury enabled the bureaucratic machine to get started. During Bismarck's chancellorship only two (Bernhard von Bülow and Karl von Hofmann) of the twenty-three officials who occupied the highest rank, that of state secretary, were non-Prussians. Eighty percent of the officials of secondary status, that of reporting counselor (*Vortragender Rat*), stemmed from the Prussian state ser-vice. This was true despite the fact that Bismarck made some effort to attract into the national service able officials from other states. Only among the higher officials in the diplomatic service (ministers and ambassadors), the railway office, the Reichsland administration, and the admiralty were non-Prussians present in significant numbers. The Prussian origin of the Reich bureaucracy was also evident in other respects: for example, the imperial state service regulations were modeled after those of Prussia; the form of appoint-ment and installation was Prussian; the official dress was patterned after an old Brandenburg *Waffenrock* and its colors were those of the Prussian military uniform. Like Delbrück, the Reich officials found it difficult to forget their Prussian origins. Most persisted in looking upon Wilhelm as king of Prussia and only secondarily as German Kaiser.[26]

It was not Bismarck's intention that the central government should appear to be but an extension of the Prussian. On the contrary, he strove from 1867 onward to give the government of the confederation and the Reich a distinct profile that would allay the suspicions of the other state dynasties and govern-ments that they were being Prussianized. In late August 1867 the Saxon en-voy in Berlin, Baron von Koenneritz, reported to his government, "Count Bismarck appears to turn his entire attention toward giving to the affairs of

[25] GW, VIc, 7; Goldschmidt, *Reich und Preussen*, p. 158. On Stosch see Frederic B. Hollyday, *Bismarck's Rival: A Political Biography of General and Admiral Albrecht von Stosch* (Durham, 1960); see also pp. 360–363, vol. 3, ch. 2.

[26] Morsey, *Reichsverwaltung*, pp. 36–37, 251–255.

the confederation a primary importance in every direction; he appears to desire that these affairs be given the greatest possible independence from those of the Prussian ministries." The appointment of high-ranking officials, rather than cabinet ministers, to the Bundesrat and Bismarck's retention of complete control over them "creates a large, unmistakable breach in the higher Prussian administration. The Prussian ministers are deprived of a good many attributes, which they must surrender to the confederate chancellor, meaning to the office of the confederate chancellor." It appeared, Koenneritz wrote in September, that "Prussia will eventually merge into Germany and not the reverse." An important Prussian official repined, "Bismarck is ruining the entire Prussian state!"[27] In the summer of 1868 the Hessian minister-president, Baron von Dalwigk, recorded in his diary that the Prussian ministries were seething with envy and dissatisfaction. Their influence was being "completely paralyzed by the chancellor's office. The burden of business placed on the chancellor's office is enormous, moreover, and without Delbrück and his capacity for work the entire complicated machinery would eventually go to pieces."[28]

These fears, and perhaps the reports of them as well, were certainly exaggerated. While desiring an independent confederate executive, Delbrück was eager to avoid any development that would cripple the Prussian bureaucracy or antagonize former colleagues in the Prussian service. For a time, moreover, some of the most vital functions of the confederate-Reich government were in fact performed by Prussian ministries. We have seen that the conduct of foreign affairs remained within the Prussian cabinet until 1869. The Prussian war ministry handled confederate military affairs, and the Prussian finance ministry and superior accounting office had significant roles in the management of confederate finances. These latter areas are most critical for an understanding of the developing relationship between the central government and Prussia.

Under the constitution the confederation had a very limited tax power. Its independent sources of income were the customs, surpluses from the post and telegraph, and certain indirect taxes. What these sources did not provide was to be supplied by assessments paid by the states according to population. This meant that the confederate-Reich government was largely dependent upon the Prussian assessment, which soon became the greatest single burden in the Prussian budget. For this reason the financial affairs and problems of the central and Prussian governments were interlocked. The national budget had to be drafted in close collaboration with the Prussian Ministry of Finance, and without the latter's approval no financial measure could be introduced into the confederation. The dependence of the confederate government upon

[27] Goldschmidt, *Reich und Preussen*, pp. 136–139.
[28] GW, VIa, 418–420; Morsey, *Reichsverwaltung*, pp. 55ff.

Prussia in financial matters was a subject of frequent criticism in the German Reichstag, usually coupled with demands for the creation of a national cabinet, including a ministry of finance.

The issue was sharpened by the fact that in the beginning the Prussian minister of finance did not sit in the Bundesrat. Earlier we have seen that only high-ranking officials below ministerial rank were made Prussian delegates to that body. Lacking a seat in the Bundesrat, the minister could not appear in the Reichstag to defend the budget unless he happened, as did August von der Heydt, to be an elected member. Naturally this circumstance was regarded as unsatisfactory by Reichstag liberals, whose debates on this subject will be discussed later. But it also created problems for the relationship between Bismarck and his Prussian colleagues and between the chancellor's office and the Prussian Ministry of Finance that required clarification and adjustment during the early years of the German union. A one-sided consideration of the financial needs of the confederation could endanger the financial stability of the Prussian state, and, in reverse, the pursuit of strictly Prussian interests by its Ministry of Finance could harm those of the confederation. How closely the financial affairs of the central government were meshed with those of Prussia was clearly evident in the financial crisis of 1868–1869 recounted earlier.[29]

During 1867–1869 Bismarck's relationship to his colleagues in the Prussian cabinet steadily deteriorated. Bad health and long absences from Berlin (more than five months in both 1868 and 1869) made it difficult for him to isolate the king and prevail over the ministers. His long struggle (recorded earlier)[30] with the ministers over the policy to be followed in the annexed regions and, with the cabinet and conservatives over the Hanoverian provincial fund, the failure of his attempt to liquidate the state assessments, the general retreat of the unity movement in southern Germany, and the collapse of his hopes for evolutionary unification—all combined to increase his general irritability and heighten the scorn he felt for those seven men whose permission he had to seek "whenever I want to take a pinch of snuff."[31] In May 1869 he vented his anger openly to the Reichstag in opposing a national liberal–free conservative bill calling for creation of a Reich cabinet of collegial character. "Whoever has once been a minister and headed a cabinet and been compelled to make decisions on his own responsibility no longer shrinks from that responsibility. What he does shrink from is the necessity of convincing seven people that what he wants is really the right thing to do. That is different kind of work than governing a state! All cabinet members have their own firm and honest convictions. The more honest and industrious they are, the more difficult it is for them to conform. Each is surrounded by a group of argumentative coun-

---

[29] See vol. 1, pp. 416–422.

[30] See vol. 1, pp. 392–434.

[31] BP, II, 52; see also GW, VII, 179, 218, 267–268; XIV, 748–749; AWB, I, 126; Kohl, ed., Anhang, II, 411–413.

selors, who also have their convictions. . . . I consider the collegial cabinet structure to be a constitutional failure and a mistake. . . . Prussia would make immense progress, if it would accept the principle of the North German Confederation and have just one responsible minister!"[32] Lacking the power to effect such a change, Bismarck's only course was to build up still further the chancellor's office at the cost of the cabinet.

When Heydt resigned under fire as Prussian finance minister in October 1869, a possible replacement was Delbrück, who would have assumed that ministry in addition to the presidency of the chancellor's office. But Delbrück had no ambition to hold a political office, and, furthermore, such an "accumulation" of offices contradicted his conception of confederate-Prussian relationships. In accepting this decision, Bismarck stressed, nevertheless, that the new minister of finance, whoever he might be ("a more or less arbitrary, lottery-like choice"), would have to subordinate himself to the chancellor's office. "If we succeed in building up your position as a kind of 'confederate minister of finance' to the point where you gain the necessary influence over the Prussian financial administration, there will be less danger of failure; the control would be in your hands."[33] Winner of the lottery was Otto Camphausen, president of the Prussian maritime bank (*Seehandlung*). Bismarck was pleased with the choice ("finance ministers do not grow wild here"), for Camphausen was experienced in public finance and his liberal reputation made him persona grata to the parliamentary majority. Yet he was determined to make Camphausen's position less powerful than Heydt's had been.

To this end he proposed that Delbrück in addition to his position as president of the chancellor's office, be appointed Prussian minister without portfolio, with the right to participate in all cabinet sessions dealing with confederate affairs, and the right of cosignature with the chancellor on all confederate documents dealing with confederate finances. The immediate aim, he informed Delbrück, was to enhance the "moral authority" of the president's position by giving it a more "ministerial character." The ultimate aim was gradually to rebuild the central executive into a cabinet structure on the English model, beginning with ministries of war and finance followed by a ministry of commerce. Naturally such a development would not remain a secret from the allied governments. "But the *douce violence*, which would gradually be done to them by this route, seems to me much more acceptable than a constitutional amendment aiming at the same result. Nevertheless, a constitutional amendment will have to be forced through sooner or later if the waters aren't diverted quietly into the channels I have sketched out."[34]

Bismarck's long-range plan for an imperial cabinet structured on the En-

[32] BR, IV, 184–185; GW, VIb, 15–16, 148–149, 541–542.

[33] Bismarck to Delbrück, Oct. 11, 1869. GW, XIV, 762–765. Also Delbrück to Bismarck, Oct. 23 and 26, 1869. GSA, Berlin-Dahlem, Rep. 94, Nr. 1162.

[34] GW, XIV, 764–765; VIb, 155–157, 169.

glish rather than the Prussian pattern ran counter to Delbrück's own conception of his office. While accepting appointment to the Prussian cabinet, Delbrück rejected the right of cosignature. Instead he proposed that Camphausen be appointed to the Bundesrat, where he would be given the power, as chairman of the finance committee, to cosign documents dealing with confederate finances. Bismarck acquiesced, although with obvious reluctance, trusting that Camphausen would not be influenced by the Prussian collegial principle in his handling of confederate finances.[35] Yet the primary effect of these reforms proved to be the opposite of what Bismarck intended. Camphausen gave more weight to his role in the Prussian cabinet than to his duties in the Bundesrat. Although his skill in juggling Prussia's finances solved the immediate financial crisis, the greater problem of the relationship between the central and Prussian governments remained unsolved.[36]

Later we shall see that during 1872–1873 a crisis like that of 1868–1869 disturbed Bismarck's relationship to the Prussian cabinet and the Conservative party. His conflicts with ultraconservatives over clerical influence in the schools, reform of county government, and reconstruction of the House of Lords also involved him in sharp differences with the ministers.[37] He forced the resignation of Heinrich von Mühler as *Kultusminister* (minister of education and religious affairs) but failed to unseat Minister of the Interior Friedrich zu Eulenburg, who evaded Bismarck's attempt to transform the House of Lords. These frictions and frustrations coincided with another severe illness that kept Bismarck away from Berlin during most of the year. In December 1872 the climactic point was reached when Roon decided to resign as minister of war. His health, Roon declared, had suffered from frustrations arising from the collegial necessity of having to accept actions of the cabinet majority of which he disapproved, the "rhapsodic and eccentric pressure for legislation in the present governmental program," and lack of leadership in the cabinet owing to Bismarck's extended absences. To general astonishment Bismarck's response was to resign as minister-president and persuade Roon to assume that post as of January 1, 1873.[38]

On January 25 he explained this decision to the Prussian Chamber of Deputies. In contrast to the chancellorship, the minister-presidency was a post with great responsibility and little power. This "honorific post" lacked the means with which to make any impression on the other ministers. Supported by their subordinate officials, they put up a passive resistance that had com-

---

[35] GW, XIV, 765–766.

[36] Morsey, *Reichsverwaltung*, pp. 58–60.

[37] See pp. 207–219 and Goldschmidt, *Reich und Preussen*, p. 159.

[38] Roon to Bismarck, Dec. 10, 1872. GSA, Berlin-Dahlem, Rep. 94, Nr. 1162. Bismarck to Roon, Dec. 13, 1872. GW, XIV, 844–845. Roon, *Denkwürdigkeiten*, III, 328ff.; BR, V, 356ff.; Goldschmidt, *Reich und Preussen*, pp. 160ff.; GW, VIc, 24, 27, 29; Kohl, ed., *Anhang*, I, 233. Morsey, *Reichsverwaltung*, pp. 67ff.

pelled him to admit his own powerlessness. Like a walker in loose sand, he felt exhausted from the effort. To Roon he also complained about the "treasonable desertion of the conservatives in the Catholic question," the loss of old friends, the impositions and declining favor of the king, and expressed the conviction that he had not much longer to live.[39] By resigning as minister-president he hoped to rid himself of the frictions without diminution of his real power.

If the monarch, as Kaiser, had confidence in the chancellor, Bismarck told the Chamber of Deputies, it was inconceivable that, as king of Prussia, he would allow the cabinet to launch a policy to which the chancellor was opposed. "For the king of Prussia and his cabinet to oppose the policy of the Reich chancellor is an utter impossibility; instead it is a necessity that his policy be supported." By remaining in the cabinet as minister of foreign affairs with the power to instruct Prussia's delegates to the Bundesrat, furthermore, he would be in a position to preserve the connection between Prussia and the Reich. The separation of the chancellorship and minister-presidency, he continued, would accentuate the German character of the former and thereby contribute to the growth of a "true German unity."[40] To Hohenlohe he remarked, "The Kaiser must above all become accustomed to seeing that he is more important as Kaiser than as king of Prussia."[41] The discarded Mühler saw the matter in a different light, complaining to Wilhelm, "What Prince Bismarck was not able to achieve as minister-president he now seeks with redoubled force and hate to accomplish through the importance of his position as Reich chancellor. As far as he is concerned, the Prussian cabinet is to sink steadily into nullity."[42]

The actual course of events corresponded, however, neither to Bismarck's hopes nor Mühler's fears. During Bismarck's absence from the minister-presidency the internal problems of Prussia and the Reich increased. In 1873 the Kulturkampf reached a new peak, the breach with the ultraconservatives grew worse, a financial scandal involved key figures in government and society, and the crash of the bourse introduced a business depression. Roon, asthmatic and seventy years old, was even more ill than Bismarck and spent much of the year on leave. When he did preside over the cabinet, his military manner grated upon the other ministers. Bismarck, on the other hand, found his burdens unreduced. Because he remained in the cabinet as Prussian foreign minister he continued to share collegial responsibility. He still had to familiarize himself with the issues and documents but without help from the counselors attached to the minister-president. That Delbrück voiced Bismarck's views and cast his proxy in cabinet meetings gave little relief. In May–June 1873

[39] GW, XI, 277–287; XIV, 844–845.
[40] BR, V, 361ff.
[41] GW, VIII, 75.
[42] Vietsch, Politische Bedeutung, pp. 50–51.

Bismarck wanted to withdraw completely from the Prussian cabinet.[43] But the ministers objected in view of the upcoming Landtag elections. According to Lucius, no one could see how the system would operate without his presence.[44]

Within a few months Bismarck himself was compelled to recognize that the experiment had failed. When bad health compelled Roon to resign on November 9, 1873, as both minister-president and minister of war, Bismarck returned to the former office, explaining to Wilhelm that his absence had diminished neither his burdens nor his responsibility; it had only "increased the difficulty of making my opinion felt in cabinet meetings." (In the hope of reducing the burdens of the office he secured Wilhelm's consent to the creation of a "vice-presidency," to which Camphausen was appointed.)[45] He had completely erred, he told the Reichstag later, in believing that the chancellor alone was "strong enough" to govern successfully. Without the "Prussian root" he had "no greater influence than any other person."[46]

After six years of experimentation it was already evident that the political machinery Bismarck had devised was not adequate for governing a large country. The improvisations of its origin prejudiced its later development. In the debate on January 25, 1873, the progressive deputy Rudolf Virchow teased Bismarck with the suggestion that in view of the "dissonances" within the government perhaps the time had come to convert to a parliamentary system. In reply the chancellor lamely denied the existence of frictions, of which he had himself publicly complained, and charged that the multiplicity of parties, the sharp conflicts between them, and the lack of "feeling for the state" made it impossible for Prussia to copy the English system of parliamentary responsibility.[47] In future years Bismarck never ceased to lecture his colleagues and parliamentary deputies on the nature and functioning of the Prussian-German governmental system. It will be shown, however, that his explanations shifted constantly. Year after year he wrestled continually with a problem that he never solved. Neither, for that matter, did his successors.

The Prussian-German Military System

Those clauses of the constitutions of 1867 and 1871 that dealt with military affairs made seemingly far-reaching concessions to federalism. The "united

---

[43] GW, VIc, 37–38.

[44] Freiherr Lucius von Ballhausen, *Bismarck-Erinnerungen* (Stuttgart, 1920), pp. 30, 35–56.

[45] Roon, *Denkwürdigkeiten*, III, 360ff.; GW, VIc, 42–43; VIII, 113–117; Kohl, ed., *Anhang*, I, 244–245; II, 448–451.

[46] GW, XI, 496. During 1890–1894 Bismarck's successor, Caprivi, also tried to separate the chancellorship and minister-presidency by surrendering the latter. But Hohenlohe, who succeeded Caprivi, assumed both offices, as did his successors to the end of the Second Reich.

[47] BR, V, 371–378.

army" was to be composed of state contingents. There was no German general staff or command structure and no Reich military administration, although military expenditures were borne by the national budget. These concessions, however, were illusory. Nowhere in the entire structure was Prussian hegemony so evident as in the provisions concerning the military. The king of Prussia (after 1871 the German Kaiser) was commander-in-chief, to whom officers and men swore obedience. Uniforms, insignia, organization, administration, weapons, and training were to follow the Prussian model. Prussian laws and ordinances governing the military were to be adopted by state governments when the constitution went into effect, including those on military justice, length of service, quartering, mobilization, and the like.

Prussia's hegemonic position in military affairs soon grew in ways not provided by the federal constitutions of 1867 and 1871. Beginning in 1867 during the Luxemburg crisis, Prussia negotiated military conventions with other German states that resulted in a largely unitary army. Ultimately they resulted in Prussia's incorporation (in varying ways and degrees) of twenty-two out of twenty-five contingents of the imperial army.[48] Only Saxony, Württemberg, and Bavaria maintained separate contingents. Even without these acquisitions the Prussian contingent would have been by far the largest in the German army; with them Prussia possessed by 1875 thirteen out of eighteen German army corps. Saxony, Baden, and Württemberg each had one and Bavaria two. Of the 418,872 men in Germany's standing army in 1881, the Prussian contingent alone supplied 324,766 men. Seven small contingents (Schwarzburg-Sondershausen, Waldeck, the two Lippes, and the three Hanseatic cities) were completely absorbed into the Prussian contingent; ten others (Oldenburg, Brunswick, Anhalt, and seven Thuringian states) formed separate regiments within the Prussian contingent; four (Baden, Hesse-Darmstadt, and the two Mecklenburgs) were separate contingents only in outward form, the latter three retaining their distinguishing insignia. After conscription was introduced into the Reichsland, the troops of Alsace-Lorraine were also integrated into the Prussian contingent.[49]

The military conventions circumvented the imperial constitution and were negotiated and signed without the participation of either the Bundesrat or Reichstag. Even so, the unitary principle was firmly grounded in the constitutional powers of the Kaiser (until 1871 the king of Prussia) as commander-in-chief. In this capacity he had the "duty and right" to establish and oversee

---

[48] Most of the conventions between Prussia and the north German states were signed in 1867–1868, but were renegotiated in 1872–1875. That with Baden was signed in 1870 and the last with Braunschweig in 1886. Georg Meyer and Gerhard Anschütz, *Lehrbuch des deutschen Staatsrechts* (7th ed., Munich, 1919), pp. 851–852 (fn.); Ernst Rudolf Huber, *Deutsche Verfassungsgeschichte seit 1789* (4 vols., Stuttgart, 1957–1963), III, 992–1000.

[49] Ludwig R. von Collenberg, *Die deutsche Armee von 1871 bis 1914* (Berlin, 1922), p. 9; Curt Jany, *Geschichte der königlichen preussischen Armee* (Berlin, 1928–1933), IV, 270.

the unity and conformity of the entire army, to determine the internal organization of all contingents, and to locate all garrisons; in wartime he assumed
direct command of all contingents.[50] The staff work necessary to carry out
these and other command functions was performed by the organs of the Prussian contingent. The Prussian military cabinet continued to advise the commander-in-chief on personnel matters relating to the officer corps. The Prussian general staff assumed the function of strategic planning. The Prussian
minister of war communicated directly with his counterparts in those states
that retained separate contingents and tended to wield a superior influence
over them.[51] He also acted as a Reich minister of war.

Nowhere was the problem of coordination between the Reich and Prussia
more difficult than with regard to military affairs. Here reappeared, moreover,
the problem of the relationship between civil and military leadership that had
plagued the wars of 1864, 1866, and 1870–1871. In effect there were two
Reich ministers of war: the Reich chancellor and the Prussian minister of war.
Bismarck maintained that the chancellor was responsible for all military affairs pertaining to the Reich. Yet neither he nor his office was equipped to
perform the administrative functions that followed from that responsibility.
They were actually performed by the Prussian minister of war supported by his
ministry. *De jure* the ministerial activity of the Reich was carried out by the
Bundesrat committee for military affairs, headed in the beginning by a high
official of the Prussian war ministry and after 1869 by the minister himself.
Roon was *de facto* an imperial as well as Prussian minister of war.[52]

The general was, however, dissatisfied with this state of affairs. As Prussian
minister of war he had a special status in the Prussian cabinet, which he
lacked in the Reich. In the former capacity he was the only official, except
the minister-president, who had the right of direct access to the king. Under
the cabinet rule of 1852 all other ministers could only approach the king
through the minister-president. Where military affairs of the Reich were concerned Roon did not have an equivalent right. He found it galling that Bismarck, a civilian, was as chancellor the Reich's only minister and hence
countersigned all administrative documents emanating from the Kaiser as
commander-in-chief of the German army. From 1867 onward Roon strove for
the creation of a Reich minister of war who would have the right of countersignature. Naturally Bismarck steadfastly resisted this demand, which would
have led logically to the creation of a Reich cabinet of collegial character. Yet
he found it expedient to compromise with his Prussian colleague and close

---

[50] Meyer and Anschütz, *Staatsrecht*, pp. 851–853; Paul Laband, *Das Staatsrecht des deutschen
Reichs* (5th ed., Tübingen, 1911–1914), IV, 9–10.

[51] Collenberg, *Deutsche Armee*, pp. 8–9; Rudolf Schmidt-Bückeberg, *Das Militärkabinett der
preussischen Könige und deutschen Kaiser* (Berlin, 1933), pp. 105ff.

[52] Gordon Craig, *The Politics of the Prussian Army, 1640–1945* (Oxford, 1955), pp. 223–224;
Morsey, *Reichsverwaltung*, p. 228.

collaborator of the "conflict era." While retaining the right of countersignature for all national laws dealing with military affairs, he yielded to Roon the
right to cosign all reports (*Immediatberichte*) dealing with confederate-Reich
military affairs that were destined for the ruler. In this way Wilhelm was assured, without the necessity of inquiry, that the contents had the approval of
the Prussian minister of war. In August 1868, furthermore, the latter was
made the chancellor's deputy (*Stellvertreter*) in all military and naval affairs.[53]

There were still other thorns for Roon in the thicket. The duty of the chancellor's office to supervise state governments in their execution of national
laws related to military as well as civilian affairs. As such the office was superior to the Ministry of War and had legally the right to oversee its activities.
Through the power that it assumed over the national budget, furthermore,
the chancellor's office controlled the army's source of financial support. As a
military man, Roon was doubly sensitive about his prerogatives and in the
Prussian tradition disinclined to bow to civilian leadership or control. During
Delbrück's period, however, the problem did not arise, for the president of
the chancellor's office routinely deferred to the Prussian war minister in all
matters touching military affairs. As a result the relationship was "astonish-
ingly" frictionless.[54]

Nevertheless, the effort to create a Reich war minister, parallel to the chancellor, did not cease. In 1871 (in connection with the amendment of the
constitution) and in 1873 (in connection with a new military bill) Roon
raised the issue in the Prussian cabinet. Bismarck replied that the Prussian
Ministry of War was already in fact a Reich ministry of war and that this was
enough. To attempt to give it the formal status of a Reich ministry would
unnecessarily antagonize other German governments, which were sensitive
to the "Prussianization" of the Reich. What Roon, Bismarck's long-time
friend and colleague, failed to accomplish was clearly impossible for Georg
von Kameke, his successor as war minister after 1873. On Delbrück's suggestion, Kameke proposed in August 1873 that he be given the right of direct
access to the Kaiser and of countersignature on all imperial orders dealing
with military matters. This earned him a sharp rebuke from the chancellor,
and a year later he received yet another when Bismarck learned that the general had discussed the Reich military budget bill first with the Kaiser rather
than with the chancellor. It was impermissible, he wrote from Varzin, for
Kameke, as the "actual possessor of the Reich military administration," to
ascertain the views of the emperor before coming to terms with the chancellor
as the sole responsible official for the Reich's executive affairs.[55]

Undoubtedly the principal aim of both Roon and Kameke was to enlarge

---

[53] Morsey, *Reichsverwaltung*, pp. 228–229; Vietsch, *Politische Bedeutung*, pp. 28–29.

[54] Morsey, *Reichsverwaltung*, pp. 53, 229; Vietsch, *Politische Bedeutung*, pp. 29–30.

[55] GW, XIV, 864; Goldschmidt, *Reich und Preussen*, pp. 165–169; Morsey, *Reichsverwaltung*, p. 71.

their prerogatives and establish that direct relationship with the ruler to which the Prussian military had always aspired and which in Prussia they had largely attained. Their effort was the bureaucratic counterpart of the attempt of Moltke and the military "demi-gods" during the wars of 1864, 1866, and 1870–1871 to assert their freedom to direct military strategy without regard to those political considerations that were Bismarck's primary concern. Still, the position of Roon and Kameke under the constitutional order Bismarck had devised was by no means easy. It lacked the kind of clarity that military minds tend to prize. In his relationship to the monarch the war minister had to distinguish between purely Prussian administrative matters, which he could take directly to Wihelm as king, and imperial administrative matters, which he could not take directly to Wilhelm as Kaiser. But this was not all. Where the Kaiser was concerned, the minister had to distinguish between administrative matters, which had to go through the chancellor, and command matters, which did not.

His relationship to the Reichstag was likewise ambiguous. Officially he appeared in that body as a Prussian delegate to the Bundesrat and as chairman of the Bundesrat committee on military affairs. In this capacity he was compelled to reply to questions concerning bills and policies for which he was actually, though not formally, responsible. "In a strictly legal sense he was not bound to answer such questions; in practice it was always difficult, and sometimes inexpedient, to refuse. Even a man of such determination as Roon had not always succeeded in distinguishing between questions bearing upon the forces of the empire (which he could answer) and questions dealing with the Prussian army (which he could not) or between administrative matters (which he could discuss) and command questions (which the emperor considered none of the Reichstag's business). Kameke affected liberal political views, and in parliamentary halls he was inclined to be more compliant than Roon."[56]

The Decline of Federalism

The imperial constitution granted to the Reich an extensive legislative competence—chiefly in economic, legal, and judicial affairs. The Reich, moreover, steadily increased the range of its own competence at the cost of the state legislatures. The only distinction made in the constitution between ordinary legislation and constitutional amendments was the provision that fourteen negative votes in the Bundesrat could defeat the latter. Since all Bundesrat decisions were announced as "unanimous," no statute passed by both Bundesrat and Reichstag could later be called "unconstitutional." Whether a bill conformed to or amended the constitution was threshed out on the floors

[56] Craig, *Prussian Army*, p. 224.

of the Reichstag and Bundesrat in the course of debates on the bill in question.[57] The meaning of the power known as *Kompetenz-Kompetenz* (that is,
the power of the Reich to extend its own competence) was the subject of
endless controversy among German authorities on constitutional law. According to one view, it was so elastic that the national parliament could have
amended the constitution to the point of wiping out the legislative competence of the states.[58] Yet the possibility was purely theoretical, for the Bundesrat would have rejected any such drastic amendments. Nevertheless, the
power of *Kompetenz-Kompetenz* did result in significant changes in the constitution. Some of these amendments were formally written into the constitution, but most were not. As a consequence, the actual scope of the German
constitution was soon larger than the wording of the document indicated.[59]

As already noted, the decade 1867–1878 was most fruitful in the number
of statutes passed that dealt with fundamental economic and legal affairs.
Many of these laws directly affected the population at large and brought it
increasingly into direct relationship to the central government. Those dealing
with justice were the most important in this regard. The constitution of 1867
did not provide for a national judiciary. No use, furthermore, was made of the
jurisdiction that it did grant to the Superior Court of Appeals in the Hanseatic cities, in cases of high treason, and to the Bundesrat, in cases alleging
denial of justice in state courts. (To become effective the latter provision
would have required a law of implementation, which was never passed.)[60]
Nevertheless, the constitution did grant to the Reich the power to legislate
codes of commercial law, criminal law, and judicial procedure. In 1868 the
Reichstag requested bills for all three codes and, in addition, a bill establishing a common judiciary for their enforcement. The commercial code became
law in 1869 and in the same year an appellate court, the Superior Court of
Commerce (*Reichsoberhandelsgericht*), was established to enforce the code.
The latter act was a constitutional amendment, by far the most important
during the period of the North German Confederation and a significant extension of the authority of the central government.[61] The haste to establish a
central court, even before there was a procedural code, was owing to Bismarck's eagerness to seize "every *vinculum*, even the smallest, as a cement for

---

[57] Lothar Frede, *Die an der Reichsverfassung vorgenommenen Änderungen* (Jena, 1912), pp. 26–
28, 72–74; Heinrich Triepel, *Die Kompetenzen des Bundesstaats und die geschriebene Verfassung*
(Tübingen, 1908), p. 278.

[58] Laband, *Staatsrecht*, I, 129.

[59] Paul Laband, "Die geschichtliche Entwicklung der Reichsverfassung seit der Reichsgründung," *Jahrbuch des öffentlichen Rechts*, 1 (1907), pp. 1–46; E. Bornhak, "Wandlungen der Reichsverfassung," *Archiv für öffentliches Recht*, 26 (1910), pp. 373ff.

[60] Eduard Kern, *Die Überleitung der Justiz auf das Reich* (Freiburg i. Br., 1934), p. 9.

[61] *BGB* (1869), pp. 201–210. Hermann Müller, *Die Entstehungsgeschichte des Gerichtsverfas-
sungs-Gesetzes* (Tübingen, 1939), pp. 13–15; Laband, *Staatsrecht*, III, 362–363.

German unity."[62] In 1871 its jurisdiction was extended to the entire Reich. It became, furthermore, the supreme court for Alsace-Lorraine and for cases arising from extraterritorial consular courts.[63]

The statute of June 21, 1869, establishing the universal validity of judicial decisions was another instance in which the constitution was extended. While the constitution had only granted authority for legislation on "the reciprocal execution of judicial sentences in civil matters," this statute was drafted to cover, with certain limitations, criminal cases as well. Under its provisions no court could disregard decisions of courts situated in other states. Requests for judicial aid (*Rechtshilfe*) went directly between the courts concerned; no court could refuse to comply. No state could give refuge to a criminal convicted by the courts of another state. Bankruptcy proceedings begun in one state were effective in every other. By this means the state courts became in effect national courts.[64] The foundations had been laid for a single, integrated judiciary acting on the basis of common law codes, following common procedures, and crowned by a common court of appeals.

One of the last deeds of the North German Confederation was enactment in May 1870 of a code of criminal law, laying down the principles to be followed by state courts in the definition and punishment of criminal offenses.[65] Bismarck, who followed the deliberations on this statute with considerable impatience, regarded it as very important for the "organic growth" of the confederation and its institutions.[66] In 1877 no less than four statutes were enacted that were of great significance for the integration of the German legal system: the judiciary code (*Gerichtsverfassungsgesetz*), bankruptcy code, and codes of civil and criminal procedure.[67] The first of these statutes established the imperial court (*Reichsgericht*) at Leipzig, which assumed jurisdiction over both criminal and civil law (except for commercial law). Its judges were nominated by the Bundesrat and appointed by the Kaiser. Through the power of judicial review the imperial court dominated the German judiciary, a vital contribution to the uniform interpretation of law. In a few types of litigation, such as high treason, the imperial court became the tribunal of first instance. Although the lower courts in the judicial hierarchy were state institutions, the statutes of 1877 imposed upon them common patterns of organization and procedure and in criminal law a common imperial code. After 1877 civil law was the one remaining gap in the development of an integrated German legal system. Civil law had not been included in the legislative competence of the

---

[62] GW, VIII, 76.

[63] Kern, *Überleitung*, p. 8.

[64] BGB (1869), pp. 305–315; Laband, *Staatsrecht*, III, 414–423; Heinrich Triepel, *Unitarismus und Föderalismus im deutschen Reiche* (Tübingen, 1907), pp. 59ff.

[65] BGB (1870), pp. 195–273.

[66] GW, XIV, 759–760, 775.

[67] Statutes of Jan. 27 and 30, Feb. 1 and 10, 1877. RGB (1877), pp. 41–394.

central government under the constitution. After 1869 Reichstag liberals agitated for a constitutional amendment to remedy this lack,[68] and in 1873 the
amendment was finally approved by the Bundesrat.[69] Codification was not
complete until 1896.

Undoubtedly the establishment of common law codes and a unified judiciary had a strong impact upon the development of a German national consciousness. Henceforth all Germans regardless of their states of origin were
subject to the same law enforced by courts whose decisions were universally
enforceable and subject to review by national courts. The consolidation of
the German judicial and legal systems affected the daily lives of nearly every
citizen, but it also had a deteriorating effect upon the federal structure of the
Reich. "The permanent unification of law and justice and the retreat of state
citizenship behind Reich citizenship," wrote the historian Heinrich Triepel,
"had the further result that from decade to decade the special territorial rights
of the states lost their actual importance and that, apart from the customs and
commercial affairs, the borders of the states ceased more and more to play any
part within the Reich."[70] "The direction of this development," wrote the political scientist Paul Laband, "must be characterized as decidedly unitary. The
borders of the states have lost their importance for domicile and settlement,
financial relief (except for Bavaria and until now Alsace-Lorraine), business
occupations, and the administration of justice." Through laws of the Reich
the autonomy of the states was in his opinion being steadily absorbed.[71] In
1871 a uniform coinage was established based on the gold standard. An "imperial gold coin" (Reichsgoldmünze) worth ten marks replaced the Prussian
thaler and all other coins; on one side it bore the imperial eagle and on the
other the likeness of the monarch of the state that minted it—the only concession to particularism.[72] In 1870 limitations were placed on issuance of new
banknotes in preparation for the introduction in 1874 of a new currency by
the imperial treasury.[73]

The bank statute of March 1875, which completed the creation of a single
monetary system, was one of the most important fruits of Bismarck's collaboration with the national liberals. On the Reichstag's insistence the bill prepared by the Prussian Ministry of Finance was rewritten to transform the Bank
of Prussia into an imperial bank (Reichsbank), the principal repository for public funds. It provided banking facilities for the entire country, opening
branches and subbranches in every community of importance. As the favored
bank of issue, the Reichsbank controlled the quantity of currency in circulation

[68] SBR (1869), I, 445ff.
[69] Statute of Dec. 20, 1873. RGB (1873), p. 379.
[70] Triepel, Unitarismus, p. 59.
[71] Laband, "Entwicklung," p. 8.
[72] Statute of Dec. 4, 1871. RGB (1871), pp. 404–408.
[73] Statute of Apr. 30, 1874. RGB (1874), pp. 40ff.

and regulated discount and interest rates. Such strict limitations were placed upon the issue of private banknotes that nearly half of the thirty-three banks possessing that authority quickly renounced it. The *Reichsbank* was the crowning institution of the integrated banking system that developed in the 1870s. It was a semigovernmental body possessing a standing in both public and private law. Control was in the hands of the chancellor who presided over a supervisory *Bankkuratorium* and "directed" the *Bankdirektorium*, which administered the institution. Located in Berlin, the imperial bank was a centralistic institution not provided by the constitution; its creation signified an important extension of the authority and functions of the central government and an equivalent sacrifice on the part of the states.[74]

In 1868 Bismarck told Eulenburg that the Reichstag was the parliamentary body "whose reinforcement is at present the most important task of Prussian policy."[75] Toward this end he permitted and even encouraged the expansion of its legislative competence and the exploitation of that competence in the first decade of its existence. The consequence of the strengthening of the Reichstag was a corresponding decline in the importance of other legislative organs. Earlier it has been shown that the system of government created under the constitution was one of checks and balances, modelled on the balance of power principle in foreign affairs.[76] Reichstag and Bundesrat, Zollverein parliament, Prussian Chamber of Deputies and House of Lords—these three legislatures represented alternative paths for the passage of legislation desired by the government. The strengthening of any one of these channels weakened the others. Yet the attempt to enlarge the competence of the Zollverein parliament was unsuccessful before its liquidation in 1871; the Reich inherited its legislative powers over tariffs, sugar, and tobacco. During the Kulturkampf of the 1870s the Prussian Landtag remained an important legislative channel, but thereafter its importance declined. Since imperial statutes took precedence over state laws, the importance of the Reich grew and that of Prussia and the other states shrank with the passage of every major bill through the Reichstag and Bundesrat.

[74] Statute of Mar. 14, 1875. *RGB* (1875), pp. 177ff.; Karl Maass, *Fünfundzwanzig Jahre deutscher Reichs-Gesetzgebung* (Leipzig, 1898), p. 111; Johannes Ziekursch, *Politische Geschichte des deutschen Kaiserreiches* (Frankfurt, 1927), II, 290; Laband, *Staatsrecht*, I, 401–405.

[75] Quoted in Egmont Zechlin, *Staatsstreichpläne Bismarcks und Wilhelms II, 1890–1894* (Stuttgart, 1929), p. 18.

[76] See vol. 1, 341–363.

CHAPTER SIX

Bismarck and Parliament

What Bismarck Expected of Parliament

FOR ME there exists but a single compass, a single polar star toward which I steer: *Salus publica!* . . . I have never been doctrinaire in my life. All of the systems through which the parties feel themselves divided and bound are for me of secondary rank. In the first rank comes the nation—its position toward the outside, its independence, our organization in the sense that we can breathe freely as a great nation in the world. Everything that may follow after that—whether the constitution is liberal, reactionary, or conservative—is of secondary importance. This I confess to you, gentlemen, very candidly. Furnishing the house is a *luxus*, which has its place once the house itself has been solidly built."[1] In this, one of the most famous of all quotations from his collected works, Bismarck sketched his favorite self-image: that of "the man of the state and the king" standing above the chaos of social and political life, seeking without fear or favor, prejudice or partisanship, the ideal line of policy dictated by the reasoned interest of state.[2]

While believing Germany's exposed position in the middle of Europe necessitated authoritarian control over foreign policy and military affairs, he regarded absolutism as "the most unfortunate of all forms of government." Where the king possessed full power, ministers were likely to lose the contest for royal favor to the queen, mistresses, a clever valet, or other members of the "court crowd." By occasional protests, reinforced by threats of resignation, Bismarck strove to isolate Wilhelm from "nonresponsible" advisers, but he could never completely seal off bedchamber and antechamber from alien influences. In his political thinking the function of parliament was to force the ruler to depend upon ministers who publicly defended his policies. The monarch must be constantly aware that the ministers could resign, if frustrated on an important issue, leaving him exposed as in 1862 to the attacks of the chamber. They were his shield against pressures that might lead to parliamentary government.[3]

Bismarck equated republicanism with parliamentary rule and monarchism

[1] *BR*, VIII, 328–329. "There are times for liberalism and times for reaction, also for authoritarian rule," Bismarck wrote to Prince Wilhelm of Prussia, Jan. 6, 1888. *GW*, VIc, 383.

[2] See also *BR*, VI, 129–131; XI, 292; XII, 85; Moritz Busch, *Bismarck: Some Secret Pages of His History* (London, 1898), II, 259–260, 297.

[3] *GW*, VII, 172; VIII, 384; XIV, 15; *BR*, XI, 292.

with the constitutional system of mixed powers. The last was for him the only possible system of government in Germany. "Of all the experiments that have taken place in the sphere of politics since Montesquieu and others," he declared in 1884, "the only truly useful result is the [concept of the separation of powers] between the executive, legislature, and judiciary." Yet the three branches were hardly equal in his constitutional thought. While acquiescing in the use of the courts to discipline members of parliament and his own recalcitrant subordinates (for example, Harry von Arnim), he did not yield to the judiciary the power to try impeached ministers under the "responsibility" clauses of the Prussian and Reich constitutions. Nor did he concede to parliament full partnership with the monarchy in the business of government. In the same speech of 1884—a time when his relationship with the Reichstag was at a low ebb—he lectured the deputies on the "correct use" of power. "The parliament should be able to prevent harm" by exercising its right to "veto" impractical measures proposed by armchair bureaucrats. "It should be able to prevent bad laws from being passed; it should be able to prevent the waste of public money; but, gentlemen, it cannot govern."[4] The function of the legislature was to ward off evil rather than initiate good.

How was parliament to distinguish between what was harmful and what was beneficial, what was to be opposed and what accepted? Bismarck considered himself, as a "man of state" beyond all partisan interest, to be the best judge of what constituted the public welfare. It irritated him that many deputies, frequently a majority, were unwilling to accept him in this role, that they tended to see in him a defender of special interests (the aristocracy, the propertied classes, and especially the agrarians).[5] As long as he was in power, Bismarck could see no reason for parliament to exercise its power of prevention. When it did so in the 1860s and 1880s, he considered a coup d'état to revise the electoral base and change the composition of the chamber. But not even this can be regarded as a departure from his belief that the essence of constitutional monarchy was "the working together of the monarchical will with the convictions of the governed population."[6] Almost to the end of his career Bismarck retained the conviction that at least 90 percent of the German people were monarchist in sympathy. The voting public had been misled by demagogues, whose influence had to be excised by abolishing universal male suffrage.[7]

In any conflict with parliament Bismarck believed that the monarch's will must be decisive. The boundary line between monarchism and republicanism

<hr/>

[4] BR, VI, 334; X, 46, 56.

[5] This was a constant theme of Bismarck over the years; he returned to it again in the opening chapter of his memoirs. GW, XV, 14–15.

[6] GW, XIII, 469.

[7] Hans Rothfels, ed., Bismarck und der Staat (2d ed., Darmstadt, 1953), p. 326. See his similar remarks to Carl Schurz, Jan. 28–29, 1868. GW, VII, 235–236.

would be crossed if the ruler were ever compelled by parliament "to do something that he could not willingly do." Yet in moments of extreme exasperation Bismarck was capable of reflecting on the advantages of republicanism. Wilhelm's objections to the Dual Alliance in 1879 were, he believed, entirely sentimental—sympathy for Russia, prejudice against Austria. "I know neither hate nor fear nor love," the chancellor confided. "From the human standpoint that would be laughable, but it is the way that states should be governed. . . . After experiencing how difficult ruling monarchs make it for their ministers to serve the country, one could almost become a republican." The man whom he had borne on his shoulders to the throne now thought he knew everything better than his minister and wanted to do it all himself. The huge fund of royalism and veneration for the king with which he had assumed office, he declared, was steadily declining.[8]

The English parliamentary system had a fascination for Bismarck, as it did for most German liberals. But he contended that it could not be replicated. "Until now it has not been proven in practice," he wrote in February 1870, "that parliamentary government, as it developed in England during its long and most unique history, can be naturalized in another large state, and it is likewise an error to assume that a similar apparatus of elections, votes, and caucuses could be employed elsewhere with the same lasting results as in England." He believed that parliamentary government in the English tradition was only possible under certain conditions: "when an entire people is satisfied with the essentials of an existing constitution, when the propertied and educated classes have long had a definite share in the powers of the state, when the parties within those classes chiefly fight over which among them should administer the whole and enjoy the advantages that come with that administration, when party leaders have learned how to govern and their party comrades how to let themselves be led." Even in England the sovereign and "governmental machine" together were, when a fundamental issue was at stake, still decisive in determining who would form a cabinet—"not party traditions, election platforms of the candidates, and votes in the lower chamber."[9]

By 1885 Bismarck had concluded that even in Britain the parliamentary system was doomed. Its powerlessness had cost the monarchy "its hold on the consciousness of the nation; the aristocracy, which replaced the monarchy in the course of party struggles, has lost the majority . . . and can regain it only in union or in alliance with radicals, who must be rewarded with antimonarchical concessions. The final consequence of such concessions is a republic; the consequence of a republic in a large nation is necessarily civil war."[10]

Bismarck's admiration for the British system—as it was before the second

[8] GW, VIII, 325, 333–334.

[9] Bismarck to Schweinitz, Feb. 12, 1870. GW, VIb, 241–242. See also BR, V, 371ff; GW, VIb, 209, 224–225.

[10] Bismarck to King Ludwig II of Bavaria, July 1, 1885. GW, XIV, 961.

reform bill—was genuine, and his comprehension of how it functioned more accurate than that of most German students of the English system. Yet he undoubtedly teased the deputies when he assured them at a parliamentary soirée in March 1878 that the British system was his "ideal." "This system is possible in England, where they have two large parties, but not here, where seven or eight parties exist, all of them organized differently in different law-making bodies."[11] At that moment he was plotting to split the National Liberal party.

Occasionally Bismarck spoke of the desirability of reshaping the party structure, molding political fragments into larger parties capable of supporting his program. But his favorite tactic, that of providing for alternative majorities, was divisive, for its success depended upon the multiplicity of parties as well as parliaments. Domination of the Prussian Chamber of Deputies by a single party in 1862–1866 had frustrated that tactic and presented him with the greatest internal challenge of his career. The government's duty, as Bismarck conceived it, was to "create a majority for itself in parliament."[12] "We draw, as the possibility presents itself, the diagonal of forces that are actually present," he told the deputies in 1870. "If one force becomes greater, then the diagonal takes another direction."[13] Only those parties that participated in the government's majority could hope to influence its policy; attempts to coerce the government on a substantial issue were met by maneuvers to reconstitute the majority. Compromise, Bismarck was fond of saying, is the essence of constitutional government. Yet the only compromises acceptable to him on fundamental issues were those that yielded the appearance of concession without the substance.

Bismarck was one of the most effective parliamentary speakers of his time, although he disdained oratory and was suspicious of those who excelled at it.[14] On his appearance tension mounted in the chamber. When he ordered a mug of beer, the deputies knew he was getting ready to speak. As word spread, they streamed from the halls and committee rooms to their seats.[15] What they heard was a thin, high-pitched voice that contrasted oddly with the massive head and body. He groped for words, which came out in spurts but were usually on target. He was frequently witty, often sardonic and sarcastic, but rarely dull.

Behind the scenes Bismarck was usually active in the interest of his legislative program, at least while he was in Berlin, conferring privately with important deputies, applying persuasion, pressure, and threats as he judged the situation required. Prominent members were invited to formal dinners at the

[11] BP, I, 139.
[12] BR, V, 230, 243, 251–252, 259; X, 239; GW, VIc, 165.
[13] BR, IV, 375.
[14] Busch, Secret Pages, I, 294–295, 402–403.
[15] BP, II, 214 (fn.).

BISMARCK (LEFT CENTER) IN THE REICHSTAG CHAMBER, 1889. (BILDARCHIV PREUSSISCHER KULTURBESITZ.)

BISMARCK CONVERSING WITH DEPUTIES IN THE REICHSTAG LOBBY, 1889. (BILDARCHIV PREUSSISCHER KULTURBESITZ.)

chancellery. Health permitting, he held a weekly openhouse while parliament was in session. His guests at these soirées found him a jovial and considerate host, his table laden with food, wine, and the best Munich beer. Who and how many attended—the number varied from twenty-five to five hundred—and what was said by him to whom was usually reported in the daily press and regarded as a political barometer. The appearance of Alsatian autonomists in March 1877 heralded negotiations for Reichsland autonomy and of centrists in May 1879 the approaching end of the Kulturkampf.[16] In early years there was a genuine exchange of opinion between him and his guests, but as time passed the dialogue became a monologue, in which Bismarck expounded his views, reminisced about his experiences, and told stories usually about his triumphs and others' follies. Wherever he stood or sat, a thick corona of deputies gathered, straining to hear what the great man had to say. If he tarried in one room, the others emptied. Since he generally remained nowhere very long, the deputies were in constant motion, either following in his wake or trying to anticipate where he would go next. "Everyone wanted to warm himself in [Bismarck's] sun."[17]

Honoratioren *Politics during the Early Empire*

The fracturing of German political parties during the Bismarck period was in part a reflection of the divisions in German society. Yet the history of modern politics shows many examples of parties that have endured despite acute internal frictions, held together by common ideology, force of tradition, capacity for compromise, and the necessities of political competition. In Germany these centripetal influences were not strong enough to withstand the pressures that arose from Bismarck's successes in foreign policy and his exploitation of them in domestic affairs. Earlier it has been shown that both the liberal and conservative parties divided following the Prussian victory in 1866, the assumption by Prussia of the German national cause, passage of the indemnity act, and drafting of the constitution of 1867.[18] Victory over France and the completion of German unification led to the creation of the German Center party to protect Catholic interests in a predominantly Protestant country.

It is true that the divisions of 1866–1867 did not for the time being liquidate the tradition of a single liberal and a single conservative party.[19] In the

---

[16] The scattered records of these affairs were collected and published in three volumes by Poschinger in *BP*. See also Heinrich Brockhaus, *Stunden mit Bismarck, 1871–1878* (Leipzig, 1929). The soirées began in 1869 and in 1883 were converted into *Frühschoppen*. Until 1874 the entire chamber was invited, thereafter only those who deposited their cards with the portier of the chancellery. Brockhaus, *Stunden mit Bismarck*, pp. 89–90.

[17] Arthur von Brauer, *Im Dienste Bismarcks* (Berlin, 1936), pp. 33–34.

[18] See vol. 1, pp. 328–338.

[19] For the general structure and character of German political parties in this period see Thomas Nipperdey, *Die Organisation der deutschen Parteien vor 1918* (Düsseldorf, 1961); Hans Fenske, *Wahlrecht und Parteiensystem: Ein Beitrag zur deutschen Parteiengeschichte* (Frankfurt a. M., 1972);

early years of the empire the term "party" had a dual meaning in the German political vocabulary. In the broad sense it continued to mean the liberal and conservative movements as a whole; in the narrow sense it meant the new caucuses into which those general movements were divided within the Reichstag and other parliaments. In parliament, in other words, the terms party (*Partei*) and caucus (*Fraktion*) were used interchangeably (as they are in these volumes). At election time candidates usually ran as "conservatives" or "liberals" rather than as "Prussian conservatives," "free conservatives," "national liberals," and "progressives." As yet neither the party proper nor the party caucus had a political organization extending down to the grass roots. While the former was based upon an ideology or complex of ideas and feelings, the latter was based programmatically upon a "founding manifesto" and successive "election manifestos" drafted by a central committee and detailing the party's positions on major issues. Candidates were chosen by local committees or, in districts that were politically more advanced, by associations (*Vereine*), both composed of prominent citizens sharing the general political orientation of the party. The political composition of the local club or association tended to determine the political coloration of the candidate chosen and hence the particular caucus in parliament he was likely to join if elected.

Because of this arrangement it was rare for conservative and free conservative candidates to oppose one another at the polls, and the two liberal parties put up rival candidates for the same seat only in larger cities. (In the Reichstag election of 1871, 13 districts had a single candidate, while 221 districts had only two candidates.)[20] On entering the chamber the newly elected member decided which caucus best represented his brand of liberalism or conservatism. Since the political base of the deputy was in the local committee or association, the caucus had difficulty enforcing party discipline. Leadership was vested in a committee rather than a single individual, although one or two persons in each caucus generally came—by virtue of personality, speaking ability, or political sagacity—to be regarded as its chief spokesmen.

During the early years of the empire, the conservative and liberal parties were still "parties of notables" (*Honoratiorenparteien*) rather than "parties of the masses" (*Massenparteien*). Their elected representatives, like the committees and associations that chose the candidates, were men of local or national prominence belonging to the bureaucratic, propertied, and intellectual castes. The genus *Honoratiorenpartei* reflected an older society divided into status and occupational groups with a recognized elite that was expected to

---

and James J. Sheehan, "Political Leadership in the German Reichstag, 1871–1918," *American Historical Review*, 74 (1968), pp. 511–528, and *German Liberalism in the Nineteenth Century* (Chicago, 1978).

[20] Fenske, *Wahlrecht und Parteiensystem*, pp. 107–111. In the following decades, the average number of candidates per election district rose from 2.43 in 1871 to 4.15 in 1893, increasing the importance of run-off elections necessary to secure an absolute majority. *Ibid.*, pp. 115–134.

provide political leadership. Campaigning was often minimal—in northeastern rural districts dominated by the conservatives it was almost nonexistent. But prominent national liberals, like Rudolf von Bennigsen, also rarely appeared in their constituencies at election time. Their claim to political leadership rested not on their "agitating skills" but on the deference owed them because of their status. Such efforts as national liberals made to extend their electoral base were aimed not at the newly enfranchised in the lowest social stratum of the electorate but at the *Mittelstand*, which most still regarded as the only reservoir of informed political judgment in civil society.[21] To *Honoratioren* the deputy, like the cabinet minister, was above politics. He was chosen precisely because of his independence and freedom from contamination by special interests. In Max Weber's words, he lived "for" and not "off politics."[22] This was also Bismarck's view of the deputy's proper role, which explains his irritation and even rage at "party particularism."

The elitist character of German politics was not unique in Europe. On the contrary, French and English political parties had similar characteristics and were to undergo a like transformation. The *Honoratioren* character of German political leadership was reinforced by the constitution's prohibition against compensation for service in parliament (repealed in 1906). In contrast to the Prussian Chamber of Deputies, whose members were paid a per diem allowance of three (after 1873 five) thalers, Reichstag deputies had to support themselves during the many months they spent in Berlin on public business. Repeatedly the Reichstag passed and the Bundesrat rejected a bill providing for per diem allowances. Bismarck was adamant in opposing any benefit other than free railway passes (begun in 1873 and rescinded a decade later). He hoped to keep professional politicians and working-class radicals out of the chamber. In this he did not succeed. Many deputies for whom politics was the primary calling made their living from occupations easily combined with it; for example, journalist, lobbyist, and party official. Radical deputies of modest means were subsidized from party sources.[23]

Another factor influencing the composition of both the Reichstag and Chamber of Deputies was the failure to reapportion electoral districts. Rural areas became overrepresented and urban areas underrepresented in both parliaments. Under the constitution of 1871 the Reichstag represented "the entire population," its members chosen by universal, direct, and secret male suffrage and unbound by instructions or commissions from constituents. Elec-

[21] Sheehan, "Political Leadership," p. 515, and *German Liberalism*, pp. 142–157. On the social composition and traditional politics of the German *Mittelstand* see vol. 1, pp. 13–14, 121–125, 330–340.

[22] H. H. Gerth and C. Wright Mills, eds., *From Max Weber: Essays in Sociology* (New York, 1958), pp. 84–85. Quoted by Sheehan, "Political Leadership," p. 515.

[23] Gerhard Stoltenberg, *Der deutsche Reichstag, 1871–1873* (Düsseldorf, 1955), pp. 59–60, 161. Cabinet meetings of Feb. 8 and Nov. 20, 1873. DZA Merseburg, Rep. 90a, B, III, 2b, Nr. 6, Vol. 85.

tion districts were distributed by state according to population, with 100,000 inhabitants and one deputy the norm for each district; small principalities with fewer inhabitants were guaranteed at least one district. The periodic expansion of the Reichstag to keep pace with population growth was to be regulated by future legislation. But no such law was ever passed with the consequence that with time the Reichstag ceased to represent the "entire population" other than symbolically.[24] The first Reichstag election of the German Reich (in March 1871) should have functioned like a national plebiscite, but only 52 percent of the electorate voted. In later German elections the turnout hovered slightly above 60 percent (except for 1881—56.3 percent) until 1887 when it jumped to 77.5 percent. Prussia's suffrage was far more restrictive: a three-class system, indirect election, oral voting, and election districts that had not been reapportioned since they were established in 1849. Their unequal voice, the slowness of oral voting, and its social hazards kept most lower class voters away from the polls. But even the upper classes were negligent. In 1866, 27.6 percent of eligible voters in class I (low income), 47.5 percent of class II (middle income), and 60.4 percent of class III (high income) cast their ballots. The electoral colleges chosen in this way selected the deputies by majority vote, a procedure that further reduced the chances of left-liberal and socialist candidates.[25]

The failure to reapportion and the denial of remuneration to Reichstag deputies buttressed *Honoratioren* politics for a time, but the dynamics of social change eventually produced a new kind of politics. Industrialization, urbanization, and "flight from the land" broke down "the major clusters of old social, economic, and psychological commitments."[26] New allegiances soon arose more in accord with the German's altered perceptions of his needs. Simultaneously demographic concentration, faster communication, mass education, and mass journalism opened the way for new kinds of political agitation. A few perceptive individuals (most notably, Hermann Wagener among the conservatives and Hermann Schulze-Delitzsch among the liberals) were already trying—without much success—to convince their colleagues of the need to politicize the lower classes through the nurture of their material interests. Not until the Center and Social Democratic parties (the first *Massenparteien*) had established themselves and survived the assaults of Bismarck and

[24] Alfred Milatz, "Reichstagswahlen und Mandatsverteilung 1871 bis 1918: Ein Beitrag zu Problemen des absoluten Mehrheitswahlrechts," in Gerhard A. Ritter, ed., *Gesellschaft, Parlament und Regierung: Zur Geschichte des Parlamentarismus in Deutschland* (Düsseldorf, 1974), pp. 207–223.

[25] Bernhard Vogel, Dieter Nohlen, and Rainer-Olaf Schultze, *Wahlen in Deutschland: Theorie-Geschichte-Dokumente, 1848–1970* (Berlin, 1971), pp. 286, 291. For analyses of the election laws see *ibid.*, pp. 95–128, and Nils Diederich, "Germany," in Stein Rokkan and Jean Meyriat, eds., *International Guide to Electoral Statistics* (Hague, 1969), p. 154.

[26] Karl W. Deutsch, "Social Mobilization and Political Development," *American Political Science Review*, 55 (1961), p. 494, quoted in Sheehan, "Political Leadership," p. 516.

the older parties was it fully realized that universal male suffrage and social change required a different kind of politics.

Occupational statistics show that in the 1870s Germany's most important elected bodies were still dominated by the old agrarian and bureaucratic elites, despite annexations, unification, and industrialization. Of 484 members of the Prussian Chamber of Deputies during 1870–1873, 170 (35 percent) were state officials, including 76 belonging to the judiciary, and 129 (26.7 percent) were landowners (whether farmers or estate owners, small or large landowners is undetermined). In addition, there were 19 (4 percent) retired state officials and 6 army officers, along with 30 (6.2 percent) local officials, 21 (4.3 percent) educators and 21 pastors (including 17 Catholics). The chamber contained 34 (7 percent) businessmen and rentiers, 21 (4.3 percent) lawyers, 8 journalists, and 3 physicians; 151 persons (31.2 percent) were noblemen, including 21 barons, 19 counts, and 3 princes. Three members listed themselves as "independent workers."[27] Of 384 deputies in the first German Reichstag (1871–1873), 97 (25.3 percent) were state officials, including 45 from the judiciary, and 104 (27.1 percent) were landowners, including 80 big estate owners, 22 estate owners, and 2 small farmers. Retired state officials and army officers numbered 20 (5.2 percent), local officials 11 (2.9 percent), educators 29 (7.5 percent), pastors 13 (3.4 percent). Forty-five (11.7 percent) lawyers and 30 (7.8 percent) businessmen (17 merchants and 13 industrialists) were elected. In the Reichstag sat one artisan and no factory workers.[28]

In the Prussian election of November 1870 the parties of the right suffered minor losses, conservatives electing 114 deputies as against 125 in 1867, free conservatives 41 as against 48, the old-liberals 11 as against 15. The national liberals grew from 99 to 123, the progressives from 48 to 49. The Reichstag, whose election was delayed by the war until March 1871, was larger (384 instead of 297) owing to the inclusion of the south. Here the two right-wing parties suffered a decline in numerical as well as relative strength, the conservatives sinking from 64 to 57, the free conservatives rising only from 34 to 37. The major gainers from the expansion were the national liberals (from 78 to 125) and progressives (from 29 to 46). Although the old-liberal caucus had disappeared, its place was taken by a new and short-lived Liberal Reich party, composed of about 30 members, mostly statesmen of the lesser states. Both elections were notable for the appearance in significant numbers of a new Catholic party, the Center, with 58 members in the Chamber of Deputies and 61 in the Reichstag.[29]

Most of the deputies who listed themselves as state officials and estate own-

[27] The author is indebted to Ronald Snell for these statistics. The figure includes 52 deputies elected in by-elections.

[28] Ludwig Rosenbaum, *Beruf und Herkunft der Abgeordneten zu den deutschen und preussischen Parlamenten, 1847–1919* (Frankfurt a. M., 1923), pp. 23–26.

[29] Vogel et al., *Wahlen in Deutschland*, pp. 287–290.

ers were concentrated in the Conservative and Free Conservative parties, which they dominated overwhelmingly. Despite differences in attitude toward the revolution Bismarck had effected, both parties were closely linked to the old Prussian establishment—monarchy, army, bureaucracy, Protestant church, nobility, and agrarian landlords. The National Liberal party, generally believed to have been the spokesman for big business, was composed of deputies with a wide range of occupations—estate owners, officials, judges, city officials, professors, lawyers, businessmen. Each of these groups was modest in size when compared to the total strength of the party. In 1871–1873 the Reichstag caucus, for example, had only fifteen deputies who identified themselves as businessmen (three industrialists, two bankers, six merchants, two insurers, one shipper, and one publisher), as against sixteen judges, seventeen lawyers, and five writers. The Reichstag caucus of the Progressive party, often considered to have been the spokesman for mercantile interests and light industry, contained three merchants, two factory owners, and one railway director, compared to nine professors, seven estate owners, seven lawyers, four city officials, four jurists, and three writers. The first Reichstag caucus of the Center party showed the wide distribution of listed occupations to be expected of a party created primarily for the protection of Catholic interests. The largest groups were seventeen estate owners (big and small in almost equal numbers), twelve priests, nine lawyers, nine officials (five retired), and twelve judges (four retired).[30]

On the basis of listed occupations it is impossible to explain why so many statutes of the period 1867–1878 favored the interests and growth of industrial capitalism. Certainly the commitment of the deputies, particularly of the national liberals, to business interests has been exaggerated in recent historical works.[31] But it is also true that the occupations they claimed often reflected the social status deputies preferred more than the character of their financial involvement—a factor often difficult to trace.[32] Nor does a listing such as "factory owner" reveal the amount of capital invested and what other interlocking financial and managerial commitments it may have produced. After the crash of 1873 the German public, fed by denunciations from the press, became more conscious of the frequency with which the names of certain deputies, particularly those of high title, appeared on the boards and founding committees of corporate enterprises. According to one, admittedly hostile, source, 62 members of the Prussian House of Lords, 90 members of the Cham-

[30] Willy Kremer, *Der soziale Aufbau der Parteien des Deutschen Reichstages von 1871–1918* (Düsseldorf, 1934).

[31] See, for example, the works of Helmut Böhme, *Deutschlands Weg zur Grossmacht: Studien zum Verhältnis von Wirtschaft und Staat während der Reichsgründungszeit 1848–1881* (Cologne, 1966), and Hans-Ulrich Wehler, *Bismarck und der Imperialismus* (Cologne, 1969).

[32] On this problem see particularly Lenore O'Boyle, "Liberal Political Leadership in Germany, 1867–1884," *Journal of Modern History*, 28 (1956), pp. 338–340.

ber of Deputies, and 105 members of the Reichstag were involved in varying degrees in the great corporate boom of the early 1870s.[33]

To assume, however, that deputies who happened to be bankers, industrialists, merchants, or estate owners "represented" those business interests in the chamber is rather misleading.[34] If their attitudes and votes were predictable on tax and other economic legislation, most of the important bills before the Prussian and German parliaments in these years dealt with other matters. Consider, for example, the long debates on capital punishment in the Reichstag in 1870 and the Kulturkampf laws of the next decade in both the Reichstag and Chamber of Deputies. Nor was the tradition that deputies were chosen to represent the nation rather than constituencies of no consequence. In their interpretation of that ethic, the deputies were probably no more free of cant and self-delusion than is common in all human affairs. The ranks of the free conservatives, national liberals, and progressives were filled with men who, whether or not they were in business, approved the rush toward modernity that industrialization offered and assumed that what was good for business was also good for the country. For most of them German national unity, material progress, and laissez-faire served moral as well as material ends. Idealism and self-interest are not always opposed, and politicians are happiest when they coincide.

The Dynamics of Party Politics

The material explanation of political behavior fails, moreover, to take into account the dynamics of the power struggle in a parliamentary system. In a multiparty system many other factors can influence or determine party behavior: for example, relative size and position in the political spectrum; skill in fashioning compromises; bargaining at election time; hunger for participation in a winning coalition; and the search for viable majority capable of enduring brief crises for long-term objectives. A constitution of mixed powers, furthermore, frees neither the government nor the parties from concern over their mutual relationship. The desire to maintain or establish contact with the government can be a powerful influence on party conduct. Consider, for example, how the participants in the struggle over the tariff act of 1879 explained their actions. Baron Georg von Franckenstein, the centrist deputy who fashioned the compromise that eased passage of the statute, said afterward "that his motion was based on a question of power and that the Center party had allied with the conservatives simply for the purpose of forcing the National Liberal party out of its relationship with the government and ripping away its

[33] Otto Glagau, *Der Börsen- und Gründungsschwindel in Deutschland* (Leipzig, 1877), pp. 493–519. For membership in various parliamentary bodies see Max Schwarz, *Biographisches Handbuch der Reichstage* (Hanover, 1965).

[34] For example, Böhme, *Deutschlands Weg*, pp. 262–263.

previous influence. . . . To choose the lesser of two unavoidable evils is to do nothing more than to act according to the cardinal virtue of Christian wisdom."[35] Eduard Lasker, on the other hand, judged that national liberals gave up their resistance to the bill "purely out of tactical considerations: because the momentary current in the population was favorable to the indicated direction and was extraordinarily strengthened by the mighty influence of Prince Bismarck; because the Center party was ready for an alliance with the government, thereby securing a majority; and because persistence in the minority under such circumstances did not appear to be in the party's interest. The same considerations, I fear, will lead to the same result whenever Prince Bismarck sets the game of party politics in motion similarly in any other political area."[36]

For a decade after 1867 the National Liberal party held the key position in the Reichstag—a result less of its size than of its location in the constellation of political forces in the chamber. Situated in the center of a polarized body, the caucus had the capability of producing majorities by combining either with the left or the right. Only four of the original twenty-four schismatics who had left the Progressive party in September 1866 were still in the Reichstag after 1871, along with a few other former progressives who had joined them in the following year to found the National Liberal party. The party was now overwhelmingly composed of deputies who had not participated in the constitutional conflict—"old-liberals" who had their own caucus until 1870 and newcomers from the regions annexed by Prussia in 1866 and from the lesser states north and south of the Main. This influx had greatly strengthened the right wing at the cost of the left.[37] After the departure of Karl Twesten from politics in July 1870 ("with a shattered arm, loss of position and income, completely eroded in health—without having attained or influenced anything whatever"),[38] leadership of the left fell to Eduard Lasker. A lawyer and journalist, Lasker possessed a sharp intellect, boundless energy, and total dedication to politics; he was one of the most able and feared debaters in parliament. Also prominent on the left were Max von Forckenbeck (mayor of Breslau, later of Berlin), Baron Franz Schenk von Stauffenberg (a Bavarian landowner), Hans Victor von Unruh (railway entrepreneur), and Ludwig Bamberger (banker and journalist). The most important leaders of the right wing were two veteran leaders of the old Nationalverein, Rudolf von Bennigsen and Johannes Miquel, both new-Prussians from Hanover. Bennigsen was a noble landowner, lawyer, and judge, who through political prominence had become involved in the founding of the Hanover-Altenbecken railway com-

---

[35] At a political rally, Aug. 17, 1879. SEG (1879), p. 222.

[36] To his constituents, March 1880. HW, II, 309.

[37] Gordon Mork, "The National Liberal Party in the German Reichstag and the Prussian Landtag, 1866–1874" (Ph.D. dissertation, University of Minnesota, 1966), pp. 278–283.

[38] Twesten to Gustav Lipke, July 12, 1870. HW, I, 470.

pany, which collapsed in 1874—one of the doomed ventures of "railway baron" Bethel Henry Strousberg. For Miquel politics was good business. Trained in law, he became mayor of Osnabrück, later of Frankfurt am Main, and was deeply involved after 1869 in the affairs of the *Disconto-Gesellschaft*, including the founding of new railway and banking companies. Also prominent on the right wing were Wilhelm Wehrenpfennig (journalist and after 1879 counselor in the *Kultusministerium*), Eduard Stephani (lawyer and municipal deputy in Leipzig), and Karl Braun (Wiesbaden lawyer, writer and journalist, and businessman).[39]

During the period of the North German Confederation there was little difference in the basic objectives of right and left wings of the National Liberal party, despite occasional conflicts over tactics and immediate goals. Miquel was no less forthright than Lasker in pressing for "development" of the constitution. Bennigsen, on the other hand, was a moderate by temperament. He became the dominant figure in the party as a whole through his capacity for patient negotiation and skillful compromise. Despite the stark contrast in their backgrounds, Bennigsen, the Protestant nobleman, and Lasker, the Jewish bourgeois, established a close relationship after 1870. While sharing the common ideals of liberalism and nationalism, they differed in emphasis. Bennigsen was the "idealist of the *Nationalstaat*," Lasker the "idealist of the *Rechtsstaat*." "They represented once more the two sides of the old double ideal: the unity and freedom of the nation." In the two wings of the National Liberal party can again be seen the conflicting claims of the Hegelian and humanistic traditions of German idealistic philosophy. To the right wing, the best guarantee for freedom and cultural progress was to be found in the power and independence of the state; to the left wing, it was to be found in civil liberty and parliamentary power.[40] Paradoxically, the internal cleavage of the National Liberal party, ultimately fatal for its unity, gave it a pivotal position in parliament, able through its left wing to combine with the progressives on liberal issues or through its right wing with the free conservatives and the Liberal Reich party.

In spirit the Progressive party remained true to the ideals for which it had fought during the constitutional conflict and which in its view the national

---

[39] For information on the lives and careers of national liberal leaders see Richard W. Dill, *Der Parlamentarier Eduard Lasker und die parlamentarische Stilentwicklung der Jahre 1867–1884* (Erlangen, 1956); James F. Harris, *A Study in the Theory and Practice of German Liberalism: Eduard Lasker, 1829–1884* (Lanham, Md., 1984); Martin Philippson, *Max von Forckenbeck: Ein Lebensbild* (Leipzig, 1898); Stanley Zucker, *Ludwig Bamberger: German Liberal Politician and Social Critic, 1823–1899* (Pittsburgh, 1975); Hans Herzfeld, *Johannes von Miquel* (2 vols., Detmold, 1938); Hermann Oncken, *Rudolf von Bennigsen* (2 vols., Stuttgart, 1910); Friedrich Böttcher, *Eduard Stephani* (Leipzig, 1887); and Winfried Seelig, "From Nassau to the German Reich: The Ideological and Political Development of Karl Braun (1822–1871)" (Ph.D. dissertation, University of Minnesota, 1975).

[40] Oncken, *Bennigsen*, II, 248ff.

liberals had betrayed by accepting the indemnity bill and the constitution of 1867. More than half of the progressives elected to the Reichstag in 1871 were Prussian, many of them veterans of the conflict years. The party regularly captured the six seats allotted to Berlin and four seats in the East Prussian district of Gumbinnen, which had once been the nucleus of the party. One of the latter was Baron Leopold von Hoverbeck (estate owner and judge), who remained the party's dominant figure until his death in 1875. Hoverbeck remained true to the conviction he had expressed early in his political career that it was "better to do nothing than to do something wrong." National liberals, he believed, were permitting themselves to be exploited by Bismarck, who would eventually return to a conservative course. Yet he avoided severing the connection with the National Liberal party. His death and the defection of Wilhelm Löwe-Kalbe (physician with conjugal connections to heavy industry) weakened the moderate wing of the Progressive party at the end of the 1870s. Leadership of the "committed liberals," as they called themselves, then passed to Albert Hänel (political scientist at Kiel University) and Eugen Richter (journalist). The more radical was Richter, whose personal ascendancy in the party eventually amounted to near dictatorship. Under his leadership the progressives adopted in December 1876 a party platform calling for parliamentary government, the most extreme demand yet advanced by any major political party. Richter's rigorous scrutiny of the budget and other fiscal legislation in search of hidden expenditures and irregular procedures became legendary.[41]

While willing to support some liberal aims, such as limited improvement in parliament's budget rights and creation of an imperial cabinet, the free conservatives were essentially a "government" or "Bismarck party." Many of its members were closely associated with the chancellor (Keudell, Lucius, Friedenthal), while others had close connections at court (Prince of Pless, Duke of Ujest, Count Münster). On election to the Reichstag Bismarck's own sons, Wilhelm and Herbert, became free conservatives. The party had many prominent members, but no definite leaders, unless they were Count Eduard von Bethusy-Huc (*Landrat*) and Wilhelm von Kardorff (estate owner and industrialist). Geographically the centers of free conservative strength were in Silesia and the Rhineland. The Liberal Reich party was distinguishable from the Free Conservative party chiefly because of its strong emphasis upon federalism. The caucus came into existence in March 1871 and expired in 1874. Leading figures were former ministers of southern governments such as Prince Chlodwig zu Hohenlohe-Schillingsfürst of Bavaria and Baron Franz von Rog-

[41] For portraits of progressive leaders see Ludolf Parisius, *Leopold Freiherr von Hoverbeck: Ein Beitrag zur vaterländischen Geschichte* (2 vols., Berlin, 1879–1900); Felix Rachfahl, "Eugen Richter und der Linksliberalismus im neuen Reiche," *Zeitschrift für Politik*, 5 (1912), pp. 261–274; Ina Suzanne Lorenz, *Eugen Richter: Der entschiedene Liberalismus in Wilhelminischer Zeit 1871 bis 1906*, *Historische Studien*, vol. 433 (Husum, 1980).

genbach of Baden. Many were liberal Catholics who opposed the Center party
or southern liberal nationalists antagonistic to their counterparts in the National Liberal party.[42]

Increasingly isolated on the right of the chamber was the Conservative
party. The "old conservatives," as they were called, failed in their aspiration
to become a national party in the Reichstag elections. Almost all of the deputies were from Prussia, the great majority from rural Brandenburg, Pomerania, and East Prussia. At election time the great landowners made resolute
use of their local economic and political dominance to shut out the opposition. The dependence of local pastors, schoolteachers, and innkeepers upon
them enabled estate owners and county officials (the Landrat was often the
conservative candidate) to dominate public opinion. Secrecy of the ballot was
poorly maintained, and the peasantry voted as they were told. Good speakers
and effective politicians were rare among the conservatives. Accustomed to a
privileged position in government, they found it difficult to adjust to the new
era of parliamentary politics. Two who did were Moritz von Blanckenburg
(Pomeranian landowner and Landrat) and Hermann Wagener (journalist,
state official, and railway "founder"). The "old conservative" movement operated on three fronts: Reichstag, Chamber of Deputies, and House of Lords.
Its strength mounted in each chamber; in the third it was dominant. The
conservative members in the first two chambers were not identical, nor were
their politics. Albeit reluctantly, Reichstag conservatives were inclined to
accept German unification. Believing that Prussian particularism was a lost
cause, they advocated Prussianization of the national government by adoption in the Reich of a cabinet system on the Prussian model and conversion
of the Bundesrat into a Prussian-style House of Lords. Those who sat in the
Landtag, on the other hand, were increasingly inclined toward resistance to
centralization and to revolt against Bismarck and his policy of collaboration
with national liberals.[43]

The most dramatic event of the 1870–1871 elections was the emergence of
a Catholic party, the Center, as the second strongest caucus in the Reichstag.
Although Catholics had representation earlier in both chambers (dating back
to the 1850s in the Chamber of Deputies), the Center party was a new phenomenon. It was the product of a popular religious revival in German Catholicism that began in the 1850s; fears for the faith engendered by small-
German unification under Protestant leadership; the advantages of universal

[42] See Siegfried von Kardorff Wilhelm von Kardorff: Ein nationaler Parlamentarier im Zeitalter
Bismarcks und Wilhelms II., 1828–1907 (Berlin, 1936).

[43] See Gerhard Ritter, Die preussischen Konservativen und Bismarcks deutsche Politik, 1858–1875
(Heidelberg, 1913); Robert Berdahl, "The Transformation of the Prussian Conservative Party,
1866–1876" (Ph.D. dissertation, University of Minnesota, 1965); Herman von Petersdorff,
Kleist-Retzow: Ein Lebensbild (Stuttgart, 1907); Nipperdey, Organisation der politischen Parteien,
pp. 241–264.

and equal male suffrage; agitation by the priesthood under orders from the bishops; and an effective network of local, regional, and national organizations. In March 1871 fifty-eight centrist deputies were elected to the Reichstag, of which thirty-six came from Prussian constituencies, twenty-one of them located in the Rhineland. Eighteen deputies stemmed from Bavaria. No other caucus had so broad a social and electoral base: poor and well-to-do peasants, factory and mine workers, all middle-class strata, and wealthy landowners, including many aristocrats.

The emergence of the Center threatened the previous outlines of German politics and created for a time a climate of uncertainty in both chambers. Party program and leadership were conservative, stressing particularly the virtues of federalism. The vital question was whether the Center would ally with conservatives to create a new bloc in the chamber. It will be shown, however, that its first actions isolated the Center in the Reichstag and relieved the anxiety of the old middle parties. For a time the Center could be discounted as a factor in the parliamentary balance of power. Increasingly dominant in the party by virtue of his debating and tactical skills was Ludwig Windthorst, a lawyer, former minister of Hanover, and vigorous supporter of the rights of the deposed King Georg. Other luminaries were the brothers August and Peter Reichensperger, the former president of the Cologne city council, the latter a superior court judge (*Obertribunalsrat*) in Berlin, and Hermann von Mallinckrodt, a Westphalian estate owner.[44]

The Liberal Challenge, 1871–1873

From the political standpoint Bismarck's task of consolidating the German Reich was twofold. On the one hand, the empire had to be welded together by new laws and institutions that served concrete needs of the population. To this end the Reichstag had to become the most important arena of German politics and within it a "diagonal of forces" had to be found among parties of national and liberal viewpoint. On the other hand, it was necessary to solidify the federal system of mixed powers and the aristocratic-monarchical order that the system was designed to protect. Paradoxically, success in the first of these dual enterprises jeopardized the second. Centralization was a threat to federalism as well as particularism, and the destruction of federalism would have upset the institutional equilibrium that was the essence of Bismarckian government, leaving crown and chancellor face to face with parliament. The

---

[44] Jonathan Sperber, *Popular Catholicism in Nineteenth-Century Germany* (Princeton, 1984), pp. 156–206. For the general history of the party and its leadership see Karl Bachem, *Vorgeschichte, Geschichte und Politik der deutschen Zentrumspartei* (9 vols., Cologne, 1927–1933); Margaret Lavinia Anderson, *Windthorst: A Political Biography* (Oxford, 1981); Eduard E. Hüsgen, *Ludwig Windthorst* (Cologne, 1907); Ludwig Pastor, *August Reichensperger, 1808–1895* (2 vols., Freiburg, 1899); Otto Pfülf, *Hermann von Mallinckrodt: Die Geschichte seines Lebens* (Freiburg, 1901).

obvious goal of the liberal parties was to make themselves indispensable to the chancellor and thereby exact a price for his dependency. Would his need of their support force him to yield a significant redistribution of power under the Prussian and German constitutions? If so, the day might come, by evolution if not by design, when the parliamentary majority would form the executive, rather than the reverse. Or could Bismarck appease the deputies by paying "blackmail" only in the less vital areas of civil liberties and economic freedom?

Earlier it has been shown that the Reichstag of 1867–1870 was hardly docile.[45] Neither liberals nor conservatives were content to be the mere instrument of Bismarck's policy. Repeated attempts were made by the former to regain some of the ground lost in the compromises of the constituent Reichstag. Liberal deputies found great satisfaction in strengthening the unitary aspect of the governmental structure (in cooperation with Bismarck and Delbrück); they did succeed in strengthening civil liberties (most notably in modernizing the criminal code); but they were sharply rebuffed in their efforts to "build out" the constitution by adding to the powers of the legislature at the cost of the executive. Each failure led the liberals to look forward all the more to the elections of 1870 and the review of the iron budget in 1871. Bismarck was to be confronted with the necessity of deciding whether to purchase the continued cooperation of the liberal parties by a significant enlargement of parliamentary budget rights and a fundamental reorganization of the confederate executive (an objective that had support, although for different reasons, in both conservative parties). Whether they would have been any more successful in this contest than they were during 1862–1866 is doubtful. Yet it is unquestionable that the inclination to make the challenge extended throughout the liberal front, although in differing degree.

Once again, as in 1866, a dramatically successful military campaign and a fresh anointment of the Prussian establishment with the moral unction of German nationalism frustrated the aspirations of liberal deputies for a greater influence in government. The revision that did occur in late 1870 was one that strengthened the federal rather than the unitary and parliamentary side of the constitutional structure. His talks with southern statesmen and politicians in September 1870 finally convinced even Lasker, the liberal leader who was most active in 1870 in trying to shape Germany's future, that the problems of bringing the southern states into the union precluded any attempt to liberalize or centralize the constitution.[46] Ultimately the national liberals were compelled to surrender even the lingering hope for a constitutional amendment committing the Reich to future legislation establishing the judicial responsibility of ministers. In the final debates and negotiations of November 1870 the great issue was what concessions had to be made to partic-

---

[45] See vol. 1, pp. 410–426.
[46] Dill, *Lasker*, pp. 59–69.

ularism, not liberalism. The only influence liberals could exert on the final outcome was as a pressure group mobilized by Bismarck against lingering resistance in Bavaria and Württemberg.

Northern liberals had always presumed that the completion of German unification would present them with the opportunity, in alliance with their southern counterparts, to reopen the basic issues of constitutionalism. Yet only a small group of deputies (chiefly progressives and socialists) voted against the treaties with the south that established the Reich constitution.[47] For right-wing liberals disappointment over the outcome was far outweighed by exultation over the final attainment of a German national state. Heinrich von Sybel expressed the general euphoria in a letter to Hermann Baumgarten, written soon after the Kaiser proclamation at Versailles. "How have we deserved God's grace to be permitted to experience such great and mighty things? And for what shall one live hereafter? That which has been for twenty years the object of all our wishes and efforts has now been achieved in such a bounteous, wonderful way. Where shall I at my age find a new purpose for living?"[48] Not every liberal, however, was convinced that nothing remained to be striven for. Still alive was the thought that Lasker had inscribed in the founding program of 1867: "The German state and German freedom must be won simultaneously with the same means. . . . Every step toward constitutional unity is also progress in the realm of freedom, or bears the impulse toward such progress within itself."[49]

Soon after the first Reichstag of the German Reich convened Bismarck got a chance to gauge the chamber's temper—and vice versa. In May 1871 two veteran employees of the imperial postal service at Hamburg petitioned the Reichstag in behalf of their colleagues on a matter of wages and were abruptly transferred to remote posts in East Prussia. In reply to an interpellation of the progressives, Delbrück refused any explanation, denying the right of parliament to interfere in affairs of the executive branch. The consequence was that national liberals also became alarmed over this act of "bureaucratic despotism"; they too regarded the act of petition as a fundamental right of the citizen. Southern liberals, reflected Julius Hölder (Württemberg), were "unaccustomed to this manner of conduct by a minister"; he doubted that they would be able to tolerate it for long. "We cannot sacrifice constitutional rights just for Bismarck's sake." Bismarck saw the matter differently. "The Reichstag," he remarked to Lucius, "regards the government like a snarling dog."[50]

---

[47] On the left-liberal attitude concerning the revised constitution see Ludolf Parisius, *Deutschlands politische Parteien und das Ministerium Bismarck* (Berlin, 1878), pp. 136–138.

[48] HW, I, 494. Sybel solved his problem by reliving the recent past in a multivolume history of German unification, atoning for his earlier opposition to Bismarck by celebrating the chancellor's achievements in foreign affairs. Heinrich von Sybel, *Die Begründung des deutschen Reiches durch Wilhelm I.* (7 vols., Munich, 1889–1894).

[49] Felix Salomon, *Die deutschen Parteiprogramme* (Leipzig, 1912), I, 78, 82; HW, II, 9–10.

[50] BR (1871), II, 762–770; Gerhard Stoltenberg, *Der deutsche Reichstag, 1871–1873* (Düssel-

During May 1871 the Reichstag deliberated on a bill formally uniting Al-sace-Lorraine with the German Reich. The government bill provided for a period of dictatorship to last until January 1, 1874, when the Reich consti-tution was to go into effect. Meanwhile, the Kaiser, acting through the chan-cellor, was to exercise the executive power, and the Bundesrat the legislative power. The Reichstag would have had no voice. In explaining the bill to the deputies on May 2, Bismarck seemed to invite amendments, urging the dep-uties to "have the courage to shape the future." The allied governments, he declared, were willing "to let themselves be taught, if we receive a better proposal of any kind." The liberals took him at his word, amending the bill to terminate the dictatorship on January 1, 1873, and to require Reichstag approval of any loans or fiscal guarantees incurred for Alsace-Lorraine. The latter amendment, introduced by Lasker and Stauffenberg, received the sup-port of progressives, national liberals, members of the Liberal Reich party, and prominent free conservatives—a combination that produced something of a sensation. Echoing through the discussion was the old concern over ex-cessive concentration of authority under the chancellor and the desire for an imperial cabinet. Even Treitschke protested: "It exceeds the strength of one individual, to perform simultaneously the functions of an imperial chancellor and of a regent for Alsace."[51]

Returning to the chamber on May 25, 1871, after an absence of more than three weeks, Bismarck denounced the Lasker–Stauffenberg amendment as a "painful" attack on his personal integrity. "I am represented to the country as a frivolous contractor of debts."[52] Prince Chlodwig zu Hohenlohe-Schillings-fürst, a deputy from Bavaria and member of the Liberal Reich party, expressed the general consternation when he wrote in his diary that, while it was absurd for the Reichstag to give the chancellor a vote of no confidence on such an issue, Bismarck was presumptuous to expect the chamber to reverse itself merely because, after three weeks of silence, he had finally made his objec-tions known. The centrists and progressives (who had argued for more radical amendments) wished to force the issue and were joined by some national liberals. But the matter was referred back to committee by a narrow margin. Bismarck appeared there, "at first very surly," according to Hohenlohe, but was handled with such finesse that in the end he "quite forgot why he had got angry." A compromise required Reichstag approval only for fiscal obligations that "burdened the Reich."[53]

Bismarck's conduct reveals the bad state of his nerves and his general sen-

---

dorf, 1955), pp. 61–62; Freiherr Lucius von Ballhausen, *Bismarck-Erinnerungen* (Stuttgart, 1920), p. 11.

[51] *SBR* (1871), I, 517ff.; II, 813ff.

[52] *SBR* (1871), II, 921ff.

[53] Friedrich Curtius, ed., *Memoirs of Prince Chlodwig of Hohenlohe-Schillingsfuerst* (New York, 1906), II, 54–56; Julius Heyderhoff, ed., *Im Ring der Gegner Bismarcks* (Leipzig, 1943), 109–112; Stoltenberg, *Reichstag*, pp. 82–83.

sitivity on matters that concerned his own prerogatives, but also his alarm over the appearance of a coalition of the four middle parties interested in protecting parliamentary power. In late May 1871 the same formidable combination proposed to allocate part of the French war indemnity for the aid of needy veterans of the reserve and *Landwehr*; Bismarck regarded the measures as an invasion of the Kaiser's prerogatives in military affairs; yet he felt compelled to accept it rather than face trouble with the Reichstag over a government bill that distributed part of the French *Milliarden* to the generals in the form of dotations. "The gentlemen are starting to get troublesome," he commented to Count Waldersee. "The temptation to want to govern some also is altogether too great; those flat-headed free conservatives stand out in this regard."[54]

In the fall of 1871 the Reichstag finally faced the issue awaited by "committed liberals" since 1867—the military budget. But now the circumstances were, as Forckenbeck saw it, "the most unfortunate conceivable." The defeat of France had not only heightened the prestige of the military; it had also left the Germans with a sense of isolation in Europe, of being surrounded by defeated enemies and envious powers eager to reverse the results of the wars of unification. How radically the climate had changed was evident on November 6 when the deputies voted 170 to 121 (centrists, progressives, and left wing of the national liberals in the negative) to accept a government bill allocating 40,000,000 thalers from the French war indemnity for a Reich war chest without reserving for the Reichstag any control over its use or increase. Forckenbeck could not even recall that in late 1866 he had taken a contrary position with regard to the creation of a Prussian war chest.[55]

The proposed imperial budget for 1872 reached the Reichstag in November 1871, less than two months before it was to go into effect. Of total expenditures amounting to about 117,000,000 thalers, nearly 90,000,000 were destined for the army. The latter sum was requested as a lump sum (*Pauschquantum*), leaving undefined the specific military purposes for which it was to be spent. In view of the short time left for consideration and the fact that German troops still remained in France, there was little dissent about the lump-sum feature of the bill. What the deputies objected to was the amount, which represented an increase over the 225 thalers per soldier set in the constitution. By insisting on the old rate, national liberals wished to save 1,421,000 thalers; the progressives advocated a much larger economy (6,200,000 thalers), to be gained by reducing the length of military service from three to two years.[56]

[54] *SBR* (1871), II, 861ff.; Stoltenberg, *Reichstag*, pp. 67–69; GW, VIII, 67.

[55] *SBR* (1871, 2d session), I, 24ff., 117ff., 148ff.; Philippson, *Forckenbeck*, p. 226; Stoltenberg, *Reichstag*, pp. 82–83.

[56] *SBR* (1871, 2d session), II, Nos. 109 and 121; Philippson, *Forckenbeck*, pp. 227–228; Böttcher, *Stephani*, pp. 125–126; Zucker, *Bamberger*, pp. 90–92.

Once again the government and parliament in Berlin faced the prospect of conflict over the critical question of the chamber's budgetary power in military affairs. The conflict that ensued, however, was not between the executive and legislative branches, but between the wings of the National Liberal party. The opposing fronts dissolved and reformed over a proposal advanced by the free conservative Bethusy-Huc—acting in behalf of Bismarck, Roon, and the Prussian cabinet—that accepted the reduced amount desired by the national liberals in return for a renewal of the iron budget for three years. Bismarck wished to postpone for the time being conflicts with the Reichstag over "great issues of principle," while Roon liked the lump-sum provision which left him unrestricted in allocating money.[57] Conservatives and free conservatives followed the government in accepting Bethusy-Huc's motion, while progressives and centrists were adamantly opposed. The split went down the middle of the chamber, dividing both the Liberal Reich and National Liberal parties, particularly the latter.

The critical caucus of the National Liberal party occurred on November 26, 1871. Many deputies evaded the problem by staying away. Those who came heard an impassioned debate, chiefly between Bennigsen and Forckenbeck, who were for the compromise, and Lasker, Stauffenberg, and Bamberger, who were against it. The majority sided with Bennigsen and Forckenbeck, 46 to 25. So sharp was the disagreement, so acrimonious the atmosphere that the party appeared on the verge of dissolution.[58] On November 29 the polemic spilled over on to the floor of the Reichstag. Treitschke defended the iron budget as the palladium of parliamentary freedom; Germany had never been more free than under the North German Confederation whose parliament had not debated the military budget. "Naked absolutism," Lasker replied, was preferable to "sham constitutionalism"; if the three-year budget were adopted, Germany would be one-fifth constitutional state, four-fifths military dictatorship. After a futile attempt at compromise (a two-year military budget), the national liberals split in the decisive vote: 51 voting in the majority of 152 for the three-year budget, 44 in the minority of 128 against it.[59]

The National Liberal party survived the dispute of November–December 1871; yet the conflict, by revealing basic differences in political philosophy

---

[57] Cabinet meetings of June 18, Oct. 8, and Nov. 24, 1871. *DZA* Potsdam, Reichskanzleramt, 1452, pp. 150–152, 162–165, 182–183. The ministers divided over the issue, which was resolved in favor of Bismarck and Roon by the king in a meeting of the Crown Council on Oct. 10. Wilhelm was assured that his ministers would not waver in their determination not to surrender to parliament on any critical issue relating to the army. Crown Council of Oct. 10, 1871. *DZA* Merseburg, Rep. 90a, B, III, 2c, Nr. 3, Vol. 3. Stoltenberg erred in attributing the compromise to the statesmanship of Bethusy-Huc. Stoltenberg, *Reichstag*, pp. 94–95.

[58] Stoltenberg, *Reichstag*, pp. 95–101; Böttcher, *Stephani*, pp. 123ff.

[59] *SBR* (1871, 2d session), I, 599–658.

and temperament and by generating personal animosities not easily forgotten, presaged the split that clove it apart a decade later. The most significant aspect of the affair was the revelation that the party holding the pivotal position could not exploit it to consolidate parliamentary power. No other area was so critical for such consolidation as that of annual control over the budget. By chance the Reichstag had found in the state assessments (*Matrikularbeiträge*) a means with which to control the income side of the fiscal ledger, but control over outgo would never be secure until the parliament possessed the right annually to approve military expenditures item by item. Had they been willing to accept the increase in the rate of military expenditures proposed by the government for 1872, the national liberals might at least have established a precedent for annual control upon which they could have built in the following year. What they actually did was to confirm the precedent established in 1867; thereafter, the iron budget became a permanent feature of public finance in the German Reich.

While standing firm on this major issue, Bismarck yielded on another of significance to liberals. In the final stages of their deliberations on the imperial budget for 1872, the national liberals sponsored a resolution calling upon the government to present a bill in the next session creating an imperial agency to audit government revenues and expenditures for their conformity to law. Under the confederate constitution this obligation had fallen to the Prussian superior accounting office (*Oberrechnungskammer*), whose deficiencies had long been a source of irritation to liberal critics. During the constitutional conflict of the 1860s the office had presented no obstacle to the government's willingness to rule without a legislated budget. The bill drafted by the chancellor's office and presented to the Reichstag in the session of 1872 would have created for the Reich a mere replica of it. In the chamber Lasker sponsored amendments intended to give the new auditing agency some teeth. One of them required that reports from the Reich's superior accounting office concerning the revenues and expenditures of the imperial government be presented to the Bundesrat and Reichstag "for their examination and approval." This amendment, which the government accepted, gave to the Reichstag a role in reviewing and approving the government's fiscal performance, a power that the Prussian Chamber of Deputies had never possessed.[60]

While this concession was not insignificant, the major redistribution of political power effected by Reichstag of 1871–1873 altered the relationship not between the executive and parliament but between the Reich and the German states. Here the national liberals shared the basic objective of the chancellor, that of consolidating the Reich. More than thirty laws of the North German Confederation became imperial statutes. New laws of unitary

---

[60] SBR (1871, 2d session), pp. 20–22, 37–45, Anlagen, Nos. 14 and 15; (1872), 53–61, 201–217, 511–540, 726–741, 826–833, 853, Anlagen, Nos. 10, 36, 66, 85, 153.

import were passed, the most important of which was the introduction of a new coinage based on the gold standard. The mark replaced the thaler as the new unit of currency, bearing on one side the imperial eagle and on the reverse the image of the ruler of the issuing state.[61] The constitution was amended three times: the provision for *itio in partes* was abolished; the legislative power of the Reich was extended to include certain maritime affairs and "the entire civil law." The latter amendment, stemming from an initiative taken by Lasker, met considerable opposition among the medium states of the south, which was only overcome with Bismarck's support. Like the liberal parties, the chancellor felt that common courts and common codes of law were particularly important for the work of consolidation.[62] Bismarck was chiefly responsible, however, for the defeat of another constitutional amendment that would have compelled state governments to modernize their constitutions by introducing popularly elected assemblies. Initiated by the liberal parties in the Reichstag, the amendment, which gained some support in the Bundesrat, was aimed at the two principalities of Mecklenburg, whose diets were based on a system of corporative representation that dated back to the Middle Ages. But here Bismarck drew the line, arguing for states' rights and preservation of the federal system.[63]

Collaboration with Bismarck, the liberal deputies learned, could only be on his terms. In the spring of 1872 Eduard Brockhaus wrote in his diary: "He is said to have renewed his old lament: the national liberals demanded that he go with them, and he had verily done just that; but the national liberals did not reciprocate, did not behave like a government party should, etc. Yet he also shares the blame, which as a consequence lies on both sides. . . . Stephani said recently that he believes Bismarck will soon give us another 'kick,' in order to keep us from becoming too powerful and because his whole policy consists in never depending on any one party for support, but in holding each in check with another, making a protégé of first one, then another. I am not entirely of this opinion, but there is certainly some truth in it."[64]

During the legislative period 1871–1873 German liberals failed, once again, to press the issue of parliamentary power. The reasons were many. Bismarck's accumulated successes in diplomacy and war had so heightened his prestige that the deputies were even more reluctant to cross him than they had been during 1867–1870. Furthermore, their collaboration with him was producing in other areas legislation that corresponded with their ideas and interests. But the most persuasive reason of all for being unaggressive was the

---

[61] *Ibid.*, 226–262, 318–361, 418–489, Anlagen, Nos. 50 and 122; *RGB* (1871), p. 404; *SBR* (1872), Anlagen, No. 52.

[62] *SBR* (1872), pp. 457–462, 683–688, Anlagen, No. 79; pp. 596–632, Anlagen, No. 63; pp. 746–749, 769–771, Anlagen, No. 89; (1873), pp. 167–182, Anlagen, No. 19.

[63] *SBR* (1873), pp. 623–656, 912–919.

[64] Brockhaus, *Stunden mit Bismarck*, p. 52.

fact that Bismarck and the liberals became deeply engaged after 1871 in a common struggle against German Catholicism. The liberals permitted themselves to be drawn into an attack upon the right of the Catholic minority to organize politically and of the Catholic church to conduct its affairs without interference from the state. It was a struggle from which Bismarck, the practitioner of *Realpolitik*, could extricate himself without damage to his *Weltanschauung*, but from which the liberals, who had long preached the cause of civil liberty, could only emerge badly compromised.

CHAPTER SEVEN

The Kulturkampf

URING the 1870s Bismarck suffered the first significant defeat of his political career when he failed to liquidate Catholicism as a major force in German politics. His attack upon political Catholicism became an assault on the Catholic church; this aspect of the affair gave it the popular title of Kulturkampf ("struggle for culture"), a polemical term invented not by Bismarck but by his liberal allies. The Kulturkampf was a kaleidoscope, altering its shape with each angle of observation. It can be seen as a conflict between church and state, Catholic doctrine and German idealism, faith and materialism, conservatism and liberalism, traditionalism and modernism, universalism and nationalism, particularism and consolidation. In most of these aspects the Kulturkampf was not merely a Prussian but also a German and even European phenomenon. Even without Bismarck, Prussia and Germany would have been affected by it to some degree. Yet he made the decisions that launched the nationwide struggle in Germany. While not responsible for all that happened, he set the course that others were only too glad to follow.

Paradoxically the Kulturkampf resulted from a collision between two forces, both of which acted defensively in purpose, but offensively in practice. On the one hand, the Vatican, threatened by the advance of liberal modernism and the growth of nation-states, sought to strengthen its spiritual authority through the Syllabus of Errors and the doctrine of papal infallibility. Cut off from Austria as a consequence of the war of 1866 and finding themselves a minority in what was generally regarded as a "Protestant state," German Catholics organized for the purpose of protecting their values and interests through the political process. Bismarck, on the other hand, was affected by a sense of insecurity typical of successful revolutionaries, even conservative ones. What had been created by violence had to be protected by coercion until consolidated by laws and institutions and legitimated by time and the development of a moral consensus. By early 1870 he was deeply concerned about the "Polonization" of Germans in eastern Prussia and about the role of Catholic clergy in cultivating Polish separatism. To him the founding of the Center party was further evidence of a Catholic "mobilization against the state."[1] To most Catholics the state's defense against that "mobilization" looked like an assault on freedom of faith and an assertion of the omnipotence of the state.

[1] BR, V, 233.

In the case of liberal nationalism, the third force involved in the Kulturkampf, the offensive motivation clearly predominated. *Nationalstaat, Rechtsstaat, Machtstaat,* and *Kulturstaat* were for German liberals simultaneous goals. The attainment of a national state, the advance of civil liberties, the sharing of political power with the bureaucratic state, the realization of the power-state through three victorious wars fought for an ideal cause were logically linked to the quest for that other, peculiarly German, liberal ideal—the "culture state," that is, a state separated from the church and freed from clerical influence, yet harnessed for the achievement of secular cultural objectives such as the advancement of education, promotion of science, and cultivation of the arts. For liberal nationalists, Lutheran Protestantism and German idealism were the sources of Germany's moral and intellectual greatness, while Roman Catholicism was an alien force, hostile to the sovereign state and an impediment to the spiritual unity of the nation. To persons of this conviction the Kulturkampf was a logical extension of the wars of 1864, 1866, and 1870. Following the expulsions of Denmark, Austria, and France, ultramontanism was to be ousted from Germany's soil and soul. Until this was accomplished, the work of liberation and unification would remain incomplete.[2]

Background of the Struggle

During the nineteenth century the Catholic church was confronted with the problem of adapting to a rapidly changing society. Temporarily buoyed by Romanticism and the religious revival early in the century, the church was soon washed by other currents that threatened to erode both its faith and institutional structure. The secularization of church property under both absolutism and revolution weakened its finances. The centralized, bureaucratic state jeopardized its control over the ecclesiastical hierarchy. New ideologies—liberalism, democracy, nationalism, socialism—competed with religion for loyalties. The popularization of science spread doubts about the validity of Catholic doctrine, while historical research weakened the church's supernatural aura. The industrial revolution raised social problems that required new policies lest the lower classes be alienated from the church. The unification of Italy threatened the papacy's temporal rule and even its independence.

These multiple problems produced within the church two points of view eventually identified as "liberal Catholicism" and "ultramontanism." Liberal Catholicism was a European movement of intellectuals and political leaders who urged the church to come to terms with the new age, maintaining that

[2] Ernst Deuerlein, "Die Konfrontation von Nationalstaat und national bestimmter Kultur," and Rudolf Lill, "Die deutschen Katholiken und Bismarcks Reichsgründung," in Theodor Schieder and Ernst Deuerlein, eds., *Reichsgründung 1870/71: Tatsachen, Kontroversen, Interpretationen* (Stuttgart, 1970), pp. 226–258, 345–365; Theodor Schieder, *Das deutsche Kaiserreich von 1871 als Nationalstaat* (Cologne, 1961), pp. 55–87, 125–132.

there was no basic contradiction between modernism and the traditional faith. But the papacy and hierarchy responded negatively. Over centuries the church had been in a state of almost constant siege. Like most predecessors, Pius IX (1846–1878) met the crisis by rejecting the new and reaffirming the old. In the Syllabus of Errors (1864) the papacy listed, for the guidance of the faithful, eighty propositions that were contrary to Catholic dogma. The final defeat of liberal Catholicism came when the first Vatican Council on July 18, 1870, defined the doctrine of infallibility. Almost simultaneously with the loss of its temporal sovereignty, the papacy advanced its greatest claim to spiritual power: the claim that the pope, when speaking *ex cathedra* on matters of faith and morals, was incapable of error.

The tension within the Catholic church was particularly apparent in Germany. Here, more than in any other European country, Catholicism had to compete in the marketplace of ideas and loyalties. In German idealism Catholicism encountered a secular religion of Protestant origin that had won general acceptance by the educated class. At the universities of Tübingen and Munich Catholic historians and theologians strove to demonstrate the compatibility of their faith with German idealism and, after the latter's decay, with the new scholarship.[3] Its greatest figure was the priest-historian Ignaz von Döllinger, whose three-volume history of the church treated Christianity as a historical rather than a supernatural phenomenon. Politically Döllinger was a conservative, but he saw that constitutionalism could be valuable to the church by guaranteeing its freedom from the state. He recognized that the church, in claiming its own freedom, must yield it to others as a universal right.[4]

Germany was a major center of opposition to the decision of the Vatican Council to clarify the dogma of infallibility. Meeting at Fulda in September 1869, the German bishops declared the time "inopportune" for action on the dogma. Important laymen (Peter Reichensperger, Hermann von Mallinckrodt, and Ludwig Windthorst) likewise questioned the wisdom of the step. Thirteen of seventeen German bishops attending the church council opposed the declaration. Knowing that it would pass, twelve left Rome rather than participate in the final voting. Yet all of the German bishops soon submitted to the authority of the church, as did the great majority of the German priesthood and lay Catholics from all classes in the population. Not every German Catholic chose silence rather than schism. At the universities of Munich, Bonn, and Breslau a number of Catholic professors refused to submit. Foremost in the resistance was Döllinger, who had sharply opposed the Vatican declaration in a number of writings during 1869. When Döllinger was excom-

[3] See particularly Donald J. Dietrich, *The Goethezeit and the Metamorphosis of Catholic Theology in the Age of Idealism* (Berne, 1979).

[4] Johann Joseph Ignaz von Döllinger, *Geschichte der christlichen Kirche* (3 vols., Landshut, 1833–1835).

municated in 1871, his colleagues elected him rector of the university. The Bavarian king and government publicly sympathized with his cause. Döllinger's fate galvanized a movement of liberal Catholics who, regarding themselves as the guardians of the true faith, became known as "Old Catholics."[5]

Most European governments, whether Catholic or Protestant, feared that the decisions of the Vatican Council would upset existing church-state relationships. This was true in Prussia despite the fact that here the Catholic church had attained after sharp struggles a degree of freedom unknown elsewhere in Germany.[6] Earlier in the century (1837–1841) church and state had become embroiled in controversy (the so-called "Cologne strife") over the issues of mixed marriages and heresy on the theological faculty at the University of Bonn. After ascending the throne in 1840, Friedrich Wilhelm IV ended the dispute by yielding on both points. Furthermore, he dismantled many of the controls over the church established in the age of absolutism, ending the state's monitoring of communications between curia and bishops and largely abandoning the requirement of an official placet for ecclesiastical laws. In addition, he granted to the bishops the right to approve (through the grant of the *missio canonica*) those teaching Catholic doctrine in public schools and universities and created within the Ministry of Education and Religious Affairs (*Kultusministerium*) a separate department for Catholic affairs that became the spokesman for Catholic interests within the government.[7] The Prussian constitution of 1848–1850 appeared to consolidate still further the relative independence of the Catholic church. Under it the relationship between church and state approached that stage of co-ordination (*Gleichordnung*)—each autonomous within its own sphere—that had long been the goal of the Catholic hierarchy.[8] The attempt of *Kultusminister* von Raumer in 1852 to inhibit Catholic missionary activity and restrict the right of clergymen to study in Rome produced a vigorous reaction among Catholics. Again the government capitulated. For nearly two decades thereafter the successive governments of Manteuffel, the new era, and Bismarck adhered to the constitution.

There remained one vital area where the authority and functions of church and state overlapped, an area that was critically affected by the dispute within the Catholic church over the doctrine of infallibility. Catholic theologians at

---

[5] Karl Bachem, *Vorgeschichte, Geschichte und Politik der deutschen Zentrumspartei* (9 vols., Cologne, 1927–1933), III, 32ff.; Karl Bihlmeyer, *Kirchengeschichte* (Paderborn, 1926–1930), III, 392ff.; H. E. Feine, *Kirchliche Rechtsgeschichte* (Weinheim, 1954), I, 600; Erich Schmidt-Volkmar, *Der Kulturkampf in Deutschland, 1871–1890* (Göttingen, 1962), p. 23. On the old Catholic movement see C. B. Ross, *The Old Catholic Movement* (London, 1964) and Victor Conzemius, *Katholizismus ohne Rom* (Cologne, 1969).

[6] Joseph Schmidlin, *Papstgeschichte der neuesten Zeit* (Munich, 1934), II, 164.

[7] Bachem, *Zentrumspartei*, I, 97–100; Feine, *Rechtsgeschichte*, pp. 568ff.

[8] Feine, *Rechtsgeschichte*, p. 574.

the universities and teachers of Catholic doctrine in the upper schools were simultaneously state officials and, with diminishing exceptions, priests. Whether priests or laymen, they were as teachers subject to the discipline of the bishop owing to his right to grant and withdraw the *missio canonica*. Initially the policy of the Bismarck government was to take no official notice of the Vatican decree on infallibility and to avoid involvement in clashes between bishops and recalcitrant teachers and professors.[9] The policy of nonintervention worked in three cases (Bonn, Cologne, and Breslau), but failed in a fourth (Braunsberg in Ermeland), where the bishop was more aggressive in pursuing the issue. The refusal of a certain Chaplain Wollmann to read to his students a pastoral letter elucidating the dogma led to the withdrawal of his *missio canonica* and to the excommunication of both Wollmann and the director of the *Gymnasium* who supported him. The government not only refused to dismiss the heretical teacher and administrator, but also insisted that students either attend Wollmann's classes or be expelled.[10] The Braunsberg case established a precedent for the entire monarchy. To the government the bishop's action was an invasion of state authority; to Catholics the government's action was an invasion of church authority.[11] Although the problem was thorny, the dispute over religious instruction in the schools and universities could not in itself have produced the Kulturkampf. That the issue became magnified into a full-scale struggle between church and state was owing to other factors of greater significance.

Founding of the Center Party

Despite a Hohenzollern tradition of religious toleration dating back to the Great Elector, Catholics had never felt secure in the Prussian state. The "Cologne strife" of 1837–1841 and the Raumer directives of 1852 were forceful reminders that an authoritarian bureaucracy, accustomed to dominate the Evangelical church, could not be depended upon to respect Catholic autonomy. Both affairs, even though they ended favorably for Catholics, left behind a sense of wary distrust. During the 1850s the conservative press continued to trumpet the virtues of the "Prussian evangelical state" or "Protestant military state." If "co-ordinate" under the constitution, there was no real "parity" between Catholic and Protestant in Prussia. Civil service, officer corps, and university faculties remained overwhelmingly Protestant. Financial support appeared more plentiful for the Protestant than the Catholic

---

[9] Bismarck to Wilmowski, Oct. 30, 1890. Adelheid Constabel, *Die Vorgeschichte des Kulturkampfes* (Berlin, 1956), p. 40.

[10] Schmidt-Volkmar, *Kulturkampf*, pp. 60–63; Constabel, *Vorgeschichte*, pp. 58–59, 66–71, 88–101.

[11] See the debate in the Chamber of Deputies, Nov. 27, 1872. *SBHA* (1872–1873), I, 153–181.

church and for Protestant rather than Catholic elementary schools.[12] Beginning with the election of 1852, Catholic deputies formed a separate caucus in the Prussian Chamber of Deputies to defend Catholic interests. During the 1850s the party (numbering sixty-four deputies) made common cause with the liberal opposition on such matters as civil liberties. The great issues of the early 1860s, however, were those of military reform and the integrity of the constitution. Upon these issues Catholic deputies could not take a firm stand, probably because of their diverse social and political interests. As the electorate polarized over the constitutional conflict, the Catholic caucus (called the "Center party" after 1859) collapsed and dissolved.[13]

The events of 1866 were thoroughly demoralizing for Catholic politicians. For many Germans, Catholic as well as Protestant, the conflict between great-Germanism and small-Germanism, between Austrian and Prussian leadership in Germany was simultaneously a conflict between Catholicism and Protestantism. Those Catholics who saw the conflict in this light had to regard themselves as among the defeated of Königgrätz. Their political leaders reacted in varying ways. August Reichensperger stopped reading newspapers, dropped out of politics, for a time, and immersed himself in art history (he was an authority on Gothic art).[14] His brother, Peter, reluctantly accepted the North German Confederation as a necessity, being convinced that only Prussia could construct a new "roof" over Germany. On the other hand, Mallinckrodt, who had lost his seat in the Chamber of Deputies in 1863, was elected to the constituent Reichstag, where he risked his career as a Prussian official by charging that Prussia, not Austria, had been responsible for the recent war.[15] The most influential Catholic cleric, Baron Wilhelm Emmanuel von Ketteler, bishop of Mainz, advised Catholics in a widely read book to accept what they could not change and to cooperate in the completion of a *kleindeutsch* unification.[16] The failure of the constituent Reichstag to incorporate in the north German constitution clauses on religious liberty from the Prussian constitution caused many Catholic deputies (including Mallinckrodt, Windthorst, and Peter Reichensperger) to join progressives in voting

[12] Ludwig Bergsträsser, ed., *Politischer Katholizismus: Dokumente seiner Entwicklung* (Munich, 1921–1923), I, 186–190, 211ff.; Ludwig Pastor, *August Reichensperger, 1808–1895* (Freiburg, 1899), I, 356ff.; Bachem, *Zentrumspartei*, I, 146ff.

[13] August Reichensperger judged that the victory of either the Progressive party or the Bismarck government would be a "calamity"—the former because it would lead to parliamentary government, the latter because it would lead to absolutism. Pastor, *Reichensperger*, I, 424, 455, and 467–468. On the social, political, and clerical currents in Catholic politics in this period see Jonathan Sperber, *Popular Catholicism in Nineteenth-Century Germany* (Princeton, 1984), pp. 39–155.

[14] Pastor, *Reichensperger*, I, 578ff.

[15] Otto Pfülf, *Hermann von Mallinckrodt: Die Geschichte seines Lebens* (Freiburg, 1901), 318ff.; Bachem, *Zentrumspartei*, III, 17. Mallinckrodt's punishment was a transfer from Catholic Paderborn to Protestant Merseburg. Pfülf, *Mallinckrodt*, pp. 319ff.

[16] Wilhelm Emanuel von Ketteler, *Deutschland nach dem Kriege von 1866* (Mainz, 1867).

against the constitution as a whole. So disparate were their views that Catholic deputies were unable to find common ground upon which to form a caucus in either the Reichstag or Chamber of Deputies after 1867. Many entered the Free Conservative party; some joined conservative Protestants in a short-lived caucus, the Federal-Constitutional union; others remained uncommitted.[17]

During the years that followed Catholics continued to feel isolated and on the defensive. Bismarck's collaboration with liberals, the seeming dominance of the liberal-national *Zeitgeist* in the Reichstag, the public's adverse reaction to the summoning of the Vatican Council (June 29, 1868) and to the ensuing public discussion of the dogma of infallibility—all tended to heighten their sense of vulnerability. In August 1869 there were other warning signals. A small, newly constructed Dominican chapel in Moabit, a working-class district of Berlin, was sacked by a mob soon after its dedication on August 4. The *Berliner Arbeiterverein* and various liberal organizations petitioned the Chamber of Deputies either to abolish all cloisters or to enforce strictly a statute of 1810 restricting their expansion. The committee on petitions, Rudolf Gneist reporting, recommended the latter course.[18] But the Prussian cabinet, on Bismarck's advice, refused to support disabilities against Catholics (February 1870), and the committee report was tabled, despite attempts by Mallinckrodt, supported by about eighty Catholic deputies, to force debate on the issue.[19]

During June 1870 the first steps were taken to draft a Catholic political program in view of the coming elections for the Reichstag and Chamber of Deputies. The outbreak of war in July and the coming completion of German unification added urgency to the task. Assemblies of leading Catholics at Münster (June 14, 1870) and Soest (October 28, 1870) produced programs stressing religious demands (autonomy of the church, freedom of faith, church marriage, confessional schools, and "actual" parity of "recognized religions"), political demands (preservation of federalism, rejection of the unitary state, reduction of military expenditures), and social demands (harmonization of the interests of capitalists and landowners, strengthening of the middle class, and legislative action to improve the condition of factory workers).[20] The parliamentary caucuses of the Center party, organized after the November and March elections of 1870–1871, reached fifty-eight deputies in the Prussian Chamber of Deputies and sixty-one in the Reichstag.[21]

By choosing the name "Center party," some founders hoped to avoid iden-

[17] Bachem, *Zentrumspartei*, III, 10ff.

[18] *SBHA* (1869–1870), Anlagen, II, No. 221.

[19] Crown Council of Feb. 2, 1870. *DZA* Merseburg, Rep. 90a, B, III, 2c, Nr. 3, Vol. III. *SBHA* (1869–1870), III, 2039–2043.

[20] Wilhelm Mommsen, ed., *Deutsche Parteiprogramme* (Munich, 1960), 212ff.

[21] Bernhard Vogel, Dieter Nohlen, and Rainer-Olaf Schultze, *Wahlen in Deutschland: Theorie-Geschichte-Dokumente, 1848–1970* (Berlin, 1971), pp. 287, 290.

tifying the new caucus as Catholic, even though the title had already been used by Catholic deputies in the Prussian Chamber of Deputies during the early 1860s. But the new party quickly became identified in the press and public mind as a Catholic party and its deputies were often designated as "clericals." In parliament a few Protestant deputies were accepted as *Hospitanten* (for example, Ludwig von Gerlach and the Hanoverian Guelph Ludwig Brüel), but the party as a whole never attracted a significant number of Protestant voters.[22] Catholic members of the Free Conservative party refused with few exceptions (most notably Karl Friedrich von Savigny), to join, as did many liberals (notably Max von Forckenbeck). Many of the newly elected Catholic representatives from southern Germany joined the Liberal Reich party and, after its dissolution, the Free Conservative and National Liberal parties. Polish deputies, furthermore, insisted on maintaining their own caucus, as did the deputies from the Reichsland. Nor did the Center succeed in capturing the whole of the Catholic vote. Although 36.2 percent of the electorate was Catholic, the Center received only 17 percent of the ballots cast or less than half of the Catholic vote.[23]

The first parliamentary démarche of the Center was poorly chosen for a party desiring to widen its confessional base. On February 18, 1871, the Center caucus in the Prussian Chamber of Deputies sent an address to Kaiser Wilhelm at Versailles requesting his intervention for the restoration of the temporal rule of the papacy. Wilhelm did not reply, but the speech from the throne opening the Reichstag on March 21 contained a passage that bore on the problem: "The respect that Germany demands for its own independence it willingly pays to other states and peoples, the weak as well as the strong." In a responding address the Reichstag declared, "The day of intervention in the internal life of other peoples will, we hope, never recur under any pretext, in any form." Leaders of the Center attacked this passage as unacceptable and voted against the entire address. But the centrists remained almost alone in their protest (six Polish deputies abstained from voting) and the address passed, March 30, by an overwhelming majority (243 to 63).[24]

Unquestionably the Center made a bad tactical error in raising this issue. The address, which had been approved in advance by all other parties of the Reichstag, was intended as a patriotic demonstration of national unity and retroactive approval of all that Bismarck, the Kaiser, and the armies had accomplished in the recent war.[25] Certainly the passage to which the centrists objected was an unnecessary slap by the liberals at "ultramontanes." By refusing to accept it, however, the Center exposed itself to the charge of seeking military intervention by the new Reich in behalf of the papacy in the tradition of the early medieval empire. At the moment of final achievement of

---

[22] Bachem, *Zentrumspartei*, III, 126ff., 142ff.
[23] Schmidt-Volkmar, *Kulturkampf*, p. 25; Vogel et al., *Wahlen in Deutschland*, p. 290.
[24] *SBR* (1871), I, 2–3, 49–72; III, Nos. 11 and 17.
[25] Schmidt-Volkmar, *Kulturkampf*, p. 31.

German unification the Center went on record as opposing the cause of national self-determination in Italy. It was a quixotic effort. Like the progressives during 1862–1866 and national liberals during 1867–1870, the centrists had no real possibility of influencing Bismarck's foreign policy. They tilted at windmills.

This disastrous debut prejudiced the success of the Center's attempt on April 1–4, 1871, to incorporate into the Reich constitution six articles from the Prussian constitution guaranteeing (with some elasticity) freedom of speech, press, assembly religious belief, and the autonomy of ecclesiastical institutions. If they thought to enjoy the support of liberals on this issue, the centrists were soon disabused. Their opponents pointed out that the amendment was centralistic in import and hardly consonant with the federal emphasis in the program of the Center party.[26] But the Center's list of civil liberties was also somewhat limited. It did not include, Treitschke noted, freedom for science and learning or the right to civil marriage. If centrists were inconsistent, liberals were more so. In venting their spleen against "clericals," liberals of all stripes (except the extreme left) repudiated their traditional support of civil liberties under the constitution. In 1848, declared Miquel, an inexperienced liberal party had erroneously believed that every reduction in state power was a gain for freedom. As a result, article 15 of the Prussian constitution had granted to the Catholic church "an unheard-of special position." Again the Center found itself isolated in the chamber. Its bill was rejected 223 to 59.[27]

For liberals the debates of March 30–April 4, 1871, were the beginning of the Kulturkampf. They occurred in an atmosphere of crisis over the doctrine of infallibility. In Bavaria Döllinger and the archbishop of Munich had reached the fork in the road (March 28 and April 2), and on April 3 the faculty of the university came out for Döllinger, as did a public mass meeting on April 10.[28] Simultaneously the Braunsberg school controversy reached its climax. "The conflict between church and state," Stauffenberg told the Reichstag, "has now passed from theory into reality." Robert Römer, a Württemberg national liberal, charged that for centrists the highest authority was not the German Kaiser but the pope. "The issue today is: Rome or Germany."[29]

Bismarck's Decision to Attack

The perception of the Catholic church and its political ambitions that ultimately led Bismarck into the Kulturkampf was formed during the 1850s. On hearing of the founding of the Catholic caucus in 1852, he wrote to Otto

[26] Ludwig Hahn, *Geschichte des Kulturkampfes in Preussen* (Berlin, 1881), pp. 47–48.

[27] *SBR* (1871), I, 104–155; III, No. 12.

[28] *SEG* (1871), pp. 103–107.

[29] *SBR* (1871), pp. 67, 141.

Manteuffel, "The lust for conquest in the Catholic camp will not allow us to avoid indefinitely an open struggle with it." As long as the right-wing parties in the chamber held together, the "ultramontane party" would be compelled to make common cause with liberals. This coupling of "Jesuitry with liberalism," if properly exploited by the government press, could cost the liberals such sympathy as they still enjoyed in the eastern provinces. He advised Manteuffel against withdrawal of the Raumer directives on the grounds that "no secure alliance can be formed with the ultramontane party," for which every concession was but an installment, and a further incitement, toward the ultimate goal of complete domination.[30]

During 1853–1854 Bismarck followed a controversy between the government of Baden and the bishop of Freiburg and concluded that the conflict had more than local significance. It was indicative of the "militant, insatiable, and irreconcilable spirit" that for a decade had driven "part of the Catholic clergy" to seek domination over all Protestant sovereigns. Concessions would only lead to new demands, until the clergy attained their ultimate goal of "unlimited rule."[31] Ludwig von Gerlach's defense of the bishop in the *Kreuzzeitung* so incensed Bismarck that he feared the violence of his own un-Christian emotions. It was then that he wrote to Leopold von Gerlach the letter, previously quoted,[32] describing the struggle against Catholicism as one of his most difficult tasks in Frankfurt, equating "Catholicism" with "enemy of Prussia" in southern Germany, and denying that Catholicism ("a hypocritical, idolatrous papism full of hate and cunning" whose "presumptuous dogma falsified God's revelation and nurtured idolatry as a basis for worldly domination") was a Christian faith.[33] In June 1855 he discussed with a Prussian police officer the evidence of Catholic subversion in southern Germany, particularly in connection with the festival at Fulda on the eleven hundredth anniversary of the death of St. Boniface, and came to the conclusion that "these conspirators are more dangerous for us now than democrats."[34]

Bismarck's aversion to political Catholicism was so strong that he failed to assess correctly the position of the Catholic caucus (now called the Center party) at the beginning of the constitutional conflict. While annoyed by Prussian recognition of the kingdom of Italy, the Center was divided over the army bill and, because of this ambivalence, strove to steer a moderate course between the government and parliamentary opposition. In a dispatch to Rome (October 24, 1862) Bismarck asserted that the Center, a party held together less by political than by religious conviction, was even more hostile to the government than were extreme democrats. For many reasons, but par-

[30] *GW*, I, 257–258, 264.
[31] *GW*, I, 392–393.
[32] See vol. 1, p. 368.
[33] *GW*, XIV, 340.
[34] *GW*, II, 54.

ticularly because of its religious character, he would regret having to fight the party with "kindred weapons." Rome too ought to avoid such a struggle, in view of the privileges enjoyed by the church under the constitution of 1848–1850. The state had a right to expect that Prussian Catholics would be guided by their "obligations to king and country" rather than by "political partisanship." It was obvious, he concluded, that this advice also applied to the Polish clergy. If the archbishop of Posen-Gnesen should "mix religion and politics," the government expected Rome to give him no encouragement or protection.[35]

During the years 1866–1870 Bismarck's suspicions of Catholic hostility and aggression rose again to the surface. In the fall of 1866 the Landtag's Catholic caucus, in the final months of its existence, voted against a number of critical measures presented by the government: the indemnity bill, the annexations, a large government loan, and the dotation bill rewarding Bismarck and the generals for the recent victory. While unable to block any of these statutes, the oppositional stance of the Catholic deputies, coupled with that of the progressives, disturbed the picture of internal solidarity that Bismarck wished to project before southern Germany and Europe. The Catholic caucus, he complained to Rome in December 1866, was "the most hostile in the chamber," its attacks on the government "exceeding in animosity those of the democrats themselves."[36] Nor were Bismarck's fears dimmed by the dissolution of the first Center party and obvious signs of confusion in the Catholic camp. The struggle over civil liberties in the constituent Reichstag, the association between Catholic and Guelph particularists, the danger of a Catholic league of European powers, the role of the ultramontanes in strengthening southern resistance to the completion of unification, and particularly the part played by the Catholic clergy in nurturing the spirit of Polish nationalism[37]—all of these developments, real and imagined, reinforced Bismarck's belief in the existence of a widespread Catholic conspiracy that posed a threat to both his German and European policies.[38]

In 1868–1870 Bismarck repeatedly appealed (as he had in 1862 and 1866) to the pope to exercise his influence to halt this "continuing secret and open

---

[35] GW, IV, 5–6.

[36] GW, VI, 185.

[37] For the role of the "Polish problem" in Bismarck's view of Catholicism and the Center party see pp. 106–114, and vol. 1, pp. 194–196.

[38] During most of his years in office Bismarck was firmly convinced that the conspiracy reached as far as the palace and even to the Kaiser's bedchamber, where Kaiserin Augusta, secretly prompted by ultramontane clerics and by the French ambassador, Viscount Gontaut-Biron, sought to prejudice the Kaiser against his chancellor's politics. For just a few of the many sources documenting this conviction see GW, VII, 213; VIII, 195–197, 202–204, 214; XIV, 776; Freiherr Lucius von Ballhausen, *Bismarck-Erinnerungen* (Stuttgart, 1920), pp. 91, 93; Moritz Busch, *Bismarck: Some Secret Pages of his History* (London, 1898), II, 231, and *Tagebuchblätter* (Leipzig, 1899), I, 439, 442, 473; II, 420, 426ff., 431ff.

war of circles in the Catholic church against Prussia." Clergy had combined with "democrats and radicals" in an "unnatural alliance" willing to indulge in "every slander, defamation, and lie" to defeat the national party in the recent Zollverein elections. Southern Catholic newspapers, supplemented by the Catholic press in France and Belgium, had competed with one another in printing this "filth." Yet the Catholic church enjoyed in Prussia and northern Germany a freedom unrivaled anywhere in the rest of Germany and Europe. While personally well disposed toward the Catholic church, Bismarck warned, he could not continue to defend its interests in the face of such hostility. Those who contended that the Catholic church was a danger to Prussia and the confederation and that lasting peace with the Catholic church was impossible would gain in influence. By exerting its powers to moderate and halt this agitation, on the other hand, Rome could prove its willingness to ally with Berlin against revolution, rather than the reverse.[39]

In these documents one can see the familiar characteristics of Bismarck's political technique—the litany of benefits accorded and injuries received, the revelation of his own pivotal position and of the options at his disposal. But they also show (like their predecessors in 1862 and 1866) Bismarck's continuing conviction that the key to his political difficulties with German Catholics lay in Rome. Despite the efforts of Harry von Arnim, the north German representative at the Vatican, to disabuse him on this point, the chancellor remained unshaken in his belief that Rome did possess the power to control not only the political conduct of the ecclesiastical hierarchy and the priesthood in general, but also that of Catholic laymen and the Catholic press everywhere in Europe. During the late 1860s he sought continually to get the Vatican to see that its true interest was to use that power to get German Catholics to accept Prussian leadership.[40] His vision of the Catholic church was that of a "tightly organized" monarchical institution capable of commanding "unquestioned obedience" from the faithful, both clerical and lay, not only in matters of faith but also in matters of political conduct.[41]

Undoubtedly Bismarck did believe that Prussia was the target of an ultramontane crusade, so unremitting in its hostility that normally conservative clergy, serving a conservative institution, were willing to make common cause with political and social radicals and with national revolutionaries in Prussian Poland. What he wrote to Rome on this score might have been exaggerated for political effect, but he repeated the charge within the councils of the Prussian government and in private conversation.[42] As long as German unification remained incomplete, nevertheless, he was in a poor position to carry out the threats in his dispatches to Arnim. Every overt struggle either

[39] GW, VIa, 344–349; see also VIb, 141–142, 643, 672.
[40] GW, VIa, 399–400; see also VI, 181ff., 215ff.; VIa, 72–73; XIV, 721–722.
[41] GW, VIb, 59–60; also 20–22.
[42] GW, VIb, 60; Busch, *Tagebuchblätter*, I, 187, 188.

with the north German clergy or with the papacy itself had to be avoided lest moderate Catholics, particularly in the south, be mobilized by the ultramontanes against Prussia.[43] In February 1870 Bismarck joined the Prussian cabinet in rejecting the initiative of the Chamber of Deputies in the Moabit affair, refused to back Governor-General von Horn in his conflict with the Archbishop Ledóchowski of Posen-Gnesen, and dispatched the Prussian Duke of Ratibor as Wilhelm's personal representative at the jubilee of Pius IX.[44] But the most striking examples of Bismarck's hands-off policy toward the church before 1871 are to be seen in his attitude toward the Vatican Council in 1869–1870 and toward the "Roman question" during 1870–1871.

As the Vatican Council approached and the preliminary debate within the church on the subject of infallibility gained in heat, Bismarck took the view that the affair was an internal concern of the church that need not involve the north German government unless the council should "transgress on the area of the state." He hoped, nevertheless, that friction within the church would weaken the ultramontanes and hence mitigate the effectiveness of their agitation against Berlin. Hence he willingly supported the unsuccessful efforts of Catholic governments (first Bavaria, later France and Austria-Hungary) to form a common front of European powers toward the Vatican Council.[45] Yet he firmly rejected Arnim's pleas that Berlin initiate such an action on the grounds that any intervention by a Protestant power would consolidate rather than divide the council. The government had no cause to fear the results of the council, he instructed Arnim, for it possessed the legislative power with which to counteract any ensuing invasion of the rights of the state. In mastering such a crisis the government could rely on the "developed state consciousness of the nation"—among the majority of Catholics as well as the predominant majority of Evangelicals.[46] "To take up the struggle over Catholic dogma on Roman terrain," he wrote to Abeken at the time of the Vatican Council in June 1870, "would be like attacking the Leviathan in water; we will let him come on dry land first, that is, onto the floor of practical execution of the dogma under Prussian state law; there we are superior to him."[47] He was willing to lend sympathy and support to the oppositional German bishops, but only if they requested it, which they did not. Bismarck correctly foresaw that the German bishops would eventually submit to the will of the

[43] GW, VIa, 72–73, 165.

[44] Cabinet meeting of Feb. 26, 1869. DZA Merseburg, Rep. 90a, B, III, 2b, Nr. 6, Vol. 81. Meeting of Crown Council, Feb. 2, 1870. DZA Merseburg, Rep. 90a, B, III, 2c, Nr. 3, Vol. III. GW, VIa, 20–21, 119–120, 283; VIb, 37ff.

[45] GW, VIb, 33–34, 66–67, 70–71, 90–91, 255–256, 281ff., 299ff., 313ff., 333; VII, 296ff.; Busch, Tagebuchblätter, I, 15ff.

[46] GW, VIb, 197–200; also VIb, 84ff., 283ff., 292ff.; XIV, 754; also Constabel, Vorgeschichte, pp. 17ff. and George O. Kent, Arnim and Bismarck (Oxford, 1968), pp. 5–19.

[47] GW, XIV, 779.

council, whatever their personal views on infallibility. Yet he did expect that the controversy would "loosen" the "compact organization" of the church and disrupt the unanimity of the Catholic press in its hostility toward Berlin.[48]

The Roman question became acute in 1870 when Napoleon III was compelled to withdraw the French garrison that had since 1860 preserved the pope's rule over the city. Desperately the curia surveyed the European scene for support against Italian occupation of the holy city. For Bismarck, intervention in behalf of the pope (a policy urged upon Wilhelm by the Empress Augusta in numerous letters)[49] was unthinkable, since it would have driven Italy into the arms of revolutionary France. Yet he did believe that political benefits might be derived from limited assistance to the papal court. He sought to persuade the government in Florence to treat the pontiff respectfully and, after some hesitation, he renewed an offer (first extended in 1866) of asylum of the pope in Germany, either at Fulda or Cologne.[50] It ought to be useful, he remarked to Busch, to demonstrate to German and Polish Catholics that Berlin was the "sole power now existing that is capable of protecting the head of their church."[51] Although Pius remained in the Vatican, Bismarck continued to seek in Rome leverage to be used against German Catholics. When it appeared that the "clerical party" in Bavaria might succeed in defeating the treaty for union with the north, he wired Arnim (December 21, 1870) to point out to the curia that such an action would not halt German unification, but would merely force him "to seek and find the basis for Kaiser and Reich in the public opinion" that demanded their creation, identifying Catholicism with those elements that had successfully opposed the new Germany. Would this accord with the wishes and interests of the curia? "Such a situation would be contrary to our desires, but we shall have to face the facts."[52] Again the results were disappointing. On January 18, 1871, he telegraphed Arnim that clerical influences were still active in Bavaria against the treaty despite the "unquestionable sympathy exhibited by the pope for us."[53]

Throughout the winter and spring Bismarck persisted in a policy of neutrality on the Roman question, seeking to avoid alienating either the papacy or the Italian government, while exploiting their mutual hostility to extract favors from both.[54] To all entreaties, including personal letters from the pope to Wilhelm and the sending of a papal emissary (Archbishop Ledóchowski) to Versailles, he replied that Germany would only participate in a common

[48] GW, VIb, 290–291, 295–296.
[49] Constabel, Vorgeschichte, pp. 29ff.
[50] GW, VIa, 72–73; VIb, 458, 470, 491–492, 496–497, 503, 620. On the issue of asylum see GW, VIb, 553, 556, 589; XIV, 721–722.
[51] Busch, Secret Pages, I, 220–221.
[52] GW, VIb, 643.
[53] GW, VIb, 672.
[54] GW, VIa, 72–73, 165.

step initiated by the European powers, an event of which there was little likelihood. In February he agreed to Arnim's suggestion that, in view of the failure to gain assistance against ultramontanism, the connection with Rome ought to be loosened. Arnim was withdrawn at the beginning of March and the Reich's representation at the Vatican left to the Bavarian envoy, Count Tauffkirchen. Yet Bismarck continued (on March 31, May 1, and May 19, 1871) to urge the Italian government to avoid unnecessary affronts to the pope.[55] He still believed, in other words, that good relations with the papacy might have some usefulness in German politics.

Bismarck claimed later that his initial reaction to the founding of the Center party was not hostile.[56] One of the founders, after all, was Karl Friedrich von Savigny, the high-level Prussian diplomat who had helped steer the constitution of the North German Confederation through the council of ministers and constituent Reichstag. His presence held out the prospect that the party's conservatism would outweigh its Catholicism and that the party would support "common national interests." According to the chancellor, the party's position on the address to the Kaiser and on a bill of rights in the imperial constitution destroyed these expectations. The clerical caucus, he wrote to the Prussian envoy in Munich, had become a purely confessional party, whose voters were willing to sacrifice national for Catholic interests. The aggressiveness of the clericals compelled the government itself to take the offensive, as a matter of self-defense.[57] But Bismarck ordered the envoy, nevertheless, not to become identified with the Döllinger movement. While its relations with the Catholic church had become more difficult, the Reich must maintain neutrality in disputes over dogma.[58]

There was another reason for caution. Bismarck had launched yet another attempt to get the papacy to change the course of the Center party. On April 17, 1871, he instructed Tauffkirchen to find an opportunity to inform the curia that the aggressive conduct of the Center had increased antipapal sentiment in Germany. Four days later he was gratified to receive a telegram from Tauffkirchen stating that the papal secretary of state, Cardinal Antonelli, had "disapproved and deplored the conduct of the Catholic, so-called Center caucus in the Reichstag as tactless and untimely." On May 10, he could report that the pope himself had characterized the Center's actions as "inopportune

---

[55] GW, VIc, 6–7; Schmidt-Volkmar, *Kulturkampf*, pp. 11–23; Kent, *Arnim and Bismarck*, pp. 39–46.

[56] Busch, *Tagebuchblätter*, III, 148; GW, VIc, 3–4.

[57] Bismarck to Werthern, Apr. 17, 1871. GW, VIc, 3–4. In late March Bismarck set out to know his enemy. At his direction aides prepared during April an elaborate set of maps and statistics, showing the distribution of Catholic and Polish voting strength, district by district, with a color code to show which deputies had voted against the address to the king. DZA Potsdam, Reichskanzleramt, 1438.

[58] GW, VIc, 4–6.

and impractical" in an interview with the Austrian envoy, Count Gustav von Kálnoky.[59] One can imagine with what elation Bismarck must have received these messages. They seemed to confirm the wisdom of the policy he had followed for so many months. Surely the Center party must respond to the pope's displeasure. If not, it was now at least completely isolated, cut off from Rome as well as from other political parties, and hence exposed and vulnerable.

On May 14, 1871, Bismarck empowered Count Frankenberg, a free conservative leader, to make known what he had learned from Rome in a speech to Silesian constituents, which was widely reported in the German press. When the accuracy of the report was challenged by Catholic journalists Bismarck wrote a letter confirming it to Frankenberg that was published in the *Nationalzeitung* on June 23.[60] No sooner had it appeared than it was disavowed. Bishop Ketteler released to the press a letter of June 5 from Cardinal Antonelli that contained a far different account of his remarks to Tauffkirchen. According to the state secretary, he had merely criticized as "premature" what he had understood to be an attempt of the Center to get the parliament to declare itself in favor of intervention on behalf of the papacy. The Center, Ketteler pointed out, had made no such attempt; hence even Antonelli's mild criticism was beside the point. Antonelli's letter went on to urge Catholic deputies, as a matter of conscience, to "seize every opportunity" to preserve and defend their religion and the rights of the papacy against all attempts at intimidation.[61] When Tauffkirchen gained another interview with Antonelli on June 26, the cardinal clung to the position outlined in the letter to Ketteler and explained away the earlier impression he had given the envoy as a misunderstanding.[62]

Sometime during June, days before he learned of Antonelli's retraction, Bismarck decided to take the offensive against clerical and ultramontane influences in Prussian and German public life. In his diary Prince Hohenlohe wrote that on the evening of June 19 Bismarck read to him the letter to Frankenberg, asking him whether he approved. "I said that I could raise no objection, though the clericals would not be altogether pleased." Bismarck replied that he did not care to please them. He found the clericals' alliance with such democrats as Schröder-Lippstadt exceedingly irritating; it might have "knocked the bottom out of the cask." He proposed to proceed "more vigorously against them and in particular to expel the Krätzig clique" from the government.[63]

[59] *BR*, V, 204.
[60] *GW*, XIV, 819.
[61] *SEG* (1871), pp. 177–178.
[62] Schmidt-Volkmar, *Kulturkampf*, pp. 39–40.
[63] Friedrich Curtius, ed., *Memoirs of Prince Chlodwig of Hohenlohe-Schillingsfuerst* (New York,

Adalbert Krätzig was head of the Catholic department of Prussia's *Kultus-ministerium*. The Catholic and Protestant departments were twin agencies through which the Prussian government exercised its powers over religious affairs. Bismarck believed that under Krätzig the Catholic department had become a Trojan horse within the walls. Instead of representing the interests of the government toward the Catholic church and Polish population, the department had become their advocate and protector within the government.[64] On June 26 the Prussian cabinet accepted Bismarck's decision, with the reluctant acquiescence of *Kultusminister* Heinrich von Mühler, to unite the two departments under a Protestant head and transfer Krätzig to a harmless post in the judiciary. At the same meeting the cabinet reluctantly rejected as too far reaching a proposal to resolve the Braunsberg school controversy by ending compulsory religious instruction in all *Gymnasien*; instead it upheld school regulations compelling Catholic students to attend the dissident Wollmann's classes.[65]

Four days earlier the German public had already been informed of the general significance of what was to come. On June 22, 1871, the *Kreuzzeitung* published a sensational article, generally believed to have been written by Hermann Wagener and to have a semiofficial character. By choosing the title "Center Party," the article charged, the clericals had attempted to disguise its sectarian character. Its members and allies had used every means at their disposal to hinder German unification. By raising the religious issue they had now reopened another fissure dividing the German people. In the face of such aggression the German Reich could not remain on the defensive. In the near future it must decide to confront aggression with aggression, "abroad as well as at home." Three hundred years ago Germanism had proven stronger than Romanism. How much stronger must it be now that Rome was no longer capital of the world and the German imperial crown was worn by a German rather than a Spanish prince.[66]

Bismarck neither planned nor foresaw the extent of the long struggle between church and state that began in the summer of 1871. He appears to have believed that a show of force would impress the Vatican with his seriousness, compelling the pope to use his allegedly absolutistic powers to halt the ultramontane crusade against the German Reich. "I do not want war with the church, not even with the Catholic church," Mühler recorded him as saying in June 1871, "but in order to have a just peace, those on the other side must first recognize that we will permit ourselves to be oppressed and trod upon

---

1906), II, 60; also *GW*, VIII, 9–10. For Bismarck's animus toward Krätzig see Constabel, *Vorgeschichte*, pp. 120–121.

[64] The Catholic department had, he told the Chamber of Deputies in 1886, "the character of a Polonizing organ within the Prussian administration," *GW*, XIII, 158.

[65] Cabinet meeting of June 26, 1871. *DZA* Merseburg, Rep. 90a, B, III, 2b, Nr. 6, Vol. 83.

[66] *SEG* (1871), p. 175. On dating this article see Schmidt-Volkmar, *Kulturkampf*, p. 37.

only to a certain degree and that we have the power and the will, when necessary, to defend ourselves." In October he spoke to Mühler of the ultramontanes as merely "outposts." "The actual army stands on the other side of the
Alps."[67]

Motivation

Historians have long disputed over what motives led Bismarck into the morass
of the Kulturkampf, particularly over whether they are to be found in foreign
or domestic politics—whether the Kulturkampf, in other words, was a product of the *Primat der Aussen-* or *Innenpolitik*. The issue, however, is misconceived, for Bismarck did not in this case separate foreign from domestic politics. His motivation in the Kulturkampf was composed of a complex of
mutually supporting ideas, prejudices, and circumstances, no one of which
would have been adequate to produce the end result. At the base of the complex was his earlier conviction that Prussia was the object of a malevolent
crusade on the part of ultramontane clergy and laymen. Their ultimate goal
was domination over all governments, particularly over the Hohenzollern
monarchy as the chief Protestant power in Europe. Evidence of this crusade
could be seen in the unanimity with which the Catholic press throughout
Europe attacked Prussia, the efforts to forge a hostile alliance among Catholic
powers in Europe, Catholic support for German particularism and Guelph
resistance, the nourishment of Polish nationalism by Catholic clergy, the formation of the Center party on a purely confessional basis, the willingness of
conservative Catholics to make common cause with democratic radicals and
even socialists, and the church's demand for blind obedience under an infallible pope.

All of these concerns were connected with the general problem of consolidation, the solution to which was Bismarck's principal goal after 1867. Seen
in this light, his attack on political Catholicism in the Kulturkampf was intimately related to all of his other foreign and domestic policies during this
period: the reconstruction of the eastern alliance; collaboration with liberal
and national parties; the Germanization of ethnic minorities; the development of Reich institutions; expansion of industrial capitalism; and passage of
integrating legislation. While interwoven with these many other policies of
the period, the Kulturkampf differed in character. They were constructive
policies, aimed at building economic, institutional, and psychological unity,
but the Kulturkampf was primarily destructive, aimed at the elimination of
the Center party (or at least of its confessional base), the liquidation of clerical influence within the Prussian government and public schools, the wid-

---

[67] Walter Reichle, *Zwischen Staat und Kirche: Das Leben und Wirkens des preussischen Kultusmi-
nisters Heinrich von Mühler* (Berlin, 1938), pp. 323–325.

ening of the schism within the Catholic church produced by the infallibility controversy, the weakening of the relationship between the universal church and its German branch, and the rupture of an old alliance between clericalism and Polish nationalism and of an incipient alliance between clericalism and social radicalism. Having excised Austrian and French influence in German affairs through the military arm of the state, Bismarck now strove to excise ultramontane influences through its legislative and executive arms. As in 1866 and 1870, he waited to strike until the foe appeared isolated and vulnerable.

Bismarck was not alone in exaggerating the Catholic menace. Throughout Europe statesmen, liberals, and Protestants shared the fears generated by the attempt of the curia to meet the challenges of the century by heightening papal authority through the Syllabus of Errors and Vatican Council. Yet Bismarck was unique in that he viewed himself as a complete realist, an observer of the actual world and the forces that moved it, unprejudiced by personal motives or ideological passions. Where political Catholicism was concerned the capacity for objective judgment that had led him earlier from triumph to triumph in foreign and domestic affairs deserted him. Events were to prove, furthermore, that he overvalued the capacity of the state (at least within the means he possessed) to mold reality through its power to legislate and administer, and he undervalued the tenacity with which men cling to their ideals and traditions in the face of political persecution. The Leviathan proved to be nearly as formidable on dry land as in water.

Bismarck's judgment in the summer of 1871 was clouded by sheer hubris. His unbroken series of triumphs, climaxed by the favorable treaty with France signed at Frankfurt, left him in an exultant mood. On appearing in the Reichstag to announce the treaty on May 12, he was greeted with tumultuous applause by the deputies. On the same day Count Waldersee found him "decidedly proud" of his achievement.[68] Four days later, lubricated by much beer and May wine, he regaled Prince Hohenlohe with the tale of how he had outfoxed Thiers and Favre in the negotiations. "He treats everyone with a certain arrogance, . . ." Hohenlohe wrote in his diary, "He is the terror of all diplomatists."[69] Another contemporary and associate, Gustav von Diest, found Bismarck's "whole nature" changed after the war of 1870–1871: "He no longer tolerated contradiction; he was accessible to flattery; even the smallest, alleged disregard for his ego and his position exasperated him."[70] His pointless quarrel with the Reichstag (related earlier)[71] over the governance of Alsace-Lorraine was symptomatic of his mood.

[68] GW, VII, 512.
[69] Hohenlohe, Memoirs, II, 52–53.
[70] Gustav von Diest, Aus dem Leben eines Glücklichen (Berlin, 1904), p. 420. Kultusminister Mühler had a similar impression. See Reichle, Staat und Kirche, pp. 335ff.
[71] See p. 173.

In all of Bismarck's writings and recorded remarks it is necessary to distinguish where possible between what he believed and what he said for tactical purposes. Certainly he was conscious of the propaganda value of associating "black and red" in a common conspiracy against the government. We have seen him advise Manteuffel in 1852 to couple "Jesuitry with liberalism" in the government press in order to frighten liberal Protestant voters. During the Reichstag election campaign in February 1870 he instructed his *Leibjournalist* Busch to write, whenever opportunity offered, of the "Savigny-Bebel" or "Liebknecht-Savigny" party.[72] There can be little doubt, nevertheless, that Bismarck actually believed that the Catholic opposition was willing to ally with any subversive force, of whatever character, in order to "undermine the authority of the government."[73] We have seen that he regarded the clergy as chiefly responsible for the growth of Polonism and the decline of Germanism in the eastern provinces and that his policies toward the Poles were based on this conviction. It is also apparent that he regarded the Center party as an abnormal phenomenon in party politics owing to its inclusion of men of disparate views (conservatives and democrats) and social classes (aristocrats, bourgeois, workers). He could not comprehend how August Reichensperger, a conservative Prussian official, could associate for any normal political end with Schröder-Lippstadt, a barricade fighter of 1848, and with Windthorst, the Hanoverian Guelph. He concluded that the only bond was religious fanaticism, which ought to play no role in politics, "What do you intend with this party?" he asked Reichensperger.[74]

Bismarck's sensitivity to a black and red alliance also arose from an awareness of the vulnerability of his regime on the "social question." Earlier we saw that his discussions with Hermann Wagener and Ferdinand Lassalle during the constitutional conflict led him to speculate on the advantages of state socialism as a means of winning working-class votes.[75] In 1866, however, he turned in another direction, finding in German nationalism moral justification for Prussian expansion and in the bourgeoisie the social support for German consolidation. By 1871 he had begun to fear that the Catholic opposition might seize the opportunity he had passed up in 1866. Since 1848 the "Christian-social" idea had made steady progress in the Catholic church. Bishop Ketteler's greatest achievement was to ground social reform in Catholic theory and to make it a Christian moral imperative. In the period that saw the triumph of Manchesterism in Prussian government and party politics, the bishop borrowed from Lassalle the idea of productive associations. While his understanding of the social problem was limited (the artisans were his primary concern, and he rejected state aid), Ketteler's contention that Chris-

[72] Busch, *Tagebuchblätter*, II, 148, 160.
[73] BR, V, 209–211; GW, VIc, 9, 14–16, 21–22, 31–33, 176–179; VIII, 103–105.
[74] Pastor, *Reichensperger*, II, 63–65.
[75] See vol. 1, pp. 223–233, 284–286.

tian love and charity must cope with general social problems opened the way for other clergymen to attack the social ills of the factory system.[76] By the end of the 1860s there had begun to develop in the Ruhr and Rhineland a Christian-social movement organized in Catholic workers associations and supported by its own press. By March 1870 the associations were able to hold at Elberfeld their first general convention. Whereas Catholic clergymen had earlier attacked socialists and communists as subversive of church, government, and society, those involved in the Christian-social movement aimed at a new target—atheistic liberalism and laissez-faire capitalism. Despite all that divided them in matters of religion, socially concerned Catholics had found common ground with socialists.[77] Bismarck's sharp reaction to this development shows his sensitivity to the fact that collaboration with liberals and people of property had left his regime with a highly exposed left flank. The counterattack he launched in June 1871 was directed at both Catholics and socialists. During that crucial month he not only took the first steps toward the Kulturkampf, but he discussed with Russia and Austria-Hungary joint action against the Socialist International.[78]

For Bismarck the Kulturkampf was primarily an "internal preventive war" against dangers, real and imagined, that threatened the consolidation of the German Reich. Yet there was a secondary motivation of more positive character; namely, the desire to reconstruct the relationship between church and state in Prussia. Bismarck's distaste for bureaucratic government led him in the early 1870s to seek greater autonomy or "self-administration" in local, provincial, and church government. In each case the first signs of this intention can be seen in his rejection of the plans of his fellow Prussian ministers to integrate the provinces annexed in 1866 into the Prussian state. Earlier it was shown how he defeated the projects of Eulenburg, Lippe, and Heydt. Now Mühler suffered the same fate. By imposing a common church constitution, the minister intended to integrate the Lutheran and Calvinist churches in the new provinces into the Prussian Evangelical church under the supreme headship (Summepiskopat) of the king. In the course of time he expected the Lutheran and Calvinist congregations would voluntarily accept the "Evangelical union" that had been imposed on the old provinces by King Friedrich Wilhelm III. King Wilhelm, on the other hand, looked upon the union as a "sacred inheritance" from his father and brother whose extension into the new provinces could not wait. Bismarck succeeded in delaying and

---

[76] See his Die Arbeiterfrage und das Christentum (Mainz, 1864); also Bachem, Zentrumspartei, II, 57ff.

[77] Schmidt-Volkmar, Kulturkampf, pp. 44–45. See also P. Jostock, Der deutsche Katholizismus und die Überwindung des Kapitalismus (Regensburg, 1933) and E. Naujoks, Die katholische Arbeiterbewegung und der Sozialismus in den ersten Jahren des Bismarckschen Reiches (Giessen, 1939).

[78] Schmidt-Volkmar, Kulturkampf, p. 45.

defeating both plans on the grounds that the resentments created by coercion would increase resistance to Prussian rule.[79]

Bismarck's opposition was more than a matter of political expediency. He held convictions about the proper relationship between church and state in stark contrast to those of Wilhelm I, Mühler, and most conservatives. It was not the task of the state, he believed, to intervene in affairs of the church by legislating on matters of belief or ecclesiastical structure. In harmony with his pietistic faith he judged that the state could not elevate religious life, although it could further the work of the church through financial support. The implications of this philosophy were nothing less than radical: the sovereignty exercised by the monarch over the Protestant church for four hundred years should be abolished; the state must no longer impose the Evangelical union; the church must govern its own affairs on the provincial level; clergymen should no longer act as supervisors in the public schools; religion should no longer be a subject of instruction in the educational system.[80]

While he favored separation of church and state, Bismarck's conception of that term was not as far-reaching as that obtaining in the United States or even in Great Britain. It was not his intention to disestablish the Protestant church, which would continue to receive support from the treasury; nor did he propose that the last remaining manorial right of the estate owners, that of naming the local pastor, should be abolished; needless to say, he did not intend to sever the ideological bond between throne and altar that had made the Protestant church for four centuries the chief moral bastion of the aristocratic-monarchical order. Bismarck appears to have arrived at his basic position on church and state sometime after 1866. Just when is difficult to say, for he was absorbed in other tasks in these years, and naturally he was chary about making all of his views known to either the Kaiser or the *Kultusminister*. The first basic discussion with Mühler occurred in early 1869, and the result was mutual frustration. As a consequence, Bismarck's first stroke for the separation of church and state (the fusion on July 8, 1871, of the Catholic and Protestant departments of the *Kultusministerium* under a Protestant director) was aimed at the Catholic rather than the Protestant church. "Since you hindered me in executing [my plans] in the Evangelical church," he subsequently told Mühler, "I must enter by way of Rome."[81]

[79] Reichle, *Staat und Kirche*, pp. 223ff.

[80] *Ibid.*, pp. 236ff.; Heinrich Bornkamm, "Die Staatsidee im Kulturkampf," *Historische Zeitschrift*, 170 (1950), pp. 276ff. Both Reichle and Bornkamm detect the influence of Friedrich Fabri, chief of the Protestant Rhenish Mission, whose views on the revision of church-state relationships were similar, but neither author is able to establish any direct contact between the chancellor and the inspector. Klaus Bade has shown that Fabri, a frequent petitioner to the foreign office for colonial projects in the 1870s, only came into direct contact with the chancellor over these matters in the 1880s. *Friedrich Fabri und der Imperialismus in der Bismarckzeit* (Freiburg, 1975).

[81] Reichle, *Staat und Kirche*, pp. 243–244; Constabel, *Vorgeschichte*, pp. 100ff.

In August 1871 at Bad Ems, where these words were spoken, Bismarck finally revealed to the minister his full intentions: "struggle against the ultramontane party, especially in the Polish regions . . . ; separation of church and state, of church and school altogether; transfer of school inspection to laymen, abolition of religious instruction from the schools, primary as well as secondary; transfer of religious affairs to the minister of justice." The pious Mühler was shocked by this Godless proposition, and his eavesdropping wife went down on her knees to pray that her husband would not agree to it. Had Bismarck, Mühler asked, revealed to Wilhelm the extent of his plans? "No," was the wrathful answer, "I know where the Kaiser stands. If you do not make him shy for me, I will lead him, despite it all, whither I will."[82] Mühler had only two choices: either resign or execute Bismarck's will. Instead he chose the middle road, the most dangerous of all, hoping to protect the Evangelical church from Bismarck's plans, while yielding to his demands for more energetic measures against ultramontanes. Bismarck forced him into one compromise after another, harassing him all the while with accusations of inactivity: "In this struggle we need a commander. . . . For a minister you are too correct. . . . Are you secretly a Catholic?" Mühler's compromises alienated his conservative friends, while Bismarck's complaints isolated the hapless minister in the cabinet and undermined Wilhelm's trust. Behind the scenes the chancellor mobilized liberals and free conservatives for a vote of no confidence in the Landtag. In mid-January 1872 Mühler resigned.[83] Bismarck had rid himself of another of those "useless old men."

In his successor, Adalbert Falk, Bismarck found a more suitable instrument for the pursuit of his objectives. Born in Silesia, the son and grandson of Protestant pastors, Falk had been trained in law, had served as a state's attorney, and had been since 1868 a privy counselor in the Prussian Ministry of Justice; he had had political experience as a deputy in the Landtag, member of the constituent Reichstag, and Prussian delegate to the Bundesrat. His political orientation was national liberal, and his appointment strengthened the reputedly liberal wing (Camphausen, Delbrück, Leonhardt) of the "cabinet of two souls," as it was known in the liberal press.[84] Falk's appointment came as a surprise, for he was not widely known. His appointment reflected Bismarck's desire ultimately to place church affairs under the control of the Ministry of Justice, from which he expected a more "nonpartisan" treatment.[85] Falk shared with Bismarck the conviction that the sphere of the state had to be made secure against incursions by the church. No more than Bismarck did

[82] Reichle, *Staat und Kirche*, pp. 332ff.
[83] Reichle, *Staat und Kirche*, pp. 349ff., 359ff.; Constabel, *Vorgeschichte*, pp. 100ff., 127ff.; Hermann Oncken, *Rudolf von Bennigsen* (Stuttgart, 1910), II, 236. Bismarck had never had a high opinion of Mühler's capacity. GW, VII, 267–268.
[84] Reichle, *Staat und Kirche*, p. 411.
[85] Reichle, *Staat und Kirche*, pp. 444ff.

he conceive the Kulturkampf as a conflict of religious or world views. Unlike the chancellor, however, he conducted it as a legal rather than a political struggle. He did not doubt that the legislative and police power of the state would suffice to achieve the end in view. The function of the state was to legislate, the duty of the citizen to obey. But he seems also to have been sincerely convinced that none of the laws he fostered actually invaded the proper sphere of the church and that obedience to them could not justly be regarded by Catholics as contrary to conscience. He judged the Catholic conscience from the standpoint of a Protestant.[86]

The Kulturkampf Laws

"What is expected of me?" Falk asked Bismarck when they discussed his new assignment. Bismarck's reply was succinct: "Reestablishment of the rights of the state against the church and with the least possible noise."[87] It was the tragedy of the German Kulturkampf that the actions of Falk and Bismarck went far beyond the mere reestablishment of the rights of the state against the Catholic church and that they were accompanied by an uproar that reverberated throughout Germany and Europe for most of a decade. In seeking to drive the church out of the sphere of the state, they seriously invaded the sphere of the church and the rights of the individual. Far from separating church and state, they heightened the authority of the state over the Catholic church.

A few Kulturkampf laws did, it is true, contribute to the separation of church and state—most notably the school supervision and compulsory civil marriage statutes. While inspired by the immediate problems of Prussian Poland and the Braunsberg school controversy, the school supervision act of 1872 clarified the right of the state to control education in both public and private schools. By confirming the state's power to appoint and remove county and local school inspectors, it curbed the traditional, fiscally beneficial, practice of appointing clergymen to supervisory and teaching posts without remuneration.[88] Obligatory civil marriage was introduced in Prussia in March 1874 and, on the initiative of Reichstag liberals, in the entire Reich in February 1875.[89] While an avid supporter of the school supervision act, Bismarck resisted compulsory civil marriage, foreseeing that it would alienate Protestants as well as Catholics. He acquiesced only when Falk threatened to resign.

Most Kulturkampf legislation reinforced the supremacy of the state over the church. The so-called "pulpit paragraph," an amendment to the Reich penal

---

[86] On Falk see Erich Förster, *Adalbert Falk: Sein Leben und Wirken als preussischer Kultusminister* (Gotha, 1927).

[87] Förster, *Falk*, p. 75.

[88] GS (1872), p. 183.

[89] GS (1874), pp. 95–109; RGB (1875), pp. 23–39.

code in December 1871 initiated by an anticlerical Bavarian government, made clergymen punishable by two years imprisonment for political statements "endangering the public peace."[90] An imperial statute of July 1872, launched by the Reichstag, expelled the Jesuit order from the Reich.[91] Most of the "conflict laws" were Prussian, not imperial statutes. In April 1873 two amendments to the Prussian constitution made the Evangelical and Catholic churches "subject to the laws of the state and to the legally established supervision of the state" and gave to the state the power to enact statutes regulating the education, employment, and dismissal of clergymen, and to establish the "limits of the disciplinary authority of the church."[92] This prepared the way for the "May laws" of 1873 which: (1) stipulated that future clergymen of both confessions must be "Germans" who had graduated from a German *Gymnasium*, studied for three years in a German university, and passed state examinations in philosophy, history, and German literature (an experience intended to guarantee loyalty to Germany rather than Rome); (2) declared that only German ecclesiastical authorities could exercise disciplinary power over clergy and subjected such disciplinary actions to review by the provincial governor-general and by a new "royal court for church affairs"; (3) made appointments to ecclesiastical offices subject to the approval of the governor-general; (4) subjected church officials guilty of violating the law to fines, imprisonment, and removal from office; (5) regulated and eased the conditions under which a citizen might end his church affiliation.[93]

These statutes, which were roundly condemned by the Prussian bishops, failed of their purpose. Rather than submit to state supervision of the training of priests, the bishops closed the seminaries. Prospective priests neither attended the universities nor took the prescribed state examinations. Instead of seeking the government's approval of their nominees, the bishops left ecclesiastical offices vacant. When fines were imposed, they went to jail rather than pay. Confiscated property was repurchased at auction by loyal Catholics, who restored it to the church. Diocesan financial records were hidden or destroyed in order to keep them out of the hands of royal commissioners appointed to administer vacant dioceses. Although Catholic *Landräte* were dismissed, the resistance of local and low-ranking state officials (including the police) was too massive to be punished or terrorized. They disobeyed orders from on high and openly sympathized with the priesthood.[94]

By April 1874 Bismarck had already commenced to shift the blame for failure onto his colleagues. It had never been his intention to engage in a campaign against the Catholic church, he asserted to the Saxon minister Baron Richard von Friesen. "I wanted to fight the Center as a political party,

---

[90] *RGB* (1871), p. 442.
[91] *RGB* (1872), pp. 253–254.
[92] *GS* (1873), p. 143.
[93] *GS* (1873), pp. 191–208.
[94] Sperber, *Popular Catholicism*, pp. 240–252.

nothing more! If they [the ministers] had limited themselves to that, it would certainly have been successful. I am completely blameless for the fact that they went further and aroused the whole Catholic population." He had been too ill to read the "thick drafts" of prospective bills and cut out the "dumb stuff" they contained.[95] Yet legislation that Bismarck himself fostered in 1874–1875 alienated the Catholic population even more, without bringing the government any closer to its goal.

Bismarck, it is often asserted, lacked an appreciation of moral forces in public life.[96] This is hardly true, for we have seen that after 1858 he came to the conclusion that Prussian expansion could not be achieved without the moral sanction of German nationalism and that his policies after 1866 were based on that assumption. In the Kulturkampf he, paradoxically, both overestimated the moral force of Catholicism (the danger of an ultramontane crusade against Germany) and underestimated it (the tenacity with which Catholics would cling to their faith and church under political persecution). But he also overestimated the immediate value of German nationalism (as an ally in the struggle against political Catholicism) and underestimated it (as a force for the eventual reconciliation of the Catholic opposition to the German Reich). Indeed, Bismarck's tendency to look upon the papacy as a foreign power commanding an ultramontane army and his frequent use of military terminology in referring to the Kulturkampf explain why the struggle has been likened to an "internal preventive war." Against Rome, as earlier against Vienna and Paris, he deliberately mobilized and exploited forces whose views and passions he did not fully share, calling upon German national sentiment to support and justify a policy conceived, or rather misconceived, in the interest of state.

The wars of unification, Syllabus of Errors, Vatican Council, and dogma of infallibility had produced a steadily widening stream of religious controversy in Germany; the actions of Bismarck and Falk in 1871–1873 brought it to flood stage. The press, public meetings, and parliaments were filled with contention, charges, and countercharges. In the views of the Kulturkämpfer can

---

[95] GW, VIII, 115–117. See also his letter to Crown Prince Friedrich Wilhelm. Horst Kohl, ed., Anhang zu den Gedanken und Erinnerungen von Otto Fürst von Bismarck (Stuttgart, 1901), II, 447–478. Bismarck was unenthusiastic about the law providing for compulsory civil marriage, which he had publicly opposed in 1849, and yet he accepted Falk's bill, and defended it in the chamber on Dec. 12, 1873. GW, VIII, 49; XIV, 838; VIc, 43–47; BR, VI, 120–152. Although not minister-president in early 1873, Bismarck participated in the deliberations of the Prussian cabinet on the May laws and defended them in the House of Lords. BR, V, 381–409; GW, VIII, 50. There is no contemporary evidence of his disapproval. On May 26, 1873, Lucius recorded him as saying, "I am happy that Falk has conducted himself so well, but I have to support him in his church legislation—the only cabinet member who does." Lucius, Bismarck-Erinnerungen, p. 30.

[96] The Protestant theologian Willibald Beyschlag, for example, said of Bismarck, "He has never demonstrated that he knows how to weigh ideal forces." Quoted in Wilhelm Lütgert, Die Religion des deutschen Idealismus und ihr Ende (Gütersloh, 1923–1930), IV, 57.

be seen all of the successive layers of the German intellectual experience from the bedrock of religion to the topsoil of materialism. To liberal Protestants (for example, Theodor Mommsen) the goal of the conflict was to complete the Reformation and free 20 million German Catholics from the embrace of ultramontanism. Nurtured in the philosophy of German idealism (often called "the secret religion of the German educated class"), German nationalists viewed the conflict as a cosmic struggle between the German and Latin spirits, between the German idea of freedom, manifested in the Protestant Reformation and the neohumanism of the age of Goethe, and Roman authoritarianism, manifested in an absolute, infallible pope in search of world dominion. Having achieved political unity, Germany must now attain spiritual unity, perhaps even a new national religion (Paul de Lagarde). Others of the idealistic school (for example, Constantin Rössler) regarded the Kulturkampf as a defense of the state, seen in the Hegelian tradition as the vessel of the *Weltgeist* and embodiment of morality, a state that had reached its fullest realization in the German Reich of 1871 under a Protestant monarchy. For adherents of *Realpolitik*, who had discarded Hegelian metaphysics, on the other hand, the issue was preservation of the authority of the sovereign state and of positive law against a rebellious corporation and refractory individuals within civil society. Although many realists were religious men (for example, Heinrich von Treitschke), their position on the Kulturkampf was essentially political, based on the presumed needs of the state rather than upon any ideal or religious conception. For them the question was simple: which was to be dominant over the state, the government or the Roman church?

Since mid-century realism, secularism, and materialism had been on the ascent among the educated, fed by the simultaneous acceleration in German industrial development, successive triumphs on the battlefield, and expanding awareness of advances in scientific knowledge. The materialistic viewpoint had been nourished by the popular writings of David Friedrich Strauss depicting Christianity as a historical phenomenon, of Ernst Haeckel on social Darwinism, and of Ludwig Büchner popularizing the natural sciences. A renewed faith in human progress had arisen, confident that the new scholarship and new science would steadily unlock the secrets of history, society, and the universe, banishing ignorance and superstition. To liberals of this conviction the Syllabus of Errors and dogma of infallibility were a declaration of war against progress, modern science, and even civilization itself—an intolerable reversion to a medieval value system that the western world had long outgrown. It was in this sense that Rudolf Virchow, eminent scientist and parliamentary leader, dubbed the conflict a "struggle for culture."[97]

[97] Virchow to Chamber of Deputies, Feb. 8, 1872. SBHA (1871–1872), II, 663–669. For liberal and national views of the Kulturkampf, see particularly the debates of 1873 on the May laws. SBHA (1872–1873), III, 1488ff. On general attitudes in Germany see Lütgert, *Religion des deutschen Idealismus*, IV, 49–89; Bornkamm, "Die Staatsidee im Kulturkampf," pp. 48–72; Erich Förster, "Liberalismus und Kulturkampf," *Zeitschrift für Kirchengeschichte*, 47 (1928), pp. 543–

Germany did not divide in the 1870s cleanly into two camps, for and against ultramontanism. Some liberals, much to the surprise and distress of their own colleagues, were of the opinion that the liberal parties were seriously compromising their own credo by supporting exceptional laws (*Ausnahmegesetze*) against Catholics. It was true that many statutes could be interpreted with some elasticity as an intervention by the state to protect civil liberties—the rights of the citizen against the churches (civil marriage statute), of renitent Catholics against the clergy (law on church affiliation), of the lesser Catholic clergy against the higher (limitation of the church's disciplinary power). Yet this did not blind a small minority of national liberals (Lasker, Bamberger) and progressives (about twelve, including Hoverbeck, Richter, Franz Duncker) to the fact that most Kulturkampf laws, beginning with the pulpit paragraph of November 1871, were an unjustifiable infringement of civil liberty and an unfortunate precedent for liberals and democrats. "The hand that turns the skewer to the right," Richter warned, "can also turn it to the left."[98]

The most serious cleavage produced by the Kulturkampf was among conservatives. Protestant theologians who joined the struggle in the early months became disillusioned in varying degrees by the company in which they found themselves. Increasingly the Kulturkampf appeared to be a liberal rather than a Protestant undertaking, a struggle of realists for the omnipotent state and of materialists against all Christianity, rather than a renewal of the faith Luther had begun. They were incensed by the apparent penetration of these attitudes into the government itself. From Heinrich Friedberg, Prussian under secretary in the Ministry of Justice and delegate to the Bundesrat, they heard, for example, that "mere morality" had to be considered secondary to what was expedient and necessary under existing circumstances.[99] Through Mühler, furthermore, they learned that there was more to the government's policy than met the eye, that Bismarck's campaign against Catholics masked an ulterior purpose—a separation of church and state that would affect the Protestant as well as the Catholic church.[100] Once more the piper in the Wilhelmstrasse appeared to be leading conservatives toward the sacrifice of their most cherished principles.

---

559. Of the thousands of pamphlets, newspaper articles, and speeches that could be cited, a good example of the anti-Catholic viewpoint is J. C. Bluntschli, "Römische Weltherrschaft und deutsche Freiheit," in *Rom und die Deutschen* (Berlin, 1872), in the series Fr. v. Holtzendorff and W. Oncken, eds., *Deutsche Zeit- und Streit-Fragen: Flugschriften zur Kenntnis der Gegenwart* (Berlin, 1872), I, 291–329.

[98] Eugen Richter, *Im alten Reichstag: Erinnerungen* (Berlin, 1894–1914), I, 43.

[99] SBR (1874–1875), II, 1039; also Lütgert, *Religion des deutschen Idealismus*, IV, 56.

[100] Reichle, *Staat und Kirche*, pp. 411ff.

CHAPTER EIGHT

Climax of the Liberal Era

Alienation of the "Old Conservatives"

SINCE the beginning of the nineteenth century Prussian conservatives had repeatedly compromised, willingly and unwillingly, their twin ideals of the corporate society and Christian state. Under Bismarck the rate of sacrifice accelerated. In 1866 they swallowed the indemnity bill and universal male suffrage and bit into the principle of legitimacy by accepting Prussia's annexations. During the North German Confederation they watched Bismarck's flirtation with liberal nationalists, his many favors to industrial capitalism, and a flood of unifying legislation that depreciated the importance of Prussia, the power base of the conservative order. We have seen that the conservative reaction to these developments varied from total opposition (Ludwig von Gerlach) to full acceptance (the free conservatives). The cost was disunity, not only through the departure of the free conservatives, but also through the internal fracturing of the Conservative party itself. After 1867 each of the three caucuses of the Conservative party (Reichstag, Prussian Chamber of Deputies, and Prussian House of Lords) had its own political complexion.[1] While Reichstag conservatives tended to cooperate with the government, Landtag conservatives balked in 1867–1869 and were bludgeoned into submission by Bismarck's threats and Wilhelm's disapproval.[2] In 1872 two issues—the school supervision and county government reform acts—renewed their resentment.

The school inspection bill had been one of the chief bones of contention between Bismarck and *Kultusminister* Mühler. On Bismarck's insistence it was separated from the context of a general education reform bill and presented to the Landtag in February 1872 as an "emergency law." The bill affirmed that school inspection was a function of the state, not the churches, and clarified the right of the state to appoint and dismiss school inspectors throughout the monarchy, not merely in the eastern provinces. Eulenburg had warned Bismarck that the wide scope of the bill would cause many conservative Protestants to side with Catholics in opposition.[3] And so it did. Conservatives

---

[1] Robert Berdahl, "Conservative Politics and Aristocratic Landholders in Bismarckian Germany," *Journal of Modern History*, 44 (1972), pp. 5–6, and "The Transformation of the Prussian Conservative Party, 1866–1876" (Ph.D. dissertation, University of Minnesota, 1965).

[2] See vol. 1, pp. 422–426.

[3] Adelheid Constabel, ed., *Die Vorgeschichte des Kulturkampfes* (Berlin, 1956), p. 138. For the bill see *SBHA* (1871–1872), Anlagen, Nos. 5 and 175.

sensed correctly that Bismarck's purpose was to remove all clerical influence, Protestant as well as Catholic, from the school system. In the debates of the Chamber of Deputies in February 1872 they listened to the leaders of the left-liberals—Lasker, Richter, Virchow—praise the bill as a blow for freedom and for separation of church and state. In the voting on February 13, many conservatives joined Center and Polish deputies against the measure, which passed 207 to 155. Passage was never in doubt owing to the support of the free conservatives, national liberals, and progressives, but the size of the conservative opposition boded ill for the measure in the House of Lords. During the debate Bismarck warned that he would use "every constitutional means" to secure passage in the upper chamber. This was a thinly veiled threat that the king would name enough peers to overcome any opposition. On March 8 the bill passed the House of Lords by a vote of 126 to 76.[4]

Landtag conservatives feared not only for the survival of the "Christian state," jeopardized by the school inspection law, but also for that of the corporate state (Ständestaat), jeopardized by the county reform bill. Since early in the century few changes had occurred in county and local government in the "old provinces" of Prussia. While losing their judicial power in 1848, the owners of noble estates (Rittergutsbesitzer) had retained control over village government and local police. In addition, each owner of such an estate possessed a seat in the county assembly (Kreistag), which controlled local taxes and nominated three candidates from whom the king, acting through the Ministry of Interior, chose the Landrat. The Landrat was both a royal official and a representative, usually a member, of the local gentry. Since 1860 liberal legislators and publicists had constantly called for reform; many conservatives found the system difficult to defend.[5]

During the dispute on the Hanoverian provincial fund Bismarck had threatened conservatives with a reform bill that would break their stranglehold on rural government. Whether he would have carried out the threat is doubtful. He wanted to expand the dominant social group by including men of "social prominence," whose wealth was derived from sources other than estates and to reduce bureaucratic control through greater local autonomy in such matters as roads, social welfare, and local finance. Yet he balked at the idea of granting to rural counties and communities the degree of autonomy that cities had enjoyed since the Stein reforms early in the century. In many cities, he maintained, the election of mayors had resulted in financial and political corruption. Hence the "chief officials" of the county must be royal appointees.[6] Bismarck was too much the Junker and too much the authoritarian to become the heir of Stein.

[4] SBHA (1871–1872), II, 654–757; SBHH (1871–1872), I, 225.

[5] On the history of local government in Germany see particularly Heinrich Heffter, Die deutsche Selbstverwaltung im neunzehnten Jahrhundert (Stuttgart, 1950).

[6] GW, VIb, 143, 157; VII, 226–227, 268–270.

While his aims were moderate, Bismarck had considerable difficulty in launching a reform. His first obstacle was Count Eulenburg, whose Ministry of Interior was responsible for drafting the bill. He respected Eulenburg's ability (a rare concession), but thought him lazy (a foible exploited by his subordinates to delay action) and too independent (not the best attribute for longevity in the Bismarck cabinet).[7] When finally presented to the Landtag in late 1869, the bill was too conservative for liberals and too liberal for conservatives. The debate dragged out: war intervened; the issue was shelved. After the war Eulenburg found himself in the same dilemma as Mühler. In view of Bismarck's pressure, something had to be accomplished; yet nothing could be achieved in the Chamber of Deputies without support from the national liberals. Eulenburg's instinct for survival as a minister outweighed his conservatism, but he also relished the prospect of being ranked with Stein and Hardenberg as one of the great reformers of the Prussian political order. At any rate the bill he introduced in the Landtag in December 1871 met the wishes of national liberals and free conservatives and finally won, although for purely tactical reasons, the votes of progressives.[8]

The statute abolished the police and administrative powers of the owners of knights estates (*Rittergutsbesitzer*). Local and county government was reorganized on three levels: (1) the village, administered by a chairman (*Gemeindevorsteher*) and two aldermen (*Schöffen*) elected by the village and approved by the *Landrat*; (2) the district, whose chairman (*Amtsvorsteher*) was elected by the county assembly and appointed by the provincial governor-general (*Oberpräsident*); and (3) the county, governed by a *Landrat* selected in the traditional manner and assisted by an executive committee (*Kreisausschuss*) chosen by the county assembly. The assembly was to be elected by a three-class voting system (large landowners, burghers, and small farmers and laborers). The system combined in a unique way popular election, representative bodies, and higher authority.[9]

Despite the enthusiasm of liberals, the reform was hardly revolutionary, and many conservatives in the Chamber of Deputies found they could support it. Hence the measure passed by an overwhelming majority (256 to 61) on March 23, 1872, the minority consisting chiefly of estate owners and *Landräte* from the eastern provinces (including Bismarck's brother Bernhard!). In the House of Lords, however, archconservatives of this type constituted the majority. After long debate the bill was overwhelmingly defeated (145 to 18) on

---

[7] On Bismarck's efforts to move the Ministry of Interior to undertake county reform see Freiherr Lucius von Ballhausen, *Bismarck-Erinnerungen* (Stuttgart, 1920), p. 25; BP, II, 72ff.; GW, VIa, 490–491, 561, 564; VIb, 8; XIV, 747, 757.

[8] Heffter, *Selbstverwaltung*, pp. 546ff.; R. R. Reininghaus, *Graf Friedrich zu Eulenburg: Preussischer Minister des Innern 1862–1878* (Tübingen, 1932), p. 25.

[9] GSP (1872), pp. 661–716.

October 31, 1872.[10] In the attacks of Kleist-Retzow, Count Lippe, and other hotspurs of the "Stahl caucus," as the ultras called themselves, it is evident that what disturbed the Junkers was not only loss of power, but also loss of ideology. Since the beginning of the century every successive conservative thinker had sought to buttress the concept of the *Ständestaat* and preserve institutions that were believed still to embody it. To accept abolition of manorialism was to admit the futility of the effort. What the ultras resisted was not merely the sacrifice of special privileges, but also the whole transformation from status to class society that was the inexorable consequence of industrial and urban development.[11]

From Varzin, whence he had retired in May on the verge of collapse, Bismarck followed the struggle in the Landtag with mounting wrath. He had anticipated, to be sure, that county reform would encounter greater difficulty than the school inspection act. "That concerned questions in which the evangelical Junker had *no* direct interest; this is a question of money and influence in daily life." He was particularly outraged that *Landräte* and provincial governors who sat in the Chamber of Deputies had dared vote against the bill in league with "revolutionary" elements "hostile to the government."[12] Still, he sniffed among the odors of adversity the perfume of opportunity. What mattered now was not Eulenburg's bill, which in any case was not entirely to Bismarck's taste, but a reform of the House of Lords itself. In messages to Berlin he contended that the upper chamber was not fulfilling its proper function as a protector of monarchical interests; instead it had become "antigovernmental" and "dangerous to the state." To pack the chamber with enough new peers to secure passage of Eulenburg's bill would be a mere "palliative." Needed was a fundamental change in the composition of the chamber that would make it "similar to a state council [*Staatsrat*],"[13] not a pale imitation of the British House of Lords. While willing to permit hereditary members in the chamber, he wished to replace other aristocratic peers with high officials, generals, provincial governors, mayors, and representatives of bourgeois landowners and wealthy businessmen ("a curia of millionaires"). Such a chamber would speak for the most important interests in Prussian society; it would carry greater weight in the Chamber of Deputies, and would be inclined to support the government, particularly if its elective segment were subject to dissolution.[14]

[10] SBHA (1871–1872), III, 1497–1500; SBHH (1871–1872), I, 365–576.

[11] See particularly the speech by Count Lippe, on Oct. 23, 1872. SBHH (1871–1872), I, 382–383. For the ultras' views see Berdahl, "Conservative Politics and Aristocratic Landholders," pp. 1–20.

[12] GW, XIV, 839, 843; VIc, 24. For Bismarck's experiences with and views on the reform of county government see pp. 77–91.

[13] GW, VIc, 24–27; XIV, 840–841; Waldemar von Roon, *Denkwürdigkeiten aus dem Leben des General-Feldmarschalls Kriegsministers Grafen von Roon* (4th ed., Breslau, 1897), III, 323–326.

[14] Moritz Busch, *Tagebuchblätter* (Leipzig, 1899), II, 380, 385–391. See also his remarks at a parliamentary dinner, Jan. 25, 1873. GW, VIII, 53–54; Lucius, *Bismarck-Erinnerungen*, pp. 24–

By giving reform of the House of Lords priority over county reform, Bismarck also hoped to unseat Eulenburg, another of those independent colleagues who obstructed his domination of the Prussian cabinet. In late October 1872 the minister appealed to Bismarck for assistance, explaining that he was determined to bring about the county reform or fall in the attempt.[15] Bismarck's reply was a harsh letter of the kind that often preceded the departure of a hapless minister. He excoriated his "honored friend" for having failed to discipline and purge officials (*Landräte* and provincial governors) who had opposed the school inspection and county reform statutes; the *Landrat* for Varzin, for example, had characterized the chancellor as "an incompetent and unchristian minister." "I believe that your leniency has contributed not inconsiderably to the debasement of society." Instead of performing his duties, Eulenburg was "beating on the skull of a sick man, in the hope of striking off a phosphorescent spark."[16]

Eulenburg, however, knew how to help himself. Ignoring the poisoned darts flying from Varzin,[17] he pushed through the cabinet, over the opposition of ministers Roon and Selchow, slight modifications of the county reform bill sufficient to meet conservative objections and an agreement to force its passage through the upper chamber by naming twenty-four new peers (loyal generals and high officials). By this *Pairschub*, Eulenburg wished "to break the opposition once and for all," easing passage not only of the county reform act but also of upcoming Kulturkampf laws that were unpopular among conser-

26. Ernst Feder, ed., *Bismarcks grosses Spiel: Die geheimen Tagebücher Ludwig Bambergers* (Frankfurt, 1933), p. 200. Under a statute of May 30, 1855, the House of Lords was composed of (1) royal princes of the house of Hohenzollern appointed by the king (none was ever appointed); (2) hereditary members drawn from the high nobility, including heads of the south German families of Hohenzollern-Hechingen and Hohenzollern-Sigmaringen, 22 mediatized (that is, former imperial) houses, and 51 other noble houses; (3) heads of noble families possessing noble estates and granted hereditary membership by the king (41 seats by 1911); (4) members appointed for life (largely high officials, officers, and clerics, numbering 88 by 1911); (5) members chosen by certain organizations possessing the right of representation. In the latter category were chapters of three evangelical cathedrals, associations of nobles bearing the hereditary title of "count" in each of the eight provinces, certain distinguished noble families with such names as Alvensleben, Arnim, Bredow, Kleist, and Schwerin (18 seats by 1911), fifty-six associations formed by owners of noble estates that had been in the possession of the same family for at least fifty years (altogether 90 seats), professors of ten Prussian universities, and certain city governments (51 by 1911). In 1911 the chamber was composed of 347 members, of whom 260 were noblemen, 87 were burghers. Of the burghers most were officials, academicians, mayors, and businessmen, but no representatives of farmers or laborers, except for one artisan (appointed in 1911). Ernst Rudolf Huber, *Deutsche Verfassungsgeschichte seit 1789* (Stuttgart, 1963), III, 83–85. For Bismarck's views on reform of the House of Lords see Werner Frauendienst, "Bismarck und das Herrenhaus," *Forschungen zur brandenburgischen und preussischen Geschichte*, 45 (1933), pp. 286–314.

15 Horst Kohl, ed., "Aus der Korrespondenz des Grafen Friedrich zu Eulenburg mit dem Fürsten Bismarck," *Deutsche Revue*, 25 (1900), pp. 190–191; Heffter, *Selbstverwaltung*, p. 552.

16 GW, XIV, 839, 843–844.

17 To put pressure on Eulenburg and the other ministers Bismarck launched a discussion of the problem in the *Kölnische Zeitung*. Busch, *Tagebuchblätter*, II, 382–391.

vatives.[18] Wilhelm was agreeable. He feared that a reformed House of Lords would become "a skiff bobbing in the wake of the Chamber of Deputies battleship," and Bismarck was too far away to change the Kaiser's mind.[19] After repassing the lower chamber comfortably, the bill was approved by the House of Lords on December 7 by a margin of twenty-five votes. Eulenburg rejoiced that he might go down in history as the "rejuvenator of Prussia."[20]

The county reform bill proved in practice to be less of a change than its liberal supporters imagined and its conservative opponents feared. It ended manorialism by severing the formal connection between political privilege and ownership of noble estates, but did not liquidate the power of the gentry as such. Big landowners continued to dominate county assemblies in the eastern provinces and tended to monopolize the new office of district chairman, which controlled the police. While county governments enjoyed greater autonomy, ultimate authority still rested with the central government acting through the *Landrat*. Increasingly the position of *Landrat* was held by professional officials rather than by members of the local gentry, who generally lacked the legal and administrative training the post now required. Still, more than half of those who held the office in 1914 were Junkers.[21]

The struggles of 1872 shattered the unity of the Conservative party. Embarrassed by the position of Landtag conservatives on the school inspection bill, the Reichstag caucus renamed itself the "Monarchical-National party" and announced its intention to work "hand in hand" with the Bismarck regime.[22] In the Landtag those deputies who voted for the county reform bill adopted the title "New Conservative party" to make clear their disagreement with the "old conservatives," who sided with the intransigents of the House of Lords. The most dramatic consequence of the school inspection and county reform acts, however, was the open break that now ensued between Bismarck and ultraconservatives, some of whom, like Kleist-Retzow, had been lifelong friends and associates. To the ultras the conduct of Bismarck and Eulenburg constituted a betrayal of trust highly damaging not only to the gentry, but also to the "Christian state" and the monarchy itself.[23] To Bismarck, on the other hand, it was utterly incomprehensible that conservatives could think of op-

[18] Cabinet meetings of Oct. 29, Nov. 3, 9, and 17, 1872. DZA Merseburg, Rep. 90a, B, III, 2b, Nr. 6, Vol. 84.

[19] Crown Council of Nov. 8, 1872. DZA Merseburg, Rep. 90a, B, III, 2c, Nr. 3, Vol. III. For the effect of Bismarck's absence on these deliberations see his exchange of letters with Wilhelm in Horst Kohl, ed., *Anhang zu den Gedanken und Erinnerungen von Otto Fürst von Bismarck* (Stuttgart, 1901), I, 228–232.

[20] SBHA (1872–1873), I, 22–53, 68–141; SBHH (1872–1873), I, 15–55, 64–71; Heffter, *Selbstverwaltung*, p. 553.

[21] Heffter, *Selbstverwaltung*, pp. 553–556; Herbert Jakob, *German Administration since Bismarck: Central Authority versus Local Autonomy* (New Haven, 1963), pp. 47–51.

[22] Felix Salomon, *Die deutschen Parteiprogramme* (Leipzig, 1907), II, 1.

[23] Herman von Petersdorff, *Kleist-Retzow: Ein Lebensbild* (Stuttgart, 1907), pp. 418ff.

posing the government. In his vocabulary the ultras were now "enemies of the state," a phrase he previously reserved for democrats, socialists, ultramontanes, and Guelphs.

Deteriorating Health

Bismarck's struggles with cabinet, king, and ultraconservatives during 1872 left him in a state of nervous exhaustion. On May 3 his physician, Heimrich Struck, penned a dire warning. The chancellor was suffering, he wrote, "from functional disturbances in almost all bodily organs." Declining strength and nervous exhaustion could lead to a "premature marasmus." The patient had lived for many years off the "capital of his nervous system." Income and outgo were not in balance. Against his own better judgment the doctor had frequently sought to assist either with stimulants or depressants. "But now I must tell you that I have reached the end of what medicine can accomplish with palliatives." Struck advised the prince to take a leave of absence lasting at least six months, during which time he must be relieved of all duties.[24]

How Bismarck diagnosed his problem can be seen in a number of sources. Lucius had never seen him "more grim and out of sorts" than at a parliamentary soirée on May 4. "My oil is used up; I can't any more," he complained. "It is too much to work alone with such colleagues and against the influence of the queen." Parliament also caused him distress by its "incomprehension of conditions." Foreign powers lacked initiative. "We now make the events in Europe and, if we do nothing, then nothing happens." "My sleep gives me no rest. I dream about what I have thought about while awake, if I go to sleep at all. Recently I saw a map of Germany in front of me, on which one rotten spot appeared after another and then fell away."[25]

One week later his mood had not improved. At the soirée on May 11 Gustav von Diest—government official, conservative deputy, and frequent guest in the Bismarck household—approached the chancellor and chanced to remark that his host must be feeling better. "It is just my misfortune that I never find sympathy!" was the response. He had paced the floor all night, the prince declared, falling asleep only at 8:30 in the morning, awaking at 3:00 P.M. "But the sleep was not refreshing. And now [I have] this pressure on my brain that makes everything that lies behind my eyes often seem like a glutinous mass. I am not able to hold on to my thoughts continuously. In addition, there is this unbearable pressure on my stomach, with unspeakable pains." Diest advised cold compresses on head and torso. Bismarck replied, "I know that [treatment]; they call it 'Neptune's belt.' I used it carefully, as prescribed, but the only results were new colds and nervous symptoms." Diest proposed

---

[24] Bismarck to Wilhelm, May 9, 1872. GW, VIc, 19.
[25] Lucius, *Bismarck-Erinnerungen*, pp. 21–22.

yet another remedy. Being "much more choleric" than other men, Bismarck should "lie face down for eight days," which might bring him "eight weeks of good health." At this, the prince became furious. "I tell you that my nerves are at the breaking point, and the doctors have forecast a nervous breakdown, if I do not take some months now to relax completely."[26]

On May 14, 1872, Diest met the chancellor in an anteroom of the Reichstag and found him confused about the day of the week. Didn't the prince feel better, he asked, now that a vacation was in prospect? "With a deep tragic-melancholic expression," Bismarck replied, "No, I feel worse than ever today; I fear a stroke. It is all over with me." With a deep sigh he shook the deputy's hand and left him to enter the chamber, where a few minutes later, to Diest's astonishment, he delivered two highly effective (judging from frequent laughter and applause) attacks against the ultramontanes. It was on this occasion that he spoke those ringing words, "Don't worry; we are not going to Canossa, neither physically nor spiritually," which resonated in the daily press but later returned to haunt him.[27] Small wonder that Diest and others concluded that Bismarck's ailments were laced with hypochondria.

Wilhelm granted Bismarck's request for an extended leave, and on May 18 he left Berlin for Varzin, where he remained, with but one interruption, for nearly seven months. In his absence Delbrück transacted the routine business of the empire, and Roon assumed Bismarck's duties in the Prussian cabinet. With Bucher's secretarial help, Bismarck continued to conduct foreign affairs. In late June he wrote to his daughter that he could dispose of Europe in ten to fifteen minutes every morning at breakfast, "since no one is here to make matters difficult." Letters to his family tell of long walks and rides to inspect the timber, of sleeping eleven hours "like a sack," of Sultan's adventures (chained up at night so as not to disturb his master, the mastiff bit and clawed his way to freedom), of his plans for adding a new wing to the mansion, and of Struck who seemed to bring his illnesses with him. The doctor was besieged in "this normally healthy region" by patients with broken bones, hemorrhages, and other ailments. "Only Bucher and I refuse obstinately to take any of his medicines."[28]

In late July he had a visitor, John Lothrop Motley, who found his old Göttingen friend "little changed in appearance since '64, which surprises me. He is somewhat stouter and his face more weather-beaten, but as expressive and powerful as ever. . . . He looks like a Colossus, but his health is somewhat shattered. He can never sleep until four or five in the morning. Of course, work follows him here, but as far as I have yet seen it seems to trouble him

[26] GW, VIII, 37–38.
[27] GW, VIII, 39; BR, V, 336–345.
[28] GW, XIV, 832–835.

but little. He looks like a country gentleman entirely at leisure."[29] Indeed Bismarck had become stouter. A suit ordered for his silver wedding anniversary (July 28) proved too small, being based on measurements taken in 1868. This may have cost the tailor himself some sleep, for he received from the mighty chancellor of the German Empire a sharp rebuke: "You . . . assume that I become smaller and thinner with age, which is seldom the case. . . . I did not expect that a business such as yours, ordinarily so intelligently conducted, could have studied so little the natural history of the human body."[30]

As the summer neared its end, Bismarck asserted that his health was not much better than in the spring. "Until now," he confessed, "I have been unable to work." Johanna too was ailing, though she sought to hide it, and Bismarck anticipated that they would remain at Varzin "for most of the winter." In September he was compelled to attend the Berlin meeting at which the three emperors formed their league. He endured the negotiations, banquets, and other festivities, but sped back to Varzin on September 19. During October he felt stronger and, disregarding the instructions of his physician, entered at long distance into the fray over the county reform bill—only to suffer a severe relapse. The conduct of the ultras made him boil with anger, as did Eulenburg's success in evading the trap set for him. That Wilhelm followed Eulenburg's advice, not Bismarck's, in packing the House of Lords was doubly upsetting.[31] Bismarck's vexation was self-defeating, for it made him too ill to undertake a journey to Berlin in November, when his presence alone could have altered the situation. Instead Struck had to be summoned to Varzin by telegraph on November 10. "I fear that I am more used up than I have admitted to myself," the prince wrote to Wilhelm three days later. "I am ashamed not to be at my post at such an important moment."[32]

On December 14, 1872, the news of a fresh cabinet crisis compelled Bismarck, despite his poor condition, to leave the quiet of Varzin for the clamor of Berlin. Piqued on being outvoted by the other ministers, Roon and Selchow wanted to resign. Their departure would have jeopardized the delicate balance in the cabinet between conservatives (Roon, Selchow, Itzenplitz, Eulenburg) and liberals (Camphausen, Falk, Leonhardt). It would have confirmed the prejudices of those Prussian conservatives who believed that Bismarck had sold out to liberalism. There was no reason to regret Selchow's

[29] George W. Curtis, ed., *The Correspondence of John Lothrop Motley* (New York, 1889), II, 340, 342–343.

[30] Horst Kohl, ed., *Fürst Bismarck: Regesten zu einer wissenschaflichen Biographie des ersten Reichskanzlers*, (Leipzig, 1892), II, 50; GW, XIV, 836.

[31] Bismarck to Countess Eberhard zu Stolberg-Wernigerode, Aug. 9, 1872. [Hans Goldschmidt, ed.], "Neue Briefe von und über Bismarck," *Deutsche Allgemeine Zeitung* (July 9, 1937) Vol. 76, Nr. 312–313, Beiblatt; Kohl, ed., *Bismarck-Regesten*, II, 52–54; Hans Goldschmidt, *Das Reich und Preussen im Kampf um die Führung von Bismarck bis 1918* (Berlin, 1931), p. 159.

[32] Kohl, ed. *Bismarck-Regesten*, II, 54; GW, XIV, 836, 841–842.

exit, to be sure, for his was a modest talent. But the departure of Roon—after Bismarck the cabinet's most prestigious member—would have been highly damaging. Faced with this threat, the prince made a decision he had contemplated for months: to lighten his burdens by resigning as Prussian minister-president in order to concentrate his energies on imperial affairs. By handing over to Roon the highest office in the Prussian government, moreover, he pumped up the general's ego and kept him in the cabinet.[33]

Yet this is not all that was at stake. On the day before his departure from Varzin, Bismarck wrote a revealing letter to Roon. "My profession is such that one makes many enemies, but no new friends." Honesty and fearlessness had cost him old friendships. "I am in disfavor among all members of the royal house, and the trust of the king in me is declining. Every intriguer finds his ear." The treasonable desertion of the Conservative party in the Catholic question had deprived him of the political base he preferred. "Given my age and my conviction that I do not have long to live, there is something discouraging in *this* world about the loss of old friends and associations. When coupled with concern about [the health] of my wife, which has returned in increased measure in recent months, this discouragement is crippling. My springs have lost their tension from being overtaxed. . . . The king hardly knows how shamelessly he has ridden a good horse. . . . The influences that counter my efforts are too powerful for me, and the malicious vanity and political uselessness of the conservatives have deprived me since last year of all joy in the struggle. Nothing can be done with the conservatives; they follow 'speakers' like Kleist and intriguers like Bodelschwingh. I can't do anything against them."[34]

Except for brief excursions to Friedrichsruh and Varzin and a two-week official visit to St. Petersburg in May, Bismarck remained at his post in Berlin from December 14, 1872 to June 27, 1873. From January to May he was plagued by pains in leg, hip, and throat; at times he could neither walk nor stand. At the end of June he retired, "drained of all energy and will," to Varzin, "where I don't need to see or speak to anyone for fourteen days at a stretch." Bismarck had not succeeded, despite his surrender of the minister-presidency, in ridding himself of the burden of Prussian affairs, and Wilhelm refused his request to be relieved of his last remaining cabinet post, that of Prussian minister of foreign affairs. Instead he tried to recover his strength once more during a lengthy vacation in the country. Thrice it was interrupted by unavoidable travels: to Berlin in early September 1873 for the unveiling of the victory column in the Königsplatz; to Berlin again in late September, despite "rheumatic-nervous pains," to receive the king of Italy and his foreign

[33] On the cabinet crisis of November–December 1872, see Roon, *Denkwürdigkeiten*, III, 321–340.

[34] GW, XIV, 844–845.

minister; to Vienna in October with Wilhelm on a state visit. Afterward he returned to Varzin "acutely sick." In November he was besieged by a throat ailment; the doctors suspected diphtheria.[35]

Since mid-October 1873 Bismarck had been depressed by the news that Roon, now seventy-one years old and asthmatic, had finally resigned on grounds of poor health. After less than a year of experimentation, it was evident that the attempt to separate chancellorship and minister-presidency was a failure. Reluctantly Bismarck again became the presiding officer of the Prussian cabinet. But Roon's departure was also a keen personal blow to the prince. It was upon Roon's shield that he had been elevated into office in 1862, and the two had been closely associated for nearly a dozen years. Since 1866 Roon had not always been happy over the course steered by his friend in domestic affairs, particularly over Bismarck's collaboration with German liberals and "Verdeutschung a tout prix." Yet Roon had accepted the school inspection and county reform acts and, as minister-president, had even presided over the drafting and passage of the May laws of 1873. The letter Bismarck wrote to Roon on hearing of the latter's resignation shows genuine pathos. The general was, he said, the "one remaining feeling heart" among the ministers. "The longer I remain in office the more lonely I become; the old friends die or become enemies and one makes no more new ones."[36]

Bismarck's sense of loss and isolation was heightened by yet another disappointment—his failure to bring into the cabinet Moritz von Blanckenburg, his old friend of Kniephof days, with whom he had once shared a love for Marie von Thadden. Blanckenburg was perhaps the most effective of those moderate conservative leaders in Reichstag and Landtag who had, despite frequent grumbling and dissent, refused to follow the ultras in breaking with the Bismarck government. A description of his attitude written by his sister-in-law in these years mirrors the ambivalence of moderate conservatives in general: "Vexed though he is at Bismarck, he is too attached to be able to break with him entirely. Moreover, he has had too much opportunity to get to know the conservatives and appreciate their intellectual poverty, their egoism and incapacity, not to see blame on both sides." When Selchow resigned in the fall of 1872, as minister of agriculture, Bismarck proposed that he be replaced by Blanckenburg, hoping through him to cement his relationship to the moderate conservatives. Blanckenburg, who was initially favorable to the appointment, expected to push the government in a conservative direction. Since 1869 Blanckenburg and Hermann Wagener had been urging Bismarck to create a new conservative party based on landowners, artisans, and proletarians; such a party, they argued, would enable the government to ditch its

[35] Heinrich von Poschinger ed., *Bismarck-Portefeuille* (Stuttgart, 1898), II, 174; VIII, 47, 76; XIV, 846, 854–855, 857–858; Lucius, *Bismarck-Erinnerungen*, pp. 30, 35–36.

[36] Roon, *Denkwürdigkeiten*, II, 361–370; GW, XIV, 856–857.

alliance with the national liberals. But Falk ended Blanckenburg's candidacy by threatening to leave the cabinet rather than accept him as a colleague.[37]

Count Königsmarck, who received the appointment, lasted less than a year, and in November 1873 Bismarck succeeded in getting even Falk to accept Blanckenburg's candidacy. But by this time Blanckenburg had changed his mind. The May laws had made him more critical of the government's course, which, he now realized, he could not change as a cabinet member. He was not impressed, furthermore, by Bismarck's argument that as a minister he need concern himself only with agriculture, not politics. The presence of Camphausen as minister of finance seemed to guarantee that economic policy would continue to favor industry and trade rather than farming. Blanckenburg not only refused to become Bismarck's colleague, but also gave up his seat in the Reichstag to return "like salmon from the sea" to his estate in Pomerania. "For the time being," he wrote to Roon, "nothing is to be accomplished with political parties. Bismarck has destroyed every bridge in Pomerania that I could have still rebuilt." Bismarck was bitter over this fresh apostasy. "Blanckenburg's party loyalty," he complained to Roon, "is greater than his devotion to king and country." "God has permitted the desertion of our Junkers from throne and faith and thereby badly damaged our armor."[38]

By the end of 1873 Bismarck was chronically ill and doubted that he had long to live; he felt isolated and alone, deserted by his oldest friends and by most of his social class. The forced resignation of Hermann Wagener (discussed later) was another cruel blow, costing him the services of "the only person around me with whom I can speak without restraint."[39] Although severely depressed, Bismarck's narcissistic self-assurance was unshaken; he firmly believed that the path he followed was the only viable one, that those who opposed him were malevolent, and that those who failed to help him were lacking in loyalty and patriotism. The self-image he painted in the letter to Roon was that of his paternal ancestors, of a feudal warrior standing in the breach determined to hold the wall against all assailants. "Sick or healthy I will hold up the flag of my feudal lord against my factious cousins as firmly as against Pope, Turks, and Frenchmen."[40] In mid-December he returned to Berlin "to undergo the chronic suffering of parliamentary activity," calling on God to provide the "armor of disdain" needed to protect him from the attacks of his fellowmen. "Our opponents," he wrote to Julius Andrássy, "are infinitely superior to us because they lack education and knowledge of affairs, goodwill and patriotism, and they have the advantage that they serve only

[37] Hermann Witte, ed., "Bismarck und die Konservativen: Briefe aus Trieglaff," *Deutsche Rundschau*, 149 (1911), pp. 381–386; Petersdorff, *Kleist-Retzow*, pp. 415–416; Wolfgang Saile, *Hermann Wagener und sein Verhältnis zu Bismarck* (Tübingen, 1958), pp. 106–111.

[38] Roon, *Denkwürdigkeiten*, III, 367–372.

[39] GW, XIV, 828.

[40] GW, XIV, 856–857. See also Petersdorff, *Kleist-Retzow*, pp. 447–448.

BENNIGSEN: "WHY IS IT THAT THE MACHINE WORKS SO SLOWLY?" DELBRÜCK: "THE MECHANIC IS SICK. WE WOULD PREFER TO STOP THE FACTORY ALTOGETHER." WILHELM SCHOLZ IN *KLADDERADATSCH*, 1874.

themselves and the party to which they belong, not the country and not the king. The struggle is very unequal, but it must be fought."[41]

The Elections of 1873–1874

His feud with the conservatives made Bismarck all the more dependent upon the National Liberal party. Without its support there was no prospect of winning the Kulturkampf or continuing the consolidation of the Reich. By 1874 this dependency began to seem ominous owing to the growing power of the party's left wing and of its principal spokesman, Eduard Lasker.

Lasker was born in 1829 at Jaroscyn in Posen. His family was Jewish and middle class, his father a small manufacturer. As a student in Vienna Lasker fought at the barricades in the ranks of the Academic Legion. The coming of the new era in 1858 enabled him to begin his career as a Prussian official (judiciary) at Berlin. He soon became prominent as a journalist in the liberal press and was elected to the Prussian Chamber of Deputies in 1865 and to the Reichstag in 1867. In both parliaments he quickly established his reputation as a fearless and effective speaker, particularly upon issues of civil rights and parliamentary power. Although eagerness for national unity led him from the Progressive into the National Liberal party in 1866–1867, he remained close in political temperament to the progressives. Many moderate liberals regarded

[41] GW, XIV, 857–858.

him as far too radical for the National Liberal party; yet he maintained a close personal relationship with Bennigsen.[42]

During 1873 Lasker reached the peak of his career as a deputy. In January–February his revelations in the Prussian chamber of corruption in the granting of railway concessions forced the resignation of Hermann Wagener, who was morally and financially ruined by the charge. Another victim was Count Itzenplitz, whose Ministry of Commerce was responsible for granting the concessions. In April the Reichstag passed, by overwhelming majority, a bill long advocated by Lasker to include civil law within the legislative competence of the Reich. On June 13, the Reichstag resolved on his initiative to begin its annual sessions in October rather than February, and on the following day the government bill creating an Imperial Railway Office was passed only after he had put through significant amendments. These achievements and the publicity they received made Lasker the most discussed German politician of the year.[43]

Naturally this did not endear him to Bismarck. To be sure, the two men were of one mind concerning the necessity of much of the centralizing legislation of the period, and Bismarck considered the imperial law codes to be a highly important contribution to national unity. Yet he had hardly forgotten Lasker's interference in the delicate negotiations with south German governments during 1870. He resented, furthermore, the loss of Wagener (but not Itzenplitz!), and was inclined to interpret Lasker's assault on the *Geheimrat* as an attack upon himself. ("You came within a hair of hitting me.")[44] What irritated Bismarck the most, however, was Lasker's persistent success in amending government legislation. Until a Lasker amendment had been accepted, he later complained, government bills had no chance of passage.[45]

How sensitive Bismarck was to Lasker's growing influence was evident during the Reichstag debate of June 16, 1873, on the government's bill for an imperial press act. Lasker objected to the brief time allotted for discussing a measure involving "the rights of the people" and added that the bill had no chance of passage; fewer than two dozen deputies favored it. Coming from Lasker, who was seconded by Windthorst, this assessment of the bill's chances was devastating. It provoked Bismarck to denounce Lasker's "declamation" about civil rights as "outmoded talk." "All who sit here are representatives of

---

[42] Richard W. Dill, *Der Parlamentarier Eduard Lasker und die parlamentarische Stilentwicklung der Jahre 1867–1884* (Erlangen, 1956). On Lasker's relationship to Bennigsen see Hermann Oncken, *Rudolf von Bennigsen* (Stuttgart, 1910), II, 248–254.

[43] Dill, *Lasker*, pp. 97–114.

[44] To Lasker at a parliamentary dinner, Feb. 1, 1873. *BP*, I, 69. In order to demonstrate his continued loyalty to Wagener, Bismarck visited him at his quarters "in full uniform, in the full light of day, before all the people." Saile, *Wagener und Bismarck*, p. 115; Siegfried von Kardorff, *Wilhelm von Kardorff: Ein nationaler Parlamentarier im Zeitalter Bismarcks und Wilhelms II., 1828–1907* (Berlin, 1936), pp. 96–97. See also Roon, *Denkwürdigkeiten*, III, 351–356.

[45] *BR*, X, 21.

EDUARD LASKER. (COLLECTION OF GORDON MORK.)

LUDWIG WINDTHORST. (ARCHIV FÜR KUNST UND GESCHICHTE, BERLIN.)

EUGEN RICHTER. (BILDARCHIV PREUSSISCHER KULTURBESITZ.)

RUDOLF VIRCHOW. (ARCHIV FÜR KUNST UND GESCHICHTE, BERLIN.)

the people; we all belong to the people; I too have civil rights; his majesty the Kaiser also belongs to the people; we are all people." In rebuttal Lasker interpreted the chancellor's attack as an attempted "put down" and a denial of parliament's right to oppose the government. "We are on a footing of complete equality here." Each deplored the "tone" that the other had imparted to the discussion, and Bismarck spoke of his sense of "injury" that any deputy could talk to him in this acidulous way. Hohenlohe judged that both men were in the wrong, "but particularly Bismarck."[46]

That Bismarck came to hate Lasker as much as he did Windthorst shows how threatened he felt by a parliamentary leader who was not overawed by his achievements, who refused to be impressed by his claims of bad health and injured nerves, who possessed debating skills equal to his own, who was moved more by principle than expediency, and who, because of the following he attracted, threatened the chancellor's power and influence over the internal political life of the country. When not carried away by anger, as was obviously the case on June 16, Bismarck understood the necessity of getting along with Lasker, at least for the time being. Five days later he sent Lasker a special invitation to his parliamentary soirée, where he ostentatiously engaged the "little doctor" in a lengthy conversation that was duly reported in the public press.[47] By the end of the year he had even more cause to fear this man, whose abilities he privately respected.[48] The elections held in Prussia in October–November 1873 and in Germany on January 10, 1874, created for Lasker—or appeared to create for him—a commanding position in German politics.

In these elections, held nearly three years after the start of the Kulturkampf, Bismarck and his liberal allies had their first chance to judge the effectiveness of their attack upon the Center party and Catholic hierarchy, while conservatives learned the consequences of being at odds with the Bismarck government, which failed, for the first time since 1862, to intervene in behalf of conservative candidates.[49] In both legislatures the Conservative party virtually collapsed, sinking from 55 to 22 seats in the Reichstag and from 114 to 30 seats in the Chamber of Deputies (the most severe loss being that of the old conservatives, who sank from 71 to 4). Even the free conservatives suffered losses, declining from 41 to 35 in Prussia and 37 to 33 in the Reich.

[46] SBR (1873), I, 1175–1184; Dill, Lasker, pp. 112–113.

[47] BP, I, 73–74.

[48] BP, II, 211–214.

[49] Ludolf Parisius, Deutschlands politische Parteien und das Ministerium Bismarck (Berlin, 1878), p. 162. Bismarck ordered official action against Prussian Landräte who were sympathetic to "Jesuits and Poles" and to "enemies of the state." GW, VIc, 39–40, XIV, 854–856. He was relentless in pushing Minister of Interior Eulenburg into action against "conservative conspirators." Bismarck to Eulenburg, July 8, Aug. 1, Nov. 5 and 21, 1873, June 29 and Aug. 5, 1874. F. Eulenburg Papers, courtesy of Wend Graf zu Eulenburg-Hertefeld and John C. G. Röhl. See also Lucius, Bismarck-Erinnerungen, p. 39; Petersdorff, Kleist-Retzow, pp. 454–466.

Catholic voters rallied to the defense of church and party, with the consequence that the centrists increased from 58 to 88 in the Chamber of Deputies
and from 61 to 91 in the Reichstag. The liberal parties were the biggest win-
ners, the national liberals rising from 123 to 174 in Prussia and from 125 to
155 in the Reich; for the progressives the increase was from 49 to 68 and 46
to 49. Among smaller parties, the Poles held their old strength at 18 seats in
the Chamber of Deputies and 14 seats in the Reichstag, while the Reichsland
sent 15 deputies to the Reichstag, where they formed a separate caucus of
"protesters." The Liberal Reich party, composed of 30 southern deputies in
1871, disappeared from the Reichstag. In both elections it was evident that
the Kulturkampf had polarized the voters. Protestants voted for liberals
(chiefly national liberals); Catholics, for centrists. For the first time since
1866 the two liberal parties had an absolute majority in both parliaments (242
out of 432 in the Chamber of Deputies, and 204 out of 397 in the Reichstag).[50]

   In the Reichstag, however, there were other conceivable combinations.
Since the Kulturkampf had driven the Center into an attitude of "decisive
opposition," progressives had the possibility of hammering together a coalition of dissidents (progressives, centrists, Poles, social democrats, and other
assorted "*Reichsfeinde*") numbering 184 deputies. When joined by only fifteen
national liberals, such a coalition could, if incapable of constructive action,
at least block legislation proposed by the government. In other words, the left
wing of the National Liberal party (about eighteen deputies) led by Eduard
Lasker held the pivotal position in the chamber. By combining either with
the moderate-conservative or the radical-oppositional side of the chamber, it
might swing the chamber. "In such situations," wrote Eugen Richter, "the
decisive role had passed from Bennigsen and his followers to Lasker and his
followers. More than any previous deputy, Lasker dominated both the Reichstag and Chamber of Deputies during the ensuing legislative period."[51]

Renewal of the Iron Budget

The great issue of German politics in the mid-1870s was whether and how
Lasker would exploit the pivotal position he appeared to have gained in national politics. Would this dedicated liberal seek to enlarge the range of parliament's authority at the risk of splitting the National Liberal party? The
crucial test was not long in coming, for the first great task of the empire's
second Reichstag was to decide on whether the "iron budget" of Germany's
military establishment, granted for three years in 1867 and again for three

---

[50] Bernhard Vogel, Dieter Nohlen, and Rainer-Olaf Schultze, *Wahlen in Deutschland: Theorie-
Geschichte-Dokumente, 1848–1970* (Berlin, 1971), pp. 287, 290.
   [51] Eugen Richter, *Im alten Reichstag: Erinnerungen* (Berlin, 1894–1914), I, 75; Parisius, *Parteien*, pp. 176–177; Oncken, *Bennigsen*, II, 256.

years in 1871, was to be renewed. No other issue was so close to the heart of the problem of parliamentary power.

Wilhelm and the Prussian War Ministry proposed to regain the ground lost to the constituent Reichstag in 1867. Under the bill presented to the Reichstag in February 1874 the strength of the peacetime army was established indefinitely at 401,659 men. Until the government requested a further increase, the size of the army and therefore its cost (constituting 90 percent of the imperial budget) was to be outside parliament's control. The bill's opponents had some reason for confidence. In 1871 all of the deputies in the Progressive, Center, and Polish caucuses had voted against the iron budget and had been joined by a number of national liberals, including Lasker. Given the new composition of the chamber, the prospects of this combination were good. Hoping for a quick decision, the progressive leader Hoverbeck proposed that the bill be discussed in plenum without being referred to committee. But the Reichstag chose the latter course and the bill did not reach the chamber until after the Easter vacation. During the interim members of the Free Conservative and National Liberal parties sought escape from the approaching confrontation by proposing compromises in the form of substantially lower figures than that proposed by the government. The conservative and official press agitated vociferously for passage without compromise.[52]

During most of March and April 1874 Bismarck was confined to his quarters too lame to walk. According to Struck, the illness stemmed from the old leg injury and began as an "abnormal" attack of gout. "Initially swelling of the veins, inflammations, great pain, later the passing of much sediment and uric acid, etc. No fever, pulse never above 64, heart beat and tone are constantly weak." The doctor prescribed morphine (one-twelfth of a gram) to induce sleep and whiskey and gin as a diuretic.[53] Bismarck's diagnosis was different. What made him sick, he told Baron von Friesen, the Saxon envoy, was vexation—"vexation not at his enemies and political opponents, with whom he knew how to cope, but at those who ought to support him in their own interests and for the good of the country, but who everywhere harmed him and left him in the lurch."[54]

Unlike November 1872, Bismarck's illness in 1874 did not render him politically ineffective. Through two friendly deputies he issued what amounted to an ultimatum to the liberal opposition. Apparently the time had come, the *Spenersche Zeitung* quoted him as saying, to take back those confident words he had uttered in March 1867: that Germany, if lifted into the saddle, would know how to ride. "The Reichstag seems to want to prove that Germany can *not* ride." Prominent deputies appeared to think themselves bound by earlier

[52] SBR (1874), III, No. 9; Parisius, *Parteien*, pp. 182–188.
[53] Lucius, *Bismarck-Erinnerungen*, pp. 43–44, 55; also GW, XIV, 860.
[54] GW, VIII, 114.

commitments to abolish the iron budget. By contrast, he, Bismarck, had always sought to learn and had never hesitated to change his opinions when the situation demanded, "for I have always placed the fatherland above myself." Deputies chosen by the electorate expressly to support the chancellor were now betraying their constituents. "I cannot accept this situation. I cannot sacrifice my European reputation. As soon as I am able to grasp the pen, I shall submit my resignation." But at the end his choices were stated somewhat differently: "either my resignation or the Reichstag's dissolution!"[55]

Bismarck, dissatisfied with the report in the *Spenersche Zeitung*, launched a clarification of his position in the semiofficial *Norddeutsche Allgemeine Zeitung*: "The strength and position of the Progressive party and of the portion of the National Liberal party that goes with it has made the situation intolerable"; fifty to sixty deputies chosen by districts loyal to the Reich were "operating against the imperial government, and this at a time when parties hostile to the Reich are so strong that majorities are bound to fluctuate." This "bad situation" was destined to grow worse rather than better during the coming legislative period. Hence the chancellor had come to the opinion that the only solution was an appeal to the voters, which, if unsuccessful, would prove that "a constant majority upon which any government can support itself is totally impossible." In another "correction" written for the *Spenersche Zeitung*, Lucius wrote, "[Bismarck] no longer feels strong enough to overcome official frictions and the difficulties created by a fluctuating majority in the Reichstag." Again the prince threatened resignation.[56] The Kaiser also made his sentiments known. On the occasion of his birthday (March 22), he told his generals how sad it made him in the "evening of life" to have his authority in military affairs questioned again by a parliamentary opposition. On the same day he told a Reichstag delegation that he was firmly resolved, if necessary, once more to take up the struggle against parliament.[57]

Again the liberal front buckled under the weight of the chancellor's displeasure. Most liberals (including some progressives) still considered him indispensable, at least in foreign affairs. They were impressed by his claim that the state of his health (the *Spenersche Zeitung* carried a full report of his ailments) was too precarious to put up with internal opposition on crucial matters. No one relished having to appeal to the country on such an issue as the size and support of the German army only three years after war with France. It was evident that in the recent elections the public had reacted to the issues of the Kulturkampf; they had voted for liberal rather than conservative candidates under the assumption that to do so was to support Bismarck in his struggle against the "foes of the Reich." The chancellor was probably accurate

[55] *BP*, II, 93–94.

[56] *BP*, II, 194–196.

[57] SEG (1874), p. 98 (Mar. 22); Martin Philippson, *Max von Forckenbeck: Ein Lebensbild* (Leipzig, 1898), p. 257.

in judging that fifty to sixty national liberals would lose their seats in any earnest contest with the government over the military issue. They had been sent to the Reichstag to support the government in its struggle against ultramontanes, not to seek an enlargement of the chamber's budgetary power. The pivotal position gained by Lasker and his allies did not stem from the will of the electorate but from an accident of party politics. It existed in the structure of the chamber, not in the minds of German voters.[58]

As the days passed, the weakness of the liberal position became increasingly evident. A flood of petitions from all parts of Germany and all social classes (including peasants, workers, and day laborers), advised the Reichstag to accept the bill.[59] Gradually the national liberal press joined conservative and official journals in urging settlement. Not since 1848, declared Bennigsen, had he witnessed a popular political movement "so strong and primitive." One party colleague, Eduard Stephani, detected "a veritable fanaticism for unconditional acceptance of the statute." Richter, leader of the unconditional opposition, was likewise impressed by passions that the statements from Bismarck and Wilhelm aroused and the press tendentiously exploited. When the entire governmental apparatus (from top to bottom) beat the drums, he remarked, the noise was loud enough to deafen some and shatter the weak nerves of others.[60] Once again, liberals were compelled to face the truth: the German public was basically unconcerned about the issue of parliamentary power, especially when the issue had to do with the army. "Most voters," reported the *Spenersche Zeitung*, "want no conflict with the government and have made this wish clear to their deputies."[61]

By April 9, 1874, when the deputies reassembled after the Easter vacation, the opposition bloc had begun to dissolve. Lasker found that his group of thirty followers had shrunk to about fifteen. Progressives, furthermore, informed him that six of their members could not be relied upon. Seven members of the Alsace-Lorraine "protest party" were boycotting the parliament.[62] Still, the great majority of the national liberals would probably have stood with the progressives against the bill, if the government had continued to insist on a permanent military budget. On March 30, however, the Kaiser had summoned Forckenbeck, president of the Reichstag, and hinted at his willingness to compromise on this issue.[63] During the next ten days Forcken-

---

[58] For assessments of the weaknesses of the liberal position see Parisius, *Parteien*, pp. 190–193; Oncken, *Bennigsen*, II, 258–259; Hans Herzfeld, *Johannes von Miquel* (Detmold, 1938), I, 276–280.

[59] *SEG* (1874), p. 102 (Apr. 4).

[60] Parisius, *Parteien*, p. 192; *SBR* (1874), II, 768; Friedrich Böttcher, *Eduard Stephani* (Leipzig, 1887), p. 141.

[61] Parisius, *Parteien*, p. 193 (fn.).

[62] *Ibid.*, pp. 193–194; *SEG* (1874), pp. 87–88.

[63] Lucius, *Bismarck-Erinnerungen*, pp. 49–50, 529–530; *HW*, II, 102–103. For Wilhelm's view

beck, Miquel, Bennigsen, and the Kaiser were repeatedly in Bismarck's sickroom. At the critical caucus of the National Liberal party on the evening of April 9, these three leaders proposed a "compromise" in the form of a seven-year military budget, which was unanimously approved.[64] Eduard Stephani described the scene among national liberals on the following day, when word arrived that the Kaiser had accepted the offer: "jubilation without precedent, much running about hither and yon. I ran to Miquel; we rejoiced greatly. . . . Everyone was happy that the conflict wanted by the Center and conservatives and feared by us had been avoided. The conservatives are outraged."[65]

During the first week in April 1874 Lasker faced his moment of truth. He too decided to desert Richter and the progressives in their demand for a yearly military budget. He wanted a four-year period, but yielded without joy to the "compromise" that his colleagues obtained. Dedicated liberal though he was, he recognized that the cause was lost; he could not command the votes with which to insist on a more generous settlement. But he also was plagued by the thought that, by persisting in opposition, he would only precipitate the split within the party that had nearly occurred over the same issue in 1871.[66] On April 14, the new iron budget or *Septennat* was approved in the Reichstag by a vote of 224 to 146. The majority was composed principally of conservatives, free conservatives, national liberals, and some progressives. The minority was composed of progressives, centrists, social democrats, Poles, and Guelphs.[67]

To Bennigsen Bismarck appeared, despite his illness, "as fresh, energetic, and full of genius as ever, and in this affair he has executed a masterpiece from his sickbed."[68] Indeed the chancellor had cause for satisfaction. He had no real desire to dissolve the Reichstag. Such a course, he confessed to Lucius, would greatly embitter the minority and split the majority, both of which he needed for the rest of his legislative program. "I cannot depend upon the conservatives alone, without making concessions to the Center; yet I would do it, if what I would win thereby were a real gold coin and not just a shiny penny." By surrendering the *Aeternat*, on the other hand, he was assured of a secure majority. The *Septennat*, furthermore, would extend beyond the next two Reichstag elections, and it was difficult to make definite plans for a longer time. But he also confessed to Lucius that, in forcing the military to accept the *Septennat*, he had been compelled to threaten resignation. A seven-year

---

of the problem see his letter to Roon on May 8, 1874. Johannes Schultze, ed., *Kaiser Wilhelms I. Weimarer Briefe* (Berlin, 1924), II, p. 300.

[64] Philippson, *Forckenbeck*, pp. 257–258; Oncken, *Bennigsen*, II, 259–260; GW, XIV, 859–860; Herzfeld, *Miquel*, I, 278–280.

[65] Böttcher, *Stephani*, pp. 141ff.

[66] See the exchange of letters, Lasker and Stauffenberg, Apr. 1 and 3, 1874, in *HW*, II, 101–103.

[67] SBR (1874), II, 747–805. Lucius, *Bismarck-Erinnerungen*, p. 530. The thirteen progressives who voted against the compromise bolted the party to form the "Löwe caucus."

[68] Oncken, *Bennigsen*, II, 261.

military budget would enable him to keep some control over the army, that "state within a state." The military cabinet would be less inclined to ignore the chancellor and Prussian Ministry of War if it knew that in the not too distant future the generals would again need their support against parliament.[69] Here is to be seen the familiar pattern of balance and counterbalance characteristic of Bismarckian *Realpolitik*.

Again Bismarck had triumphed over a seemingly formidable parliamentary opposition. The result showed that in any serious confrontation with his liberal "allies" on the issue of military defense versus parliamentary power he held the upper hand, because he, not they, had the greater backing of vocal public opinion. If unequal to him on such an issue, there was always the possibility, even likelihood, that the liberal majority would prove troublesome on other issues, such as civil rights, in which the emotions of the public were not so deeply engaged. During the same session, however, the government succeeded in maneuvering the Reichstag liberals into still another "compromise." The imperial press act, over which Bismarck and Lasker had quarreled in 1873, was reintroduced in 1874. On the occasion of its second reading in March, the Reichstag accepted amendments that limited the power of the police to confiscate printed material without prior court approval and the power of state's attorneys to prosecute publishers, pressmen, journalists, and distributors. In return for abolishing the stamp tax and publishers' bonds, however, the parliament restored most of the offending clauses, which in any case many national liberals favored as a check on socialist as well as on ultramontane agitation. In this form the bill was finally passed.[70]

Bismarck's need for consolidating legislation, his struggle against the Center and Polonism, his increasing concern over socialist agitation, and his deepening quarrel with ultraconservatives had created a constellation of forces in parliament potentially dangerous to the mixed constitutional order. Yet the performance of the liberals in the spring of 1874 belied their strength and certainly left him with no just cause for alarm. On the "Siamese twins"— iron budget and press act—he got essentially what he wanted.

The Arnim Affair

The discord between Bismarck and the ultraconservatives was heightened during 1874–1875 by his difficulties with Harry von Arnim. A Pomeranian

---

[69] To Lucius, Apr. 9, 1874. Lucius, *Bismarck-Erinnerungen*, pp. 49–52. Through Lucius Bismarck hoped to influence the free conservatives, of whom the baron was a member, to accept the compromise he had just negotiated with the national liberals. Many free conservatives and progovernment conservatives found the compromise a bitter pill. Moritz von Blanckenburg wrote to Roon of the "compromise catastrophe." Roon, *Denkwürdigkeiten*, III, 404–406; also Poschinger, ed., *Bismarck-Portefeuille*, II, 177–178.

[70] SBR (1874), I, 374–537; II, 1083–1145; III, Anlagen, Nos. 23, 67.

Junker, Arnim had entered the Prussian foreign service in 1851, the same year as did Bismarck, with whom he was well acquainted. After serving as secretary of legation in various posts, Arnim was appointed Prussian envoy to the Vatican in 1864 on Bismarck's recommendation. At the time Bismarck appears to have thought highly of him. Arnim's performance in Rome raised some questions about his ability to stay within his instructions; nevertheless, he became Berlin's principal negotiator at the peace conferences with France at Brussels and Frankfurt in 1871. After the treaty was signed, he was sent to Paris as German ambassador, then the most important post in the German foreign service. Here he soon outraged the chancellor by carrying on unauthorized, although not ineffective, negotiations with President Thiers over the execution of the Frankfurt treaty. Acute disagreement developed between the two men, moreover, over whether Berlin should favor a republic (Bismarck's position) or a Bourbon restoration (Arnim's position) in France. Yet the eventual consequences of their dispute were out of proportion to the cause. In February 1874 Arnim was recalled from Paris, then jailed, tried, and convicted for misappropriating official documents. Ultimately he was also convicted of treason and lese majesty.[71]

Arnim's principal offense never appeared in the indictments—that of competing with Bismarck for influence with the Kaiser and aspiring to replace him as chancellor. Arnim was certainly not alone in speculating that Bismarck's days were numbered, that either recurrent bad health or the death of the Kaiser would soon end the chancellor's career.[72] He was simply more foolish and more vulnerable than others who engaged in the same sport. By bringing his views on policy directly to the Kaiser, he threatened the prince's weakest flank. Theoretically all German envoys were the personal representatives of the Kaiser and as such had the right of direct access to him. Bismarck himself had made use of this right during his years as Prussian minister in Frankfurt, St. Petersburg, and Paris. Now he expected German diplomats to wheel and turn at his command like troops on parade. To Arnim it seemed that the chancellor wanted the reports of his ambassadors to reflect his own instructions rather than the actual situation.[73] Bismarck was deeply annoyed by Arnim's persistence in advocating support for a monarchical restoration in France and by his presumption in attempting, not without success, to influence the Kaiser. But he also suspected that Arnim had, on at least one occasion, delayed carrying out instructions to benefit his speculations on the stock market, and he firmly believed that the ambassador was secretly opposing the

---

[71] On the Arnim affair see George O. Kent, *Arnim and Bismarck* (Oxford, 1968).

[72] See, for example, Friedrich Curtius, ed., *Memoirs of Prince Chlodwig of Hohenlohe-Schillingsfuerst* (New York, 1906), II, 103ff.

[73] Perhaps it would be simpler, Arnim suggested, "to compose the reports of the ambassadors in Berlin." Kent, *Arnim and Bismarck*, pp. 74–75; Harry von Arnim, *Pro Nihilo! Vorgeschichte des Arnim'schen Prozesses* (Zurich, 1876), p. 37.

policy of his own government in the German and European press. Yet he was compelled to undergo the humiliation of contending with this vain and presumptuous man for influence at the royal palace.[74] The longer the humiliation, the greater the punishment. The chancellor bided his time, steadily playing out the rope, while Arnim fashioned his own noose.

In May 1873 the Thiers government finally fell—to Bismarck's distress and Arnim's delight—and was replaced by a promonarchist regime under Marshal MacMahon. Bismarck suspected Arnim's complicity, for the ambassador had often advocated intrigues to this end. Despite the ambassador's denials, he persisted in insinuating this to Arnim, to the Kaiser, and in the public press. In June 1873 he drafted a memorandum to Wilhelm, painting an exaggerated picture of the consequences for Germany's domestic and foreign policy of Arnim's machinations at Paris and suggesting that the Kaiser, since he seemed more impressed by Arnim's recommendations than by Bismarck's, find another minister to direct his foreign policy. But the document was never sent.[75] Presumably the time was not yet ripe. On a visit to Berlin in early September, Arnim spoke with both Wilhelm and Bismarck; the former, he said, was reassuring, the latter wrathful to the point of incoherence. Why, Arnim asked, did Bismarck "persecute" him? "I," the prince replied, "am the persecuted. For eight months—for a year—you have injured my health, robbed me of my rest. You conspire with the empress [against me], and you will not rest until you sit here at this desk, where I sit, and find out for yourself that this too is not enough. I have known you since youth. You regard every superior as a natural enemy; you said that yourself, years ago. I am the enemy at the moment. You delayed the conclusion of the convention of March 15 to bring about the fall of Thiers, and I must bear the responsibility for this political mistake. You have accused me before the Kaiser. You have connections at court that have long hindered me from recalling you."[76]

The ease with which Bismarck finally obtained Arnim's recall belies the seriousness of the threat he posed. Two days after that savage interview the chancellor sent a dispatch to Paris protesting a pastoral letter of August 3, 1873, by the bishop of Nancy, who called upon the faithful in his diocese (to which German Lorraine belonged) to pray for the reunion of Metz and Strassburg to France. Although the new French government went far in trying to assuage him, Bismarck became steadily sharper in his rebukes and demands. He was assisted in keeping the issue alive by the archbishop of Paris, who issued a similar pastoral letter on September 9, and by an assembly of French bishops at Bourges, which endorsed the pope's condemnation of the Kultur-

[74] Kent, *Arnim and Bismarck*, pp. 63–116.

[75] *Ibid.*, pp. 121–122; GP, I, 182–191.

[76] Arnim, *Pro Nihilo*, pp. 76–79. That Arnim's account of the interview was reasonably accurate can be assumed from Bismarck's marginalia on the copy of *Pro Nihilo* in the archives of the foreign office. Kent, *Arnim and Bismarck*, pp. 123–124.

kampf. In substance the issue was nothing but a routine friction of the postwar period, but Bismarck actually described it to the Kaiser on October 11 as a grave crisis that threatened European peace. It may be that his purpose was to point up the international ramifications of the Kulturkampf and perhaps even to derive some benefit from it in the coming elections and in the debate over the military budget that was to follow. At any rate he also repeatedly—and untruthfully—charged that Arnim, who had returned to his post at the end of September, was seriously derelict in pressing the German point of view on the French government. By February 24, 1874, Wilhelm was sufficiently impressed to order Arnim recalled from Paris.[77]

Except for Arnim's own folly, his recall would probably have ended the affair. Stung by defeat and maltreatment, the ambassador secretly released to a Viennese newspaper, Die Presse, documents written during his period in Rome, purporting to show that he, in contrast to his government, had foreseen the consequences of the Vatican Council and the doctrine of infallibility and implying that Bismarck, had he only heeded Arnim's advice, could have avoided the Kulturkampf. In view of the widespread comment that followed in the European press Bismarck published in the Norddeutsche Allgemeine Zeitung other documents that tended to prove the contrary. This inspired Arnim to defend himself in an open letter to Döllinger, which revealed still more details about German policy toward the Catholic church. The German and Austrian press began to choose sides as to who had shown the greater wisdom, chancellor or ambassador.[78] The contest was hardly equal, for the chancellor was the mechanic of German foreign policy, the ambassador its tool. For Bismarck to release official information to the press was legal and legitimate, for Arnim to release it without authorization was illegal and insubordinate. Still the case against Arnim might have resulted merely in reprimand and retirement,[79] had not Friedrich von Holstein, secretary of legation at Paris, discovered that eighty-six documents were missing from the embassy files.

Accused of theft, Arnim put up a lame defense: many of the missing papers were private letters and had never been part of the embassy papers; others had been taken by mistake and would be returned; some he did not have and had never possessed. Meanwhile, Arnim sought to secure his political future by purchasing a newspaper and campaigning for election to the Prussian House

[77] Kent, Arnim and Bismarck, pp. 124–128.

[78] Ibid., pp. 129–136.

[79] Arnim denied releasing the documents to Die Presse, and the case against him could not be proved at the time, but it was established that he had launched a false report in a Belgian newspaper in 1872 and, in denying responsibility for it, had made a false statement to the foreign office. Kent, Arnim and Bismarck, pp. 137–139. On the legal proceedings against Arnim see Gerhard Kratzsch, Harry von Arnim, Bismarck-Rivale und Frondeur: Die Arnim-Prozesse 1874–1876 (Göttingen, 1975).

of Lords.[80] On legal advice Bismarck recommended to the Kaiser that Arnim be prosecuted on criminal charges—the only secure way to obtain speedy return of the missing papers. On October 4, 1874, Arnim was arrested at Nassenheide, his estate in Pomerania, on a warrant issued by the Berlin City Court. An Austrian diplomat described the general reaction: "First impression: painful. Form of proceedings: shocking. Arrest unusual for this kind of offence. It comes as a surprise that the city court here has been chosen. Antagonism [between Bismarck and Arnim] still too fresh in everybody's mind not to interpret the trial as a personal affair."[81] Correspondence seized at Nassenheide yielded interesting details on Arnim's relationship to journalists but none of the missing documents. The preservation of official secrets was in any case no longer the main purpose of the action. Backed by the Kaiser, Bismarck was now bent on the total ruin of Harry von Arnim. He insisted on a public trial.

By its verdict on December 19, 1874, the Berlin City Court proved its professional competence and immunity to pressure from the government. The judges cleared Arnim of several charges of misbehavior while in office, accepted his view that many of the documents taken were personal, but convicted him of purloining thirteen that were unquestionably official. Instead of thirty months imprisonment demanded by the prosecutor, the court sentenced him to three. Both sides appealed the conviction, and in the Court of Appeals the government had better luck—the sentence was increased to one year (June 24, 1875). But Arnim was already out of reach. Released on bail owing to his acute diabetes, he fled the country after his first conviction and never returned. From Switzerland he petitioned the Kaiser, pleading less for clemency than for "protection" against Bismarck's hatred. No sooner had the petition arrived, however, than its effect was nullified. An anonymous pamphlet published in Switzerland appeared in Berlin bookstalls with the provocative title *Pro Nihilo: The Prelude to the Arnim Trial*. The pamphlet, which the Prussian police tried vainly to suppress, defended and glorified Arnim but vilified Bismarck, Wilhelm, and the courts. In addition, it disclosed information on German relations with France since 1871. That Arnim was the author was obvious and soon proven. In new proceedings before the Prussian Supreme Court Arnim was convicted of treason and lese majesty (October 1876) and sentenced to five years in prison. The hapless diplomat died in exile in 1881.[82]

---

[80] *Ibid.*, pp. 147–149; Norman Rich and M. H. Fisher, eds., *The Holstein Papers: The Memoirs, Diaries, and Correspondence of Friedrich von Holstein, 1837–1909* (4 vols., Cambridge, Eng., 1955–1963), III, 31–39. On being recalled from Paris, Arnim was reassigned to Constantinople, but he was delayed by illness and the death of a daughter. Judging from the publication in *Die Presse*, he may have decided sometime during the two months after his recall to retire from the foreign service and begin a political career.

[81] Quoted in Kent, *Bismarck and Arnim*, p. 153, from E. Wertheimer, "Der Prozess Arnim," *Preussische Jahrbücher*, 222 (1930), p. 274.

[82] Kent, *Arnim and Bismarck*, pp. 144ff.

Arnim was not without friends and defenders. Although he stemmed from the lesser Pomeranian gentry, he had powerful connections. His first wife was an illegitimate daughter of Prince August of Prussia, his second a daughter of Count Adolf Heinrich von Arnim-Boitzenburg, once Prussian minister of interior, briefly minister-president in 1848, and thereafter leader of the conservatives in the House of Lords until his death in 1868. The count's son and heir, Arnim's brother-in-law, was a free conservative deputy, who on December 8 (the day before Arnim's trial began in Berlin!) accepted appointment as governor-general of Silesia, replacing a man regarded as too lenient in pursuing the Kulturkampf.[83] This branch of the Arnim family was both numerous and influential. Even Bismarck was distantly related to it through his sister's marriage to Oskar von Arnim-Kröchlendorff. Members of the Arnim clan petitioned the Kaiser to pardon Harry, but Bismarck and Minister of Justice Leonhardt pointed out that the sinner was impenitent, and the request was refused.[84]

Among ultras Harry's prosecution was regarded as persecution, a vicious attack by Bismarck upon a personal rival and yet another betrayal of his own caste. After initial doubts liberal journalists and deputies were impressed by the government's case against Arnim, but within the aristocratic opposition his fate was regarded as another example of Bismarck's ruthlessness.[85] Bismarck's motive in destroying Arnim was not entirely personal. The foreign service of the German Reich was young, and its tradition still unformed despite its Prussian roots. One of Bismarck's intentions may have been to consolidate his authority over it by making an example of Arnim. Certainly Arnim possessed, despite some gifts, serious deficiencies as a diplomat. In addition, he was vain, ambivalent, often contradictory, and sometimes mendacious. If his end was the consequence of his character, it was also revelatory of Bismarck's. Arnim dug his own grave, but Bismarck armed him with pick and shovel.

Kullmann and Majunke

During 1874–1875 the Kulturkampf mounted in intensity. Bismarck prodded Falk for new statutes authorizing punishment of contumacious bishops and the dismissal of seminary directors, educators, and officials unwilling to conform to the "new shape" of Prussian policy.[86] In the spring of 1874 came a new series of "May laws": a Reich "expatriation statute," authorizing the states to

[83] SEG (1874), pp. 238–239; Kardorff, *Kardorff*, p. 75. In October the Kaiser had sent the count a message of sympathy and awarded him the Order of the Red Eagle, third class, with ribbon. Lucius, *Bismarck-Erinnerungen*, p. 56.

[84] Kent, *Arnim and Bismarck*, p. 182.

[85] Petersdorff, *Kleist-Retzow*, p. 417. Said Kleist-Retzow, "Arnim dared to harbor the thought that he could replace Bismarck—for that he was to be destroyed."

[86] GW, VIc, 39–40, 48–51.

expel refractory priests and deprive them of citizenship, and Prussian statutes permitting the removal of church property and vacant benefices from the control of contumacious bishops and strengthening state control over clerical education.[87] On January 14, 1874, the archbishop of Posen-Gnesen was imprisoned, on March 7 the bishop of Trier, on March 31 the archbishop of Cologne, and on August 4 the bishop of Paderborn. Church officials who took over their administrative functions were arrested, as were priests who refused to leave parishes vacated by the courts; some were taken at the altar itself. Among their parishioners tempers flared. On March 22 thousands packed the square in front of Cologne cathedral to cheer the archbishop before his arrest. Similar demonstrations were accorded the other bishops.[88]

On July 13, 1874, Eduard Kullmann, a twenty-one-year-old cooper's journeyman from Magdeburg, fired a pistol at Bismarck as the chancellor's carriage drove into the street outside his quarters at Bad Kissingen; at that moment Bismarck turned to greet someone, and the movement may have saved his life. The bullet only creased his right hand. Kullmann was seized on the spot and interrogated shortly afterward by his intended victim. He had acted, the culprit declared, in anger over the May laws and Bismarck's treatment of the Center party. That evening at a torchlight celebration of his escape the chancellor said, "The blow aimed at me was directed not at me personally, but at the cause for which I have dedicated my life: the unity, independence, and freedom of Germany."[89]

Although belonging to a Catholic journeyman's association, Kullmann acted alone; there was no evidence of conspiracy. Yet the official press depicted him as the natural fruit of priestly fanaticism,[90] and Bismarck exploited the episode by insisting that the Prussian government take sharper measures against both Catholic and socialist agitators, including the closing of numerous Catholic associations and prosecution of newspapers.[91] In early December the Kullmann affair led to a rancorous scene in the Reichstag. During an attack on Bismarck's foreign policy, the Bavarian centrist Edmund Jörg referred in passing to Kullmann's deed as the "crime of a half-crazy man." After replying to Jörg's criticisms of his policies, Bismarck produced an uproar by twice hurling at centrists sitting in front of him the charge: "Try to free yourselves from this murderer as you wish, he clings firmly to your coattails. He calls you *his* party!" Amid the storm of applause and protest that raged through the hall was heard a loud "Phooey!" from centrist deputy Count Bal-

[87] *RGB* (1874), pp. 43–44; *GSP* (1874), pp. 135–142.

[88] *SEG* (1874), pp. 98–99, 543–548.

[89] Kohl, ed., *Bismarck-Regesten*, II, 92–93.

[90] *SEG* (1874), p. 154.

[91] Arthur von Brauer, *Im Dienste Bismarcks* (Berlin, 1936), p. 38. A secretary in the foreign office, Brauer was charged with the task of urging other German governments to take similar measures, but with scant success.

lestrem. Bismarck reached for the pistol in his pocket, measured the distance, and considered whether to aim at the stomach or between the eyes. But he settled for a verbal bullet. "Phooey is an expression of loathing and scorn. Don't think that such feelings are foreign to me; I am just too polite to express them."[92] The tumult that followed lasted for minutes, the deputies applauding, hissing, gesticulating. Lucius feared a fistfight would erupt. So did Forckenbeck, who was presiding, and sent for his hat. But the clamor finally subsided. "That evening," Lucius reported, "Bismarck was in a particularly good mood, as after a satisfying action."[93]

With Bismarck it is never easy to distinguish between tactic and belief, calculation and sentiment. Certainly he exploited Kullmann's deed to win public sympathy, as he had that of Ferdinand Cohen-Blind in 1866.[94] To the same end he kept the courts busy during 1874–1875 trying cases of libel and slander. The cases were so numerous that Arthur von Brauer, the official charged with initiating these cases, drafted a standard form that could be quickly filled out and dispatched to the prosecutor's office. No offender who came to Bismarck's attention, not even the lowliest, escaped. Brauer could remember only one case that was not processed, that of a drunken Catholic reported to have said, "Bismarck can kiss my arse." The report came back from the chancellor's desk with a reply: "He mine also!" Again personal and political motives were mixed. Bismarck wanted to show the country how shamelessly its greatest statesman was being abused, but also to cripple the ultramontane and socialist newspapers with fines.[95]

By this time threatening letters were common in Bismarck's mail, and he felt his life was in constant danger. No more did he sally forth from his quarters in the Wilhelmstrasse without an armed guard. The pistols of his two would-be assassins fascinated him. Blind's had been purchased by Delbrück and given to the chancellor as a present; Kullmann's was purchased by Bismarck himself from the Bavarian state's attorney. The two weapons lay on his desk, and he often regaled vistors with detailed accounts of both episodes. They were not, however, mere souvenirs. In December 1874 a guest at a parliamentary soirée picked up Blind's pistol for a closer look, and the weapon discharged.[96] The prince, it appears, no longer knew what to expect of people

[92] BR, VI, 214–223; Heinrich Eduard Brockhaus, Stunden mit Bismarck, 1871–1878 (Leipzig, 1929), pp. 116–117.

[93] Lucius, Bismarck-Erinnerungen, pp. 59–60.

[94] Since the court proceedings against Kullmann, who was sentenced to fourteen years imprisonment, did not reveal his party affiliation, Bismarck sought out witnesses who had heard the culprit say that the center was "my party." Their testimony was released to the press. GW, XIV, 866; SEG (1874), pp. 208–242. On the Cohen-Blind affair see Julius H. Schoeps, Bismarck und sein Attentäter: Der Revolveranschlag, Unter den Linden am 7. Mai 1866 (Berlin, 1984).

[95] Brauer, Im Dienste Bismarcks, pp. 30–31.

[96] BP, I, 83–84, Lucius, Bismarck-Erinnerungen, pp. 60–62, 68. The room was crowded, but no one was hit. On entering Bismarck's quarters at Bad Gastein (Sept. 17, 1877), the Italian

who entered his office. His reaction to Ballestrem's "Phooey!" shows what was on his mind. His next assailant would receive a bullet from the pistol of the first.

Evidently Bismarck genuinely believed that ultramontanes were guilty of having spurred Kullmann to his deed. Otherwise he would not have reacted so strongly, a few days after the altercation with Jörg, to the Reichstag's action in the Majunke affair. Paul Majunke was a priest, parliamentary deputy, and editor of *Germania*, which had become the chief voice of the ultramontanes. In the latter capacity he had been sentenced to a year's imprisonment for slandering the Kaiser, Bismarck, and other ministers, but evaded jail by going abroad. When the Reichstag session began, he took advantage of his presumed immunity as a parliamentary deputy and returned. On December 11, 1874, he was arrested by the Berlin police on orders from the same city court that was trying Harry von Arnim. Next day Lasker brought the matter to the attention of the Reichstag, which voted without debate or dissent to refer the case to its rules committee for quick investigation. In the committee there was doubt whether the wording of the constitution actually foreclosed an arrest on a conviction that had preceded the opening of the session. But it was also evident that many national liberals had begun to have second thoughts about the issue. On December 16, the committee reported itself unable to make a recommendation. By a narrow vote, 158 to 151, the chamber rejected a motion to table and then approved Hoverbeck's motion for a constitutional amendment that would "preserve the dignity of the Reichstag" by making impossible the arrest of a deputy during the session without its permission. Lasker's group joined progressives and centrists to form the majority.[97]

Bismarck's reaction to these events was astounding. On December 13, 1874, Lucius reported him "extremely indignant" over the vote to refer the Majunke case to committee. By its "tactless" failure to ascertain beforehand the government's position, the Reichstag "has confirmed my conviction that one cannot govern with such parliamentary bodies and my intention to withdraw from all [governmental] affairs in my sixtieth year. Lasker is not happy unless he can execute a freedom caper against the government."[98] On Decem-

---

statesman Francesco Crispi was startled to note "a small pistol with a white grip on the table." *GW*, VIII, 216.

[97] *SBR* (1874–1875), I, 628–629, 725–757; IV, No. 125. Ludolf Parisius, *Leopold Freiherr von Hoverbeck* (Berlin, 1897–1900), II, 308–311.

[98] Lucius, *Bismarck-Erinnerungen*, pp. 62–63. At the Crown Council held on Dec. 18, Wilhelm gave his view of the gravity of the situation: "for the first time the leaders of the extreme parties have succeeded on an important issue in creating a majority, from which the formation of a cabinet would be impossible." *DZA* Merseburg, Rep. 90a, B, III, 2c, Nr. 3, Vol. 4. Unrequited overtures to the Progressive party may also have been one of the reasons for Bismarck's anger over the Majunke episode and the Hoverbeck motion. According to one source, the chancellor had made an effort at rapprochement with the progressives during 1874 in the hope of building a new base of support in both liberal parties against the Center and conservatives. If so, it came to an abrupt end. Parisius, *Parteien*, p. 200; *BP*, I, 85–87.

ber 16, Bennigsen found the chancellor "in a frightful turmoil, such as I have never seen before. He said repeatedly that he must resign, that he could not put up any longer with the annoyances at court and with an uncertain Reichstag majority. 'I have already been shot at twice. Daily I receive warnings from the police not to go walking any more or to travel in an open carriage. Now let another chancellor be shot at by fanaticized Catholic workmen.' " Bismarck's wife and daughter, Bennigsen concluded, were exciting him more and more with their cares and anxieties. Princess Bismarck, with whom the deputy had a long talk, "seriously believes there is a great ultramontane murder conspiracy, which could order new attempts at assassination at any time."[99] Next day the deputy Frankenberg recorded in his diary: "This morning the news spread like wild fire: Bismarck has handed in his resignation. The Reichstag looked like a disturbed beehive."[100]

At a parliamentary dinner held on December 17 in the chancellor's quarters, Bismarck spoke to deputies Bennigsen, Miquel, Wehrenpfennig, and Löwe about "the grave occurrence in the Reichstag." He would resign, he was quoted as saying, because the previous day's vote had shown that he no longer had a majority in the Reichstag. "The National Liberal party lacks a firm leadership and has no recognized leader. Bennigsen would be incomparably preferable in that capacity to Lasker, whom the prince holds for a good soldier, but a bad general. He demanded that the majority seek contact with him and that he be able to depend upon it with greater certainty than previously." In voting for the Hoverbeck resolution, Lasker and forty members of the National Liberal party had sided with his "most extreme opponents, the Center party." The deputies tried to assuage him, pointing out that the issue was the Reichstag's internal affair, that the chancellor was in no way bound by the Hoverbeck resolution, and that in any case the matter was not of an "urgent nature." But Bismarck continued to insist that his request to step down was a fait accompli. Since there was no likelihood that the Kaiser would let Bismarck go, the deputies left the Wilhelmstrasse knowing that they must either appease "sulking Achilles" or face a dissolution and reelection of the Reichstag.[101]

Unwittingly Ludwig Windthorst provided them with a solution. Undisputed leader of the Center party since Mallinckrodt's death in May, Windthorst was on the alert for issues that, like the Hoverbeck resolution, might spark another oppositional majority. On December 18, he moved that the foreign office's "disposition fund" be abolished. Like the notorious "Guelph fund," this appropriation was secretly dispensed by the chancellor to influence the press (Windthorst spoke of "the general purchase of public opinion"). In the past it had often been the target of liberal criticism. But this time the

[99] Oncken, *Bennigsen*, II, 274.
[100] Poschinger, ed., *Bismarck-Portefeuille*, II, 179.
[101] BP, I, 84–85.

centrist leader blundered, for Bennigsen seized the chance to deliver a rousing defense of Bismarck's achievements in foreign affairs. He treated the chancellor's "extreme irritability" not as a personal weakness, but as a natural consequence of malicious attacks upon him by those seeking to undermine the "institutions of the German Reich and German national policy." He converted the retention of the disposition fund into a general vote of confidence in Bismarck's leadership. Windthorst's motion was overwhelmed, 199 to 71, the minority being composed of centrists, Poles, socialists, and one maverick democrat. Apprised of the result, Bismarck, resplendent in full uniform, strode into the chamber, mounted the dais, and grasped the speaker, Forckenbeck, by the hand. The chamber erupted in "stormy applause."[102]

Windthorst and Lasker

There was no rational motive for Bismarck's violent reaction to the Reichstag's conduct in the Majunke affair. The unanimity of the decision to refer the matter to committee shows that the action was procedural, not substantive. The Hoverbeck resolution had no binding effect on the government; without Bismarck's consent no constitutional amendment could have passed the Bundesrat. Whether even the Reichstag would have passed it was dubious.[103] Nor was there any evident reason why at the time a parliamentary crisis would have been useful to Bismarck. In recent years the Reichstag and Prussian Chamber of Deputies had, with some compromises, passed the statutes he considered vital. Majorities had been found for the Kulturkampf laws, iron budget, and press act. By initiating a statute creating an imperial bank, the Reichstag had contributed significantly to Bismarck's program for the consolidation of the Reich. Progress was being made in drafting imperial law codes that would further the same purpose. Barring a dissolution, the next parliamentary election was two years distant. On December 11–14, 1874— that is, during the days when the Majunke affair boiled over—the Reichstag deliberated on military appropriations in the annual budget. On the Reichstag's insistence the appropriation was discussed for the first time by item rather than as a lump sum (*Pauschquantum*); yet the debate went smoothly, and even the Kaiser was satisfied with the result.[104] At dinner on December 13 Bismarck himself said repeatedly, "Everything has been going well." "Then sud-

[102] SBR (1874–1875), II, 806–812; Oncken, *Bennigsen*, II, 275–278.

[103] In Jan. 1875, the progressives introduced a constitutional amendment to eliminate the loophole that had permitted Majunke's arrest. But the bill did not reach the floor of the chamber before adjournment. SBR (1874–1875), IV, No. 156; Parisius, *Hoverbeck*, II, 310–312. During the next session the bill was defeated, 142 to 127. Eighteen members of the National Liberal party's left wing followed Stauffenberg in abstaining. SBR (1875–1876), I, 472–499; SEG (1875), p. 205.

[104] SBR (1874–1875), I, 597–672; BP, I, 67; Lucius, *Bismarck-Erinnerungen*, p. 61.

denly," he continued, "a sharp wind blows out of a side alley and upsets everything."[105]

Bismarck's conduct in the Majunke affair shows how subject German politics had become to his physical and mental health. The letters of his wife to their eldest son, then on the staff of the Prussian legation in Munich, provide an intimate account of the fluctuations in his health during the critical winter of 1874–1875. During the autumn months at Varzin she reported his condition as "fairly good," but complained repeatedly of a "terrible, never-ending cough."[106] At Berlin in late November the weather turned frigid. "It's freezing here, stone and bone, as they say" and *Papachen* caught cold, producing abdominal pains "as earlier in Varzin." After a Reichstag speech on December 1, his condition worsened—acute stomach disorder "accompanied by severe and unceasing heartburn." What physicians prescribed seemed merely to worsen his condition. Buoyed perhaps by his fierce response to the ultramontane attack (Jörg) on his foreign policy on December 4, he was "much better" for a few days,[107] but the improvement did not last. During the rest of December and into January 1875, Johanna reported, her husband suffered "difficult nights—just a few hours sleep in the morning, not enough to rid him of fatigue, which remains in his limbs the entire day. No desire to eat whatever, absolutely no interest in wine, and frequent heartburn as before. All of this distresses and upsets me very much and, in addition, hate letters and newspaper clippings constantly arrive threatening my beloved's life."[108] The hand wounded by Kullmann continued to ache, a constant reminder of danger.[109] From the physician Struck, Lucius heard, "The princess influences him also with her fears of assassination and makes him anxious."[110] "For weeks he has suffered from insomnia," Johanna confided to Tiedemann. "He can't sleep because he gets so angry, and then he gets very angry because he can't sleep."[111]

"Anger and hate are bad counselors in politics, and I pray to God for humility and forgiveness," Bismarck had written to the Kaiser, shortly after Kullmann's attack.[112] Yet the anger welled up in him and affected both his health and his political judgment. By recording in his diary what he observed in the

---

[105] Lucius, *Bismarck-Erinnerungen*, p. 62.

[106] Johanna von Bismarck to Herbert von Bismarck, Aug. 28, Sept. 9, 14, 19, 24, 28, Oct. 22, 24, 25, and Nov. 5, 1874. BFA, Bestand C, Box 6.

[107] Johanna to Herbert, Dec. 4 and 8, 1874. *Ibid.*

[108] Johanna to Herbert, Jan. 16, 1875. *Ibid.* Bismarck, she reported, was being treated with "Animi powder for strength" and "atropine pills for the stomach." Johanna to Herbert, Jan. 27. *Ibid.*

[109] GW, VIc, 56; XIV, 861–862.

[110] Diary entry of Oct. 27, 1875. Lucius, *Bismarck-Erinnerungen*, p. 75.

[111] Christoph von Tiedemann, *Sechs Jahre Chef der Reichskanzlei unter dem Fürsten Bismarck* (2d ed., Leipzig, 1910), pp. 13, 18. On Jan. 18, 1875, he told Tiedemann, "I have not slept for three nights and have eaten practically nothing for three days." *Ibid.*, p. 3.

[112] GW, XIV, 861.

JOHANNA VON BISMARCK IN 1873. (FÜRST HERBERT BISMARCK, ED., *FÜRST BISMARCK'S BRIEFE AN SEINE BRAUT UND GATTIN*, J. G. COTTA'SCHE BUCHHANDLUNG NACHFOLGER G.M.B.H., STUTTGART, 1900.)

Bismarck household at dinner on January 25, 1875, Christoph von Tiedemann has unwittingly given us vital clues to the interaction between anger, insomnia, appetite, and physical health as they affected Bismarck's psychic state and personal conduct at this critical time in his life. As mentioned earlier,[113] Bismarck astounded Tiedemann by complaining that he lacked appetite, then proceeding to consume two portions of every course, including

[113] See pp. 52–53.

pickled boar's head (over Johanna's protests), chased by long draughts of beer from a large silver tankard. On that occasion he had two men on his mind: Windthorst and Lasker. A philosophical discussion about Schopenhauer, Eduard von Hartmann, and Goethe came around with seeming inevitability to what was uppermost in his thoughts: "And Goethe has been almost always loved, seldom hated. Yet hate is as great a spur to life as love. Two things preserve and embellish my life: my wife and—Windthorst. The one is there for love, the other for hate." Later that evening he went through the catechism of his dislikes: those "feminine influences" that complicated the Kulturkampf; the "many privy counselors in the ministries" who were "warm friends of the ultramontanes"; those "quite cracked conservatives" who were "blind with hatred against everything that is called liberal"; and "part of the national liberals with whom nothing can be accomplished. Their doctrines work like blinders, and it is a pity that a man like Lasker can play such a role. Lasker is the real disease that infects the state; he is even more of a disease-bearing louse than Windthorst."[114]

Bismarck's rage at Windthorst reveals the degree of his frustration over his failure to overcome the resistance of the Center either by browbeating the Catholic hierarchy or by appealing to the nationalistic and patriotic instincts of Catholic voters. But it also shows the rising personal cost of the struggle. The alienation of old friends and their cries of betrayal tore at his nerves and upset his psychic balance. Their apostasy made him more dependent upon liberal allies who, although hardly a serious threat, were basically distasteful to him. In particular, it galled him that this "dumb Jew boy" Lasker had been elevated by an election that was the product of the Kulturkampf into a potentially commanding position in the Reichstag.[115] The mere fact that Lasker appeared to have that possibility of alternate choice, Bismarck's own favorite position in politics, disturbed the prince, even though the record of the preceding year did not justify the assumption that the deputy either would or could exploit it to become a serious threat. With jaundiced eye the prince watched every action in the chamber that seemed to indicate that Lasker's influence was growing. Hence he blew the Majunke affair up into a major crisis in his relationship with parliament. His emotions got the better of his political judgment.

High Point of the Kulturkampf

If not responsible for details of the May laws of 1873–1874, Bismarck was unquestionably the driving force behind the more drastic legislation of 1875. "For me," he said, "the first consideration of the moment is to fight ultramon-

---

[114] Tiedemann, Sechs Jahre, pp. 14–16.
[115] Erich Förster, Adalbert Falk: Sein Leben und Wirken als preussischer Kultusminister (Gotha, 1927), p. 485.

tanism; everything else is secondary."[116] Increasingly he was dissatisfied with the efforts of his colleagues and subordinates. "Falk believes he can fight ul- tramontanes with velvet gloves, but iron claws are appropriate." "Falk is a captious lawyer; he doesn't go for the whole, but only pulls single gray hairs out of the black pelt." "Falk proceeds too slowly and timidly; we must clear the road; that is, we want now to bring the matter to the point of bending or breaking."[117] "Daily I have to complain about the conduct of my colleagues. All too often they act as though the task were entirely that of solving legal problems. . . . The minister of interior [Eulenburg] does not generally pro- ceed with the desirable energy."[118] He urged upon his colleagues "a purifica- tion of officialdom" in the Catholic provinces. The bureaucratic "organs" of state must be staffed with men capable of pursuing with independent zeal and initiative the policy of the state against "the hostile influence of the clergy." The state must employ "every legal means within its power to break resistance to the authority of the law." To do anything less was to underestimate the severity of the struggle and responsibility of the government. What new laws, he wondered, would be "necessary to break the influence of the priests?"[119] What vexed Bismarck about the May laws was not their severity, but their failure to deploy the power of the state adequately to demoralize the foe. While keeping prosecutors and courts busy, they merely irritated Catholic clergy and laymen into greater resistance.

During 1875 the actions of the papacy and the Prussian bishops provided him with provocation for further action. On February 5 Pius IX issued an encyclical that boldly declared Prussia's May laws "invalid, since they contra- vene completely the divine dispositions of the church." The bishops were admonished to stand fast against the state's incursions. "As it is written, one must obey God more than men."[120] The answer of the Prussian government was the so-called "suspension and breadbasket act" (Sperr- und Brotkorbge- setz). Enacted into law on April 22, 1875, the statute suspended most of the state's annual subsidy (889,718 out of 1,011,745 thalers) to the Catholic church. In the hope of dividing the clergy, it provided that bishops who ob- ligated themselves in writing to obey Kulturkampf laws would have their al- locations restored.[121] In reply, Prussia's bishops petitioned the king and House

[116] To Tiedemann in Jan. 1875. Tiedemann, Sechs Jahre, p. 3.

[117] Lucius, Bismarck-Erinnerungen, pp. 57–58 (late Nov. 1874) and p. 72 (Apr. 11, 1875).

[118] To the national liberal deputy Ludwig Seyffardt, Jan. 22, 1875. BP, II, 233–234.

[119] To the Prussian cabinet, Mar. 13, 1875. GW, VIc, 56–57. See also Tiedemann, Sechs Jahre, p. 27 (Apr. 24, 1875). Ronald Ross has described in piquant detail the combination of legal and administrative obstacles, financial exigencies, and clerical evasions that frustrated effective exe- cution of government policy in the Kulturkampf. See his "Enforcing the Kulturkampf: The Bis- marckian State and the Limits of Coercion in Imperial Germany," Journal of Modern History, 56 (1984), pp. 456–482.

[120] SEG (1875), pp. 54–55, 408–411.

[121] GSP (1875), pp. 194–196; Erich Schmidt-Volkmar, Der Kulturkampf in Deutschland 1871– 1890 (Göttingen, 1962), pp. 138–140.

BISMARCK AND THE POPE AT CHESS. PIUS IX CONTEMPLATES HIS NEXT MOVE (AN ENCYCLICAL). THE
CARTOONIST PREDICTED IT WOULD BE HIS LAST—"AT LEAST IN GERMANY." WILHELM SCHOLZ IN
KLADDERADATSCH, 1875.

of Lords, deploring "disorder," but refusing to make any such pledge.[122] Bismarck found the petition "highly impertinent" and now insisted on a statute (June 18, 1875) abolishing three articles in the constitution: article 15, which granted to the Evangelical, Catholic, and other churches the right of autonomous administration; article 16, which granted to the Catholic church the right to communicate with Rome; and article 18, which abolished the power of the state to nominate, elect, and confirm candidates for church offices.[123] Another statute of June 20, 1875, removed church property from the bishop's administration and placed it under a committee elected by the congregation. The capstone of all Kulturkampf legislation was laid in early May with the passage of the "congregations statute," ordering the dissolution within six months of all cloisters not engaged in healing or teaching.[124]

In whipping these statutes through the Prussian cabinet and Landtag, Bismarck encountered his greatest problem not from legislators, but from his king and colleagues. For three years he had advocated excision of the three offending articles in the constitution. Before there could be peace, he told Hohen-

[122] *SBHH* (1875), I, 409, 657.
[123] Lucius, *Bismarck-Erinnerungen*, p. 72; GSP (1875), p. 259.
[124] GSP (1875), pp. 217–218, 241–255. The congregations (or cloisters) act also proved to be much less effective than foreseen. Two-thirds of the more than 900 religious foundations existing in the Hohenzollern monarchy provided medical and educational services that the state could not readily replace. Only 189 houses were closed during the two years that followed passage of the statute; only 340 by the end of the Kulturkampf. Ross, "Enforcing the Kulturkampf," pp. 468–472.

lohe, Prussian law had to be "purged" of all those elements that "since the time of Friedrich Wilhelm IV have confused the relationship between church and state."[125] But the ministers resisted his drastic step, which affected the Protestant as well as Catholic church. To break their resistance, Bismarck had to deploy his ultimate weapon—the threat of resignation. Properly interpreted, this was actually a threat to get the Kaiser to dismiss the other ministers by forcing the ruler to choose between them and Bismarck. When it came to dissolution of the cloisters, Wilhelm was the greatest obstacle. Visiting in Wiesbaden, the monarch was temporarily out of Bismarck's reach, but well within range of Empress Augusta, who was sympathetic to the Catholic cause. Wilhelm insisted that the law exclude nursing orders and allow teaching orders four years to dissolve. For once Bismarck let him have his way.[126]

Neither house of the Landtag presented much difficulty. In the Chamber of Deputies the Center party and its Polish and Guelph allies fought practically alone against these draconian laws. Progressives and national liberals vied with one another in baiting ultramontane deputies, particularly Windthorst, who sought to define the issue as one of religious liberty. Among liberals voting en masse for amendments to the constitution were, ironically, some who in 1848–1850 had striven mightily for inclusion and retention of clauses guaranteeing freedom of thought, expression, and religion. Bismarck, who actively defended most of the bills in both houses of the legislature, clashed sharply with old friends—Ludwig von Gerlach, now allied with centrists in the Chamber of Deputies, and Hans von Kleist-Retzow, leader of the ultras in the House of Lords. Gerlach interpreted the *Sperrgesetz* as a declaration of war against one-third of Prussia's population and an affirmation of the deified state; the state is God, and the *Kultusminister* is his prophet. But Bismarck denied any belief in the "heathen Godhead of state" and reaffirmed his faith in the trinity: "God, King, and Country." Gerlach was isolated among conservative deputies, all of whom voted for this and the other laws.[127] Even in the House of Lords the resistance was less than expected, for some "feudalists" who had voted against the May laws were unable to countenance the pope's attempted "invalidation" of Prussian statutes. In balloting on the *Sperrgesetz* on April 15, 1875, thirty peers followed Kleist-Retzow in opposing the bill, which passed with a majority of 91. Bismarck praised the majority for building "a bridge with which to reunite" the Conservative party, whose division had caused him "great injury." But the bridge was shaky. One hundred and fifteen unexcused peers did not vote. The cloister bill and constitutional amendments passed by an even smaller vote, 66 to 24 and 69 to 24. The

[125] To Hohenlohe, Mar. 26, 1875. GW, VIII, 140–141. See also his similar statement to Károlyi, Apr. 17, 1875, reported in Schmidt-Volkmar, *Kulturkampf*, p. 141.

[126] GW, VIc, 57–58.

[127] SBHA (1875), II, 839–844, 893–895.

number of abstentions was ominous—114 on the first vote, 103 on the second.[128]

Although the Kulturkampf's origin must be sought in Bismarck's genuine anxiety about the advance of Polonism in eastern Prussia and about the dangers of political Catholicism for Germany's foreign relations and internal consolidation, he sought to exploit it to build up a reliable parliamentary majority. During the debate on the *Sperrgesetz* in the lower chamber, he spoke of the Kulturkampf as "an extraordinarily useful school" for statesmen. The deputies were learning that the state must be strengthened against subversive parties. "The consequence of this will be that with time we shall have only two parties—one that negates the state and fights it, the other composed of patriotic, loyally inclined, respectable people. . . . This great party will take shape, and it will ultimately embrace all parties that want the state at all. These parties are now already coming closer together." Those on the extreme right, he continued, had become "more open, more modern"; those on the left, to "recognize the indispensability of the state." "All the earlier sins in political life have given way to repentance and conversion . . . and the patriotic majority has become larger and stronger."[129]

During the Kulturkampf it was an open question as to who was making the greater gains: Bismarck or his liberal allies. Thinking that they had the better part of the bargain, liberals of both parties were increasingly reluctant to challenge the government on any important issue of power. They watched Bismarck, Wilhelm, and most conservatives march down the broadening path of modernization in economic and cultural life and were only too happy to bulldoze away the obstacles. For Bismarck the Kulturkampf became, among other things, a tool for political consolidation. Through it he hoped to weld together a large and subservient parliamentary majority that could be used on other political fronts. By pointing to a common foe, he hoped to give liberals and conservatives, bourgeois and aristocrats a common cause. In the spring of 1875 this tactic appeared to have achieved some success.[130] Whether it would suffice to hold the majority together on major issues unrelated to the Kulturkampf remained to be seen.

[128] *SBHH* (1875), I, 219–272, 320–339, 363–383, 409–413, 651.

[129] *BR*, VI, 256.

[130] This tactic does not suffice to explain either the origins of the Kulturkampf in Bismarck's thought and action or the actual course of German politics in the 1870s and 1880s. It was the expedient by-product of a struggle begun for other purposes, another demonstration of his capacity to perceive and strike at more than one target in any developing political action. See the author's "Bismarcks Herrschaftstechnik als Problem der Historiographie," *Historische Zeitschrift*, 234 (1982), pp. 561–599.

✦ℐ⊱✦

Reconstruction in Foreign Relations

N RECENT works historians have tended to see in almost every facet of Bismarck's diplomacy, including the wars of unification, evidence that the chancellor was motivated by the "primacy of domestic policy" (*Primat der Innenpolitik*). According to this view, his foreign no less than his domestic policy aimed at consolidating the power of the German "ruling classes"—that is, the agrarian, industrial, and financial elites—against the social and political ambitions of lesser interest groups and social classes. Foreign policy was harnessed to a number of defensive strategies whose purpose was to buttress the Prussian-German establishment against social and political democratization in an age of industrialization and modernization.[1] This interpretation does not suffice in itself to explain German foreign policy before or after 1871. Seldom is hard evidence to be found that economic or social strategies were primary in determining Bismarck's course in foreign affairs. We shall see that on significant occasions the predominant evidence points rather to the contrary. "Foreign policy and economic affairs must never be combined with one another," he declared in the 1890s. "Each is balanced within itself. If one of them is burdened by the other, the equilibrium is lost."[2]

The high-level diplomatic correspondence of the great nations in the nineteenth and early twentieth centuries contains few references to the requirements of foreign trade, foreign investment, pressure from special interests, and the need to seek abroad the safety valve for domestic discontents. Instead the dispatches are full of reports and speculation on the attitudes of rulers and foreign ministers, changing alignments and realignments among states, alter-

---

[1] See Helmut Böhme, *Deutschlands Weg zur Grossmacht: Studien zum Verhältnis von Wirtschaft und Staat während der Reichsgründungszeit 1848–1881* (Cologne 1966) and "Politik und Ökonomie in der Reichsgründungs- und späten Bismarckzeit," in Michael Stürmer, ed., *Das kaiserliche Deutschland 1870–1918* (Düsseldorf, 1970), pp. 26–50; Hans-Ulrich Wehler, ed., *Der Primat der Innenpolitik* (Berlin, 1965; 3d ed., 1976), *Bismarck und der Imperialismus* (Cologne, 1969), and *Das deutsche Kaiserreich 1871–1918* (Göttingen, 1973), translated as *The German Empire, 1871–1918* (Dover, 1985); Dietrich Geyer, *Der russische Imperialismus: Studien über den Zusammenhang von innerer und auswärtiger Politik 1860–1914. Kritische Studien zur Geschichtswissenschaft*, vol. 27 (Göttingen, 1977); Heinz Wolter, *Bismarcks Aussenpolitik, 1871–1881* (Berlin-East, 1983).

[2] To Hermann Hoffmann, editor of the *Hamburger Nachrichten*, in the 1890s. GW, IX, 400. Other similar utterances spread over a period of three decades show that the separability of economic and political objectives (and the ultimate primacy of the latter over the former) in foreign affairs was for Bismarck a consistent principle. To Werther, Apr. 9, 1863, in Helmut Böhme, ed., *Die Reichsgründung* (Munich, 1967), pp. 132–133. To the Reichstag on Dec. 12, 1876; BR, VI, 450–459. To a Hungarian correspondent, Mar. 5, 1880; GW, XIV, 914. To Sidney Whitman in mid-October 1891; GW, IX, 158.

nating fears of isolation and entanglement, shifts in the balance of power engendered by those fears, and the changed margins of safety and danger those shifts produce. These concerns are not phantasmagoria, but real dangers that can affect not only the future of governments, but also the security and welfare of millions. No less than party politics in a parliamentary system, politics among states reflects a struggle for power that can transcend the demands of material interest and ideological commitment. Within such systems the competing units tend to become functions of one another; the most irreconcilable interests are compelled to take each other into account in their search for security or aggrandizement. The mastery of these dynamic, ever-fluctuating relationships is the task of statecraft. Never was any statesman more conscious than Bismarck of this task and the requirements it imposes. His first aim after the victory of 1870–1871 was to escape the isolation that was the predictable cost of a unilateral disruption of the balance of power system.

Limits of the German Nation

Nowhere was apprehension concerning Bismarck's further intentions after the victory over France more acute than in Great Britain. Suspicion of Napoleon III and belief in the justice of the German desire for national unity had prejudiced British opinion in favor of Germany at the beginning of the war, but this mood quickly evaporated after the battle of Sedan. Now the realization dawned that the eclipse of France meant the supremacy of Germany. In parliament Benjamin Disraeli, leader of the opposition, depicted in dire terms the consequences of what the Gladstone government had presumably permitted to happen. "This war represents the German revolution, a greater political event than the French revolution. I don't say a greater, or as great a social event. What its social consequences may be are in the future. Not a single principle in the management of our foreign affairs, accepted by all statesmen for guidance up to six months ago, any longer exists. There is not a diplomatic tradition that has not been swept away. You have a new world, new influences at work, new and unknown objects and dangers with which to cope. . . . The balance of power has been entirely destroyed, and the country that suffers most, and feels the effects of this great change most, is England."[3] The Germanophile Sir Robert Morier rejoiced "at this great turning-point" in the history of Europe as well as Germany. Yet he too feared that "unparalleled successes" and the "absolute power that the German nation has acquired over Europe" would tend "to modify the German national character, and not necessarily for the better. Arrogance and overbearingness are the qualities likely to be developed in a Teutonic race under such conditions, not boasting or

[3] George Earle Buckle, *The Life of Benjamin Disraeli, Earl of Beaconsfield* (New York, 1920), V, 133–134.

vaingloriousness."[4] The German demand for Alsace-Lorraine also aroused forebodings. Gladstone himself anticipated that "this violent laceration and transfer" would be "the *beginning* of a new series of European complications."[5] Odo Russell, British ambassador in Berlin after 1871, believed that the chancellor's objective was "the supremacy of Germany in Europe and of the German race in the world" and that he would "go any lengths" to achieve this end. The annexation appeared to be a step toward the unification of German-speaking Europe under the government in Berlin.[6]

Statesmen in southern Germany and Austria suspected even before 1870 that Bismarck had such a goal. For Count Friedrich von Beust, the Austro-Hungarian chancellor, the greatest danger in the union of northern and southern Germany lay not in the growth of Prussian power, undesirable as that was, but in the attraction that a unified Germany would have for the German population of the Habsburg Empire. He was convinced that Prussia, if she gained control over the south, would not halt at the Austrian border, but would inevitably seek to found a great-German empire stretching all the way to the Adriatic Sea.[7] In July 1870 the Austro-Hungarian Minister of War Baron Franz Kuhn von Kuhnenfeld expressed the fears of the war party in Vienna when he wrote, "If Prussia is victorious and we remain neutral, it will be a certainty that the Prussian king, proclaimed Kaiser of Germany immediately after the great victory, will declare that all German kings have lost their thrones and will unite the great German Reich under the scepter of the Hohenzollern. The Prussian spiked helmet will stand on the River Inn and it would perhaps be only a question of time how long the German provinces of Austria would remain under Austrian rule. Prussians on the Inn means Finis Austriae. The rule of the Hohenzollern would then stretch from the North Sea to the Adriatic over sixty million Germans. . . . Hungary alone would remain as a refuge state for the house of Habsburg, for powerful Germany will not suffer *the* German river, the Danube, to remain in alien hands. Germany will incorporate the whole stream to the Rumanian border and destroy the empire of the Magyars."[8]

Both before and after the war of 1870 the French government sought to

[4] Rosslyn Wemyss, *Memoirs and Letters of the Right Honorable Sir Robert Morier* (London, 1911), II, 165–181, 242–244.

[5] John Morley, *The Life of William Ewart Gladstone* (New York, 1903), II, 348.

[6] Edmond Fitzmaurice, *The Life of George Leveson Gower, Second Earl Granville* (London, 1911), II, 111–114; Lord Newton, *Life of Lord Lyons* (London, 1913), II, 41, 53. For further British reactions see Klaus Hildebrand, "Grossbritannien und die deutsche Reichsgründung," in Eberhard Kolb, ed., *Europa und die Reichsgründung: Preussen-Deutschland in der Sicht der grossen europäischen Mächte, 1860–1880. Historische Zeitschrift*, Beiheft, Neue Folge, No. 6 (1980), pp. 9–62.

[7] Heinrich Potthoff, *Die deutsche Politik Beusts* (Bonn, 1968), pp. 382–383.

[8] Potthoff, *Deutsche Politik Beusts*, pp. 383–384. Such thoughts were not unknown to Beust's successor, Count Julius Andrássy. Eduard von Wertheimer, *Graf Julius Andrássy: Sein Leben und seine Zeit* (Vienna, 1910–1913), II, 110.

exploit against Prussia the latent fears in St. Petersburg that Russia too would be affected by the movement for a German national state. On being posted as ambassador to Russia in October 1869, Count Émile Fleury was instructed to warn the Russian chancellor, Prince Alexander Gorchakov, that the "Germanic idea" would be a danger to Europe; if it continued to grow, the concept would "naturally encompass within its sphere of action all populations that speak German—from Courland to Alsace."[9] In July 1871 Jules Favre, foreign minister of the Thiers regime, instructed the new ambassador to Russia, General Le Flô, to point out to the Russians that the "principle of German unity" invoked by Prussia to justify her territorial aggrandizement must inevitably lead to the attempt to acquire "all peoples of German origin" on the Danube and likewise the "German provinces of Russia."[10]

From 1866, when the issue first arose, until the end of his life Bismarck consistently maintained that Berlin could not afford to display any official interest in the fate of either the German population in the Habsburg Empire or the German diaspora in Russia and the new world. Although "every German" regarded with sympathy the efforts of the Germans in Russia to preserve "their nationality and especially their language," he declared in 1870, any public display of that sympathy would be a disservice to the victims. It would merely arouse hopes for German assistance that were illusory, for "no real political interest" of Germany was involved. An attempt at intervention would merely confirm Russian suspicions that Germany had designs on the Baltic provinces. The tsarist Russification program would be intensified and German relations with Russia injured.[11] In July 1870 Hans Lothar von Schweinitz, north German envoy to Vienna, reported widespread apprehension on the Danube that Prussia, if victorious over France, would "devour" the German, and Russia the Slavic regions of the Habsburg Empire. Bismarck replied, "The suspicion that northern Germany could have the inclination or interest to destroy the Austrian monarchy is an absurdity that I have often exposed. The incorporation of so-called German Austria with its Czech and Slovenes in the North German Confederation would mean the destruction of the latter." No one, he continued, could visualize Vienna as a provincial city lying on the frontier of a German Reich. Statesmen on both sides of the Leitha must surely grasp that he regarded "every tendency toward German conquest of Austria is a folly that is outside national politics."[12]

Foreign diplomats who expected Bismarck to launch a pan-German policy were inaccurate not only in their judgment of his intentions, but also in their assessment of German public opinion and what influence it might have on foreign policy. The lively debate within the German intelligentsia between the advocates of a small-German (*kleindeutsch*) and great-German (*gross-*

9 *Les origines diplomatiques de la guerre de 1870/71* (Paris, 1910–1932), XXV, p. 377 (fn.).
10 Jules Favre to General Adolphe Le Flô, July 7, 1871. *DDF*, I, 39–40.
11 GW, VIb, 316–317. See also GW, VIb, 13; VIII, 45, 536, 567.
12 GW, VIb, 416–417. See also GW, VI, 53; VIII, 469–470, 475, 480, 567.

deutsch) unification had long since been resolved in favor of the former. The narrow victory of the small-Germanists in the Frankfurt parliament in 1848–1849, their success in capturing the academic community and the public press in the 1850s and 1860s through the activities of the Nationalverein, and the deepening economic cleavage between Austria and the Zollverein produced by Germany's rapid industrialization in the same period had all prepared the way for popular acceptance in 1866–1871 of the frontiers that Bismarck established. In common speech after 1871 "Germany" was no longer the land of Arndt ("*soweit die deutsche Zunge klingt*"), but that of Bismarck and the *kleindeutsch* movement. After the dissolution of the German confederation "Germany" and "Austria" identified two separate states, regions, and peoples.

The progressive contraction in the meaning of the term "Germany" can be traced in public documents. In the treaty of Nikolsburg in 1866 Kaiser Franz Joseph consented to "a reconstruction of Germany without participation of the Austrian imperial state." Amendments introduced into the German constitution in 1870–1871 anchored this narrower conception of the nation in the basic law of the Reich. The terms "German" and "German Reich" were substituted for "north German" and "North German Confederation." The preamble and first article defined the region of the German Reich by listing its member states, and Bismarck insisted on the title "Deutscher Kaiser" rather than "Kaiser von Deutschland." And yet later clauses identified the German Reich as "Germany." Particularly significant was article 3, which read, "For entire Germany there exists a common citizenship [Indigenat]. . . ." A Bundesrat committee charged with a final review of the amended constitution declared the expression "Germany" to be inaccurate, "for the German Reich obviously embraces regions inhabited by a population of non-German nationality, while other large regions exist next to and independent of the German Reich that are inhabited by genuinely German peoples [*Volksstämme*]." Yet the committee majority could not "bring itself" (in the words of the Baden minister Rudolf von Freydorf) to advise against using the term "Germany" in the constitution of a Reich that included most of German-speaking Europe.[13]

The expressions of the constitution were those used within the Reichstag and Bundesrat, the public press, and (one may assume) popular speech. The general public (except for ethnic minorities) quickly came to think of the German Reich as the "German national state." The word *Stamm* remained to identify subdivisions of the nation distinguished by territory, dialect and (according to tradition) tribal origin. This transformation occurred with surprising speed. In November 1871 a Bavarian particularist provoked derisive laughter in the Reichstag when he described the "German Reich" as com-

[13] Emil Meynen, *Deutschland und deutsches Reich: Sprachgebrauch und Begriffswesenheit des Wortes Deutschland* (Leipzig, 1935), pp. 75–78, 187–189.

posed of "nations" possessing "special characteristics" to be respected and pre-served.[14] To liberal-national deputies at least it was now ludicrous to apply the word "nation" to anything but the *kleindeutsch* Reich. Advocates of the "return" of Alsace-Lorraine did not necessarily look upon the German-speaking regions of Switzerland, Austria, Bohemia, and the Baltic as irredenta that must one day be recovered. On the contrary, Heinrich von Treitschke was vigorously applauded when he told the Reichstag in November 1871: "I believe that whoever works for the fall of Austria out of a fantastic sentimentality for our fellow Germans there acts, knowingly or unknowingly, as an enemy of the German Reich."[15] In later years German nationalists were sympathetic toward the struggle of Austrian Germans to maintain their traditional dominance within the Habsburg Empire, but few believed that the future of the "German nation" was involved in the outcome. Only socialists argued that separation from Austria was a tragic loss to the German people. Among Catholics there was considerable division and ambivalence. The views of some were indistinguishable from those of liberal nationalists, while others accepted, if regretfully, the irreversibility of the events of 1866–1871. Only a shrinking minority of "Reich Germans" appears to have deplored the contraction in the public mind concerning what constituted "Germany." The anguished reaction of the few who protested is itself proof that the contraction occurred. One who protested was Paul de Lagarde, who lamented that 45 million Reich Germans had tragically "forgotten" Austria-Hungary's 10 million Germans.[16] To the Austrian poet Franz Grillparzer it was an occasion for rhyme:[17]

> *Als Deutscher ward ich geboren*
> *Bin ich noch einer?*
> *Nur, was ich Deutsches geschrieben,*
> *Das nimmt mir keiner.*

Not until the emergence of "pan-Germanism" in the 1880s did the popular concept of the "German nation" begin to expand again from the region of the Reich to the region of German-speaking Europe. We shall see that Bismarck contributed, if unwittingly, to its progress.

[14] *SBR* (2d Session, 1871), p. 220. See also the discussion on Austrian Germans in the constituent Reichstag. *SBR* (1867), I, 111, 121, 125–126, 182.

[15] *SBR* (2d Session, 1871), pp. 600–601. See also Treitschke's essay "Österreich und das deutsche Reich," *Preussische Jahrbücher*, 28 (1871), pp. 667–682.

[16] Meynen, *Deutschland und deutsches Reich*, pp. 79–91; Paul de Lagarde, *Deutsche Schriften* (4th ed., Göttingen, 1903), pp. 166ff. On socialist attitudes see Hans Ulrich Wehler, *Sozialdemokratie und Nationalstaat* (Würzburg, 1962).

[17] Franz Grillparzer, "Für das Album einer deutschen Fürstin (1867)," in J. Minor, ed., *Franz Grillparzers Werke* (Stuttgart, no date), p. 128.

The Dynamics of Foreign Policy

On the evening of August 13, 1871, Bismarck granted a two-hour interview to the French chargé d'affaires in Berlin, in which he stated with brutal frankness what he expected from France. "The state of [public] opinion, the attitude of the press, and the language of the French government, which does not seem to favor good relations between our two countries, seem to indicate that you would like soon to have your revenge." France would pay 2 billion of its indemnity of 5 billion francs, he predicted, but would make war in 1874 rather than pay the rest. To fight "sooner rather than later" was best for Germany; to return to the battlefields in less than ten years would be "suicidal" for France. "But that is your affair."[18]

The French diplomat thought the chancellor had "exaggerated"; yet this was not the case. From the moment war was declared in July 1870, Bismarck firmly believed that France would never be reconciled to the loss of her position as the foremost power on the European continent. Whether history would have proved him right we cannot know, for the annexation of Alsace-Lorraine made his prophecy self-fulfilling. In order to gain a secure military barrier to the west he inflicted upon France an injury that no future French party or government could accept as permanent.

The enduring hostility of France seriously reduced the flexibility of the strategy of alternatives that Bismarck had employed with such devastating effect in the preceding decade. It was no longer possible to "hold open every door and every turning."[19] One door appeared to be permanently closed. But other factors also forced him to readjust his political tactics after 1871. During the preceding years he had exploited with great effect the fluid situation in European politics produced by the Crimean War and the upsurge of nationalism produced by the war of 1859 and its aftermath in Italy. The breach between Austria and Russia after 1855 and the fears generated by Napoleon's ambitious and blundering foreign policy after 1861 had opened the gates through which Prussia had passed. The growth of national sentiment had provided him with a moral justification for Prussia's expansion that made it palatable to German and European public opinion.

But now Germany, being a satiated state, needed time to digest what it had devoured. The task of German foreign policy was to shield the Reich from external danger during a period of internal consolidation. The moment had arrived to switch from a revolutionary to a conservative foreign policy. In Bismarck's opinion Germany no longer had any objective that could profitably be attained by war. In fact, any European military conflict involving two major powers was contrary to German interests. Whatever the origin, whoever the combatants, wherever the battlefield, Germany was likely to become

[18] Gabriac to Rémusat, Aug. 14, 1871. *DDF*, I, 61–65.
[19] See vol. 1, pp. 80–85.

involved. In such a war she would inevitably be trapped into fighting for someone else's interests. *Realpolitik* dictated that Germany strive to preserve the peace of Europe.

The dominant position achieved by Germany in European politics as a result of the victories over Austria and France and widespread suspicion of Bismarck's plans for exploiting it ought to have generated new alliances designed to redress the balance by holding Germany within its new frontiers. In his famous "Kissingen dictation," composed June 15, 1877, in the middle of the great Balkan crisis that led to the Congress of Berlin, Bismarck stated succinctly what bothered him, not only at that time, but also throughout the last two decades of his chancellorship. "A French newspaper recently said of me that I am afflicted by '*le cauchemar des coalitions*'; this kind of incubus will remain a justified concern to German ministers for a long time, perhaps forever. A coalition can be formed against us by west European powers with the addition of Austria; more dangerous still would be one composed of Russia-Austria-France. A great intimacy between two of the last named powers would provide the third at any time with the means of putting us under very painful pressure. . . . If able to work, I could develop and complete the picture that I visualize: not that of any territorial acquisition, but of a total political situation, in which all powers, except France, need us and are kept from coalitions against us as much as possible by their relations to each other."[20] The hostile alliance of Bismarck's nightmare had a significant historical precedent—the "Kaunitz coalition" of France-Austria-Russia that had come within a hair of depriving Frederick the Great of his greatness.[21]

The ideal "total situation," then, was one in which every European power (he would have included even France, if governed by an anticlerical republic) was bound to Germany more closely than to other powers. But the realities of the European balance of power tended to make such an ideal situation unlikely for more than brief intervals. Hence his usual objective in the dynamics of power politics was that which he revealed in January 1880 when lecturing the Russian diplomat Saburov about the "importance of being one of *three* on the European chessboard. That is the invariable objective of all the cabinets, and mine above all. Nobody wishes to be a minority. All politics reduces itself to this formula: to try to be one of three, as long as the world is governed by the unstable equilibrium of five great powers."[22] At one time or another Bismarck considered three possible combinations: Germany-Austria-Russia, Germany-Austria-Britain, or Germany-Britain-Russia. He preferred the first

[20] GP, II, 153–154.
[21] For his concern about a resurrected "Kaunitz coalition" see BR, IX, 398.
[22] J. Y. Simpson, *The Saburov Memoirs or Bismarck and Russia* (New York, 1929), p. 111. See also his statement to the Reichstag, Jan. 11, 1887. BR, XIII, 178ff.

coalition but was willing, in the event of necessity, to resort to either of the others.[23]

During Bismarck's two decades as Reich chancellor the basic tensions that shaped European politics were three: between Germany and France over Alsace-Lorraine; between Russia and Austria over southeastern Europe; and between Russia and Britain over conflicting interests from the Balkans to India and China. Other frictions there were, particularly in the colonial world, but these three were primary, for they determined the relationships between the great powers. The second and third areas of conflict were for Bismarck a source of both danger and opportunity. Twice, in 1876–1878 and in 1885–1887, they threatened to produce the major European war he wished to avoid. But they also provided the chance for Germany to seize the position of the fulcrum in the European balance of power, that mobile position between conflicting interests that gave Bismarck the best chance of attaining his twin objectives of isolating France and preserving the peace of Europe.

Although he believed certain "interests of state," grounded in political geography, influenced the conduct of governments, Bismarck was well aware that the interpretation of those interests differed from individual to individual and faction to faction. Naturally he followed the ebb and flow of French political life with scrupulous care. His hope was that the character of the new regime in Paris would make it incapable of alliances (*bündnisunfähig*).[24] The events that followed the conclusion of the war with Germany were reassuring. Civil war between the new government headed by Louis-Adolphe Thiers and the radical Paris Commune seemed to confirm the prejudice of European statesmen that France was still the heart of revolutionary unrest in Europe. The defeat of the commune was followed by a period of indecision, during which Orleanist and Bourbon factions disputed over which dynasty would be restored to the throne. This division within the monarchist majority in the Versailles assembly enabled Thiers to consolidate his position. Bismarck regarded this development as favorable to Germany, for he anticipated that a monarchical restoration would bring to power conservative and clerical interests that would find sympathy in Austria and Russia.[25] As long as German occupation forces remained in France, futhermore, the maneuverability of French foreign policy was limited.

Austria-Hungary was the common partner in both of the tripartite combinations that Bismarck tried to preserve as possible options for Germany. Geography, history, and ethnic relationship seemed to dictate a close relationship, once the issue of the empire's position in Germany had been resolved. Even while warring against the Habsburg monarchy in 1866, Bismarck be-

---

[23] Concerning the possibility of the third combination see GP, II, 36.

[24] See especially GP, I, 157–162.

[25] GP, I, 47–48, 65ff., 157–194; GW, VIII, 7–9, 85–87, 117–118, 160.

lieved in the necessity of ultimate reconciliation. To prepare the way he insisted on a peace at Nikolsburg that cost Austria no territory and no indemnity. For reasons already noted, however, he had little success until 1871.[26] The Prussian victory at Sedan and completion of German unity ended Austrian efforts to preserve a south German "buffer zone" against Prussia; simultaneously Russia's unilateral repudiation (with German encouragement) of the Black Sea clauses in the Treaty of Paris raised new anxieties in Vienna over Russia's aims in the Balkans. By mid-December 1870 Chancellor Beust and his subordinates in the foreign ministry had concluded that both internal stability and external security now required an Austrian-German alliance that would establish a great "central European bulwark of peace." Reassured by Bismarck's denial of all irredentist claims on Austria, Beust pursued this objective henceforth with single-minded determination. In August–September 1871 his efforts were crowned with success when Bismarck and Wilhelm I conferred with Beust and Kaiser Franz Joseph at Ischl, Gastein, and Salzburg, reaching an informal agreement to collaborate in foreign policy.[27]

Simultaneously, however, Franz Joseph was engaged in an internal reform not entirely compatible with his new foreign policy. Without consulting Beust, he had appointed on February 7, 1871, a new Cisleithanian cabinet, headed by Count Karl von Hohenwart as minister-president with Prussophobe Albert Schäffle as minister of commerce—advocates of a new federalism designed to appease the empire's Polish and Slavic populations. Hohenwart's new federalism would have elevated Bohemia, dominated by Czechs, to constitutional equality with Austria and Hungary. The logical counterpart of such an internal reform should have been a pro-Russian more than a pro-German foreign policy. Although Russian Panslavs applauded this reform, it was unpopular among Hungarians, who did not favor granting to other ethnic groups what they themselves had so recently obtained, and Austrian Germans, who saw in it yet another blow to their traditionally dominant position in the Habsburg Empire. The emotions aroused by the controversy raised the possibility of an internecine quarrel that might one day lead to German or perhaps Russian intervention in the internal affairs of the Danubian empire.

Bismarck regarded the Hohenwart–Schäffle cabinet as both black and red (ultramontane and socialist); he attacked its program publicly in the press and personally to Beust and Franz Joseph. He was particularly disturbed by the cabinet's plan to make concessions to the Poles of Galicia, a policy that promised to increase the discontent of the Polish populations of Russia and Prussia. To his gratification, Franz Joseph finally restored harmony in his government by dismissing the reform cabinet. Beust's policy had triumphed, but not he.

[26] See vol. 1, pp. 314–316, 434–445.
[27] Nicholas Der Bagdasarian, *The Austro-German Rapprochement, 1870–1879* (Cranbury, N.J., 1976), pp. 67ff.; F. R. Bridge, *From Sadowa to Sarajevo: The Foreign Policy of Austria-Hungary, 1866–1914* (London, 1972), pp. 54–57.

BISMARCK AND BEUST EMBRACE. A VIENNESE PERSPECTIVE ON AUSTRIA'S "NEWEST FRIENDSHIP." *BERG'S KIKERIKI*, VIENNA, FEBRUARY 6, 1871.

His cooperation with Austria's German liberals, who had bitterly opposed the Kaiser's course in the recent struggle, had evidently contaminated him in Franz Joseph's mind. In November 1871 he was dismissed as chancellor and sent to London as ambassador. Prince Adolf von Auersperg replaced Hohenwart as Austrian minister–president, and Hungarian Court Julius Andrássy replaced Beust as Austro-Hungarian foreign minister. Andrássy was even more committed than Beust to a pro-German policy for Austria.[28]

The most sensitive points in Bismarck's conception of German foreign policy concerned relations with Russia and Britain. Close cooperation with Russia had been central to his policy since 1862; it had helped to isolate Austria in 1866 and had prevented Austria from allying with France in 1870. Bismarck's best resource in Russia was Tsar Alexander II. Alexander was closely related to the Hohenzollern family, being a nephew of Wilhelm I. He was increasingly alarmed over the growth of revolutionary radicalism in Europe and its effects on Russia. Still, there were anti-German elements within the Russian government. The influence of German intellectual life, very strong early in the century, was ebbing. Many Russians resented the role Baltic Germans had played in Russian government. Gorchakov had long been partial to the ideal of cooperation with France. According to his colleague Count Peter Shuvalov, furthermore, Gorchakov was "jealous of the fame of his colleague in Berlin" and inclined to "advise the opposite" of whatever Bismarck proposed in order to avoid the appearance of following in his footsteps.[29]

These uncertainties made it all the more imperative for Bismarck to leave open the possibility of intimacy with Great Britain. When Odo Russell came to Versailles in November 1870 to inform him of Britain's concern over Russia's repudiation of the Black Sea clauses of the Treaty of Paris, Bismarck set the new policy in motion. He told Russell that Berlin had no secret understanding with St. Petersburg. Their relationship was "an open avowed, unconscious alliance . . . , which he not only does not attempt to deny, but also openly declares to be a national and family alliance of friendship and gratitude for past services, which it is his duty to maintain until future events bring about more advantageous alliances." Britain and Austria, he continued, were Germany's "natural allies"; for such an alliance Germany was prepared to make sacrifices.[30]

This interview signaled the beginning of the "see-saw politics" that characterized Bismarck's diplomacy at crucial moments during the next two decades. His immediate objective was evidently to drive still deeper the cleavage between France and Britain that had opened in the late years of the Second Empire. The Gladstone government (1868–1874) made no attempt to snap at the bait that Bismarck dangled. After Palmerston British statesmen were inclined to avoid continental entanglements, unless necessary to prevent the total domination of Europe by a single power. They thought of Britain as a

[28] Heinrich Lutz, Österreich-Ungarn und die Gründung des deutschen Reiches (Frankfurt, 1979), pp. 342ff.

[29] Reuss to Bismarck, Apr. 8, 1875. Hajo Holborn, "Bismarck und Schuwalow im Jahre 1875," Historische Zeitschrift, 130 (1924), p. 264. See also Hajo Holborn, Bismarcks europäische Politik zu Beginn der siebziger Jahre und die Mission Radowitz (Berlin, 1925), pp. 15ff.

[30] Fitzmaurice, Granville, II, 74.

world power, whose primary concern must be the preservation of the British Empire. Pacifistic by inclination, Gladstone and his associates wished to reduce military expenditures and concentrate upon domestic rather than foreign affairs. Continental countries, whose military expenditures were on the increase, began to look upon Britain as a secondary power.[31] "It is a favorite saying of Prince Bismarck," wrote Morier on April 1, 1874, "that he lost five years of his political life by the foolish belief that England was still a great power."[32]

Actually this development had advantages for German policy. Knowing that Britain was unlikely under normal circumstances to ally with either France or Germany, Bismarck could promote the closer relationship with Russia and Austria upon which he had now resolved. Although grounded in *Realpolitik*, the eastern connection had other attractions. In the emerging industrial age, an era of new social forces and new ideologies, it provided the best hope of stabilizing the traditional social and political order of central and eastern Europe. The upsurge of international socialism in the early 1870s offered Bismarck both a threat and an opportunity. The necessity of meeting the socialist menace was one of the principal arguments he used in Vienna and St. Petersburg for reviving the Holy Alliance.[33] The red scare, fed by the excesses of the Paris Commune, provided a basis for renewing the tripartite relationship that Bismarck had earlier denounced as an unnecessary handicap to the pursuit of Prussia's self-interest. Confronted with a common foe, the European powers would be more amenable to Berlin's new status in the European balance of power. The fear of German hegemony would yield to the comfort of German cooperation and even leadership.

The eastern alliance would also bring together the three partitioners of Poland. Through it, Berlin could acquire leverage with which to influence their policies toward their Polish subjects. Any concessions to the Poles in Russia or Austria (such as those made by Beust and Hohenwart) would inevitably have had repercussions on the Prussian side of the border. In this respect, Bismarck's effort to unite the three great empires of central and eastern Europe was the external counterpart of the Prussian Kulturkampf and the defense against "Polonization" of Germans in Prussia's eastern provinces. That the alliance served Bismarck's domestic and foreign policy simultaneously was a fortunate coincidence that reinforced its value, but was not its primary motivation.

[31] William L. Langer, *European Alliances and Alignments* (2d ed., New York, 1956), pp. 17–18.

[32] Wemyss, *Morier*, II, 330.

[33] Wolter, *Bismarcks Aussenpolitik*, pp. 90ff. On May 20, 1871, the Kaiser wrote to Kaiserin Augusta: "the reports from Paris [the commune] are steadily worse; that is, good for us." Quoted in *ibid.*, p. 92.

The Three Emperors League

Although they shared his social objectives, Andrássy and Gorchakov could hardly accept Bismarck's ambition to control the switchboard of European politics. Their interests and those of the powers they served differed from his. Bismarck hoped for Austrian support or benevolent neutrality in any future difficulties with France, and Andrássy wished to entice Germany and perhaps Britain into backing Austria in any future difficulties with Russia. In seeking the German alliance, the Austrian hoped to liquidate the close relationship between Berlin and St. Petersburg existing for nearly a decade. Gorchakov, on the other hand, coveted for himself the central position in European politics that Bismarck was beginning to occupy. Hence he refused to surrender even now the prospect that Russia might establish a working relationship with France, and he determined, by easing their differences over the Balkans, to prevent Austria-Hungary from becoming too closely allied with Germany.

These conflicting motives stood in the way of any rapid decisions on the part of the three empires. In his negotiations with Beust and Andrássy Bismarck stressed that Germany would not sacrifice its relationship to Russia for the sake of rapprochement with Austria. When Franz Joseph decided upon an official visit to Berlin that would demonstrate his acceptance of the results of the battle of Königgrätz, Alexander II and Gorchakov, apprehensive over the signs of increasing intimacy between Berlin and Vienna, invited themselves, in effect, to the same meeting.[34] In September 1872, the three emperors and their foreign ministers assembled in the German capital for a round of state dinners, parades, and conferences. Bismarck hastened to reassure the British about the results. "We have witnessed a novel sight today," he told Russell. "It is the first time in history that three emperors have sat down to dinner together for the promotion of peace.—I wanted these emperors to form a loving group, like Canova's three graces.—I wanted them to stand in a silent group and allow themselves to be admired, but I was determined not to allow them to talk, and that I have achieved, difficult as it was, because they all three think themselves greater statesmen than they are."[35] There was far more talk than Bismarck admitted. Although no written agreements emerged (the foreign ministers judged the time not yet ripe), the conference brought about the reconciliation of Alexander and Franz Joseph and negotiations between Gorchakov and Andrássy that eased Russian-Austrian friction over the Balkans.

The fact that neither Austria nor Russia could afford to permit the other to ally with Germany independently heightened the willingness of both to come to terms. In May 1873 Wilhelm, accompanied by Bismarck and Moltke, re-

[34] GP, I, 197–200.

[35] N. Japikse, *Europa und Bismarcks Friedenspolitik: Die internationalen Beziehungen von 1871 bis 1890* (Berlin, 1927), pp. 29–31.

turned the tsar's visit by journeying to St. Petersburg. The result was a military convention between Germany and Russia binding each to support the other with two hundred thousand men in the event of an attack by another European power. The document was signed by the two emperors and the two generals, Moltke and Field Marshal Berg, who had negotiated it.[36] Bismarck evaded the Russian attempt to separate Germany from Austria by insisting that the convention be invalid unless joined by Austria. But Franz Joseph and Andrássy demurred, unwilling to tie their hands in the Balkans or to guarantee, if only indirectly, Germany's possession of Alsace-Lorraine.[37] Instead they negotiated with Alexander and Gorchakov, who visited Schönbrunn in June 1873, a more general agreement to "maintain the peace of Europe" against disturbances from any direction, with more concrete decisions to be made when the disturbance occurred. This commitment was less valuable to Germany than the one signed in St. Petersburg. Yet Bismarck was satisfied, for his principal objective had been achieved. In October 1873 Germany joined the Schönbrunn convention and the "Three Emperors League" was born.[38]

Naturally Bismarck had reason to fear that the existence of the league would drive Britain into the arms of France. At every successive step in its formation he reassured London that this development was in no way harmful to British interests. The Gladstone cabinet did not respond to his suggestion that Britain associate with the league. Yet Britain and Russia, urged on by the German chancellor, did come to an agreement in the summer of 1873 demarcating their respective spheres of influence in central Asia. In September King Victor Emmanuel, concerned over the possibility that a restored French monarchy might intervene in behalf of the papacy, visited Vienna and Berlin in search of support. By the end of 1873 Italy had joined the orbit of the three eastern powers. The isolation of France appeared complete. Peter Shuvalov, Russia's ambassador to Great Britain, judged that "as long as the three emperors hold together, they can impose their will on the rest of Europe. If they forbid France to make war on Germany, the French can do nothing."[39] Small wonder that Bismarck regarded Shuvalov as Russia's ablest statesman.

In September 1872 the official *Provinzial-Korrespondenz* expressed the government's satisfaction that its diplomatic efforts had been accepted so quickly and unreservedly by neighboring states, despite the "unexpected" accretion of power Germany had gained by its victories. This was a circumstance with few parallels in world history.[40] And yet there was still considerable uneasiness among European statesmen about the events of 1866–1871. No Euro-

---

[36] GP, I, 201–204.

[37] GP, I, 203–206.

[38] GP, I, 206–207.

[39] To Reuss, Apr. 25, 1875. Holborn, "Bismarck und Schuwalow," p. 267.

[40] Wolter, *Bismarcks Aussenpolitik*, p. 121.

pean congress had been called to negotiate and ratify the redistribution of power brought about by Prussia's victories. The "European concert," which in 1815–1823, 1840, and 1856 had seemed to prove the existence of a European community of nation-states, appeared to have collapsed. And yet was Disraeli correct in his statement to the British House of Commons, so often quoted, that the European balance of power had been destroyed? Surely this judgment was premature, colored by its political purpose, which was to discredit the foreign policy of Gladstone and Granville.[41] At the time, to be sure, there could be little doubt about German hegemony in Europe. As long as it was partially occupied by German troops, France could hardly pull its weight in the balance of power system. Seen from the direction of St. Petersburg and Vienna, the Three Emperors League was a restraining net with which Germany's partners hoped to keep Germany from abusing its newfound power.

The willingness of patriotic Frenchmen to subscribe to two huge loans enabled their government to pay off the indemnity much earlier than anyone, including Bismarck, had anticipated. On September 16, 1873, the last German occupation troops withdrew across the frontier, and, on November 20, 1873, the monarchist majority in the French National Assembly installed a former Napoleonic general, Marshal Patrice MacMahon, as president for seven years. France was on its way toward the resolution of its constitutional crisis (finally accomplished through passage of the "Wallon amendment" on January 30, 1875). Under Thiers, moreover, the new regime had already begun to reconstruct the armed forces; in a message to the National Assembly in December 1871, Thiers declared that the reorganization was nearly complete for a projected army of six hundred thousand men. In Berlin, France's financial, military, and political recovery was followed with greater concern than was probably justified.[42] Moltke was persuaded that the French army would soon be strong enough to launch the "war of revenge" for which chauvinistic French patriots were already calling. In 1872 the chief of the Prussian general staff began drafting plans for preventive action that would "close at last the volcano that had shaken Europe for a century through its wars as well as its revolutions."[43] Although he accepted renewed military action as a possible option against a resurgent, vengeful France, Bismarck was inclined to believe that active intimidation and interference in France's internal affairs would suffice to keep the French weak and docile.[44]

[41] Langer's judgment, "After all, the war completely destroyed the balance of power in Europe," was also exaggerated. *Alliances and Alignments*, p. 15.

[42] See particularly *GP*, I, 69–75, 101–110, 116–117, 149ff.

[43] Gerhard Ritter, *Staatskunst und Kriegshandwerk* (Munich, 1954–1968), I, 288. See also Moltke's statements about the likelihood of war with France to Odo Russell on Mar. 1, 1873. Fitzmaurice, *Granville*, II, 113.

[44] See particularly Allan Mitchell, *Bismarck and the French Nation, 1848–1890* (New York,

"Is War in Sight?"

In Bismarck's opinion the switch from Thiers to MacMahon in France "worsened" Germany's political position in Europe.[45] "A weak, civilian, anticlerical, isolated France had been replaced by a stronger, military, ultramontane France more capable of forming alliances." Thiers had possessed too little internal support to follow the policy that French interests, if "coolly calculated," would determine. Such a policy would dictate that France "go hand in hand with Rome" and with Germany's "most active and dangerous internal foes." "Under MacMahon France has become more attractive to potential allies; under a [restored] monarchy, to which MacMahon is to be the bridge, this will be even more true."[46] Here the interaction between domestic and foreign affairs in Bismarck's political calculations is particularly evident, but it was not the needs of the German economy and of German social stability that guided him; rather it was his conception of what was needed to achieve Germany's internal consolidation. His near paranoia about the dangers of political Catholicism to the German Reich led him in foreign as well as domestic affairs into a series of unwise actions that were not only unsuccessful but also harmful on both fronts. At home the Kulturkampf disturbed civil peace and alienated a large minority; abroad it disrupted Bismarck's system of foreign relations by arousing suspicions as to Germany's intentions toward France. By 1875 Germany was in danger of isolation and Bismarck of being regarded as a bully who had to be checked before he disturbed the peace of Europe.

Initially Bismarck actually expected to find support for the Prussian Kulturkampf in foreign capitals. The Russian government had long been in conflict with the papacy owing to St. Petersburg's attempt to suppress the Catholic clergy in Russian Poland and end the church's partiality for the cause of Polish nationalism. In Vienna the new government of Auersperg-Andrássy had a liberal and anticlerical reputation. By its occupation of Rome in 1870 the Italian government had renewed its long-standing feud with the Vatican. But even the Gladstone government in London was vaguely sympathetic to the Prussian campaign against ultramontanism.[47] These events and attitudes apparently encouraged Bismarck to put pressure upon the MacMahon government to suppress anti-German agitation within the French episcopacy and the newspaper press. In August 1873 the bishop of Nancy had called upon Catholics to pray for the return of Alsace-Lorraine. The appeal was read from pulpits throughout the dioceses of Nancy and Toul, which included parts of

---

1971), pp. 73ff., and *The German Influence in France after 1870: The Formation of the French Republic* (Chapel Hill, 1979), pp. 62ff.

[45] Bismarck to Edwin von Manteuffel, commander of German occupation troops in France, June 2, 1873. GP, I, 189. MacMahon had been elected president of France on May 24, 1873.

[46] Bismarck to Lothar von Schweinitz, German ambassador in Vienna, June 4, 1873. GP, I, 189 (fn.).

[47] Langer, *Alliances and Alignments*, pp. 36ff.

Lorraine ceded to Germany. In November a number of French bishops condemned Prussia's Kulturkampf laws as discriminatory and immoral.

The Paris government went a long way toward satisfying Bismarck's protests. It urged the bishops to moderate their attacks and even suspended a journal of which Bismarck complained. Yet it could not accept Bismarck's demand that the offending bishops be prosecuted under a long dormant penal statute of 1819.[48] The French ambassador to Berlin, Viscount Armand de Gontaut-Biron, had the impression that Bismarck's complaints about the French episcopacy were motivated not only by the Kulturkampf but also by the necessity of influencing the outcome of the Reichstag election of January 1874 and of the ensuing debates over the iron budget in the spring of 1874. Bismarck's return to Berlin in mid-December 1873 coincided with a renewal of hostile attacks on France in the German press.[49] In January the semiofficial *Norddeutsche Allgemeine Zeitung* declared, "A French government that demeans itself in the service of Roman priest-politics would be hostile to us not because it is the government of France but because it would be a satellite of Rome, with which we could not live in peace. . . . As soon as France identifies itself with Rome it will become thereby our sworn enemy."[50] Soon afterward Bismarck bluntly told Gontaut-Biron that France must not permit itself to be drawn by religious fanatics into an anti-German alliance. "In that case it would be better to fight in two years [or] in one year, than to wait until you have finished your preparations." The warning was followed by a denial. He vigorously rejected accusations in the French press that he was advising the Kaiser to seek in war with France an escape from Germany's internal difficulties. That, he declared, would be a "dishonest act." "We are very far away from any idea of war. What profit could we derive from it?"[51]

Bismarck's expectation that the governments in Vienna and Petersburg would be sympathetic to the Kulturkampf was destined to disappointment. Tsar Alexander and Foreign Minister Gorchakov were more inclined to negotiate than fight in their dispute with Rome over the Polish church. They deplored the alienation of Prussian conservatives as damaging to the monarchical principle in Germany, and Gorchakov was temperamentally averse to following in Bismarck's wake on any issue.[52] But neither were Franz Joseph and his ministers disposed to follow the Prussian example, and Andrássy is said to have been repelled by the vehemence with which Bismarck denounced

---

[48] André Dreux, *Dernières années de l'ambassade en Allemagne de M. de Gontaut-Biron, 1874–1877* (Paris, 1907), pp. 5ff.; GP, I, 211–233.

[49] Dreux, *Gontaut-Biron*, pp. 2–10.

[50] SEG (1874), pp. 43–44.

[51] Jan. 13, 1874. Dreux, *Gontaut-Biron*, pp. 18–26. See also Bismarck to Reuss, Jan. 23, 1874. GP, I, 235.

[52] GW, VIc, 33–35, 51–54; Holborn, "Bismarck und Schuwalow," pp. 259–271; Dreux, *Gontaut-Biron*, pp. 41–42.

the pope while visiting Vienna in October 1873 (at a Burgtheater performance of Shakespeare's *Henry VI*, Bismarck compared the pope to Jack
Cade). Not even the Italian government wanted involvement in Prussia's
feud with the papacy, a justified caution in view of Bismarck's continuing
attempts to undercut the Center party by coming to terms with the Vatican.[53]

Bismarck's greatest failure in 1873–1875, however, was in miscalculating
the attitude of other European powers toward France. In late 1873 the British,
Austrian, and Russian governments, like their predecessors in 1814–1815,
welcomed France's return to the European balance of power. The other great
powers had no more interest in keeping France weak than in furthering German hegemony. Under these circumstances Bismarck's too obvious efforts to
isolate the French and keep them powerless had the opposite effect.

During a visit to Petersburg in February 1874, Franz Joseph and Andrássy
were struck by the increased distrust of Germany to be found in the Russian
capital. After conferring with the Russians, each took the trouble to assure
General Adolphe Le Flô, the French ambassador in St. Petersburg, that "a
powerful France is more necessary than ever for the European equilibrium."
"Bismarck," said Andrássy, "has lost his sangfroid and his self-control."[54]
Even the Italian government pleased the French by drawing away from Berlin
and toward Paris. Since late 1873 Bismarck had sought, by mediating disputes
between England and Russia over conflicting interests on the approaches to
India, to prevent a British rapprochement with France. But the effort was
appreciated by neither party.[55] In December 1873, Odo Russell reported
Bismarck as saying that "he would greatly prefer to fight it out at once and
declare war [on France] tomorrow than wait until they were prepared to attack." Russell warned that Bismarck's aim was to expand the Reich to include
all German-speaking people in Europe.[56] In a personal letter to Wilhelm
dated February 10, 1874, Queen Victoria warned against the "lamentable
consequences" that "might" result from a renewed German attempt to crush
France.[57]

These adverse signals caused Bismarck to relax his attempt to get the
French government to take legal action against the bishops.[58] But he re-

---

[53] Erich Eyck, *Bismarck: Leben und Werk* (Zurich, 1944), II, 152–154; Georges Goyau, *Bismarck et l'église* (Paris, 1911), II, 65–66. Eyck cites Goyau, who gives no source for this story. If
unsubstantiated, the episode was not out of character for Bismarck. See Wertheimer, *Andrássy*,
II, 107.

[54] *DDF*, I, 312–313; Japikse, *Bismarcks Friedenspolitik*, pp. 36–38. Dreux, *Gontaut-Biron*, pp.
47–60.

[55] Holborn, *Mission Radowitz*, pp. 26ff.; Langer, *Alliances and Alignments*, pp. 39–41.

[56] Winifred Taffs, *Ambassador to Bismarck: Lord Odo Russell, First Baron Ampthill* (London,
1938), p. 66, and "The War Scare of 1875," *Slavonic Review*, 9 (1930–1931), pp. 335–349, 632–
649.

[57] George Earle Buckle, ed., *Letters of Queen Victoria* (2d ser., New York, 1926), II, 313–314.

[58] *GP*, I, 238; *DDF*, I, 310–311.

mained full of disquiet about French intentions.[59] Over Wilhelm's protest he inserted a passage in the speech from the throne opening the Reichstag (October 30, 1874) that, while larded with assurances of Germany's peaceful intentions, warned unnamed foreign powers against letting their "partisan passions" give way to "deeds."[60] Simultaneously he became unsettled about Germany's relationship to Russia. Berlin's ambassador in Petersburg, Prince Heinrich VII Reuss, was absent from his post owing to illness, and the first secretary, Count Friedrich von Alvensleben, was an unsatisfactory substitute. Gorchakov, furthermore, seemed determined to heighten Russia's value to German policy by demonstrating his detachment from it. To this end perhaps he blocked Bismarck's attempt to get the three empires to recognize the republican Serrano government in Madrid. In February 1875, Bismarck took the extraordinary step of dispatching to Petersburg a special emissary, Joseph Maria von Radowitz.

This was the famous "Radowitz mission," of which, like the Alvensleben mission of 1863, too much has been made. As instructed by Bismarck, Radowitz appears to have limited himself to the coordination of Russian and German policy toward Serbia and Montenegro and a general reconnaissance of Russian attitudes (particularly Alexander II) toward Germany. But his visit enabled someone, apparently Gorchakov, to launch the rumor that Radowitz had come to seek Russia's alliance or neutrality in the event of a German war with France, in return for which Germany would support Russia's aims in the Balkans.[61] While his story circulated through diplomatic channels, Bismarck heightened its credibility by ill-considered actions against Belgium and France.

In late December 1874 (soon after the Majunke affair), the *Norddeutsche Allgemeine Zeitung* published a report received from the French police that a boilermaker named Duchesne in Belgium, where Prussia suffered from a bad

[59] See GP, I, 239ff., and also his remarks to the Hungarian writer, Maurus Jokai, Feb. 27, 1874. GW, VIII, 105–108.

[60] SEG (1874), p. 156. The Kaiser told Hohenlohe that "he was too old to begin another war, and feared that Prince Bismarck was trying to drag him little by little into fresh hostilities." Friedrich Curtius, ed., *Memoirs of Prince Chlodwig of Hohenlohe-Schillingsfuerst* (New York, 1906), II, 128–129.

[61] On the Radowitz mission, see Holborn, *Mission Radowitz*, pp. 53–90, and Hajo Holborn, ed., *Aufzeichnungen und Erinnerungen aus dem Leben des Botschafters Joseph Maria von Radowitz* (Berlin, 1925), I, 296–314. Holborn corrected at important points the earlier account of Hans Herzfeld in *Die deutsch-französische Kriegsgefahr von 1875. Forschungen und Darstellungen aus dem Reichsarchiv*, vol. 3 (Berlin, 1922). Martin Winckler has attempted to prove, largely through content analysis of newspaper articles, that the purpose of the Radowitz mission was a German-Russian agreement to divide Europe into spheres of influence. But his resurrection of that long refuted thesis is unconvincing. "Der Ausbruch der 'Krieg in Sicht'-Krise vom Frühjahr 1875," *Zeitschrift für Ostforschung*, 14 (1965), pp. 671–713. For a more favorable view of Winckler's thesis see Andreas Hillgruber, *Bismarcks Aussenpolitik* (Freiburg, 1972), pp. 139–140, 148–149, 214.

press owing to the Kulturkampf, had offered to kill the German chancellor if paid sixty thousand francs by the archbishop of Paris. The result was an exchange of notes between Berlin and Brussels during February 1875, in which Bismarck, whose hand still smarted from the effect of Kullmann's bullet, accused the Belgian government of tolerating ultramontane agitation against Prussia and demanded that the Belgian criminal code be amended to permit prosecution of persons whose conduct exposed the state to intervention by foreign powers.[62] Rumors began to circulate that the harshness of Bismarck's reaction presaged an effort to partition Belgium and the Netherlands.[63] On March 4 this episode was overshadowed by a startling order from the Kaiser prohibiting under his emergency powers the export of horses across Germany's borders. Bismarck had reports that German horse traders had received an order for the purchase ("without regard to price") and immediate export to France of ten thousand military riding horses. Neither Bismarck nor Hohenlohe, now German ambassador in Paris, believed that the French were planning on war "within the next year; but [the loss of] 10,000 riding horses," Bismarck wrote, "would be a blood-letting that we would still feel if compelled to mobilize in about three years."[64]

On the heels of this development came news that on March 12 the French National Assembly had approved a surprise amendment adding a fourth battalion to each regiment and a fourth company to each battalion of the French army. Although the new battalions were for the time being mere cadres, the German general staff calculated that the law would eventually add 144,000 men to the total strength of the French army. On the basis of Moltke's estimates Wilhelm concluded that by the thirteenth or fourteenth day of any future mobilization French forces would possess "a great superiority over the German army."[65] Adding to the climate of concern in Berlin was an approaching conference at Venice between Emperor Franz Joseph and King Victor Emmanuel. In Berlin, where plans were under way for a state visit to Rome, it appeared that the Italians were giving the Austrian Kaiser precedence over the German. Could the "ultramontane alliance" of Bismarck's nightmares be in the offing?[66]

Bismarck turned to the newspaper press to spread the alarm. On April 5, 1875, the *Kölnische Zeitung* carried a report "from Vienna" linking French rearmament to an approaching restoration of the French monarchy, reconciliation of the papacy and Italian government, an ultramontane plot to bring about Andrássy's fall; the ultimate goal was a "Catholic league" composed of

[62] GW, VIc, 55–56; DDF, I, 367, 371–377.

[63] DDF, I, 379–380. Wemyss, Morier, II, 333–335.

[64] GP, I, 245–247.

[65] GP, I, 248–253 (fn.); Ferdinand von Schmerfeld, ed., *Graf Moltke: Die deutschen Aufmarschpläne 1871–1890. Forschungen und Darstellungen aus dem Reichsarchiv* (Berlin, 1929), pp. 46–50.

[66] Japikse, *Bismarcks Friedenspolitik*, p. 40.

Italy, Austria, and France under the aegis of the papacy. Austria and France would join in a "revenge coalition" to undo the consequences of the wars of 1866 and 1870.[67] On April 8, Berlin's *Die Post* reiterated and expanded on these speculations in an article headed, "*Ist der Krieg in Sicht?*" War was indeed in sight, the article concluded, but "this does not exclude the possibility that the clouds may disperse."[68] These sensational articles, believed to have been inspired by Bismarck's press bureau, created shock waves in the European press and chancelleries.[69] In a dispatch to London Bismarck sought to focus the attention of the British government on French military preparations, which, it was claimed, "far exceeded the needs of a peaceful policy and the material strength of the country." To Paris, however, he telegraphed that the two articles had "surprised him" and cited a newly published statement in the *Norddeutsche Allgemeine Zeitung*, whose purpose was to quiet the uproar. But Wilhelm himself was "shocked" by the *Kölnische* and *Post* articles and complained that even the *NAZ* article was excessively alarmist.[70]

[67] "Neue Allianzen," *Kölnische Zeitung*, Apr. 5, 1875.

[68] Reprinted in Freiherr Lucius von Ballhausen, *Bismarck-Erinnerungen* (Stuttgart, 1920), pp. 531–534. The authorship of the articles in the *Kölnische Zeitung* and *Die Post* has been much discussed. The first article was sent by Ludwig Aegidi of the foreign office press bureau to the editor with the request that it be printed without change—"every word has been weighted." Aegidi to Heinrich Kruse, Apr. 4, 1875. *HW*, II, 124. See also Paul Wentzcke, "Die Kriegsgefahr von 1875," *Kölnische Zeitung*, No. 754 (Oct. 27, 1922), and Japikse, *Bismarcks Friedenspolitik*, p. 40. Constantin Rössler was known in informed circles to be the author of the article in *Die Post*. To Tiedemann Rössler denied that he had written the piece at the behest of the foreign office. Christoph von Tiedemann, *Sechs Jahre Chef der Reichskanzlei unter dem Fürsten Bismarck* (Leipzig, 1910), p. 29. But this was probably untrue. Rössler was a frequent commentator on foreign affairs for *Die Post* and may have wished to protect his reputation as an independent journalist. Without a general directive from Bismarck the press bureau would scarcely have launched such a press campaign, although the execution was probably left to the discretion of the bureau. While denying responsibility for the two articles, Bismarck expressed satisfaction over their publication. Concerning the *Die Post* article, he told Lucius on April 11, "I am pleased that it appeared in an independent—unofficial—newspaper and that I do not have to answer for it. It is quite useful if on occasion a very bright light is thrown on the confused situation. Of war there is no talk whatever." Lucius, *Bismarck-Erinnerungen*, pp. 71–72. See also his reputed remarks that same evening to his guests in *ibid.*, pp. 72–73. During these years Bismarck frequently engaged the newspaper press to fight his political battles on both foreign and domestic issues. Sometimes he dictated the exact wording of the articles, but more often he merely gave a general directive and did not see the exact wording before publication. On Bismarck's use of the press see Irene Fischer-Frauendienst, *Bismarcks Pressepolitik* (Münster, 1963); Robert H. Keyserlingk, *Media Manipulation: A study of the Press and Bismarck in Imperial Germany* (Montreal, 1977), and Winckler, "Ausbruch der 'Krieg-in-Sicht'-Krise," pp. 671–713. Later when he saw the consequences of leaving his "press lions" loose to attack at will, Bismarck dissolved the press bureau in the foreign office (May 27, 1875) and reduced, but never eliminated, his indirect use of the press for the promotion of his policies. Doubtless his later complaints about the German press's lack of discipline stemmed from the episode of 1875. Herzfeld, *Kriegsgefahr von 1875*, p. 31. But the fault was his.

[69] *GP*, I, 253.

[70] *GP*, I, 249, 254–255.

Decazes Triumphs

During the next three weeks the Paris and Berlin governments sought to cool the dispute by reassuring each other and the European powers of their peaceful intentions and mutual satisfaction that the affair was ended. But neither Bismarck nor Foreign Minister Louis Decazes was willing to relinquish the possibility of deriving benefit from the episode. Each strove to rally Europe to its cause—Bismarck for the purpose of coercing France into relinquishing its military expansion and reorganization, Decazes for the purpose of building a league of neutrals to restrain German aggression against France. That Decazes triumphed was owed primarily to Europe's reaction toward rumors of approaching war emanating from Berlin and the bullying tactics of the German chancellor.

On visiting Berlin in late March, Hohenlohe was disturbed to hear "high-placed officers, including Minister of War Kameke, assert that Germany must attack France before being attacked by her and that, if war was not already unavoidable, the best course would be to begin it next year."[71] Undoubtedly there was much loose talk on this subject in Berlin during the spring of 1875. On the evening of April 21, Radowitz, his tongue unleashed by a bibulous dinner at the British embassy, made some philosophical observations about war and peace to Gontaut of the kind that Bismarck normally despised.

Radowitz maintained that the crisis had been resolved, and yet he proceeded, according to Gontaut, to pose a rhetorical question: If Paris were bent on "revenge," why should Germany wait until France had rearmed and contracted alliances? From the "political, philosophical, and even Christian" standpoint Berlin would be justified in taking preventive action.[72] On April 26, Bismarck himself told Austrian Ambassador Count Aloys Károlyi (according to the latter's statement to Odo Russell) that, if France continued military preparations on the "present scale," it would be ready for war in 1877. Unless France slowed its rearmament, Germany's duty was "to take the initiative and put a stop to war by energetic measures."[73] In its May issue the influential *Preussische Jahrbücher*, generally a progovernment publication, carried

[71] From his soundings in Paris Hohenlohe concluded that a "convalescent" France was in no mood or condition for war and that the French government could, without damage to its popular support, refuse to fight even if German troops should cross the border. Hohenlohe to Bismarck, Apr. 21, 1875. Helmuth Rogge, *Holstein und Hohenlohe* (Stuttgart, 1957), pp. 68–72.

[72] Dreux, *Gontaut-Biron*, pp. 91–98; *DDF*, I, 415–421. Later Radowitz composed at Bismarck's request a far less harmful version of this conversation in a promemoria, dated May 12, 1875. *GP*, I, 275–277. See also the account in his memoirs: Radowitz, *Aufzeichnungen*, I, 318–332. But on May 20 Hohenlohe heard through a mutual friend that Radowitz believed Germany must "begin" a war against France and defeat her before she was ready for the conflict. Rogge, *Holstein und Hohenloke*, p. 71.

[73] Taffs, *Russell*, pp. 86–90.

an editorial dated April 12 justifying preventive war.[74] In the first days of May both Bismarck and Moltke spoke to Belgian Ambassador Baron Jean Baptiste de Nothomb about the threatening character of French military preparations; in addition, Moltke brought up the possible necessity of a preventive war.[75] On May 2, obviously at Bismarck's request, Moltke sought out Odo Russell to say that responsibility for preventive war lay not with the state that attacked, but with the state that provoked the attack.[76] War could, however, be avoided, he said, if the great powers would stand by Germany and show the French the hopelessness of a war of revenge. On May 3, State Secretary Bernhard von Bülow informed Hohenlohe of Bismarck's continuing conviction that the "end goal" of French rearmament "remained" that of preparing the army "as quickly as possible" to undertake a "military campaign against Germany."[77]

These continuing threats of preventive action did not persuade the French to abandon their military reorganization but did enable Decazes to depict Bismarck in London, Petersburg, and Vienna as a menace to European peace. In a circular dispatch sent on April 29 to French ambassadors, Decazes denounced Radowitz's "strange doctrine" of preventive war (reported by Gontaut) as disruptive of international law and a danger to the security of every European power, "if it should actually be adopted by Germany."[78] Not only that, he also gave Gontaut's report to journalist Henry Blowitz who used it to write an article for the London *Times*, on the German theory of preventive war. The article was republished throughout Europe and caused yet another public sensation, like that of the articles in *Die Kölnische Zeitung* and *Die Post* in early April.[79]

The British and Russian governments were greatly disturbed by these revelations of German attitudes and no longer inclined to accept at face value the pacific assurances they received from Berlin. Russian Ambassador Peter Shuvalov, returning from Petersburg to his post in London, stopped off in Berlin (May 5–6, 1875) to convey to Bismarck and Wilhelm the alarm of his government. The Kaiser seemed utterly unaware of Europe's fears and uncomprehending when the ambassador referred to them. From Augusta Shuvalov heard that Wilhelm was gradually weakening and was "completely in Bismarck's hands." On arriving in London he reported to Lord Derby, foreign secretary in Disraeli's new cabinet, that the German chancellor was in a "morbid state of mind." Bismarck had complained of sleeplessness and poor

---

[74] "Politische Korrespondenz," *Preussische Jahrbücher*, 35 (1875), pp. 448–459.

[75] Dreux, *Gontaut-Biron*, pp. 104–105; Newton, *Lyons*, II, 74; *DDF*, I, 441–444.

[76] Taffs, *Russell*, pp. 89–90.

[77] GP, I, 267–269.

[78] *DDF*, I, 423–428; Dreux, *Gontaut-Biron*, pp. 121–127.

[79] Eyck, *Bismarck*, II, 170–172; Henry S. Blowitz, *Memoirs of M. de Blowitz* (New York, 1903), pp. 96–115; *DDF*, I, 445–446.

health, talked of resignation as an "absolute necessity," yet "spoke of things that he meant to do as minister some months hence": he "appeared to think that all Europe was inclined to coalesce against Germany and was also much haunted by the idea of assassination." Shuvalov concluded "that fatigue, anxiety, and other causes had produced in [Bismarck] a state of nervous excitement that may explain many of his recent sayings and doings."[80]

Disraeli and Derby resolved to collaborate with Tsar Alexander and Gorchakov in establishing a common front against Germany such as Palmerston had created to hold back France in the crisis of 1840. To this end Queen Victoria wrote personally to the tsar, and Odo Russell was instructed to support a Russian peace initiative during the tsar's scheduled visit at Berlin, May 10–13.[81] Nourished by reports from Decazes of so many bellicose statements from Bismarck, Radowitz, and Moltke, Alexander and Gorchakov came to Berlin to express their disapproval. During the preceding weeks Wilhelm had

PRINCE ALEXANDER GORCHAKOV. (DIETRICH SCHÄFER, *BISMARCK: EIN BILD SEINES LEBENS UND WIRKENS*, VERLAG VON REIMAR HOBBIG IN BERLIN, 1917, VOL. 2.)

[80] Derby to Ponsonby, May 10, 1875. Buckle, ed., *Letters of Victoria*, II, 389–395. See also Newton, *Lyons*, II, 75–78. Crown Prince Friedrich Wilhelm was also inclined to attribute the crisis to Bismarck's "nervous irritation." Friedrich Wilhelm to Queen Victoria, May 24, 1875. Buckle, ed., *Letters of Victoria*, II, 401.

[81] Buckle, *Disraeli*, V, 422; Buckle, ed., *Letters of Victoria*, II, 393–394, 396. Disraeli saw in the affair a splendid opportunity to demonstrate in the first year of his ministry his decisiveness in foreign affairs—with little risk to Britain. By cooperating with Russia, he also hoped to drive a wedge between that power and Germany. Robert Blake, *Disraeli* (London, 1966), pp. 571–574.

repeatedly been surprised by journalistic excesses in Germany and nonplussed by assumptions abroad that his country was on the brink of attacking France.[82] He had no difficulty convincing his nephew Alexander that these rumors were groundless. In an acrimonious interview Gorchakov had the pleasure of witnessing Bismarck's discomfiture on being told that Europe would not sit idly by if France were attacked. According to one account, he even demanded that the German chancellor give his word that Germany did not intend to go to war against France.[83] Afterward Gorchakov telegraphed to Russia's ambassadors, "The emperor is leaving Berlin convinced of the pacific dispositions that reign here and that assure the maintenance of peace." When leaked to the press, the final words came out twisted: "that now assure peace." Bismarck gave it yet another twist: "Now peace is assured." He never forgave Gorchakov for what he believed to have been a deliberate attempt by the Russian to portray himself as an "angel of peace" who had saved France from German attack. In his memoirs Bismarck even attributed the entire war-in-sight crisis to Gontaut's distortions and Gorchakov's puffery,[84] but the archives tell a different story. If Gorchakov enjoyed putting his German "pupil" in his place, Bismarck was the chief cause of his own humiliation.

TSAR ALEXANDER II. (BILDARCHIV PREUSSISCHER KULTURBESITZ.)

[82] Langer, *Alliances and Alignments*, pp. 48–49.

[83] GP, 272–273; *DDF*, I, 452–454, 466–469; Newton, *Lyons*, II, 79; Taffs, *Russell*, pp. 98–99; GW, XV, 363–364; Eyck, *Bismarck*, II, 173–174.

[84] Gorchakov to Orloff, May 13, 1875. *DDF*, I, 456, GP, I, 283; GW, XV, 363–364; Dreux, *Gontaut-Biron*, p. 166.

The Indispensable Man

The rebuff that Bismarck experienced from other European powers in May 1875 was the greatest diplomatic defeat of his career, and historians have long puzzled over the circumstances and decisions that led him into this debacle. The diplomatic maneuvers that preceded and accompanied the wars of 1864, 1866, and 1870–1871 have long been regarded as textbook lessons in diplomatic technique—how to promote the interest of state against great odds at minimum cost. Bismarck's diplomacy during 1873–1875 can be seen as a textbook lesson in diplomatic bungling—how to miscalculate perceptions of self-interest in foreign capitals and create a hostile front by making unwise responses to foreign provocations. For once, he blundered badly in the use of his favorite political tactic—the threat of alternative choice. The option he displayed to the French—preventive war—was not one that, if defied, he was actually prepared to employ. He bluffed, and the bluff was easily called. What had happened to dull the political sensitivity of the man many regard as perhaps the most astute of all practitioners of the diplomatic art?

In the previous chapter we have seen that Bismarck's conduct of domestic affairs during the same period was also marked by serious errors in judgment. His attacks on the French bishops and the Belgian boilermaker Duchesne had their counterparts in his persecution of Harry von Arnim, confrontations with Jörg and Ballestrem, and conduct in the Majunke affair. The source of these errors has to be sought in his steadily deteriorating physical and psychological condition. His narcissistic drive for self-assertion and dominance had encountered, despite great successes, irritations and frustrations sufficient in number and magnitude to do serious damage to his mental and physical health. That he came close to murdering an opposition deputy on the floor of the Reichstag in December 1874 is the most dramatic illustration of the debilitating anger that seethed within him whenever he contemplated the remaining obstacles and hindrances to the free exercise of his will in internal affairs. Bismarck's futile journalistic and diplomatic assault on France in the war-in-sight crisis of February–May 1875 shows that narcissistic rage had also begun to affect his conduct of foreign policy.

Disproved long ago is the accusation that he actually planned a preventive strike against France in 1875 and was restrained only by warnings from Britain and Russia. Less ink would have been consumed on this problem, if historians had known that during the critical months of the war-in-sight crisis he was actually on the verge of retirement. During 1874 Bismarck often spoke of his intention to retire on his sixtieth birthday in the following year. Most of his listeners on these occasions probably assumed, as did Lasker, that the statements were "mere pretence."[85] But on May 11, 1875, the prince actually dis-

---

[85] BP, I, 86, 88; Ludolf Parisius, *Deutschlands politische Parteien und das Ministerium Bismarck* (Berlin, 1878), p. 204; Hohenlohe, *Memoirs*, II, 129–130; Newton, *Lyons*, II, 61–63.

patched to the Kaiser a request to be released from office that, in contrast to many previous "resignations," has to be taken seriously. At age sixty Bismarck doubted that he had long to live, particularly if he remained in office. He expected to fall victim either to a stroke or an assassin.

No convincing ulterior motive for the resignation of May 1875 is discernible. Unlike that of December 1874, this request was not aimed at recalcitrant parliamentary deputies, to whom it remained unknown. Nor was it an attempt to coerce the Kaiser into doing Bismarck's will on any important issue. During the preceding weeks, they had been at odds over the cloister act; yet this crisis ended in late April when the cabinet acquiesced in the Kaiser's decision.[86] Was the resignation designed to unseat another Prussian minister? When he composed the first draft in February, Bismarck was deeply vexed over the "perfidy" and "cowardice" of his colleagues.[87] Eulenburg, Achenbach, Falk, and Persius (a counselor) had ignored a cabinet decision in voting in the Chamber of Deputies for a motion by the progressive leader Rudolf Virchow to extend the Prussian county reform act of 1875 to include the western provinces.[88] Bismarck was distressed, furthermore, by the failure of Eulenburg and Falk to "purify" the ranks of government officials in the Rhineland and compel provincial governors to enforce the May laws. ("In the last analysis women govern us, and Eulenburg will do nothing against petticoats— that is the secret of our domestic politics.") As late as May 7 Bismarck spoke of forcing the Kaiser to choose between himself and Eulenburg.[89] But there was no mention of Eulenburg in the letter of resignation, and the minister remained in office until 1878.

Judging from Johanna's letters and her husband's own statements, the motives for the resignation were fatigue, ennui, ill health, and mental depression. "At the time of my return to Berlin in late autumn of last year," he wrote in the resignation, "I seemed to have justification for the hope that my health, after a long and difficult illness, had been so fortified by my leave of many months and by the cure at Kissingen that I could resume the official responsibilities given me by your majesty. Unfortunately this hope has not been fulfilled. A brief resumption of my duties sufficed to confine me after Christmas for several months to my bedroom, so that during the entire winter I was unable to fulfill more than part of my official obligations. In the belief

---

[86] GW, VIc, 57–58.

[87] Johanna von Bismarck to Herbert von Bismarck, Feb. 15, 1875. BFA, Bestand C, Box 6.

[88] Lucius, Bismarck-Erinnerungen, p. 69 (Feb. 14, 1875). In Lucius's opinion the source of this confusion was Bismarck himself: "Bismarck loses the context [of government affairs] apparently because of his ill-health or absences. He sees his colleagues too seldom, leaves them without directives, and intervenes violently once they are already engaged in a definite direction. As I judge it, all of his colleagues, except perhaps for Camphausen on occasion, have exerted themselves uprightly to further his policy."

[89] Tiedemann, Sechs Jahre, pp. 27, 32–33. For other testimony on his mood that spring see GW, VIII, 145–146.

that I was sufficiently restored, I felt duty-bound to resume my service to your majesty at the beginning of April but was compelled after a few days to go to bed again and keep to my room. . . . The doctors have told me repeatedly that my bodily strength is no longer equal to my way of life and that, if I continue the latter, I am likely to collapse before long." The step, he declared, was "very hard" to take; he would miss his "accustomed activity."[90]

In the spring of 1875 Bismarck reached a climactic point in his long career. He had expanded Prussia and created the German Reich. He had turned back the liberal challenge of the 1860s by appropriating vital parts of the liberal program. With stolen materials he had constructed a framework of laws and institutions capable of consolidating the empire he had created. In domestic affairs there appeared to be no significant threat to his position, his program, and the constitutional order. The Center party was nearly isolated in Landtag and Reichstag. With the cloister act the "fighting laws" of the Kulturkampf would soon be complete. Even in the House of Lords the number of ultraconservative foes appeared to be shrinking. Despite two years of economic depression, the coffers of the state treasury were full.[91]

For nearly a quarter of a century Bismarck had climbed the rugged face of German and European politics. Now he had reached a pinnacle from which he could look down with some satisfaction on what he believed to have achieved. But he was also worn out from the climb, his nervous system tortured by anger and anxiety. What vexed him most was his belief that those who should have joined him in the ascent were trying to drag him back from the summit. One evening, only three days after he had finished his letter to Wilhelm, Tiedemann found him ruminating about how little understanding people showed for the difficulties of his position. He expected no better from posterity. Historians always see things through their own spectacles, he declared. But he did respect Carlyle's capacity to penetrate men's souls. "For me it is especially burdensome that my personal opponents increase with every passing year. My calling demands of me that I tread on the toes of a lot of people, and no one ever forgets that. I am too old to win new friends. I also have no time for them. And the old friends disappear from view as soon as they believe I will no longer do anything for them. So eventually I will be surrounded only by personal enemies."[92]

The progress of Bismarck's resignation from conception to execution presents a puzzle. From previously unknown evidence it appears that he informed members of his family sometime in early January 1875 of his final resolve to

---

[90] For the successive drafts see Horst Kohl, ed., Bismarck-Jahrbuch, 1 (1894), pp. 87–93. The final draft is also in GW, VIc, 58–60 and Horst Kohl, ed., Anhang zu den Gedanken und Erinnerungen von Otto Fürst von Bismarck (Stuttgart, 1901), I, 251–254.

[91] GW, VIII, 149; Lucius, Bismarck-Erinnerungen, p. 75.

[92] Tiedemann, Sechs Jahre, p. 33 (May 7, 1875); see also Lucius, Bismarck-Erinnerungen, p. 78 (Oct. 31, 1875).

ON HIS SIXTIETH BIRTHDAY, BISMARCK IS DEPICTED AS A WEARY ATLAS READY TO DROP HIS BURDEN.
FRANCE AND THE PAPACY LOOK ON IN HOPE, THE GERMAN PUBLIC IN DISMAY—"HE CANNOT LEAVE!"
WILHELM SCHOLZ IN *KLADDERADATSCH*, APRIL 1875.

leave office in April. The tone of the letters Johanna wrote to her eldest son Herbert during the following weeks point to such a resolve. She quoted her husband as being "tired of living" and rejoiced that he would soon find in the forests of Varzin and Lauenburg the peace and quiet needed to restore his health and pleasure in life.[93] In mid-February she reported casually (as though Herbert knew it already) that *Papachen* was "firmer than ever on his April departure."[94] About this time Bismarck wrote the first draft of his letter to the Kaiser requesting release from office.[95] On February 26, Johanna reported that the deed was done. "Papa has handed in his request for retirement, and I think everything will go smoothly. In April we will be able to turn our backs on Berlin forever." This time she held Wilhelm ("the all-highest old man") and Augusta (his "master"), not the other ministers, responsible for her husband's condition. The dissolution of a relationship that had lasted almost thirteen years, she wrote, would not be easy. "But we are amenable to all arrangements."[96]

By March 3 Johanna was less sure. "Concerning our departure from Berlin I can say today nothing more certain than in my preceding letter. He definitely *wants to leave*, but when? He doesn't say, and you know full well that one does not ask. . . . All our acquaintances here bemoan [his decision] frightfully—whether uprightly or hypocritically who knows? I always assume the latter and am convinced that they have already put together the future cabinet with Harry [von Arnim] *à la tête!*"[97] In late March her husband spoke vaguely, as he had since January, of spending a month (now mid-April to mid-May) in the Sachsenwald drinking bottled "Kissingen water," after which they would proceed to Varzin. But continuing cold weather outweighed his need for country air. Johanna still dared not ask about the fate of his resignation but suspected that "only another long leave" was in prospect.[98] In late April she wrote that *Papachen*, after a few weeks of improved health, had again been laid low by "terrible coughing, chest pains, headaches, fever, bad nights, bad stomach."[99] Unfortunately Johanna's correspondence with Herbert lapsed during May, the actual month of Bismarck's resignation.

How can we account for the fact that Bismarck's letter of resignation, which according to Johanna was "handed in" in late February, formally bears the date of May 4 and, judging from Wilhelm's response, did not actually

[93] Johanna to Herbert, Jan. 22, 27, and Feb. 14, 1875. BFA, Bestand C, Box 6.

[94] Johanna to Herbert, Feb. 15, 1875. BFA, Bestand C, Box 6.

[95] The draft is undated. See Kohl, ed., *Bismarck-Jahrbuch*, I, 87–90.

[96] Johanna to Herbert, Feb. 26, 1875. BFA, Bestand C, Box 6.

[97] Johanna to Herbert, Mar. 3 and 6, 1875. BFA, Bestand C, Box 6.

[98] Johanna to Herbert, Mar. 22 and 25, 1875. BFA, Bestand C, Box 6. In the final draft (May 4) of his resignation Bismarck stated in fact that Wilhelm had already granted "a longer leave." Kohl, ed., *Bismarck-Jahrbuch*, I, p. 93.

[99] Johanna to Herbert, Apr. 26, 1875. BFA, Bestand C, Box 6.

reach the monarch until May 11? If Johanna's letters are to be trusted (why not?), the prince's decision was known and "lamented" among close acquaintances (Lucius and the Prince of Pless are mentioned) in early March.[100] One letter seems to suggest that the crown prince, who visited the chancellor, knew of it.[101] Did Bismarck deceive his wife and associates about having dispatched his letter to the king? Or did the letter lie on his desk those many weeks, while he pondered his decision and tinkered with the wording? What the conflicting evidence suggests is a long period of indecision and quandary, during which he discussed his personal condition and prospects informally with the Kaiser, who urged him merely to take another long leave.

Yet another factor in the delay may have been the crisis in foreign affairs. Bismarck's first information on France's reputed purchase of German horses came on February 26, and news of the intended expansion of the French army reached him sometime after March 12. Perhaps he persuaded himself that he should not leave office until he had sobered the French "with a stream of cold water."[102] At the end of April, however, came the disturbing relapse in Bismarck's health that Johanna reported to Herbert. Reminded again of his debilitated condition, the prince finished the final draft of the letter to Wilhelm on May 4. That he delayed its delivery until May 11 was owed to the diplomatic crisis. Before the talks with Alexander and Gorchakov on May 10, it would have been inappropriate to inform Wilhelm officially of his resolve to abandon the helm. Chancellor and Kaiser were both intent on keeping the decision secret (the Kaiser insisted that the scribe be sworn) in order to prevent the German public from jumping to the conclusion that the war-in-sight crisis was the reason for his departure.[103]

Bismarck did not believe that the war-in-sight crisis would do lasting damage to Germany's position in Europe. "The favorable condition of our internal affairs and of Germany's foreign relations," he wrote on May 4, "permits your majesty at the present moment to undertake changes, which must soon occur independently of every human will, but which at the present moment can be allowed to assume a form that appears purposeful."[104] But one wonders what effect the crisis may have had upon Bismarck's view of himself, whether the crisis weakened or strengthened his resolve to retire. Did he see in the diplomatic triumph of Decazes evidence that bad health was affecting his political

[100] Johanna to Herbert, Mar. 6, 1875. BFA, Bestand C, Box 6. The memoirs of Lucius, a leader of the free conservatives and usually well informed, do not mention these conversations, nor anything at all concerning the actual resignation in May. Lucius, Bismarck-Erinnerungen, pp. 68–75.

[101] Johanna to Herbert, Mar. 6, 1875. BFA, Bestand C, Box 6. Herbert told Lucius that Crown Prince Friedrich Wilhelm visited Bismarck four times in this period. Lucius, Bismarck-Erinnerungen, p. 73.

[102] Eyck, Bismarck, II, 155ff.

[103] Kohl, ed., Anhang, II, 253–255.

[104] GW, VIc, 59.

skills? Or did his humiliation at the hands of Gorchakov lead him to decide, consciously or unconsciously, to remain in office?[105] Did he prefer to stay in power rather than give enemies the satisfaction of believing that they had forced him out? If so, the greatest consequence of the war-in-sight crisis of 1875 may be one that historians have never suspected. It may have prolonged Bismarck's career by fifteen years.

Wilhelm was shocked by Bismarck's formal request for release from office. Apparently he had confidently expected their discussions of the prince's health problem in February and March to end in another extended leave. In the letter of May 4, however, Bismarck proposed to use the leave as a transitional period during which to prepare the way for a new government. But Wilhelm refused to release him, and Bismarck, who could have insisted, bowed to the decision.[106] Bismarck remained in office after 1875 because Wilhelm could not do without him and because Bismarck was inclined to the same point of view. To the grand duke of Weimar Wilhelm wrote, "I don't know how long he will be able to bear this existence, but I am convinced that he will be stronger when he returns to his positions. He himself knows and feels that he is irreplaceable as long as he lives. After him his post will be occupied, but he will never be replaced."[107] The time had come for Bismarck to retire gracefully from office—both for his own sake and perhaps for the good of his country. And he let it pass.

[105] On May 11, Gorchakov informed an incredulous Gontaut that Bismarck had handed in his resignation—on grounds of ill health—and claimed to have seen the document. Gorchakov hoped that Bismarck would revoke the decision, and Gontaut was sure that he would. *DDF*, I, 452. Apparently Bismarck showed the letter to Gorchakov on May 10, at a time when he did not yet appreciate that the resolution of the war-in-sight crisis would be interpreted abroad as a triumph for Russian-French diplomacy over Germany.

[106] Kohl, ed., *Bismarck-Jahrbuch*, I, 93–94; Kohl, ed., *Anhang*, I, 254–255; GW, VIc, 60.

[107] Wilhelm I to Karl Alexander, Grand Duke of Weimar, June 21, 1875. Johannes Schultze, ed., *Kaiser Wilhelms I. Weimarer Briefe* (Berlin, 1924), II, 118–119. How widespread the same assumption was can be seen in Eduard Lasker's remarks to Hohenlohe (Nov. 12, 1874). "Lasker . . . talked of Bismarck's projects of retiring. He regards them as mere pretence and says that Bismarck is too much of a demon to let the reins out of his hands. To my remark that the situation was ominous on account of the feeling at Court, Lasker replied that there was nothing to fear there. At the decisive moment no one would be willing to let Bismarck go, because they had no substitute for him. There were plenty of strawmen who imagined they could replace Bismarck, but the Kaiser would think twice before he put one of them in Bismarck's office." Hohenlohe, *Memoirs*, II, 130.

BOOK THREE

The Change of Front Begun,

1875–1878

He had made up his mind that under the empire the German Princes would still remain particularists, and he had therefore recommended universal suffrage in elections for the [Reichstag], believing that the mass of the people, favorable to imperial union, would act as a counterpoise. Experience, however, showed that, while the Princes rallied loyally to the new order, the weapon which he had devised to neutralize their anticipated opposition was constantly directed against himself.

—*Sir Edward Malet, quoting Bismarck in 1885*

✠

CHAPTER TEN

Economic Catastrophe and Liberal Decline

URING the late 1870s Bismarck launched changes in foreign and domestic policy so extensive in scope that some historians have written of a "refounding of the German Reich."[1] Although this is surely an overdramatization, the chancellor did execute a turnabout in internal and external affairs during these years. A list of the actions he took shows the extent and complexity of the shift: an attempt to make the Reich financially independent of the federal states and simultaneously to reduce the power of the Reichstag; the effort to reconstruct the "diagonal of forces" in parliament by reconstituting the Conservative party, splitting the National Liberal party, negotiating a truce in the Kulturkampf, and destroying the Social Democratic party; his reconstruction of the Reich executive and of its relationship to Prussia; a transition from free trade to protectionism and the forging of a new social and political link between agrarian landowners and industrial entrepreneurs; and, finally, the revision of Germany's foreign relations through negotiation of the Dual Alliance with Austria.

Bismarck's conception of the art of governing makes it unlikely that he followed any master plan in inaugurating this broad change of front. Indeed his decisions came individually over a period of years. Yet they possess a coherence that suggests they were, individually and collectively, his response to a changed perception of how to solve the basic problem with which he had long been concerned—that of the social and political consolidation of the German Reich. At the beginning of the 1870s he believed the greatest danger to that consolidation was state and regional particularism in combination with foreign foes. This anxiety explains his excessive reaction to political Catholicism. As the years passed, the Reich was welded ever more closely together by the progress of its economy, by the passage of many basic laws affecting all citizens, and by the growth of the imperial government and its various agencies. Evidence accumulated that the state dynasties and governments had come to accept their new status as federal states, while Bismarck's success in reconstructing Berlin's traditional alliance with the eastern great

---

[1] Helmut Böhme, *Deutschlands Weg zur Grossmacht: Studien zum Verhältnis von Wirtschaft und Staat während der Reichsgründungszeit 1848–1881* (Cologne, 1966), p. 419. See also Ivo N. Lambi, "The Agrarian-Industrial Front in Bismarckian Politics, 1873–1879," *Journal of Central European Affairs*, 20 (1961), p. 390; Fritz Stern, *Gold and Iron: Bismarck, Bleichröder, and the Building of the German Empire* (New York, 1977), p. 372; and James Sheehan, *German Liberalism in the Nineteenth Century* (Chicago, 1978), pp. 179, 181.

powers eased his fears of a new "Kaunitz coalition." Although his concern over particularism and ultramontanism by no means vanished, it was now overshadowed by other dangers he perceived on the domestic and international scene—by the threat of democratic liberalism and proletarian socialism. Henceforth Bismarck's principal objective was to consolidate the social and political establishments of Prussia-Germany and of its foreign allies against the possibility of internal subversion.

Bismarck's reassessment of the problem of consolidation was certainly conditioned, if not determined, by the economic depression that struck Germany and Europe after 1873. Germany's unification had taken place during a period of generally rising prosperity; its consolidation had to move forward during an era of economic crisis and social distress. To be fully understood, the events of the late 1870s, whether in domestic or foreign affairs, must be seen against the backdrop of that economic crisis.

The Depression of 1873–1879

The capital of Prussia made a poor impression on Arthur von Brauer in 1866 when he first saw it as a student newly arrived from southern Germany. Berlin was, he reported, a dull city. With the exception of the palaces and museums, its architecture was tasteless, monotonous, and boring. Most streets were badly paved with uneven stones and lined by open sewers through which oozed "a nauseous, sluggish slime" highly offensive to the senses. The hotels and restaurants were worse than those in southern Germany, and he was struck by the modesty with which most Berliners lived. Returning in 1872 at the height of the *Gründerjahre*, Brauer found the city "swimming in gold and gusto." "The hunger for profits and wealth possessed the new capital of the Reich, and even a large part of the once so solid Prussian officialdom and officer corps had joined the dance around the golden calf with no pangs of conscience. Swindlers gained large fortunes in a few days. Everyone, from princes to workers, gambled on the bourse. An obtrusive, undignified opulence predominated everywhere." When Brauer came again in 1874, the scene was again radically different. "The infamous *Gründer* millionaires had become beggars; not a few were in prison." Many officials and citizens had lost all they possessed. "Laborers were either unemployed or worked sullenly at starvation wages." Many expensive restaurants, once flowing with champagne, had been either closed or converted into beer halls. "The entire city was depressed and unhappy."[2]

The depression of 1873–1879 left a deeper imprint on German society than

[2] Arthur von Brauer, *Im Dienste Bismarcks* (Berlin, 1936), pp. 39–40. For a description of Berlin during boom and bust see Gerhard Masur, *Imperial Berlin* (New York, 1970), pp. 59ff., and Maximilian Müller-Jabusch, *So waren die Gründerjahre* (Düsseldorf, 1957).

any other economic crisis before the inflation of 1919–1923 and the crash of 1929. Although the entire capitalist world was affected, the German depression was particularly acute owing to the excesses of the *Gründerjahre*. Within six years wholesale prices in general sank by one-third, those in heavy industry by more than one-half.[3] By comparison the depressions of 1857 and 1866 had been brief interruptions in a generally upward trend. Now the German economy appeared to stagnate. "The years go by," wrote Schulze-Delitzsch in 1876, "and confidence, which is the soul of all sound commerce, does not want to return; still there is no dissolution of the spell that weighs upon our economic circumstances. The failure of corrupt enterprises is followed by the bankruptcy of others involved in their losses. Even those firms that under normal circumstances could have recovered from the damage they suffered begin to expire, since the volume of business remains behind the most modest expectations."[4] The business world was gripped by a sense of enduring crisis and even panic.

As noted earlier, the signs of approaching difficulty were also evident in German agriculture by the late 1870s. For two decades American and Ukrainian farmers had been conquering an increasing share of the European grain market. Eventually Argentina and even India joined the invasion. Cheap land, virgin soil, and superior farm machinery enabled farmers of the American Midwest to produce at low cost; new railways and steam navigation reduced the expense of long-distance transport. Russian grain, which earlier had reached western Europe largely through Black Sea ports, could now be transported more cheaply by rail to the German frontier and Baltic seaports. During the 1870s new machinery overcame difficulties in milling the hard wheat grown in Russia and America. Under these circumstances German grain growers began to lose their hold on export markets, particularly in Great Britain, which for decades had been the best foreign customer of east-Elbian estate owners. Although it threatened their domination of the domestic market as well, the inflow of Russian grain was not without benefits for eastern producers. Before it could be sold to the bakers of Germany and western Europe, Russia's hard wheat had to be mixed with the softer variety grown in Germany. Hence Prussian landowners retained an interest in the export trade even under changed conditions. It will be shown that as a consequence they were in no hurry to abandon the doctrine of free trade.[5]

[3] Alfred Jacobs and Hans Richter, *Die Grosshandelspreise in Deutschland von 1792 bis 1934. Sonderhefte des Institut für Konjunkturforschung*, vol. 31 (Berlin, 1935), pp. 44–45.

[4] Friedrich Thorwart, ed., *Hermann Schulze-Delitzschs Schriften und Reden* (Berlin, 1909), I, 641.

[5] Karl W. Hardach, *Die Bedeutung wirtschaftlicher Faktoren bei der Wiedereinführung der Eisen- und Getreidezölle in Deutschland 1879* (Berlin, 1967), pp. 73–77; also Theodor Freiherr von der Goltz, *Geschichte der deutschen Landwirtschaft* (Stuttgart, 1903), II, 390ff., and Wilhelm Abel, *Agrarkrisen und Agrarkonjunktur* (2d ed., Hamburg, 1966), pp. 257–261.

During the 1870s the expansion in American exports depressed grain prices in Europe generally. Prices plunged on the British market in 1874–1875 and did not fully recover in the following years. Germany was sheltered from this pressure by a series of bad harvests during 1875–1881 (1878 was an exception) that kept grain prices fairly constant. During these years the shortages were made good first by imports from Russia (1876–1877) and thereafter from North America. At the end of the decade the rising tide of American exports to Europe portended trouble for German landowners. Their export markets were disappearing and even the domestic market appeared vulnerable.[6] Nor did landowners like Bismarck with heavy investments in timber have much to cheer about. During the period in which Bismarck acquired Varzin and Friedrichsruh, the timber trade was in a growth stage. Between 1863 and 1872 the increase in private construction produced an expansion in sales of wood and wood products of from 3 to 5 percent per year. The collapse of 1873 led to a steep decline in construction with the consequence that by 1879 the growth rate had fallen to 0.1 percent and remained at less than 1 percent until 1883.[7] During the period 1850–1865 average lumber prices mounted steadily from seven to eleven marks per cubic meter, fluctuating during the next seven years between nine and ten marks. Between 1873 and 1875 the price climbed steeply to more than thirteen marks, but fell to about ten marks in 1877 and 1878. Fuel wood followed roughly the same curves.[8]

German grain producers of the 1870s were troubled by the price level, not because it fell, but because it failed to rise sufficiently to compensate for poor harvests and rising costs. During the prosperous decades since 1830 speculation in land had driven up property values as much as 400 percent. "Landowners became rich while asleep."[9] But indebtedness and interest charges also rose. Mortgages of 80 to 90 percent of the purchase price of the property and 100 percent of real value (in terms of yields) were not uncommon. The wages of rural workers also mounted as landowners competed with industry for their services. During the *Gründerjahre* the cost of money, labor, and farm implements climbed steeply, while agrarian incomes tended to remain constant. The collapse of 1873–1874 eased this crisis, although wages tended to decline

[6] Hardach, *Bedeutung wirtschaftlicher Faktoren*, pp. 83–84; on grain prices see Max Sering, *Internationale Preisbewegung und Lage der Landwirtschaft in den aussertropischen Ländern* (Berlin, 1929), pp. 170, 172, and *Die landwirtschaftliche Konkurrenz Nordamerikas in Gegenwart und Zukunft* (Leipzig, 1887), pp. 532, 545, 546, and 739; Walther G. Hoffmann, *Das Wachstum der deutschen Wirtschaft seit der Mitte des 19. Jahrhunderts* (Berlin, 1965), p. 522, and Ashok V. Desai, *Real Wages in Germany, 1871–1913* (Oxford, 1968), p. 118.

[7] Walther G. Hoffmann, "Wachstumsschwankungen in der deutschen Wirtschaft 1850–1967," in Walther G. Hoffmann, ed., *Untersuchungen zum Wachstum der deutschen Wirtschaft* (Tübingen, 1971), pp. 80, 90.

[8] Hoffmann, *Das Wachstum der deutschen Wirtschaft*, p. 563. For other figures derived from sales by the Prussian state forests see Sering, *Internationale Preisbewegung*, p. 173.

[9] Hardach, *Bedeutung wirtschaftlicher Faktoren*, p. 85.

more slowly than implement prices. Then came the years of poor harvests that reduced farm income, while encouraging foreign imports. Even the good harvest of 1878 had its adverse side, for the bounty depressed prices in 1878–1879. At the end of the decade there were grounds for uneasiness about the future of German agriculture.[10]

The economic crisis of the 1870s had acute consequences of a social, political, and psychological nature. To liberals who believed in the efficacy of free enterprise, periodic depressions were a natural process by which the market purged itself of inefficient and marginal businesses. To conservatives, on the other hand, the depression in industry demonstrated the folly of the Bismarck–Delbrück economic policy, which had lifted restrictions on incorporation, granted freedom of occupation, and liquidated guild and state controls. Except for those dependent upon the export-import trade, capitalists located the source of their difficulties in the policy of free trade that exposed them to foreign competition. Many workers, whose wages sank as the entrepreneurs retrenched, were convinced by the argument that the system of private ownership itself, whether of land or industry, was the cause of their distress. The threatened business class was open to insinuations by conservative writers that the depression was the consequence not only of capitalistic greed and corruption, but also of a conspiracy by Jewish bankers and entrepreneurs who had taken advantage of German innocence. During the 1870s imperial Germany experienced its first general wave of anti-Semitism, one that continued to lap at the edges of popular consciousness and to erode humanistic values even after the depression receded and prosperity returned.[11]

Academic Socialism

In *Sturmflut* the novelist Friedrich von Spielhagen depicted typical personalities of the *Gründerjahre*: a spendthrift and nearly bankrupt nobleman who gouges his farm tenants and seeks succor in an advantageous marriage; a newly rich, high-living company promoter and a dishonest official who enlist the nobleman in a scheme to gain a government charter for a new railway, whose watered stock they wish to sell to a gullible public; a general whom they attempt to corrupt in order to get his support for a naval base to be constructed at a bad location on the new railway line; a small manufacturer and supporter of the Progressive party who had fought at the barricades for the republican cause in 1848 and still feels the sting of defeat; and the dissatisfied workers

    [10] Abel, *Agrarkrisen und Agrarkonjunktur*, pp. 253–257; Goltz, *Landwirtschaft*, II, 347, 354–356, 383–394, 402–403; Arthur Spiethoff, *Die wirtschaftlichen Wechsellagen* (Tübingen, 1955), II, tab. 27.

    [11] See particularly Hans Rosenberg, *Grosse Depression und Bismarckzeit* (Berlin, 1967), pp. 88–117, and Max Nitzsche, *Die handelspolitische Reaktion in Deutschland. Münchener volkswirtschaftliche Studien* (Stuttgart, 1905), pp. 97–98.

whom he dismissed for daring to join the socialist movement. In the background we hear rumbles of dissatisfaction from the urban lower classes, who strike and threaten violence to the owners at the very height of the boom.[12]

Although their real earnings rose sharply in the years 1869–1873 (except for a brief interruption during the war against France), German workers sensed that they were not sharing fully in the general prosperity. "[Bismarck] has done nothing for the working people," Lassallean socialists charged in 1872. "He has not made our lives easier, only more sour year by year, because of the effect of the economic laws passed with his help."[13] The period 1869–1873 was marked by a "strike fever" unprecedented in Germany, as workers sought to cope with inflation and exploit the labor shortage. Their demands were chiefly for higher pay and shorter hours, the right to retain union membership on being employed, the removal of brutal work supervisors, and an end to the prosecution of striking workers and leaders. Most strikes were spontaneous and local. Many were successful, but the largest—walkouts by Berlin machinists and miners in the Ruhr and Upper Silesia in 1872—ended in failure. Although brief, the walkouts left behind an increased awareness by proletarians of the need to organize and build permanent strike funds.[14] Another symptom of the times was rioting on the outskirts of Berlin. The rapid growth of the city's population through immigration (twenty thousand to thirty thousand annually in the 1860s, peaking at fifty thousand in 1871) created a massive housing shortage for workers; rents soared and overcrowding reached crisis proportions. Tenement construction lagged while builders constructed luxury apartments and villas for the rich. Unable to find quarters, thousands of workers lived in shantytowns of their own construction on the edge of the city. Evictions by the police led to riots, one of which left 102 policemen injured and 159 workers with saber wounds. The rising cost of living also produced disturbances in the streets of Mannheim, Frankfurt am Main, Munich, Stuttgart, and other places.[15] In the upper strata of society the experience of 1869–1873 raised new doubts about the virtues of laissez-faire and unrestrained capitalism. "The gentlemen of the bourgeoisie," wrote Theodor

[12] Friedrich von Spielhagen, *Sturmflut* (Leipzig, 1877).

[13] Quoted in Heinrich von Poschinger, ed., *Fürst Bismarck als Volkswirth* (Berlin, 1889–1890), I, 69.

[14] Hedwig Wachenheim, *Die deutsche Arbeiterbewegung, 1844 bis 1914* (Cologne, 1967), pp. 136–149. SEG (1872), pp. 159, 167; Klaus Tenfelde, *Sozialgeschichte der Bergarbeiterschaft an der Ruhr im 19. Jahrhundert* (Bonn–Bad Godesberg, 1977), pp. 436–486. The files of the Prussian Ministry of Commerce show how broad the spectrum of worker discontent became in the late 1860s. Strikes were reported in the building trades, furniture manufacture, shipbuilding, lumbering, mining, textile manufacture, shoemaking, baking, and many other trades. DZA Merseburg, Rep. 120, BB, VII, 1, Nr. 1, 2, 3.

[15] Paul Kampffmeyer and Bruno Altmann, *Vor dem Sozialistengesetz: Krisenjahre des Obrigkeitsstaates* (Berlin, 1928), pp. 98–103; Nicholas Bullock and James Read, *The Movement for Housing Reform in Germany and France, 1840–1914* (Cambridge, Eng., 1985), pp. 19, 53–55.

Lohmann in June 1873, "have grown anxious [*den Katzenjammer bekommen*] about the consequences of their own legislation."[16]

Laissez-faire was the only doctrine of natural law that gained widespread acceptance in Germany during the nineteenth century. Through the writings of Adam Smith, David Ricardo, and John Stuart Mill, German economists had come to regard economics as an exact science based on the laws of supply and demand and the natural mechanism of the marketplace. Spreading outward from the universities into the bureaucracy, the business world, and the liberal press, Manchesterism triumphed over the national economics of Friedrich List, the corporative social views of Victor Aimé Huber and Hermann Wagener, and the egalitarian state socialism of Ferdinand Lassalle. During the middle decades the remarkable expansion of industrial capitalism and the wealth it produced seemed to confirm the validity of liberal economic principles.

Yet even before the collapse of 1873 some observers within those same groups in which laissez-faire had won its greatest success (academicians, government officials, and businessmen) became uneasy about the growing gap between rich and poor, capital and labor, and its possible consequences for social stability. Beginning in the late 1860s, this uneasiness led to the search for a new social policy capable of preventing or overcoming the alienation of labor. (Even Crown Prince Friedrich Wilhelm reflected in his diary that, political unity having been achieved, the next goal must be social unity.)[17] The reforms proposed were numerous and varied. They ranged from modifications of the free enterprise system to bold plans for state socialism. Ernst Engel, director of the Prussian Statistical Bureau, which in the 1860s became an important agency for the training of economists, advocated an "industrial partnership system," under which employees would gradually be given a role

---

[16] Hans Rothfels, *Theodor Lohmann und die Kampfjahre der staatlichen Sozialpolitik, 1871–1905. Forschungen und Darstellungen aus dem Reichsarchiv*, vol. 6 (Berlin, 1927).

[17] For the social views of Friedrich Wilhelm and the historians Alfred Dove and Jakob Burckhardt at this juncture see James J. Sheehan, *The Career of Lujo Brentano: A Study of Liberalism and Social Reform in Imperial Germany* (Chicago, 1966), pp. 47–48. In Feb. 1872 Ernst von Eynern, a merchant at Barmen in the Ruhr, wrote to Heinrich von Sybel, "Of necessity manufacturing and burgher circles are paying the greatest attention to the social question. But it is only too understandable that they often subordinate their judgments either to individual interests or to . . . the collective interests of those engaged in the same kind of enterprise." He called for "a scientific investigation of the question" in behalf of those "who recognize the impossibility of the present situation." *HW*, II, 43. In late 1873 the standing committee of the German Commercial Association (*Deutscher Handelstag*) was sufficiently aroused to launch a large-scale enquiry, with the cooperation of the Reichskanzleramt and German governments, into "the agitation among workers" and the "dangers it raises for German industry." *DZA* Potsdam, Reichskanzleramt, 452, pp. 2–62. Bismarck received a copy. Achenbach to Bismarck, Dec. 16, 1873. *Ibid.*, p. 60. The rising tide of general concern, especially among manufacturers, but also landowners, can be seen in the communications received by the Reichskanzleramt. *DZA* Potsdam, Reichskanzleramt, 1294, Vol. 1 (1869–1878).

in the ownership and management of the enterprises in which they worked. One of his students, Lujo Brentano, who was fascinated by British trade unionism, began in the late 1860s his life-long agitation for collective bargaining as the best way to improve labor's share in the benefits of industry. Gustav Schmoller, on the other hand, hoped to develop a socially conscious bureaucracy, independent of the class struggle, that would institute social reform, acting under the advice of experts, meaning professors like himself. Adolph Wagner likewise hoped for a "social monarchy" capable of meting out social justice to workers on an objective basis. Schmoller and Wagner were representatives of the "young historical school" of German economists that "led German economics away from the Anglo-French traditions and developed a 'German school' with roots in the romantic and Hegelian movements."[18]

This group of young professors had no sooner become aware of their common interest in social reform than they were harshly attacked by threatened Manchesterites. In December 1871 the liberal journalist Heinrich Oppenheim denounced them in the *Nationalzeitung* as *Kathedersozialisten* ("academic socialists"). "We regard as socialists," he declared, "anyone who proposes a system of state action to solve the social question." Another liberal critic charged, "They only lack the courage to be like Bebel and Liebknecht." To be branded a *Kathedersozialist* was a serious matter, for an avowed socialist had no chance for an academic career in imperial Germany. Although widely disparate in their social programs, the threatened scholars were compelled to stand together against the assault of the Manchesterites. The latter belonged, for the most part, to the left wing of the National Liberal party (most notably Oppenheim and Ludwig Bamberger), men with strong ties to financial and banking interests, who feared that the writings of the *Kathedersozialisten* might provide the ideological basis for an antiliberal coalition composed of workers, landowners, and government officials.[19]

None of the *Kathedersozialisten* was a political activist. They were primarily university professors and economic historians who hoped through their researches and writings to reorient German economic and social policy. They wished to revive and reinforce the tradition that the Prussian state was a neutral force beyond the reach of the conflicting interests in civil society and dedicated to the common welfare. Through social justice they expected to bridge the gap between the social classes and construct a more cohesive society. That they achieved public prominence and an audience for their views was largely owing to the bitterness of their quarrel with the Manchesterites.

In July 1872 a small group of *Kathedersozialisten* met at Halle to organize a

[18] See particularly Sheehan, *Lujo Brentano*, pp. 48ff.; also Gerhard Wittrock, *Die Kathedersozialisten bis zur Eisenacher Versammlung 1872*, Historische Studien, vol. 350 (Berlin, 1939), pp. 19–120.

[19] Sheehan, *Lujo Brentano*, pp. 59–66; Wittrock, *Kathedersozialisten*, pp. 121ff.

common front against their liberal foes. Out of this conference came a larger meeting at Eisenach in October to which was invited anyone interested in social reform and critical of laissez-faire. These criteria brought together 150 persons (chiefly professors, officials, and a few manufacturers) whose views were so disparate that Schmoller, who presided, had to insist that the subject of principle be avoided in favor of specific reforms.[20] The subjects discussed were: more effective administration of factory laws through permanent government agencies; prohibition of child labor; compulsory schooling for the lower classes; limitation of labor by married women; unconditional acceptance of labor's freedom to organize; legal recognition of unions and legal protection for their treasuries; and the creation of conciliation services and courts of arbitration.[21] A concrete result of the Eisenach meeting was the organization in May 1873 of the Association for Social Policy (*Verein für Sozialpolitik*) which remained the forum for the views of the *Kathedersozialisten* to the end of imperial Germany.

The influence of the association on German legislation proved to be negligible because of the disparate views of its members and the apolitical trend that developed in German academic circles after 1870. Yet the association did make criticism of laissez-faire intellectually respectable and prepared the public for the social reforms of the 1880s. The polemics between Brentano and his associates, on the one hand, and Oppenheim, Bamberger, and finally Heinrich von Treitschke, on the other, exaggerated the gulf between *Kathedersozialisten* and Manchesterites. During the mid-1870s efforts were made by Eduard Lasker, Gustav Schmoller, and Rudolf Gneist to effect a reconciliation between the association and the Congress of German Economists. At the end of the decade the two organizations made common cause against tariff protectionism and the shift to the right in Bismarck's domestic policy.[22] Yet their common front on this issue could not erase the fact that the *Kathedersozialisten*, incapable of winning the liberals as a whole to social reform, had merely introduced another crack in liberalism's fractured facade. Through them laissez-faire lost its status as the unchallenged doctrine of German "science." Their call for protection of the weakest social group in the competitive

---

[20] Sheehan, *Lujo Brentano*, pp. 67ff.

[21] *SEG* (1872), p. 205.

[22] Sheehan, *Lujo Brentano*, pp. 72ff. *HW*, II, 137–139, 143–144. In 1872 Heinrich von Treitschke recognized that the "danger" was "very great" and began to study the social question. "The need of the working classes can no longer be denied," he wrote. "Nor can it be denied that the state must intervene where the self-seeking of the propertied classes blinds them to the truth." Treitschke to Heinrich von Sybel, May 15, 1872. Max Cornicelius, ed., *Heinrich von Treitschkes Briefe* (Leipzig, 1920), II, 349. Yet he finally denounced the views of the *Kathedersozialisten* in a vitriolic pamphlet, *Die Sozialisten und ihre Gönner*, in which he appraised the bourgeoisie as a new aristocracy and expressed his fears of "bestial mob movements" that threatened "the ideal values of our culture." *Ibid.*, III, 370–371, 393–400, 410–413.

world of capitalism led easily to the conclusion that weak industries must also be protected from the brutal competition of foreign producers.

Growth of Proletarian Socialism

The grant in 1867 of universal, direct, equal, and secret male suffrage in national elections and the abolition in 1869 of anticombination laws opened new avenues for labor to realize its objectives. The depression of the 1870s provided the compulsion to exercise both rights. By 1878 wages in the iron industry, for example, had fallen below the level of 1869. The Phoenix iron works in Duisburg reduced its daily wage from 3.30 to 2.10 marks; the Heinrichshütte iron works in the Siegerland from 2.50 to 2.43 marks. Louis Baare, general director of the Bochumer Verein, reported that laborers were willing to work for 1.50 marks per day "just to keep their positions," although they could "not exist" on such a wage. The average yearly wage paid by the Bochumer Verein sank from 1,190 marks in 1874 to 875 marks in 1880. In December 1874 the Krupp concern began a drastic wage reduction, warning that "every expression of dissatisfaction" would be regarded as notice of the worker's intention to quit; by 1879 Krupp had reduced wages by half, a record by no means unique in heavy industry. The average yearly income of industrial workers and artisans sank from 620 marks in 1873 to 558 marks in 1879.

Layoffs were massive. The number of workers employed in German mining declined from 289,000 to 275,000 between 1873 and 1879. During the same period the number of miners employed in the district of Dortmund fell from 84,000 to 77,000. Individual industries were hit even harder. Between 1873 and 1879 the Hoerder Verein reduced its manpower from 4,709 to 2,604, the Bochumer Verein from 4,077 to 2,507, the Dortmunder Union reduced its work force by half, from 12,102 (1873) to 6,322 (1877); more than 4,000 were dismissed in 1874 alone. Of the 30,000 metal workers listed with the Invalidenkasse in Berlin, only 18,300 were employed in 1875. In December 1879 Berlin's chief of police warned "that the continuing loss of wages and jobs and the very depressed conditions existing in a number of regions is spreading doubt about the justice of the present economic and social order and dissatisfaction with the existing [system] in an ever larger circle of the population, a circle that is usually very calm and moderate."[23]

The effects of this catastrophe were soon evident in election statistics. In the Reichstag election of 1871 socialists of the Lassalle and Eisenach factions had polled 124,000 votes (3.2 percent of the electorate) and elected two deputies; in that of 1874 they polled 352,000 votes (6.8 percent of the electorate) and brought in nine candidates, six Eisenachers and three Lassalleans.[24] In

[23] Hans-Ulrich Wehler, Bismarck und der Imperialismus (Cologne, 1969), pp. 78–79.
[24] Heino Kaack, Geschichte und Struktur des deutschen Parteiensystems (Opladen, 1971), p. 46.

London Friedrich Engels exulted, "The election in Germany places the German proletariat at the head of the European labor movement. For the first time workers vote en masse for their own people, put forward their own party, and this is true throughout Germany."[25] This success provided a new incentive for unity in the socialist movement. Obstacles to fusion had been reduced when the Lassalleans gave up their hope of collaborating with the Bismarck government and the Eisenachers realized the futility of their agitation for a great-German federal republic. Harassment and persecution by German governments, furthermore, impressed upon the leadership of both parties and their associated unions the need for a united front. At Gotha in 1875 the two parties combined to become the Social Democratic Workers party with a common leadership and a program that reflected a compromise between Lassallean state socialism and Marxian revolutionary socialism.[26]

In the united party two former Eisenachers, August Bebel and Wilhelm Liebknecht, became the dominant figures (Lassalle's successor, Johann Baptist von Schweitzer, had been forced out of politics after 1871 and died in 1875). Neither had a firm grasp of Marxian theory. Bebel only found time to study *Das Kapital* during periods of imprisonment after 1869. They were not advocates of violence. To Marx's distress the goals outlined in the Gotha program of 1875—liberation of the working class "within the framework of the existing national state" and attainment "by all legal means of a free state and socialist society"—were democratic, but not revolutionary and not international. Yet there was no question but that the united movement, owing to its republican, egalitarian, and socialistic character, was hostile to the aristocratic-monarchical order in Germany and to the capitalistic system.[27]

The founding of the Social Democratic party did not end the cleavages within the labor movement, as the history of German trade unionism shows. We have seen that German trade unions, in contrast to those of the Anglo-Saxon world, were politically oriented from the start.[28] The Lassalleans and Eisenachers organized rival socialist unions that were merged after the parties united. Under the influence of Wilhelm Emmanuel von Ketteler, bishop of Mainz, a number of Catholic unions (including some Protestant members) were formed that amalgamated after 1890 and affiliated with the Center party. Max Hirsch and Franz Duncker organized a chain of labor unions under the influence of the Progressive party. No one political party could justly claim to represent all of the German working class. Yet two of the three trade union

[25] Georg Eckert, ed., *Wilhelm Liebknecht: Briefwechsel mit Karl Marx und Friedrich Engels* (The Hague, 1963), p. 184.

[26] August Bebel, *Aus meinem Leben* (Stuttgart, 1911), II, 330ff.; Willy Albrecht, *Fachverein-Berufsgewerkschaft-Zentralverband: Organisationsprobleme der deutschen Gewerkschaften 1870–1890* (Bonn, 1982), pp. 195–242.

[27] Karl Marx, *Kritik des Gothaer Programms* (new and enlarged edition, Berlin, 1946).

[28] See pp. 28–29.

organizations—the Hirsch-Duncker unions (left-liberal) and the "free unions" (socialist)—were affiliated with political parties either highly critical of
or fundamentally opposed to the existing political order. The Catholic Center
and Social Democratic parties apparently satisfied the need of their proletarian members for a new human association and spiritual orientation to replace
what had been lost in the shift from a rural to an urban environment. In the
industrial communities provided by employers like Karl Stumm and Alfred
Krupp some workers found a patriarchal relationship reminiscent of what they
had left behind in the eastern countryside. Both the Center and Social Democratic parties ultimately created subcultures with which workers could identify. Each in its own way provided an ideology capable of explaining the total
life experience, a party press for relating it to daily issues, and a program of
activities (youth groups, outings, meetings, and rallies) that absorbed the
workers' leisure time "from the cradle to the grave."

Yet there were, of course, significant differences between the two parties.
The Center bridged the gap between capital and labor, between the older and
newer social classes, and its leadership was essentially conservative. The social democrats, on the other hand, were outspokenly proletarian, anticapitalistic, and democratic. Their emergence from obscurity to become a significant
political force capable of polling more than 9 percent of the electorate in 1877
shows that the party expressed the aspirations of increasing numbers of urban
workers. It also shows the effect of the depression and the growing sense
among wage laborers that neither the Prussian-German establishment nor the
liberal and conservative parties of the Reichstag looked after their interests.

Like their Catholic counterparts, some Protestant clergymen appreciated
the danger of failing to grapple with the problem of social reform. When
Adolf Stöcker, a former army chaplain, arrived in Berlin to assume the post
of court preacher and director of the Berlin City Mission in 1874, he was
shocked to discover the degree of middle and lower class alienation from the
church. During 1874–1878, 80 percent of all marriages in Berlin took place
outside the church and 45 percent of all children were not baptized.[29] To meet
the threat of social democracy, which was avowedly atheistic and anticlerical,
Stöcker founded the Christian Social Labor party, "based on the Christian
faith," and "love of king and fatherland." The party program advocated obligatory craft unions, social security funds under state supervision, and arbitration courts. Legislation was to be sought abolishing Sunday labor, child labor,
employment of married women, and other abuses. The "gap between rich and
poor" was to be reduced through progressive income and inheritance taxes,
luxury taxes, a tax on the bourse, and laws against usury.[30]

But Stöcker was badly outwitted in his first attempt to organize Berlin work-

[29] Wachenheim, Arbeiterbewegung, p. 190.
[30] Wilhelm Mommsen, Deutsche Parteiprogramme (Munich, 1951), pp. 27–28.

ers. Seeking to "use workers to reach workers," he chose as his political missionary to the lower classes a tailor named Emil Grüneberg, a former social democratic agitator and "ne'er do well" who had found it advantageous to convert to Christianity. On the evening of January 3, 1878, Grüneberg sought to found the new party at an assembly of about a thousand workers—mostly committed social democrats—in a Berlin beer hall and was laughed down. Stöcker, lurking in the background, rushed to his rescue—the court preacher's first political appearance—but his pastoral eloquence evoked more laughter, ironic applause, and a point-by-point rebuttal from Johann Most, a Reichstag deputy with a razor-sharp tongue. The assembly voted for a resolution declaring that, since Christianity had not ended need and suffering in nineteen centuries, socialism was the only path to social justice.[31]

In Berlin the Social Democratic party held the field against Stöcker's Christian socialism even in the antisocialist election of 1878. Since 1874 the socialists had made deep inroads in the strength of the Progressive party, which dominated Berlin politics, and on the Hirsch–Duncker trade unions, its labor auxiliary. On March 10, 1878, they demonstrated their strength when thousands joined in the funeral procession of the printer August Heinsch, a party functionary. At the end of April even more (an estimated twelve thousand), showed their indignation by marching in another funeral procession, that of Paul Dentler, a socialist editor who had been jailed, although acutely ill of consumption, and died in prison. "Who can still speak of Berlin's 'worker battalions' in view of these thousands of marchers?" asked the liberal *Magdeburger Zeitung*. "Regiments, brigades, divisions, yes even entire army corps of mourners were mobilized to pay final honor to those who have certainly died for the cause."[32] The concentration of so many disciplined adherents of an avowedly atheistic, republican, and anticapitalistic movement in the nation's capital, the nerve center of its government, armed forces, and communications, began to produce anxiety among the wealthy and powerful—including Bismarck. By the late 1870s fear of socialism, the burgeoning fruit of a continuing economic depression, began to supplant the fear of Catholicism as the chief danger to the consolidation of the German Reich.

Repression

Like many contemporaries, Bismarck was shocked into a renewed awareness of working class discontent by the communard revolution in Paris during April and May 1871. Although without a common philosophy or program, the communards were united in opposing the return of the wealthy, generals,

[31] Walter Frank, *Hofprediger Adolf Stoecker und die christlich-soziale Bewegung* (Berlin, 1928), pp. 54–61.

[32] Bebel, *Aus meinem Leben*, II, 398–399.

monarchists, and clergy to power and influence in France. Their execution of hundreds of hostages (including the archbishop of Paris) horrified governments and people of property everywhere—far more than did the "white terror" that followed the commune's defeat by the army of the French National Assembly. At Berlin August Bebel irritated the Reichstag by declaring that the fighting in Paris was just a preliminary skirmish. "In a few decades the battle cry of the French proletariat will become the battle cry of the entire European proletariat: 'War upon the palaces, peace to the cottages, death to misery and idleness.' "[33] In London Karl Marx, speaking for the International Workingmen's Association, boldly acclaimed the commune as the first spontaneous proletarian uprising in European history and a prognosis of the coming revolt of proletarians everywhere against their capitalistic oppressors.[34]

Established in 1864, the International Workingmen's Association had become the chief spokesman for European radicals. Affiliated trade unions and socialist organizations were to be found in all European countries. By 1869 its annual congresses had developed, despite factional and philosophical cleavages, a communistic program that called for the abolition of private property. Marx's open approval of the Paris Commune and his apologia for its atrocities were not shared by most of the membership; dissent over this issue deepened the cleavages within the International and contributed a few years later to its dissolution. Yet Marx's audacious stand on the commune gave the "red terrorist doctor" in London fresh notoriety in the European press and for the first time focused the attention of Europe's governments and dominant classes upon the International as a potential source of subversion. But there was also a fresh awareness of the fact that the International and its affiliates everywhere thrived on genuine popular dissatisfactions grounded in social injustice.

Even before the drama of the commune unfolded Bismarck began (September 12, 1870) to seek a common front with the Austrian and Russian governments against subversive movements in Europe—another example of his talent for striking simultaneously at two targets with the same weapon. Although genuinely concerned about socialism, he also found it a convenient issue upon which to launch the rapprochement that ultimately led to the Three Emperors League. After the end of the war against France he proposed that the European powers exchange information on subversives and regard revolutionary activity as a criminal rather than a political offense, which would make the offenders extraditable. But Great Britain rejected the latter measure and refused to participate in a European conference proposed by Spain to consider steps against the International. Bismarck too backed away from the Spanish proposal, explaining that he was much too busy in the strug-

---

[33] SBR (1871), II, 920–921.
[34] Karl Marx, The Civil War in France (London, 1871).

gle against "ultramontane enemies of the state."[35] At Bad Gastein in August
1871 Bismarck reached agreement with Beust on a common policy but not on
joint action in the social question. They resolved: to satisfy justified wishes of
the working classes by changing "production, trade, and prices" where government action could be "harmonized with the general interests of the state";
and to "restrict agitation dangerous to the state through prohibitive penal
laws insofar as that can be done without harm to a healthy public life."[36] Here
was formulated the dual policy of reform and repression that Bismarck was to
pursue for the next twenty years.

For the time being repression was more in evidence than reform. During
the war with France both democratic and social radicals felt the heavy hand
of the police. Initially the Lassalleans and many Eisenachers (but not August
Bebel and Wilhelm Liebknecht) supported the "defensive war" against Napoleon III, as did Marx and the International. This changed quickly in early
September when Napoleon fell, the French republic was proclaimed, and the
demand for Alsace-Lorraine arose. In Hanover the central committee of the
Eisenachers issued a "Brunswick Manifesto" praising the republic and denouncing annexation. The five members were promptly arrested by the military governor of the coastal regions, General Vogel von Falckenstein, and
were transported in chains to a prison at Lötzen in East Prussia. Additional
arrests followed, including those of two democrats: Herbig, a Hamburg merchant, and Johann Jacoby, a Königsberg physician active in radical liberal
causes since 1848.[37] Although Bismarck and the Kaiser approved of the
Brunswick arrests, Bismarck found the imprisonment of Herbig and Jacoby
politically inexpedient and criticized Falckenstein's ban on the socialist press
and assemblies as an unnecessary violation of the constitution.[38]

The most notorious political arrests of 1870–1871, however, were those of
Bebel and Liebknecht carried out by the Saxon government. As Reichstag
deputies, the two Eisenacher leaders had abstained from the first vote on war
credits. In November 1870 five Lassallean deputies joined them in denouncing the annexation of Alsace-Lorraine and voting against further war loans
amid tumultuous scenes in the Reichstag.[39] After adjournment Bebel, Liebknecht, and Adolf Hepner, editor of the social democratic *Volksstaat*, were
taken into custody at Leipzig (December 17, 1870). But the Saxon police
could find no hard evidence of subversive activity. Released in April 1871,

[35] Gerhard Schümer, *Die Entstehungsgeschichte des Sozialistengesetzes* (Göttingen, 1929), pp. 4–
12; Kampffmeyer and Altmann, *Vor dem Sozialistengesetz*, pp. 72ff.

[36] *AWB*, I, 161.

[37] Bebel, *Aus meinem Leben*, II, 186–189; Hans-Ulrich Wehler, *Sozialdemokratie und Nationalstaat* (Würzburg, 1962), pp. 45–51; Kampffmeyer and Altmann, *Vor dem Sozialistengesetz*, pp.
54–68.

[38] GW, VIb, 522–524, 561–573; Schümer, *Entstehungsgeschichte*, pp. 16–18.

[39] *SBR* (1870), 2d extraordinary session, I, 9–23.

the three were, nevertheless, arraigned on charges of inciting high treason (*Hochverrat*) in March 1872, perhaps under some pressure from Bismarck. The result was conviction and two years fortress imprisonment for Bebel and Liebknecht; Hepner was declared not guilty. For lese majesty Bebel received an additional nine months and was deprived of his Reichstag seat. During their trial the socialists had some success in converting the courtroom into a forum for the propagation of their views. Their martyrdom probably increased the popularity of the socialist movement among workmen.[40] So likewise did the fate of other editors and party workers harassed and arrested during the following years by the Saxon police, who were determined, so Bebel wrote, to "put their colleagues in the rest of Germany in the shade."[41]

By the early 1870s it had become evident that Bismarck's social policy suffered from a basic contradiction. He had delivered into labor's hands two potent weapons, the ballot and the strike, but had taken no positive steps to assure that they would not be used in ways harmful to the Prussian-German establishment. None of the half-hearted discussions and attempts at social amelioration during the 1860s had gotten anywhere. Now in the early years of the empire he was faced with a disturbing combination of social and political woes: the success of the Center party in attracting labor support; signs of increasing socialist agitation among discontented workers; evidence (convincing at least to Bismarck) of an unholy "red and black alliance" between social radicals and Catholic clergy;[42] the number and dimensions of the strikes in German industry during the *Gründerjahre*; the continued emigration of farm labor from Germany; and finally reports that striking industrial workers were joining hands with farm laborers in a common struggle against the possessing classes.[43]

Initially the Bismarck government sought to meet the problem of strikes and subversion under existing statutes. In January 1871 Minister of Interior Eulenburg ordered Prussian police to keep track of "movements among the workers." As reports from police agents, many spurious, accumulated in the files, the minister sought to stretch Prussian and imperial statutes to prohibit or dissolve workers' assemblies, demonstrations, and organizations.[44] In September 1872 he directed provincial governments to be vigilant in enforcing the provision of the industrial code that guaranteed nonstrikers the right to

[40] Bebel, *Aus meinem Leben*, II, 245–258, 267; Kampffmeyer and Altmann, *Vor dem Sozialistengesetz*, pp. 74–76, 81. The convicted published the proceedings of the trial. *Der Hochverraths-Prozess wider Liebknecht, Bebel, Hepner* (2d ed., Berlin, 1894).

[41] Bebel, *Aus meinem Leben*, II, 291–292, also 261, 295–296.

[42] Bismarck to Schweinitz, Jan. 27, 1873. *GW*, VIc, 31–33.

[43] Cabinet meeting of Apr. 3, 1873. *DZA* Merseburg, Rep. 90a, B, III, 2b, Nr. 6, Vol. 85. See also *AWB*, I, 185–186, and Poschinger, ed., *Bismarck als Volkswirth*, I, 68–69.

[44] Werner Pöls, *Sozialistenfrage und Revolutionsfurcht in ihrem Zusammenhang mit den angeblichen Staatsstreichplänen Bismarcks. Historische Studien*, vol. 377 (Lübeck, 1960), pp. 30–32; Kampffmeyer and Altmann, *Vor dem Sozialistengesetz*, pp. 76ff.

work.[45] But Bismarck was dissatisfied with the results. He concluded that the rights accorded labor and its socialist advocates under existing law were too generous.[46] In September 1872 he gained the cabinet's consent to seek through imperial legislation new statutes regulating the press and the right of association (*Vereinswesen*). The government, he declared, could not remain "passive" when the social democratic press constantly aroused the workers against the government and the propertied classes.[47] Six months later, other bills were added that would have punished industrial, agrarian, and forestry workers for breach of contract and limited the right of *Freizügigkeit* by which workers evaded civil judgments for breach of contract by migrating to another state.[48]

For the time being, however, the only repressive statute that the government succeeded in getting passed was the imperial press act of 1874, which permitted confiscation of printed matter without prior approval by the courts. This statute, which was aimed at the ultramontane Catholic as well as the socialist press, heightened the power of the police to seize newspapers, books, pamphlets, and placards whenever they suspected a violation of law. The responsible editors, publishers, printers, and distributors could be fined as much as 1,000 marks and imprisoned up to one year. Although denounced by Lasker as an attack on freedom of the press, the statute finally passed in April 1874 after socialist progress at the polls had alarmed liberals as well as the government. Still the liberals sheared away some of the stronger features desired by the government, including the power to punish those connected with such publications without proof of complicity. In the final compromise, furthermore, the liberals secured abolition of the stamp tax on newspapers and the requirement that publishers be bonded.[49]

Even without the press act existing Prussian and imperial laws gave sufficient latitude for a conservative minister of interior, zealous gendarmes, imaginative prosecutors, and hostile judges to do serious damage to the socialist movement. A Prussian statute of March 11, 1850, bolstered by a high court decision of 1875, gave the police extensive powers over associations that dis-

[45] SEG (1872), p. 183.

[46] Bismarck to Kaiser, Apr. 4, 1872. Hans Rothfels, ed., *Bismarck und der Staat* (2d ed., Darmstadt, 1953), pp. 331–332.

[47] Cabinet meeting of Sept. 16, 1872. DZA Merseburg, Rep. 90a, B, III, 2b, Nr. 6, Vol. 84; DZA Potsdam, Reichskanzleramt, 1452, pp. 214–214v.

[48] Cabinet meeting of Apr. 3, 1873. DZA Merseburg, Rep. 90a, B, III, 2b, Nr. 6, Vol. 85. The bill reached the Reichstag in 1874 as an amendment to the industrial code, but died in committee and was not reintroduced. SBR (1874), I, 113–147; III (Anlagen), No. 21. It received strong support from manufacturers and many artisan guilds, but condemnation by a few workers' assemblies. SBR (1874), III (Anlagen), No. 90 and SBR (1874–1875), IV (Anlagen), No. 190.

[49] SBR (1874), pp. 148–161, 374–537, 1083–1145; statute of May 7, 1874, RGB (1874), pp. 65–72. See also Pöls, *Sozialistenfrage und Revolutionsfurcht*, p. 34. On the development of the statute within the government see DZA Potsdam, Reichskanzleramt, 1302 and 1303.

cussed "public affairs" and "political subjects."[50] Paragraph 130 of the imperial criminal code allowed fines as high as 600 marks and sentences up to two years for inciting violence between classes; other useful paragraphs were those punishing lese majesty, slander against institutions of the state, and incitement to high treason.[51] The progress of Lassalleans in Berlin was of particular concern in the early 1870s (socialists polled just over seven thousand votes there in the Reichstag election of January 1874—27.4 percent of those cast).[52] To meet this challenge the government transferred to Berlin state's attorney Hermann Tessendorff, known for his vigorous prosecution of social democrats in Magdeburg. On January 1, 1874, the day after he assumed office, Tessendorff addressed an open letter to Berlin's chief of police, Guido von Madai, declaring that "excesses of every kind, bordering on bestiality, among the lower classes of the population" had reached the point of "endangering public safety and morals and justified the strictest measures against those responsible." Criminals, rioters, and social democrat "terrorists" were listed as equally dangerous.[53] During the following months Madai arrested and Tessendorff prosecuted dozens of socialists under the criminal code and with the help of sympathetic judges sent many to prison. According to August Bebel, eighty-seven Lassalleans received jail sentences totaling more than 211 months. In June Tessendorff obtained a judgment closing the headquarters of the Lassallean General German Workers Association, although the association had already dissolved. Wilhelm Hasenclever, who had replaced Schweitzer as president, was sentenced to two months in jail. Policemen, prosecutors, and judges in other cities and states followed Tessendorff's example with the consequence that most of the branch offices of the Lassallean organization were also closed. After the fusion at Gotha, the united party was banned in Berlin by the order of the city court. But the social democrats had the foresight to locate their headquarters in Hamburg beyond the reach of the Saxon and Prussian police.[54]

Events were to prove that the incarceration of leaders and even the closing

[50] Prussian statute of Mar. 11, 1850. GS (1850), pp. 277–283; "Erkenntnis der ersten Abtheilung des Senates für Strafsachen, vom 26. November 1875," *Entscheidungen des königlichen Ober-Tribunals* (Berlin, 1876), vol. 76, pp. 394–398.

[51] Kampffmeyer and Altmann, *Vor dem Sozialistengesetz*, pp. 108–111. Eulenburg to Bismarck, Jan. 2, 1877. DZA Potsdam, Reichskanzlei, 1292/2, pp. 150–151.

[52] Wachenheim, *Arbeiterbewegung*, p. 161. In 1877 the socialist share in Berlin reached 39.2 percent. *Ibid.*, p. 188.

[53] "Tages-Chronik," *Spenersche Zeitung*, No. 24, Abendausgabe (Jan. 15, 1874), p. 1; Eduard Bernstein, *Die Geschichte der Berliner Arbeiter-Bewegung* (Berlin, 1907), I, 290–292.

[54] Bebel, *Aus meinem Leben*, II, 310–311. On the Tessendorff era in Berlin see Albrecht, *Fachverein-Berufsgewerkschaft-Zentralverband*, pp. 197–201; Bernstein, *Berliner Arbeiter-Bewegung*, I, 292ff.; Franz Mehring, *Geschichte der deutschen Sozialdemokratie* (2d ed., Stuttgart, 1904), IV, 71–84. On the activities of Berlin's political police, strengthened by contributions from the Guelph fund, see Dieter Fricke, *Bismarcks Prätorianer* (Berlin, 1962), pp. 29ff.

of political offices could not halt the growth of the socialist movement. Its progress could be measured not only by increasing strength at the polls, but also by the expansion of the party press from eleven newspapers in 1875 to forty-two in 1877.[55] More damaging were Tessendorff's actions against socialist trade unions. He exploited the resurrected Prussian statute of March 11, 1850, by prosecuting the Berlin carpenters' union, which had Lassallean affiliations, for failing to register as a political organization with the Prussian police. During 1874–1875 this and similar prosecutions in Berlin compelled Lassallean unions (carpenters, masons, shoemakers, plasterers) to close their doors, and their umbrella trade union organization (*Der allgemeine deutsche Arbeiterunterstützungsverband*) dissolved. Although their leaders attempted to evade prosecution by reorganizing and moving to safer environments (principally Hamburg), the socialist trade union movement was severely crippled for the time being. In making his case to the courts Tessendorff candidly admitted that his purpose was not to punish individual leaders, but to close the unions themselves.[56] Again his example was followed elsewhere, particularly in Saxony and Bavaria.[57] The socialist trade unions were badly handicapped during the worst years of the depression, when they were most needed to stem the decline in wages. Another consequence was that socialists, handicapped in their pursuit of purely economic objectives, concentrated their efforts on political agitation.[58]

By forcing Lassalleans and Eisenachers to unite in 1875, Tessendorff ended any prospect that the former could be played off against the latter.[59] As a consequence even more drastic steps appeared necessary to quell the socialist menace. In the Reichstag session of 1875–1876, the Bismarck government introduced a bill (*Strafgesetznovelle*) amending the criminal code in order to bring political misdeeds within the range of common crime. One of its paragraphs would have permitted imprisonment for fomenting class conflict.[60] As will be seen in the next chapter, Reichstag liberals combined with centrists

[55] Wachenheim, *Arbeiterbewegung*, p. 183; Schümer, *Entstehungsgeschichte*, p. 26. The growth of the socialist press had been expedited by abolition of the stamp tax on newspapers, a result that Bismarck anticipated when he opposed abolition in 1871. *AWB*, I, 162–163.

[56] Albrecht, *Fachverein-Berufsgewerkschaft-Zentralverband*, pp. 197–202; Wachenheim, *Arbeiterbewegung*, pp. 162–164, 186.

[57] Bebel, *Aus meinem Leben*, II, 311; Albrecht, *Fachverein-Berufsgewerkschaft-Zentralverband*, pp. 202–206.

[58] Wachenheim, *Arbeiterbewegung*, p. 193; Albrecht, *Fachverein-Berufsgewerkschaft-Zentralverband*, pp. 209ff.

[59] Bebel, *Aus meinem Leben*, II, 308ff. At the outset of his career in Berlin, Tessendorff was warned by Chief of Police Madai that this would be the consequence. Kampffmeyer and Altmann, *Vor dem Sozialistengesetz*, pp. 132–152.

[60] *SBR* (1875–1876), III (Anlagen), No. 54 (paragraph 130). Bismarck, who had already pressed the minister of justice for such a measure in 1871, was active in shaping the bill of 1875. Bismarck to Kaiser, Apr. 4, 1872. Rothfels, *Bismarck und der Staat*, pp. 331–332; Cabinet meetings of June 21 and Nov. 7, 1875. *DZA* Merseburg, Rep. 90a, B, III, 2b, Nr. 6, Vol. 87.

and socialists to defeat the "socialist paragraph," which they regarded as tantamount to a "law of exception"—a term still odious to liberals, despite the statutes they had recently passed against Catholics.

The defeat of the "socialist paragraph" did not lessen Bismarck's interest in another draconian measure aimed at both socialists and Catholics. Through the Bundesrat and Prussian envoys to the lesser states he sought throughout the 1870s to coordinate action against radical organizations under existing state statutes.[61] But the laws employed were not uniform among the larger states and were ineffective or nonexistent in some of the smaller states. In 1874–1875 Bismarck gained the approval of the cabinet and Kaiser for an imperial statute outlawing organizations "dangerous to the state."[62] Primary responsibility for drafting the bill fell to Minister of Interior Eulenburg, who, satisfied with the repression being achieved under the Prussian and other state statutes passed during the reactionary 1850s, did not push the matter. In late 1876 Bismarck failed in his effort to persuade the Hamburg senate that it had legal authority under the free city's laws to close the headquarters of the Social Democratic party.[63] Again he importuned Eulenburg to get ahead with the project for an imperial statute. But the minister produced only excuses and promises.[64]

In May 1877 Bismarck, patently exasperated, again demanded haste. To make his point, he sent Eulenburg an alarming memorandum received from Daniel Krüger, Hamburg's envoy in Berlin. The Reichstag election of 1877, Krüger declared, had demonstrated the effectiveness of socialist agitation in all of Germany. The number of socialist voters had doubled in three years, despite the reduced capacity of workingmen to give financial support to the party. "By spreading into the ranks of the so-called lower middle class [Kleinbürgertum] in the majority of German cities, the socialist electorate has reached such an importance that the destruction of bourgeois democracy and the sole domination by socialism over the lower classes of the population appears to be just a question of time." The socialist infection, Krüger continued,

[61] DZA Potsdam, Reichskanzleramt, 720/1 (entire volume). For the actions against socialists in Saxony see the exchange of correspondence between Bismarck and Kameke, Feb. 27 and Mar. 3, 1874, Philipsborn and Delbrück, June 22 and 25, 1875, Philipsborn and Hofmann, July 23 and Aug. 5, 1876. DZA Potsdam, Reichskanzleramt, 1292/2, pp. 110–122.

[62] Cabinet meetings of Oct. 22, 31, and Nov. 29, 1875. DZA Merseburg, Rep. 90a, B, III, 2b, Nr. 6, Vol. 87; Eulenburg to Bismarck, Oct. 4, 1876 (concerning Bismarck's démarche of 1874), DZA Potsdam, Reichskanzleramt, 1292/2, p. 132.

[63] Exchange of correspondence between Bülow, Hofmann, Versen, and Krüger, Sept. 17, 21, and Dec. 9, 1876; Bismarck and Eulenburg, Dec. 18, 1876, and Jan. 1 and 2, 1877; and Bismarck to the Hamburg Senate, Jan. 1877. DZA Potsdam, Reichskanzleramt, 1292/2, pp. 123–125v, 134–141v, 147–157.

[64] Bismarck to Eulenburg, Sept. 27, 1876, and Eulenburg to Bismarck, Oct. 4, 1876. DZA Potsdam, Reichskanzleramt, 1292/2, pp. 130–133. Bismarck's letter of Aug. 5, 1876, is not in the file.

had even spread to rural areas. In the union of 1875 radical socialism had won out over Lassallean socialism, with the consequence that the movement was now bent on political revolution rather than on mere economic gains. A united socialist movement, he concluded, could only be repressed by a single national statute uniformly applied by all German states.[65]

Eulenburg, however, was ailing and inactive. In the summer of 1877 Bismarck apparently shelved the project temporarily while negotiating with the national liberals over Eulenburg's replacement. Finally, in 1878 he found his chance. Two attempts to assassinate the Kaiser enabled him to flatten all opposition to the exceptional law against socialists for which he had striven with increasing urgency since 1872.

Reform

Social unrest, Bismarck told the Kaiser in April 1872, was a "sickness" affecting the entire civilized world. "The cause of this sickness is that the unpropertied classes, as their sense of self-worth and their claims on the good things in life gradually rise, strive to satisfy those claims at the cost of the propertied classes." While advocating stronger laws against striking trade unions and socialist agitation, he insisted that "repression" in itself was no cure. "That can only come very slowly from the effects of continuing education and experience and from a series of legislative and administrative measures derived from the most diverse areas of political and economic life and directed toward the effective removal of obstacles standing in the way of the earning capacity of the unpropertied classes."[66] What were the "obstacles" and how were they to be removed? At the beginning of the 1870s Bismarck's thoughts about repression were clearer than his conception of reform. Lacking information and ideas, he turned to the "experts."

Not long after his talk with Beust at Bad Gastein, Bismarck urged upon Minister of Commerce Itzenplitz (October 1871) the appointment of a committee to confer on urban working conditions, preparatory to a joint German-Austrian conference on the same subject. The "experts" he recommended were officials acquainted with social conditions, landowners managing their own estates, manufacturers, persons involved in social welfare, and authors acquainted with the main currents of social thought. "Testimony from intelligent laborers is not to be excluded." But Itzenplitz feared that an official inquiry would merely increase labor's doubts about the adequacy of existing

---

[65] Bismarck to Eulenburg, May 30, 1877, enclosing the memorandum (dated Feb. 1877) received from Krüger and presumably written by him. DZA Potsdam, Reichskanzleramt, 1292/2, pp. 166–166v and 147–165v.

[66] Rothfels, *Bismarck und der Staat*, pp. 331–332.

welfare statutes.[67] It was true that Prussia already possessed a variety of welfare chests regulated by the state: for example, guild funds for journeymen and apprentices, state funds for widows and orphans of officials, and local insurance funds for miners (*Knappschaftskassen*), factory and railway workers (*Unterstützungskassen*), to which both employer and employee contributed. Other institutions beneficial to labor were savings banks, credit associations, consumer cooperatives, and accident insurance companies (the latter necessitated by an imperial statute of 1871 establishing liability of railway, mine, and factory companies for work-related accidents and deaths).[68] In addition, various factory acts had restricted child labor (1835, 1845, 1853), established local councils to regulate hours of work (1849), provided for factory inspectors on a limited basis (1853), attempted to abolish the truck system (1849) and wage withholding (1869). Other advances (including provision for the arbitration of labor disputes) had been made in the north German industrial code of 1869, which became imperial law after 1871.[69]

Bismarck was unimpressed with Itzenplitz's argument that discussion of the shortcomings of this system would merely add fuel to socialist agitation. Socialistic theories and postulates, he replied, had already penetrated so deeply and broadly into the masses that to try to ignore the danger or exorcise it through silence would be in vain. On the contrary, the matter should be discussed as loudly and publicly as possible in order that the masses should not be misled by agitators but should come to understand which of their demands were justified and which were not. Obviously the most "burning questions"— those of hours, wages, and housing—could not be excluded from the discussion. Of the two rival socialist movements, only the Bebel–Liebknecht party was affiliated with the Socialist International. With the Lassalleans understanding was still possible. There was still time to reconcile most workers to the existing "state order" and to harmonize the interests of workers and employers.[70] Although Itzenplitz yielded to Bismarck's pressure, the committee he appointed was hardly one to propose drastic action. It met only once (November 26, 1871) and recommended more of what already existed: self-help through voluntary institutions fostered by the state.[71] Although high officials

[67] Bismarck to Itzenplitz, Oct. 21, 1871. *AWB*, I, 160–161; Poschinger, ed., *Bismarck als Volkswirth*, I, 65.

[68] Walter Vogel, *Bismarcks Arbeiterversicherung: Ihre Entstehung im Kräftespiel der Zeit* (Braunschweig, 1951), pp. 20ff. Itzenplitz drafted and sponsored the employer's liability act of 1871 only with great reluctance and under considerable pressure from Bismarck and the Bundesrat. DZA Merseburg, Rep. 120, BB, VII, 1, Nr. 16, Vol. 1, pp. 11–68.

[69] Friedrich Syrup, *Hundert Jahre staatliche Sozialpolitik, 1839–1939* (Stuttgart, 1957), pp. 58–73.

[70] Bismarck to Itzenplitz, Nov. 17, 1871. *AWB*, I, 164–165.

[71] The committee was composed of three industrialists (Liebermann, Stumm, Hammacher), a physician-politician with close ties to industry (Löwe), two city officials, one owner of a noble

of the Ministry of Commerce were not of one mind, the dominant views—
laissez-faire and corporative self-help (particularly the views of Victor Aimé
Huber)—militated against state intervention.[72]

Bismarck was not dependent upon Itzenplitz and his colleagues, however,
for ideas on social reform. Close at hand was Hermann Wagener, an official
of the Prussian *Staatsministerium*, who was in contact with two conservative
writers with strong views on the social question: Rudolph Meyer and Karl
Rodbertus. Since 1869 Wagener and Moritz von Blanckenburg had been urging the chancellor to take the lead in a reconstruction of the Conservative
party that would combine agrarian, artisan, and proletarian interests and relieve the government of its dependence upon the national liberals.[73] In January 1872 Wagener addressed to Bismarck a memorial pointing out that to
fight ultramontanes and socialists concurrently was a "dangerous enterprise,"
"for it would drive the socialists even more, and irrevocably so, into the clerical camp. . . . A social Kaiser would be stronger than a social pope in opposing the materialistic tendencies of the present." Although repressive measures
might be necessary against "antinational" elements in the socialist movement
(the Eisenachers), the movement itself could be won, if the monarchy satisfied "justified aspirations" of the lower classes. "Whither the masses turn is of
decisive importance not only for political and parliamentary life, but also for
the character of the army." Conscripted workers would be reliable soldiers
only if their loyalty to the Reich was cemented by concrete benefits.[74]

In October 1872 Bismarck dispatched Wagener to observe the Eisenach
congress of the *Kathedersozialisten* and ordered full publicity on the proceedings in the official press. During November 1872 the privy counselor presided
over the thirteen sessions of a German-Austrian conference of technical experts on the social question and socialist agitation that was the outgrowth of
Bismarck's talk with Beust at Bad Gastein. The Austrians came with instructions to discuss only the Socialist International, but Wagener managed to
open up the greater issue of social reform. Although the participants agreed
on a number of moderate proposals, the intentions of the two governments
were so divergent that no practical result was achieved insofar as Austro-German cooperation was concerned.[75] During the following year Wagener,
scarred by Eduard Lasker's revelations of official corruption, was compelled to

---

estate, one professor (Wagner), and several high officials from the Ministry of Commerce (including the future minister Achenbach). *AWB*, I, 167–168.

[72] Vogel, *Arbeiterversicherung*, pp. 26–27; Rothfels, *Theodor Lohmann*, pp. 27–30.

[73] Wolfgang Saile, *Herman Wagener und sein Verhältnis zu Bismarck: Ein Beitrag zur Geschichte
des konservativen Sozialismus. Tübinger Studien zur Geschichte und Politik*, vol. 9 (Tübingen, 1958),
pp. 106–111; Herman von Petersdorff, *Kleist-Retzow: Ein Lebensbild* (Stuttgart, 1907), pp. 461–
462.

[74] Horst Kohl, ed., *Bismarck-Jahrbuch* (Berlin, 1899), VI, 209–214.

[75] Vogel, *Arbeiterversicherung*, pp. 27–28. Wagener's detailed report of the conference sessions
is in *DZA* Potsdam, Reichskanzlei, 1292/2, pp. 3–55.

resign. Conservatives like Rudolph Meyer thought Wagener to be the only "statesman" in the Prussian government "who knows and understands the social question from the ground up."[76] Bismarck spoke of him as his "most industrious worker," but Wagener's usefulness had limits. Ordered to draft a statute, the *Geheimrat* was likely to write a newspaper article.[77] He lacked the capacity to translate ideas into action.

Wagener's departure did not, however, immediately sever his relationship to the chancellor. They continued to confer and correspond until 1877, when Bismarck suspected Wagener of participating in attacks upon him by *Die Deutsche Eisenbahn Zeitung*. Until that time the chancellor used his old friend for various missions, helped him financially, and continued to request from him memorials on the social question.[78] Marginalia on one such document of January 1874 shows that Bismarck, though interested, was skeptical of Wagener's ideas. The memorial advocated: "abolition of the dominant economic system" (Bismarck: "How?") through the reintroduction of usury laws (Bismarck: "does not suffice") and prohibition of excessive promises of high interest rates and dividends; introduction of a normal workday defined in terms of the quantity of work (Bismarck: "difficult to determine") rather than the number of hours; an agrarian reform that would slow emigration by "transforming the landless worker into a small landowner," preference to be given to soldiers; a voice in community government for rural laborers in order to prevent formation of labor unions; aid to industrial labor, including artisans, by replacing the guilds with corporative bodies to be organized on the initiative of the workers themselves, but to be regarded as "state institutes"; obligatory health, unemployment, and old age insurance; compulsory arbitration of labor disputes by courts composed of representatives of workers and owners; and reconciliation agencies to mediate agreements on wages, hours, and working conditions.[79] In October 1874 Bismarck again sent Wagener, accompanied by Rudolph Meyer, to the annual congress of the *Kathedersozialisten*. Their report is studded with Bismarck marginalia testifying both to his interest and his continuing skepticism. "For me," Wagener wrote, "the chief concern and final aim is to recombine the *disjecta membra* of the masses of the population and insert them correctly into the organism of the state" (Bismarck: "*ubi, quomodo, quando, quibus auxiliis?*").[80]

Bismarck's intervention into social policy and his appointment of Wagener to head the German-Austrian conference of November 1872 must have an-

[76] Vogel, *Arbeiterversicherung*, p. 118; Saile, *Hermann Wagener*, p. 118.

[77] GW, VIII, 660.

[78] The destitute Wagener also became demanding in money matters and appeared even to threaten revelations that would embarrass Bismarck. Saile, *Wagener*, pp. 119ff.

[79] Kohl, ed., *Bismarck-Jahrbuch*, VI, 214–226.

[80] Arnold Oskar Meyer, *Bismarck: Der Mensch und der Staatsmann* (Stuttgart, 1949), p. 532; Vogel, *Arbeiterversicherung*, p. 157.

noyed Itzenplitz. But it also jarred him into action. In early November he penned a statement intended to guide Prussian officials participating in the conference. In contrast to his earlier notes to Bismarck, it called for full publicity in the government press to "clarify the interests of workers and employers." While insisting that the conference not stray from the "fundamentals of the state and civil [*bürgerlich*] society," Itzenplitz called for discussion of Sunday labor, female employment in factories, trade school education, the housing shortage, urban transportation, and social insurance.[81] In March 1873 he sent to his cabinet colleagues a series of concrete proposals for imperial statutes on: the prohibition of child (under twelve) labor in factories; restriction of older children (twelve to fourteen) to half-day shifts; application of the factory acts on child labor to all employment outside the home; extension of the state's power to compel employers to safeguard the life and health of workers; obligatory appointment of factory inspectors in all regions; expansion of their authority to enforce the factory laws; and an official enquiry into the conditions of female labor for the purpose of drafting new legislation.[82] Itzenplitz had reversed course, but not soon enough to satisfy Bismarck. In June 1873 he was replaced by a subordinate, Heinrich Achenbach, who was more sympathetic toward reform.

During 1873–1874 mounting concern within the government, parliament, and public led to a remarkable series of enquiries into working conditions and labor-owner relationships. In response to petitions, the Reichstag resolved on April 30, 1873, to ask the chancellor to investigate whether additional legal protection was needed for child and female factory workers.[83] The Bundesrat followed suit, and the result was a massive investigation during 1875–1876.[84] Other petitions complained that the industrial code of 1869 had produced an adversary relationship between master artisans and journeymen and had left unsolved many problems of industrial labor, including labor disputes and social insurance. The result was yet another general enquiry, formally launched by Bismarck, during 1875–1876 into the relationships between employers (master artisans and factory owners) and employees (journeymen and factory workers).[85]

---

[81] Itzenplitz, Nov. 3, 1872. *DZA* Merseburg, Rep. 120, BB, VII, 1. Nr. 2., Vol. 3, pp. 24–25.
[82] Itzenplitz to cabinet, Mar. 12, 1873. *DZA* Merseburg, Rep. 120, BB, VII, 4, Nr. 1, Vol. 1. For other preparations for reform see Itzenplitz to Eulenburg and Falk, May 7, 1873, *ibid.*, and cabinet meeting of May 25, 1873. *DZA* Merseburg, Rep. 90a, B, III, 2b, Nr. 6, Vol. 85.
[83] *DZA* Merseburg, Rep. 120, BB, VII, 3, Nr. 2, Vol. 2. *SBR* (1873), pp. 395–405, Anlagen, No. 60.
[84] *Protokolle über die Verhandlungen des Bundesraths des deutschen Reiches* (1873), Drucksachen, No. 147; (1874), Proceedings of Jan. 31, 1874, pp. 34–35; (1876), Proceedings of Nov. 17, 1876, p. 231; (1876), Drucksachen, No. 83. The results of the enquiry are also to be found in *DZA* Merseburg, Rep. 120, BB, VII, 3, Nr. 2, and *DZA* Potsdam, Reichskanzleramt, 443, 444, 446.
[85] *DZA* Merseburg, Rep. 120, BB, I, 1, Nr. 12, Vol. 8; *DZA* Potsdam, Reichskanzleramt, 435/

Nor did rural labor escape the attention of the Bismarck government in the 1870s. The flight of peasants to German cities and foreign lands, the resulting labor shortage on the farm, frequent breaches of contracts by workers, the penetration of socialist agitation into the countryside, and the vulnerability of regions dominated by large estates to their propaganda led the Prussian cabinet to institute an investigation into agrarian labor conditions. But the enquiry consisted only of a series of conferences held by the Ministry of Agriculture. All participants were officials, except for two "practical experts" (the landowners Moritz von Blanckenburg and Friedrich von Wedell-Malchow), who were included on Bismarck's insistence.[86] The conference discussed how to slow down the migration by imposing written, legally binding work contracts, by increasing the number of landowning peasants through internal colonization, and by extending to landlords the same financial liability for accidental injuries and deaths that had been imposed on factory owners in 1871. Bills were drafted, but no legislation resulted.[87] In 1875–1876 Bismarck, responding to a petition from the Congress of German Landowners, attempted to launch a new and more thorough investigation into the real wages of rural workers, but the other ministers were dubious, and no action resulted.[88] To some conservatives this failure was another demonstration of the Bismarck government's disinterest in agrarian problems.[89] But the real explanation lay in the decline of the labor shortage in the 1870s and the easing of the problem that had produced the discussion.[90]

The enquiries into factory working conditions, on the other hand, were more productive. Conducted by the state governments under the supervision of the Imperial Chancellor's Office, the dual investigations of 1875–1876 provided information that became the basis for two major reforms: the two imperial social insurance acts of April 7–8, 1876, and the industrial code act (*Gewerbegesetznovelle*) of July 17, 1878. In the spirit of laissez-faire the industrial code of 1869 had freed welfare chests from bureaucratic control and had

---

1, pp. 2–2v, and 440/1. With official cooperation the German Commercial Association (*Deutscher Handelstag*) conducted during 1873 through local chambers of commerce an enquiry into strikes (including the gathering of statistics) and agitation among workers to determine "what dangers were growing out of them for German industry." DZA Potsdam, Reichskanzleramt, 452, pp. 2–62.

[86] Cabinet meeting of May 25, 1873. DZA Merseburg, Rep. 90a, B, III, 2b, Nr. 6, Vol. 85. Poschinger, ed., *Bismarck als Volkswirth*, I, 69; AWB, I, 187–189, 201–202, 227–229; BP, I, 180–181.

[87] DZA Merseburg, Rep. 120, BB, VII, 5, Nr. 3, pp. 7–190.

[88] Bismarck (as chancellor) to Bismarck (as minister president), May 14, 1875. DZA Merseburg, Rep. 120, BB, VII, 5, Nr. 3, pp. 191–193, also pp. 220–261; DZA Potsdam, Reichskanzleramt, 1294, Vol. 1, pp. 70–71v, 102–108v, 125–125v.

[89] Rudolph Meyer, *Politische Gründer und die Corruption in Deutschland* (Leipzig, 1877), pp. 69–74, 188–189.

[90] On rural labor conditions in the 1870s see Goltz, *Landwirtschaft*, I, 364–369.

abolished compulsory membership where the worker already belonged to a voluntary fund. The effect was chaotic. The two statutes of April 1876 reintroduced state regulation by regional authorities and limited the chests to two types: voluntary funds under state supervision and compulsory funds organized by the state.[91] Nevertheless, most workers were still without insurance protection, since existing chests covered only those working in a few heavy industries. When in need, the uninsured had to resort to poor relief, a humiliating and denigrating experience.[92]

Except for Bismarck's obstructionism the second significant social reform act of the 1870s—a statute amending the industrial code (*Gewerbegesetznovelle*)—might also have reached the Reichstag in 1876. From Varzin Bismarck questioned the necessity of new legislation limiting child and female labor. The enquiry, he declared, had been launched during the boom when industry was driving its workers hard. "Today the situation has changed significantly. Supply exceeds demand." Many manufacturers were renouncing profits, even absorbing losses, just to keep their work forces intact until prosperity returned. If burdened by new governmental restrictions, they would discharge workers, especially women and young people. He also opposed the imposition of general restrictions without regard to varying circumstances in different industries and regions. By shortening the working day and reducing the paychecks of women and young people, the statute would diminish their capacity to feed themselves and lead to malnourishment. Bismarck's objections forced the cabinet to set the matter aside.[93] But in March 1877 free conservatives of the Reichstag interpellated the government on the status of the legislation. Resolutions from many quarters—free conservatives, national liberals, progressives, and socialists—called upon the Reichstag to demand new factory legislation as soon as possible.[94]

Under this pressure the machine began to move again. Aided by Achenbach, Karl von Hofmann, Delbrück's replacement as chief of the Chancellor's Office, drafted three related reform bills, one of which was a factory act.[95] But before he could distribute the bills to the Bundesrat, he received an abrupt telegram from Varzin ordering him to halt all action.[96] Bismarck had learned of the bills "by accident." They had been prepared, he said, without his knowledge, without prior discussion in the Prussian cabinet, and in contra-

---

[91] *RGB* (1876), pp. 125–136. On the origin of this legislation see Rothfels, *Theodor Lohmann*, pp. 41–43.

[92] Vogel, *Arbeiterversicherung*, pp. 21–24.

[93] Bismarck *Votum* to cabinet, Sept. 30, 1876. *AWB*, I, 233–237.

[94] *SBR* (1877), pp. 286–320, 1031–1200, 1383–1492; Anlagen, Nos. 20, 23, 74, 77, 92, 107.

[95] For Hofmann's account of the origins of the three bills see Hofmann to cabinet, Oct. 20, 1877. *DZA* Potsdam, Reichskanzlei, 436, pp. 196–200v. The draft of the proposed factory act (Entwurf B) is *ibid.*, pp. 119–127.

[96] Telegram, Kurowsky to Hofmann, July 27, 1877. *DZA* Potsdam, Reichskanzlei, 436, p. 135. Also telegram, Bismarck to Hofmann, Aug. 3, 1877, *ibid.*, p. 141.

diction to his opinion (*Votum*) of the preceding September.[97] The outraged "hermit of Varzin" fired off stiff rebukes to both Hofmann and Achenbach. Most of his ire was directed at the factory act. In their zeal for the bodily safety of workers, sparing young people, separating the sexes at work, keeping the Sabbath holy, he declared, the ministers proposed to interfere inordinately in private enterprise. If compelled to protect workers against every danger, some industries (gunpowder, dynamite, glass, poisonous chemicals) would have to go out of business; others would only survive under the most unusual circumstances. If factories could be invaded by inspectors, why not homes—in search of loaded weapons, explosives, acids, and poisons? More effective for the solution of the social question would be reinforcement of the statute on the liability of employers for job-related accidents and its extension to protect workers from disability arising from sickness and exhaustion.[98]

Hofmann had erred on procedure, but he was also the victim of a coincidence. Since his appointment in 1873 Achenbach had set out to enforce the industrial code of 1869 by appointing factory inspectors even in rural areas like Pomerania. On July 12, 1877, Bismarck's paper factories at Varzin were inspected for the first time. Inspector Hertel did not like what he saw: belt-driven wood saws and drills without protective covers and running free while unattended; papermaking machines unequipped with safety shields; elevated walkways and staircases without guard rails; a gas-operated machine housed in the same room with an open fire; a technically deficient gasworks in danger of explosion. He directed the Behrend brothers, who operated the plants, to correct the deficiencies by August 15.

Bismarck reacted by inspecting the inspector. He discovered that Hertel was merely carrying out instructions handed down from Achenbach's ministry.[99] In his reprimand to Achenbach Bismarck challenged the right of any official to make such discretionary judgments. Factory owners subjected to such inspections would seek redress by voting for opposition candidates. In

[97] Kurowsky to Hofmann, Aug. 1, 1877, and Hofmann to Kurowsky, Aug. 3, 1877. *Ibid.*, 136–140.

[98] Bismarck to Hofmann, Aug. 11, 1877. *Ibid.*, pp. 143–144v.; Bismarck to Achenbach, Aug. 10, 1877. *AWB*, I, 258–265. Apparently puzzled by Bismarck's sudden distaste for factory inspectors, Achenbach appears to have directed a subordinate to search the archives for Bismarck's prior attitudes. He found that since 1868 Bismarck and those responsible to him (Wagener in the Austro-German conference of November 1872) had repeatedly supported the extension of the factory inspection system, first authorized for Prussian industrial regions in a statute of May 16, 1853. The memorandum dated Oct. 9, 1877, never left the ministry. If Achenbach intended it for Bismarck, he had second thoughts. *DZA* Merseburg, Rep. 120, III, BB, VII, 4, Nr. 1, Vol. 2, pp. 89–115.

[99] Hertel to Georg and Moritz Behrend, July 24, 1877. *DZA* Merseburg, Rep. 120, III, BB, VII, 4, Nr. 1, Vol. 2, pp. 84–85. Moritz Behrend to Hertel (no date), and Hertel to Moritz Behrend, July 31, 1877. *Ibid.*, pp. 86–87. Bismarck to Achenbach, Aug. 10, 1877. *Ibid.*, pp. 88–89.

brief, Bismarck not only vetoed the imposition of new restrictions on factory owners that would hinder production, but also chastised the responsible minister for having gone too far in implementing existing legislation for the protection of labor.[100]

When Hofmann presented (October 20, 1877) a revised draft of the factory act, from which the offending paragraphs had been removed, Bismarck still found the bill too strong. Government officials, he insisted, must be given the power where appropriate to except manufacturers from the restrictions on the employment of young people between fourteen and sixteen years of age.[101] As finally passed the factory act of July 17, 1878, banned child labor in factories, mines, and construction work under the age of twelve and limited youths between twelve and fourteen years to six hours labor daily (exceptions to be permitted by action of the Bundesrat). The Bundesrat received the power to restrict employment of women and young people in hazardous industries. Youths under sixteen were required to attend elementary school for three hours daily. Trade schools (*Fortbildungsschulen*) were made obligatory for youths under eighteen. Workers under twenty-one were required to carry work books listing their places and types of employment, but without reference to performance. The prohibition of the truck system was extended and reinforced.

Many provisions of the government bill were significantly stiffened by Reichstag amendments. The most critical amendment was the reinsertion, without significant opposition, of obligatory factory inspection (including dangers to life and health), which Bismarck had vetoed. Last-ditch efforts by Westphalian industrialists to delay and water down the statute were ignored. During that same summer that brought the liberal era to an end, the Reichstag, shortly before its dissolution over the antisocialist act, passed a statute significantly increasing the authority of the state to protect industrial labor.[102]

When the Prussian cabinet accepted these changes, Bismarck had to decide whether to gain the king's veto, secure the defeat of the bill in the Bundesrat, and start the legislative process all over again. He turned for advice to Albert Maybach, who had replaced Achenbach at the Ministry of Commerce. Maybach reminded Bismarck that, despite the opposition of the Bundesrat's representatives at every stage in the discussion, the great majority of the Reichs-

[100] AWB, I, 258–265; DZA Potsdam, Reichskanzleramt, 436, pp. 151–160. See also Hofmann's record of his conference with Bismarck, Sept. 24, 1877. DZA Potsdam, Reichskanzleramt, 436, pp. 163–163v.

[101] Hofmann to cabinet, Oct. 20, 1877. DZA Potsdam, Reichskanzleramt, 436, pp. 196–200v. Tiedemann to Hofmann, Nov. 20, 1877. DZA Potsdam, Reichskanzleramt, 437, pp. 41–42v.

[102] SBR (1878), III, 500; IV, 1185–1187; RGB (1878), pp. 199–212. In the same session amendments to another government bill for the creation of arbitration courts allowed under the industrial code of 1869 made the bill unacceptable to the governments, and it failed of passage in the Bundesrat. SBR (1878), Anlagen, Vol. III, No. 110.

tag (including the industrialists Karl Stumm and Wilhelm Büchner) had supported the amendments. Nothing could be gained by reopening the discussion. Whatever one thought of its value, factory inspection was an established institution that could no longer be abolished. Inspectors could be used, furthermore, to keep track of radical agitation among workers. If properly instructed, they need not be an irritant to businessmen. They must be told not to conduct themselves like policemen but as tactful advisers and mediators.[103] Bismarck capitulated.[104]

The social crises of the early 1870s had reawakened Bismarck's old interest in the problem of social reform. No less than Wagener and many others he grasped that concrete action was needed to keep the loyalty of the lower classes. Their loyalty was, in fact, vital to the social consolidation of Germany's new empire. Why, then, did he not do more at this critical juncture?

Generally the answer is that his collaboration with liberals dedicated to laissez-faire and the dominance of laissez-faire doctrines within the Prussian and imperial governments prohibited any dramatic change in social policy. But there are other explanations. Bismarck's sympathy for employers, reinforced by his own experiences, limited severely what he was willing to accept in the way of protective legislation. In the area of safety regulations and restrictions on child and female labor even Itzenplitz was more progressive than Bismarck. The officials who drafted the statutes of 1876 and 1878 and the Reichstag majority that amended that of 1878 deserve far more credit than the chancellor for what was accomplished. This raises the further question why Bismarck was not more active during the 1870s within that area—employers' liability and social insurance—in which he did have positive views on reform.

The answer here is twofold. On the one hand, Bismarck's health was poor during much of this decade, particularly in the critical years 1872–1876. His debilitating illnesses exhausted his nerves and reduced his energies. In domestic affairs he squandered what energy he possessed on an unworthy and self-defeating project, the Kulturkampf. He misconceived the primary problem facing his government in internal affairs. By the time he reversed priorities in the 1880s the chance to prevent the alienation of labor, either through suppression or reform, had passed.

[103] Hofmann to Maybach, May 31, 1878, and Maybach to Hofmann, June 4, 1878. DZA Potsdam, Reichskanzleramt, 438, pp. 217–220v; also DZA Merseburg, Rep. 120, BB, I, 1, Nr. 12, Vol. 11. Hofmann to Tiedemann, DZA Potsdam, Reichskanzleramt, 438, pp. 225–225v.

[104] Hofmann to Tiedemann, June 28, 1878, and Tiedemann to Hofmann, June 30, 1878. DZA Potsdam, Reichskanzleramt, 438, pp. 228–229. Bismarck satisfied himself with a Bundesrat resolution establishing "common standards" for factory inspectors throughout the Reich along the lines Maybach had proposed. *Ibid.*, pp. 227–227v and 230. Bismarck to king, July 9, 1878. *Ibid.*, 231–239.

Toward Protectionism

Until the late 1870s the powerful financial interests in Germany were divided on the issue of free trade versus protectionism.[105] Manufacturers of finished products who exported their wares or who were dependent on imports of raw materials, merchants (particularly in the coastal cities from Bremen to Memel), shipbuilders and owners, and shippers in general were naturally for free trade; they found support in state officials and political economists imbued with laissez-faire economics. These groups dominated the Congress of German Economists established in 1859, which backed government policy during the heyday of free trade in the 1860s. But they had important support until the mid-1870s from eastern landowners who exported their crops, particularly to Britain, and wanted low prices on farm implements. In the Congress of German Landowners established in 1868 and the German Council on Agriculture founded in 1872, they acquired organizations with which to advance agrarian interests. This combination of interest groups, government officials, and economic theorists made laissez-faire in tariff policy long seem invincible.

Yet protectionism was never without adherents. Since the 1840s the cotton spinners of Saxony, Bavaria, and Württemberg and the pig iron producers of Rhineland-Westphalia—industries suffering from foreign competition in the domestic market—had rowed against the current. While free traders found their holy writ in Adam Smith's *Wealth of Nations* and in the writings of his German disciples, particularly the emigré John Prince-Smith, protectionists drew spiritual nourishment from Johann Gottlieb Fichte's *The Closed Commercial State* (1800) and Friedrich List's *National System of Political Economy* (1841). Yet Fichte wrote before Germany's industrial age and List at its beginning. The latter argued, furthermore, that tariff walls were necessary only to protect infant industries in the early stages of industrialization and that they could be reduced once domestic manufacturers were able to meet foreign competition—a stage that, it could be argued, Germany had now reached. But List also opposed duties on imported raw materials and agrarian products. So the protectionists turned in the late 1860s to the writings of an American economist, Henry C. Carey. A translation of Carey's *Manual of Social Science* was published in Germany in 1863 and was widely read and quoted by the end of the decade. Basically his view was that protectionism alone would permit coordination of the interests of industry, agriculture, and commerce. Protected from outside competition, industry would grow prosperous and pro-

---

[105] On the early struggle between business and agrarian interests over the tariff issue see Ivo N. Lambi, *Free Trade and Protection in Germany 1868–1879, Vierteljahrschrift für Sozial- und Wirtschaftsgeschichte*, Beiheft 44 (Wiesbaden, 1963), pp. 1–54; Walther Lotz, *Die Ideen der deutschen Handelspolitik von 1860 bis 1891* (Leipzig, 1892), pp. 28–145; Nitzsche, *Handelspolitische Reaktion*, pp. 1–114.

vide markets for agrarian products, relieving the farmer of dependence upon exports.[106]

The natural battleground for the advocates of free trade and protectionism were the semiofficial chambers of commerce composed of delegates elected by businessmen in towns throughout Germany. Since 1860 the Prussian (later German) Commercial Association (*Handelstag*) had held national conventions at which the delegates deliberated on national economic policy. In 1868 the convention majority called for a reduction in iron tariffs, but only on the basis of reciprocity with France, Belgium, and Austria. Dissatisfied with this compromise, the extreme free traders, led by the maritime cities, held annual conferences at Berlin during 1868–1870 to agitate for abolition of duties on pig iron and reduction of duties on rolled and forged iron. The threatened interests petitioned the chancellor and the Zollverein parliament through their chambers of commerce and manufacturers' associations (particularly iron, cotton yarn, paper, and chemicals).[107] Within the upper chamber of the Zollverein parliament the governments divided on the tariff issue, the maritime states for free trade, the southern states for protection, while Prussia and the remaining states took an intermediate position. In the lower, elective chamber the issue cut across party lines, the opposing sides forming caucuses to defend their positions. The tariff act of May 1870 gave the free traders half a loaf—the reduction of the duty on pig iron by 50 percent (from 5 to 2.50 groschen per ton), the loss in revenue to be made up by increased duties on coffee.[108]

During the boom years that followed, protectionists were hard pressed to argue that either their prosperity or imperial finances required perpetuation of the iron duties. In the Reichstag the free-trade caucus, led by agrarian conservatives, agitated for their abolition, but for preservation of the remaining duties on farm products such as starch. The imperial government responded by introducing in June 1873 a bill that would have abolished on October 1, 1873, import duties on pig iron, farm machinery, and starch, while reducing the import duties on other iron and steel products, also on soda and some textiles, and ending the export duty on rags (beneficial to the paper industry). The bill expressed the free-trade philosophy of Rudolf Delbrück but had the approval of Bismarck and Wilhelm I; only the Bavarian government opposed it in the Bundesrat. The motivation was practical as well as doctrinaire. At the height of the *Gründerjahre* it seemed impossible for German industry to supply the voracious demand for iron, steel, and machines; foreign imports were needed.[109]

[106] Carl Adler, ed., *Die Grundlagen der Sozialwissenschaft von H. C. Carey* (3 vols., Munich, 1863).

[107] See *DZA* Potsdam, Reichskanzleramt, 1603.

[108] *BGB* (1870), pp. 123–142.

[109] *SBR* (1873), III, No. 88; IV, No. 192. Lambi, *Free Trade and Protection*, pp. 55–72.

Even as the Reichstag deliberated, the balloon began to deflate. The collapse of the Vienna bourse in May, accompanied by bankruptcies and suicides, was followed by a summer of uncertainty on the Berlin exchange. The chancellor's office and the Bundesrat were inundated with petitions and letters from the affected interests, particularly in Lorraine, Westphalia, the Rhineland, and Upper Silesia. (Among the letters addressed to Bismarck was one from his own financier, Gerson Bleichröder, opposing the bill.)[110] During the boom, manufacturers who could not get enough raw iron to feed their machines had petitioned the government in favor of free trade.[111] But now that both the producers and consumers of iron in heavy industry were threatened, they closed ranks in favor of continued protectionism. Landowners and merchants were left to continue the battle for the tariff act.

For the time being victory in parliament belonged to the free traders. All that spokesmen for the iron and steel industry (Deputies Stumm, Kardorff, Varnbüler, Hammacher, Miquel, Löwe) could achieve in the Reichstag was a compromise that delayed repeal of the duties on starch and some finished iron products until January 1, 1877. The rest of the bill remained intact, including the abolition of the tariff on pig iron.[112] If a subsequent bill should abolish textile duties, as seemed possible, the prospect arose that Germany would become completely free trading in three-and-a-half years.

During those years, as the depression deepened and lengthened, the pendulum of vocal public opinion began to swing toward protectionism. Although the price of industrial products fell sharply, the mines, furnaces, and machines continued to spew forth their products, for heavy industrialists were reluctant to curtail output. It was better to sell at a slight profit or even a loss than to let equipment stand idle. To reduce costs they cut wages, executed mergers, and erected cartels. They hoped to dispose of their surplus products on foreign markets and had some success. The textile industry had not fully shared in the boom and was not as badly affected by the bust. Although the price of cotton yarn fell, so did the cost of raw cotton. Increases in the export trade took up the slack of reduced sales at home. By 1877, nevertheless, textile manufacturers began to experience lower profits, losses, idle equipment, and laid-off workers.[113]

Germany was not, of course, the only country so affected. Wars, diplomatic crises, and the decline of tax revenues during the depression created fiscal

[110] Bleichröder to Bismarck, May 15, 1873. DZA Potsdam, Reichskanzleramt, 1604, pp. 96–99. See also Louis Baare to Bismarck, June 10, 1873, ibid., pp. 101–105v, and the earlier petition from Der zollvereinsländische Eisenhüttenverein to Bismarck, Jan. 27, 1868, containing the signatures of Haniel, Mulvany, Hammacher, and many others. Ibid., 1603, pp. 4–18.

[111] Typical petitions of this kind are those of Sept. 15 and 16, 1869, and Jan. 14, 1870, from Coeln, Hagen, and Deutz. Ibid., 1603, pp. 159–165.

[112] SBR (1873), pp. 1266–1305, 1385–1421; RGB (1873), pp. 241–293.

[113] Nitzsche, Handelspolitische Reaktion, pp. 30–40.

emergencies in many countries. Higher tariffs were the easiest solution and, once adopted for fiscal purposes, they were boosted further to achieve protectionism. Civil War debts led the United States to adopt higher tariffs in 1866–1867, which initiated a climb to full protectionism in the following decades. The cost of the wars of 1859 and 1866, when coupled with the effects of the depression, forced the Habsburg Empire to undertake "tariff reform" in 1874–1875, 1878, 1882, and 1887, and Italy in 1878, 1887, and 1891. The approach of war with Turkey led the Russian government to demand all customs payments in gold after January 1, 1877, increasing costs to importers by 33 percent. During the peace negotiations of 1870 Thiers warned that France would require higher tariffs to pay for the war indemnity. To this end he obtained a "most favored nation" clause in the Treaty of Frankfurt that constituted a retreat from the earlier free-trade treaty with the Zollverein. Export subsidies (*titres d'acquit à caution*) gave French iron exporters a competitive edge in Germany. During 1877–1878 protective tariffs were under discussion in the French National Assembly; statutes in 1881, 1885, 1887, and 1892 gave France its protective wall. Only Great Britain remained true to the principle of free trade.[114]

Under these circumstances it was only natural that protectionism should have gained new advocates in Germany. Whether the last iron duties would be abolished on schedule (January 1, 1877) came to be regarded as a test of the continuing power of the free traders. Within weeks after passage of the tariff act of 1873 the affected industry began to organize to protect its interests. In November–December 1873 the first steps were taken to found the Association of German Iron and Steel Industrialists. By 1876 the association was nationwide, representing 214 firms subdivided into six regional groups. The northwestern group of Rhineland-Westphalia, composed of seventy-two firms, tended to predominate. The driving force within the organization was Louis Baare of the *Bochumer Verein*. Beginning in 1875, the association's executive council, headed by secretary-general August Rentzsch, decided to establish liaison with other interested groups in the business community (local chambers of commerce and machine building and railway companies) and even to approach "some intelligent landowners," whose complaints about the land tax could be supported as a quid pro quo. But the agrarians were unsympathetic, and the industrialists retaliated by calling for repeal of the remaining duties on agricultural products.

Another tactic was to infiltrate free-trade organizations. In September 1875 the association collaborated with the Association of South German Cotton Manufacturers in committing the Congress of German Economists to a protectionist resolution by a vote of sixty-two to fifty-eight. But in the following year the free traders succeeded in getting the decision reversed. An attempt

[114] *Ibid.*, pp. 3–17.

in 1875 to swing the Association for Social Policy into the protectionist camp also failed. Their successful collaboration with the south German textile manufacturers added fuel to a decision by Ruhr industrialists to found a national organization representing all manufacturing interests sympathetic to protectionism. In November 1875 Wilhelm von Kardorff—Silesian industrialist, leader of the Free Conservative party, and author of a highly effective pamphlet, *Gegen den Strom*, defending extreme protectionism—seized the initiative by summoning to Berlin a group of German entrepreneurs to discuss such an organization. The result was the Central Federation of German Industrialists. Although iron interests predominated, the Central Federation included many other interest groups (cotton, woolen, and linen textiles, leather, soda, paper, porcelain, and matches). Yet divergent purposes compelled the federation to formulate its original program of 1876 in vague terms.[115]

As the deadline for legislative action on the iron tariff approached during 1876 the Association of German Iron and Steel Industrialists and allied bodies deluged the Reichstag, Bundesrat, governments, Kaiser, and chancellor with petitions, statistics, and delegations expounding their cause. Sympathetic members of the Reichstag were lobbied and the press mobilized. Workers in the affected industries and the communities dependent upon industrial prosperity gathered petitions containing thousands of signatures. On the tariff issue class conflict gave way to interest-group solidarity. The breadth and vigor developed by the protectionist movement during 1874–1876 took the free traders by surprise. They hastened to counterattack through the Congress of German Economists, Congress of German Landowners, German Council on Agriculture, Association for Social Policy, and various local bodies and conventions. In turn, the free traders of agrarian and mercantile regions (chiefly the seaboard towns and their hinterlands and the eastern farmlands) inundated parliaments and governments with petitions and appeals. The bulging files in the archives of the chancellor's office give mute testimony to the dimensions of the popular mobilization over the tariff issue.[116] Never before in modern German history, not even in the era of unification, had so many Germans become involved on a question of public policy. In the struggle over the tariff the interest groups, never completely absent from Prussian and German politics, became fully organized and their tactics more blatant as they reached for the levers of power. A battle of economic interests had begun that shortly was to overshadow the traditional cleavages in German politics.

Later we shall see that in 1876 the free traders won the first engagement:

[115] Lambi, *Free Trade and Protection*, pp. 73ff.; Nitzsche, *Handelspolitische Reaktion*, pp. 117ff.; Böhme, *Deutschlands Weg*, pp. 359–409.

[116] DZA Potsdam, Reichskanzleramt, 1604–1608. The free traders had the active support of the Prussian cabinet, which resolved to reiterate its determination to abolish the iron tariff and make that position known in the press. Cabinet meeting of Sept. 22, 1875. DZA Merseburg, Rep. 90a, B, III, 2b, Nr. 6, Vol. 87.

the remaining iron duties fell as scheduled on the first day of 1877. But it was soon evident that this was not the final battle. As the depression continued the number of adversely affected interests grew and likewise the discredit of laissez-faire. The stream of petitions continued to flow, calling now for the reestablishment of the abandoned duties.[117] The Central Federation of German Industrialists expanded its protectionist program to include the whole of German industry. Protectionists succeeded, furthermore, in committing the German Commercial Association to their cause, despite virulent protests from much of the membership.

The conflict over tariff policy, like that over academic socialism, had implications for German political life that were much broader than the issue itself. German liberals had linked economic freedom (freedom of occupation, freedom to incorporate, freedom from state regulation and paternalism, freedom of international trade) to political freedom (constitutionalism, civil rights, the *Rechtsstaat*, ministerial responsibility, popular control over the legislative process). For a quarter of a century economic and political freedom had been seen as Siamese twins with a common heart. To discredit free trade was to discredit political freedom.[118] Germany's entrepreneurial elite, thousands of white-collar employees, and the owners of securities, whose common welfare was dependent upon the health of the capitalistic system, appeared to be faced with the necessity of choice between a political liberalism inseparably linked to free trade and a return to the old policy of state interventionism linked to Prussian authoritarianism. The first road seemed to lead to financial ruin, the other to financial survival. Bismarck soon discerned the options and offered the choice.

The "Era of Libel"

In December 1874, *Die Gartenlaube*, a monthly magazine with a circulation of about four hundred thousand and a readership estimated at two million, began publication of a series of articles purporting to tell the true story about the "bourse and corporate swindles in Berlin and in Germany." The author, Otto Glagau, reiterated and enlarged his charges in two sensational books published in 1876 and 1877, which were widely discussed, even on the floor of parliament.[119] He did not limit himself to the sordid story of dubious and

---

[117] DZA Potsdam, Reichskanzleramt, 1609–1617.

[118] Max Nitzsche pointed out that the union between free trade and liberalism had not always existed either in Germany or in other countries. In 1845 H. Brüggemann, a well-known writer on economic subjects, wrote, "To be liberal in outlook and for protective tariffs was for most people one and the same thing." Bismarck condemned protectionists in his early years in parliament as men of liberal and "revolutionary" sentiment. Nitzsche, *Handelspolitische Reaktion*, p. 70.

[119] Otto Glagau, *Der Börsen- und Gründungs-Schwindel in Berlin: Gesammelte und stark vermehrte Artikel der "Gartenlaube"* (Leipzig, 1876) and *Der Börsen- und Gründungs-Schwindel in Deutschland* (Leipzig, 1877).

fraudulent transactions in securities. By tracing the personal connections between the owners and managers of corporate enterprises, on the one hand,
and liberal newspapers, journalists, deputies (particularly those of the National Liberal party), on the other, he depicted parliament and press as dominated by the special interests of big business. But he also indicted the bourgeois class, free enterprise, the joint-stock company, the bourse, and the
whole system of liberal economics, which he held responsible not only for the
recent excesses but also for the depression itself and for all social and moral
ills of his time.

"The history of company foundings and security issues during 1870–1873,"
he wrote, "is the history of an unprecedentedly big and impudent, crafty and
intensive swindle such as has never before occurred." Losses suffered by investors he estimated at 1.5 billion thalers, a sum far greater than the French
war indemnity. "But these financial losses are small compared to the wounds
that the swindle has inflicted on the general welfare, to the crisis in commerce
and industry that has ravaged Germany for years and whose end is not in
sight, to the distress that burdens the people, who are filled with a dissatisfaction and bitterness that drives them in ever greater numbers into the arms of
social democracy and has already produced rioting and revolts in several
places! How much prestige and repute have the German people forfeited!
How quickly has the glory so recently won paled and vanished! How much
has been lost in honesty and morality, virtue and religion, industry and thrift-
iness, discipline and ethics! The worst and most unnatural crimes have become common. Murder and robbery, break-ins and thievery make city and
country unsafe. Deceit and embezzlement spread like the plague. Suicide has
become epidemic. Beggars and vagabonds wander about in droves; prisons
and penitentiaries are overfilled; civil and criminal cases, bankruptcies, auc-
tions, and seizures are legion. All of this is the immediate consequence of the
company and stockmarket swindles that are chiefly the work of Jews and semites."[120]

Glagau was not impressed by the fact that the first revelations of corruption
had come in February 1873 from a liberal Jewish deputy. Lasker, he charged,
had found his culprits only among the conservatives—"dilettantes like Privy
Counselor Wagener, Prince Putbus, Prince Biron, etc." Actually the guilty
speculators belonged primarily to Lasker's own people—"to the children of
Israel and to your own party, the national liberals." Ninety percent of the
stock market and corporate speculators of the "founding years," he claimed,
were Jewish. Many influential newspapers were owned by Jews, and those still
in Christian hands employed Jewish journalists, who constituted one-half of
the entire journalism profession. "I do not wish to kill or slaughter the Jews;
nor do I wish to drive them out of the country. I wish to take nothing from

[120] Glagau, *Schwindel in Deutschland*, pp. xvii–xviii.

them that they possess, but I do wish to hold them in check, fundamentally in check." No more, he cried, should Christians let a "false tolerance and sentimentality" prevent them from throwing off "domination" by this "physically and psychically most degenerate race."[121] In a final book published in 1879 Glagau called for a Kulturkampf against Jews.[122]

Glagau took credit for having introduced the issue of corruption into the public press, which, he maintained, had largely ignored or suppressed it after Lasker's initial revelations. Actually he was preceded by the *Die Deutsche Eisenbahn Zeitung*. This obscure Berlin journal, edited by Joachim Gehlsen, set out in 1874 to prove that the chief offenders were not Wagener and conservative aristocrats, toward whom Lasker had pointed his accusing finger, but Jewish capitalists and their liberal allies in the Prussian ministries and in the Prussian and German parliaments. As his notoriety grew, Gehlsen attracted anonymous contributors reputed to be in "the highest circles of society." Among them were the conservative journalist Rudolph Meyer and perhaps Hermann Wagener. Renamed the *Deutsche Reichsglocke*, the journal printed "revelations" concerning the "plundering" of various Prussian state funds by Bleichröder and the *Disconto-Gesellschaft* in collaboration with Camphausen, the Prussian minister of finance. Finally Gehlsen dared to insinuate that Bismarck himself was one of the profiteers. Repeatedly jailed for libel, Gehlsen finally fled to Switzerland. Two successors in the editor's chair were arrested and at the end of 1876 the journal ceased publication.[123]

Although a few other newspapers (*Deutsche Landes-Zeitung* and *Staatsbürgerzeitung*) followed the *Gartenlaube* and *Reichsglocke* into the muck, none was as important as the *Kreuzzeitung*, since 1848 the principal organ of Prussian conservatism. In June–July 1875 the *Kreuzzeitung* published a series of articles signed by Franz Fürchtegott Perrot on "the era Bleichröder, Delbrück, Camphausen and the new German economic policy." A Rhinelander of French extraction, artillery officer during the war of 1870–1871, former business manager of a Rhenish railway, and currently secretary-general of the Mecklenburg Trade Association, Perrot had earlier published a number of articles and pamphlets attacking the note-issuing privilege of private banks as an exploitation of the public for private gain. His campaign against banknotes was motivated by a deep distrust of capitalism in general. "We possess," he wrote in October 1871, "a number of state agencies that work systematically to favor mobile big capital in an unnatural way, to allow it to accumulate in an uneconomic way, and to give it privileges dangerous to the state, and to confer

---

[121] Glagau, *Schwindel in Deutschland*, pp. 441ff., and *Schwindel in Berlin*, pp. x–xi, xxv, xxx, 240ff. For statistics on and a general description of the role of Jews in German business and the professions by the 1870s see P. G. J. Pulzer, *The Rise of Political Anti-Semitism in Germany and Austria* (New York, 1964), pp. 3ff.

[122] Otto Glagau, *Des Reiches Noth und der neue Culturkampf* (Osnabrück, 1879), pp. 265ff.

[123] R. Meyer, *Politische Gründer*, pp. 146–171.

upon it a position and tendency within the state that quite obviously pro-
motes socialism as a kind of self-defense. . . . *Corporations are legalized arrangements for the exploitation of all by some.*"[124]

Perrot might have remained obscure had not Philipp von Nathusius Ludom, editor of the *Kreuzzeitung* since 1872, engaged him to write the "era
articles." These essays, revised by Nathusius, charged that Germany was governed by the "consortium Delbrück-Camphausen-Bleichröder" aided by Jewish deputies and journalists in the interest of the banking industry (five-sixths
of which was allegedly controlled by Jews). "If the financial and economic
policy of the new German Empire and previously that of the North German
Confederation gives impartial observers the impression of being purely that of
a banker (that is, a policy by and for bankers), that impression is certainly not
strange in view of the relationships in these matters among the leading personalities. Herr von Bleichröder is himself a banker; Herr Delbrück is related
to a banker (Delbrück, Leo & Co.); and Herr Camphausen is the brother of
a banker (Camphausen & Co.). And if the monetary and economic policy of
the German Empire always gives the impression of being *Judenpolitik* (that is,
a policy and legislation directed by and for Jews), that too is easily explain-
able, since the intellectual author of this policy, Herr von Bleichröder, is himself a Jew. . . . Messrs. Lasker, Bamberger, and their close friend, H. B. Op-
penheimer . . . are also Jews and are the actual leaders of the so-called
'national-liberal' majority in the Reichstag and Prussian lower chamber. . . .
Yes, we are at this time actually governed by Jews" and "almost exclusively
for the advantage of our citizens of Hebrew faith and Jewish nationality."
Perrot and Nathusius charged, furthermore, that all major legislative acts of
recent years (uniform weights and measures, common coinage, the incorporation statute) as well as the government's railway policy and its use of the
French war indemnity had been for the exclusive benefit of Jewish banks and
stock market interests. In conclusion, the article referred to the close relationship between Bismarck and Bleichröder, insinuating that the chancellor
himself had been corrupted by the power of capital.[125]

Glagau was merely the most prolific of several pamphleteers who exploited
the scandals of the "founding years" to discredit liberal ministers and deputies
as the spearhead of a great Jewish and capitalistic conspiracy. One of the most
daring was Rudolph Meyer, son of a Pomeranian landowner, disciple of Hermann Wagener, editor of the conservative *Berliner Revue*, and recent contrib-
utor to the *Reichsglocke*. In his *Politische Gründer und die Corruption in Deutschland*, published early in 1877, Meyer followed Glagau in depicting Bismarck
as the dupe of German capitalism. By unnecessarily abandoning "traditional

[124] L. Feldmüller-Perrot, ed., *Franz Perrot: Bismarck und die Juden. "Papierpest" und "Aera-
Artikel von 1875"* (Berlin, 1931), pp. 119–120.
[125] *Neue Preussische [Kreuz-] Zeitung*, June 29, 1875. Republished with minor editorial
changes—and favorable comment—by Feldmüller-Perrot, *Bismarck und die Juden*, pp. 271–280.

Prussian policy" and imitating the "caesaristic socialism" of Napoleon III, he had unwittingly created a "political and financial power" of banking and industrial interests that he could no longer control. Although all financiers were regarded as sinister (except for a few older private banking houses that had not lost their propriety in the founding years), the two special villains of Meyer's story were Gerson Bleichröder and David Hansemann (the *Disconto-Gesellschaft*). With their many capitalistic associates these two giants of the banking world had competed with one another in plundering not only the investing public but also the state treasury. With lucrative stock options and directorships they had bribed high Prussian officials (Scheele, Wilckens, Wehrmann, Schumann) and leading deputies of the free conservative (Kardorff, Münster) and national liberal (Miquel, Bennigsen, Bamberger, Rönne, and others) parties. Dominated mostly by Jews, the great banking houses were but vehicles of "speculation and usury" engaged in "legalized deceit."

One of their greatest swindles, Meyer averred, was the *Preussische Central-Boden-Credit-Aktiengesellschaft*, ostensibly founded for the benefit of Prussian landowners, but actually for their exploitation. Only the centrists and old conservatives had generally escaped corruption. The safeguards against such abuses had been demolished since 1867 by liberal legislation, for which Bismarck, his ministers and officials (Delbrück, Camphausen, Achenbach, Michaelis), and the liberals in parliament were solely responsible. But Bismarck bore the chief responsibility, for "the man of the century" had not used his immense power to halt the depredations of that "king of the rats," German capitalism. "As long as Prince Bismarck remains the sole powerful idol, the German nation will be sacrificed to the empire and the empire to the chancellor—as for the chancellor, he belongs to the Jews and the swindlers." The only solution was "removal of the present system and of its bearer."[126]

Since the beginning of the century bureaucratic reformers had expedited the development of German capitalism by moving progressively toward economic freedom. After 1867 Bismarck's cooperation with the liberals brought about the final triumph of laissez-faire. Now at the moment of apparent victory in the economic sphere, a triumph that many hoped was but the prelude to new political and constitutional conquests, the liberals suddenly found themselves the targets of widespread popular dissatisfaction. In 1876 Wilhelm Wehrenpfennig described the ironies of the situation in the *Preussische Jahrbücher*. "Whoever invested his fortune in bad securities does not find fault with his own incaution but with the incorporation statute. Whoever lost money on solid company shares does not put the blame on the transitional character of everything earthly—which since the time of the Pharaohs has alternated lean with fat years—but on our false economic policy. The indus-

---

[126] R. Meyer, *Politische Gründer*. On Meyer see William O. Shanahan, *German Protestants Face the Social Question: The Conservative Phase, 1815–1871* (Notre Dame, 1954), pp. 375–379.

trialist complains about tariff policy, the landowner deplores the free migration of labor [*Freizügigkeit*]; both complain about freight rates on the railways,
whose shareowners attribute their losses to the false policies of the state. Arrangements that other civilized peoples have had for centuries (for example,
features of our industrial code) are attacked as harmful innovations. Even the
most pressing and successfully executed reforms, such as our currency and
banking laws, are subjected to a most astonishing mishmash of reproaches and
complaints. . . . Agrarians, protectionists, conservatives, and democratic socialists—all have prescriptions for curing the ills of the world. The prescriptions cancel each other out. If one were chosen, the majority of the nation
would denounce it. None of the dissatisfied groups has a program that is politically and economically feasible, but all deplore the existing laws and the
factors that have brought them about."[127]

Throughout central Europe liberalism had been struck by a crisis of confidence of near catastrophic proportions, not only with regard to the doctrines
of classical economic theory, but also with regard to its individualistic social
ethic. What surfaced here was not just a dispute about public policy and a
search for scapegoats. The attack on liberals and Jews was a symptom of the
uneasiness felt by many Germans about the economic and social revolution
of their time. They lived in an era of accelerating change in which a familiar
environment, sanctified by tradition, was being rapidly eroded and replaced
by another filled with unknown hazards. Bourgeois and aristocrats alike feared
that the liberal era had produced in industrial capitalism a monster that would
devour its progeny. The crash and ensuing depression brought out many latent anxieties—hatred of the Jew, particularly of Jewish politicians and businessmen, *Mittelstand* fears of impoverishment and proletarianization, apprehension over socialist subversion of the economic and social order, suspicion
of the wealthy and their ambitions to enrich themselves at the cost of the
many—of the kind that in a later age were to culminate in National Socialism.

[127] Wilhelm Wehrenpfennig, "Politische Korrespondenz," *Preussische Jahrbücher*, 37 (1876),
pp. 97–98.

Transition in Domestic Policy,
1875–1876

N JUNE 4, 1875, Bismarck, his request for retirement refused, went on an extended leave that lasted until November 20. In past years he had often begun his recuperation in the baths at Bad Kissingen. But in 1875 he decided against returning to the scene of Kullmann's attack and spent summer and fall at Varzin. There he tried to follow the Kissingen routine; yet six weeks of saline baths left him weak and scarcely able to walk, much less ride. So he undertook a new regimen of "malt and brine baths" that seemed to be more successful. In early September Hohenlohe found him looking "fairly well" and walking, although still complaining that his health was poor in comparison with the previous year. Lucius, who was summoned to Varzin at the end of October, wrote that the prince "looked well" but complained of rheumatism in shoulder and chest and of intensive heartburn. Struck reported that his patient was also bothered by phlebitis, which hindered standing.[1] Delbrück and others shouldered many of the routine burdens in Berlin, but the chancellor was not able to separate himself completely from the cares of office. In June the attacks of Perrot in the *Kreuzzeitung* disturbed his peace; in August and September rebellions against Turkish rule in Bosnia and Herzegovina began to trouble Europe's chancelleries; and the work of the commission drafting imperial law codes also caused concern.[2] Still, his working hours were greatly reduced. In the solitude of Hither Pomerania Bismarck had time to think.

As related, Bismarck's request for release from office in May 1875 cannot be dismissed as a charade or political maneuver. Yet it may be doubted whether, if the Kaiser had granted it, Bismarck would have been satisfied to remain idle for long. Even in his debilitated condition, he was still driven by the same restless energy, the same insatiable need to dominate and control, that he had always displayed. While he sat under the oaks and beeches at Varzin, ideas moved about in his mind like molecules in solution. They centered upon two problems: how to continue consolidation of the imperial government, but in a conservative rather than liberal direction, that is, at the

---

[1] Horst Kohl, ed., *Anhang zu den Gedanken und Erinnerungen von Otto Fürst von Bismarck* (Stuttgart, 1901), I, 260; GW, VIII, 150–151; Freiherr Lucius von Ballhausen, *Bismarck-Erinnerungen* (Stuttgart, 1920), pp. 75–76.

[2] GW, VIc, 60–63.

cost of the Reichstag more than of the states; and how to consolidate his own authority over the executive organs of Prussia and the Reich, while strengthening their coordination. Most of his actions during the next four years in domestic affairs stemmed from perceptions formed and initial decisions made during his Pomeranian recuperation of 1875.

Two Basic Decisions

Sometime during the winter of 1875–1876, Bismarck sketched his mood and intentions for the benefit of a group of friendly deputies. "I am bored. The great tasks are done. The German Reich has been erected. It is recognized and respected by all states and nations. We will know how to prevent coalitions of the kind that are usually formed against a state that has achieved great things. If France should have ideas of revenge, it will find no allies against us, and without them it will dare nothing. In view of these circumstances what is left for me to do?" He was, he declared, "too tired" to hunt rabbits, but "a big and powerful wild boar, perhaps an Erymanthian," would be a different matter. "To give the German Reich a powerful, unshakable fiscal foundation, which would provide the Reich with a dominating position and bring it into organic union with all public interests in the state, province, county, and community—that would be a great and worthy task that could stir me to expend the last of my declining strength. The task is difficult in itself. Actually I am not an expert in these areas, and my present advisers, industrious though they may be in conducting day-to-day business, have no creative ideas. They move on worn-out tracks. I have no other recourse than to conceive the reform ideas myself and to use whatever instruments I can find to execute them."[3]

The implications of this new goal were enormous. To strengthen the Reich financially was to heighten the unitary principle at the cost of the federal. Ordinarily this would have been applauded by liberal nationalists and deplored by conservatives and by state governments. But much more was involved than merely a shift from federalism to centralism. New sources of income for the Reich would reduce and perhaps abolish the state assessments (Matrikularbeiträge), which in the late 1860s and again in the late 1870s disordered the finances of the states. Their abolition would also gravely reduce the power of the Reichstag, which had found in the assessments a surrogate for its inadequate power over the purse. Since imperial taxes could be collected indefinitely once granted and since tax laws could only be changed

[3] BP, I, 86–88. Poschinger gives no source and no exact date for these remarks. But they are descriptive of the mood in which Bismarck returned from Varzin in late 1875. On Apr. 21, 1873, he told Lucius, "Everything is now unexciting and boring, but the nation will again one day experience an intense heat that will bring the brittle metals to the melting point." Lucius, Bismarck-Erinnerungen, p. 29.

with the approval of the Bundesrat, Kaiser (who signed), and chancellor (who countersigned), the Reichstag had no effective control over the income of the Reich except through its power to set the amount of the state assessments in the annual budget. Those same assessments were also a surrogate for the Prussian Landtag's inadequate authority over appropriations. Through the Reichstag's power to legislate the Prussian assessment the liberals had acquired leverage on the Prussian government. In some degree they could plug the loophole in the Prussian constitution that had enabled the Bismarck government to expend state revenues for four years without a legal budget. In 1875 Bismarck returned to the program of "fiscal reform" that had failed in 1868–1869.[4]

In October 1875 Bismarck's old friend, the conservative leader Moritz von Blanckenburg, spent a few days in Varzin and on his return exulted to Roon that the "collapse of the liberal domination of parliament and cabinet" and of the prevailing economic policy (Manchesterism) was in prospect. While prophesying a "rosier" future, Blanckenburg admitted that he was baffled about how to attain it; he feared this was true of Bismarck as well. In December, after seeing Bismarck again in Berlin, Blanckenburg confirmed his earlier impressions. "Politically the situation is very confused. Bismarck is honest in his desire to be free of the spirits that he evoked; yet I cannot see the hole through which they will vanish. If it were just a matter of the old Prussia, then it would not be difficult to believe in the possibility of a healthy restoration . . . but in Germany the parties jostle one another so violently and in so many ways that I don't know how Bismarck will get rid of the present majority."[5]

To be rid of one majority required creation of another. Despite frequent grumbling, the Reichstag conservatives, "new conservatives" of the Landtag, and free conservatives in both chambers had never ceased to support what Bismarck wanted, even in the Kulturkampf. Ways had to be found to restore the strength these caucuses had lost by reconciling the "old conservatives" and by disabusing the voters who in the elections of 1873–1874 had mistakenly assumed that they were supporting Bismarck's aims in the Kulturkampf by voting for liberal rather than conservative candidates. Nevertheless, it was obvious that the conservative parties and factions could never supply by themselves the majority Bismarck required. Thus far all attempts to expand the conservatives from a Prussian party identified exclusively with the interests of the eastern gentry into a national party representing a broader spectrum of the population had failed. Hence the new majority had to be composed of liberals as well as loyal conservatives. In December 1875 Bismarck revealed his aims to Lucius: "a division of the national liberals, strengthening of its

[4] See vol. 1, pp. 418–422.

[5] Waldemar von Roon, *Denkwürdigkeiten aus dem Leben des General-Feldmarschalls Kriegsministers Grafen von Roon* (4th ed., Breslau, 1897), III, 423–425.

right wing, and weakening of the Progressive party."[6] By driving the Lasker wing out of the National Liberal party, Bismarck intended to sever the party's connection with the progressives and make it a suitable partner for the conservatives. Even if this combination did not produce a majority, it would hopefully provide a solid base from which to construct temporary alliances with other parties and political fragments on specific issues.

To achieve these objectives issues were needed, issues capable of reshaping both the party structure and constitutional relationships. During the next four years Bismarck probed steadily for the hidden valves and sluices that would release the forces he needed simultaneously to solidify the Reich financially, depress the powers of the Reichstag, and create a new majority. In the past the forces he had tapped were idealistic and ideological as well as material and social, but now most belonged to the latter categories. Out of the channels that Bismarck discovered in the late 1870s flowed a new combination of economic and social interests that dominated Germany long after he departed from the scene. A distinction must be made, however, between the problem as he originally conceived it, the means he found (as he progressed) for its solution, and the intended and unintended effects produced by his employment of those means. The problem with which he began in the fall of 1875 concerned the distribution of power between the Reich and the states and between the Reich executive and the Reichstag. His solution required the reconstruction of the Reichstag majority. In his search for a reconstructed majority, he altered the relationships between leading interest groups in German society. Yet the original problem remained unsolved, for he never succeeded in building an enduring new majority that would accept the solution he intended or in giving the Reich an independent financial structure. This will be shown as the rest of Bismarck's story unfolds.

That Bismarck was primarily concerned in the last half of 1875 with matters of power is also shown by his conception of another issue—that of his relationship as chancellor to the executive organs of the Reich and Prussia. Now that he had resolved to stay in the driver's seat, he was determined to improve his grip on the reins. During 1875 his complaints about the lassitude, independence, and even obstructionism of his ministerial colleagues multiplied. Falk, Achenbach, Camphausen, and Eulenburg were his chief targets; only Friedenthal, the minister of agriculture, seemed to perform to his satisfaction, which Bismarck attributed to the fact that Friedenthal, like himself a wealthy landowner, was a man of practical affairs. This was an old song, now sung more often.[7] Yet the most notable development of 1875 was the prince's increasing dissatisfaction with Rudolf Delbrück. In the spring he

---

[6] Dec. 17, 1875. Lucius, *Bismarck-Erinnerungen*, p. 80.

[7] Christoph von Tiedemann, *Sechs Jahre Chef der Reichskanzlei unter dem Fürsten Bismarck* (2d ed., Leipzig, 1910), pp. 9–10, 27, 32–33; *BP*, II, 233–234; Lucius, *Bismarck-Erinnerungen*, pp. 69, 72, 76, 78.

"complained bitterly" to Baron von Friesen, the Saxon envoy in Berlin, that Delbrück "entirely misconceives his position. He is nothing more than his [Bismarck's] subordinate and as such has to carry out Bismarck's orders and ideas, not his own ideas and decisions. But he fails completely to understand this. Outwardly he always acts as though he himself were the authoritative and decisive personality, and as a consequence he has also brought it about that others, including the press, actually see him as such. But he, the Reich chancellor, cannot let that be, for it damages his [Bismarck's] prestige and makes his position more difficult. He would have willingly broken with Delbrück long ago, but he cannot yet do it, for Delbrück is still indispensable, and he has at the moment no one whom he can put in his place."[8] Delbrück cast a shadow and Bismarck found it chilling—even though it reached no higher than the rim of his boots.

By August Bismarck had changed his mind about Delbrück's indispensability. On a visit to Varzin Baron Hermann von Mittnacht, leading member of the Württemberg delegation to the Bundesrat and chief representative of his government in Berlin, heard from the chancellor that Delbrück wished to retire—on grounds of health! Mittnacht was dismayed, protesting that members of the Bundesrat would regard Delbrück's departure as a "great loss." But Bismarck's view was different. "The prince said that too much had been concentrated in the Imperial Chancellor's Office rather than in the imperial chancellor, who must remain the solely responsible top leader. The machine has become too powerful in Bismarck's opinion. Departments must be established with greater independence; for example, the judicial section [of the chancellor's office] could be independent. The personality of the president of the chancellor's office [Delbrück] is imprinted on all the office's affairs. Bundesrat committees should exercise more active control over it. If we create independent departments without reducing the competencies of the Bundesrat, imperial ministries will not be needed. More ministries are also needed in Prussia. The ministries of finance and commerce could be divided, and there should be one minister of justice for legislation and a second for judicial administration."[9] Bismarck had decided to heighten his control over the executive apparatus of both the Reich and Prussia by applying the classic principle of *Realpolitik: divide et impera.*

The Program's Debut

Bismarck did not return to Berlin in late October 1875 as scheduled. Instead he requested several weeks additional leave ("every year the colder period has

---

[8] GW, VIII, 146.

[9] August 20, 21, and 22, 1875. GW, VIII, 149. See also Bismarck's remarks to Lucius on Oct. 31, 1875, and to deputies at a parliamentary soirée on Dec. 4, 1875. Lucius, *Bismarck-Erinnerungen*, pp. 76, 78; BP, I, 90–92.

done me the best service"). On October 27 the Reichstag convened amid doubts that the prince was any longer capable of carrying out his functions. Eugen Richter charged that the chancellor was "becoming more and more for us a mythical person." Only his underlings were visible during much of the year. How wise was an arrangement that made the orderly transaction of government business dependent upon the "nerves of a single man?"[10] On November 20 Bismarck reached the Wilhelmstrasse and two days later made his first appearance in the Reichstag. He looked worn and tired, spoke in a low voice, made grammatical mistakes, and groped even longer than usual for the right words. At last the Vesuvius of German politics appeared exhausted. "He will do us no more harm!" exulted a liberal deputy.[11]

Obviously stung by Richter's assault, Bismarck uttered a few self-righteous words about the sense of duty that had kept him in office for a quarter of a century, despite bad health, to which Richter and his ilk had contributed. Then he began what appeared to be a spontaneous discourse on taxes. Under debate were government bills for new stamp taxes on stock market transactions and securities and for an increase in the brewing tax—all for the purpose of covering an anticipated deficit in the imperial budget for 1876. The Reich, Bismarck declared, was still young; it needed to be further consolidated with new institutions and to be made financially independent of the states if it was to conquer particularism (especially Prussia's) and weather future storms. There was a way to achieve simultaneously the financial independence of the Reich and "tax reform" (that is, a shift from direct to indirect taxes). Increases in the indirect taxes allotted to the empire would reduce and eventually abolish the state assessments (*Matrikularbeiträge*); this in turn would make possible the reduction of direct taxes levied by the states. "Whatever one may say about indirect taxes from the theoretical standpoint, the fact is that one feels them less. It is hard for the individual to say how much he pays, how much he shifts to his fellow citizens." Yet everyone knows exactly how much income or class tax he pays. The resentment of the taxpayer would be less if the burden were hidden rather than open.

While the poor man had no way to reduce the amount of his class tax, he could, if indirect taxes were substituted for it, reduce his tax burden by consuming less tobacco, drinking less beer, or turning down his lamp in the evening. Indirect taxes and tariffs should be limited to ten to fifteen articles that were massively consumed, yet not vital to life—the "luxury items of the great masses," such as tobacco, coffee, sugar, petroleum, beer, and brandy. The luxuries of the wealthy should be taxed very high, but little income could be expected from them. Income taxes ought to be imposed only on the wealthi-

[10] SBR (1875–1876), I, 28, 115–116.
[11] Felix Rachfahl, "Eugen Richter und der Linksliberalismus im neuen Reiche," *Zeitschrift für Politik*, 5 (1912), p. 288.

est citizens, more as a "prestige" than a "finance tax." Taxes on real estate were basically unjust, for they were confiscatory. If direct taxes could be levied only by urban governments, the flight from the land would eventually cease.

The deputies, Bismarck continued, ought not to regard state assessments as "a question of parliamentary power. The power of the Reichstag rests on law, justice, and the constitution." Its right to grant or withhold taxes was secure. If the deputies wished more power they should seek it within the states, not the Reich, which was not yet strong enough to endure "tests of strength." Contrary to what Richter demanded, a collegial cabinet was impossible for the Reich; group responsibility was no responsibility at all; only one minister, the chancellor, could be responsible. On the other hand, it was possible to have imperial "ministries" of another kind: that is, separate departments directly under the control of the chancellor, an arrangement "corresponding to that of an English prime minister." Some already existed—those for foreign affairs, naval affairs, railway affairs, the post and telegraph; others were desirable, including one for Alsace-Lorraine.[12]

To Richter Bismarck's discourse appeared to be nothing more than a "harmless, uninhibited chat."[13] The chancellor's physical condition seemed to be more significant than his words; it was difficult to believe that a man in his debilitated condition was actually announcing a major reversal in policy that might require years to effect. Bismarck, however, had shot his first arrow into the target. At his parliamentary soirée on December 11, he split it with the shaft of a second. He had become, he told his startled guests, a zealous advocate of nationalization of the German railways. The Kaiser was "greatly interested" in the project;[14] the Prussian cabinet had discussed it "academically," and none of the ministers was opposed in principle. A unified railway system was as urgent and necessary as a unified postal service. It would be administered by one of the new imperial "ministries," the need for which he had justified to the Reichstag. A reorganization of the Reich executive would

---

[12] BR, VI, 292–308; SBR (1875–1876), I, 248ff. Bismarck's preference for indirect over direct taxes was not a sudden idea conceived in the late 1870s. On the contrary, he argued the advantages of indirect taxation in the research paper he wrote on political economy as a university student preparing for the state examination and again in a speech of 1851 in the Prussian Chamber of Deputies. Horst Kohl, ed., Bismarck-Jahrbuch, II (1895), II, 21–47, and BR, I, 207. He derived it from a study of French tax theory, particularly the views of J. B. Say. Georg Brodnitz, Bismarck's nationalökonomische Anschauungen (Jena, 1902), pp. 78ff.

[13] Eugen Richter, Im alten Reichstag: Erinnerungen (Berlin, 1894), I, 124; Rachfahl, "Richter," p. 288; also Geffcken to Roggenbach, Nov. 27, 1875, in Julius Heyderhoff, ed., Im Ring der Gegner Bismarcks (Leipzig, 1943), pp. 169–170.

[14] As in the case of the protective tariff in 1876, the Kaiser brought the matter independently to Bismarck's attention. Italy's conversion of its northern railways to state ownership suggested to Wilhelm that the German government might well revive Heydt's proposal of the 1850s for a publicly owned network. See his letter to Bismarck, Dec. 8, 1875, in Friedrich Jungnickel, Staatsminister Albert von Maybach (Stuttgart, 1910), pp. 30–31.

create imperial "ministries" for commerce, customs, communications, finance, justice, and Alsace-Lorraine that would administer imperial affairs under the general responsibility of the chancellor. This time, however, he drew a distinction between the English system and that which he proposed. The authority of the English prime minister over the cabinet rested on his power to force the resignation of ministers opposed to his policies; that of the chancellor, on his right to intervene in imperial agencies and make decisions "at any stage." The heads of these bodies in other words, were not to be ministers at all in the English sense. They were to be mere state secretaries acting under the direction of the chancellor, the empire's only minister. "Naturally," he concluded, "all of this will not be accomplished without a diminution of Delbrück."[15]

The news of these remarks reverberated through the German press and was the subject of widespread speculation. Obviously Delbrück's days in office were numbered, not only because he could not accept a reduced status but also because he had to oppose on principle such a state-socialist scheme as public ownership of the nation's railways.[16] But what would his departure in this context mean for the future of the government's relations with the liberal parties? The issue was unclear. With Delbrück's exit liberals would lose the man who for two decades had done more than any other to promote liberal causes within the government—low tariffs and free trade, liquidation of restraints on industrial capitalism, and growth of the imperial government at the cost of the states. Yet the liberal deputies had since 1867 persistently advocated establishment of imperial ministries and an imperial cabinet. Now the chancellor was at least using their terminology, and, although his meaning was different, the reorganization he proposed could be seen as at least a step toward ultimate realization of their aspirations. While a publicly owned railway system would violate the principle of laissez-faire and was certain to alarm some capitalists, it would be a step toward the unitary state, another oft-proclaimed goal of many liberals and of extreme nationalists like Treitschke.[17] Eventually it might provide the imperial government with yet

---

[15] BP, I, 94–96. Bismarck had already begun to make life uncomfortable for Delbrück, as is shown by an entry in Bamberger's diary dated "end of November." "Bennigsen has just told me something very notable. Standing in the Reichstag close to Delbrück, Bismarck had complained: that Delbrück opposes him everywhere by his need to dominate, that he [Bismarck] would like to provide the Reich with an organization composed of large, independent offices, such as we want, but Delbrück is unwilling to give up anything. In saying these things, Bismarck uttered such vehement comments about Delbrück that Bennigsen did not wish to repeat them—of all Bismarck's fantasies full of suspicion they were the strongest!" Ernst Feder, ed., *Bismarcks grosses Spiel: Die geheimen Tagebücher Ludwig Bambergers* (Frankfurt, 1932), p. 314.

[16] Heinrich von Poschinger, ed., *Erinnerungen aus dem Leben von Hans Viktor von Unruh* (Stuttgart, 1895), pp. 353–355.

[17] HW, II, 145–148, 152–153; Karl Schiller, ed., *Heinrich von Treitschke: Aufsätze, Reden, und Briefe* (Meersburg, 1929), III, 363ff.

another source of income beyond control of parliament and conceivably reduce those state assessments that had become for liberals the palladium of
parliamentary power over the purse. Ill or not, Bismarck had a great talent for
finding the issue with which simultaneously to advance his policy, mask its
direction, and create confusion and divisiveness among those affected by it.

For the time being Bismarck had to conceal his intentions. A premature
confrontation, or one based on the wrong issue, would consolidate the National Liberal party and cement its relationship with the progressives. Not
until the elections due in the winter of 1876–1877 was there any prospect of
altering the composition of the chamber. Hence Bismarck strove for months
to quell persistent rumors that his affection for "his friends of the majority
parties was no longer as warm as in earlier times."[18] In late November 1875
Bennigsen reported that Bismarck denied any desire for "conflict with us."[19]
At the soirée on December 18 he averred that he had no intention of turning
away from the national liberals, of conducting a "quiet war" against them
until the elections, or of trying to build a new party. "To be sure, it would be
alright with him if in the elections the so-called 'right wing' of the National
Liberal party and the free conservatives gained in strength. But he immediately went on to assure his listeners that he did not attribute much importance
to party differences." He would be satisfied if the same persons were reelected—that is, after they had learned from the voters that the public favored his policies. "He harbors great and far-reaching plans for the future
domestic policy of the Reich and in realizing them would not be able to dispense with the support of the Reichstag majority that had been loyal up to
now."[20] A few days later he summoned the deputy Wilhelm Wehrenpfennig
to reinforce the point. "Everything that is being said about his desire to break
with the national liberals," Wehrenpfennig reported him as saying, "is idle
maliciousness and nonsense. He asserts that he is more than ever resolved to
depend upon them alone for support; they are the only possible political party,
etc."[21]

Naturally these blandishments were not reassuring to everyone, particularly
not to the party's left wing. "The thought of a reorganization of the liberal
party according to our point of view," Heinrich Oppenheim wrote to Lasker
on November 10, 1875, "is so prevalent that it constantly reappears—with
all kinds of references in the press to the affected persons. Miquel spoke with
me quite spontaneously about it and expressed most decisively the desire to
emancipate himself from Bismarck!"[22] During most of 1875 Lasker had been
seriously ill of typhus, from which some thought he never fully recuperated.

[18] See an account of the soirée of Nov. 27, 1875, in BP, I, 89–90.
[19] Hermann Oncken, *Rudolf von Bennigsen* (Stuttgart, 1910), II, 286–287.
[20] BP, I, 101–102.
[21] Bamberger, *Bismarcks grosses Spiel*, p. 315.
[22] HW, II, 137.

But in late October he was back on station in the Reichstag,[23] harried by the feeling that time was running out for men of his conviction.[24] On December 27 he caucused with three close associates (Ludwig Bamberger, Max von Forckenbeck, and Baron Franz von Stauffenberg) to consider "steps toward the development of the constitution." "Lasker," Bamberger wrote in his diary, "wants to introduce a motion in the chamber that will forcefully [mit Gewalt] bring the issue to a head and must lead to a clash with Bismarck. He asked whether we were ready to go so far with him." All three shrank back from such a confrontation. Bamberger was inclined to interpret the issue as personal. Animosity between Bismarck and Lasker, he wrote, had reached the level of that earlier between Bismarck and Twesten. "They hate each other openly. Lasker believes Bismarck is now very dispensable."[25]

Lasker was correct in sensing at the end of 1875 that the liberals had reached the last crossing in their relations with Bismarck. As the economic crisis continued, liberalism as an economic theory lost ground and with it liberalism as a political ideology. The time was coming when those who prided themselves on "committed liberalism" were to be on the defensive, able only to react to Bismarck's initiatives and subject to the divisive manipulations by which he sought to reshape the structure of parliament to fit his own authoritarian ends. Important members of the national liberal left, which was presumed to hold the balance of power in German parliamentary life, had grown accustomed to dealing with Bismarck and likewise to the periodic crises it involved. Among them was Forckenbeck, who, by virtue of his general prestige as president of the Reichstag and lord mayor of Breslau (later Berlin), was regarded as a logical candidate for the chancellorship and hence essential to the success of any liberal revolt against Bismarck.[26]

Under the influence of Bismarck's charisma, Forckenbeck and his associates were inclined to share the presumption of his indispensability. Since 1866 they had traveled a long and tortuous road from compromise to compromise, which, despite the sacrifices it imposed, had achieved economic and national objectives they valued. Most important of all, they were evidently inclined to the belief that, although straws flew in the wind, no gale was in prospect. Even if Bismarck were bent on a new policy, it was not certain that it would be disadvantageous to the liberal cause or that by collaborating with him they could not, as so often in the past, shape it somewhat to their own designs. They were inclined to accept Bismarck's word that the National Liberal party was still vital to his program, that he had no intention of striking bargains

---

[23] Richard W. Dill, *Der Parlamentarier Eduard Lasker und die parlamentarische Stilentwicklung der Jahre 1867–1884* (Erlangen, 1956), pp. 130–131; Lasker to Forckenbeck, May 16, 1875, and July 3, 1875, DZA Merseburg, Rep. 92 (Nachlass Forckenbeck, B3, pp. 38–41).

[24] Lasker to Hermann Baerwald, Nov. 1–Dec. 27, 1875. HW, II, 140.

[25] Bamberger, *Bismarcks grosses Spiel*, pp. 314–315.

[26] Heinrich Oppenheim to Lasker, Nov. 10, 1875. HW, II, 137.

with the Center party or of calling off the Kulturkampf, and that he could do nothing with the conservatives "who, if restored to favor at court, would merely conspire to bring about his fall."[27]

Delbrück's Fall

Indeed, there was concrete evidence for the accuracy of these assumptions. Judged by actions as well as words, the Bismarck government seemed eager to avoid alienating the national liberals during the German and Prussian legislative sessions of 1875–1876. The policy was evident in the debates on three major issues: the imperial budget for 1876, the imperial penal code act, and the plan for railway nationalization.

In the Reichstag debates on the budget during November 1875, both Camphausen and Bismarck stressed the desire for harmonious relations with parliament. The proposals for increasing the brewing tax and introducing a new stamp tax on securities, they stressed, were not to be regarded as "cabinet questions," involving the possibility of a dissolution. Camphausen actually asserted that, if disagreement should develop between government and parliament, "then the men who lead the government must retire; others must take their places; harmony must be reached."[28] Camphausen's constitutional theory was startling, but even Bismarck tantalized the deputies with visions of future power. If the Reichstag exercised its unchallenged right to refuse new taxes, he declared, the government would simply come back again with other proposals until either the ministers or the deputies changed their minds "or other persons take over the tiller."[29] In the budget committee Eugen Richter, the parliament's keenest fiscal expert, whittled away until a new shape emerged that the deputies avidly accepted. While rejecting new taxes and preserving the state assessments at the previous level, he proposed to balance the budget by ending certain fiscal practices that in recent years had enabled the government to pile up treasury surpluses by underestimating the Reich's income. But the Reichstag majority also rejected a number of new positions for staff officers in the militia that were in excess of the iron budget. Then the deputies waited to see how the government would take the news. To general surprise Delbrück announced (December 16, 1875) that the amendments would stand, although the Reichstag would have to assume responsibility for any undesirable consequences in the budget for 1877.[30]

[27] Bamberger to Wehrenpfennig in late Dec. 1875. Bamberger, *Bismarcks grosses Spiel*, p. 315.
[28] *SBR* (1875–1876), I, 223.
[29] *BR*, VI, 307. Heinrich Geffcken wrote to Baron Roggenbach on Nov. 29, 1875. "The speeches by Camphausen and Bismarck have taken away the first conflict-anxiety of the liberals; whether Bismarck is happy with Camphausen's constitutional views seems questionable to me." Heyderhoff, ed., *Im Ring der Gegner*, p. 169.
[30] *SBR* (1875–1876), I, 694ff., 725–726.

From November 1875 to February 1876 the Reichstag and the press were even more concerned about the contents of a government bill (*Strafgesetznovelle*) to amend extensively the penal code of 1870, one of the great achievements of the North German Confederation. Some proposed changes in the code were political in character and a serious threat to civil liberties. In a speech lasting two-and-a-half hours (December 3, 1875) Lasker excoriated "rubber paragraphs" that could be stretched to include liberal critics as well as ultramontane and socialist opponents of the government. Paragraphs threatening to freedom of speech, assembly, and the press were struck out of the statute by a coalition of national liberals, progressives, centrists, socialists, and other fragments. Among the excised clauses was a so-called "socialist paragraph," which would have exposed to fine and imprisonment the organizers and members of secret societies and anyone threatening the public peace by stimulating class conflict or attacking the institutions of marriage, family, and property.[31]

In the debate on December 3, the progressive leader Albert Hänel openly charged what many thought—that the bill had been deliberately designed to cleave apart the two wings of the National Liberal party. Everyone expected a harsh reaction to the liberal amendments.[32] But again, to general astonishment, Bismarck shied away from conflict. His duty, he declared, was to request laws whether or not passage was likely. He wanted to open a dialogue with parliament, between the parties in the parliament, and between the deputies and the voters. While the majority had the right to amend government bills, it must not expect the issues to disappear. "Some worms don't die."[33] He did insist, however, on some paragraphs, which finally passed when the national liberals, after heated caucuses, deserted the opposition to join conservatives and free conservatives. Thus were passed: the "pulpit paragraph" directed against ultramontane clerics who "endangered public peace" by discussing "affairs of state"; the "Duchesne paragraph" aimed at agitators who impelled others to commit illegal acts; and the "Arnim paragraph" providing for the imprisonment of diplomats guilty of communicating official information to unauthorized persons or of misleading their superiors with false or distorted information. Although divided on the "pulpit paragraph," the National Liberal party remained intact. If the national liberals made compromises, so did Bismarck. The only issue he raised to the status of a cabinet question was the "Arnim paragraph," to which they attributed little importance.[34]

Nationalization of the German railways was not a sudden decision for Bismarck. A frequent traveler and shipper of grain and timber, he was sensitive

---

[31] SBR (1875–1876), I, 386–399.
[32] SBR (1875–1876), I, 408–410; Richter, *Im alten Reichstag*, I, 129; BP, II, 224–225.
[33] BR, VI, 309–325.
[34] BP, II, 225; HW, II, 145; BR, VI, 318–323.

to such matters as poor service and inequitable charges. During the *Gründer-jahre* he prodded his colleagues, particularly Minister of Commerce Itzenplitz, to halt the abuse of government loan guarantees and to strengthen competition by preventing monopolistic mergers and concessioning parallel lines.[35] By early 1873 he had reached the conclusion that "big corporate railway powers" could be brought under control only if the Prussian government constructed competing railways and bought the major lines radiating from Berlin, the hub of the German railway system.[36] For years he had also been distressed by the failure to implement clauses in the imperial constitution granting the Reich the power to regulate the nation's railways. He desired an imperial agency equipped with strong regulatory authority, but the medium states resisted. Passage in the Bundesrat being doubtful, he turned to the Reichstag. Apparently with the chancellor's connivance, the liberals produced a bill creating an Imperial Railway Office, which Bismarck pushed through the Bundesrat (June 1873).[37] Nevertheless, other statutes were needed if the agency was to have any effective authority over rates and services, and here again Bismarck encountered frustration. Two presidents of the agency, Friedrich Scheele and Albert Maybach, resigned in succession when they failed to obtain from the Bundesrat a regulatory statute. Behind the existing abuses stood too many vested interests—both private and state-owned railway enterprises.

Since 1866 Bismarck had been of the conviction that an active railway policy would pay big dividends in the consolidation of the Reich. In January 1870, at a moment when the movement for national unity was at a low ebb, he wrote that use of the North German Confederation's regulatory power would "strengthen national sympathies for confederate institutions. Every satisfaction of the public's wishes, every redress of widely shared grievances about the operation of one or more railway lines, every improvement in service that is attributed to the confederation will gain their thanks."[38] After six years of further frustration in his efforts to establish effective regulation, he concluded that "the national idea" could best be served by imperial ownership. Sinews of steel would bind the nation together.[39] Railway profits and railway shares had not recovered from the crash of 1873 and ensuing depression. Whether

[35] *AWB*, I, 126, 131–134, 152–154, 157–160, 170–171, 193–199; *GW*, VIb, 222, 412–413; Tiedemann, *Sechs Jahre*, pp. 45–50; Heinrich von Poschinger, ed., *Neues Bismarck-Jahrbuch* (Vienna, 1911), I, 60ff.; Alfred von der Leyen, *Die Eisenbahnpolitik des Fürsten Bismarck* (Berlin, 1914), pp. 147ff.

[36] *AWB*, I, 172–182.

[37] *AWB*, I, 181; *BR*, VI, 47–55. Contrary to Bismarck's assertions to Lucius on Apr. 12, 1873 (*Bismarck-Erinnerungen*, p. 29), neither Itzenplitz nor Camphausen opposed creation of an imperial railway agency. Leyen, *Eisenbahnpolitik*, pp. 57–64, 169–176.

[38] *AWB*, I, 146–148, 150–151; also Leyen, *Eisenbahnpolitik*, pp. 158–160.

[39] *BR*, VI, 424, 429–434; also *GW*, VIc, 57, and VIII, 149; *AWB*, I, 200, 216–222. Bismarck first mentioned the idea to Baron von Mittnacht on Aug. 20–22, 1875, and on Sept. 11, 1875, he outlined the proposal to Maybach. Leyen, *Eisenbahnpolitik*, pp. 95–96.

or not shareholders would welcome nationalization was disputed. But there was no doubt that both big landowners and big industrialists, the chief users of railway freight transport, favored it. Like Bismarck, they deplored the multitude of freight rate schedules (no less than 1,357 in 1875), the frequency with which they were changed, and the "differential rates" that favored foreign shippers. A nationalized system might also eventually provide a new source of imperial revenue with which to reduce the Reich's dependence upon the state assessments subject to Reichstag approval.[40] Bismarck expected both economic and political dividends from this venture into state socialism. Here again he was destined to disappointment.

In January 1876 the Prussian cabinet approved the sale of Prussian state railways to the Reich, despite the reservations of Camphausen.[41] In May the bill passed the Prussian Chamber of Deputies, where it was opposed by centrists as a danger to federalism and by progressives as a threat to the free-enterprise system. Richter feared the concentration of economic power that would result from a "Bismarck railway" and its possible consequences for parliamentary power over the budget.[42] In the House of Lords ultraconservatives unsuccessfully opposed the measure as a sacrifice of Prussian autonomy. Weeks before the statute was enacted, however, it was already evident that the medium states were unwilling to match Prussia's sacrifice. Although Prussian national liberals (Lasker in the lead) favored nationalization, most party colleagues from the medium states were violently opposed, as were many free conservatives from the same regions.[43] So also were their governments. Saxony, Bavaria, Württemberg, and Baden objected to loss of control over their own state and private railways and to the concentration of economic and social power that a nationalized system would bring to the Reich.[44]

Although the prospect for full nationalization was slim, Bismarck was determined to execute at least the decision of the Prussian cabinet and Landtag to offer Prussia's state-owned railways to the Reich. But even this was denied him. The Prussian ministries of finance and commerce could not agree on terms to be presented to the Bundesrat and Reichstag. Month after month,

---

[40] Conservatives had already begun to promote publicly the idea of nationalization—Count Udo zu Stolberg in the Prussian House of Lords on Mar. 19, 1875, and Karl Stumm and Wilhelm von Kardorff in the Reichstag on Nov. 24, 1875. *SBHH* (1875), I, 200; *SBR* (1875–1876), I, 308–311, 316; Richter, *Im alten Reichstag*, I, 130–131. Albert Maybach, a former Prussian official who had been appointed president of the Imperial Railway Office, proposed nationalization to Bismarck on Oct. 4, 1875. On Oct. 23, 1875, he reported to Bismarck that the proposal was financially "feasible." Annual surpluses and "savings" of about 206,480,000 marks produced by Germany's railways would suffice to float at 5.81 percent bonds worth 3,530,000,000 marks to defray the purchase. Jungnickel, *Maybach*, pp. 30–31, 50–52.

[41] Jungnickel, *Maybach*, pp. 53–54; Leyen, *Eisenbahnpolitik*, pp. 100–103, 196–201.

[42] *SBHA* (1876), II, 1134–1162.

[43] *HW*, II, 145–149.

[44] *GW*, VIc, 68–70; Leyen, *Eisenbahnpolitik*, pp. 108ff.

the impasse between ministers Camphausen and Achenbach continued, while Bismarck fumed, unable even to get a clear picture of the status of the discussion.[45] In March 1878 he described the situation to the Chamber of Deputies. "I had the agreement in principle of my colleagues; I had the agreement in principle of the entire Landtag; and yet, although minister-president, I found myself absolutely unable to bring the matter one step further along. Agreement does not help me at all when passive resistance—from what direction in this complicated machine is impossible to learn—is conducted with such success that I am scarcely in a position after two to three years to answer even the most basic questions. The Prussian cabinet has never even reached the point of discussing the question of how Prussia is formally to offer its railways to the Reich—and presumably be refused. Nor has the cabinet discussed with the Ministry of Finance the evaluation of Prussia's rail properties and the price that could be asked from the Reich."[46] Privately Bismarck concluded that Camphausen was the actual obstructionist. "The bankers, with whom he is befriended, would never have pardoned him."[47]

For all its frustrations the nationalization proposal may have helped extract at least one thorn from Bismarck's flesh. On April 25, 1876, one day before the crucial debate on it in the Chamber of Deputies, the news broke that Rudolf Delbrück had resigned—on grounds of poor health. Only Bismarck had played a greater public role in the early years of the German Reich. The chancellor's long absences from Berlin had heightened Delbrück's importance. In the press, Reichstag, and Bundesrat his departure was lamented as a great loss to the orderly operation of government. Naturally there was widespread speculation about the actual reason for his retirement. Had he disagreed with the nationalization scheme? Was the Bismarck government veering away from the free-trade and free-enterprise policies with which Delbrück was so closely identified? Was this the beginning of a purge of liberals from high office? Bismarck was quick to deny everything. For nearly a year he had pushed and shoved in the effort to unseat Delbrück. But now he delivered in the Reichstag a glowing eulogy. "Not a shadow of a difference of opinion concerning any of the pending questions of the day has appeared between him and his majesty, between him and me."[48]

Attacks by Ultraconservatives

During 1876–1877 Bismarck steadily advanced his pieces on the chessboard of German politics, pulling back his knights and rooks from exposed positions only to redeploy them later in other directions. Despite disturbing signs, the

---

[45] AWB, I, 230–232, 252–253, 281–282; Leyen, Eisenbahnpolitik, pp. 115–118.
[46] BR, VII, 214–215.
[47] Bismarck to Poschinger, May 6, 1889. GW, VIII, 659.
[48] BR, VI, 387–388.

national liberals felt reassured when successive crises were surmounted without a serious break with the government. Once again they had succeeded in leaving their imprint on critical legislation. Rumors spread of attempts by ultramontanes to negotiate with Bismarck; yet there was no apparent relaxation of the chancellor's determination to pursue the Kulturkampf. Although Delbrück had departed, the liberal ministers Falk and Camphausen remained in office. The depression continued, and agitation for protectionism grew; yet the government's position on free trade appeared unchanged. Equally lulling was the fact that Bismarck's personal relations with the ultraconservatives, instead of improving as seemed possible during deliberations on the May laws of 1875, appeared to deteriorate.

Earlier it has been shown that the indemnity act of 1866, the Hanoverian provincial fund of 1868, the school inspection and county reform acts of 1872, and the appointment of new peers in 1872 were successive wedges that widened the gap between Bismarck and the ultraconservatives and split the conservative movement into pro- and antigovernment factions in the Prussian Landtag.[49] In September 1872 the ultras came into control of the principal mouthpiece of conservative interests, the *Kreuzzeitung*. The newspaper founded and long edited by Hermann Wagener, to whose columns Bismarck himself had once contributed and which had vigorously supported his policies in the constitutional conflict, was now in the hands of a hostile editor, Nathusius Ludom. Through the "era articles" Nathusius hoped to "cause a sensation" that would win over to the ultra cause "agrarians and others" who had sided with the government on the Kulturkampf. But moderate conservatives like Moritz von Blanckenburg, who had been seeking a reunion of conservative factions on an agrarian program, were "astounded" that the *Kreuzzeitung* had resorted to libel.[50] Bismarck's first thought was to prosecute, but the articles had been composed with a careful eye on the laws against libel. Neither he nor Heinrich von Friedberg, chief of the Imperial Office of Justice, could find adequate grounds for suit.[51] Instead, the chancellor denounced the "reptile press" in the Reichstag during the debate on the *Strafgesetznovelle* (February 9, 1876). "Everyone who receives and pays for [the *Kreuzzeitung*] shares indirectly in the lies and slander that are published in it, in slanders such as the *Kreuzzeitung* contained last summer against the highest officials of the Reich, without the slightest hint of proof."[52] But this attempt to destroy the newspaper by alienating its readership backfired. Beginning on February 26, hundreds of conservative readers signed a "declaration" supporting the *Kreuzzeitung* and ostentatiously renewed their subscriptions. Among them were some of Bismarck's oldest acquaintances, including Adolf von Thadden, the

[49] See pp. 168–169, 207–213.

[50] Herman von Petersdorff, *Kleist-Retzow: Ein Lebensbild* (Stuttgart, 1907), pp. 461–462.

[51] GW, VIc, 61–62; XV, 350.

[52] BR, VI, 351–352.

owner of Trieglaff where Bismarck had first met Marie von Thadden and Moritz von Blanckenburg. Whatever sympathy Bismarck may have gained in the reaction against the "era articles" he lost in the attempt to crush the *Kreuzzeitung*. Even Blanckenburg, who was not a signer, evidently felt that he had reached a turning point in his relationship with the chancellor. One evening he pulled out of his desk letters received from Bismarck over a period of forty years, and, after reading passages to Roon, tossed them one by one into the blazing hearth.[53]

As noted earlier, the Perrot articles were but one of several attempts by conservatives and muckraking journalists to discredit liberal ministers and incriminate Bismarck personally in financial scandals.[54] Even as Bismarck considered his change of course in domestic policy at Varzin, two Pomeranian neighbors, Ludwig von Wedemeyer and Otto von Diest-Daber, were plotting to do him serious injury. At Diest-Daber's suggestion Wedemeyer wrote a pamphlet insinuating that Bismarck had received a "gratuity" (his profit from speculation in *Boden-credit* shares reserved for him at the issuing price) in return for his assistance in gaining special privileges for the company. They intended to distribute fifteen thousand copies of the document to landowners, but the unstable Wedemeyer committed suicide (November 25, 1875), and it was not until September 1876 that the brochure appeared in an abbreviated form edited by Diest-Daber. On October 6 the *Kreuzzeitung* reported that the first printing was already exhausted, and a second was in preparation.[55] The charges of Wedemeyer and Diest, like those of Perrot and Nathusius, were so cleverly phrased that the state's attorney could find no grounds for suit under the libel laws. The editors of *Die deutsche Reichsglocke*, a weekly journal, with which Harry von Arnim was connected, and Rudolph Meyer, editor of the

---

[53] Hermann Witte, ed., "Bismarck und die Konservativen: Briefe aus Trieglaff," *Deutsche Rundschau*, 149 (1911), pp. 386–387. In 1863 Thadden had said of Bismarck, "He is a hero from head to toe." On Bismarck's order the entire list of *Deklaranten* was published in the official *Staatsanzeiger* in order to show that he had indeed broken ("cut the tablecloth") with the signers. On the identity of the *Deklaranten* see BP, II, 201–202.

[54] See pp. 316–321.

[55] Otto von Diest-Daber, *Der sittliche Boden im Staatsleben: Auseinandersetzung mit dem Abgeordneten Lasker* (Berlin, 1876), pp. 49–56, and *Entgegnungen auf die Angriffe des Herren Lasker, von Bennigsen u. A. nebst Aufklärung über die Privilegien der Central-Boden-Credit-Gesellschaft* (Berlin, 1876), pp. 30–34, 44–63, and *Zur Klarstellung des anonymen Schriftstückes und der Angriffe des Abgeordneten Lasker: Einige Worte der vorläufigen Abwehr* (Diest-Daber, Selbst Verlag des Verfassers, 1878). As the titles indicate, the greater part of Diest-Daber's attack was directed at Lasker, whom he accused of having failed to include national liberals (particularly Bennigsen) and free conservatives among the culprits in the scandal. On the Diest-Daber affair see Siegfried von Kardorff, *Wilhelm von Kardorff: Ein nationaler Parlamentarier im Zeitalter Bismarcks und Wilhelms II., 1828–1907* (Berlin, 1936), pp. 97–110. For Diest-Daber's own version of events that led to his imprisonment and discharge from the officer corps see *Bismarck und Bleichröder: Deutsches Rechtsbewusstsein und die Gleichheit vor dem Gesetze. Lebenserfahrungen aus Acten, Tagebüchern und Briefen* (Munich, 1897).

weekly *Sozialpolitische Korrespondenz*, came to the prosecutor's assistance by deliberately repeating the insinuations in a form that made them, and ultimately Diest-Daber as well, vulnerable to indictment.[56] As previously described, the result was a series of trials in January–February 1877 that, while they vindicated Bismarck, revealed the depths of the bitterness that now divided the chancellor from the ultras and their journalistic allies. What his detractors published had long been bruited in the aristocratic clubs of Berlin.[57]

Bismarck never fully recovered from the wounds inflicted by his fellow aristocrats in the mid-1870s. In dictating his memoirs in the 1890s, he tried again to categorize those who had opposed him and dissect their motives. Many readers of the *Kreuzzeitung*, he declared, were motivated by principles that outweighed their Prussian and German national feeling, but some, of whom Harry von Arnim was a prototype, opposed him out of personal ambition. Members of his own caste (*Standesgenossen*) among the landed nobility, on the other hand, were personally envious that his career had elevated him above them. "That I advanced from *Landjunker* to minister they would have been able [to] forgive, but not the dotations and not the princely title that was accorded me much against my will." The predicate *Excellenz* was within the limits of what was customarily attainable, but the predicate *Durchlaucht* "aroused criticism." It was, furthermore, in the nature of politics, as in religion, for men to deny validity to the convictions of others and to identify their own cause with the public welfare. "My political convictions are right and yours false; my belief is pleasing to God and your unbelief leads to damnation." Self-righteousness led men in the political struggle to commit acts that in their private lives they would regard as improper and unjust.

"After they had joined in Perrot's disgraceful attacks on my honor, there was no longer any possibility of a personal relationship between me and the *Deklaranten*, many of whom had until then been acquaintances, even friends. Suddenly to break off contact with all or almost all friends and acquaintances is a hard test for the nerves of a man of mature years. At that time my health had long been weakened, not by the work that burdened me, but by the continuing awareness of my responsibility for major events in which the future of the fatherland was at stake." Statesmen can never know for sure whether the course they set is correct; yet they are compelled to make decisions and to act on those decisions, often over the opposition of those whom one is accus-

---

[56] Rudolph Meyer, *Politische Gründer und die Corruption in Deutschland* (Leipzig, 1877), p. 154.

[57] Kardorff, *Kardorff*, p. 106. Bismarck did not appear in person to testify at the trial. Yet he was represented by an unsigned and anonymous statement read by the state's attorney, which denied Diest-Daber's charges. The court permitted the statement to be read after the conclusion of the proceedings, but before the judges rendered their decision, on the word of the state's attorney "that he had been authorized to read it by a high personage [*von hoher Stelle*] and that he vouched for the authenticity of the contents." Diest-Daber, *Zur Klarstellung*.

tomed to take seriously. "The source of the problem is not work but doubt and concern," and the necessity of making grave decisions in times of crisis without anything to fall back upon but one's own conviction and willpower. "Intercourse with others whom one regards as equals makes easier the mastery of such crises," but, when the responsible minister suddenly finds himself boycotted and treated as an enemy by his former friends, for motives that are more personal and ignoble than objective and honorable, the consequence was damaged nerves and shattered health. One would have thought, he continued, that "the national party," in whose behalf he had incurred the wrath of former conservative party comrades, would have sprung to his defense and made clear that they did not share the views of the libelers. But the national liberals only seemed to take satisfaction in the quarrel and to want to intensify it. "Liberals and conservatives were united (each in behalf of their own partisan interests) in their determination to exhaust me, discard me, and attack me."[58]

By the late 1870s Bismarck—the unifier of Germany, minister-president of Prussia and chancellor of the German Reich, the dominant figure in German and European politics—thought of himself as deserted, libeled, and slandered by foes and former friends alike. He felt isolated and unappreciated (except by his immediate family) because he had pursued with single-minded determination, without fear or favor, the objective interests of the Prussian and German state.

Birth of the German Conservative Party

In February and March 1876 the *Kreuzzeitung-Deklaranten* affair appeared to widen the following of ultraconservatives among the Prussian gentry. While some deplored Perrot's attack on personalities, the long list of *Deklaranten* showed that the gentry shared the *Kreuzzeitung's* hostility toward the government's economic policies and its favoritism toward the interests of industrial capitalism. Nevertheless, the ultimate effect of the affair was to accelerate a movement for conservative renewal already under way. In the winter elections of 1873–1874 all conservative factions, ultras as well as moderates, had suffered disaster at the polls. Obviously the cost of the quarrel with Bismarck and of divisiveness within the conservative movement was considerable. But it was also apparent that the Prussian, particularistic, reactionary image that the conservatives projected limited their effectiveness with the voters. To prosper under universal male suffrage, it seemed, the conservatives had to enlarge their geographical and social radius by becoming a national party representing national interests. Even ultras were now willing to yield to tactical necessity. In 1876 the approach of new elections made action imperative.

[58] GW, XV, 346–353.

Months of correspondence and two preliminary caucuses by prominent conservatives in Berlin and Frankfurt am Main led in July to establishment of the "German Conservative party" and publication of an election manifesto, which served as a program until 1892. Issued by Otto von Helldorff-Bedra, a leader of the "Stahl faction" in the Prussian House of Lords, the manifesto was signed by twenty-seven prominent conservatives—thirteen from Prussia, five from Bavaria, and three each from Saxony, Baden, and Hesse. The new program and party have often been credited by historians with having converted the conservative movement: from a Prussian-particularistic to a German national basis; from an ideological to an agrarian basis; and from an oppositional to a progovernment party.[59] Actually the achievement of 1876 was not so spectacular. What the new party and program represented was not the sudden conversion of the conservative movement, but the final and decisive stage in its reorganization under a program fashioned by moderates at the cost of ultras. What had begun with the founding of the Free Conservative party in 1867 and continued with the founding in 1872 of the Monarchical-National party of the Reichstag and the New Conservative party of the Prussian Chamber of Deputies reached fruition in the German Conservative party of 1876. That the German conservatives became a pro-Bismarck party was owed as much to his turn to the right as their turn to the left.

In the first paragraph of the manifesto Helldorff and associates declared their intent to work "in a national sense" to strengthen German unity on the basis of the imperial constitution. Yet this was not a new posture for moderate conservatives. In their program of 1872 Reichstag conservatives had used the title "national" and stressed their desire to work "hand in hand" with the government in promoting "German interests." Even the New Conservative party of the Prussian Chamber of Deputies stressed that its "basic view" was national, as well as monarchical and conservative, and pledged "to support with complete dedication the policy through which Germany has attained unity, power, and freedom." Yet the Prussianism of the conservatives was by no means dead. It lived on under the guise of federalism. In 1876, as in 1872–1873, the conservatives stressed their opposition to the unitary state and their desire to preserve "the justified independence and character of the individual states, provinces, and peoples [Stämme]."[60]

The attempt of the German Conservative party to widen its geographical representation was largely a failure. Like its predecessors, the party continued to be identified with Prussia and the Prussian establishment until its demise

---

[59] See Hans Booms, Die deutschkonservative Partei (Düsseldorf, 1954), pp. 9–10, and Robert Berdahl, "Conservative Politics and Aristocratic Landholders in Bismarckian Germany," Journal of Modern History, 44 (1972), pp. 1–3.

[60] Felix Salomon, Die deutschen Parteiprogramme (Leipzig, 1907), II, 1–7. The election program of the "new conservative party" in the Chamber of Deputies is misdated in this source (1873, not 1872).

in 1918. Although the program of 1876 denounced the Kulturkampf as a "misfortune for Reich and people," the party never succeeded in enticing Catholic conservatives away from the Center party. Hanoverian Guelphs, though conservative in social and political outlook, voted either for centrists or for deputies who joined the "Hanoverian-German" caucus in parliament. Free conservatives maintained their separate party and retained the support of their constituents in Silesia. In southern and western Germany conservatives who did not vote for centrists supported the right wing of the National Liberal party. Outside Prussia the German Conservative party gained the loyalty of only small groups of voters in Saxony and Mecklenburg. It remained essentially an east-Elbian, Lutheran, and rural party. While adopting publicly a more positive attitude toward the Reich, its voters and deputies remained essentially Prussian in outlook and loyalty. From one-half to two-thirds of the party's Reichstag delegation were noblemen. Heavily represented in its ranks were big landowners, former army officers, and Prussian officials.[61]

It is also inaccurate to attribute to the new party and program of 1876 the sudden transformation of conservatism from an ideological to an agrarian program. Before and after 1876 the party never ceased to place "decisive weight on the monarchical foundations of our state and a strong authoritarian power." While confessing the need to do justice to the "needs of the present," the manifesto of 1876 stated that new legislation must be based on "real and historically established foundations," thereby "securing the continuity of our entire political, social, and spiritual development." The document called for "civil liberties for all" and for "an effective participation by the nation in legislation," yet avoided an endorsement of universal male suffrage in national elections and advocated "self-administration in province, county, and community based not on universal male suffrage but on the natural groups and organic divisions of the people." It recognized the right of the state to regulate church-state relationships but defended the internal autonomy of both Catholic and Protestant churches. The "confessional Christian grammar school" was termed "the most important barrier" to social chaos.[62] The ideology of "throne and altar" and the organic view of society remained alive in the thought and politics of Prussian conservatism. Still, the program represented a shift away from the patently worn-out feudal corporatism of ultras like Ludwig Gerlach and Count Lippe.

Agrarianism was hardly new in conservative politics. Since its inception the Prussian Conservative party had never failed to defend agrarian interests wherever they came into conflict with capitalism and industrialism. Yet it is true that the concern of conservative leaders over the "excesses of capitalism" and over the increasing weight of industry as against agriculture in the Ger-

---

[61] Booms, *Deutschkonservative Partei*, pp. 6–8.
[62] Salomon, *Parteiprogramme*, II, 7–9.

man economy increased in the mid-1870s. That concern was a primary impulse behind the decision to found a new party and draft a new program. "Here nothing whatever can be accomplished with a conservative program and a conservative agitation," wrote Baron von Mirbach-Sorquitten to Kleist-Retzow in early July 1876, "but only by moving forward in the sense of the agrarians."[63] Naturally landowners participated in the growing disillusionment with liberal economics and the free-enterprise system after the crash of 1873. The manifesto of 1876 called for "an ordered economic freedom" in contrast to the "unlimited freedom of liberal theory." It demanded the "step-by-step abolition of the privileges of big capital" and an end to the "severe damage" inflicted by excessive economic concentration and by the lack of "firm regulations for agriculture and small manufacturing. We demand especially the revision of the industrial code and of the poor law [Unterstützungs-wohnsitz] in accord with experience." Unrestrained individualism could not lead to "sound economic development"; the honest man had to be protected against speculators.[64]

For Hermann Wagener the manifesto of 1876 was a disappointment. During the early 1870s he had worked with Rudolph Meyer, editor of the conservative Berliner Revue, and Johann Karl von Rodbertus, a Pomeranian landowner and publicist, in agitating for a "social conservative" party capable of forging an alliance between agrarians and proletarians. In 1872 Wagener had a hand in the drafting of the program of the Reichstag's Monarchical-National party, to which the new conservatives adhered in 1873.[65] His influence can be seen in the program's focus on the interests of proletarians rather than artisans, its assertion that for a healthy development the German Reich must meet the needs and justified demands of the masses, and its insistence that the social question could only be solved by "the strong arm" of an authoritarian government. The state must foster institutions and corporative bodies "suitable for securing and furthering the material and spiritual position of the workers' estate" and create agencies for the arbitration of conflicts between employers and employees.[66] Yet Wagener did not succeed in introducing the word "social" into the party title. His disgrace in 1873 left him in no position to influence the manifesto in 1876, which contained only faint echoes of these clauses. While the German Conservative party largely abandoned the traditional quixotic interest of the conservatives in protecting artisans and reconstructing guilds, it made no serious attempt to expand its political influence by taking up the cause of factory workers. Wagener and other conservative social thinkers persisted, moreover, in thinking of proletarians as an es-

---

[63] Petersdorff, Kleist-Retzow, p. 464.

[64] Salomon, Parteiprogramme, II, 8–9.

[65] Walter Vogel, Bismarcks Arbeiterversicherung: Ihre Entstehung im Kräftespiel der Zeit (Braunschweig, 1951), pp. 87–92.

[66] Salomon, Parteiprogramme, II, 1–11.

tate (*Stand*) rather than a class and in seeking a solution to their problems in terms of an updated corporatism.

Naturally Bismarck was deeply interested in attempts to unite and reconstitute the conservative movement. From a letter of Blanckenburg to Kleist-Retzow of August 1872 we know that he "edited sentence by sentence" the program of 1872 and "discussed it in detail with Wagener."[67] Yet he had no part in drafting the program of 1876. That prominent ultras like Kleist-Retzow stayed out of sight during the preliminary discussions[68] led him to hope that a united, progovernment party was in prospect. But he was thoroughly disillusioned when the full membership list was published in mid-July. It included Nathusius Ludom and so many *Deklaranten* that the new party appeared to be merely the "old feudal party of the *Kreuzzeitung*" in disguise.[69] On July 18, 1876, Bismarck warned his brother Bernhard against letting the New Conservative party, of which the latter was chairman, be absorbed by the German conservatives. It was not to be expected, he wrote, that the *Deklaranten* had changed their views. If the party was to be dominated by *Kreuzzeitung* conservatives, then the government, as in 1872, would be forced to move more to the left in order to gain support against the right. Barring some "compelling need," Bernhard should not join and should advise associates against sailing "under the flag of Nathusius Ludom and his political friends."[70]

For many months Bismarck held the German Conservative party at arm's length. In late July 1876 the official *Provinzial-Korrespondenz* announced that the government had nothing in common with the new party, and national liberal deputy Georg Jung, who visited the chancellor at Bad Kissingen, reported him as saying that he would not be able to go along with the German conservatives, because they were headed by men whose views on the Kulturkampf would cost him the services of Falk.[71] In early August the *Norddeutsche Allgemeine Zeitung* and other journals reputed to be "semiofficial" mounted a lively campaign in support of the new party, but perhaps not at Bismarck's instigation. Since the war-in-sight crisis of 1875 he had loosened his contacts with the *Norddeutsche Allgemeine* and reduced somewhat his attempts to influence the press—or so he said.[72] In the November elections the new conservatives ran as a separate party, seemingly in accord with Bismarck's advice to Bernhard. The continuing tension between the chancellor and German Con-

---

[67] Petersdorff, *Kleist-Retzow*, p. 461.

[68] *Ibid.*, pp. 463–464.

[69] SEG (1876), pp. 165, 167; Ludolf Parisius, *Deutschlands politische Parteien und das Ministerium Bismarck* (Berlin, 1878), p. 218. Although Kleist-Retzow readily signed, some ultras whom he approached refused to do so, including Count Lippe, to whom a "German" conservative party made no sense. Petersdorff, *Kleist-Retzow*, p. 464.

[70] Hans Rothfels, ed., *Bismarck-Briefe* (Göttingen, 1955), pp. 391–392.

[71] SEG (1876), p. 167; BP, I, 101.

[72] SEG (1876), p. 171; BP, I, 92–93, 100; Tiedemann, *Sechs Jahre*, p. 35; BR, VI, 336–352; Moritz Busch, *Tagebuchblätter* (Leipzig, 1899), II, 423.

servative party was evident in February 1877, when he reacted strongly to an interpellation by its caucus in the House of Lords concerning the Guelph fund. Bismarck consulted with his colleagues in the cabinet on how to reply as roughly as possible, yet without inflicting injuries. Two days later the prince was still bent on having it out with the German conservatives. "The incivilities that he had thought out burdened his stomach; he had to get rid of them." But finally he handed the task over to Tiedemann, much to the disappointment of centrists and national liberals, who crowded the galleries in the hope of witnessing more friction between the government and the conservatives.[73]

In September 1877 Bismarck was still inclined to demand the expulsion of the *Deklaranten* as the price of a closer relationship between himself and the German conservatives.[74] By that time, however, his need of the party's support outweighed, while it did not expunge, the hatred he felt toward those whom he believed had betrayed him and stabbed him in the back. Bismarck and the German conservatives came to terms with one another during 1876–1877 not out of love but mutual need. Their collaboration during the next decade was dictated by the coincidence of mutual interests: a new parliamentary majority; a strengthened imperial government; a reduction in the power of parliament; and a new economic policy favorable to agriculture. Even so it was not until 1879–1881 that the *Deklaranten* became reconciled to the chancellor, establishing an uneasy truce that collapsed at the end of the decade.[75]

Parting of the Progressives and National Liberals

Despite the divorce of 1867 the progressives and national liberals continued to think of themselves as but two caucuses of a common liberal party based on the same general *Weltanschauung*. While the two caucuses had often differed on crucial issues such as the iron budget and civil rights, they never ceased to collaborate in other significant areas of legislation such as the unifying statutes, economic legislation, and the Kulturkampf. On the local level the common liberal party continued to exist in the committees and associations that picked liberal candidates for parliament. Only in larger cities did

[73] Tiedemann, *Sechs Jahre*, pp. 116–118. No evidence substantiates the view of Hans Booms that Bismarck "obviously" cooperated in the founding of the German Conservative party. Booms, *Deutschkonservative Partei*, pp. 15–19.

[74] Petersdorff, *Kleist-Retzow*, p. 466.

[75] See the exchange of correspondence in Hans Leuss, *Wilhelm von Hammerstein* (Berlin, 1905), pp. 25–34. Symbolic of the ending of an era for the conservatives was the death in mid-February 1877 of Ludwig von Gerlach. The most bitter, irreconcilable foe of Bismarck's unification of Germany and collaboration with liberals was run over by a wagon of the imperial postal service as he crossed the Potsdamerplatz in Berlin. Lucius, *Bismarck-Erinnerungen*, p. 102.

progressives and national liberals nominate rival candidates at election time.[76]

During 1876 liberals began to detect attempts by the Bismarck government, particularly by Eulenburg, to dissolve the relationship. The conservative press, *Provinzial-Korrespondenz*, and the *Norddeutsche Allgemeine Zeitung*, which continued to be regarded as "semiofficial" despite Bismarck's disclaimers, openly agitated for the demolition of the liberal majority in Reichstag and Landtag in the coming elections. In June one of Eulenburg's subordinates, *Landrat* Hermann von Knobloch, dispatched a circular urging fellow *Landräte* to work for the election of a "Bismarck party" composed of conservatives and national liberals ("particularly if the candidate happens to be a landowner"). Eulenburg expressed it bluntly in a speech to the Chamber of Deputies: "We fight the Progressive party and, if it were possible to repress that party and put the National Liberal party on its own feet, then we would be satisfied."[77]

In June 1876, nevertheless, the two caucuses held together in forcing the defeat of Eulenburg's urban government bill in the reactionary form given it by the House of Lords. In August the *Nationalzeitung* declared that the National Liberal party, for which it generally spoke, would never enter a "conservative-liberal governmental majority" as long as ministers were chosen without regard to the views of the parliamentary majority and as long as the nation's leading statesman raised the threat of reaction whenever the majority insisted on liberal principles inconsonant with what he was willing to permit for his own purposes.[78] As the election campaign got under way in September, Eugen Richter asserted that the government's attempt to split the National Liberal party and destroy the progressives had only brought the two caucuses closer together. Bismarck's purpose, he recognized, was to strengthen the conservatives and weaken the liberals, producing a parliamentary balance subject to the chancellor's control. Again there was talk of reuniting the two caucuses in order to produce a "firm liberal party capable of governing," but Richter concluded that it was better to march in two columns.[79]

Although the liberal parties preserved their traditional united front during the Prussian election campaign ending on October 27, 1876, each lost 5 seats, the progressives shrinking from 68 to 63 seats, the national liberals from 174 to 169. The conservatives gained eleven seats (from 30 to 41), while the free conservatives remained constant at 35 seats. Prussian voters appeared relatively constant in their loyalties, despite mounting pressures from the government, conservatives, and economic interest groups.[80] The first of the blows

[76] See pp. 159–161.

[77] SEG (1876), pp. 154, 157.

[78] SEG (1876), pp. 171–172.

[79] SEG (1876), p. 183; HW, II, 152.

[80] Bernhard Vogel, Dieter Nohlen, and Rainer-Olaf Schultze, *Wahlen in Deutschland: Theorie-Geschichte-Dokumente, 1848–1970* (Berlin, 1971), p. 287.

that was to cleave apart the liberal movement came neither from the voters nor from the government, but from within the ranks of the Reichstag liberals. As the economic depression dragged on and the degree of their vulnerability on economic policy widened, the progressives and national liberals parted company once more over the issue that had plagued the liberal movement practically from its inception—that of freedom versus unity.

When the Reichstag met in early November 1876, an ugly dispute erupted between the two liberal parties over the election of the chamber's presiding officers.[81] Yet this was but a prelude to the conflict that arose in mid-December over amendments to statutes establishing a common judiciary and imperial codes of civil and criminal procedure. Bismarck had long believed that unity in law and justice would contribute greatly to the consolidation of the Reich,[82] a conviction shared by most liberals. Since 1869 Lasker and Miquel, to whom a common system of law and justice were a precondition for the durability of the Reich and second only to common language as a builder of national sentiment, had repeatedly sponsored Reichstag bills extending the legislative competence of the Reich to include civil and criminal justice.[83] In 1873 they finally succeeded when a constitutional amendment was passed over the opposition of centrists and particularists in the Reichstag and of Saxony, Württemberg, and Bavaria in the Bundesrat. Although the civil code was not achieved until 1897, the statutes on judicial organization and the codes of civil and criminal procedure reached the floor of the Reichstag in November 1876. For two years these drafts had already been subjected to intense and often heated debate within the government, Bundesrat, and a special committee on the judiciary (Reichsjustizkommission) created by the Reichstag.[84]

Many points at issue were purely technical in nature, but some were loaded with political significance. In the committee and in the Reichstag the progressives and national liberals stood firmly together for amendments that: (1)

---

[81] Forckenbeck and Stauffenberg (both national liberals) were reelected first and second presidents (speakers) of the Reichstag. But the national liberal caucus refused to support the reelection of Hänel (progressive) as third president, voting instead for Wilhelm Löwe, defector from the progressives. Löwe refused to serve, and the national liberals finally accepted Hänel. The incident left resentments among the progressives, the political consequences of which were soon evident on other issues. SEG (1876), p. 94; Dill, Lasker pp. 151ff.

[82] BR, VI, 475–476, also IV, 151, 301; GW, VIb, 184; VIII, 76; Hans Goldschmidt, Das Reich und Preussen im Kampf um die Führung von Bismarck bis 1918 (Berlin, 1931), pp. 169–170, 177–179, 181–183.

[83] SBR (1869), III, 175; (1871), II, 71; (1872), III, 260; (1873), III, 138.

[84] For the background of the legal and judicial statutes that became law in 1877 see Ernst Rudolf Huber, Deutsche Verfassungsgeschichte (Stuttgart, 1963), III, 974–979. Bavaria exacted a price for yielding—exemption of Bavarian courts from the jurisdiction of the Reich Supreme Court. The medium and small states got their revenge on Feb. 28, 1877, when they majoritized Prussia—and Bismarck—for the first time by voting 30 to 28, to locate the Supreme Court in Leipzig instead of Berlin.

specified jury trials in cases dealing with the press; (2) abolished the requirement that journalists and publishers reveal their sources of information; (3)
severely limited the right of the government to open mail; (4) provided that
officials who violated the law and the rights of citizens be tried in ordinary
rather than administrative courts; and (5) gave to the Reich Supreme Court
the power of decision in jurisdictional disputes between administrative and
regular courts.[85] In view of his difficulties with the Catholic, conservative,
and muckraking press, Bismarck was sensitive on the first two points. But the
last three threatened prerogatives of the Prussian police state that had permitted authoritarian rule by the Manteuffel government in the 1850s and by
the Bismarck government during 1862–1866. The government's draft, on the
other hand, threatened to take away liberties already enjoyed in southern
states. In July 1875 Bismarck instructed Delbrück to make absolutely sure that
no concessions or commitments were made by any representative of the government in the deliberations of the special committee on the judiciary. At
the end of November 1876 he returned from Varzin to Berlin prepared to
accept failure of the judicial reform "for the time being" rather than yield
what the liberals demanded.[86]

Nothing in the prior history of the National Liberal party, however, justified the assumption that it would, in the name of principle, sacrifice statutes
it regarded as vital for the completion of German unity. Before leaving Varzin
Bismarck received from Tiedemann an accurate appraisal of the situation.
The liberal majority, Tiedemann predicted, would stand fast during the second reading of the bills. Not even the right wing of the national liberals would
have the courage to capitulate too easily on such an issue immediately before
the Reichstag election due on January 10, 1877. But on the third reading
these men, "just as careful as they are brave," would reverse themselves if the
government stood firm. Their tactic was obvious. They wanted to be able to
tell the voters, "We fought like lions to the last second for liberal principles;
only when we saw that, owing to the stubbornness of the government, the
entire reorganization of the judiciary would fail unless we gave way, did we
sacrifice with bleeding hearts some liberal postulates. Only the coercive situation in which we found ourselves is to blame."[87]

Tiedemann's scenario was accurate. On December 2, the second reading
was completed with the important amendments still intact.[88] On December
12, Bismarck exercised for the first time in years his prerogative of presiding
over the Bundesrat, which rejected eighteen amendments, including the "political" ones. The government, Bismarck told Bennigsen, had given in on a
hundred points; now it was the Reichstag's time to yield. Three days later the

[85] SBR (1876–1877), III, Nos. 5–10.
[86] GW, VIc, 60–61; Tiedemann, Sechs Jahre, pp. 91–92, 95.
[87] Tiedemann, Sechs Jahre, pp. 93–95.
[88] SBR (1876–1877), I, 135–569.

"fathers of compromise"—Miquel, Bennigsen, and Lasker—negotiated with Bismarck and Prussian Minister of Justice Leonhardt an agreement in which the government yielded little and the Reichstag much.[89] In the third reading on December 18–21, the national liberals joined conservatives and free conservatives in passing the new version over the bitter opposition of progressives, centrists, and social democrats. August Bebel denounced the bill as a "surrender of the people's rights," while the progressive spokesman Saucken charged that the national liberals had lost their independence—they had become a government party.[90] As in 1866 and 1871, national liberals eased their consciences by arguing that half of a loaf was better than none, that the achievement of national unity in such a vital area as the judiciary was worth the sacrifice of liberties that Prussian liberals had vainly struggled for most of the century to gain.

Because of his strategic position in parliament, Lasker alone could have put together a majority to defeat the bill. Instead, he was an impassioned defender of the compromise. Since 1867 Lasker, a Prussian judge, had pushed relentlessly for the establishment of unity in law and justice. Now he praised what had been attained as a great gain "in a national sense" for liberty as well as for unity. He described himself in Bismarckian terms as a realist who in 1876, as in 1867 and 1871, was willing to accept the better, which was achievable, rather than insist on the best, which was not. In the air was a strong odor of suspicion that the liberal era was about to end and a feeling that this last major legislation must be achieved before the door was shut. Both Lasker and Miquel believed that the public as a whole was uninterested in the issues posed by the political amendments.[91] "I become more and more convinced," wrote Miquel, "that we can lose all support among the people by excessive insistence on principles."[92]

To the progressives, on the other hand, the compromise was yet another spineless capitulation on the part of politicians who lacked confidence in the voters, whose liberties they needlessly bargained away. Leading the progressive attack on the compromise were Eugen Richter and Albert Hänel. Both were of the opinion that the National Liberal party had by successive compromises "steadily lost the capacity to achieve liberal demands against the government."[93] The death of Hoverbeck in 1875 and the defection of Wilhelm Löwe in 1874 had thinned the ranks of the moderates in the Progressive

---

[89] BP, I, 120–121; Lucius, Bismarck-Erinnerungen, p. 95; Oncken, Bennigsen, II, 290–296; Dill, Lasker, pp. 130–133; Hans Herzfeld, Johannes von Miquel (Detmold, 1938), II, 300–303. For the points in disagreement and full terms of the compromise see SEG (1876), pp. 214–215, 219–220.

[90] SBR (1876–1877), II, 849–1005.

[91] SBR (1876–1877), II, 864–871; Dill, Lasker, pp. 130–133.

[92] Herzfeld, Miquel, p. 299.

[93] SEG (1876), p. 194.

party, leaving the more aggressive Hänel and Richter as its principal spokes-men. Neither was inclined to tolerate any more "betrayals" of liberalism. In the election campaign that ended on January 10, 1877, progressives and na-tional liberals ceased to cooperate for the first time since 1867. In fact, they fought each other as aggressively as they did conservatives, centrists, and so-cial democrats. National liberals campaigned on their record of practical achievement during the era of collaboration with Bismarck, but denied that they had become a "government party." Progressives, on the other hand, prided themselves on being the only liberal party that had stood by its prin-ciples. Successive compromises, they declared, had seriously injured the Reichstag's prestige and led the government to count on its weakness. For the first time the progressives unequivocally called for parliamentary govern-ment—"a Reich cabinet politically and legally responsible to the Reichstag for the course of legislation and administration."[94]

Both liberal parties suffered on January 10. The national liberals lost 27 seats (155 to 128), the progressives 14 (49 to 35), while the new German Conservative party enjoyed its first triumph by winning 18 new seats (22 to 40). Other parties made minimal gains: the center 2 seats (91 to 93), free conservatives 2 (36 to 38), the social democrats 3 (9 to 12). Together the two liberal caucuses (163 out of 397 seats) could no longer control a majority even if they had been in a mood to cooperate.[95] The Lasker wing of the National Liberal party had lost, and was never again to regain, the pivotal position it had putatively enjoyed, but which Lasker had been either unable or unwilling to exploit. Even before Bismarck inflicted his first real blow, the liberal pha-lanx had begun to dissolve.

As so often in the past, the German liberals were in an unenviable situa-tion. The necessity of working under a semiauthoritarian governmental sys-tem headed by a highly effective, autocratic statesman and staffed by a func-tioning bureaucracy compelled them to make one of two choices: either to cooperate as political realists and thereby, for the sake of gains in the area of national unity and centralization, run the risk of opportunism and loss of ide-ology; or to adhere rigidly to principle regardless of the cost and run the risk of doctrinairism and political impotence. Neither course was attractive. For progressives the only possible escape would have been the development of a large popular following capable ultimately of forcing, by sheer numbers and perennial persistence, the democratization of the system. But the election of 1877 confirmed once more that neither the social foundation nor the political conviction existed for the achievement of such a goal. Left-liberals had no prospect of conquering the liberal movement as a whole, and they lacked, despite Schulze-Delitzsch, the social comprehension and political imagina-

---

[94] SEG (1876), pp. 222–231.
[95] Vogel et al., *Wahlen in Deutschland*, p. 291.

tion that would have enabled them to enlarge their base of support and voter appeal by bringing into the liberal camp the new legions of factory workers crowding the industrial towns of Saxony, Silesia, and the Ruhr.

Progress of the Transition

By January 1877 Bismarck had made some progress in implementing the plans formed at Varzin in 1875. Delbrück had been maneuvered out of office and his replacement as chief of the chancellor's office, Karl von Hofmann, had begun to reorganize the Reich executive according to Bismarck's wishes. On January 1, 1877, two divisions of the chancellor's office became separate bureaus headed by state secretaries directly under the chancellor's authority: the Imperial Office of Justice and the Imperial Chancellery for Alsace-Lorraine. As independent agencies, these bodies were not parallel to the foreign office, the admiralty, the railway office, and the chancellor's office itself. The latter now functioned as a kind of "imperial ministry for trade and finance,"[96] since these were the only functions remaining to it. The liquidation of Delbrück's old position as de facto vice-chancellor increased the personal authority of Bismarck, to whom the heads of the various parallel Reich agencies were now directly subordinate.

Bismarck also heightened his influence within the Prussian cabinet by securing the appointment of Hofmann and Bernhard von Bülow (state secretary of the Imperial Foreign Office) as voting members without portfolio. The appointment of two non-Prussians (Hofmann was a Hessian, Bülow a Mecklenburger) as Prussian ministers was a sensational development. More importantly, as imperial officials they were directly accountable to Bismarck, a fact that must certainly influence their behavior in the cabinet. Although a Prussian minister without portfolio, Delbrück had possessed no vote in the cabinet and was, furthermore, a career official who respected the lines of authority under the Prussian system. Naturally the Prussian ministers, particularly Camphausen, objected to this turn of events.[97] That they were impotent to prevent it is a measure of their declining power (and that of the cabinet itself) vis-à-vis Bismarck. The ministers would have been even more upset had they known that the chancellor contemplated a still more drastic step. When Lucius visited Varzin in late September 1876, he found his master toying with the idea of giving the "Reich ministries" (a term he increasingly applied to the various parallel agencies of the empire) more "substance" by appointing some of their chiefs as Prussian ministers *with* portfolio; he thought the Prussian Ministry of Finance should be excepted, although its function should be limited henceforth to fiscal administration.[98]

[96] BR, VII, 47.
[97] Lucius, *Bismarck-Erinnerungen*, p. 90; Kohl, ed., *Anhang*, II, 486.
[98] Lucius, *Bismarck-Erinnerungen*, p. 91.

Personal union between the executives of the Reich and Prussia would have meant, in effect, complete subordination of the Prussian cabinet to the chancellor and destruction of the Prussian tradition of ministerial collegiality. It would have ended Prussian resistance to Bismarck's will and solved the enduring problem of coordinating the Reich and Prussian governments, but it would also have greatly increased the unitary over the federal principle in the German constitutional balance. Perhaps for this reason Bismarck did not pursue the idea at that time. Instead, he sought to reinvigorate the Bundesrat by urging non-Prussian governments to take a more active policy in imperial affairs. Rather than strike for greater direct authority, he employed his old technique of mobilizing a countervailing power to overcome what he liked to call "Prussian particularism."[99]

The drift of German domestic politics during 1876 was also in the general direction Bismarck had charted. His effort to seduce the National Liberal party and to divorce it from the Progressive party was evident in remarks made to the national liberal deputy Robert von Benda in July 1876 at Bad Kissingen. Bismarck denied the accusation that the resignation of Delbrück presaged a shift to a conservative policy. Delbrück himself, he asserted, had recommended Hofmann as his successor. The Hessian was, furthermore, the most liberal of all candidates proposed. As before, Bismarck wanted to depend, he said, upon the National Liberal party for support; rumors that he wished to divide it were false. The Center, extreme conservatives, and progressives were his enemies. His major concern was that national liberals would permit themselves to be taken in tow by the progressives. Confronted by a hostile majority under progressive leadership, he would have no choice but to seek a majority on the right that would include the Center and the agrarians, whose complaints of economic injustice had some justification.[100]

Bismarck's denial that he wished to split the National Liberal party may have been genuine at this time. In September 1876 he told Lucius that he favored "further cooperation with the national liberals, who were still the most reasonable party."[101] Their conduct in fashioning the compromise on judiciary legislation in December was further proof of their "reasonableness." During these months Bismarck even had kind remarks to make about Lasker. At tea one evening in late November he surprised his aides by not joining in the general laughter at a joke told on Lasker. "I would gladly have Lasker at my side in the cabinet," he actually said. "The problem is that he is too many-sided. *Wahl macht Qual.* I don't know whether he should be entrusted with justice, finance, interior, or commerce."[102] Obviously the prince jested, de-

---

[99] GW, XIV, 879–880.

[100] GW, VIII, 174–175.

[101] Lucius, *Bismarck-Erinnerungen*, p. 94.

[102] BP, II, 211–214. Lasker was a frequent butt of contemptuous jokes in the privacy of the prince's household. See, for example, Tiedemann, *Sechs Jahre*, p. 123. According to an oft-told

spite his serious demeanor. Yet Lasker gave him no cause for complaint that winter, and Bismarck was probably gratified to hear through Lucius that the deputy was as antagonized as were the right-wing national liberals by the attacks of the progressives during the January election campaign.[103]

After the election the official *Provinzial-Korrespondenz* predicted that the new Reichstag would be dominated by a majority composed of the three parties on the right of the chamber. The only change produced by the election, it declared, had occurred within the ranks of the progovernment parties (conservatives, free conservatives, and national liberals), not between them and the antigovernment parties (progressives, centrists, Poles, particularists, and social democrats). As before the government had a "reliable majority of forty to fifty votes for the most essential interests of the Reich."[104] When the Reichstag met, there seemed to be concrete proof of the existence of such a majority coalition. In recent years the election of the presiding officers had always been taken as proof of the continuing solidarity of the liberal front. Customarily the president and first vice-president were national liberals (Forckenbeck and Stauffenberg), the second vice-president a progressive (Hänel), but in February 1877 the national liberals cast their ballots not for Hänel but for a free conservative (Hohenlohe-Langenburg), who was elected. The Reichstag appeared to have a new majority composed of those parties that in 1874 had pushed through the compromise on the iron budget and in 1876 the compromise over the law codes.[105]

Beyond question important changes were under way within the National Liberal party during the winter of 1876–1877. The steady growth of the socialist movement from election to election revealed an unsettling degree of social alienation and protest. Limited as they were by the narrowness of their class and group interests and by their perception of what policies of social reform were possible within the boundaries of liberal ideology, the national liberals were inclined to turn to the right, to seek in the Prussian-German establishment rescue from the dangers of proletarian unrest. The major unifying laws, furthermore, were now in the statute books and so also were the Kulturkampf laws. Hence Bismarck no longer had any need of the progressives. His warning to Benda that he would, if necessary, dispense with the support of both liberal parties (another classic example of the tactic of balanced options) had to be taken seriously. If national liberals wished to remain in contact with the Bismarck government and hence in a position to influence

---

story, possibly apocryphal, Bismarck once remarked in jest to Lasker that the two might one day sit together in the Prussian cabinet. "That prospect," Lasker replied, "was cut off only a few days after my birth." Robert von Mohl, *Lebens-Erinnerungen, 1799–1875* (Stuttgart, 1902), II, 1761.

[103] Lucius, *Bismarck-Erinnerungen*, p. 100.
[104] SEG (1877), p. 53.
[105] *Ibid.*, p. 55.

its policy, even to a limited degree, they had to sever their connections with democratic liberalism. Yet they were aware that a compact with Bismarck was perilous for the weaker partner. They might be forced, once they had turned their backs on the left-liberals, to accept reactionary and protectionist measures that would deprive them of the tattered remnants of their liberalism.

Forckenbeck, a good weather vane, sought escape from the dilemma by advocating neutrality. The time had come, he told a gathering in Breslau, to stand still and hold fast to what had been attained. "Whereas at one time legislation lagged too far behind the wishes of the people, now it has perhaps gone too far ahead of them." Much had been accomplished, but now the people needed time to catch up. The national liberals, he warned, were being invited to dine with old foes. "They sit down with us at the table only to cut the tablecloth between us more easily." "Therefore," he cried, shifting his metaphors, "no follies, no excessive haste! Back to the trenches for a manly defense of what has been accomplished up to now! Everything else will follow of itself!"[106]

---

[106] Martin Philippson, *Max von Forckenbeck: Ein Lebensbild* (Leipzig, 1898), pp. 282–283.

CHAPTER TWELVE

The "Chancellor Crisis" of 1877

POLITICAL progress during 1875–1876 did not improve either Bismarck's health or state of mind. In the summer of 1876 he spent six weeks at Bad Kissingen, followed by nearly four months at Varzin. In late August he complained that his nerves were so bad he could not tolerate as many as three persons at one time; he felt guilty about being inconsiderate to his family.[1] The summers did not suffice, he wrote in September, to restore the strength expended during the winter months.[2] He returned to Berlin on November 21, but immediately wanted to flee and spend the entire winter in the country. "That is the only thing that does me any good." So great was the burden of work in Berlin that he felt "on the verge of collapse."[3] During the following months he frequently complained of ill health. Facial neuralgia returned to plague him, and again he lay awake nights thinking about "everything adverse that has happened to me for thirty years." Bitter thoughts about the *Kreuzzeitung* conservatives and the *Deklaranten* still coursed through his mind, causing Lucius to conclude that he "was more angry than sick."[4] What appears to have bothered him most that winter, however, was the fear that he might be losing his hold on the Kaiser.

Struggle for the Kaiser's Mind

One year after he assumed the imperial crown Wilhelm's health began to deteriorate, and in the summer of 1873 he suffered a paralytic stroke. His recovery was slow, and, as Bismarck later recalled, the ruler's power of concentration declined. Whether speaking or listening, the monarch frequently lost track of the discussion.[5] To clear up misunderstandings that arose from his daily reading of despatches and other state documents cost the chancellor time and effort. "It would be more useful," Bismarck told Lucius, "if the Kaiser spent his time playing patience." When the chancellor argued a point,

[1] GW, VIII, 176–177; also Christoph von Tiedemann, *Sechs Jahre Chef der Reichskanzlei unter dem Fürsten Bismarck* (2d ed., Leipzig, 1910), p. 38.

[2] GW, XIV, 878–879.

[3] GW, VIII, 186–187.

[4] Tiedemann, *Sechs Jahre*, p. 116; BP, I, 127. Freiherr Lucius von Ballhausen, *Bismarck-Erinnerungen* (Stuttgart, 1920), p. 100; BR, VII, 27.

[5] Karl Heinz Börner, *Wilhelm I., Deutscher Kaiser und König von Preussen, 1797 bis 1888: Eine Biographie* (Berlin and Cologne, 1984), p. 272; GW, XV, 428.

KAISER WILHELM I. (BILDARCHIV PREUSSISCHER KULTURBESITZ.)

Wilhelm would say, "I know I'm becoming senile, and I can't help it that I live so long."[6]

In this condition the Kaiser became more susceptible to the influence of Empress Augusta, court officials, and the aristocrats and foreign diplomats (particularly French Ambassador Viscount Gontaut-Biron) who frequented the palace. In his memoirs Bismarck relived his suspicions of these years in a fascinating chapter titled "intrigues." Empress Augusta, he wrote, had a strong liking for Frenchmen and Catholics acquired in her youth. Before the railway came, German Protestant courts relieved the boredom of small-town

[6] Lucius, *Bismarck-Erinnerungen*, p. 70; also pp. 28, 31, 91.

KAISERIN AUGUSTA. (BILDARCHIV PREUSSISCHER KULTURBESITZ.)

life by offering hospitality to English and French noblemen, some with shad-
owy antecedents; Catholic noblemen and church dignitaries were also regarded as "exotic" and "interesting." Customs had changed in the new age of
fast transportation, but Augusta still clung to the attitudes of the Weimar
court of her childhood. "A Catholic priest seemed to her more impressive
than a Protestant cleric of equal rank and importance, the friendship of a
Frenchman or Englishman more attractive than that of a fellow German, and
the applause of Catholics more satisfying than that of fellow Protestants."
Hence Gontaut-Biron had ready access to the imperial court. Perhaps on his
recommendation the empress, who preferred French-speaking servants, en-

gaged as her "reader" Auguste Gérard, whom Bismarck suspected of being a French agent.[7]

Augusta, Bismarck believed, had regarded the "new era" government as "her cabinet" and she remained unreconciled to its fall. Whatever course was steered thereafter—whether liberal or conservative, anti-Austrian or pro-Austrian—she was sure to veer in the opposite direction. In this she was strengthened by Alexander von Schleinitz, former foreign minister and now house minister to the Kaiser. For years Bismarck suspected Schleinitz of heading a "kind of kitchen cabinet" (Gegenministerium) in the royal palace that supplied the empress with political reports, based on dubious sources, with the purpose of influencing the Kaiser. Through this channel, so the chancellor believed, numerous copies of the Reichsglocke and other slandering publications reached the palace and related courts. Whenever the enfeebled Wilhelm balked at his advice, Bismarck suspected that the empress had supplied her spouse with pleas and arguments at the breakfast table. Finally the chancellor, knowing that Augusta listened from an adjacent room, complained to Wilhelm about the conduct of his wife. That same evening at a court festival he told Augusta herself that she endangered her consort's health by the advice she gave him. He could not forget, he wrote, how her back stiffened and her eyes flared. She broke off the conversation and swept away, leaving him impenitent but impressed. Never had he seen her "so beautiful."[8]

Bismarck believed that Augusta was the "crystallization point" of the opposition within the Prussian-German establishment. "All of the foes whom I had unavoidably made in the most disparate areas in the course of my political struggles and in the interest of my governmental service found in their common hatred of me a bond that was for the time being stronger than their mutual antagonism. They postponed their hostility in order to gain strength against me."[9] In December 1876 he even appealed to Gontaut-Biron for help in his "continuing struggle against persons of both sexes at court."[10] A month later Lucius found him uncharitable toward the Kaiser, even offensively so. Wilhelm, the chancellor griped, treated his ministers no better than did other monarchs. "He is as hard as stone and as cold. Gratitude is alien to him. . . . He keeps me in office only because he thinks I can still do something for him."

[7] GW, XV, 89–90, 360–362; VIII, 197–198. For Gontaut-Biron's view of these relationships see André Dreux, Dernières années de l'ambassade en Allemagne de M. de Gontaut-Biron, 1874–1877 (Paris, 1907), pp. 291–316. Confirmation of Augusta's liking for Frenchmen and Catholics is to be found in: Jules Laforgue, Berlin, la cour et la ville (Paris, 1922), pp. 39–51, and Count Paul Vasili, La société à Berlin (Paris, 1883), pp. 54–65, 73–74. Vasili was a pseudonym; authorship has been attributed to both Catherine Radziwill and Juliette Adam.

[8] GW, XV, 432–435. For the origins of Augusta's hostility toward Bismarck during the 1848 revolution, see vol. 1, pp. 57 (fn.), 175.

[9] GW, XV, 434.

[10] GW, VIII, 186.

Need of appreciation, Bismarck confessed, was his own "most vulnerable point."[11]

Bismarck's sense of isolation had reached a new level. He felt abused and betrayed by members of his own social caste and unappreciated by the man whom he had boosted to power and glory. Anger at his colleagues in the Prussian cabinet and their subordinates in the ministries also reached a new peak. On March 10, 1877, he appeared in the Reichstag for the first time that session and, after listening to an attack by Richter on the government for tardy presentation of the budget bill, astonished the deputies by joining in the assault. For officials and agencies to quarrel while preparing the budget bill, he declared, was only natural, but afterward the frictions continued and peace was not easily restored. Officials preferred to write memoranda rather than turn to the chancellor for a quick decision. Prussian ministries were particularly prone, he declared, to the bureaucratic particularism peculiar to Germans. "I can say that the Reich's tide is running backward. An ebb is approaching." He claimed that he alone among Prussian ministers supported the interests of the Reich. If no progress was made toward reform, that was not because capacities were lacking. "On the contrary, there are too many men; what I lack is agreement by the men who are there, without which nothing can be done. . . . Friction behind the scenes . . . takes up three-fourths of my time."[12]

Again anger and self-pity impaired Bismarck's political judgment. Most of the charges he enunciated in the Reichstag were couched in general terms but not all. In late 1875, he declared, he had struggled for months to persuade and finally to compel the Imperial Admiralty to reduce its budget requests for 1876; then to his astonishment the admiralty yielded without a struggle to a further cut demanded by Richter in the Reichstag. He had not expected, he mocked, to find Richter's influence within the government greater than his own.[13] The chief target of this attack was General Albrecht von Stosch, chief of the Imperial Admiralty and Prussian minister without portfolio. But Stosch was merely the point man of an entire enemy company whom the chancellor wished to annihilate. Behind the general stood, so Bismarck believed, Empress Augusta, Crown Princess Victoria, and the rest of the faction at court with whom he struggled for influence over the Kaiser.

Bismarck's relations with Stosch had become increasingly acrimonious

---

[11] Lucius, *Bismarck-Erinnerungen*, pp. 97–98.

[12] BR, VII, 18–19, 35, 55. Bismarck's outburst of Mar. 10 was aimed primarily at Camphausen with whom he had differed, in a cabinet meeting on the preceding day, on the goals and strategy of finance reform. Instead of drafting the large-scale tax reform program that Bismarck demanded, Camphausen proposed to present tax bills piecemeal for the avowed purpose of balancing Prussia's budget by reducing its annual subsidy to the Reich (*Matrikularbeitrag*). Cabinet meeting of Mar. 9, 1877. DZA Merseburg, Rep. 90a, B, III, 2b, Nr. 6, Vol. 89.

[13] BR, VII, 21; also Tiedemann, *Sechs Jahre*, p. 44.

since the latter's appointment as head of the admiralty in 1872. The general was strong willed, ambitious, and independent—qualities that Bismarck did not appreciate. Stosch's difficulties with the chancellor also arose from the ambiguity of his position. For his command functions the chief of the admiralty was responsible to the Kaiser, for his administrative functions to the chancellor. The line of distinction was not always clear, but Stosch compounded the problem by occasional carelessness where the chancellor's prerogatives were concerned. The general, on the other hand, complained of Bismarck's interference in command functions and of the demands his foreign policy made on a fleet that was starved for funds. Stosch was also an intimate friend of Crown Prince Friedrich Wilhelm, on whose staff he had served in two wars and to whom he regularly reported what was said in meetings of the Prussian cabinet. In addition, he was closely associated with Karl von Normann, secretary to Crown Princess Victoria, and with Franz von Roggenbach, political adviser to Empress Augusta.[14] In private Bismarck spoke of the general as "an intriguer and spy who does not open his mouth in cabinet meetings, but then tells everything to the crown prince and to his majesty."[15] The chancellor suspected that Stosch aspired to participate in a "Gladstone cabinet" composed of liberal officials and deputies.

If true, this would have been only natural, given the precarious state of Bismarck's health, the advanced age and declining powers of the Kaiser, and the likelihood that Friedrich Wilhelm would soon succeed to the throne. Yet Bismarck, despite his constant and rather careless talk of resignation, treated speculations of this kind as proof of disloyalty and perfidy. His memoirs are spiced with paranoiac charges of intrigue and conspiracy that, judging from contemporary evidence, accurately reflected his mood during his last two decades in power.[16] Even without proof, Bismarck seems to have presumed that men whose personal connections seemed threatening *must* be plotting against him. To them he attributed that same burning need to have "disposition over the whole" with which he himself had been consumed during the long years before his appointment as the king's first minister in 1862.

Bismarck had often attempted to force Stosch to resign. In 1876 he even tried to repeat the destruction of Arnim by charging the general with treason, but he was deterred by Heinrich von Friedberg, chief of the Imperial Office of Justice, who told him the accusation could not be substantiated.[17] Obviously Bismarck hoped that a denunciation in parliament would make the general's position untenable. Indeed it was widely assumed in the press and Reichstag

---

[14] On Stosch and his relationship to Bismarck see Frederick B. M. Hollyday, *Bismarck's Rival: A Political Biography of General and Admiral Albrecht von Stosch* (Durham, 1960), pp. 99–215.

[15] Lucius, *Bismarck-Erinnerungen*, p. 105; Tiedemann, *Sechs Jahre*, p. 130.

[16] GW, XV, 338, 373, 379.

[17] Hollyday, *Bismarck's Rival*, p. 161.

that Stosch was a "dying man."[18] Yet the Kaiser had a high opinion of the general, who, furthermore, was able to prove inaccuracies in Bismarck's charge. In messages, whose skillfulness belies Bismarck's presumptions of senility, Wilhelm pointed out that both had erred: Stosch by yielding to Richter without the chancellor's consent, Bismarck by delaying for fifteen months to bring the dereliction to the Kaiser's attention. On March 24, 1877, Wilhelm asked Stosch to remain in office, and so the general did, much to Bismarck's chagrin, until 1883.[19]

No sooner had Wilhelm rejected Stosch's resignation than he faced another—Bismarck's. This was the famous request for retirement of March 27, 1877, which Wilhelm rejected on April 7, reportedly with the marginal note: "Never!"[20] Unlike that of 1875, this request was patently insincere. Thoughts of retirement, to be sure, were never far from Bismarck's mind in these years. What a relief it would be, he mused, to exchange the ugly sights and smells of industrializing Berlin for the bucolic peace of Varzin and Friedrichsruh! How satisfying it would be to swap roles with his carping critics, to let *them* wrestle with the cares and responsibilities of office, while he sat in the Reichstag and gave vent to his hostility. Let the nation see how incompetent and dishonest the blackguards were! Then perhaps he would return in triumph fully rested and health restored, brought back by a grateful monarch grown deaf to boudoir and backstairs intrigues, supported by a massive coalition of docile deputies elected by appreciative citizens (including a sobered gentry that now comprehended he was their only salvation), and instantly obeyed by servile ministers and quaking officials who no longer had any aim other than to discern and execute the chancellor's will.[21]

The master of *Realpolitik* did not confuse daydreams with reality. Perhaps the threat of resignation could be made to accomplish the same effect. Unlike the request of 1875, that of 1877 was quickly reported in the public press where it produced consternation. "Thousands of rumors and combinations for

---

[18] Hollyday, *Bismarck's Rival*, pp. 164–167.

[19] Tiedemann, *Sechs Jahre*, pp. 135–137. Tiedemann was impressed with the clarity and skill with which the Kaiser presided over a crown council session on Dec. 3, 1876. *Ibid.*, pp. 99–108.

[20] GW, XV, 379–380, 438. The editors of Bismarck's collected works were unable to locate this document in the archives and concluded, as a consequence, that it may never have existed—perhaps too great a tribute to the thoroughness and efficiency of German archivists. GW, VIc, 79. It is difficult to accept Erich Eyck's judgment that Bismarck did not commit the request to paper because he feared it would be accepted if formally presented. Erich Eyck, *Bismarck: Leben und Werk* (Zürich, 1944–1947), III, 199. After visiting Johanna on Apr. 4, 1877, the Baroness von Spitzemberg confided to her diary, "The written request for release from office now lies before the Kaiser." Rudolf Vierhaus, ed., *Das Tagebuch der Baronin Spitzemberg* (2d edition, 1961), p. 165.

[21] This mood may be deduced from several sources: Lucius, *Bismarck-Erinnerungen*, p. 106; GW, VIII, 187; Spitzemberg, *Tagebuch*, pp. 164, 166.

replacing him quickly filled the air."²² Privately, Bismarck spoke more of an extended leave than of retirement, and on March 29 he summoned the Prussian cabinet (except for Stosch) to discuss arrangements for running the government in his absence.²³ That Wilhelm took several days to reply to the request left the public under the impression that a change in regime was imminent. Yet Lasker's surmise that the delay caused the chancellor "great concern" was probably incorrect.²⁴

Bismarck knew full well how Wilhelm would react, for he had already tried him out. On December 8, 1876, the prince had confided to the Kaiser his wish to flee Berlin and the burdens of office. Wilhelm's face grew red with anger, the prince reported to Gontaut-Biron. "Look at me," he said, "I am eighteen years older than you and still holding out." "That doesn't surprise me, your majesty," Bismarck replied. "The horse always tires faster than the rider."²⁵ In April Wilhelm's reaction was the same. "Shall I make myself ridiculous in my old age? You will be unfaithful, if you desert me." From Johanna, the Baroness Spitzemberg heard on April 14 that the Kaiser had "cried like a child and spoken of abdication."²⁶

Bismarck's request for retirement in 1877, unlike those of 1872 and 1875, stemmed more from political than physical distress. According to reports, his health in March–April 1877 was actually better than during the preceding winter.²⁷ When Moritz Busch told him on April 11 how well he looked, Bismarck would have none of it. "Yes," he said, "others think so too. People misjudge me in three respects: they consider me healthier, wealthier, and more influential than I really am—particularly more influential."²⁸ A number of political reverses in recent months had left him "obviously in bad humor." For the first time the lesser states had willfully outvoted Prussia in the Bundesrat and, ignoring Bismarck's personal wishes, located the new Imperial Supreme Court in Leipzig rather than Berlin. The Reichstag had approved the decision by a large majority, despite Friedberg's protestations in behalf of the government. To Bismarck's annoyance Lasker used the occasion to attack him for failing to attend the debate. The budget debate had also left a bitter taste in Bismarck's mouth. "Richter and Hänel scolded the government like uncouth youngsters, as one might rebuke a lazy servant." Wilhelm's refusal to

---

²² SEG (1877), p. 84.

²³ Lucius, *Bismarck-Erinnerungen*, p. 106; Tiedemann, *Sechs Jahre*, pp. 129–131.

²⁴ Lasker to Bennigsen, Apr. 7, 1877. Hermann Oncken, *Rudolf von Bennigsen* (Stuttgart, 1910), II, 303.

²⁵ GW, VIII, 187. This relation to the French ambassador had, of course, a political purpose. Paris had to be told that Bismarck was still firm in the saddle.

²⁶ GW, XV, 438; Spitzemberg, *Tagebuch*, p. 166; Lucius, *Bismarck-Erinnerungen*, p. 108.

²⁷ According to an obviously well-informed article in the *Kölnische Zeitung* on Apr. 7, 1877. SEG (1877), p. 85. This would seem to be confirmed by the absence of any recorded complaints of bad health and shattered nerves during Feb.–Apr., 1877.

²⁸ Moritz Busch, *Tagebuchblätter* (Leipzig, 1899), II, 423.

part with Stosch inflicted yet another injury,[29] which Bismarck himself compounded by a gratuitous remark to deputies at a parliamentary soirée on March 17. He would not, he declared, retract the accusation made in parliament concerning Stosch's conduct in 1875, despite the documentary evidence Stosch had produced to disprove it.[30] This statement, widely disseminated in the press, had strengthened the public assumption that Stosch was doomed. When he survived, the world could see that there were, after all, limits to Bismarck's power.

Hence Wilhelm had to be reminded once more how dependent he was upon the services of his Brandenburg vassal. That a crisis loomed in foreign affairs—Russia's attack on the Ottoman Empire—made the moment particularly opportune. Ministers, officials, deputies, palace "intriguers," foreign governments, and the public had also to be shown that Bismarck's position was unshaken and would remain so at least as long as Wilhelm lived. Bismarck's aim was to renew his grip on the governmental apparatus in preparation for a fresh assault on the interconnected problems of the Reich's financial dependence on the states, Prussian particularism, railway policy, and the fiscal power of parliament. In January 1877 Lucius recorded him as saying that only the desire to bring order in the "muddled economic situation" held him in office.[31] At the height of the "chancellor crisis" in early April the free conservative *Post* claimed to know that the prince would remain "if adequately supported in his intended reforms by his Prussian colleagues or if supported by a Reichstag majority capable of freeing the ministers from their scruples." The *Kölnische Zeitung* recalled Bismarck's recent words: "When a hunter is exhausted from tramping about in the potato fields and wants to go home, no one will stop him by telling him that partridges can be shot in the neighborhood. To inform him of a wild boar in a nearby wood is another matter. For a boar hunt he will find new strength."[32] Before joining the chase, however, he required some months off the scene. In the warmth and security of his family circle he expected to reassemble the bits and pieces of his nervous system in preparation for a fresh attack upon those who still resisted his will.

Bismarck's request of 1877 for release from office, the Kaiser's refusal to release him, and the grant of another extended leave were fully reported in the German press. Bismarck himself made sure of that. Before departing from Berlin, he summoned Busch and gave him material for a series of seven articles that were published in *Grenzboten* between April 7 and June 27. The so-called "friction articles" appealed directly to German public opinion to assist the chancellor in removing the persons and influences whose intrigues and

---

[29] Lucius, *Bismarck-Erinnerungen*, pp. 104–107.

[30] BP, I, 128–129.

[31] Lucius, *Bismarck-Erinnerungen*, p. 99.

[32] *Die Post*, Apr. 7, 1877, XII, Nr. 82, p. 1. BP, I, 122–123. For a somewhat different version of the hunting story see Tiedemann, *Sechs Jahre*, pp. 132–133.

incompetencies had brought him to the point of resignation. They outlined in some detail Bismarck's charges against mostly unnamed but easily identifiable persons in the cabinet, at court, and in parliament—particularly against the "high-born lady" who sympathized with Catholics and undermined the government's position in the Kulturkampf, the Prussian ministers committed to Manchester economics who failed to produce necessary railway and tax legislation, and specifically against the sinister influence of Schleinitz whose political activities exceeded his proper duties as chief administrator of royal properties. Unless changes occurred in persons or attitudes, one article warned, Bismarck would not return to office. His extended leave would become a permanent retirement.[33]

Another "Extended Leave"

Bismarck left Berlin on April 16, 1877, and did not officially return to duty for ten months. During his absence two old problems—those of the Reich's executive structure and the delegation of authority—again became acute. As related earlier, the power of the Imperial Chancellor's Office (*Reichskanzleramt*) had been reduced, following Delbrück's dismissal, by the conversion of a number of its departments into independent agencies. Under Hofmann's presidency the office had retained authority only over the Reich's financial and commercial affairs. This decentralization made the position of chancellor all the more important, for he was the only "responsible" official to whom all the agencies of the Reich were subordinate. If Bismarck was actually to be relieved of the routine functions of his office while on leave, someone had to be deputized to act for him. The prince proposed that Camphausen, who was vice-president of the Prussian cabinet as well as minister of finance, be empowered to substitute for him as chancellor and to countersign official documents dealing with domestic affairs. But Wilhelm doubted the constitutionality of delegating the chancellor's power of countersignature, was distrustful of Camphausen's liberalism, and reluctant to take any step that might "make difficult the prince's resumption of his duties." Instead the Kaiser appointed Hofmann to act as the chancellor's deputy (*Stellvertreter*) in domestic affairs and Bernhard von Bülow, the top official in the Imperial Foreign Office, to be his deputy in foreign affairs. Neither was granted authority to countersign documents. Their role was to take care of routine business, not to formulate policy.[34]

These arrangements did not entirely relieve Bismarck from the burdens of office during the next ten months. This is clear from the log of his activities: April 16–May 20, 1877, at Friedrichsruh (conference with the Russian am-

---

[33] Busch, *Tagebuchblätter*, II, 413–447; *Grenzboten*, Apr. 7, 19, and 26; May 6 and 14; June 9 and 27, 1877.

[34] Lucius, *Bismarck-Erinnerungen*, pp. 107–108, 120; Tiedemann, *Sechs Jahre*, pp. 134, 138.

bassador); May 20–24 at Berlin (audiences with the Kaiser and crown prince); May 25–June 30 at Bad Kissingen (conferences with Bavarian Minister von Pfretzschner, Hofmann and Privy Counselor Huber, and five Württemberg pastors); July 1 at Berlin (audience with the crown prince); July 2–3 at Schönhausen; July 4–5 at Friedrichsruh; July 6 at Berlin (conference with the British ambassador); July 7–August 20 at Varzin (conferences with Bennigsen, Privy Counselor von Radowitz); August 21–23 at Berlin (audience with Kaiser, conferences with the U.S. minister to France, the Russian ambassador, and Camphausen); August 25–September 18 at Bad Gastein (conferences with the German ambassadors to Rome and Vienna and Italy's Minister of Interior Francesco Crispi); September 18–20 at Salzburg (consultations with Count Andrássy); September 22–24 at Berlin (conferences with Prussian cabinet ministers, Bavarian Minister von Rudhardt, and Crispi); September 24–October 5 at Friedrichsruh; October 6–7 at Berlin (cabinet meeting); October 8–February 14 at Varzin (conferences with Friedenthal, Lucius, Friedberg, Lehndorff, Bennigsen).[35]

The diaries of Tiedemann and Lucius also show that during this time he continued to be occupied with governmental business. Tiedemann and Bis-

THE CHANCELLOR ON SICK LEAVE. "WHAT A LOSS FOR CARICATURISTS—IF THE SICK MAN SHOULD TEAR OUT HIS FAMED THREE HAIRS!" *BERG'S KIKERIKI*, VIENNA, APRIL 12, 1877.

IN PASSING THROUGH BERLIN. BISMARCK TO HIS PHYSICIAN: "WAIT A SECOND HERE, DOCTOR; I MUST PUT OUR INTERNAL AFFAIRS IN ORDER. I'LL BE RIGHT BACK." WILHELM SCHOLZ IN *KLADDERADATSCH*, 1877.

[35] Horst Kohl, ed., *Fürst Bismarck: Regesten zu einer wissenschaflichen Biographie des ersten Reichskanzlers* (Leipzig, 1892), II, 142–150.

marck's sons, Herbert and Bill, were busy with dictations and drafts even at Kissingen and Gastein. In the fall, they were assisted at Varzin by Friedrich von Holstein, privy counselor for foreign affairs. The developing war in the Balkans, difficulties over Nicaragua, and commercial negotiations with Austria claimed Bismarck's attention. But there were also issues in internal affairs that he could not or would not escape. Much of his time and energy was spent in calculating the next steps toward fulfillment of the plan he had drafted in 1875. When winter came he set about the execution of his decisions while still at Varzin. Here the volume of business must have approximated what he would have encountered had he been in Berlin.

The public saw little of Bismarck on his travels. To be sure, his presence in large towns and summer resorts generated excitement and curiosity. In avoiding the crowds he detested, Bismarck found useful the private railway car presented to him by several railway companies. At Bad Kissingen he occupied an apartment in the *Obere Saline* at some distance from the bath house and hotels. In the morning he walked down the long winding path to the *Kurhaus*, a route heavily guarded by police. Later in the day, hundreds of vacationers gathered "in rows like a regiment of soldiers" at the *Kurhaus* entrance, where a carriage lent by King Ludwig waited. But their hopes of seeing the chancellor were dashed when the driver, acting on a signal, drove off smartly to another entrance to pick up his passenger.[36]

Bad Kissingen lies in a wide valley surrounded by cultivated fields and forested hills. Its waters, heavily impregnated with salt and iron, were considered healthy for both internal and external use, including a variety of ailments. Bad Gastein, on the other hand, is situated in the Austrian Alps on a steep northern slope 3,500 feet above the sea. The baths, which are fed by hot mineral springs bubbling from caverns beneath towering granite cliffs, were recommended for nervous afflictions, general disability, skin diseases, gout, and rheumatism.[37] Bismarck disliked mountains and abhorred Gastein with its thundering waterfalls. But Gastein was Wilhelm's favorite spa and in the past the Kaiser's presence there had dictated Bismarck's. In the autumn of 1877 the prince's doctors recommended Gastein for medical reasons. He dreaded the trip and sought to evade it by one excuse or another. (At one point he even insisted that the journey would tire his old dog Sultan, who could not be left behind!) But family and physicians prevailed.[38]

The diary and letters of Tiedemann contain a delightful record of this cure and vacation in the Alps. Among his vignettes are descriptions of a day-long excursion with the Bismarck family by wagon, horse, and foot up a misty vale to the Nassfelde atop the Tauern range, from which could be seen the snow-

---

[36] Tiedemann, *Sechs Jahre*, p. 154.
[37] *Encyclopedia Britannica* (1911 edition), vol. 15, p. 837; vol. 11, p. 504.
[38] Tiedemann, *Sechs Jahre*, p. 194.

covered peaks and glaciers of the Alpine massif; of afternoon *Spaziergänge* along the slopes of the Gastein valley during which the prince showed him points of interest, such as the bench where he had briefed Wilhelm on the Gastein Convention of 1865; of Bismarck's gracious reception of Count Beust, the old foe whom he had so thoroughly defeated; of the evening meals alone with the Bismarcks and Princess Odescalchi, a lively Hungarian brunette with "piquant face," who firmly believed in table-rapping poltergeists; of the seance during which a "long dead diplomat" rapped out "the most unbelievable political secrets," which the chancellor, struggling to hide his mirth, duly recorded. To witness Bismarck under these relaxed circumstances, secure and serene in the bosom of his family, was a revelation to Tiedemann, by no means an uncritical observer. "Our descendants will not doubt in the least that he was one of the greatest men whom the old and new worlds have produced. But only a few will be able to testify that he was also the most charming, because his proud and distant manner allowed few to see him as he actually was. That I belong to those few will remain the pride of my life."[39]

Bismarck's extended leave of 1877 was not an unqualified success. According to Tiedemann, he returned from Friedrichsruh on May 20 looking "fresh and well, very tanned." After Bad Kissingen he looked "excellent" and "very well, but thinner."[40] In July he caught a cold that delayed the departure for Gastein. But germs were not his only problem. As he grappled with issues that would face him on his return to duty, he was again besieged by anger and nervous disorders. On August 11, 1877, he wrote to Wilhelm that he felt weaker now than before the cure in Kissingen. The least work affected his nerves so adversely that he could not sleep. Domestic rather than foreign affairs were the cause. In his absence the ministers at Berlin were drafting ill-considered legislation. Hofmann, Eulenburg, Camphausen, and Achenbach were the targets of his wrath. Only Friedenthal had his confidence.[41]

At Gastein the pendulum swung toward health again, and Bismarck returned to Varzin at the end of September "relatively eager to work and reorganize."[42] Tiedemann had never seen him in a better mood. "Obviously he felt unusually well and comfortable when alone with Herbert, Holstein, and me; he let himself go completely and was from morning to night in good humor, accessible to every joke. Much work was accomplished. But we found time to ride many hours every day, and after the noonday meal engaged in the most interesting and pleasant chats." The atmosphere was so exceptional that both Holstein and Tiedemann doubted it could last. They were right.

On the evening of October 25, the two privy counselors heard a commo-

---

[39] Ibid., pp. 199–206.

[40] Ibid., pp. 147, 180; Lucius, *Bismarck-Erinnerungen*, p. 111.

[41] Horst Kohl, ed., *Anhang zu den Gedanken und Erinnerungen von Otto Fürst von Bismarck* (Stuttgart, 1901), I, 272–276.

[42] Lucius, *Bismarck-Erinnerungen*, p. 114.

tion below and raced downstairs. They found the chancellor sitting on the floor with Sultan's head in his lap. The dog had disappeared for several hours, and, on his return, Bismarck had punished him so severely that internal injuries resulted. Overcome with remorse, Bismarck whispered tenderly to the dying animal, seeking to hide his tears from the onlookers. When Sultan stopped breathing, Bismarck stood up and retired alone to his bedroom. Next day, after a sleepless night, he rode off in streaming rain, silent and morose, to retrace the paths where he had last been with the dog. Under way he confessed to Tiedemann, "It is sinful to lose one's heart as I have to an animal. Nothing in the world was dearer to me." Holstein summed it up: "The prince has lost a friend and feels isolated." For days the chancellor mourned for Sultan and bitterly reproached himself for having whipped the mastiff so hard. "He accuses himself of having a violent temper, of being brutal, and of giving pain to everyone who comes in contact with him. Then, he again reproaches himself for mourning so long and deeply the death of an animal."[43]

One misfortune followed another. Not long after Sultan was buried, one of the prince's estate managers killed himself when exposed for embezzling over 30,000 marks. Bismarck's daughter Marie caught a severe cold, and Johanna, while nursing her, stumbled in the darkened room and sustained a bad cut under the eye. During November a stream of visitors, not all of them welcome, invaded the prince's privacy and left him unhappy.[44] Friedenthal, whom Bismarck had praised so highly to the Kaiser in August, came to discuss a reorganization of the government and angered the prince by seeking greater power for himself. Again Bismarck, "discouraged and out of sorts," talked of "resigning" and was supported in this mood by his wife, daughter, and doctors.[45] Tiedemann gained the impression that Germany was on the brink of the greatest crisis of the decade in domestic affairs. The air was full of incendiary material. On December 10, he wrote that the prince had decided to remain in office, but only if his wishes were met regarding changes in personnel and organization of the government; if denied, he would "abdicate." This time he would not take partial payment; if either the Reichstag or "another

[43] Tiedemann, *Sechs Jahre*, pp. 210–213. A postmortem examination by a veterinarian showed that Sultan had "probably received a heavy blow or kick or punch because an artery ruptured and the whole stomach cavity filled with blood." Marie von Bismarck to Heinrich von Kusserow, Oct. 26, 1877. Heinrich von Poschinger, "Aus den Denkwürdigkeiten von Heinrich von Kusserow," *Deutsche Revue*, 33 (1908), p. 190. Dogs, however, are replaceable, and within a few days Count Holnstein, the Bavarian court official who had supplied Sultan, sent Tyras, a worthy substitute.

[44] Ernst Westphal, *Bismarck als Gutsherr: Erinnerungen seines Varziner Oberförsters* (Leipzig, 1922), pp. 96–100; Tiedemann, *Sechs Jahre*, pp. 216–220. The embezzlement came at a time when Bismarck was very discouraged about the financial return on his investments at Varzin. That fall he resolved to spend future summers at Friedrichsruh, which had a better climate, greater profitability, and readier accessibility. Busch, *Tagebuchblätter*, II, 479–480.

[45] Lucius, *Bismarck-Erinnerungen*, pp. 114–115.

still more important place" rejected his proposals, they would have to go on without him.[46]

The changes upon which Bismarck insisted were intended to execute the general purposes he had formulated during his leave of 1875. They were many and complex and appear in no one source but can be deduced from his actions, letters, official documents, and recorded remarks. His basic aim was to get a firmer grip on the levers of power in order to force the bureaucratic and political machine onto a track that he believed would consolidate the Reich. Where the executive was concerned, he hoped simultaneously to reduce his own involvement in routine affairs and to increase his personal authority over the Prussian cabinet. By lowering the visibility of the imperial executive through decentralization and by bringing Prussian ministers into imperial affairs, he hoped to gain both the cooperation and subordination of the latter. Previously Prussian bureaucratic self-interest had dictated resistance and obstructionism; under the new system he expected it to dictate participation and cooperation in imperial affairs. As imperial state secretaries the Prussian ministers would come under Bismarck's direct control and no longer be in a position to evade his authority. Obstructing ministers would have two choices: either resign or yield.

The issues that could compel the ministers to make these choices were chiefly those intended to establish a firm fiscal foundation for the Reich—by continuing nationalization of the German railway system and securing new indirect taxes for the Reich, including an increased levy on tobacco sales that would lead ultimately to a state monopoly. More income for the Reich would mean reduction of the annual assessments levied on the states. Abolition of those assessments would deprive the Reichstag of a financial and political weapon. Bismarck hoped, furthermore, to achieve these ends with the cooperation of national liberals (at least its right wing), for whom he now actually conceived a role within the Prussian and imperial executives. By finding a place for Rudolf von Bennigsen in the government he aimed to bind the moderate majority of that party to the government. Hopefully the result would be a durable coalition between new conservatives, free conservatives, and national liberals that would give his government a firmer base of political support in the Reichstag and Prussian Chamber of Deputies. If all of this could have been accomplished, Bismarck's influence would have been secure in every arena except one—the imperial court. That, Bismarck had to admit, was outside his reach.[47]

[46] Tiedemann, *Sechs Jahre*, pp. 220–222; also Lucius, *Bismarck-Erinnerungen*, p. 111; GW, VIII, pp. 205–206.

[47] Hans Goldschmidt, *Das Reich und Preussen im Kampf um die Führung von Bismarck bis 1918* (Berlin, 1931), p. 197.

Another Chancellor Crisis

Bismarck's "resignation" and "extended leave" reawakened doubts about the stability of the governmental system he had devised for Germany. It came at a time of deepening crisis in both foreign and domestic affairs. The economic difficulties that had begun with the crash continued to depress the capitalistic system throughout the world. The wait for a decisive upswing in the business cycle stretched out from year to year far beyond the expectations of employers, workers, and governments alike. In the Balkans new tensions developed between Austria and Russia over the fate of an independent Bulgaria that would soon threaten the harmony of the Three Emperors League. Bismarck's confessed incapacitation and his long absence from Berlin caused many of those concerned with public affairs to wonder whether the prince and the governmental system that depended upon him were equal to the problems the country faced. The time appeared to have come, only six to seven years after founding of the Reich, for a major change in its constitutional order.

"Naturally Bismarck's retirement is our chief interest," wrote Eugen Richter. "That will produce changes in party relationships so colossal that they cannot be predicted. The tariff protectionists, who have become especially dangerous, have the greatest cause to mourn. If he actually remains away from all business for a full year, that will be the equivalent of a complete retirement."[48] In the Reichstag budget debates of March–April 1877, liberals rebuked Hofmann for presenting a tardy budget bill and for failing to present a comprehensive plan for tax reform. They revived the dormant demand for a cabinet form of government in the Reich. Lasker, seconded by Richter and Hänel, went even further, asserting that only a parliamentary system could end this isolation and lack of coordination between government and parliament; otherwise the two institutions would continue to be "impenetrable mysteries" to each other. The Reichstag's attitude must be the government's. Only a cabinet based on a parliamentary majority could achieve this. In April Hänel decried the "modest" role given parliament in the chancellor crisis. All Europe was aroused by the news of Bismarck's resignation, but the Reichstag had to defend its right even to discuss the matter. Even Bennigsen warned that the national liberals would raise the issue of cabinet government on Bismarck's return to duty, seeking in harmony with the chancellor to fill the holes in the imperial constitution.

In reply Bismarck lectured the deputies about the evils of impatience, about the hazards of shaking the tree before the roots of the empire were firmly planted. The imperial agencies, he declared, already possessed the characteristics of ministries and the chancellor that of an "imperial prime minister." Ministerial organization as such was not objectionable, only the collegial form

---

[48] Eugen Richter to Paul Richter, Apr. 5, 1877. DZA Potsdam, Richter Collection. I thank James Tent for bringing this document to my attention.

of it. The Prussian example showed that a *Collegium*, because it proceeded by majority vote, was more inclined toward the negative than the positive. Under the Reich's federal system, moreover, imperial ministries would always "hover in the air" because they lacked the power and function of direct administration. The real power would always reside in the state ministries, particularly the Prussian, which commanded the bureaucratic structures that actually governed Germany. An imperial cabinet of Prussian type would only drive the Reich and Prussian governments apart.

He did not deny, however, that changes were advisable and proceeded, in seemingly impromptu fashion, to expound his views on what form they might take. The reduction of the Imperial Chancellor's Office should be completed by the separation from it of two more agencies, one for finance, the other for trade. Prussian ministries (he mentioned those of finance, commerce, and justice) ought to be divided, separating their administrative and legislative functions. The legislative ministries thus created should be brought into relationship to their counterpart agencies in the Reich. Apparently this was to be accomplished through "personal union," that is, appointment of the same person to head both bodies.[49]

Though Bismarck described these ideas as "dreams," his experiences while on leave only strengthened his conviction about the necessity of major changes in government organization. In the letter of August 11 to the Kaiser (previously quoted), he attributed his nervousness and sleeplessness to the necessity of fighting against legislation injurious to industry being drafted by colleagues during his absence. If he gave up the struggle in the interest of recuperation, the result would be an "incurable schism" between himself and his colleagues in domestic affairs. Even more distressing was the fact that the ministers gave him no support in preparing necessary reforms in tariffs, taxation, and railway affairs. As property owners he and Friedenthal were the only ministers who belonged both to the government and the governed and "felt the shoe where it pinched." Ministers, officials, and most legislators were "educated people" without property and uninvolved in industry and trade. Their bills were impractical and harmful. Unfortunately, the few businessmen in parliament were more active in politicking than in representing their material interests.[50]

In October 1877 the Prussian cabinet voted, six to three (Hofmann, Bülow, and Friedenthal in the minority), to locate a new regional court of appeals in the Prussian city of Celle (Hanover) rather than in the free city of Bremen, which was the chancellor's choice. For nearly two years Bismarck had argued that the government must, in implementing the new imperial statute on judicial organization (*Gerichtsverfassungsgesetz*), give precedence to

[49] SBR (1877), I, 44–90, 122–136, 417–425; BR, VII, 31–59.
[50] Kohl, ed., *Anhang*, I, 275–276.

imperial over Prussian interests. Now he viewed the final vote in the cabinet
as further proof that even reputed liberals, once they became Prussian ministers (for example, Camphausen, Falk, and Leonhardt), tended to be infected
with the virus of Prussian particularism. Through Bülow, Bismarck informed
his colleagues that he did not regard the decision as binding on himself as
chancellor and that he would seek remedy through imperial legislation that
would preserve the interests of the Reich.[51]

Bülow had become Bismarck's most trusted lieutenant even in domestic
affairs, for Hofmann was no longer in high regard. The prince complained
increasingly of the latter's "weakness," "helplessness," and "tactlessness." "A
capacity for public speaking always makes me doubtful about the judgment
and understanding of the person concerned. Most people are burdened with
a considerable mortgage of pride. Their capital worth is what remains after
subtracting that mortgage."[52] When the Hessian did exercise some initiative,
on the other hand, Bismarck accused him of exceeding his authority, of failing to consult, and of exaggerating, like Delbrück before him, the importance
of the chancellor's office in his dealings with the Bundesrat and the state
governments.[53] "Hofmann has given me more trouble in recent months than
all other ministers together," Bismarck said in early December 1877. "Prussian particularism is the worst enemy of the Reich. The most influential imperial offices must be united with the Prussian ministries. The vice-chancellor
must be Prussian vice-president. The Imperial Chancellor's Office in its present form must come to an end. What to do with Hofmann is a difficult question."[54]

By the fall of 1877 Bismarck had decided upon a new tactic in his struggle
to force the governmental machine along the charted course. In the Delbrück
era he had built up the Reich executive at the cost of Prussian and other state
governments. Now he proposed to reduce the profile of the imperial bureaucracy and increase Prussia's role in imperial affairs. Beginning in September
1877 he issued a series of directives ordering imperial officials to avoid the
expression "imperial government" in official correspondence, to cease the
long-standing practice of drafting "presidential" bills for consideration by
Bundesrat and Reichstag, and to prepare (through budgetary arrangements)
for the separation of the financial department from the Imperial Chancellor's
Office. Simultaneously he renewed his efforts to force his Prussian colleagues
to produce bills providing for new taxes and giving real regulatory power to
the Imperial Railway Office. In January 1878 he ordered the Prussian minister

---

[51] *DZA* Merseburg, Rep. 90a, B, III, 2b, Nr. 6, Vol. 89; Goldschmidt, *Reich und Preussen*, pp.
29–31, 177–179, 181–188.

[52] Lucius, *Bismarck-Erinnerungen*, pp. 112, 120; Rudolf Morsey, *Die oberste Reichsverwaltung
unter Bismarck, 1867–1890* (Münster, 1957), pp. 92–94.

[53] See pp. 307–309, 351–352.

[54] Lucius, *Bismarck-Erinnerungen*, p. 116.

Camphausen, rather than the imperial official Hofmann (much to the latter's distress), to represent him at the opening of the Reichstag.[55]

If Hofmann led Bismarck's blacklist, Camphausen came close behind. "Slay Augusta, Camphausen, Lasker, and their cliques for me," he told the Baroness Spitzemberg in April 1877, "then I can continue in office."[56] In Bismarck's view Camphausen, as Prussian minister of finance and vice-president of the cabinet, had the primary responsibility for initiating the needed tax and tariff legislation.[57] But Camphausen resented Bismarck's domineering ways and prided himself on being the only minister who was not "in flight" before the chancellor.[58] As a Manchester liberal, furthermore, he was understandably reluctant to assume responsibility for a "reform" that might include protective tariffs, a state tobacco monopoly, nationalization of railways, and reduction of the budgetary power of the Reichstag.[59] So Camphausen procrastinated. The only tax bill Bismarck received while at Varzin came from Hofmann—for an increase in the tobacco tax—and it fell far short of the chancellor's intentions. In early December Lucius got the impression that Bismarck was biding his time, waiting for Camphausen and company to "suffer the shipwreck" that would enable him to return to Berlin and form "a homogeneous cabinet and, if possible, a conservative Reichstag majority."[60]

In mid-December 1877 Bismarck began to set the stage for his return to duty by sending an ultimatum to his Prussian colleagues. He directed Bülow to inform Camphausen and Achenbach that his resumption of his tasks was dependent upon new arrangements that would secure the "energetic and *voluntary*" cooperation of Prussian ministers and officials in imperial affairs. The "more ideal attempt at an independent development of the Reich" had to be regarded as a failure. Henceforth he would seek to extend the system of personal union by appointing Prussian ministers to imperial offices. The "vice-presidency" of the Prussian cabinet must be combined with the "vice-presidency of the Reich in internal affairs." "The representation of the imperial chancellor (minus foreign affairs) must be identical at all times with the representation of the minister-president." ("Hofmann . . . is not weighty enough for that and we should seek another acceptable position for him.") In order to implement the constitutional powers of the Reich in railway affairs, the

---

[55] GW, VIc, 84–85, 88–89, 99–100; Goldschmidt, *Reich und Preussen*, pp. 188–191.

[56] GW, VIII, 199.

[57] Goldschmidt, *Reich und Preussen*, pp. 209–213.

[58] Tiedemann, *Sechs Jahre*, p. 126. "He only needs to nod or shake his head and the whole cabinet, except me, does what he wants." As vice-president of the cabinet, he (Camphausen) had to do all of the "dirty work" while Bismarck reserved the right to intervene at any moment and make the minister "superfluous."

[59] Goldschmidt, *Reich und Preussen*, pp. 217–218.

[60] Lucius, *Bismarck-Erinnerungen*, pp. 117, 120; Goldschmidt, *Reich und Preussen*, pp. 188–189.

Prussian "railway minister"[61] or his deputy had to be appointed head of the Imperial Railway Office. "In addition to tax reform and the completion of those railways on the western border required for military purposes, the fulfillment of those clauses of the imperial constitution dealing with railway affairs is one of the tasks whose execution must be the condition for my lasting return to office. If I cannot secure the adequate and *spontaneous* assistance of all competent organs of the Prussian government for the execution of what is recognized as necessary in these areas, I will, if my health permits, appear in the next session of the Reichstag, but only in order to present publicly the reasons for my definite retirement." To Bülow he denied that his purpose was to force Camphausen's resignation. He would prefer to see the desired reforms undertaken by his present colleagues. If that proved to be unattainable, then he "wanted to leave."[62]

While the idea of personal union was old, the form that Bismarck gave it at the end of 1877 was new. In 1876 he had talked of giving imperial "ministries" more "substance" by appointing imperial state secretaries as Prussian ministers with portfolio.[63] Yet this plan was never carried out, for Hofmann and Bülow were Prussian ministers without portfolio. Now the chancellor proposed to attack the problem via the opposite route. Henceforth he would seek to extend the system of personal union by appointing Prussian ministers to imperial offices. By this means he hoped to engage his Prussian colleagues in imperial affairs and "smoke out" their particularism.[64] "Prussia," he said, "is in greater need of Germanization than Germany of Prussianization."[65] The Saxon envoy at Berlin, Oswald von Nostitz-Wallwitz, recognized another aim: "By this route Bismarck will seek to attain for himself a privileged and decisive position within the Prussian cabinet of the kind that he possesses as chancellor in the empire."[66]

Bismarck also resolved to insist on two other related measures: the final dissolution of the *Reichskanzleramt* as the prelude to personal union, and a permanent system of deputization. In January 1878 he composed a long memorandum to the Kaiser in which he formally proposed the first of these steps. As administered by Delbrück, he now tactfully admitted, the *Reichskanzleramt* had proved a useful and indispensable "nursery" for the training of imperial officials. But its growth had threatened the state governments, put their ministers on the defensive, and led to their virtual withdrawal from the affairs of the Bundesrat—with the consequence that "the empire is stranded."

---

[61] The creation of a separate Prussian ministry for railway affairs was apparently under consideration. Goldschmidt, *Reich und Preussen*, p. 215.

[62] Goldschmidt, *Reich und Preussen*, pp. 191–197.

[63] Lucius, *Bismarck-Erinnerungen*, p. 91.

[64] Goldschmidt, *Reich und Preussen*, p. 198.

[65] BP, I, 127.

[66] Goldschmidt, *Reich und Preussen*, p. 215.

To refloat it, he proposed to divide the *Reichskanzleramt* into an Imperial Treasury (*Reichsschatzamt*) and an "administrative office" (*Verwaltungsamt*), from which later an "office of commerce" might be separated. An imperial executive divided into departments would appear less formidable and more accessible to the counterpart ministries in the states, spurring their cooperation. In particular, he expected a harmonious relationship to develop between the Imperial Treasury and the Prussian Ministry of Finance, without which the "basic reform of our tariff and tax system," the most pressing need of the Reich, was impossible. Roon was his model. Although insistent on protecting his prerogatives as Prussian minister of war, the general had effectively nourished the interests of the Reich.[67]

The need for a permanent system of deputization had become apparent in April 1877 when the progressives, particularly the political scientist Hänel, attacked the deputization of Hofmann and Bülow as unconstitutional. Although he did not accept their interpretation of the constitution, Bismarck came to appreciate the wisdom of clarifying the issue. He had more in mind than merely the need to provide for future leaves of absence or incapacitation. The expansion of administrative functions and the division of the *Reichskanzleramt* into separate agencies had made it impossible for one individual, particularly one who was frequently sick, to exercise actual control over day-to-day operations of the imperial bureaucracy. Under these circumstances the "responsibility" imposed on the chancellor under article 17 of the constitution had become fictional. In conjunction with the proposed final liquidation of the *Reichskanzleramt*, therefore, Bismarck proposed to establish a permanent system for delegating the chancellor's right of countersignature either to a vice-chancellor or to individual state secretaries. Such an arrangement would enable him to shift to subordinates some of the burdens of his position, without sacrificing his own final authority. But it might also appease somewhat those liberals who charged that the business of state was suffering because the Reich lacked a cabinet. When deputized, imperial state secretaries would have some of the attributes of ministers, but not the kind of independence enjoyed by members of the Prussian *Collegium*.[68]

The Bennigsen Candidacy

On April 6, 1877, at the height of the "chancellor crisis" Tiedemann recorded in his diary a startling remark by Bismarck: "In all questions that have to do with personnel the Kaiser is difficult, but, when it comes to substituting one person for another, he is almost impossible. When I proposed to him

---

[67] To the Kaiser, Jan. 22, 1878. Goldschmidt, *Reich und Preussen*, pp. 222–230. See also the draft of *Immediatbericht* of Dec. 18, 1877, composed by State Secretary Friedberg and extensively revised by Bismarck, but never sent. *Ibid.*, pp. 199–209.

[68] Goldschmidt, *Reich und Preussen*, pp. 201–203; BR, VII, 151–153.

recently that Bennigsen be made Prussian minister of interior, he looked at me as though he were talking to a drunk."[69] Once again Bismarck had conceived, in the spirit of *Realpolitik*, one of those tactical zigzags that Wilhelm's linear mind could not follow. To Wilhelm the turn to a conservative policy meant very simply the abandonment of the liberal alliance. But Bismarck was not one to assume that men could not be brought to act against their interests or, at least, to substitute a lesser for a greater interest. Had he not persuaded Austria, for example, to cooperate against Denmark for objectives that were more Prussian than Austrian? Until he had made the effort, he did not presume that liberals could not be seduced into cooperating with the government for conservative purposes.

At the end of April he confided his intentions to Lucius. He was determined, he said, to insist on certain changes before resuming his duties: "I can't carry Eulenburg any further and perhaps not Camphausen either." As a Prussian minister Bennigsen "would at least offer the guarantee that we will not lose the support of the liberal party, which we still need very much. . . . It would be good if now some rulers succeed [to German thrones] who are not overly strong and if the more important personalities would leave the Reichstag and enter the government. This will be the easiest way to accomplish the consolidation of the Reich. I will not allow the weakening of the small states and the Bundesrat."[70] By bringing Bennigsen into the government he proposed, in other words, to gain the cooperation of national liberals for a reduction in the powers of the Reichstag.

Wilhelm's negative reaction did not deter Bismarck from wooing Bennigsen. In the past he had always been able to bring the monarch around to his point of view at the crucial moment. In mid-July 1877 he invited Bennigsen to Varzin for several days during which they sounded each other out on a number of issues. In September they may have conferred again when Bismarck halted briefly in Berlin en route from Bad Gastein to Friedrichsruh. In November Friedenthal acted as go-between in the continuing discussions. On the day after Christmas Bennigsen was again at Varzin for a three-day visit, which this time was widely publicized. At the end they agreed to talk again on Bismarck's return to Berlin. We do not know exactly what was said on these occasions. But they seem to have discussed Bismarck's plans for reorganizing the government, the need for new taxes to reduce the deficit in the imperial budget, and the conditions for Bennigsen's entry into the cabinet.[71]

Apparently Bismarck offered Bennigsen the Prussian Ministry of Interior, whose incumbent, Eulenburg, was in bad health and expected to retire, and

[69] Tiedemann, *Sechs Jahre*, p. 134.

[70] Lucius, *Bismarck-Erinnerungen*, pp. 110–111.

[71] See particularly Oncken, *Bennigsen*; Goldschmidt, *Reich und Preussen*, pp. 32–50, 188–232; Morsey, *Reichsverwaltung*, pp. 91–100; Dietrich Sandberger, *Die Ministerkandidatur Bennigsens. Historische Studien*, vol. 187 (Berlin, 1929).

the vice-chancellorship of the empire, which was to be wrested from Hofmann. Bennigsen appreciated that this was a trap. As minister of interior, he would have headed a conservative bureaucracy composed of tenured officials, who would have limited his effectiveness. He preferred the Ministry of Finance which, in view of the coming budget crisis, was the most critical post in the government. But he also realized that his influence even in this post would be minimal without the support of at least one other minister from the ranks of the national liberals. Hence he proposed as minister of interior Max von Forckenbeck, president of the Reichstag, who, as a close associate of Lasker, could also guarantee the unity of the National Liberal party. After consultation with other party leaders, he added a third candidate, Baron Franz von Stauffenberg, who would have headed the projected Imperial Treasury. Bennigsen, furthermore, had no intention of helping Bismarck weaken the Reichstag. While agreeing to increases in indirect taxation that would have liquidated state assessments, he specified that the future taxes must be renewed each year. The budgetary power that parliament had unexpectedly found after 1867 in the state assessments would be perpetuated in a new guise.[72] Even so, the negotiations of 1877 marked a major change in the tax program of the National Liberal party. No longer did the party insist on direct taxes (*eine quotisierte Einkommensteuer*) for the Reich. It abandoned that issue to the progressives.[73]

Since the rebuff in March 1877 Bismarck had left Wilhelm uninformed about his negotiations with Bennigsen. By the end of December, however, rumors were rife in the German press; on December 29, the *Norddeutsche Allgemeine Zeitung* carried the story of major changes to come in the Prussian cabinet. To allay suspicion, Bismarck directed Count Lehndorff to give the Kaiser "some information" about the "soundings" he had undertaken with Bennigsen. In a letter dated December 30, Bismarck misled his sovereign by intimating that the only subject discussed had been that of taxation. As a result of the Bennigsen talks he anticipated, so he claimed, a favorable reception in the Reichstag for a general tax reform that would raise "large sums" from new indirect taxes on tobacco, beer, and the like.[74]

This letter crossed one penned by Wilhelm on the same day. In it the Kaiser took the chancellor sharply to task for not informing his master of the approaching "great upset" in the royal cabinet, about which the press seemed to know so much. Eulenburg had asked whether it was really true that his position had been offered to Bennigsen. "Must I therefore beseech you to give

---

[72] Oncken, *Bennigsen*, II, 320–321, 327–337; Lucius, *Bismarck-Erinnerungen*, p. 121; Goldschmidt, *Reich und Preussen*, pp. 28–29.

[73] Karl Zuchardt, *Die Finanzpolitik Bismarcks und die Parteien im Norddeutschen Bunde* (Leipzig, 1910), p. 79.

[74] *Norddeutsche Allgemeine Zeitung*, Dec. 29, 1877, XVI, Nr. 306; Kohl, ed., *Anhang*, I, 276–277.

me information on what is actually going on? Where Bennigsen is concerned, I would not be able to respond trustingly to his entry into the cabinet, for, talented though he is, he would not be able to follow the quiet and conservative course of my government that you yourself have told me so very decisively you intend to pursue." Opposite "follow" Bismarck wrote into the margin a single word that encapsulated his intentions with regard to the Bennigsen candidacy: "*doch*" ("to the contrary").[75]

December had been a good month for Bismarck's health. During Bennigsen's visit, however, he contracted the grippe, now complicated by anger. The Kaiser's letter, which arrived on New Year's Eve, cost him a sleepless night marked by attacks of biliousness. Struck had to be summoned from Berlin to attend him. In a letter to Hohenlohe the prince complained that the Kaiser's "lack of consideration" had irritated his nerves and delayed his recovery from "this insignificant cold."[76] Nor was his condition improved by receipt of a conciliatory letter from Wilhelm, who said that he now realized, after hearing Lehndorff's report and reading Bismarck's letter of December 30, that Bennigsen was "not a candidate."[77] For three weeks the chancellor was confined to his room and bed, subject to painful and exhausting fits of coughing and unable to sleep without opium. He lay there depressed and "pathologically sick with anger"[78] at the thought that the Kaiser could write him a critical letter, even though the deception that the letter implied was true.

After the collapse of the "Bennigsen candidacy" liberal journalists and politicians—and in their wake historians—debated at length: whether the chancellor could have been sincere or whether the contact with Bennigsen had not been from the start a conscious deception that had no other purpose than to tantalize and mislead, and whether, assuming the offer was sincere, Bennigsen made a fatal mistake in not seizing the chance to participate in the government and thereby gain the leverage with which to prolong the liberal era now drawing to a close.[79] There appears to be no good reason to assume that Bismarck's overtures were insincere. Wilhelm's opposition was not insuperable, particularly at a time when Europe was involved in a major crisis in foreign affairs. By threatening resignation Bismarck had often succeeded in overcoming the ruler's resistance on critical issues because Wilhelm could not do without him. To gain Bennigsen's consent, the prince was prepared to make concessions. He would have yielded to the deputy's desire for the Ministry of Finance, and the two men were agreed that this ministry should be

---

[75] Kohl, ed., *Anhang*, I, 277–279.

[76] Tiedemann, *Sechs Jahre*, p. 225; GW, XIV, 892; Gerhard Ebel, ed., *Botschafter Paul Graf von Hatzfeldt: Nachgelassene Papiere, 1838–1901* (Boppard am Rhein, 1976), I, 314.

[77] Kohl, ed. *Anhang*, I, 277; Oncken, *Bennigsen*, II, 338, 342.

[78] Lucius, *Bismarck-Erinnerungen*, p. 124.

[79] See particularly Oncken, *Bennigsen*, II, 334ff.; Sandberger, *Ministerkandidatur Bennigsens*, pp. 178–182.

closely linked to the projected Imperial Treasury. He probably described the deputization statute to Bennigsen as a concession to the liberal demand for responsible ministries. It is even possible, moreover, that he showed a willingness to grant yearly renewal of taxes as a substitute for the Reichstag's right to establish the amount of the state assessments.[80] What he could not concede was the inclusion of Forckenbeck and Stauffenberg and the "change of system" that the appointment of three national liberal deputies would imply. His aim was a ministerial parliament, not a parliamentary ministry.

Among some national liberals the news of the pourparlers aroused euphoric expectations. In view of Wilhelm's advanced age and Bismarck's failing health, perhaps their moment had actually come. At last Bismarck's need of *them* appeared to outweigh their need of *him*. What they had vainly striven for thirty years to achieve from outside the government might now be achieved from within. At a parliamentary dinner on January 27, 1878, Bennigsen confided to Lucius his views on the strength of the liberal position. The liberals held two trumps: "(1) The rising need for new money, which cannot be satisfied without our help; (2) the approaching end in two years of the *Septennat*. We sense how unpleasant it is for Bismarck to work with parliament as a power factor. He has only a superficial understanding of taxation and domestic questions and exaggerates his influence on the legislature in these matters. It could happen that he will be overwhelmed, if he does not come to an understanding with parliament. . . . If an understanding is now reached between parliament and government, a steady development will be assured for the next twenty years; if not, incalculable complications could ensue."[81]

How high the expectations of the national liberals soared during these weeks can be seen in the reports of Bennigsen and Bamberger to the Reichstag's national liberal caucus on February 18, 1878. According to the south German, left-liberal deputy Julius Hölder—whose diary is the only account we have of this important meeting—the two leaders described the disarray in the Prussian and imperial executive bodies as "insufferable" and a "thorough tax reform" as imperative. "For that reason a truly responsible government is necessary, one in close touch with the Reichstag's majority." Bismarck himself, they declared, was aware of this necessity and had talked about it with Bennigsen. Imperial ministries, the chancellor maintained, were unattainable because of "difficulties." As a substitute he had ordered the drafting of a "deputization statute." "Something or other is to be attained in this direction. The grant of new taxes must be kept in hand as a means of pressure not only against the Bundesrat but also (as it appeared to me, at least according to the sense of their remarks) against Bismarck and the Kaiser in order (briefly said)

[80] GW XV, 369; Kohl, ed., *Anhang*, I, 277; Tiedemann, *Sechs Jahre*, p. 225.
[81] Lucius, *Bismarck-Erinnerungen*, pp. 125–127.

RUDOLF VON BENNIGSEN IN 1872. (HERMANN
ONCKEN, *RUDOLF VON BENNINGSEN*, DEUTSCHE
VERLAGS-ANSTALT, STUTTGART AND LEIPZIG,
1910, VOL. 2, P. 240.)

BARON AUGUST VON STAUFFENBERG IN 1871.
(BILDARCHIV PREUSSISCHER KULTURBESITZ.)

to force a parliamentary administration of the Reich. In particular, the finances of the Reich and Prussia must come into one person's (Bennigsen)
hands."[82]

The Reichstag that opened in February 1878 was dominated by a majority
coalition composed of national liberals, free conservatives, and conservatives,
whose leaders (Bennigsen, Lucius, Seydewitz) established in advance a com-

---

[82] Dieter Langewiesche, ed., *Das Tagebuch Julius Hölders, 1877–1880* (Stuttgart, 1977), pp.
78–79. Judging from the seemingly careful wording of Hölder's diary entry (recorded on Feb. 20),
parliamentary government, although never explicitly stated as the goal of the negotiation, was
what the participants in the meeting had in mind. In the caucus on Feb. 20 Hölder made his
own aim explicit: "For parliamentary government, since the necessity of the matter is pushing us
in that direction." *Ibid.*, p. 81. The conviction that Germany was on the verge of converting
from a mixed to a parliamentary system of government existed in every branch of the liberal
movement during 1877–1878, from the national liberal right to the progressive left. See S. E.
Köbner, "Die Kanzlerkrise," *Deutsche Rundschau*, 14 (1878), pp. 302–318, and Ludolf Parisius,
Deutschlands politische Parteien und das Ministerium Bismarcks (Berlin, 1878), pp. xxxvi–xxxvii.
Bismarck himself was sensitive to this radicalization of liberal expectations. See his dictation of
May 29, 1878, published anonymously in the *Norddeutsche Allgemeine Zeitung* (GW, VIc, 113–
114), and his remarks during the soirée on Mar. 23 in which he described the English system as
his "ideal," but declared it practicable only under a two-party system. *BP*, I, 139.

MAX VON FORCKENBECK, ABOUT 1878. (BILDARCHIV PREUSSISCHER KULTURBESITZ.)

mon position on major issues.[83] Yet the left wing of the National Liberal party did not feel comfortable in this combination. Hence Forckenbeck, Lasker, and their associates set about the task of rebuilding their relationship to Hänel and the right wing of the Progressive party in the interest of a "partnership of liberal parties, which [Forckenbeck] held at this moment to be required in

[83] Lucius, *Bismarck-Erinnerungen*, pp. 127–218.

behalf of the continued development of freedom." Privately, Forckenbeck hoped for collapse of the Bennigsen–Bismarck negotiations, which he presumed were a trap for liberals of his conviction, as indeed they were.[84] Once in the cabinet, Bennigsen and his associates would have faced the necessity of either shedding or abiding by their convictions. The former course meant capitulation, the latter resignation. His experiences with the national liberals over more than a decade led Bismarck to gamble on their capitulation.

In his memoirs Bismarck wrote that Bennigsen's insistence on the appointments of Forckenbeck and Stauffenberg in their December 1877 talk at Varzin left him with the "impression" that the negotiation had failed and that Wilhelm's sharply negative reaction had ended any further consideration of it.[85] Yet Bill Bismarck, during a visit to Berlin on January 11, 1878, told Tiedemann: "The negotiations with Bennigsen are not at all to be regarded as having failed."[86] During January–February 1878, Bismarck followed a double course, unwilling to discard either option as long as benefit might be derived from it or, to use his own words, to throw out muddy water until he had pure. As long as the Bennigsen candidacy remained alive, Camphausen, out of anxiety over his own status, would be under pressure to supply the tax bills the chancellor demanded of him. There was always the possibility, moreover, that national liberals might drop their demands in their eagerness to "spring into the ship and help steer."[87] Even if they did not, their hopes and anticipations of power might be exploited to gain their cooperation in legislative matters.

Bennigsen left Varzin with the impression that the negotiation would resume on Bismarck's return to Berlin.[88] But Bismarck delayed his return, exploiting his relapse in health as an excuse. Through Herbert he indicated to Bennigsen that press sensationalism and Eulenburg's intrigues at court had antagonized Wilhelm and complicated his task.[89] By January 18 his "good humor" and "capacity for work" had returned; yet he clung to Varzin. In a letter to Tiedemann Lucius described the consequences: "Neither Bundesrat nor Reichstag will get its work under way until he is here, and the present state of confusion is simply unbearable." Not until February 14 did the chancellor depart for Berlin impelled, to his great irritation, by the necessity of answering an interpellation in the Reichstag concerning the Balkan crisis.[90] He would have preferred to temporize even longer.

[84] *Ibid.*, pp. 125–126; also Oncken, *Bennigsen*, II, 353.
[85] GW, XV, 369–371.
[86] Tiedemann, *Sechs Jahre*, p. 225.
[87] GW, XV, 369; Tiedemann, *Sechs Jahre*, p. 234.
[88] Oncken, *Bennigsen*, II, 334.
[89] *Ibid.*, II, 342–343.
[90] Tiedemann, *Sechs Jahre*, pp. 226–232.

The Deputization Statute

The principal fruit of the Bennigsen negotiation was the deputization statute passed in March 1878. The government's bill provided that the Kaiser, on the proposal of the chancellor, could delegate the chancellor's duties and functions to one or more officials. While the deputized official had the right of countersignature, he acted under the constitutional "responsibility" of the chancellor, who retained the right to intervene at any moment and to reassert his power of decision. In the debates on the deputization bill, progressives seized the opportunity to renew their attacks on the Bismarck system. The executive functions of the chancellor, they charged, had multiplied and diversified to the point that his "responsibility" was meaningless. Under "the most powerful statesman that Germany had ever seen" contact between government and parliament had become "only accidental, irregular, and from case to case." Only a parliamentary system, Hänel declared, could assure the harmony between executive and majority that was essential for consistent government. For the Kaiser and chancellor alone to decide who would be deputized—and when—was "a kind of dictatorship."

In reply, Bismarck maintained that the Kaiser already possessed the power to deputize and could exercise it even if the bill, which merely clarified the procedure, were not passed. Again he disputed the practicability of a cabinet system for the Reich and asserted that the new structure of the Reich executive, with its single responsible chancellor and multiple agencies, now approximated the English cabinet system. Again he teased the deputies with the thought that, if they were patient, the new system might evolve in the direction they desired. In Bundesrat and Reichstag, delegates of the state governments reinforced his arguments, opposing a ministerial system in the Reich as injurious to the federal principle. Bennigsen, seconded by Lasker, rejected Hänel's call for revolutionary changes in the governmental system. Still under the illusion that he might enter the government, Bennigsen accepted the bill as an important step in the right direction and carried his entire party with him. National liberals, conservatives, and free conservatives combined to pass the statute against centrists, progressives, and socialists.[91] Bismarck's flirtation with Bennigsen had eased the passage of a major item in the chancellor's legislative program.

Another accomplishment was the "change in personnel" at which he had aimed for months. As the Stosch affair showed, Wilhelm was not easily persuaded to dispense with the services of a minister or official to whom he had grown accustomed, and, as his sharp reaction to Bennigsen's candidacy revealed, finding a replacement acceptable to him was equally difficult. Hence Bismarck pushed for the execution of policies rather than dismissal of minis-

[91] SBR (1878), I, 321–348, 373–420, 431–441; RGB (1878), pp. 7–8. On the drafting of the bill see Goldschmidt, *Reich und Preussen*, pp. 230–232, 235–238.

ters.[92] After the ultimatum delivered through Bülow in December, he pressed Camphausen and Achenbach relentlessly to produce those bills on financial and railway affairs that he had declared to be the condition of his continuance in office. Camphausen, besieged in recent months by anxiety about the security of his position, was flattered by the thought that Bismarck's new policy of bringing Prussian ministries into imperial affairs heightened his own importance. Yet he was troubled by the realization that Bismarck's aim was a finance reform that would reduce the power of the Reichstag, an objective contrary to his liberal convictions and likely to alienate liberal allies in parliament.[93] He also realized that one of the financial measures upon which Bismarck was most insistent, a state tobacco monopoly, was for him political dynamite, since most liberals opposed it. Yet new income had to be found if the growth in imperial expenditures (up 25 percent since 1872) was not to be covered by increased state assessments. Earlier surpluses with which the Reich had balanced its budget in 1875 and 1876 were exhausted. Camphausen sought to escape from this dilemma by proposing not the tobacco monopoly, but a large increase in the tobacco tax and a new stamp tax on securities, Lombard loans, business contracts, and lottery tickets. Ironically this "middle course" was the same taken by his predecessor Heydt in 1869. And as in Heydt's case it led straight to disaster.[94]

Since Heydt's failure the "bourse tax," as the second of these levies was commonly called, had been repeatedly resurrected and rejected. It was favored by agrarians in the House of Lords as a means of equalizing the tax burden and was opposed naturally by the business community. As in 1869 left-wing national liberals, led by Lasker and Stauffenberg, insisted in the Reichstag debate on February 22, 1878, that the grant of new imperial taxes must be part of a general tax reform and include guarantees for parliament's budget power. Camphausen tried to cope with his critics by describing the difficulties that lay in the way of a tobacco monopoly. But Bismarck undercut him, saying outright that he favored the monopoly and considered the tobacco tax increase to be but a transitional stage toward it. Bismarck's disavowal of Camphausen created consternation in the chamber. It was, Lasker judged, the most dramatic and suspenseful parliamentary session he had ever attended.[95]

Camphausen should have resigned that evening, but he could not bring

[92] Bismarck to Bülow, Dec. 15, 1877. Goldschmidt, *Reich und Preussen*, pp. 196–197.

[93] Bülow to Bismarck, Dec. 26, 1877. GSA, Berlin-Dahlem, Rep. 94, Nr. 1162. Goldschmidt, *Reich und Preussen*, pp. 190–191, 209–213; Lucius, *Bismarck-Erinnerungen*, p. 120; Morsey, *Reichsverwaltung*, p. 96.

[94] Camphausen to Bismarck, Dec. 29, 1877. DZA Potsdam, Reichskanzlei, 2080, pp. 42–46; for the ensuing exchange of letters see *ibid.*, pp. 50–57, and Goldschmidt, *Reich und Preussen*, pp. 216–218. SBR (1878), I, 118–120; III, Nos. 20 and 22.

[95] SBR (1878), I, 120–144, 156.

himself to abandon the post he had held for nearly a decade. Next day (February 23) he tried to erase the impression that he and the chancellor were at odds by quoting a memorandum he had written in February 1877 favoring the monopoly in principle. That brought him the satisfaction of hearing Bismarck praise his professional competence, "firmness of character," and "decisiveness." He hoped, Bismarck said, to continue with Camphausen "on the same path further than I could have foreseen a few years ago." The two men shook hands, Camphausen tearfully, in full view of the astonished chamber.[96] By clinging to his position "like a drowning man to a straw," Camphausen ruined his relationship to the liberals (even Bennigsen was firmly opposed to a tobacco monopoly), without whose support he had publicly declared he could not remain in office. After watching the Reichstag reject all of his bills, except for an insignificant levy on playing cards, the minister finally resigned.[97]

On February 22–23 Bismarck demonstrated how to slaughter a colleague without being charged with murder. He put Camphausen's head on a block, but liberals wielded the axe. Camphausen was not the only victim. In view of his opposition to the tobacco monopoly, Bennigsen terminated his candidacy for the cabinet.[98] (Bismarck never had to tell him that he was no longer under consideration.) Achenbach, whom Bismarck had denounced to the Chamber of Deputies on March 23 for "passive resistance" on railway reform, also resigned.[99] By coincidence still another ministry became vacant. Eulenburg, long at odds with Bismarck and in bad health, resigned in March at the end of a six-month leave. Since the Landtag approved Bismarck's request that the vice-presidency of the cabinet, hitherto coupled with the Finance Ministry, be made into an independent, salaried position, the prince now had four positions to fill in his search for his "homogeneous cabinet."[100] At his parliamentary soirée on March 23, he remarked, "In large states like Prussia and Germany it is not so important whether a cabinet is inclined either to the right or left on different questions, for the legislature will compensate. It is much more important that the government proceed in one direction. If six horses are harnessed to the wagon, they must all obey one will or never go forward."[101]

Bismarck now had the opportunity to select four new horses. His first choice was Count Otto zu Stolberg-Wernigerode, who had proved his capacity as an administrator in Hanover after its annexation and been rewarded with the embassy in Vienna. Stolberg became Bismarck's chief deputy in do-

[96] SBR (1878), I, 147–164; Lucius, Bismarck-Erinnerungen, p. 130.

[97] Lucius, Bismarck-Erinnerungen, p. 130; Friedrich Böttcher, Eduard Stephani (Leipzig, 1887), pp. 198–199.

[98] Oncken, Bennigsen, II, 352–353.

[99] BR, VII, 213–215.

[100] Lucius, Bismarck-Erinnerungen, p. 117.

[101] BP, I, 141.

mestic affairs as vice-president of the Prussian cabinet and vice-chancellor of the Reich. The new minister of interior was Count Botho zu Eulenburg, a career Prussian official and cousin of the departed minister (Count Friedrich zu Eulenburg). Albert Maybach, former president of the Imperial Railway Office and an ardent advocate of public ownership or regulation of railways, assumed the Ministry of Commerce. But the critical post was the Ministry of Finance, and no qualified person, it appeared, wanted to succeed Camphausen. After nine or more refusals (including Bennigsen and possibly Delbrück!), Tiedemann proposed in desperation a candidate no one had thought of because he was so little qualified—Arthur Hobrecht, the national liberal lord mayor of Berlin.[102]

During the period of the "Bennigsen candidacy," Heinrich von Treitschke wrote to Gustav Freytag, "Bismarck cannot tolerate independent characters near him, and I advise no friend of mine to put his head in the noose."[103] Rudolf Virchow told the Chamber of Deputies, "The minister-president is said . . . to be an iron man who can put anything across, and yet he presents himself in parliament as the weakest of all, as though he were utterly unable to direct even the smallest of his colleagues to do what the state's situation and politics demand." But this was mere theater, which masked the injuries the chancellor inflicted by his penchant for "ruining" those who worked with him. "One after the other is brought down, not only kicked out but also showered afterward with spite and contempt. The number of personalities willing to offer themselves as possible ministers is becoming steadily smaller. Obviously we are facing a complete bankruptcy of personalities in the German Reich."[104]

What Treitschke, the national liberal, and Virchow, the progressive, saw from a distance Lucius, the free conservative, observed close up. "The inclination to blow every petty matter up into a conflict is almost pathological and leads to constant frictions. In view of his nerves he can preserve himself for the Reich and the state only if he relinquishes a large part of his activity and allows some room for independent personalities working with him. In quiet moments he sees that himself and is resolved to permit it."[105] But Bismarck's quiet moments were few, and by mid-June 1878 Lucius was shocked to find him already complaining about all of his new colleagues except Maybach. "Hobrecht is a groveler, who always seeks contact with the national liberals. Botho Eulenburg is a state's attorney, who can always cite six statutes to explain why something cannot be done. Stolberg complains about having nothing to do, although he can order everything laid before him." In October

[102] Tiedemann, *Sechs Jahre*, pp. 235ff. Lucius, *Bismarck-Erinnerungen*, pp. 130–135.
[103] Quoted in Oncken, *Bennigsen*, II, 336.
[104] *SBHA* (1877–1878), II, 1965–1966.
[105] Lucius, *Bismarck-Erinnerungen*, p. 134.

Lucius reported, "He is again unrestrained in talking about ministerial colleagues and is somewhat unjust to them. At least Count Stolberg and [Botho]
Eulenburg, who entered the cabinet with great reluctance, do not deserve his
displeasure."[106]

With the "Bennigsen candidacy" Bismarck and the national liberals entered a critical stage in their relationship. Once the courtship was over, both
sides found reasons why it was a poor match. The prince was dismayed to
discover that Bennigsen was not a statesman, but just another "institutional
doctrinaire," who lacked the "independence" to enter the government alone
and was too much under Lasker's influence.[107] Bennigsen and his associates,
on the other hand, felt relieved to be rid of temptation. "We all said: thank
God!" reported Eduard Stephani.[108] Bennigsen began to see how unrealistic
his prospects had been. "I can congratulate myself and my friends on having
gotten safely out of this affair. In view of Bismarck's present nervousness and
the irrational way in which he has recently conducted business and handled
political parties, it would not have been possible to get along with him for as
much as half a year."[109] Having rejected Bismarck's caress, the national liberals were wary of his foot. They began to prepare for a dissolution of the
Reichstag.

Nevertheless, they decided against "systematic opposition," resolving to
consider each issue on its merits.[110] Hence they accepted the deputization
statute, but stood firm against the government's tax program and plan to reorganize Prussian ministries. On March 2, 1878, the chancellor twisted the
arms of Bennigsen and Forckenbeck in favor of the tobacco monopoly, beginning with "inducements" (did he again offer Bennigsen a ministry?) and ending with "threats" (he would dissolve the Reichstag and, "if necessary," govern without it; the military conventions between Prussia and the other states
would be adequate to secure the power of the Reich).[111] At the end of the
month he told Kardorff that a dissolution was "unavoidable," for he could not
govern with a Reichstag that refused funds and was dominated by ideologues.[112] But then he appears to have reverted to an earlier opinion—that it

---

[106] Ibid., pp. 141–146. Before accepting the appointment, Stolberg tried to get Bismarck to
define his functions and responsibilities. Bismarck was miffed by the request. He held out the
prospect of a Prussian ministry with portfolio, but it did not materialize. Goldschmidt, Reich und
Preussen, pp. 239–240; Lucius, Bismarck-Erinnerungen, pp. 133–136.

[107] Tiedemann, Sechs Jahre, pp. 233–234; Lucius, Bismarck-Erinnerungen, pp. 131–132; GW,
VIII, 249.

[108] Böttcher, Stephani, p. 200.

[109] Bennigsen to his wife, Mar. 18, 1878. Oncken, Bennigsen, II, 360.

[110] BP, II, 272.

[111] Martin Philippson, Max von Forckenbeck. Ein Lebensbild (Leipzig, 1898), p. 295; BP, II,
273.

[112] GW, VIII, 254. Conversation with Kardorff, Mar. 31, 1878.

would do no good to dissolve over the tax issue. "We must now draft an eco-nomic program and seek to imprint it on the consciousness of the voters—then, after a year and a half, it will be possible to vote on economic, not political, issues."[113] Julius Hölder was right to suspect "fire in the attic."[114]

Reorganizing the Reich Executive

Passage of the deputization act in March 1878 expedited the final dissolution of the Imperial Chancellor's Office (*Reichskanzleramt*). In May was established the Imperial Chancellery (*Reichskanzlei*), the chancellor's personal secretar-iat, whose first chief was Tiedemann. In 1879, the two remaining divisions of the *Reichskanzleramt* were renamed the Imperial Treasury (*Reichsschatzamt*) and the Imperial Office of the Interior (*Reichsamt des Innern*). The problem of what to do with Hofmann was solved when he agreed to head the latter agency in combination with the Prussian Ministry of Commerce. The sepa-rate agencies of the Reich were now eight: foreign office, admiralty, post and telegraph, Alsace-Lorraine, railway office, judicial office, treasury, interior office. The *Reichskanzlei*, consisting of only three, later four officials, was the channel through which the chancellor communicated with heads of the seven agencies dealing with domestic affairs; the state secretary of the foreign office reported directly to the chancellor. Bismarck's extended absences from Berlin made the chancellery an important agency, but it never achieved the status of the old *Reichskanzleramt*; nor did its chief attain the power Delbrück had enjoyed.[115]

Bismarck's plans for restructuring the Prussian ministries ran into trouble in the Landtag at the hands of centrists, progressives, and national liberals. All were generally resentful over the bill's form (a supplement to the budget), the haste with which the chamber was expected to pass it, and the absence of a finance minster to defend it. In December 1878 the national liberals, shaken by recent experiences, changed sides and passed a revised bill.[116] Yet the lesser states grumbled at the "personal union" for which these measures were in-tended to lay the groundwork. They feared "conflicts of interest" and the "open Prussian hegemony" that would result if Prussian ministers with port-folio should act simultaneously as chiefs of imperial agencies, Prussian dele-gates to the Bundesrat, and countersigning deputies of the chancellor.[117]

During 1876–1879 Bismarck took a long step toward undisputed and unob-

[113] GW, VIII, 250.

[114] BP, II, 272.

[115] Morsey, *Reichsverwaltung*, pp. 224ff.

[116] SBHA (1877–1878), II, 1956–2030; Anlagen, II, No. 299; SBHA (1878–1879), I, 142–162, 433–455, 479–480; Anlagen, I, Nos. 30 and 56.

[117] Goldschmidt, *Reich und Preussen*, pp. 42–43, 213–216, 218–222, 232–238.

structed control over the executive branches of the German and Prussian governments. For that reason he became less interested in structural changes that
might have made a more efficient instrument of government out of the un-
gainly machine he had fashioned in 1866–1867. During the years that followed he continued to shift gears from time to time, but without attaining a
clear and lasting solution to the problem of coordination between the Reich
and Prussia that was to be one of his unfortunate legacies. In early 1879 he
returned to a policy of accentuating the importance of the Reich administration by initiating "regular conferences" among heads of the imperial agencies
to establish "common principles of policy"—but only two were held. At the
second meeting (April 9, 1879) he announced his intention to establish a
sharper separation between the Prussian and imperial executive bodies, ordering that "presidential bills" (that is, those prepared in imperial agencies)
be sent directly to the Bundesrat without prior approval by the pertinent Prussian ministers. At the same time he reasserted his right as Prussian foreign
minister to instruct the votes of Prussian representatives in the Bundesrat and
to monitor all communications between the Prussian and German governments.[118] This new emphasis upon the Reich executive at the cost of the
Prussian cabinet can also be seen in his appointment of Hofmann as Prussian
minister of commerce (March 1879). Maybach, who now became minister of
public works (Bismarck's new "railway ministry"), did not combine that post
with the presidency of the Imperial Railway Office. Friedberg, moreover, was
not permitted to remain chief of the Reich Office of Justice when he became
Prussian minister of justice, on the grounds that this would constitute a "mediatization of the Reich."[119] Evidently Bismarck now considered the accumulation of offices through personal union hazardous both to the principle of
federalism and to his own personal power as the holder of the constitutional
balance.

Where governmental relationships were concerned, Bismarck shifted constantly from one expedient to another, unable to find an adequate and lasting
structure. His attempts along the way to explain and elucidate legal and constitutional relationships were often contradictory. He was consistent only in
his unceasing quest to heighten his own authority by juggling persons, offices,
parties, and governments. In this he was driven by a narcissistic quest for
personal power, by enduring uneasiness about the solidity of the German social and political order, and by his continuing search for the means with
which to advance its consolidation. About the realities of the dangers he
sensed there can be no doubt. That those dangers ultimately materialized was

---

[118] *Ibid.*, pp. 245–246, 250–258.

[119] *Ibid.*, pp. 262–265. Maybach, however, was appointed chief of the imperial agency that
administered the publicly owned railways of Alsace-Lorraine. F. Jungnickel, *Staatsminister Albert
von Maybach* (Stuttgart, 1910), pp. 64ff.

owing not only to their evolutionary force but also to the limitation of Bismarck's own vision. He left Germany with a governmental machine whose cogs and wheels were poorly meshed, of whose working relationships he himself was never clear—a machine that was increasingly oriented toward the satisfaction of his own need to dominate and control.

CHAPTER THIRTEEN

The Antisocialist Statute

NE OF BISMARCK'S more than four hundred guests at a parliamentary soirée in March 1878 described him as he was at age sixty-three. "The prince's hair is almost white, his face reddish, but his corpulence is especially evident. He was the bulkiest man in the gathering, although others were not lacking in *embonpoints*. When talking, the prince is often noticeably afflicted by a nervous sweat. He also appears to suffer from an asthmatic condition; at times he stops talking in order to take a deep breath. Unfortunately our chancellor is not healthy. Willpower alone permits him to surmount his suffering and fulfill the difficult tasks of his high office."[1] That evening, while guzzling Munich beer in "the genuine student manner," Bismarck asked a guest for advice on how to get rid of podagra and take off weight. "I'm becoming so fat that I have to purchase new uniforms and wardrobe every year."[2] Between 1874 and 1879 Bismarck's weight increased by 45 lbs. (227 to 272).[3]

Physically Bismarck profited little from the ten months' leave of 1877–1878. In February and March 1878 weakness compelled him to sit during his longer speeches in parliament, and once he had to break off before finishing.[4] The foreign policy speech of February 19, in which he depicted himself as Europe's "honest broker," was rhetorically one of his best performances, although extemporaneous. Later he said that he had been nearly overcome by exhaustion—"the heads [of the deputies] seemed like black points." That evening he could neither eat nor sleep. Next day, when Lucius came to dinner, his appetite was back: "He devoured half of a turkey-hen, slicing everything himself with his knife, and drank one-quarter to one-half of a bottle of cognac mixed with two to three bottles of Apollinaris. During the day he enjoys neither beer nor champagne; cognac mixed with water suits him best. He insisted that I drink with him so that he couldn't tell how much he consumed. There is concern that his dietary mistakes could suddenly lead to a stroke."[5] On

[1] *BP*, I, 141.

[2] *BP*, I, 139.

[3] Augustin Cabanès, "La Médecine Anecdotique: Bismarckiana," *La Chronique Medicale*, 5 (1898), p. 534. At age 32 Bismarck had weighed 200 lbs. Georg Schmidt, *Schönhausen und die Familie von Bismarck* (2d ed., Berlin, 1898), p. 5. See also Ernst Schweninger, *Dem Andenken Bismarcks* (Leipzig, 1899), p. 25.

[4] *BR*, VII, 81, 207, 211, 242.

[5] Freiherr Lucius von Ballhausen, *Bismarck-Erinnerungen* (Stuttgart, 1920), pp. 128, 130.

March 27, he confessed to the Chamber of Deputies that he could work but a few hours a day and was compelled to curtail contacts with other ministers. Yet he complained bitterly that people treated him like a "basically healthy person, of whom everything was expected that an active and healthy person can accomplish by day and night." His was a "thankless profession."[6]

Two visitors found Bismarck in a resentful and cynical mood at this time. His services to the state, he grumbled to Busch, had robbed him of his health. "People should be grateful to me for this, instead of electing to the Reichstag men of vanity and ingratitude."[7] To Lucius he spoke of "envy and conceit" and told the fable about a man who was promised the fulfillment of any wish— with one condition: his most bitter enemy would receive double the same. The man's wish was to go blind in one eye. "One of Bismarck's more notable characteristics," Lucius reflected, "is the tendency to harbor deep thoughts of revenge or retaliation for injustices he has suffered or presumes to have suffered. In his pathological excitability he conceives many things to be unjust that others probably do not intend to be such." Lucius could see why a capable person like Stolberg would hesitate to join Bismarck's government. The "abruptness and violence" with which business was transacted kept "tranquil and rational persons" from working with the chancellor.[8]

In April 1878, Bismarck planned to spend two weeks in Friedrichsruh, but his departure was delayed until April 17 by an attack of rheumatism. Three days after arriving in the Sachsenwald, he fell ill of shingles, and Dr. Struck had to be summoned from Berlin.[9] On May 6, the forestry expert, John Booth, found him able to walk in the woods to inspect new plantings but very weak and unable to stand for long. That evening at dinner the prince was abnormally quiet, talking mostly to his physician about his health and what could be done to deaden the neuralgia that returned each night to plague him.[10] While still in this convalescent condition, he received shocking news from Berlin that required a new burst of activity. Suddenly the new era in German politics toward which he had been groping since 1875 seemed attainable.

Hödel and Nobiling

On the afternoon of May 11, 1878, a worker named Max Hödel fired three shots from a revolver on the avenue *Unter den Linden* as Kaiser Wilhelm and his daughter, the Grand Duchess of Baden, rode by in an open carriage. Nei-

[6] BR, VII, 229–230.

[7] Moritz Busch, *Tagebuchblätter* (Leipzig, 1899), II, 210–211.

[8] Lucius, *Bismarck-Erinnerungen*, pp. 129, 134.

[9] GW, XIV, 893; Horst Kohl, ed., *Fürst Bismarck: Regesten zu einer wissenschaflichen Biographie des ersten Reichskanzlers* (Leipzig, 1891), II, 161.

[10] GW, VIII, 259–260.

ther was hit, and Hödel was apprehended while running from the scene. Less than three weeks later, on June 2, the Kaiser, while riding on the same avenue, was struck by two shotgun blasts from a second story window. This time his assailant was Karl Nobiling, Ph.D., who shot himself in the head before being arrested. Wilhelm was driven to the palace, bleeding profusely from pellet wounds in the cheek, throat, shoulder, and hand. "I do not understand," he sighed, "why I'm always being shot at."[11] Though painful, his injuries would not have been serious except for his age (eighty-one). Hödel was tried, condemned, and executed on August 19, while Nobiling succumbed of his wounds on September 10.

Hödel and Nobiling were psychopaths eager for attention and notoriety—a type known all too well in recent history. Both may have been syphilitic. A twenty-year-old journeyman tinsmith from Dresden, Hödel had a long record of petty crime. It is not certain that he aimed to kill, and his deed may (his explanations were inconsistent) have been purely demonstrative, intended to dramatize either himself or, as he claimed, the fate of the poor. Nobiling had studied agriculture and economics at the universities of Halle and Leipzig. At the age of thirty he was professionally unsuccessful. His father had died a suicide, and one of his brothers had a criminal record. It was difficult to obtain testimony from either man, Hödel because of his imbecility and Nobiling because his head wound left him seldom lucid. There was no evidence that the two men knew each other or that either had coconspirators.

The news of these crimes sent shock waves through the German press and public and aroused general indignation. To many they were proof of a widespread conspiracy against the monarchy and the prevailing social order; others believed that they were at least influenced by the poisonous atmosphere produced by socialist agitation. That the German socialist movement, like Karl Marx, eschewed individual acts of violence as counterproductive to their goals was disregarded or disbelieved. The conspiracy thesis was reinforced by Hermann Tessendorff, the red-baiting state's attorney, who investigated both cases and generally suppressed evidence that did not fit the theory that Hödel and Nobiling had socialist connections. Hödel had once belonged to the Social Democratic party in Leipzig and had sold subscriptions to party journals and distributed its literature. But he had been expelled from the party on a charge of embezzlement. Later he signed up with the Anarchist League and with the new Christian Social Labor party of court preacher Adolf Stöcker, both deadly enemies of the social democrats. Although he had expressed some socialist views in early years, Nobiling had most recently presented himself as a national liberal and attended socialist meetings only to heckle speakers. In one of his few coherent moments he explained that he had wanted to remove

[11] Christoph von Tiedemann, *Sechs Jahre Chef der Reichskanzlei unter dem Fürsten Bismarck* (2d ed., Leipzig, 1910), p. 267.

Wilhelm in order that Crown Prince Friedrich Wilhelm, who was "more in-dependent and less easily influenced," could ascend the throne.[12] The readi-ness of the public to believe that the deeds of two madmen were proof of a socialist conspiracy is evidence of the growing social tensions and fears pro-duced by five years of economic depression, the growth of socialist agitation, and recent successes of the Social Democratic party at the polls. The mood of the country can be seen in the following account, written by a socialist, of what happened on the evening of May 11 in the provincial city of Halle, when news arrived of Hödel's act: "Thousands of people poured into the streets and wandered about; the marketplace was a wildly simmering, bub-bling kettle full of excited people. Some prayed, others sang, '*Nun danket alle Gott.*' Many did not yet know the details of the attempted assassination and kept asking, 'Is he dead? Is he dead?' Bells rang from all churches, and many persons ran about bareheaded, as though out of their minds, knocking the hats off of others in a blind rage." Persons emerging from a restaurant known to be a meeting place for radicals were attacked by a frenzied crowd, which continued for days to roam the streets.[13]

At Friedrichsruh Bismarck received the news of Hödel's shots within an hour after the event. That evening in Berlin, as Tiedemann drafted a report on a socialist conspiracy based on testimony from an unreliable informer,[14] a telegram arrived from Friedrichsruh asking, "Should we not use the attempted assassination as grounds for immediately presenting a bill against the socialists and their press?" Two days later, as the Prussian cabinet debated the issue, Herbert brought another message from Friedrichsruh. "Our duty and obliga-tion to the country require that we at least attempt to seek remedy through legislation. If the legislature hampers us in this, we have at least discharged our duty. . . . If the Reichstag refuses to assist the government in suppressing social democracy, we must renew the effort in the next session. At any rate it would be advantageous in the next election, if the Reichstag were compelled, in view of the attempted assassination, to take a position with regard to a bill against socialist subversion."[15] Since the collapse of the Bennigsen candidacy, Bismarck had been considering the dissolution of the Reichstag. Now Hödel had provided him with a superb issue on which to fight the election that would follow.

---

[12] Paul Kampffmeyer and Bruno Altmann, *Vor dem Sozialistengesetz: Krisenjahre des Obrigkeits-staates* (Berlin, 1928), pp. 157–176. This is a partisan account by two socialists who had access to the documents of the official investigation. For more sober versions, see Gerhard G. Schümer, *Entstehungsgeschichte des Sozialistengesetzes* (Göttingen, 1929), and Wolfgang Pack, *Das parlamen-tarische Ringen um das Sozialistengesetz Bismarcks 1878–1890* (Düsseldorf, 1961).

[13] Kampffmeyer and Altmann, *Vor dem Sozialistengesetz,* pp. 176–177.

[14] Tiedemann, *Sechs Jahre,* pp. 260–262.

[15] GW, VIc, 108–109. Also Tiedemann to Hofmann, May 19, 1878. DZA Potsdam, 1291/1, pp. 78–79.

The issue was not new, although it had taken a dramatically new turn. During the winter of 1875–1876 the government had sought and failed to gain passage of an amendment to the penal code that would have permitted the fining and imprisonment of persons threatening the public peace by stimulating class conflict or by attacking the institutions of marriage, family, and property. On that occasion, too, Bismarck's purpose had been to force the Reichstag to take a position on the problem of subversion. In 1878, however, Bismarck's first obstacle was not the Reichstag but the cabinet. Friedenthal and Leonhardt were outspoken in their opposition to Bismarck's proposal. But Hobrecht, Falk, and Eulenburg also doubted the wisdom of proposing an exceptional law against socialists. They expected the Reichstag to reject the bill and preferred a more intensive use of existing laws to combat subversion. Friedenthal carried their views to Friedrichsruh, but "as usual" drew the shorter end of the argument. "The prince . . . firmly insisted that the social-democratic movement can be effectively combatted only if we gain the right to surmount the barriers established in the so-called civil rights clauses of the constitution out of excessive concern for the protection of individuals and political parties. The state finds itself in a state of emergency vis-à-vis socialists. In an emergency one cannot be hypersensitive about methods—à *corsaire corsaire et demi!*"[16]

On May 16, Botho Eulenburg, after a roundtrip to Friedrichsruh, gave the cabinet the draft of an "exceptional law," whose presentation to parliament the chancellor declared to be the government's "unavoidable duty." It provided that the Bundesrat be empowered to suppress "publications and organizations that pursue the aims of social democracy," subject to later approval by the Reichstag; that local police be authorized to dissolve socialist meetings and forbid distribution of socialist literature in public places; and that participants in forbidden clubs and meetings be imprisoned. Faced with this ultimatum from Friedrichsruh, only Hobrecht clung to his objections.[17] Without a formal ballot the bill was dispatched to the Bundesrat, which approved it on May 17 over minor opposition (Bremen and Hamburg).[18] In the Reichs-

[16] Tiedemann, *Sechs Jahre*, pp. 263–264. Cabinet meeting of May 14, 1878. DZA Merseburg, Rep. 90a, B, III, 2b, Nr. 6, Vol. 90.

[17] Eulenburg's draft provided that the chancellor should exercise the power of suppression, but Bismarck, in accord with his new emphasis on federalism, insisted that the Bundesrat be given that authority. Cabinet meeting of May 16, 1878. DZA Merseburg, Rep. 90a, B, III, 2b, Nr. 6, Vol. 90.

[18] Other governments had doubts about the bill but voted for it. Schümer, *Entstehungsgeschichte*, pp. 33–34. For the bill see *SBR* (1878), IV, No. 274. Bismarck instructed Hofmann to tell the Reichstag that the issue of socialist subversion was not new. Hödel's deed had merely reaffirmed the necessity of legislative action to strengthen the powers of the state. The new bill was merely another such effort, like the penal code act of 1875, whose "rubber paragraphs" Lasker and the left-liberals had excoriated. Tiedemann to Hofmann, May 19, 1878. DZA Potsdam, Reichskanzleramt, 1292/1, pp. 78–79. See also p. 333.

tag, however, the steamroller broke down. At a caucus on May 21 the national liberals divided over the issue. Again Bennigsen's gift for compromise filled the breach. The caucus agreed to oppose the bill, but left open the possibility for other legislation.[19]

In the chamber Bennigsen shouldered the responsibility for explicating the party's position. Like the government, he insisted, liberals appreciated the danger posed by growing socialist agitation and the necessity of taking action against excesses committed by the movement. What they objected to was the desire of the government to proceed on the basis of an exceptional rather than common law. Many of the "aims" that the law was intended to proscribe were shared by nonsocialist scholars and "humane legislators" insofar as they concerned general improvement in working class conditions. Exceptional laws like the Carlsbad decrees had done little to prevent the spread of subversive ideas but merely poisoned the relationship between government and people. The "dictatorial power" demanded by the government would only arouse sympathy for its victims. At no time since its creation, furthermore, had the German government appeared less capable of exercising such a power. "The important man who, as minister-president of Prussia, stands at the head of the responsible government and who, as chancellor, is alone responsible for the affairs of the German Reich has not been well for a long time. Despite great effort and self-sacrificing devotion to duty, he has not been able as a consequence of his health to conduct more than part of the business that is entrusted to him by law and the constitution. . . . I am sorry to have to say it, but I cannot avoid stating that in Prussia the ministerial crisis is permanent." On May 24 the two conservative parties alone voted for the bill, which was overwhelmingly defeated (251 to 57).[20]

Tiedemann, who meanwhile had been summoned to Friedrichsruh, was astonished at Bismarck's "indifference" to the news of this defeat. "When the Reichstag majority disturbs his plans, he usually does not lack caustic remarks in airing his displeasure. But this time he limited himself to a few joking remarks about the unfortunate ministers whose duty it had been to defend the ill-fated bill. Whether he would have been so indifferent if he had himself been compelled to stand in the breach during the fight is another matter. Obviously he believes the fruit is not yet ripe enough to be shaken from the tree and that public opinion must be given time to prepare itself for further, more far-reaching measures. There was no talk of dissolving the Reichstag as an answer to the abrupt rejection of the bill." Perhaps, Tiedemann speculated, information received on May 21 had had a calming effect on the

[19] Otto Bähr to Friedrich Oetker, June 15, 1878, HW, II, 197–198; less informative is the diary of Julius Hölder, BP, II, 280–281, and Dieter Langewiesche, ed., Das Tagebuch Julius Hölders, 1877–1880 (Stuttgart, 1977), pp. 107–108.

[20] SBR (1878), II, 1495–1554; Hermann Oncken, Rudolf von Bennigsen (Stuttgart, 1910), II, 362–369.

prince's ego: Russia had agreed to meet the other powers in Berlin to search for a peaceful settlement of the Balkan crisis. Although unburdened by the "mortgage of conceit," Bismarck took satisfaction in knowing that he was shortly to be the arbiter of Europe.[21]

When the telegraph reported Nobiling's attack on June 2, Bismarck, his health improving daily, was walking in the woods with two newly acquired dogs, Tyras and Rebecca. Tiedemann found him returning across an open field. The prince was in a good mood; the forest air, he said, had soothed his nerves. When he paused, Tiedemann told him briefly that the Kaiser had been shot and "severely wounded." "The prince halted abruptly. He drove his oaken walking stick into the dirt with a heavy thrust and, breathing deeply as though struck by a flash of inspiration, said, 'Then we will dissolve the Reichstag!' " Only then did he ask for details. With quickened step the two men hurried home, where Bismarck ordered preparations for the return to Berlin on the following morning. During the journey on June 3, it became evident what fantasies Nobiling's deed had aroused throughout Germany. At each station, the train was met by excited crowds bearing the "wildest and most unbelievable rumors": the crown prince had been fired on; Prince Friedrich Karl was wounded; mines had been discovered under the royal palace. By the time they reached Berlin, Bismarck was sufficiently alarmed to dispatch Tiedemann to inquire of Minister of War Kameke whether steps had been taken to strengthen the Berlin garrison against insurrection. That evening the chancellor spent a few minutes with the Kaiser, who was cheerful but indignant at being the target of shotgun pellets rather than an "honorable bullet." For a monarch to be hunted down like a rabbit or pheasant was humiliating.[22]

Dissolution of the Reichstag

In the summer of 1878 Bismarck reached another peak in his reputation as Europe's greatest diplomatist. For one month (June 13 to July 13) Berlin was Europe's capital, as statesmen of the great powers strove under his "honest brokerage" to resolve their differences over the Balkans without war. In foreign affairs his talents seemed indispensable to Germany and even Europe. At the same time, his reputation for effective statesmanship in domestic affairs touched bottom. To competent observers of widely disparate political convictions, it appeared that the governmental machine was breaking down. Years of depression had brought social distress to a dangerous level; workers were restive and bourgeois fearful; a crisis loomed in public finance. The man

---

[21] Tiedemann, *Sechs Jahre*, pp. 265–266.

[22] *Ibid.*, pp. 266–270. On May 17, 1878, Tiedemann reported to Bleichröder that the prince's health was improving "day by day"; although diminishing, the neuralgia was still evident and likewise its consequence—sleeplessness. *Bleichröder Archive*, Kress Library of Business and Economics, Harvard, Box I, Folder 14.

whose primary responsibility it was to master these problems was perennially sick, usually absent from Berlin, and able to spend at best only a few hours a day on public business. He was, furthermore, often out of touch with his colleagues in the Prussian cabinet. His attacks upon them in the press and in parliament had created a seemingly permanent ministerial crisis. To find qualified replacements for them had become increasingly difficult. The chancellor appeared unable to make the complicated machinery of the Prussian-German state operate effectively, although it was his own design. His chief solution to the problem was authoritarian—to heighten his own power at the cost of his colleagues and of parliament.

Under these circumstances even right-wing liberals were willing to consider whether the machine required reconstruction, whether a parliamentary democracy could achieve new efficiency and momentum by bringing fresh blood into the government and closing the gap between the Reichstag and imperial executive. To be sure, the octogenarian Hohenzoller who sat on the dual thrones of Prussia and the Reich seemed blissfully unaware of the internal crisis of his regime and more attached than ever to the man who had steered him past the reefs and shoals of the 1860s to a preeminent position in Germany and Europe. But Wilhelm's time seemed short and, given his physical condition, perhaps Bismarck's as well. Furthermore, the growing fiscal crisis and the need for new taxes seemed to provide liberals with the means of coercion necessary to bring about constitutional reform. At this moment came the shots of Hödel and Nobiling. For days stunned opponents could only mutter, "That Bismarck has incredible luck [Schweineglück]."[23]

Tiedemann's account of the scene that afternoon in the field at Friedrichsruh has often been analyzed for what it reveals about the chancellor's character and purposes. After hearing only the bare fact that the Kaiser had been wounded, he made instantaneously the crucial decision to dissolve the Reichstag. At that moment he did not know the identity of the assassin, the nature of the man's political connections, or even the extent of Wilhelm's injury. That he thought of politics first and of Wilhelm second was characteristic, but not necessarily proof of cold-blooded indifference.[24] On June 3 he paid his "liege lord" a brief visit, and, on leaving the room where the dignified old man lay swathed in bandages, unable to speak or sign his name, the iron chancellor stood for a time in a window niche and wept. On the following day Baroness Spitzemberg found him still visibly shaken.[25] There is no reason

[23] Kampffmeyer and Altmann, Vor dem Sozialistengesetz, p. 176.

[24] Erich Eyck, Bismarck, Leben und Werk (Zurich, 1944), III, 228–229; Walter Bussmann, Das Zeitalter Bismarcks in Leo Just, ed., Handbuch der deutschen Geschichte (3d ed., Constance, 1956), vol. 3/II, p. 181.

[25] Memoirs of Gustav von Wilmowski. DZA Merseburg, Hausarchiv, Nachlass Kaiser Wilhelms I., Rep. 51, F, III, 10, p. 49; Rudolf Vierhaus, ed., Das Tagebuch der Baronin Spitzemberg

to doubt the depth of Bismarck's concern at the time about the twin problems of social distress and subversion. The sources show that he had never completely lost sight of the social question since his talks with Wagener and Lassalle in 1862–1863 and that his concern increased after 1871. Furthermore, his solution had been consistently dual: social reform and police repression.[26] Still, it is undeniable that the first thought that raced through his mind in the meadow at Friedrichsruh was how to exploit the incident against left-wing liberals. For weeks he had wrestled with the problem of how to gain a majority in the Reichstag more amenable to his wishes on the matter of new taxes. Suddenly the opportunity was there. "Now I have the rascals where I want them!" the chancellor is said to have exulted. "Does your highness mean the social democrats?" he was asked. "No! The national liberals!"[27]

Characteristically, Bismarck opened the cabinet meeting on June 4—the first since Nobiling's attack—with remarks about his own health. His condition, he said, was still too poor to allow the full resumption of his duties. In May, the Reichstag majority's declaration of no confidence in the government during the debate on the antisocialist bill had caused him again to consider resigning. But retirement was no longer possible in view of Nobiling's attack. Required was a new and more far-reaching exceptional law, including provisions for "protection of property, marriage, and family" (similar to those proposed earlier in the so-called "rubber paragraph," authority to ban socialists from certain places and districts and to intern them, and denial of their right to possess and bear arms without permission from the police. Finally, he favored immediate dissolution of the Reichstag in order to exploit public indignation over Nobiling's deed and because the National Liberal party had withdrawn its trust in the government. But he would, he declared, accept the will of the cabinet majority if the ministers wished to attempt this legislation with the existing parliament. When it became apparent, however, that indeed the majority did favor the latter course, Bismarck adjourned the meeting, ostensibly to await the arrival of Count Stolberg, the cabinet's new vice-president, and to consult with the Kaiser or crown prince. Next day only Friedenthal, Eulenburg, and Hobrecht still argued against immediate dissolution; collegial procedure, nevertheless, permitted Bismarck to present that course to the crown prince as the will of the entire cabinet.[28] He had to

---

(Göttingen, 1961), p. 171. See also Hajo Holborn, ed., *Aufzeichnungen und Erinnerungen aus dem Leben des Botschafters Joseph Maria von Radowitz* (Berlin, 1925), II, 16.

[26] See pp. 293–310.

[27] There is no firsthand source for this frequently cited quotation. But see Oncken, *Bennigsen*, II, 370. Like many unverified quotations from famous people, the quotation is at least in character. For months, Bismarck had been on the alert for a reason to dissolve the Reichstag. *GW*, VIII, 254.

[28] Cabinet meetings of June 4 and 5, 1878. *DZA* Merseburg, Rep. 90a, B, III, 2b, Nr. 6, Vol. 90.

"wring" the antisocialist bill out of his colleagues, he complained later to Lucius.[29]

The ministers opposed to dissolution argued that it was unnecessary because the existing Reichstag, shaken by Nobiling's attack, would now readily approve the antisocialist bill if reintroduced. Crown Prince Friedrich Wilhelm, upon whom the final decision rested, tended to share this opinion. Friedrich Wilhelm had hurried home from England on hearing the news of Nobiling's attack, expecting perhaps to govern as regent during his father's incapacitation. But Wilhelm's injuries did not justify a regency, and the Kaiser directed, probably on Bismarck's advice, that his son be appointed deputy (*Stellvertreter*), a status that he had himself once held during the incapacitation of Friedrich Wilhelm IV. Although he accepted this role, the crown prince was deeply offended that Bismarck had not summoned him to participate in the audience on June 4, in which the decision was reached. An unpleasant confrontation occurred in which, according to one account, the crown prince reminded Bismarck "to take heed of whom he was addressing." Yet Friedrich Wilhelm approved the Reichstag's dissolution in a meeting of the Crown Council on June 5. Although opposed to capital punishment, he also signed the death warrant for Hödel.[30] Once he had defended the dignity of his position, Friedrich Wilhelm, like his father on so many occasions, yielded to Bismarck's will. Much had happened since his act of defiance in 1863; evidently he was no longer capable, at least under these circumstances, of precipitating an open breach with "that man."

Under the constitution the Bundesrat had the power to dissolve the Reichstag on the motion of the Kaiser (or his deputy). Like most Prussian ministers, some ministers of other state governments (including Bavaria and Baden) doubted the necessity of dissolution. Bismarck raised the issue to the level of a vote of confidence in his leadership. Before resigning, so he told the Bavarian government, he would as his last official act advise the Kaiser to declare martial law over an area "yet to be determined." For Prussia to be in the minority on this issue, moreover, would demonstrate the necessity of revising the imperial constitution—with obvious consequences for the federal system. The consequences of a defeat on the issue of dissolution in the Bundesrat would, he hinted darkly to the government of Baden, affect "individual governments" more than it would the Reich and its institutions. Under these threats the reluctant governments yielded; the Bundesrat voted unanimously

---

[29] GW, VIII, 281.

[30] Crown Council of June 5, 1878. DZA Merseburg, Rep. 90a, B, III, 2c, Nr. 3, Vol. IV. The evidence does not support the assumption (Eyck, *Bismarck*, III, p. 229) that the crown prince was angered because Bismarck had cheated him out of a regency. It was patent that Wilhelm's wounds did not justify a regency. On the confrontation see Erich Förster, *Adalbert Falk: Sein Leben und Wirken als preussischer Kultusminister* (Gotha, 1927), p. 494; Spitzemberg, *Tagebuch*, p. 171.

CROWN PRINCE FRIEDRICH WILHELM, ABOUT 1875. (BILDARCHIV PREUSSISCHER KULTURBESITZ.)

KAISER WILHELM I, RECUPERATING FROM NOBILING'S ATTACK AT BAD EMS IN THE SUMMER OF 1878.
ATTENDING HIM IS DR. ERNST SCHWENINGER, WHO LATER BECAME BISMARCK'S PERSONAL PHYSICIAN.
(BILDARCHIV PREUSSISCHER KULTURBESITZ.)

for dissolution.[31] Nevertheless, Bismarck did not get everything he desired. The minister of war blocked his demand that martial law be imposed on Berlin and that six regiments patrol the streets to "impress the mob"—so he told Baroness Spitzemberg. Nor did ministers support his demand for one thousand additional policemen and for imposition of controls (passports) to inhibit migration into the capital. Bismarck complained of their "cowardice," "irresolution," and "obstructionism." "Unless I stage a coup, I can't get anything done."[32]

In his memoirs Bismarck reported what sinister thoughts invaded his mind when the ministers voted against dissolution. They appeared so well informed concerning the willingness of the national liberals to reverse themselves on the antisocialist bill that it confirmed his suspicion that an agreement had already been struck for the "division of my legacy." The successive moves of his opponents were like "lightning flashes," each illuminating part of the landscape, "allowing me to comprehend the entire situation." His enemies were planning a "Gladstone cabinet," whose potential members were Stosch, Eulenburg, Friedenthal, Camphausen, Rickert, and possibly even Windthorst. Whether such a cabinet, if assembled, would have been stable, was a question the plotters never considered. "The chief purpose was negative—to get rid of me—and on that subject the partners in this enterprise were united for the time being. Each could hope, once that objective was achieved, to force the others out. That is the way things go in all heterogeneous coalitions, whose only bond is dislike of what exists. The entire combination had no success at that time because neither the king nor the crown prince could be won for it."[33]

The passage, written in the 1890s, was obviously intended to put Wilhelm II in a poor light in comparison with his father and grandfather—loyalty to himself being for Bismarck the criterion of political wisdom. But it was probably also an accurate recall of his thoughts in the summer of 1878. Once again he was beset by a sense of isolation and a near paranoiac suspicion that dark conspiracies were being hatched by a most improbable combination of polit-

[31] Bülow to Werthern, June 7, 1878. DZA Potsdam, Reichskanzleramt, 412, pp. 6–14. Bülow to Flemming, June 15, 1878. Ibid., pp. 15–19. GW, VIc, 114–115; Heinrich von Poschinger, ed., Fürst Bismarck und der Bundesrat, 1867–1890 (Stuttgart, 1897–1901), III, 438–443.

[32] Spitzemberg, Tagebuch, pp. 172–173. For differences among the ministers on the contents and phraseology of the antisocialist bill see Eulenburg to Hofmann, July 11, 1878. DZA Potsdam, Reichskanzleramt, 1292/1, pp. 91–132.

[33] GW, XV, 372–373, 378–379. When officials failed during this period to acquire his signature on state documents—not strange in view of his long absences—Bismarck saw in this a "symbol" of the fate they were preparing for him. Another signal, he thought, was a resentful letter he received in mid-August from Botho Eulenburg, who threatened to resign because Bismarck had sent "an underling," Tiedemann, to reprove him for a mistake in procedure, namely, publishing the new antisocialist bill before the Bundesrat had acted on it. GW, XV, 374–376, 378.

ical foes.[34] At the diplomatic dinner that ended the Congress of Berlin on June 24, he regaled his guests with a discourse on Prussian history intended to prove that "every sovereign" (sic!) since the Great Elector had been joyfully received at the start of his reign and hated at the end. "So it will be in my case." He recounted the story of his political career and declared that he was glad to be "unpopular again."[35]

Election of 1878

Earlier elections had shown German liberals the advantages of universal male suffrage; that of 1878 revealed its dangers. National patriotism, which from 1867 to 1874 had reinforced their appeal to the electorate, now became a weapon of the government and their conservative foes. Bismarck defined the issues for voters in a manifesto published in the official *Provinzial-Korrespondenz* on June 27 under the title, "The purposes and wishes of the governments concerning the election." Originally composed by a press secretary, this document was twice painstakingly revised by the chancellor for maximum effect.[36] The final version declared bluntly that the aim of "the governments" was to gain a "reliable majority" in the Reichstag at the cost of the National Liberal party. Because it could form majorities either with the right, middle, or left of the chamber, that party had a "dominating position," which was tolerable only as long as it gave heed to the wishes of "the governments."[37] Since the beginning of 1878, however, the attitude of the national liberals had changed. Instead of cooperating with the government, they demanded the right to review and approve government bills before their introduction into the chamber. No government could accept that kind of "tutelage" from a party that did not possess a majority.

Then the manifesto zeroed in on a still smaller target. Within the National Liberal party, it asserted, the left wing had established its "leadership," with the consequence that the party regularly allied itself with the progressives. For years this coalition had obstructed government efforts to check radical agitation, culminating in the rejection of the antisocialist bill in May. It was "indisputable" that the Progressive party had prepared the way for socialism since

---

[34] Oncken, *Bennigsen*, II, 387.

[35] GW, VIII, 263.

[36] Horst Kohl, ed., *Bismarck-Jahrbuch* (Leipzig, 1894), I, 97–121; SEG (1878), p. 103. Bismarck's systematic assault on Lasker actually began in the debates of March on the deputization statute. Lasker, he asserted, had caused him more difficulty in the execution of his tasks than any other member of the Reichstag. GW, XI, 576. The chancellor was accurately informed about the division within the national liberal caucus in the discussion of May 21 on the Lex Hödel. Schümer, *Entstehungsgeschichte*, p. 38. His intent to widen the cleavage can be seen in an anonymous press release of May 29, 1878, to the *Norddeutsche Allgemeine Zeitung*. GW, VIc, 113–114.

[37] The use of the plural was in execution of Bismarck's new policy of emphasizing the federal aspect of the constitution, after a decade of unitary emphasis.

1862 by "systematically undermining all pillars of the monarchical state."
Along with ultramontane attacks upon the "authority of the state," it had set
the stage for the socialist assault upon law, order, and morality. People who
lived in this atmosphere and from this "nourishment" lost their sense of values
and respect even for a "venerated and beloved Kaiser." Not until the ruler
was wounded had the National Liberal party concluded, under the pressure of
public opinion, that legislation was necessary. Whether the governments
continued their relationship to the moderates in the party depended upon
whether the moderates severed their links with the progressives and threw off
the "domination" of Lasker, Bamberger, and their associates, who were actually progressives masquerading as national liberals. Moderate national liberals
must clearly establish in the election campaign that they firmly supported the
governments not merely because of the exigencies of the moment but also for
the "lasting security of the state."

In order to prevent the "collapse of our monarchical and political order,"
Bismarck was determined to face a "series of difficult struggles." The Reichstag
would be dissolved repeatedly until the voters repudiated attempts by left-
wing liberals to seize power. The deputies' incomprehension of the government's program for reducing direct taxes, a tobacco monopoly, and liquidation of state assessments was evidence of their impracticality. Jurists, officials,
and academicians were incapable of feeling or understanding the ills of industry and commerce. They were men of "philosophical, humanistic orientation" without "productive occupations," inexperienced in practical affairs,
and inclined toward rhetoric, doctrinairism, and party politics. They had
"neither an interest in nor an understanding of the economic needs of their
producing constituents."

Bismarck's election manifesto of June 1878, which hardly mentioned socialism, was an open declaration of war upon the left wing of the National
Liberal party. In effect, it called for their expulsion from the party, the sub-
servience of the moderate majority to the government, and repudiation by
the voters of all democratic liberals. What Bismarck had been unable to accomplish with a lump of sugar (his offer to Bennigsen in 1877) he now proposed to achieve with a whip. He judged that five years of economic depression, anxieties over the spread of socialism, and general revulsion over the
deeds of Hödel and Nobiling had produced a mood in the country that would
enable him simultaneously to liquidate the liberal era, which had outlived its
usefulness and become a political liability; to break up the combination of
foes within parliament and government that he believed to be plotting his
downfall; and to provide a docile majority in the Reichstag that would enable
him to gain that secure grip on the entire apparatus of government for which
he still grappled. But the manifesto also served to convert the election of 1878
into a plebiscite. The voters were asked to choose between Bismarck, the
unifier of Germany and master of European diplomacy, and the "conspirators"
who wished to supplant him. The ministers, deputies, and courtiers, whose

"obstructionism" and "procrastination" had tortured his nerves and injured his health, were to be cowed by a convincing demonstration of his political clout. Yet the master of *Realpolitik* did not rely on mere personal charisma to achieve that end. On the contrary, he appealed to special interests—to hard-pressed landowners and farmers, bankers, industrialists, merchants, and shop-keepers—by indicating his wish to jettison liberal economics in favor of the interventionist state.

Bismarck's manifesto set the tone for the election campaign. Following his lead, the conservative and official press loosed a torrent of abuse against Bennigsen, Stauffenberg, Lasker, and other leaders. "Socialism is . . . one of the worst and yet just one of many horrors spawned by liberalism" was a typical accusation by the *Kreuzzeitung*. Centrist newspapers rejoiced that their moment of revenge against liberal persecutors had finally arrived, charging that the liberal attack on the church had weakened resistance to subversive doctrines.[38] Indeed the liberals had fallen into an evil situation. For six years they had voted with enthusiasm for exceptional laws against Catholics, the Reichstag's expulsion of the Jesuit order in 1872 being the most notable example. In voting against the *lex Hödel*, however, they went on record for the civil rights of socialists and other subversives.[39] In defending the liberal position before the Reichstag on May 23, Bennigsen sought to reconcile this contradiction by arguing lamely that the anti-Jesuit law had affected only hundreds, while the *lex Hödel* would affect hundreds of thousands.[40] After Nobiling's shots the contradiction could no longer be maintained, and the national liberals were eager to reverse themselves. By dissolving the chamber, Bismarck deprived them of the opportunity. Their political gyrations made the national liberals vulnerable to charges from the right of being "soft on radicalism" and from the left of being inconsistent and unprincipled.

By interpreting the election to voters as a struggle between the government and the liberals, Bismarck's manifesto aggravated the liberals' predicament. If moderates in the National Liberal party accepted the oppositional role thrust upon them by the chancellor and right-wing press, they would lend credence to Bismarck's charge that they had abdicated party leadership to the Lasker group. By repudiating that role, on the other hand, they would expose themselves to the charge of again capitulating to Bismarck and of sacrificing the remaining shreds of their liberalism. Both choices threatened the unity of the party. For moderates the first course was distasteful, for Lasker and his associates the latter.

Yet the need to preserve party unity triumphed for the time being over

---

[38] *Norddeutsche Allgemeine Zeitung*, No. 135, June 20, 1878; *Kreuzzeitung*, Nr. 176, Aug. 1, 1878. See the summaries of press opinion in Schümer, *Entstehungsgeschichte*, pp. 59–62, and in Pack, *Ringen*, pp. 57–73.

[39] See Tiedemann's remarks to Wehrenpfennig on this point. Tiedemann, *Sechs Jahre*, pp. 274–275.

[40] Oncken, *Bennigsen*, II, 369.

"THE BILL IS AIMED AT THE SOCIAL DEMOCRATS, BUT WHAT IF IT SHOULD FLY OVER ITS TARGET?"
WILHELM SCHOLZ IN *KLADDERADATSCH*, 1878.

Bismarck's effort to drive in the fatal wedge. Under Bennigsen's urging the party press moderated the polemical tone in which it replied to the provocations of the government and the right-wing press. Appalled by the consequences of his brief flirtation with the idea of constitutional reform, the Hanoverian strove to reassert his leadership over the party without alienating the left wing. In the interest of unity Lasker, under pressure from Stauffenberg and Stephani, permitted the election platform he had composed for the party to be defused of its "oppositional tendency." The national liberals, Stephani wrote to Bennigsen, must avoid giving the impression that the election contest was personal: Lasker contra Bismarck. Otherwise the result would be a fiasco, for on such an issue "we do not have the nation behind us." Bismarck's success in the Congress of Berlin had "mightily" increased his "authority and popularity." To attack him personally would make the national liberals the laughingstock of the country. The defeat would be so catastrophic that the "moderate middle parties" would lose their position of leadership for an indefinite time. "Unknown figures will replace each other in continuing fluctuation and change." Once they surmounted their initial panic and confusion, the national liberals fought the election against the socialists rather than against Bismarck, as a contest between parties supporting the state (*staatserhaltende*) and those inimical to it (*staatsfeindliche*).[41]

On July 30, 1878, the voters dealt the liberal parties another severe, although not a catastrophic defeat. In three elections (1874, 1877, and 1878)

[41] Oncken, *Bennigsen*, II, 374–380; Pack, *Ringen*, pp. 68–69.

the national liberals had declined from 155 to 128 to 99 seats, the progressives from 49 to 35 to 26. By contrast the conservatives had risen from 22 to 40 to 59, the free conservatives from 33 to 38 to 57, the centrists from 91 to 93 to 94. Distressing to Bismarck and liberals alike was the surprising success of the Guelph party, which grew from 4 to 10 seats, conquering more than half of the nineteen constituencies in the province of Hanover. Naturally the fortunes of the social democrats were scrutinized closely. Under the circumstances the decline in their voting strength was small (from 493,288 in 1877 to 437,158 voters in 1878). The decline in constituencies captured was proportionately greater (12 to 9); again cooperation among "bourgeois parties" in runoff elections robbed the social democrats of a representation (2.3 percent of the chamber) commensurate with their voting strength (7.6 percent of the electorate).[42]

Of equal interest was the fate of the left wing of the National Liberal party. Following Bismarck's lead, Lasker was made the general whipping boy of the conservative and official press. Carl Braun described the scene: "Whenever anything goes wrong somewhere, whenever someone loses money on a speculation, whenever business is bad, whenever someone has corns or suffers from a badly made shoe, he is told, 'Lasker is the cause of it. He made those bad laws under which you suffer.' "[43] In the attempt to unseat Lasker the free conservatives chose as their opposing candidate none other than Herbert von Bismarck, who ran with his father's blessing. The constituency, however, was in the duchy of Sachsen-Meiningen, outside the direct reach of the Prussian bureaucracy. Lasker won by a wide margin.[44] Stauffenberg too was singled out as a special target with the consequence that he lost in his old constituency at Munich; in the runoff election Bennigsen found for him a safe district in

---

[42] Bernhard Vogel, Dieter Nohlen, and Rainer-Olaf Schultze, *Wahlen in Deutschland: Theorie-Geschichte-Dokumente, 1848-1970* (Berlin, 1971), pp. 290–291.

[43] Quoted in Richard W. Dill, *Der Parlamentarier Eduard Lasker und die parlamentarische Stilentwicklung der Jahre 1867–1884* (Erlangen, 1956), p. 166.

[44] Bismarck vented his displeasure to the Duke of Sachsen-Meiningen, maintaining that the local *Landrat* had supported Lasker, with whom he was befriended. GW, VIc, 117–119. In the runoff election Herbert sought a seat at Ratzeburg in Lauenburg, where Friedrichsruh is located. But Bismarck's neighbors elected by a narrow margin the national liberal industrialist Friedrich Hammacher. Bernstorff to Bismarck, Aug. 1 and 3, 1878. DZA Potsdam, Reichskanzlei, 1825, pp. 1–2. Again, Bismarck intervened, blaming the result on unenthusiastic support by the local *Landrat* and on unfair tactics of the national liberals. His official protest was eventually rejected by the Reichstag's election commission. Bismarck to Boetticher, Aug. 11, 1878. *Ibid.*, pp. 3–4, and Bericht der Wahlprüfungs-Kommission, Mar. 27, 1879. *Ibid.*, pp. 26–27. Bismarck was no less interested in the election of his other son, Wilhelm, who was also defeated in the regular election. With Lucius's help, Tiedemann found him a seat at Langensalza in the runoff election, after securing the withdrawal of the free conservative candidate. Exchange of letters, Tiedemann and Wilhelm von Bismarck, Aug. 13, 20, and 21, 1878. *Ibid.*, pp. 5–14. This time Bismarck himself gave the order to make sure that government officials (*Landräte*) did their duty. Bismarck to Lucius, Aug. 23, 1878, and to Stolberg, Sept. 1, 1878. *Ibid.*, pp. 17–18.

Braunschweig. The other major figures of the left wing—Forckenbeck, Bamberger, Rickert—also survived the onslaught. Yet the left wing suffered proportionately greater losses than the right. Within the National Liberal party occurred in 1878 the same shift to the right that was evident in the electorate as a whole.[45]

Although its losses were not as great as some expected, the National Liberal party experienced in 1878 a severe psychological blow. For the first time since 1866 Prussia's moderate liberals had felt the full fury of Bismarck's assault and witnessed its effect on the voters. To non-Prussians among them the experience was totally new. Bred and educated in the idealist tradition, many did not relish the experience of being at odds with the "state," symbolized by Bismarck, the Kaiser, and the ruling order. Some were troubled by genuine doubt that the *Rechtsstaat* could protect society against radical subversion. Bismarck stated his price—by purging the party of Lasker and associates, the national liberals could return to that comfortable and fruitful relationship with the government that they had enjoyed for a decade. To many the price had begun to look worth paying.[46]

The Lex Nobiling

After returning to Berlin on June 3, 1878, Bismarck, who had barely recovered from his recent bouts with shingles and rheumatism, had to endure for four weeks the wear and tear of a European congress. At the outset the man upon whose skill, more than that of any other person, the peace of Europe depended, thought that his condition would not permit him to attend more than two or three sessions. Official business of any sort, he complained, robbed him of sleep.[47] Afterward, somewhat fortified psychologically by the success of the congress, he spent one month at Bad Kissingen followed by another at Bad Gastein. At the Bavarian spa he exchanged visits with the British Marquess of Lorne, who recorded his impressions. "He has grown stouter but still holds himself as erect as ever. He was very breathless after coming up the stairs, his eyes watered a great deal, and his look of a gallant great mastiff filling up the sofa was more marked than of old." Although Bismarck's eyes were blue, the impression they left on Lorne was "yellow brown."[48]

The prince was satisfied with the results of his Kissingen cure; to one of his visitors there he looked "physically strengthened." But Falk, who saw him later at Gastein, found him "uncommonly nervous and excited," full of com-

[45] Oncken, *Bennigsen*, II, 380–389.

[46] See particularly the quandary of Julius Hölder, as expressed in his diary. Hölder, *Tagebuch*, pp. 109–116.

[47] GW, VIII, 265.

[48] Duke of Argyll, *Passages from the Past* (London, 1907), I, 251–252.

plaints about the long-standing "conspiracy" (for which he cited dates and details) of the national liberals against him, about his earlier breach with the conservatives that had left him "a lonely man in old age," and about the "ingratitude of the world" that most statesmen experience. "I am tired and embittered; it would be for the best if the bullet of an assassin should kill me."[49]

Returning to Berlin on September 16, Bismarck plunged into the Reichstag debate on the new antisocialist bill and promptly fell ill. The medical diagnosis was urticaria, a skin inflammation arising either from infection or diet.[50] But Bismarck preferred another explanation: "The shorthand stenographers [of the Reichstag] turned against me in connection with my last speech [September 17]. As long as I was popular that was not the case. They garbled what I said so that there was no sense in it. When murmurs were heard from the Left or Center, they omitted the word 'Left,' and, when there was applause, they forgot to mention it. The whole bureau acts in the same way. But I have complained to the president. It was that which made me ill. It was like the illness produced by oversmoking, a stuffiness in the head, giddiness, a disposition to vomit, etc."[51] Although he was out of bed again after two days, the resumption of business soon wore him out. Despite a week at Varzin (September 23–29) and nearly two weeks at Friedrichsruh (October 22–November 3), he felt compelled to request another extended leave. "My health leaves much to be desired," he wrote to Wilhelm on November 9. "I need absolute quiet for a while; I haven't had that for a long time."[52] Since May 14, 1875, the German chancellor had spent 772 out of 1,275 days either at a spa or on one of his estates. To be sure, he was not always idle during those long absences. But the business of government surely suffered, and his critics were certainly justified in questioning, as did he, whether he was any longer able to govern.

As Bismarck anticipated, the election of 1878 ended conclusively the possibility that the two liberal parties could dominate the Reichstag. The parliament was now divided into three major groups of approximately equal strength: liberals, conservatives, centrists. Hence Bismarck appeared to have a choice between two majorities: the conservative parties could be combined with either the Center party or National Liberal party.[53] The former course required the liquidation or, at best, moderation of the Kulturkampf.

To the master of *Realpolitik* it had long been evident that the assault on the Center party and the Catholic church could not be conducted simultaneously

---

[49] See Falk's relation to Bennigsen in Oncken, *Bennigsen*, II, 382, 387–388; Förster, *Falk*, pp. 490–492.

[50] *BR*, II, 166–167.

[51] Busch, *Tagebuchblätter*, II, 535.

[52] Horst Kohl, ed., *Anhang zu den Gedanken und Erinnerungen von Otto Fürst von Bismarck* (Stuttgart, 1901), I, 281–282.

[53] Oncken, *Bennigsen*, II, 389.

with the opening of new fronts against socialists and left-liberals. Hence it was hardly coincidental that the first positive signs of a willingness to settle the Kulturkampf appeared in late 1875 when he first formulated his new objectives in domestic affairs at Varzin.[54] Yet his determination not to "go to Canossa" was genuine; what he wanted was reconciliation without surrender. The news that Pius IX was dead, telegraphed to Varzin on February 8, 1878, put Bismarck in a good mood. "We must drink to that," he exclaimed, ordering a bottle of Nordhäuser.[55] A second telegram that arrived in Berlin on February 20 announced the election (as Pope Leo XIII) of Cardinal Pecci, who was rumored to be conciliatory. But Bismarck was skeptical: "When lions change into lambs, the waves will flow backwards."[56] In March Leo announced his succession to Wilhelm in a friendly message, to which the Kaiser replied in kind. By mid-April there was considerable optimism in the German diplomatic corps and among high church officials over the prospect of a settlement, but Bismarck was less sanguine. A second message from the Vatican dated April 17 seemed to confirm his suspicion that the pope's price for peace was too high; namely, repeal of the May laws and restoration of articles 15, 16, and 18 in the Prussian constitution. Yet Leo sent out so many peace feelers in May and June that it became impossible to doubt his desire to treat.[57]

While at Bad Kissingen Bismarck conferred repeatedly with the papal nuncio, Cardinal Aloisi Masella (July 30–August 16). Although the discussions were cordial, both men realized that their positions were irreconcilable. The Nuncios spoke for the restoration of the relationship between church and state existing before 1870, the chancellor for that existing before 1840. Instead of seeking a general settlement, they discussed a truce, Bismarck offering to go "a little way toward Canossa," by moderating execution of the May laws, if the Vatican would exert a favorable influence on the centrists, Poles, and ultramontane press.[58] Actually the prince believed that even this modus vivendi could only be achieved "very gradually, a drop at a time." For the time being, the Vatican must be given the impression that Berlin was happy with the status quo and had no need to change it.[59]

His experiences in the Kulturkampf had made Bismarck less optimistic than

---

[54] See his remarks to Heinrich von Sybel and Edwin von Manteuffel as quoted in Erich Schmidt-Volkmar, *Der Kulturkampf in Deutschland, 1871–1890* (Göttingen, 1962), pp. 202–203. See also Bismarck to Gossler, July 22, 1881. GW, VIc, 218–219.

[55] Tiedemann, *Sechs Jahre*, p. 231.

[56] Lucius, *Bismarck-Erinnerungen*, p. 128.

[57] Förster, *Falk*, pp. 529ff.; Schmidt-Volkmar, *Kulturkampf*, pp. 226–227; GW, VIc, 115. The rapprochement began gingerly on both sides. Bismarck refused to receive the pope's first message to the Kaiser, because it came through the wrong channel—the papal nuncio at Munich, not the Bavarian government. The pope on the other hand, took umbrage at the delay in the Kaiser's reply and at its language—German.

[58] Schmidt-Volkmar, *Kulturkampf*, p. 235.

[59] To Falk, Aug. 8, 1878. Förster, *Falk*, pp. 535–536.

he had been in 1871 about the authority of the pope over Catholics in other than religious matters. "The Center party is a force that he can use to attack us but not to support us, even if he should honestly and lastingly intend to do so." If the Center party should dissolve, he reasoned, most of its fragments would reemerge as Guelphs, south German particularists, progressives, pro-Austrian great-Germanists, pro-French Alsatians, and other malcontented groups. Their hostility toward Prussia and the German Reich had other

MODUS VIVENDI. LEO XIII, OFFERING HIS FOOT FOR KISSING: "NOW, PLEASE, DON'T BE SHY ABOUT THIS!" BISMARCK, RETURNING THE COURTESY: "YOU LIKEWISE, PLEASE!" WINDTHORST PEERS ANXIOUSLY THROUGH THE CURTAINS. WILHELM SCHOLZ IN *KLADDERADATSCH*, 1878.

grounds than merely their Catholicism. "The pope," he told Falk in late August, "does not have the least influence on the Center party." Hence the Kulturkampf would have to continue for a time. Perhaps in ten to fifteen years the German schools would create by their work of "national education" a better basis for ending it. For the time being, however, it would be unwise to let the public know that there was no prospect of a settlement. "In my opinion the uncertainty must be maintained as long as possible. The belief in an approaching reconciliation between state and curia will unquestionably be beneficial for the conduct of the curia, the Center, and the liberal parties."[60]

That Bismarck had met with Masella in Kissingen was reported in the German press, and the *Kreuzzeitung* jumped to the conclusion that the chancellor had conclusively broken with the National Liberal party.[61] But this was not at all the case; the Kissingen talks with Masella had merely confirmed that the chancellor was still dependent, at least for the time being, upon the national liberals for his legislative program. In mid-August he found an opportunity to present his terms to Bennigsen and colleagues through Robert von Benda, a right-wing liberal deputy who happened to be in Kissingen. Violating his own instructions to Falk (did he expect Bennigsen not to believe him?), he admitted to Benda that the centrists were "unusable" and that the talks with Masella, although "very serious" in intent, could produce nothing more than a modus vivendi. Yet he expressed satisfaction over the results of the election. "Now we have learned that the country thinks much differently than did the old Reichstag." What he hoped for, he said, was a firmer cohesion between the "three parties friendly to the government" and the expulsion from the National Liberal party of about two dozen deputies who really belonged among the progressives. "Always the same old song," commented Benda. The deputy objected that the loss of so many members would jeopardize the majority, but the chancellor insisted on the accuracy of his calculation. Finally, Bismarck reiterated three times another "old song." "On the whole . . . the party caucuses, whether conservative or liberal, are for him completely indifferent, today more than ever. He will go his own way. Those who go with him are his friends; those who oppose him are enemies—to the last breath." If the goal was not attained now, there could be a second and even third dissolution. "I do not want it, but it could come to that."[62]

What Bismarck wanted of the National Liberal party was what he demanded of his colleagues in the Prussian government: unconditional subordination. The language he used and attitudes he displayed are reminiscent of his arguments for the reorientation of Prussian foreign policy during the decade before he came to power in 1862—indifference to political idealism,

[60] Bismarck to Falk, Aug. 8, 1878, and conversation with Falk on Aug. 29–30, 1878, at Bad Gastein. Förster, *Falk*, pp. 533–536, 538–541. See also *GW*, VIII, 268.

[61] Oncken, *Bennigsen*, II, 383 (fn.); *Kreuzzeitung*, Nr. 182, Aug. 7, 1878.

[62] Robert von Benda to Bennigsen, mid-August 1878. Oncken, *Bennigsen*, II, 382–383, also *GW*, VIII, 269.

resolute pursuit of self-interest, and ruthless use of the tactic of alternative choice. Yet his range of options had been seriously narrowed by the folly of the Kulturkampf. The prejudices and near paranoid fears that had led him into the attack on the Catholic church had caused him to violate his own philosophy of political realism. In the 1850s he had contended that Prussia could not afford to leave covered any squares on the chessboard of European politics. But the Kulturkampf had removed nearly one-third of the Reichstag from the field of play. For all his talk of "complete indifference" about allies, Bismarck was still dependent upon national liberals for the execution of his policies. Hence he had to hammer away at the party's contours in order to reshape it to fit his needs.

When the Reichstag convened on September 9, 1878, the national liberals, chastened by recent experiences, were ready to vote for an antisocialist bill.[63] The only issue was to what degree they would follow Lasker and his left-wing allies in seeking to limit the bill's infringement of civil rights. Even Lasker favored strengthening the criminal code against subversives; yet he was as opposed on principle to an "exceptional law" against socialists as he had been against the Jesuit law of 1872. Although hostility toward him was growing within the party, Lasker was too important not to be included among the seven national liberals chosen for the ad hoc committee of twenty-one members, chaired by Bennigsen, that was established to consider the government's bill. During its sessions in late September he introduced a number of amendments intended to mitigate the bill's more draconian features. This earned him a sharp attack in the Norddeutsche Allgemeine Zeitung (obviously stemming from Bismarck), which shook the deputies by threatening another dissolution. Hurrying back and forth between the chancellor and national liberal caucus, Bennigsen produced another of those familiar "compromises" that had marked the course of the moderates since 1866—it gave the chancellor most, although not all, of what he wanted. In the crucial party caucus on October 9, Lasker complained bitterly that Bennigsen had left him uninformed and unconsulted. But the Hanoverian had so outmaneuvered Lasker that only two other deputies (Stauffenberg and Bamberger) came to his support.[64]

The antisocialist law of October 21, 1878, outlawed "social-democratic, socialistic, and communistic" organizations that aimed to overthrow the ex-

[63] Needing their support, Bismarck avoided conflict by advising conservatives to vote for the reelection of Forckenbeck as president. More suprising was the reelection of Stauffenberg as first vice-president, but this was owing to the tactical situation in the voting. The first ballot showed a three-way division between Stauffenberg, a conservative, and a centrist. The conservative candidate withdrew, and Stauffenberg received the liberal and free conservative votes, the latter in return for the reelection of Hohenlohe-Langenburg as second vice-president. The conservatives either withheld their votes or voted for the centrist—an ominous development. Oncken, Bennigsen, II, 390.

[64] Oncken, Bennigsen, II, 387–393; Dill, Lasker, pp. 167–168.

isting political and social order or whose activities endangered the public peace, "especially harmony between the social classes." Publications could be forbidden and assemblies dissolved in which such tendencies became evident. Officers of, and even landlords providing quarters for, prohibited organizations could be imprisoned up to one year, organization members up to three months plus a fine of 500 marks. Convicted agitators could be refused sojourn in "designated districts and places" and denied residence where they had lived for less than six months. Offending proprietors of inns, taverns, liquor stores, publishing houses, bookstores, lending libraries, and reading rooms could be fined, imprisoned, and put out of business. With Bundesrat approval "limited martial law" could be declared in "endangered" districts, permitting police to prohibit public meetings, halt the distribution of printed matter, and deport agitators. Lasker's only achievement was a clause limiting duration of the statute to March 31, 1881—a concession extracted from Bismarck by Bennigsen in the interest of preserving party unity. In the final vote on October 19, the national liberals—Lasker included, albeit reluctantly—joined with conservatives and free conservatives to outvote, 221 to 149, an opposition composed of centrists, progressives, and social democrats.[65]

Although too much for Lasker, the antisocialist law did not go far enough for Bismarck. He was sharply critical of the way Botho Eulenburg managed the bill in the Bundesrat and of certain features incorporated in it even before it reached the Reichstag. He would have preferred, for example, a clause providing for the dismissal, without pension rights, of government officials who were socialists. "The majority of the poorly paid subaltern officials in Berlin and, in addition, the railway signalmen, switchmen, and workers in similar categories are socialists, a fact of obvious danger in the event of uprisings and troop movements. If the law is to be effective, I do not believe it possible to let citizens, legally proven to be socialists, retain the right to vote, the right to stand for election, and the pleasure and privilege of sitting in the Reichstag."[66] In the Reichstag during October 1878, Bismarck continued publicly to express confidence in the efficacy of universal male suffrage,[67] but privately he had already begun to speculate on its abolition. "I consider the [antisocialist] statute just a first step," he told Lucius, "which must be followed by others."[68]

[65] SBR (1878), I, 387–389; RGB (1878), pp. 351–358.

[66] GW, VIc, 116–120; GW, VIII, 268. Also cabinet meeting of Apr. 24, 1879, DZA Merseburg, Rep. 90a, B, III, 2b, Nr. 6, Vol. 91.

[67] BR, VII, 261.

[68] Lucius, Bismarck-Erinnerungen, p. 143; Förster, Falk, pp. 489–490. According to a Bavarian delegate to the Bundesrat, Hofmann admitted (June 7, 1878) that "further measures" against social democrats were being considered, including a "reform" of the election law. For the time being, however, it was inadvisable to "put the question into the foreground." Ivo Lambi, Free Trade and Protection in Germany 1868–1879. Vierteljahrschrift für Sozial- und Wirtschaftsgeschichte, 44 (Wiesbaden, 1963), pp. 173–174.

CHAPTER FOURTEEN

Balkan Crisis and Congress of Berlin

URING his extended leave at Varzin in the summer and fall of 1875, Bismarck had the chance not only to rethink his internal policy but also to absorb the lessons of the war-in-sight crisis. The attempt to isolate and bully France into abandoning the rebuilding of its army had failed, as had the effort to garner support abroad for the Prussian Kulturkampf. The only consequence of these actions had been to give the French and Russian foreign ministers the opportunity to demonstrate to Bismarck that an aggressive, threatening foreign policy could only end in Germany's isolation and that the great powers of Europe would close ranks to prevent any additional disruption of the balance of power system. Although the German chancellor remained irritated by the diplomatic defeat he had suffered in May 1875 and the manner of its infliction, he realistically concluded that his tactics, although not his grand strategy, had to change.

His basic objective remained the same, that of isolating France, assuring Germany of at least two allies in an unstable equilibrium of five and finding those allies preferably in Russia and Austria. He remained as convinced as ever that the French were a volatile and vengeful people, whose friendship could not be won. Much depended, however, on who governed France and under what form of government. A republic, particularly one established by the narrowest of margins, was of no advantage to Germany unless governed by republicans. As long as the monarchial and clerical faction under Mac-Mahon held power, he considered France an active danger to Germany.[1] Yet the new policy Bismarck adopted toward France after 1875, that of distraction and diversion, had the virtue that it could be pursued toward a conservative as well as a radical republican government. The greatest danger to Bismarck's grand strategy in 1875–1880 came, however, not from a resurgent France but from the prospect that Russia would become involved in a war against Austria or England or both.

Emergence of the Eastern Crisis

The embroilment that produced this threat was again the "eastern question," the most persistent source of international friction in Europe from 1815 to 1914. After twenty years of relative quiescence, the problem again became

---

[1] Freiherr Lucius von Ballhausen, *Bismarck-Erinnerungen* (Stuttgart, 1920), p. 113.

acute owing to a series of rebellions and wars by Balkan peoples against the Ottoman Empire that began in July 1875 with an uprising in the provinces of Bosnia and Herzegovina.[2] The rebels had mixed motives: religion (Christian versus Moslem), nationalism (southern Slavs against Turks), government (corruption, inequitable taxation, an incompetent judiciary), and economics (poor peasants against Moslem landlords). Without outside help and encouragement the insurgency would scarcely have become important. But German and Italian unification had aroused nationalistic aspirations everywhere. Serbia aspired to unite the southern Slavs into a single state; for two decades Slavic nationalists in Russia had fostered a Panslav movement calling for the union of all European Slavs under Russian leadership, an objective that could only be achieved through dissolution of the Habsburg and Ottoman empires. Within the Habsburg monarchy some groups were eager to annex Bosnia and Herzegovina—military men, who desired a more defensible frontier behind Austria's exposed Dalmatian coast, and Croats, who longed for a southern Slav union that would lead to the conversion of the Dual into a Triple Monarchy. Like fellow Magyars, Andrássy was opposed to the incorporation of more Slavs in the Habsburg Empire. The Ottoman Empire, he believed, was a necessary barrier to the advance of national movements in the Balkans, movements that, if successful, would "ruin" the Dual Monarchy and make it the "sick man" of Europe.[3] The monarchy's German liberals also believed that the Ottoman Empire had to be preserved if Austrian business interests were to succeed in developing the lower Danube and controlling the railway route to Saloniki. The empire's disintegration, furthermore, would open opportunities for Russian economic and political penetration into the Balkans. With strong support from Germans and Magyars, neither of whom wished to include more Slavs in the Habsburg Empire, Andrássy sought to dampen the revolt by securing concessions from Constantinople for the rebels. On his initiative the European powers instructed their consuls in August 1875 to try to settle the dispute, and, when this failed, Andrássy gained the support of the powers for a reform program to be forced upon the government in Constantinople. But the reforms demanded in the "Andrássy note" (December 30, 1875) came to naught, for they were too much for the Porte and too little

[2] On the origins of the Balkan crisis of the late 1870s and the reactions of the European powers toward it see: Richard Millman, *Britain and the Eastern Question, 1875–1878* (Oxford, 1979); David MacKenzie, *The Serbs and Russian Pan-Slavism, 1875–1878* (Ithaca, 1967); Mihailo D. Stojanovic, *The Great Powers and the Balkans, 1875–1878* (New York, 1939); B. H. Sumner, *Russia and the Balkans, 1870–1880* (Oxford, 1937); George H. Rupp, *A Wavering Friendship: Russia and Austria, 1876–1878* (Cambridge, Mass., 1941); David Harris, *A Diplomatic History of the Balkan Crisis of 1875–1878: The First Year* (Stanford, 1936); R. W. Seton-Watson, *Disraeli, Gladstone and the Eastern Question: A Study in Diplomacy and Party Politics* (London, 1935); and Nicholas Der Bagdasarian, *The Austro-German Rapprochement, 1870–1879* (Cranbury, N.J., 1976).

[3] Rupp, *Wavering Friendship*, p. 39; Bagdasarian, *Austro-German Rapprochement*, pp. 183ff.

for the insurgents. During the spring of 1876 the Turkish army made little progress against the rebels, and the rebellion began to spread.[4]

The conflicting counsels and interests that characterized the Habsburg Empire were evident also in Russia and Britain. Since the Crimean disaster Russia had satisfied its imperialistic hunger in the east, expanding its borders on the weaker Asiatic front and remaining on the defensive in the west. Tsar Alexander II and his closest advisers believed that this policy must be continued until Russia had completed the internal consolidation that began with the social and political reforms of the 1860s. Without that consolidation Russia was not powerful enough, fiscally and militarily, to contest with the great powers of central and western Europe for control over the Balkans. And yet Panslav agitation, which penetrated the most diverse groups within the middle and upper strata of Russian society, subjected the government to pressures it could not ignore. Although Alexander made the chief decisions in foreign policy, he was dependent for counsel and execution upon Chancellor Gorchakov, who, now in his late seventies, was disinclined to be adventurous. Gorchakov was subject to contradictory pressures and persuasions by his subordinates, including two whom he suspected of wanting to succeed him: Count Peter Shuvalov, ambassador to Britain, and General Nikolay Ignatyev, ambassador to the Ottoman Empire. The former was a conservative supporter of Russia's partnership in the Three Emperors League; the latter, a dedicated Panslav.[5]

The developing crisis in the Near East became a testing ground for Disraeli's resolve, on taking office in February 1874, that Britain must play a more active role in continental affairs. Since completion of the Suez Canal in 1869, the eastern Mediterranean had become the most sensitive region in British foreign policy. That Suez was the "key to India" had become the undisputed dogma of British strategic thinking. In November 1875 the Egyptian Knedive put his share (46 percent) of the Suez Canal Company up for sale, and, while French financiers haggled, Disraeli acted. Although the controlling interest in the company remained with Ferdinand de Lesseps's company, the prime minister exulted that France was no longer in a position to shut up the canal in any future crisis, severing Britain's shortest route to India. By the same token, he was convinced that Britain must seek to preserve the Ottoman Empire, especially Constantinople and the Straits, from Russian penetration. The empire must stand as a buffer protecting the eastern Mediterranean from

---

[4] Eduard von Wertheimer, *Graf Julius Andrássy: Sein Leben und Seine Zeit* (Vienna, 1910–1913), II, 252–277; Theodor von Sosnosky, *Die Balkanpolitik Österreich-Ungarns seit 1866* (Stuttgart, 1913–1914), I, 127–149; Harris, *Balkan Crisis*, pp. 132–287.

[5] Dietrich Geyer, *Der russische Imperialismus: Studien über den Zusammenhang von innerer und auswärtiger Politik 1860–1914. Kritische Studien zur Geschichtswissenschaft*, vol. 27 (Göttingen, 1977), pp. 56–66; MacKenzie, *Serbs and Pan-Slavism*, pp. 27–29; B. H. Summer, *Russia and the Balkans*, pp. 18–35, 56–80.

Russian expansion. And yet Disraeli's unfortunate choice as foreign secretary, Lord Derby, was a mistrustful and withdrawn man, who tended to oppose any decisive action that might result in war.[6]

Initially Bismarck welcomed the Balkan uprising, for it diverted attention of governments and the public away from the "French-German question" and the drubbing he had recently suffered in the war-in-sight crisis.[7] His basic premise was that Germany had no direct interest in the Balkans; the problems of the Ottoman Empire were of importance to Germany only for their effect upon the relationships between the other great powers. If Austria and Russia came to blows over the issue, Germany might have to choose between them, and the rejected suitor would very likely seek support in France. Again and again he insisted that Germany would agree to no proposition by Austria or Russia regarding the Balkans until those powers had reached an agreement with each other. War between Britain and Russia over the Turkish legacy was less dangerous for Germany than one between Austria and Russia, but only relatively so, for Austria might be tempted, as in the Crimean War, to enter the conflict.[8] To avoid such a chain reaction, Bismarck naturally supported Andrássy's peace initiatives in the Ottoman Empire. Since Alexander and Gorchakov also cooperated, the Three Emperors League appeared to have found a new common purpose. In fact, all of the signatory powers of the Paris treaty of 1856 (including France, Italy, and, albeit reluctantly, Britain) supported the Andrássy note. Superficially, the old concert of Europe had been reborn. And yet there was general skepticism that the decline and dissolution of the Ottoman Empire could be halted. Now the question was what should take its place.[9]

In late November 1875 Bismarck returned to Berlin with a partial answer to this question that would have enabled Berlin to recover the central role in the European balance of power so laboriously established during 1864–1873. His objective was obviously that which he later described in the "Kissingen dictation": "a total political situation, in which all powers, except France, need us and are kept from coalitions against us as much as possible by their relations to each other."[10] His first step was an attempted rapprochement with Britain. In November he warmly approved London's purchase of Suez Canal Company shares, and on January 2, 1876, he told Ambassador Odo Russell of his desire for a "frank and cordial understanding" with the Disraeli cabinet

[6] On Derby see especially Millman, *Britain and the Eastern Question*, pp. 1–12, and Robert Blake, *Disraeli* (London, 1966), pp. 581–587.

[7] Bismarck to Wilhelm I, Aug. 13, 1875. Horst Kohl, ed., *Anhang zu den Gedanken und Erinnerungen von Otto Fürst von Bismarck* (Stuttgart, 1901), I, 260.

[8] GW, VIII, 182–183.

[9] Harris, *Balkan Crisis*, pp. 140–153; MacKenzie, *Serbs and Pan-Slavism*, pp. 69–73; GP, I, 207–208.

[10] GP, II, 153–154.

on the Balkan problem. Germany, he explained, could neither afford to let Austria and Russia "become too intimate behind her back" nor "let them quarrel with safety to herself." Peace depended, he declared, upon the cooperation of those powers, but there was danger that Andrássy might be swept aside by annexationists in Vienna eager to intervene in the Balkans. Three days later he suggested to Russian Ambassador Paul d'Oubril that the best way to buttress Andrássy's position would be to arrange an "arrondissement" for Austria in Bosnia in exchange for "advantages" for Russia in Bessarabia. He believed that Britain would accept "similar bagatelles" in order to fulfill her objectives at Suez. "I ask for just one thing—to be charged with preparing the English cabinet and getting its agreement for this combination."[11] On February 19 Bismarck advised the British that war could be avoided in the Balkan crisis only in two ways: cordial cooperation among the powers to maintain the territorial status quo and, if that were unsuccessful, an amicable settlement among the powers concerning "what should be done with Turkey." Being "territorially saturated," Germany had no interest in the matter other than to preserve the peace in Europe. But the British response to these overtures was cool and dilatory, and Gorchakov declined to concede to Bismarck such a brilliant role. The Russian chancellor wrote to Oubril that Bismarck, like Napoleon III in his time, reminded him of *le grand tentateur sur le montagne.*[12]

The failure of the Andrássy note, followed by the spread of the Balkan rebellion to Bulgaria and the murder of the German and French consuls at Saloniki, gave new urgency to the Balkan crisis in April–May 1876. On May 11–14 the foreign ministers of the Three Emperors League met in Berlin to consider what further steps should be taken against Turkey. Moved by rising Panslav agitation, Gorchakov arrived with a proposal for a European conference to force Turkey to accept reforms in the insurgent region—to be supervised by an international commission backed by a military occupation. In a private conference before the tripartite meeting Bismarck repeated to Andrássy his proposal for a mutual rectification of frontiers, for Austria in Bosnia and Russia in Bessarabia. But Andrássy rejected such drastic steps, and the three powers accepted his program (the "Berlin memorandum"), calling for a European initiative to effect a two months' armistice for the execution of reforms and a naval demonstration at Constantinople by the six signatory powers of the 1856 Treaty of Paris.

On May 13, Gorchakov, as the eldest of the three chancellors, presented their joint proposal to the ambassadors of the other three nations—Britain,

[11] Winifried Taffs, *Ambassador to Bismarck* (London, 1938), pp. 116–122; Millman, *Britain and the Eastern Question*, pp. 60–73; Serge Goriainov, *Le Bosphore et les Dardanelles* (Paris, 1910), pp. 314–315, and *La question d'orient a la veille du traité de Berlin, 1870–1876* (Paris, 1948), pp. 65–66.

[12] Taffs, *Ambassador to Bismarck*, pp. 130–131; Goriainov, *La Question*, p. 66.

France, and Italy—in his polished, oratorical French (Bismarck doodled: "Pompon, pompo, pomp, po!"). He would like an affirmative answer, Gorchakov declared, before his and Andrássy's departure from Berlin on May 15. Although France and Italy complied, Disraeli and his colleagues were offended by the subordinate role London was expected to play in the affair and by the peremptory treatment (May 13–15 was a weekend, hardly a time to get action out of a British cabinet). They refused to "put a knife to Turkey's throat," a country whose survival was still an axiom of British policy. Gorchakov returned to Russia outraged by the British attitude, a mood that influenced his conduct in the following months. Bismarck, however, "fell into a fit of laughing" over the Russian chancellor's discomfiture.[13]

An Untimely Question

As so often in the past, events in the Balkans had a way of forcing the powers to engage in actions contrary to their original intentions. The seeming paralysis of the sultan's government encouraged other Balkan peoples to join the attack. In the late spring of 1876 the Bulgarians rebelled, and at the end of June Serbia and Montenegro were emboldened to declare war against Turkey with the aim of uniting the southern Slavs under a single crown. The future of the Ottoman Empire was no longer a hypothetical problem. The European powers were now compelled to cope with what they apparently could no longer avoid. In contemplating the possibilities of the Balkan situation, the powers were beset by fear tempered by avarice. The task of preserving peace among the great powers, still Bismarck's primary objective, became more difficult. In October, he summarized the problem: "The question whether we are to be brought into permanent friction with England, even more with Austria, and most of all with Russia over the Eastern tangle is infinitely more important for Germany's future than all the relations of Turkey to her subjects and to the European powers."[14]

The Serbian-Montenegrin attack on Turkey brought Panslav agitation in Russia to a new peak. Russian volunteers and contributions of goods and money began to flow toward Belgrade. Officially Alexander and Gorchakov held to a policy of nonintervention despite mounting public pressure. But secretly they approached Austria in search of an agreement for the protection of their respective interests whoever the victor, Turk or Slav. Andrássy now accepted the likelihood that his policy of promoting Turkish reform had failed and that Austria must assure for itself a proper share of Bosnia-Herzegovina in view of the expected victory of the Serbs. On July 8, 1876, Franz Joseph

[13] Harris, *Balkan Crisis*, pp. 276–376, 447–456; Millman, *Britain and the Eastern Question*, pp. 87–101; W. F. Monypenny and G. E. Buckle, *The Life of Benjamin Disraeli* (London, 1910–1920), IV, 897, 904; Sumner, *Russia and the Balkans*, pp. 164–165.

[14] *GP*, II, 64.

and Alexander met at Reichstadt in Bohemia, where their foreign ministers worked out a secret agreement—or thought they did (there was no common text)—on how to protect Balkan peoples if the Turks won and how to divide Balkan soil if the Slavs triumphed. Subsequently the participants disputed what each had obtained or yielded at Reichstadt. What had seemed so obvious in July that it need not be written down became obfuscated within weeks by the unexpected victory of the Turks and the enlarged objectives of the contracting parties.[15]

Their eagerness to come to terms at Reichstadt had been stimulated by the failure of both to reach agreement with Britain. Following its rejection of the Berlin memorandum in May 1876, the British government ordered a naval unit to Besika Bay at the mouth of the Dardanelles. But otherwise the London cabinet temporized, Derby out of timidity and indecision, Disraeli because he was too old and decrepit to take over the Foreign Office, with whose performance he was increasingly dissatisfied. But as the summer progressed the shifting current of British public opinion made it increasingly difficult for the British government to continue the traditional policy of supporting the integrity of the Ottoman Empire.

In October 1875 the Balkan rebellions had upset the precarious balance of the Turkish treasury, compelling the Porte to default on huge loans obtained over decades from British and French banks at high rates of interest. While this pained the financiers, the public was inflamed by rumors of the severity with which Turkish irregular troops quickly put down the Bulgarian uprising. In June, July, and August 1876 newspapers carried lurid accounts of Turkish atrocities against the Bulgars and in July Disraeli and Derby answered parliamentary interpellations by claiming the reports were exaggerated. On September 6, 1876, Gladstone's famous pamphlet on *The Bulgarian Horrors and the Question of the East* was published, of which forty thousand copies were quickly sold. Violence and brutality had occurred on both sides in the Ottoman embroglio, but the British public had ears only for the sins of the Turks. As popular hostility toward the Turks rose, the British government, like its counterparts in Petersburg and Vienna, began to consider what Britain must gain from the seemingly inevitable partition of the Ottoman Empire.[16]

In July and August 1876 the Turkish army scored a series of victories over the Serbs. The defeat of the Serbs, despite the help of Russian volunteers (including a Russian general, who assumed command), increased the pressure of Panslavs and imperialistic army officers for Russian armed intervention, if

[15] George H. Rupp, "The Reichstadt Agreement," *American Historical Review*, 30 (1925), pp. 503–510, and *Wavering Friendship*, pp. 111–151. For both Austrian and Russian versions of the "agreement" see Sumner, *Russia and the Balkans*, pp. 583–588.

[16] Millman, *Britain and the Eastern Question*, pp. 27–30, 101–191; David Harris, *Britain and the Bulgarian Horrors of 1876* (Chicago, 1939); R. T. Shannon, *Gladstone and the Bulgarian Agitation, 1876* (London, 1963).

not in behalf of the Serbs, whose performance had been disappointing, then of the Bulgars, whose fate had aroused the sympathies of all Europe. Popular revulsion in Britain against Turkish atrocities raised doubts in Petersburg that England would stand in the way, particularly if Russia's actions were proclaimed as necessary to save Christian peoples from Moslem barbarism.[17] In bucolic Varzin Bismarck followed this development with detachment. He believed that a Russian war on Turkey was not only an inevitable but also a desirable outcome of the crisis—as long as Russia acted in harmony with Austria in planning its objectives in the struggle. On September 13, he learned from Andrássy for the first time the extent of the Reichstadt "agreement"—as the Austrians understood it.[18] The powers appeared to be adopting the solution Bismarck had repeatedly urged: mutual compensation through partial dismemberment of the Ottoman Empire.

And yet Bismarck was uneasy that autumn about German relations with Russia. In late August he began to fear that frequent charges in the Russian press that Germany was "cool" toward Panslav aspirations, in conjunction with other "unfriendly" (Gorchakov) influences at the Russian court, might adversely affect the tsar's attitude. He was compelled, furthermore, to risk offending Gorchakov by declining the chancellor's proposal that Germany call for a European conference to deal with the Balkan problem, lest German foreign policy be engaged in behalf of purely Russian objectives. Another source of uneasiness was a hiatus in German representation at the Russian court. Ambassador Lothar von Schweinitz was on leave, hunting in the Austrian Alps, and Bismarck had no confidence in Oubril, a Roman Catholic, whom he suspected of papism and intrigue. Hence Bismarck advised Wilhelm to send Field Marshal Edwin von Manteuffel to the tsar, then attending military maneuvers at Warsaw. Manteuffel bore a personal letter from the Kaiser (dated September 2) in which Wilhelm assured his nephew, "The memory of your attitude toward me and my country from 1864 to 1870–1871 will guide my policy toward Russia, whatever comes."[19] On September 8, Manteuffel returned from Warsaw, reporting that, although Alexander and Gorchakov were nettled by Bismarck's refusal to comply with their conference proposal, the tsar was clearly touched by Wilhelm's assurances of benevolent neutrality if war proved necessary against the Turks. "I like to count on you," he wrote to Wilhelm, "as you will always be able to count on me" (Bismarck: "The only question is how far?").[20]

[17] William L. Langer, *European Alliances and Alignments, 1871–1890* (2d ed., New York, 1956), pp. 95–96; MacKenzie, *Serbs and Pan-Slavism*, pp. 112–152; Rupp, *Wavering Friendship*, pp. 152ff.

[18] GP, II, 45–47.

[19] GP, II, 34–38.

[20] GP, II, 38–45.

Manteuffel also conveyed Alexander's wish for a "declaration in some form or other to the effect that Russia has the sympathies of Germany in the eastern question." Bismarck was leery of any such declaration, which in any event could only reiterate what Wilhelm had already written. But on September 14 Oubril came to State Secretary Bernhard von Bülow, Bismarck's right arm in the foreign office at Berlin, and reported that Alexander wanted answers to two questions he claimed to have asked Manteuffel in Warsaw: What would Germany's attitude be, if Russia's "dignity" required her to act independently? What diplomatic action Bismarck would propose, since he was disinclined to accept the Russian proposal for a six-power conference?[21] Bismarck found that such questions, delivered orally and almost casually, were contrary to diplomatic form. Gorchakov, he reasoned, could not have commissioned Oubril to ask them, unless he had some ulterior purpose. In any case, the first question had already been answered in Wilhelm's letter of September 2, and the second Bismarck branded an "impertinence." He ordered that no full answer be given to Oubril, whom he believed deceitful.[22]

Two weeks later, however, it became evident that the tsar, now at Livadia in the Crimea, was getting impatient. On October 1, General von Werder, the German military attaché, telegraphed from Livadia that Alexander urgently wanted a response to another question he claimed (Bismarck: "*not true!*") to have asked Manteuffel at Warsaw: "Would Germany act as Russia did in 1870, if Russia went to war with Austria?"[23] In this most peculiar and irregular way Bismarck was suddenly confronted with the critical question he had hoped to avoid. He was being asked bluntly to choose between Germany's two allies in the Three Emperors League.

Bismarck had no way of knowing how Alexander had progressed within three weeks from concern about Germany's attitude toward Russia in the event of war against Turkey to concern about how Germany would act should Russia go to war against Austria. At Livadia the tsar was surrounded by generals, Panslavists, and imperialists eager for action in the Balkans. On September 21, he signed an order for partial mobilization in Russia's southwestern military districts. Simultaneously he dispatched to Vienna a special emissary, Count Felix Sumarokov-Elston, to seek (September 21–October 4) a redefinition of the Reichstadt agreement. In both Vienna and London (but not in Berlin) the Russians proposed that: Austria occupy Bosnia; Russia occupy Bulgaria; and the great powers send fleets to the Bosphorus to overawe the Turks. Franz Joseph and Andrássy were favorable to the first of these propositions, but not to the second; the British were opposed to the second and

[21] GP, II, 44, 47–48.
[22] GP, II, 48–52.
[23] GP, II, 52–54.

third. By sending Sumarokov-Elston back empty-handed, the Austrians decided against joining Russia in invading Turkey, but they made clear their intention to remain benevolently neutral and left open the door to further negotiations. In the superheated political climate at Livadia Alexander and his advisers concluded that, if Austria would not become their partner in war, she must intend to become their opponent.[24] Under that supposition they determined to test the loyalty of their German ally.

Bismarck had long anticipated and sought to delay the day when Germany might be faced with the question Alexander now asked.[25] Yet he was dumbfounded by the timing and tactlessness of its communication—orally through a general without diplomatic experience. Nowhere in the diplomatic communications exchanged up to this point, furthermore, had there been any hint that the Russians were considering war with Austria. Bismarck suspected Gorchakov of setting a trap. "If we answer 'no,' he will use it to prejudice Tsar Alexander against us; if we answer 'yes,' he will use it in Vienna."[26] He would have preferred an evasive reply or none at all, but Wilhelm feared to offend his nephew.[27] Bismarck recalled Schweinitz from vacation and sent him (October 23) to Livadia with the German response: In the event of a Russian-Turkish war, Germany would urge Austria to keep the peace with Russia. But if a break should occur between Russia and Austria, Germany would have no reason to abandon her neutrality. If Italy and France should enter the war, Germany might have to look after its own interests. If the whole of Europe should combine against Russia, it would not be in Germany's interest to see Russia's position as a European power seriously and lastingly damaged. Germany's interests would be just as deeply affected, if the integrity of the Habsburg Empire or its position as a factor in the European balance of power should be threatened.[28] In his memoirs Bismarck put the matter more succinctly: "We could indeed endure that our friends should lose or win battles against each other, but not that one of the two should be so severely wounded and injured that its position as an independent great power participating in European affairs would be endangered."[29]

Bismarck's famous response to Russia's "untimely" question is a classic in the history of balance of power diplomacy. Better than any other perhaps,

[24] Rupp, *Wavering Friendship*, pp. 168–184; R. W. Seton-Watson, "Russo-British Relations during the Eastern Crisis," *Slavonic Review*, 4 (1925–1926), pp. 187–191.

[25] GW, VIb, 534; VIII, 147, 155, 182–183.

[26] GW, II, 54–57.

[27] GP, II, 61–64.

[28] GP, II, 76; Wilhelm von Schweinitz, ed., *Denkwürdigkeiten des Generals von Schweinitz* (Berlin, 1927), I, 347–360.

[29] GW, XV, 388–390.

that document illustrates Bismarck's most characteristic political tactic: his exploitation of conflicting interests (within a largely closed system) for the creation of balanced options, which reserved to himself (and the interest he served) the freedom to choose, even while denying it to others.[30] In it he demonstrated to the Russians—as he did also to the Austrians, when their emissary called at Varzin—both the limits and value of Germany's political friendship.[31] Britain's return to an active role in European affairs enabled him to think realistically about other combinations that might become necessary in the continuing effort to keep Germany "one of three on the European chessboard." The options he considered at this time as alternatives to the Three Emperors League were, depending on the circumstances, Britain-Germany-Russia and Britain-Germany-Austria.[32] Russia's reaction to his message of October 23 could only have increased his readiness to consider the second of these choices.

Both the tsar and Gorchakov made clear to Schweinitz and Bismarck their dissatisfaction with the German response. "We expected great things from you," said the Russian chancellor, "and you bring us nothing that we did not know long ago." Gorchakov insisted that Germany should be willing to declare to the world that Russia had the right as the "mandator of Europe" to

[30] See vol. 1, pp. xxix, 80–84.

[31] On Oct. 3–4, 1876, Bismarck received a secret visit from Baron von Münch, sent by Andrássy to sound out Bismarck's attitude in the event of a break between Russia and Austria because of the latter's rejection of the overtures brought by Sumarokov-Elston. The chancellor's response was similar to that sent to Gorchakov via Schweinitz. Rupp, *Wavering Friendship*, pp. 194–197. What he told the Austrians he repeated to a parliamentary soirée on Dec. 2, 1876 (*BP*, I, 118–119) and to the Reichstag on the fifth (*BR*, VI, 446).

[32] *GP*, II, 36. When Schweinitz visited Varzin (Oct. 10–12, 1876) to receive his instructions for Livadia, he asked Bismarck what Germany would require "as compensation for our support in the eastern crisis." Bismarck replied, "a guarantee for Alsace-Lorraine would be acceptable." In the chancellor's written instructions (Oct. 23), however, Schweinitz read that Germany could not give "contractual assurances that would lastingly bind us" to Russia. Hence he merely sounded out Gorchakov about the possibility of a Russian guarantee for Alsace-Lorraine. Gorchakov replied that such commitments were "of little use." Schweinitz, ed., *Denkwürdigkeiten*, I, 355, 359–362. Three years later, Bismarck claimed that in Oct. 1876 Gorchakov had rebuffed his offer to go with Russia "through thick and thin" in return for the requested guarantee. *Ibid.*, II, 87–90, 224; Wilhelm von Schweinitz, ed., *Briefwechsel des Botschafters General von Schweinitz* (Berlin, 1928), p. 141; J. Y. Simpson, ed., *The Saburov Memoirs or Bismarck and Russia* (New York, 1929), p. 55. Historians have expended a lot of ink and paper discussing the seriousness of Bismarck's "alliance offer" of Oct. 1876. See the summary in Rupp, *Wavering Friendship*, pp. 202–209. Before beginning any serious action (for example, the war on Austria in 1866 and his break with the liberals in 1878), Bismarck's practice was to offer to treat with the opposition, if only to assure himself that no other option was viable. Such maneuvers were also useful for unsettling the opposition and providing himself later with a countering reproach of the following sort: "You complain about *my* conduct, but just consider how much better off you would have been, had *you* only accepted the offer I once made you!"

put an end to "unbearable conditions" in the Ottoman Empire.[33] With German help he wished to depict Russia in the coming war as the savior of Christianity and of western civilization itself. In the margin of the messages received from the tsar and Gorchakov Bismarck scrawled his reactions in three languages: "Who is Europe?" *"Qui parle Europe a tort—notion geographique."* *"Redensarten."*[34]

To the Kaiser he wrote, "I have always heard the word 'Europe' from the mouths of those political figures who demanded from other powers something that they don't dare ask in their own names."[35] As Christians Germans were certainly concerned about human suffering in other parts of the world. But Germany was being asked "to engage its power, its peace, and its European relationships" in behalf of causes in which other European powers had a far greater self-interest. England, Austria, and Russia should be left to draw their own chestnuts out of the fire. "We should not shoulder the cares of other powers. We will have quite enough of our own."[36] He assured the Russians of Germany's "understanding" and "sympathy" for their cause in the Balkans, urged them to get on with their invasion of Turkey, and pledged to assist in "localizing" the war by keeping Austria and Britain neutral.[37] He advised Russia to approve Austria's occupation of Bosnia and England's occupation of Egypt. But he resolved not to involve Germany with Russia and England in the "difficult question" of where the Russian army should halt in its advance toward Constantinople.[38]

Russia's Road to War

In late 1876 Bismarck and Germany were the center of attention among European governments. Gorchakov's inconvenient question and his effort to get Bismarck to provide Russia with moral justification for attacking Turkey were just two indications that Germany, superficially isolated in May 1875, was now the power whose support was most desired by all powers involved in the eastern crisis. As noted, Bismarck was compelled to stave off dangerous overtures from both Russia and Austria, each seeking support against the other. But he also refused Andrássy's proposal for a German-Austrian alliance to hold Italy in check, on the grounds that such a combination would be interpreted in Petersburg as anti-Russian.[39] In London Disraeli, grown distrustful

[33] GP, II, 80–83; Schweinitz, ed., *Denkwürdigkeiten*, I, 361.
[34] GP, II, 87.
[35] GP, II, 88.
[36] GP, II, 90.
[37] Rupp, *Wavering Friendship*, pp. 312–318, 328–331, 348–349.
[38] GP, II, 78–79.
[39] Langer, *Alliances and Alignments*, pp. 98–99; Wertheimer, *Andrássy*, II, 338–342.

of Russia's aims and badgered by anti-Turkish agitation from "atrocitarians," broached the possibility of an English-German agreement to preserve the status quo in the Balkans—and in Alsace-Lorraine![40]

Disraeli's démarche inspired Bismarck to describe to the Kaiser and the German foreign office his "fantasy picture" of the ideal solution: Bosnia to Austria; Bessarabia to Russia; Egypt and Suez to England; Syria to France; Constantinople, its environs, and the Straits to remain in the Ottoman Empire. "All Turkey, including the various peoples who live there, is not worth so much as a political institution that civilized European peoples should destroy themselves in great wars for its sake." He was determined, nevertheless, neither to take the initiative for such a settlement nor to put diplomatic pressure on any other power toward that end. Even though couched in the friendliest terms, such pressure could only harm Germany's foreign relations. He could not conceive of any proposal that would elicit only applause from the concerned powers and antagonize no one.[41] In accordance with this viewpoint, he gave the British only a hazy outline of his "fantasy," reproached them for having ignored earlier proposals that Britain restrain Russia in collaboration with Austria and Germany, and warned that their refusal had compelled him to support Gorchakov's plan for joint diplomatic action by the European powers against the Turks.[42] Disraeli and Derby had to be shown the cost of failing to respond to Bismarck's overtures.

On October 31, 1876, Russia gave the Porte, whose victorious army was advancing on Belgrade, forty-eight hours in which to accept an armistice of six weeks in the war with Serbia. The Porte yielded, and, on Britain's proposal, the great powers sent plenipotentiaries to a conference at Constantinople, ostensibly for the purpose of settling the Balkan war. Before the first plenary session was held on December 23, Lord Salisbury and Ignatyev, the British and Russian plenipotentiaries, hammered out on agreement, whose principal terms would have preserved Serbia, given Montenegro its conquests, united Bosnia and Herzegovina into a single province, and divided Bulgaria laterally into two provinces. The three provinces were to be autonomous, with elected assemblies and governors appointed by the Porte but approved by the European powers.[43] Neither Britain nor Russia was sanguine about the probable success of this program. Salisbury's purpose is said to have been to split the Three Emperors League and deprive Bismarck of his central position in European affairs, while Ignatyev strove to buy time for Russia's

[40] Taffs, *Ambassador to Bismarck*, p. 158; Millman, *Britain and the Eastern Question*, p. 193.

[41] GP, II, 69–72.

[42] Taffs, *Ambassador to Bismarck*, pp. 159–161.

[43] Millman, *Britain and the Eastern Question*, pp. 208–231; R. W. Seton-Watson, "Russo-British Relations during the Eastern Crisis," *Slavonic Review*, 4 (1925–1926), pp. 432–462; Lady Gwendolyn Cecil, *Life of Robert Marquis of Salisbury* (London, 1921–1932), II, 89–125.

lagging financial mobilization and obtain for Russia a European mandate to make war on Turkey. The Porte had accepted the conference only under duress. On December 23, 1876, even as the conference began its first plenary session, Turkish liberals headed by Grand Vizier Midhat Pasha proclaimed with thundering cannon a liberal constitution for the entire empire. The new governmental order, the Turks declared, would make the reforms planned for the new Balkan provinces unnecessary. On these grounds an assembly of Turkish notables, meeting in Constantinople on January 18, 1877, rejected the Salisbury–Ignatyev program. The course of Balkan events had served to stimulate not only a Panslav convulsion in Russia but also a national revival in Turkey. On neither side was there now any mood for compromise. [44]

Oddly enough, Bismarck, representing the country least involved at Constantinople, became the scapegoat for the conference's failure. Alexander II complained bitterly over Germany's "platonic" support at Constantinople. The Panslav Ignatyev, whose skill as a negotiator won over Salisbury, insinuated that Bismarck, whose suggestions for dismembering the Ottoman Empire were widely known, was responsible for stiffened Turkish resistance. [45] If Ignatyev was the inventor, Decazes was the propagator of this charge. The French plenipotentiary at Constantinople lost no chance to demonstrate French support for the Salisbury–Ignatyev plan. At Paris Decazes intimated to British Ambassador Lord Lyons that the German chancellor planned to attack France in the hope of dissolving an incipient British-French-Russian entente. Again Gorchakov saw his chance to make Bismarck the whipping boy of European opinion. Europe was soon inundated with inspired newspaper articles accusing the German chancellor of deliberately frustrating Russia's just ambitions in the Balkans. [46]

In analyzing the European scene for his subordinates on October 20, 1876, Bismarck declared that a rapprochement between England and France was not injurious to the interests of Germany and the European balance of power—"on the contrary." [47] But a few months later he had begun to view with concern the evidence of growing intimacy between those powers and Russia. He suspected Gorchakov of intrigues in Vienna aimed at the fall of Andrássy and inclusion of Austria in an anti-German coalition. [48] These concerns were heightened by reports of continuing Russian and French troop concentrations on Germany's borders. In January and February 1877 the Prussian general staff worked on plans for a two-front war against both countries. France required only five days to mobilize five hundred thousand troops, it

[44] Roderic H. Davidson, *Reform in the Ottoman Empire, 1856–1876* (Princeton, 1963), pp. 358–395.

[45] GP, II, 125–131; GW, XIV, 881–885; Schweinitz, ed., *Denkwürdigkeiten*, I, 378ff.

[46] Langer, *Alliances and Alignments*, pp. 109–110; Rupp, *Wavering Friendship*, pp. 320–321.

[47] GP, II, 72.

[48] GP, II, 128–130; also GP, I, 317.

was believed, while Germany needed ten. Moltke anticipated a decisive bat-
tle in Lorraine and a negotiated peace with France, after which German forces
could be turned against Russia.[49] Despite Bismarck's warning, backed by
Moltke and Kameke, Wilhelm was disinclined to believe in the threat of a
French-Russian attack and agreed only with reluctance to strengthen the gar-
risons at Metz and Strassburg.[50] A flurry of recriminations appeared in the
French and German press reminiscent of 1875. Again there was talk among
German military men of the advisability of a preventive strike against France.
And again Bismarck declined "to play God" by trying to predict the future.
"Every war, even a successful one, is a misfortune. . . . To try to drive out the
devil with the help of Beelzebub would be a dangerous game."[51]

In view of these uncertainties Bismarck turned again to Britain, inquiring
what the Disraeli government would do in the event of war between Germany
and France. Could London be expected to mediate? If Germany supported
British aspirations in the east, would Britain support Germany in the west?[52]
But again the British were unresponsive. Neither Derby nor Disraeli believed
in the likelihood of a French attack, and they concluded that the German
chancellor was whipping up another war scare like that of 1875. Did he look
upon Russian involvement in the Balkans as an opportunity to crush the
French? This suspicion was no more justified in 1877 than in 1875. Although
documentation on the episode is thin, it seems apparent that Bismarck was
again genuinely concerned that the French might seek to exploit Germany's
seeming isolation to launch a war of revenge. The fall of the MacMahon
government on May 16, 1877, did not assuage his fears. But he welcomed the
victory of Gambetta and the republicans at the polls in December, which
began a new era of reconciliation and even cooperation in German-French
relations.[53] Among the first benefits for Bismarck was the resignation of Decazes as foreign minister and the removal of Gontaut-Biron, the much distrusted and probably maligned French ambassador, a favorite of Empress Augusta.

Even before the beginning of the Constantinople conference, the Russians
had begun to speculate on its failure. Bismarck's unwillingness to back Russia
against Austria had forced St. Petersburg to give up any thought of war against

---

[49] Ferdinand von Schmerfeld, *Die deutschen Aufmarschpläne 1871–1890. Quellen und Darstellungen aus dem Reichsarchiv*, vol. 7 (Berlin, 1929), p. 65; Gerhard Ritter, *Staatskunst und Kriegshandwerk: Das Problem des "Militarismus" in Deutschland* (Munich, 1954–1968), I, 292–293;
Wolfgang Windelband, *Bismarck und die europäischen Grossmächte, 1879–1885* (2d ed., Essen,
1942), pp. 45–47.

[50] Friedrich Curtius, ed., *Memoirs of Prince Chlodwig of Hohenlohe-Schillingsfuerst* (New York,
1906), II, 194–195.

[51] Kohl, ed., *Anhang*, II, 497. See also *ibid*., I, 258–261 and GW, VIc, 62–63.

[52] GP, I, 312, 310–328; Taffs, *Ambassador to Bismarck*, pp. 177–187.

[53] Kohl, ed., *Anhang*, II, 494–505; André Dreux, *Dernières années de l'ambassade en Allemagne
de M. de Gontaut-Biron, 1874–1877* (Paris, 1907), pp. 264–289.

both Austria and Turkey. The Russians appeared to have two options: either come to terms with Austria over the fruits of a Russian war against Turkey or give up the idea of such a war. By January 1877 the heat of public opinion and Panslav agitation both inside and outside the government had made the second option unviable. At Budapest on January 15, 1877, representatives of Russia and Austria signed a military convention and on March 18 a political convention, in which Andrássy exacted his price for benevolent neutrality in the coming war. Under the first agreement Austria might occupy Bosnia and Herzegovina but not extend its military operations into Rumania, Serbia, Bulgaria, and Montenegro. The second agreement dealt with the political settlement that would follow either a Russian victory or the dissolution of the Ottoman Empire. Austria might annex, at a time of her own choosing, Bosnia and Herzegovina (but not the Sanjak of Novi-Bazar, whose disposition was left to subsequent agreement), while Russia would reacquire Bessarabia and the frontier lost in 1856. No "great, compact Slavic or other state" was to be erected in the Balkans. Bulgaria, Albania, and the rest of Rumelia "might be constituted into independent states." Greece "might" annex Thessaly, Crete, and part of Epirus, while Constantinople "might become a free city."[54]

Without going to war or even mobilizing, the Dual Monarchy was assured of territorial acquisitions that would frustrate Panslav ambitions to unite the southern Slavs. By assuming control later over Novi-Bazar, Austria-Hungary could keep Serbia and Montenegro apart and also preserve for herself a sally port into the Balkans; by foreclosing the creation of a large Bulgaria, she left open the route for Austrian commercial expansion toward Salonika. The gains Russia could make from the war were limited, regardless how complete the victory and how great the sacrifice.

Through Ignatyev, who toured Europe's capitals in March 1877, Alexander and Gorchakov made a final, vain effort to organize European powers either to force the Porte to yield without war or to give Russia the mandate to conduct a crusade in behalf of Christianity and humanity.[55] Bismarck urged them to go to war but in their own interest. He recognized that some outlet had to be found for the anger and frustration of Russian imperialists and Panslavists. But he also wanted to prove to Russia Germany's loyalty as an ally, and he expected that Russia's invasion of the eastern Balkans would trigger a division of Turkish soil—the only way to resolve the crisis without a European war. Neither the tsar nor his chancellor was eager to attack. Yet they had, under the prodding of the Panslavists, followed a course that made war hard to avoid when the Turks refused to yield to diplomatic pressure. Their military preparations, Bismarck sneered, had put the Russians in the position of the diner

[54] A. F. Pribram, *The Secret Treaties of Austria-Hungary, 1879–1914* (Cambridge, Mass., 1920–1921), II, 190–203; Rupp, *Wavering Friendship*, pp. 326–351.

[55] Wertheimer, *Andrássy*, II, 390–395; Rupp, *Wavering Friendship*, pp. 326–351.

who no longer wants the steak he ordered but feels compelled to eat it because
he has to pay for it.[56] On April 24, 1877, the tsar declared war on Turkey.

Europe's Road to Berlin

Bismarck could regard the Russian invasion of the Balkans with relative equa-
nimity. He had repeatedly assured Petersburg of Germany's benevolent neutrality and of his willingness to do what he could to block an anti-Russian
coalition.[57] That Austria had exacted favorable terms from Russia for its neutrality meant that the Three Emperors League was as secure as could be expected in the ever-quivering balance of power. Russia's military involvement
in the Balkans diminished the possibility of her collaboration with France
against Germany. The only acute danger for Germany would come if England
should go to war against Russia to protect Constantinople and the Straits. To
avoid this, Bismarck continued during the first weeks of war to push for a
limited partition of Turkey. He seconded Shuvalov's advice to his government that Russia restrict its objectives to the annexation of Bessarabia, autonomy of Bulgaria, and expansion of Montenegro. To Austria he recommended
annexation of Bosnia, Herzegovina, and perhaps other districts. France, he
declared, had already received her compensation in Algeria, but might take
Tunis as well, if she finally abandoned Alsace-Lorraine. Italy might have a
"portion" of Tripoli.[58] Through Münster and Russell he suggested that Britain
accept Egypt and possibly even Syria, Crete, and Cyprus. To limit Russia's
advance he advised the British to occupy the Dardanelles. Again he assured
Derby of his desire for "an intimate and lasting alliance" with Britain, but
spoke of a "cordial and intimate understanding between England and Russia,
to which Germany would become a party."[59] These suggestions merely filled
Disraeli and his colleagues with distrust. They suspected Bismarck of seeking
to embroil Britain in war with Russia in order to gain for Germany the freedom to attack France and perhaps annex the Netherlands.[60] "There must finally be an end to this," Disraeli burst out. "I find him everywhere in my way.
. . . The man is a European nuisance. Bismarck, more than Russia, is my
problem, and I am firmly resolved to thwart him."[61]

[56] Wertheimer, Andrássy, II, 367; Lucius, Bismarck-Erinnerungen, p. 94; Goriainov, Bosphore
et Dardanelles, pp. 321–322. On the Russian decision for war see MacKenzie, Serbs and Russian
Pan-Slavism, pp. 187–193, and Geyer, Der russische Imperialismus, pp. 64–66.

[57] See, for example, GP, II, 137–138, 146–147.

[58] Schweinitz, ed., Denkwürdigkeiten, I, 424–428; Langer, Alliances and Alignments, p. 123;
Rupp, Wavering Friendship, p. 375.

[59] GP, II, 149–150, 153–154; Taffs, Ambassador to Bismarck, pp. 190–197.

[60] Taffs, Ambassador to Bismarck, pp. 197–198; Millman, Britain and the Eastern Question, p.
251.

[61] Wertheimer, Andrássy, III, 48–50.

During the rest of 1877 Bismarck largely withdrew from attempts to steer the Balkan crisis. Comparative inactivity suited not only the diplomatic situation but also the precarious state of his health. We have seen that, after another of his celebrated "resignations" (this one a charade), he left Berlin (April 16) on another extended leave that lasted ten months. At Friedrichsruh, on brief visits to Berlin, and on travels to Kissingen, Gastein, and Salzburg he conferred with foreign diplomats as the Balkan drama unfolded but made no serious effort to influence its direction. In June he drafted the famous appraisal of Germany's situation in Europe known as the "Kissingen dictation," in which he described the "*cauchemar des coalitions*" that disturbed his sleep, the "most dangerous" of which was Russia-Austria-France. Too great an "intimacy" between any two of these powers would enable the third to place Germany under "very painful pressure." "Because of my concern over these eventualities I would regard it as desirable if the eastern crisis produced the following results, not immediately but in the course of years: (1) gravitation of Russian and Austrian interests and mutual rivalries toward the east; (2) cause for Russia to assume a strong defensive position in the east and on its coasts and to need our alliance; (3) for England and Russia a satisfactory status quo, which will give them the same interest that we have in the maintenance of existing arrangements; (4) a separation of England from France, which remains hostile to us, because of their frictions over Egypt and the Mediterranean; (5) such relations between Russia and Austria as will make it difficult for them to launch an anti-German conspiracy to which centralistic or clerical elements in Austria might perhaps be inclined." As he watched and waited, Bismarck hoped that out of the confusion of motives and conflicting interests would emerge a "total situation" in which all European great powers "except France" would need Germany and be kept from coalitions against her by their conflicting interests.[62] Short- and long-term objectives were fused in a clear yet flexible plan for the pursuit of Germany's interests, as Bismarck perceived them.

During the spring and early summer of 1877 Russian troops crossed Rumania and invaded Ottoman territory more quickly than anticipated. In London the Russian advance was followed with mounting anxiety, scarcely mitigated by Gorchakov's assurances that Russia had no designs on Egypt, Suez, and (somewhat more vaguely) Constantinople and the Straits. Nor was an exchange of views between the British and Austrian governments on what the two powers could accept in the way of a Balkan settlement imposed by Russian arms very reassuring; the British began to suspect the existence of an Austrian-Russian understanding on the outcome of the war. On July 21,

---

[62] GP, II, 154. For the general context of the quotation see pp. 252–254.

1877, the Disraeli cabinet resolved to declare war on Russia, if Russian armies should defy British warnings by occupying Constantinople more than briefly; preparations were begun for ordering the British fleet to Constantinople.[63]

But then, to universal surprise, Turkish resistance stiffened. At the fortress of Plevna, Osman Pasha and his troops put up a resistance that stalled the entire Russian advance from July 20 to December 10. The long delay embarrassed the Russians and relieved the Austrians and British. As the siege of Plevna came to an end, the Porte turned to the neutral powers requesting their mediation. Bismarck replied that Germany would mediate only if requested to do so by Russia. "In view of the long border we share with the tsarist empire, our relationships with Russia are much more important to us than all of Turkey."[64] Although increasingly anxious about Russian intentions, the Austrian government was reluctant to join Britain in any action until certain that Russia would not honor its secret commitments to Vienna.[65] On January 27, 1878, the Porte accepted Russia's peace terms and four days later signed an armistice that halted the fighting, but not the advance of Russian troops toward Constantinople.

Within the British government there was no consensus about how to react to Russia's progress toward the Straits—much to the distress of Queen Victoria, whose anxiety over the Russian threat and British inaction reached a feverish pitch. "In a cabinet of twelve members," Disraeli told her, "there are seven parties or policies as to the course which should be pursued."[66] Disraeli favored a naval demonstration at the Straits in order to stop the Russian advance on Constantinople, which he now perceived as the "key to India." But the lethargic Derby was immovably opposed to any warlike action—to the point of collaborating secretly with Russian Ambassador Count Peter Shuvalov to halt the drift toward war in both London and St. Petersburg. That Lady Derby was known to be relaying cabinet decisions and indecisions within hours to Shuvalov heightened the confusion. The prime minister found it necessary to bypass his foreign secretary by secretly warning Petersburg in August 1877 that Britain would go to war if Russia should resume the advance on Constantinople. But the tsar and Gorchakov, knowing the disarray within the British government, could see no reason to halt after the fall of Plevna. Having decided to go to war, Alexander had put aside his doubts about its wisdom, comfortable in the thought that the monarchy was now united with the Russian people in a fight for a holy, national cause. On January 23, 1878,

[63] Wertheimer, *Andrássy*, III, 40–41, 44–45; Millman, *Britain and the Eastern Question*, pp. 274–316.

[64] GP, II, 160–163.

[65] Wertheimer, *Andrássy*, III, 55–59; Rupp, *Wavering Friendship*, pp. 399ff.

[66] Blake, *Disraeli*, p. 634.

Disraeli succeeded in getting the cabinet to order the fleet to sail through the Dardanelles. But even now the confusion in London continued. Twice the fleet was ordered back to Besika Bay before it finally reached Constantinople on February 15. Derby's resignation was accepted and then revoked. Embarrassment over this vacillation and the adverse reaction it produced from a public already inflamed by "jingoism" forced the Disraeli government to assume an ever more belligerent stance. For weeks Europe teetered on the edge of a major conflict.[67]

In the end the Balkan conflict did not become a European war because no great power wanted it and all exerted themselves to prevent it. At San Stefano Ignatyev succeeded in wresting from the Porte a victor's peace, which delighted Russia's Panslavists but seemed excessive to political realists like Shuvalov. Britain and Austria found the treaty an intolerable affront to their interests; to the latter it was also a betrayal of secret agreements and often reiterated promises. Both governments were prepared to fight rather than accept Russian domination of the Balkans and the Straits. Since its army and finances were in no condition to engage in such a war, the Russians had no choice but to accept a European conference to revise the treaty. On March 6, Andrássy formally called upon the powers to meet at Berlin. After some haggling, they accepted, and the congress was scheduled for June.[68]

That Berlin was selected as the site for the international congress that concluded the Balkan crisis was symbolic of the position to which Bismarck's diplomacy had elevated the Prussian capital in merely fifteen years. The last previous European congress had been held at Paris in 1856 to conclude the Crimean War. On that occasion the choice of Paris had been looked upon as a recognition of the new prestige of France under Napoleon III. To go to Berlin—a difficult decision for the French government—was to recognize the change wrought by German victories over Austria and France. But it was also proof that the war-in-sight crisis of 1875 had been but a passing episode in European politics. The neutral course Bismarck had steered since the fall of that year in the eastern question had left him the only statesman in Europe who, despite British distrust and Russian dissatisfaction, was presumed to have the authority and relative impartiality capable of presiding over a congress to resolve the Balkan crisis and preserve Europe's peace.[69]

---

[67] Millman, *Britain and the Eastern Question*, pp. 335–402; Monypenny and Buckle, *Disraeli*, IV, 1090ff.; Blake, *Disraeli*, pp. 623–628, 632–641; Geyer, *Der russische Imperialismus*, pp. 66–67, 70–71.

[68] Wertheimer, *Andrássy*, III, 69–87; GP, II, 207–209; Rupp, *Wavering Friendship*, pp. 427ff. For the treaty of San Stefano see Imanuel Geiss, ed., *Der Berliner Kongress 1878: Protokolle und Materialien. Schriften des Bundesarchivs*, vol. 27 (Boppard am Rhein, 1978), pp. 15–21.

[69] Langer, *Alliances and Alignments*, pp. 140–142.

The Honest Broker

The task of presiding over a European congress could scarcely have fallen upon Bismarck at a more inconvenient time. While relatively inactive on the diplomatic front during the preceding year, he had been deeply engaged in major actions in internal affairs. These were the months of his effort to reorganize the Prussian-German government, his futile negotiations for Bennigsen's entry into the government, and his continuing effort at "tax reform" that ultimately produced the protective tariff. Immediately before the congress met occurred the two attempts on Wilhelm's life that led to dissolution of the Reichstag and the beginning of an election campaign. As observed, Bismarck's long leave (April 1877 to February 1878) had done little to restore his health. He returned to Berlin too weak either to stand or work for long, afflicted by sleeplessness, rheumatism, neuralgia, and shingles. He was not eager to assume the task now thrust upon him, but accepted chiefly on the insistence of Tsar Alexander. He anticipated being blamed by whichever power was dissatisfied with the results.[70] On February 19, he described the role he intended to play in words long remembered. He would act, he said, not like a referee but like "an honest broker, who really wants to get the business settled."[71]

The business to be settled was a revision of the Treaty of San Stefano in a manner favorable to the interests of Britain and Austria. Since Russia had declined to go to war against those powers in defense of the treaty, she had no choice but to permit such a revision, while trying to retain as many gains as possible. For Russia the necessity of accepting the congress was itself a humiliation. If in Berlin the Russians were compelled to surrender at the bargaining table too much of what Russia's soldiers had won on the battlefield, the tsarist regime would suffer a catastrophic loss of prestige. Before the congress met the Russians maneuvered to separate their foes by sending Ignatyev to Vienna to learn Austria's terms. Franz Joseph and Andrássy flatly refused to retreat from their interpretation of the Reichstadt and Budapest conventions. The Treaty of San Stefano had created a single Bulgarian state which, roughly following the ethnic maps of the period, extended in the south to the Aegean Sea and to the west across Macedonia to Albania. To Andrássy this "greater Bulgaria" violated the prohibition in the Budapest convention against a "great, compact Slavic or other state." A Russian occupation lasting two years seemed to assure that the new Bulgaria would become a Russian client state. The treaty, furthermore, provided for the enlargement of both Montenegro, which was to receive a strip of Dalmatian coast, and Serbia, which was allotted part of the Sanjak of Novi-Bazar. Andrássy objected stren-

---

[70] Geiss, *Kongress*, p. xii; Wertheimer, *Andrássy*, III, 86–87.
[71] *BR*, VII, 92.

uously to both of these arrangements. Austria, he maintained, must have the right to occupy and annex not only Bosnia and Herzegovina but also the entire Sanjak of Novi-Bazar, including the town of Mitrowitza. The Austrian aim, he frankly explained, was to construct a railway to Saloniki and hence secure Austrian political and economic dominance over the western Balkans. To the same end the weakened Ottoman Empire must be left in possession of Macedonia. In view of the bellicose attitudes in Britain against Russia, Andrássy expected to exact from Petersburg a high price for Austrian friendship. But he merely drove the Russians to settle with Britain.[72]

After months of divisiveness and indecision in the British cabinet, Disraeli took a firmer grip on British foreign policy. Although his old friend Derby still clung to the post of foreign secretary, the prime minister in effect took over the management of the Foreign Office. Steps were taken to strengthen the army and to move forces from Britain and India to the Mediterranean. Within the government there was talk of acquiring new bases in the Aegean, eastern Mediterranean, and even the Persian Gulf. All of this was too much for Derby, who appeared to be on the verge of alcoholism and a nervous breakdown. He resigned on March 28, to be replaced by Salisbury. In continuing negotiations with Russia, the British demanded that the entire Treaty of San Stefano be subject to discussion at the coming congress and that existing treaties dealing with Turkey and the Straits be regarded as still valid until expressly changed by the signatory powers.[73] In a circular dispatch of April 1 addressed to the great powers, Salisbury stated clearly Britain's objections to: (1) a greater Bulgarian state under Russian control with a large Greek minority and in possession of the Aegian littoral; (2) territorial rearrangements that would give Russia effective control of the Black Sea; (3) imposition of a large and crippling war indemnity that would give Russia coercive power over Turkey; and (4) and the whole combination of treaty provisions that would cost the Ottoman Empire its independence, shift the balance of maritime power in the region, endanger access to the Straits, and thereby damage severely British interests in the Mediterranean.[74]

Although they refused to yield to British demands that they withdraw their army from the gates of Constantinople (permitting the British fleet to withdraw to Besika Bay), the Russians finally came to terms with Disraeli and Salisbury in negotiations conducted through Shuvalov, who shuttled between London and Petersburg, stopping off at Berlin to consult with Bismarck. In an agreement completed on May 31, 1878, Britain and Russia agreed to restrict the southern and western frontiers of Bulgaria and divide the country

---

[72] GP, II, 252–257, 259–262, 273–275, 294–303; Wertheimer, *Andrássy*, III, 90–100; Rupp, *Wavering Friendship*, pp. 478–496.

[73] Millman, *Britain and the Eastern Question*, pp. 403–416.

[74] Harold Temperley and Lillian M. Penson, *Foundations of British Foreign Policy from Pitt (1792) to Salisbury (1902)* (London, 1966), pp. 363–380.

into two segments laterally along the spine of the Balkan Mountains, the southern part remaining under nominal Turkish sovereignty but without Turkish troops. In return, Britain accepted the expansion of Serbia and Montenegro and Russian annexation of Bessarabia, Kars, and Ardahan; Batum became a free port. (Meanwhile, Britain had obtained Cyprus in a secret agreement with Turkey.) Russian forces occupying Bulgaria were limited to twenty thousand men and were to be withdrawn six months after the conclusion of peace. Informed by Bismarck of what was taking place between Britain and Russia, an outmaneuvered Andrássy made haste (June 6) to accept Britain's plan for Bulgaria in return for British support for Austria's acquisition of Bosnia (but without any British commitment on the future frontiers of Serbia and Montenegro).[75]

These prior agreements eased Bismarck's task of brokering the congress, but their vagueness left many problems unresolved. As president of the body, he established the agenda and directed the flow of the deliberations. Before the congress assembled, Russia agreed that the entire Treaty of San Stefano was to be open for discussion, while Britain and the other powers agreed that decisions must be unanimous, giving Russia the right of veto. Bismarck's procedure was to raise one issue at a time, beginning with the most critical (Bulgaria), invite the delegates to state their general positions regarding it, then adjourn for private conferences between the conflicting parties at which differences were hammered out. When they had reached agreement, sometimes with Bismarck's help, the issue came back to the full congress for ratification. Although Bulgaria—its size, shape, and division—was the most important problem, there were others of significance: the military and political rights of the sultan in southern Bulgaria (Eastern Rumelia), over which the Porte retained nominal sovereignty; Austria's right to occupy and administer Bosnia, Herzegovina, and Novi-Bazar; the frontiers of Serbia, Montenegro, Greece, and Rumania; Russia's new borders in Asia Minor and particularly the status of Batum under Russian rule; Britain's prior, secret acquisition of Cyprus; and, behind the scenes, the compensation (Tunis) to be promised to France.[76]

That the Congress of Berlin produced a treaty that ended the Balkan conflict for the time being was largely owed to Bismarck's skill and effort. The

[75] Millman, *Britain and the Eastern Question*, pp. 417–451; Cecil, *Salisbury*, II, 258ff.; Monypenny and Buckle, *Disraeli*, IV, 1164–1173; Wertheimer, *Andrássy*, III, 98–107; GP, II, 277–279, 289–294, 312–321, 324–329. Bismarck was concerned that England and Russia might combine against Austria, a development contrary to Germany's interests. Walter Bussmann, ed., *Staatssekretär Graf Herbert von Bismarck: Aus seiner politischen Privatkorrespondenz* (Göttingen, 1964), p. 88.

[76] On the congress see Geiss, *Kongress*, particularly pp. ix–xxxv; Alexander Novotny, ed., *Quellen und Studien zur Geschichte des Berliner Kongresses 1878. Veröffentlichungen der Kommission für Neuere Geschichte Österreichs*, vol. 44 (Graz–Köln, 1957), and W. N. Medlicott, *The Congress of Berlin and After* (2d ed., London, 1963). For the best portraits of the participants see Seton-Watson, *Disraeli, Gladstone*, pp. 431–446.

task was not easy. "Quite apart from the importance of the negotiations," he said later, "it is extremely tiring to express one's self in a foreign tongue [French]—even though one speaks it fluently—so correctly that the words can be transcribed without delay in the protocol. Seldom did I sleep before six o'clock, often not before eight in the morning for a few hours. Before twelve o'clock I could not speak to anyone, and you can imagine what condition I was in at the sessions. My brain was like a gelatinous, disjointed mass. Before I entered the congress I drank two to three beer glasses filled with the strongest port wine . . . in order to bring my blood into circulation. Otherwise I would have been incapable of presiding."[77] As on other occasions Bismarck knew how to convert disability into asset. His health, he kept telling the delegates, would not permit a long congress. Disraeli portrayed him pithily at one such moment: "Bismarck, with one hand full of cherries, and the other of shrimps, eaten alternatively, complains he cannot sleep and must go to Kissingen."[78]

This constraint permitted him to focus attention on and limit debate to the really critical issues, those that could mean the difference between war and peace. Discussion of details made him visibly impatient and gruff to the edge of discourtesy. Where impasse threatened he was ready with compromises; if need be, he could also threaten (once he met the Turkish delegation in full uniform with spiked helmet). The forced pace brought Shuvalov and others to the point of exhaustion. "No one has ever died from work," was Bismarck's reply to their complaints. He dominated the congress—arrogant yet supple, persuasive in three languages, always forcing the tempo, yet ever mindful of his role as the honest broker. That the congress finished in twenty sessions lasting exactly one month (June 13 to July 13) was owed to his leadership. But there was, as Hohenlohe noted, a cost—a mountain of details left behind, to be worked out subsequently by multinational commissions amid considerable rancor.[79]

In contrast to Bismarck, Gorchakov appeared feeble and somewhat senile, capable of damaging but not furthering the work of his able subordinate, Peter Shuvalov. His chief concern was to hitch his own reputation to the San Stefano treaty and saddle Shuvalov with the blame for its inevitable revision. Andrássy was badly hobbled by strong opposition within Austria to his objectives. As a consequence, he supported Britain against Russia and relied on British help in gaining the right to occupy Bosnia and Herzegovina. "I have heard of people refusing to eat their pigeon unless it was shot and roasted for them," said Bismarck in disgust, "but I have never heard of anyone refusing to eat it unless his jaws were forced open and it was pushed down his throat."[80]

---

[77] GW, VIII, 280, also 265–266.

[78] Temperley and Penson, *Foundations of British Foreign Policy*, p. 389. Disraeli was himself in wretched health and barely held out to the end of the congress. Blake, *Disraeli*, p. 649.

[79] Geiss, *Kongress*, pp. xx–xxi; Medlicott, *Congress of Berlin*, pp. 36–136.

[80] Cecil, *Salisbury*, II, 281; Langer, *Alliances and Alignments*, p. 152.

Nevertheless, Andrássy achieved his most important objectives, including the right to garrison Novi-Bazar. To Bismarck's relief the French representatives at the congress—William Henry Waddington, a Protestant and moderate republican, and the Count of St. Vallier, Gontaut's replacement as ambassador to Germany—cooperated in seeking a peaceful outcome. Naturally the whipping boys of the congress were the Turks, led by Alexander Caratheodory and Sadoullah Bey. Bismarck often treated them with contempt, rudely dismissing their objections and reservations as needless impediments to the business at hand. If the congress ended in war rather than peace, he warned them, Turkey would bear the cost of the ultimate settlement, whatever the outcome of the fighting.[81]

After Bismarck the most impressive figure at the congress turned out to be Disraeli (Bismarck: "*Der alte Jude, das ist der Mann*"). Although unable to communicate in French, he advanced British interests with considerable force and skill, ably assisted in detailed negotiations by Salisbury. Under their leadership the British came away with the greatest gains of any power: Cyprus, a reduction by three-fifths in the size of Bulgaria, preservation of Turkish sovereignty over Macedonia and the coast of the Aegean. With Suez and Cyprus, British naval power now dominated the eastern Mediterranean, and the route to India was secure. Russia received Bessarabia, Kars, Ardahan, and Batum (as a free port).[82] But the liberation of Bulgaria and the enlarged frontiers and sovereignty accorded to Serbia, Montenegro, and Rumania were not enough to appease Russian imperialists and Panslav agitators. They were offended that Shuvalov had surrendered so much of what Ignatyev had extracted from the Turks at San Stefano and that the Straits remained closed to Russian warships. Above all, the Russians were indignant over the failure of Germany and Austria to shield them from this disaster. They had succeeded neither in gaining the mandate of Christian Europe for their crusade against the Turk nor in securing the active support of their allies. Instead, Bismarck had remained strictly neutral, Andrássy had followed the British lead at Berlin, and Russia had been isolated. The Three Emperors League appeared to be a broken instrument—seemingly beyond repair.[83]

Other consequences of the Balkan crisis and Congress of Berlin, nevertheless, approximated the favorable outcome Bismarck had forecast in the "Kissingen dictation" of 1877. No longer did he have to be concerned that Germany's partners in the Three Emperors League might become too intimate for Germany's good. The failure of Andrássy's attempt to collaborate with Russia in the Balkans had been replaced by the likelihood of perpetual friction between them and the consequent dependency of one or even both upon Ger-

---

[81] Geiss, *Kongress*, pp. xiv, xxiii–xxiv, 207–211.

[82] For the German and French versions of the Treaty of Berlin see Geiss, *Kongress*, pp. 369–407.

[83] For Russia's reaction to the treaty see Sumner, *Russia and the Balkans*, pp. 544ff.

THE REICHSKANZLER-PALAIS. IN 1878 THE IMPERIAL CHANCELLERY MOVED INTO WILHELMSTRASSE 77, THE FORMER PALAIS RADZIWILL, NEWLY RENOVATED TO HOUSE THE CHANCELLOR'S RESIDENCE AND OFFICIAL RECEPTION ROOMS. THE FIRST MAJOR EVENT TO OCCUR IN THE BUILDING WAS THE CONGRESS OF BERLIN, JUNE 13–JULY 13, 1878. (ULLSTEIN BILDERDIENST.)

SIGNING OF THE BERLIN TREATY, JULY 13, 1878. FRONT ROW, LEFT TO RIGHT: COUNT KÁLNOKY, PRINCE GORCHAKOV (SITTING), BENJAMIN DISRAELI (LORD BEACONSFIELD), COUNT ANDRÁSSY, PRINCE BISMARCK, COUNT SHUVALOV. PAINTING BY ANTON VON WERNER, 1881. FOR AN INTERPRETATION OF THE PAINTING SEE P. 497, FOOTNOTE 21. (ALFRED FUNKE, *DAS BISMARCK-BUCH DES DEUTSCHEN VOLKES*, W. BOBACH & CO., LEIPZIG, 1921, VOL. 2, P. 80.)

man support and mediation. The cooperative conduct of French diplomats at the congress had confirmed Bismarck's prognosis that a republican and anti-clerical government in Paris would ease the tension between France and Germany. At the congress, furthermore, Bismarck finally succeeded in dispelling the British government's perennial suspicion that the new German Reich and its chancellor were a continuing threat to European peace and stability. For a time Germany's "half-hegemony" over the European balance of power was regarded with less concern in London, Paris, and Vienna. The new question was whether Russian distrust and even hostility would become the critical weak spot in German foreign relations.

BOOK FOUR

The Change of Front Completed,

1879–1880

Everyone here pipes the same tune. Everything depends entirely on Bismarck. Never has personal rule been so complete, not merely out of fear but also out of admiration and voluntary submission.

—Lothar von Schweinitz
at Berlin in 1879

Nowhere else in the world has even the most boundless admiration for the personality of a political figure led a proud nation to sacrifice so completely its own essential convictions to him. On the other hand, it has also very seldom happened that fundamental opposition to a statesman of this prodigious dimension has unleashed such a mass of hatred as was directed against Bismarck in his time by the extreme left and the German Center party.

—Max Weber in 1918

++

CHAPTER FIFTEEN

Renewal of the Interventionist State

THE ASSASSINATION attempts of Hödel und Nobiling in 1878 were for Bismarck, though not for the Kaiser, a stroke of good fortune. At a critical time in his chancellorship they enabled him to fight an election on the issue of loyalty, patriotism, and reverence for the monarch, whose result extended by one more notch his control over the machinery of government. They demonstrate again his capacity to exploit the unexpected. Yet Bismarck was not one to depend on luck. In the economic and fiscal crisis of the late 1870s he already sensed an opportunity for a major stroke in domestic policy that might achieve the objectives he had pursued in domestic affairs since 1875. A few months before the attacks on Wilhelm's life he had found what he believed to be the common denominator for the many fiscal, social, and political fractions in his problem. It was tariff protectionism.

Fiscal Crisis and Social Ferment

The chain of thought and action that led to the tariff act of 1879 began in 1875 when Bismarck, the issue of his retirement settled, resolved to seek for the Reich a "powerful, unshakable financial foundation" that would give the imperial government a dominating position over and an organic connection with the state, provincial, and local governments.[1] During the three years that followed, a fiscal crisis developed in the Reich and in Prussia that appeared to lead away from this objective. Shrinking revenues and growing expenditures compelled the Reich to depend increasingly upon state assessments (*Matrikularbeiträge*) and borrowed money to balance its budget. Once again, however, Bismarck found in adversity an opportunity for progress toward his goal, which had acquired by now a social as well as a political dimension.

Under the constitution the Reich's independent revenues were derived from tariffs and other indirect taxes—chiefly on sugar, liquor, salt, beer, and tobacco (in order of importance). Additional sources of income were profits from the imperial post and telegraph systems, the state-owned railway of Alsace-Lorraine, imperial bank, and a few other public services (mint, printing office, and patent office). Military success produced temporary financial gains. The French war indemnity paid for the cost of the war of 1870–1871, for

---

[1] See pp. 322–332.

liquidation of debts contracted by the North German Confederation, and for extraordinary costs of the Reich during 1871–1873. Enough was left for the establishment of several special funds: a war reserve, a disabled veterans fund, a fortification fund, and a Reichstag building fund.[2]

After 1874, however, the depression began to affect imperial finances. Customs revenues declined from a peak of 122,610,000 marks in 1873 to 100,020,100 marks in 1877. Of this loss more than half (about 12,000,000 marks) was attributable to the reduction and liquidation of the iron tariffs in October 1873 and January 1877. The yield from consumption taxes (tobacco, sugar, salt, liquor, beer) remained relatively constant at about 130,000,000 marks, as did the 5,000,000 to 6,000,000 marks derived from minor sources, such as the stamp tax on bills of exchange and on foreign lottery bonds. Shrinking revenues were coupled with increased expenditures for new imperial agencies, for the publicly owned telegraph network, and, in view of the mounting crisis in foreign affairs, for the army and navy. To cover the deficit, the states were assessed 73,943,600 marks in 1873, a sum that sank to 67,144,300 in 1874 but rebounded to 81,108,500 marks in 1877–1878 and 87,345,500 in 1878–1879. In 1877 the Reich began to borrow, and by 1879 the national debt had reached 138,860,700 marks.[3]

Increasing assessments for the benefit of the Reich disrupted the budgets of federal states. Under the constitution the states were assessed according to population rather than ability to pay, which meant that small states with agrarian economies had proportionately a much greater burden than their industrializing neighbors. But larger states also felt the crunch. Prussia, which in 1873 enjoyed a surplus of 73,886,000 marks, had difficulty balancing its budget by the middle of the decade. The Prussian treasury groaned under a deficit of 30,310,000 marks in fiscal 1878–1879 and 73,240,000 marks in 1879–1880. Increasing payments to the Reich (33,383,400 marks in 1873, 41,615,100 marks in 1878) were not the only problem. The depression years brought declining revenues from state-owned forests, mines, and railways.

---

[2] Karl W. Hardach, *Die Bedeutung wirtschaftlicher Faktoren bei der Wiedereinführung der Eisen- und Getreidezölle in Deutschland 1879. Schriften zur Wirtschafts- und Sozialgeschichte*, vol. 7 (Berlin, 1967), pp. 182–183; Wilhelm Gerloff, *Die Finanz- und Zollpolitik des deutschen Reiches nebst ihren Beziehungen zu Landes- und Gemeindefinanzen von der Gründung des Norddeutschen Bundes bis zur Gegenwart* (Jena, 1913), pp. 61, 521–522; Max Nitzsche, *Die handelspolitische Reaktion in Deutschland. Münchener volkswirtschaftliche Studien*, vol. 72 (Stuttgart, 1905), pp. 141–143.

[3] *Statistisches Handbuch für das deutsche Reich* (Berlin, 1907), I, 552–558, 576; Hans Günter Caasen, "Die Steuer- und Zolleinnahmen des deutschen Reiches, 1872–1944" (Dissertation, Bonn, 1953), statistischer Anhang; Richard Müller, *Die Einnahmequellen des deutschen Reiches und ihre Entwicklung in den Jahren 1872 bis 1907* (München-Gladbach, 1907), pp. 4–5; Hans Blömer, *Die Anleihen des deutschen Reiches von 1871 bis zur Stabilisierung der Mark 1924* (Bonn, 1947), pp. 24–25, 90–91; Camphausen to Bismarck, Sept. 19, 1876. DZA Potsdam, Reichskanzleramt, 1617, p. 17. *Votum* of Hofmann, Maybach and Hobrecht, June 15, 1878. DZA Potsdam, Reichskanzlei, 2081, pp. 127–131.

More important, much of Prussia's income was derived from direct taxes (for example, class and classified income taxes) more sensitive to depression than the indirect or consumption taxes of the Reich. In good years no reserves had been built up by the federal states; instead surpluses were used to retire debts, reduce and abolish taxes, and increase the size of the bureaucracy.[4] City governments were also in fiscal difficulty. In November 1877 Bismarck received from the mayor of Berlin (Hobrecht at the time) a cry for help signed by 880 communities. First submitted without result in 1874, the petition declared that Prussian legislation had increased their burdens in many areas, particularly for higher education, without providing an equivalent increase in income. Over the years, in fact, the Prussian state had deprived the cities of many sources of income, culminating in the abolition of the milling and slaughter tax in 1873. They urged a revision of the building tax, now overdue after fifteen years of economic growth, and the transfer of one-half of its yield to the communal governments (*Gemeinden*), rural as well as urban. Only such a massive infusion of new income could keep the cities financially afloat.[5]

In order to bear their burdens both city and village governments (the latter were no less affected, merely less vocal, than their urban counterparts) were compelled to resort to a highly unpopular and inequitable device, the imposition of surtaxes on the class and classified income taxes and on land and building taxes. The amount of these surtaxes varied from region to region, depending on many factors such as the needs of the governmental units concerned and variations in the tax base from which it was taken as a percentage. In the rural east the surtax paid by landowners amounted to an additional 10 to 20 percent of the direct tax, while in the Rhineland, where tax assessments tended to be low, the surtax could reach 500 percent. Trans-Elbian estate owners, still unconvinced of the justice of real estate taxes as such, deeply resented the surtax on the land and building tax. In rural areas with little industry, estate owners had to carry a proportionately larger share of the cost for public services than did the bankers and industrialists who were their urban counterparts.[6]

In the landlords' view agriculture was the victim of the failure of the Prussian state to readjust its tax policy in harmony with the transition from agriculture to industry as the chief source of wealth in German economy. Wilhelm von Rauchhaupt, Junker landlord and *Landrat*, explained what this meant. "For about thirty years our entire system of production has been skewed so significantly toward the capitalistic side that the earlier foundation of our tax system, under which landownership was regarded as the base for

---

[4] Hardach, *Bedeutung wirtschaftlicher Faktoren*, pp. 183–184; Gerloff, *Finanz- und Zollpolitik*, pp. 521–524.

[5] *DZA* Potsdam, Reichskanzlei, 2080, pp. 1–4.

[6] On the range of surtaxes see GW, VIc, 110–111; BR, VIII, 227–285; and SBHA (1883–1884), I, 685.

our whole tax system, has likewise been skewed. Today the power of capital has become so great and has surpassed that of landownership by such a margin that landowners have even fallen into a considerable dependency upon capital. As a consequence it would in fact constitute an utter misunderstanding of the taxpaying capacity of individual classes of the population in this country if we tried to continue the present system, under which everything is in the final analysis based on landownership."[7] Landlords like Rauchhaupt resented what they regarded as triple taxation on income derived from farming, that is, the land and building tax, classified income tax, and surtaxes on both. By contrast, income derived from industry was subject only to dual taxation (industrial tax paid by business enterprises and classified income tax paid by managers and investors). They demanded an income tax on corporate income, a tax on stock market transactions (*Börsensteuer*), and a special tax on unearned income (*Kapitalrentensteuer*).

In terms of ability to pay, neither landlords nor capitalists were the chief victims of Prussia's antiquated tax system. Despite a fundamental reform of the Prussian class and classified income tax in 1873, the poorer groups in Prussian society were obviously overburdened. Although an income of 1,200 marks annually per household was regarded as necessary for a minimum standard of living, 6,242,853 persons lived in households classified by the tax collectors in 1879 at less than 420 marks. The class tax ranged from 3 marks in class one (2,697,365 persons in households classified at 420 to 660 marks annually) to 12 marks in class four (290,065 persons in households classified at 1,050 to 1,200 marks annually). Like all other taxpayers, furthermore, the poor were subject to the surtaxes imposed by local officials.[8]

The assessed incomes were generally less than actual incomes, and for that reason the class tax cannot be used as a true measure of lower class income. That workers found the class tax onerous, nevertheless, seems evident from the number of tax "executions" imposed on delinquents. During the years 1878–1881, the average number of persons subject to attachments by the tax collector was 24.6 percent of class one, 25.8 percent of class two, 18.6 percent of class three, and 10.2 percent in class four. More than half of the "executions" in classes one and two were fruitless. The statistics for the cities were even worse: in Berlin, for example, the percentages of executions in the first four classes were 70, 65.6, 41.9, and 14.3. Of 190,000 attempted attachments for tax delinquency in Berlin, 178,000 were without result.[9] No less damaging to workers' morale than the tax burden itself was the knowledge that the tax rate (at most 3 percent) paid by the richest persons in the realm was

[7] *SBHA* (1883–1884), I, 679.

[8] *SBHA* (1879–1880), Anlagen, Document No. 18.

[9] "Einkommensteuer," in *Handwörterbuch der Staatswissenschaften* (2d ed., Jena, 1900), III, 39.

not much greater than their own. (The tax rolls show five persons with incomes between 1,080,000 and 2,400,000 marks in 1879.)[10]

To Bismarck the growing fiscal crisis of the Reich and state governments was not unwelcome. It created a financial need, the satisfaction of which might achieve political and social as well as fiscal objectives.[11] By 1877–1878 the shape of the reform he intended to undertake had acquired greater definition. His fundamental aim was still the "financial consolidation" of the Reich, by which he meant the acquisition of new sources of revenue (either by publicly owned enterprises or new indirect taxes) that would permit liquidation of the state assessments (*Matrikularbeiträge*). But now he hoped not only to make the Reich financially independent from the states but also to make the states dependent upon the Reich. He sought new sources of imperial income so lucrative that millions of marks in imperial revenues could be shared with the federal governments. With these millions the Prussian government could begin step by step to liquidate (as state but not as local taxes) the class and classified income taxes, land and building taxes, and their respective surtaxes. By ending the state assessments, he would remove from the Reichstag the budgetary weapon that he had unwittingly yielded in 1867. By liquidating the Prussian system of direct taxes as state taxes, he would reduce the taxing power of the Prussian Landtag. By liquidating first the entire class tax and lower brackets of the classified income tax, he could grant tax relief to the Prussian working class and *Mittelstand*, both adversely affected by the depression. By transferring what remained of the classified income tax and the land and building taxes to local governments he could end the fiscal crises of the cities and enable eastern estate owners, who controlled the county and village governments, to relieve themselves of the hated surtaxes and conceivably reduce the tax rates on their property and income.[12]

The critical factor in this complicated equation was, of course, the source of the bounty that would make it all possible. Bismarck's solution was flexible: nationalization of a major industry, which, as a state monopoly, could produce sufficient revenue to carry the main burden of the reform; imposition of indirect taxes on mass consumption items; or a combination of both. Initially his greatest hope was for an imperial monopoly of the manufacture and sale of tobacco, whose potential income was variously estimated at 130,000,000 to 163,000,000 marks. But his negotiations with Bennigsen in 1877–1878 showed that the tobacco monopoly was politically infeasible for the time being. Although reform was his primary aim in railway nationalization, he undoubtedly expected that a railway monopoly would be fiscally lucrative. Yet

[10] *SBHA* (1879–1880), Anlagen, No. 18.

[11] Christoph von Tiedemann, *Sechs Jahre Chef der Reichskanzlei unter dem Fürsten Bismarck* (2d ed., Leipzig, 1910), p. 123; Freiherr Lucius von Ballhausen, *Bismarck-Erinnerungen* (Stuttgart, 1920), p. 106.

[12] See Bismarck to Hobrecht, May 25, 1878. GW, VIc, 110–112.

the opposition of state governments compelled him, as we shall see, to abandon the project for the Reich but not for Prussia. Reinstitution of the iron tariff was originally just one of several new indirect taxes he wished to impose. But as the protectionist movement grew in size and intensity, Bismarck seized on protective tariffs (for both industry and agriculture) as the main source of the millions he needed to institute his general tax reform.

We shall see that tariff protectionism served many purposes for Bismarck—economic, fiscal, social, and political. Recent historical writing has stressed one of those purposes to the neglect of all others—namely, his so-called *Sammlungspolitik* (a term he never used), through which he is presumed to have brought the magnates of heavy industry and big agriculture together into a coalition, which, although founded on common greed, was politically useful for the legitimation and consolidation of a traditional regime threatened by the forces of "modernization." But Bismarck's social and political objectives during the last decade of his chancellorship cannot be reduced to the contours of this model. His mental processes—above all his capacity for calculating options and combinations—were far too complex to be reduced to a single formula.

If executed, Bismarck's plans for the nationalization of important enterprises and whole industries (tobacco, liquor, railways, insurance, and coal mining) would have significantly enlarged the public at the cost of the private sector of the German economy. His invasion of the capitalistic system would have been costly not only for individual branches of the system but also for its nerve center, the bourse. Like other landowners, Bismarck believed that German capitalists did not carry a fair share of the state's fiscal burden. For reasons of social justice as well as revenue, he too wished to impose taxes on the bourse (*Börsensteuer*) and unearned income (*Kapitalrentensteuer*). "It is only equitable that income derived from sources requiring no work on the part of the owner should carry a larger share of the public burden than income whose purpose is to compensate the recipient for work performed in gaining it. The beneficiary of the first kind of income is in a position, indeed a much more favorable one, to obtain the second kind as well, without sacrificing the first. Income from capital can bear a higher taxation than that from work. When invested in landed property, capital is in principle subject to taxation as real estate, but not when invested in interest-bearing securities." The proposed tax, which was to be self-assessed, must apply to "all commercial paper paying interest or dividends with the exception of mortgage obligations, since the value of the latter has already been affected by the real estate tax on the property pledged as security for the mortgage."[13] Even as Bismarck moved

[13] Bismarck to State Secretary Karl Herzog, Nov. 1, 1877. *DZA* Potsdam, Reichskanzlei, 193, pp. 40–93. Unable to make any headway with tax proposals in Prussia because of Camphausen's resistance, Bismarck launched his plan for an unearned income tax in the Reichsland, where he was the only minister. Here he returned to an idea that he had defended as early as 1850 as a

toward tariff protectionism in 1878–1879, he planned new taxes that were highly offensive to the business community that the tariff was intended to protect.

We shall see that Bismarck never succeeded in instituting the whole, but only parts of his "tax reform." What defeated him was the resistance of special interests affected by his plans, the conflicts those plans aroused among interest groups, and particularly the unwillingness of the Reichstag and Prussian Chamber of Deputies to sacrifice the power they possessed in fiscal matters. The coupling of political with fiscal and social objectives led repeatedly to the frustration of the latter two, including Bismarck's plans to relieve the hard-pressed German working class and *Mittelstand* from the burdens of the class and classified income taxes.[14]

The resistance Bismarck was to encounter from the Reichstag can be seen in the fate of those new tax bills he finally extracted from Camphausen in 1877–1878. Only one was enacted, a playing-card excise tax of insignificant yield.[15] Although national liberals recognized the disadvantages and even irrationality of the state assessments as a permanent system of public finance,[16] they were as reluctant to part with the weapon that had unexpectedly fallen into their hands as Bismarck was eager to recover it. Bennigsen's negotiations with Bismarck show that they were not insensitive to the urgency of new taxes. But they demanded a surrogate for the parliamentary power they were being asked to surrender. To achieve his ends Bismarck had to find issues of compelling force, issues capable—either because of their appeal to patriotism or to special interests—of overcoming the kind of resistance the liberal parties showed when they emasculated Camphausen's tax program in March 1878. The attempt on Wilhelm's life provided him with one such issue, the protectionist movement with another.

Progress toward Protectionism

In the Potsdam archives of the Imperial Chancellor's Office thick folders containing hundreds of letters, petitions, and other documents still testify to the size and intensity of the debate in the 1870s over protectionism versus free trade. Naturally, most of these documents stem from interests adversely affected by existing laws, particularly the law of July 7, 1873, providing for

deputy in the Prussian Chamber of Deputies. Georg Brodnitz, *Bismarcks nationalökonomische Anschauungen* (Jena, 1902), pp. 106–107.

[14] See vol. 3, chaps. 2, 6, 7, and 10.

[15] The only other new taxes that had been imposed by the Reich since 1871 were the brewing tax of 1872 and the brandy tax for Alsace-Lorraine of 1873. Hardach, *Bedeutung wirtschaftlicher Faktoren*, p. 284.

[16] See especially the remarks by Lasker and Rickert in the Reichstag debate of Mar. 10 and 12, 1877. SBR (1877), I, 50–51, 88–89.

abolition of the remaining tariff on iron as of January 1, 1877. But the agrarian and trading interests which, in alliance with free trade advocates inside and outside of the government, had secured passage of that law were also active in defending it. Although some documents on both sides of the controversy stemmed from individuals and small groups (including the magnates of industry, banking, commerce, and agriculture), many show the steady growth of organized agitation, culminating in identical petitions from different localities with thousands of signatures. The petitions for protectionism contain the names and occupations of thousands of workers and artisans, who were apparently no less convinced than employers that their jobs and incomes depended on shielding the country from foreign imports competitive with the goods they produced. These massive files give the impression of a steadily growing struggle primarily between the western and eastern provinces, between iron producers, iron merchants, and iron consumers. The conclusion is difficult to escape that no issue since the revolution of 1848, not even that of German unification, had mobilized so many people, individuals, groups, organizations, and interest groups in the effort to influence government policy.[17]

Within the government, the Kaiser was evidently the first to question seriously the wisdom of free trade. During the summer of 1875, bombarded by contradictory petitions, he proposed a delay of one to two years in executing the law of 1873 to make time for a study of conditions in the iron industry. But Delbrück and the cabinet assured him that the complaints of the protectionists were unjustified.[18] Wilhelm mused over the "puzzle" that, while industrialists and bankers (specifically Abraham Oppenheim) wrote of "stagnation," his ministers reported "everything blooming." The government, he concluded, looked to the past, Oppenheim to the immediate future.[19] In 1876 Wilhelm spent the autumn season at his old palace in Koblenz, where he apparently consulted with Ruhr industrialists. Afterward he returned to Berlin convinced that the iron industry was faced with "ruin" if the iron duties fell on schedule. He summoned a Crown Council (October 24, 1876) to discuss the matter. While protesting that he was not a protectionist, the Kaiser again proposed a delay in implementing the law of 1873. Once more the Kaiser's ministers opposed him. Abolition of the iron duties, Camphausen declared, had been included in the statute of 1873 to provide cheap farm machinery for eastern landowners to replace farm workers who had migrated to the cities during the preceding boom. Industrialists had produced their own

[17] DZA Potsdam, Reichskanzleramt, 1603–1613.

[18] DZA Potsdam, Reichskanzleramt, 1616, pp. 18, 213, 223–229, 231–243. Cabinet meeting of Sept. 22, 1875. DZA Merseburg, Rep. 90a, B, III, 2b, Nr. 6, Vol. 87.

[19] Wilhelm I to unknown person, Oct. 10, 1875. DZA Potsdam, Reichskanzleramt, 1616, p. 230. Oppenheim had petitioned the Kaiser to delay abolition of the iron tariff pending an investigation of conditions in the iron industry. Wilmowski to Bismarck, Aug. 6, 1875. *Ibid.*, pp. 214–222.

"calamity" by an excessive expansion of plant and equipment during the boom years. To extend the tariff would merely prolong the unavoidable agony of their retrenchment. The government, Achenbach argued, would arouse the dissatisfaction of consumers and inaugurate a major "struggle among interest groups" if it reversed the position it had established in the act of 1873 and defended in 1875 with the support of an overwhelming majority in the Reichstag. Despite their expectations, the complaining interests would not benefit from a continuation of the offending tariffs. Wilhelm was patently displeased on finding himself isolated among his ministers. In the margin of the official minutes of the meeting he restated his position.[20] Never again in the ten years that remained to him on the throne did he summon another session of the Crown Council.

Bismarck was absent from Berlin on leave during both of these discussions. At Varzin during 1875, he too began to express doubts about the economic policies of Delbrück and Camphausen.[21] For him laissez-faire had always been a matter of pragmatism rather than principle. Dissatisfaction with liberal economics was one, although probably not the main reason for his decision at this time to ditch Delbrück.[22] Yet his attention at that time was more on foreign-political and fiscal than on protectionist aspects of the tariff problem.[23] Beginning in October 1875, he insisted that Germany's dignity required that its free-trade policy be reciprocated by other states. He demanded retaliation against foreign governments that discriminated against German producers with tariffs and export premiums. Otherwise his thoughts at this time about tariffs were subordinated to the larger problem of a "thorough tax reform" that would bring about a shift from direct to indirect taxes (including tariffs). The drafting of such a plan, he insisted, was the duty of Camphausen and his financial experts, not the chancellor.[24]

[20] Crown Council of Oct. 24, 1876. DZA Merseburg, Rep. 90a, B, III, 2c, Nr. 3, Vol. 4. At the end of the protocol is an addendum signed by Crown Prince Friedrich Wilhelm: "I was not informed of the meeting and was not present! 13.11.76." The chancellery copy of the protocol has Bismarck's marginalia. DZA Potsdam, Reichskanzlei, 1617, pp. 70ff.

[21] Bismarck to Friedberg, July 18, 1875. GW, VIc, 61–62.

[22] See his remarks to Kardorff, Mar. 31, 1878. GW, VIII, 254–255.

[23] This view of Bismarck's original motivation in reviving the tariff question after 1875 has been developed by Hardach, Bedeutung wirtschaftlicher Faktoren, pp. 53–60. But it was also stressed by Nitzsche, Handelspolitische Reaktion, pp. 90, 145–147, and even by Oswald Schneider, "Bismarck und die preussische-deutsche Freihandelspolitik (1862–1876)," Schmollers Jahrbuch für Gesetzgebung, Verwaltung und Volkswirtschaft im deutschen Reich, 34 (1910), pp. 193–196. French exports of heavy goods to Germany were relatively unimportant during the 1870s. French imports of iron products, for example, amounted to less than 1 percent of German production, of iron and steel hardware a little more than 1 percent, and of cast iron between 2.5 and 5 percent. Bismarck's objection was more political than economic. He regarded French export subsidies as both inequitable and degrading for Germany.

[24] AWB, I, 202–204, 247–252; Heinrich von Poschinger, ed., Bismarck als Volkswirth (Berlin, 1889–1890), I, 77–78; DZA Potsdam, 1616, pp. 258–298; 1617, pp. 13–38.

Within the cabinet a struggle developed in early 1877 between Camphausen, who clung to free trade, and Achenbach, who began to lean toward protectionism. Both agreed with Bismarck, to be sure, upon the necessity of retaliatory tariffs. A government bill to this end was passed by the Bundesrat in December 1876 but died in the Reichstag.[25] In April 1877 the cabinet took over a bill to restore the iron tariffs initiated by Reichstag protectionists (Kardorff and Löwe) and, adding the retaliatory features of the preceding bill, submitted it to the Bundesrat, where it passed with vigorous support from Bavaria and Württemberg. But again the measure was torpedoed by the free-trading majority in the Reichstag.[26]

During 1877, while Bismarck was at Varzin, protectionist agitation continued to mount. In October negotiations between Germany and Austria-Hungary for renewal of the trade treaty of 1868, under way since April, were broken off. Bismarck was determined not to accept a renewal that would leave Austrian industrialists sheltered from German imports. His instructions to the German negotiators may have been intended to shipwreck the discussions in order to leave open the way for protectionist legislation in Germany. While the Hungarians were free traders, both Bismarck and the Austrians wanted to be free of treaty commitments in order to hike tariff rates. Soon afterward Bismarck advanced toward protectionism by supporting Achenbach's proposal for a general inquiry into business conditions as the preliminary step toward unilateral revisions of Germany's tariffs.[27] In February 1878 a Prussian proposal for an inquiry into conditions in the iron industry reached the Bundesrat and resulted during the summer in the appointment of two commissions, one for iron manufactures, the other for cotton and linen textiles.[28] By that time, however, Bismarck had already openly embraced protectionism.

After ending the Bennigsen candidacy and forcing Camphausen out of office in March 1878, Bismarck moved quickly to reorient the economic policy of the government. On March 31, two months before the *Attentat*, he summoned Kardorff for a discussion in which he announced his intention to dissolve the Reichstag over the tariff issue. "Earlier I was myself a free trader, being an estate owner, but now I am a complete convert and want to make good my earlier errors," Kardorff recorded him as saying. His goal was "moderate protective tariffs and finance tariffs." "I want tariffs on tobacco, spirits, possibly sugar, certainly petroleum, perhaps coffee, and I am not afraid of

[25] AWB, I, 237–243, 245–247; Poschinger, ed., *Volkswirth*, I, 94–95, 110–111; Tiedemann, *Sechs Jahre*, pp. 105–106; Ivo Lambi, *Free Trade and Protection in Germany 1868–1879. Vierteljahrschrift für Sozial- und Wirtschaftsgeschichte*, 44 (Wiesbaden, 1963), pp. 152–153.

[26] Lambi, *Free Trade and Protection*, p. 157; SBR (1877), II, 655–841; III, Nos. 76 and 123.

[27] AWB, I, pp. 257–258, 266, 272; Hardach, *Bedeutung wirtschaftlicher Faktoren*, pp. 60–63; Lambi, *Free Trade and Protection*, p. 161.

[28] Heinrich von Poschinger, ed., *Fürst Bismarck und der Bundesrat*, 1867–1890 (Stuttgart, 1897–1901), III, 449–455.

grain tariffs, which could be right useful to us against Russia and also Austria."
He listened readily to Kardorff's plea for restoration of the iron tariffs, which
the deputy reinforced by pointing out to the owner of the Sachsenwald that
falling timber prices could be attributed to the lowered consumption of wood
in coal mining and of charcoal in iron manufacture.[29] Five days later the
chancellor called upon the Prussian cabinet to consider reinstitution of the
iron tariffs as the first step toward a total economic reform program.[30] Shortly
afterward the official *Provinzial-Korrespondenz*, to the joy of Ruhr heavy industrialists, advocated "protection for domestic industry." Free trade, it edi-
torialized, ignored "the real needs of the people" and, in the absence of reciprocity from other governments, sacrificed their interests on the altar of
principle.[31]

Freight Rates and the Price of Grain and Timber

Why Bismarck abandoned free trade for protectionism in 1878–1879 is still
hotly debated. Earlier German historians were inclined to see it as a brilliant
tactical maneuver marking his transition from liberalism to conservatism or
from Manchesterism to state interventionism. This view was popular among
those who regarded the state as the moving force in history and saw Bismarck
as the greatest practitioner of *Staatsräson* since Frederick the Great.[32] Historians imbued with a materialist or sociological viewpoint, on the other hand,
are inclined to interpret the protective tariff as a feat of social engineering.
According to this view, his purpose was to weld together a new alliance of
special interests, between big agriculture and big business, in order to establish a new social foundation for the empire.[33] Another opinion is that his
primary aim was to solve the fiscal crisis in a way that would consolidate the
Reich vis-à-vis the federal states and the German Reichstag.[34] Each interpretation has some merit, but none suffices as a single explanation. All neglect
the degree to which Bismarck's perception of the problem was derived from

[29] GW, VIII, 253–256. See also AWB, I, 249–250, 310–311.

[30] Cabinet meeting of Apr. 5, 1878. DZA Merseburg, Rep. 90a, B, III, 2b, Nr. 6, Vol. 90.

[31] Poschinger, ed., *Volkswirth*, I, 143.

[32] Ludwig Maenner, *Deutschlands Wirtschaft und Liberalismus in der Krise von 1878. Archiv für Politik und Geschichte*, vol. 9 (1927); and Georg Freye, "Motive und Taktik der Zollpolitik Bis- marcks" (unpublished dissertation, Hamburg, 1926).

[33] Hans Rosenberg, *Grosse Depression und Bismarckzeit* (Berlin, 1967), pp. 187–191; Helmut Böhme, *Deutschlands Weg zur Grossmacht: Studien zum Verhältnis von Wirtschaft und Staat während der Reichsgründungszeit 1848–1881* (Cologne, 1966), pp. 419–420, 530–586; Hans-Ulrich Weh- ler, *Bismarck und der Imperialismus* (Cologne, 1969), pp. 105–106; and from the East German point of view Lothar Rathmann, "Bismarck und der Übergang Deutschlands zur Schutzzollpolitik (1873/75–1879)," *Zeitschrift für Geschichtswissenschaft*, 4 (1956), pp. 899–949.

[34] Hardach, *Bedeutung wirtschaftlicher Faktoren*, p. 195, and Gerloff, *Finanz- und Zollpolitik*, pp. 148–149.

personal experience as a landowner and from the frustrations he experienced
in his railway policy.

During the late 1870s the prince was very disappointed by the "poor return"
from his investments in farming and forestry. "Apart from the paper mills,"
he complained to Busch in October 1877, "Varzin brings me nothing. It is
hardly possible to sell grain, since railway rates for foreign grain are too low.
The same is true of timber, which realizes very little, owing to the competition. Even the proximity of Hamburg to the Sachsenwald is of little use to me
at present."[35] A year later Busch recorded the prince's reaction to a rumor
that he was purchasing an estate in Bavaria. "Bavarian estate! I have not the
least idea of buying one. I have lost enough on the one I bought in Lauenburg,
where the purchase money eats up the income of the whole property. How
can an estate yield anything when a bushel of grain is sold at the present low
price? . . . I said that long ago and tried to find a remedy. This is ruining our
entire agriculture." Busch then relayed complaints from farmers in the vicin-
ity of Leipzig about the "intolerable competition" they suffered from Polish
and Hungarian grain "in view of the high wages paid to labor," observing that
"the people look to you for assistance." "Yes," the prince replied, "there will
be no improvement until there is an increase in railway rates or a higher duty
on grain."[36]

To assume that Bismarck consciously directed the state's economic policy
to promote personal interests would be unfair. What he did was to generalize
his personal into the common interest. He concluded that the scissors of cost
and price that sheared his profits affected agriculture as a whole—for him the
most important branch of the German economy and the economic base of its
social and political order. Experience strengthened his conviction that as an
economic producer he was in a better position to assess the empirical effects
of government policy than were the lawyers, judges, and journalists who dominated parliament and the academically trained officials who staffed the bureaucracy. *He* knew "where the shoe pinched."[37] Whatever the experience of

---

[35] Moritz Busch, *Tagebuchblätter* (Leipzig, 1899), II, 457. Disgust over his income from Varzin
was one of the factors that led to Bismarck's decision to make Friedrichsruh his principal residence in 1877. *Ibid.*, II, 480, 486. But the decline in the price of timber also kept him from
harvesting all of the trees that matured each year at Friedrichsruh. *Ibid.*, II, 524. Sering's index
for lumber prices (based on the average price paid for lumber harvested from the Prussian state
forests during 1851–1875) sank from a high of 133 in 1875 to 108 in 1879. Max Sering, *Internationale Preisbewegung und Lage der Landwirtschaft in den aussertropischen Ländern* (Berlin, 1929), p.
173. See also Heinrich Rubner, *Forstgeschichte im Zeitalter der industriellen Revolution* (Berlin,
1967), in Wolfram Fischer, ed., *Schriften zur Wirtschafts- und Sozialgeschichte*, vol. 8 (Berlin,
1967), pp. 151–152.

[36] Busch, *Tagebuchblätter*, II, 535–536.

[37] See his election manifesto of July 1878. Horst Kohl, ed., *Bismarck-Jahrbuch* (1894), I, 120–
121.

other east-Elbian landowners,[38] Bismarck himself felt the pinch of falling timber and grain prices in the late 1870s and was inclined to attribute it to foreign
competition. Initially, he blamed that ill not on low customs duties but on
lower freight rates enjoyed by foreign shippers.

During 1877–1879 Bismarck often complained about differential freight
rates, particularly for timber. In March 1878 he read to the Chamber of Deputies an official report that attributed a decline of 8,000,000 marks in timber
sales of the Prussian state forests in 1877 to long-distance rates favoring Hungarian timber merchants.[39] Differential freight rates, he argued, had the effect
of "export premiums" paid to foreign producers selling in the German market.[40] "If we do not get control of and regulate these utterly senseless railway
rates," he told the forestry expert John Booth, "we will go bankrupt in the
end."[41] "The German farming population is close to ruin," he said to Austro-
Hungarian Ambassador Széchényi in late January 1879.[42] It was a "question
of life and death." Only higher tariffs and reduction of differential freight rates
could save German grain and timber producers. "I myself have cause for complaint," he remarked at a parliamentary soirée in February. "To be sure, I have
my salary to fall back on, but agriculture must be helped."[43] In March he
intervened at the Ministry of War to suggest that German lumber be used in
military construction. The durability of imported American lumber, he declared, was questionable; the government's purchase of foreign timber, furthermore, was a bad example for the country.[44]

Since 1873 the chancellor had battled in vain to gain effective regulatory
powers for the Imperial Railway Office, and in 1875 his decision to seek nationalization of the German railways was one of the principal decisions for his
change of front in domestic affairs. His purposes were several: to end financial
abuses and achieve uniformity in rates and coordination in services; to break
the influence of the "railway powers" over the nation's economy; and to give
the nation an added material foundation for its political unity. As shown
earlier, these efforts were frustrated by vested interests and advocates of free
enterprise. The greatest obstacles proved to be the German medium states,

---

[38] Hardach, *Bedeutung wirtschaftlicher Faktoren*, p. 128.

[39] BR, VII, 237–242; AWB, I, 273–274.

[40] Tiedemann to Hofmann, Dec. 17, 1878. AWB, I, 298.

[41] GW, VIII, 289.

[42] GW, VIII, 294–295. See also his remarks at the parliamentary soirée on May 17, 1879. BP,
I, 175.

[43] BP, I, 153–156. See also Poschinger, ed., *Volkswirth*, I, 202. Differential freight rates favorable to imports were a common cause of complaint among German farmers. See Hardach, *Bedeutung wirtschaftlicher Faktoren*, pp. 102–103, 107–108, 117–118. In making its case for protectionism in February 1879, the Congress of German Farmers stated that still higher tariffs would have
to be demanded if the differential were not abolished. *Ibid.*, p. 163. The issue was also frequently
mentioned in the tariff debate of May–July 1879.

[44] GW, XIV, 900–901.

which wished to control their own railways, and, to Bismarck's great annoyance, the Prussian ministries of finance and commerce, which for nearly two years were unable to agree on terms for the cession of Prussia's railways to the Reich. His discontent over these failures was one of the motives for his threat to resign in March 1877. His determination to break the "passive resistance" of Achenbach and Camphausen led to the decision to seek a separate "railway ministry" and to the ultimatum of December 1877 to his Prussian colleagues, in which action on railway policy was made a major condition for his return to duty.[45] "Private railways must be demoted from their position," he told Baron von Mittnacht.[46]

Under Bismarck's hounding, Achenbach finally did produce a bill giving regulatory authority to the Imperial Railway Office, but the Prussian cabinet had not yet acted on it when the minister resigned in March 1878.[47] His replacement, Albert Maybach, was an energetic official who, as president of the Imperial Railway Office during 1874–1876, pressed for both nationalization and a strong regulatory statute. After failing to attain either, he had resigned to take an inferior post in the Prussian Ministry of Commerce. Now he became Achenbach's successor, first as "Minister of Commerce, Industry, and Public Works" (full title of the Ministry of Commerce) and, after the division of that ministry in 1879, as "Minister of Public Works" (Bismarck's "railway ministry"), a post he held until 1891.[48] During the recurrent cabinet crises of 1878 Maybach was the only minister who kept Bismarck's confidence. Although both preferred a nationalized rail system, they finally recognized that the resistance of the medium states was insurmountable. Sometime late in 1878 they gave up the futile attempt to sell Prussia's lines to the Reich and concentrated instead on an alternative they had already discussed in 1876: the purchase by the Prussian state of all remaining private lines within its borders.[49] Such a monopoly would, particularly in combination with an Imperial Railway Office equipped by a new statute with effective regulatory powers, have much the same capacity to effect reform as would a nationalized railway.

During those months in 1878–1879 in which Bismarck abandoned free trade in tariff policy, he pushed with equal vigor for the liquidation of free

[45] See pp. 328–336, 369–375; also Tiedemann, *Sechs Jahre*, p. 132, and Hans Goldschmidt, *Das Reich und Preussen im Kampf um die Führung von Bismarck bis 1918* (Berlin, 1931), pp. 190ff.

[46] Feb. 15, 1878. GW, VIII, 245.

[47] Goldschmidt, *Reich und Preussen*, p. 191 (fn.).

[48] See Friedrich Jungnickel, *Staatsminister Albert von Maybach* (Stuttgart, 1910), pp. 28ff.

[49] AWB, I, 216–222, 232, 281–282; GW, XIV, 897, VII, 319; Alfred von der Leyen, *Die Eisenbahnpolitik des Fürsten Bismarck* (Berlin, 1914), pp. 224–231. Conflict between the ministries of commerce and finance continued, but Hobrecht was a weaker personality than Camphausen and Maybach a more committed one than Achenbach. See Tiedemann, *Sechs Jahre*, pp. 352–354.

enterprise in railways. If akin in philosophy—the rejection of laissez-faire and revival of the interventionist state—these measures were unlike in their effects. While tariff protectionism favored the interests of heavy-industry capitalism, the regulation and public ownership of railways injured those of railway capitalism. The former harmed, the latter furthered the interests of mercantile capitalism. *Both* measures, however, benefited the interests of big agriculture as Bismarck perceived them.

In early January 1879 Bismarck renewed his campaign in the Prussian cabinet and among German governments for an imperial statute regulating railway rates. "The circumstance that such a major industry affecting the public interest as railway transport is left to private firms and individual administrations for exploitation in behalf of private interests without legislative control has an analogue in the economic history of the modern state only in the old practice of farming out the collection of taxes. If the collection of the class and income taxes in each province or the collection of customs duties on certain segments of our borders were left to exploitation by private corporations in the way that railway companies set standards, they would at least be subject to rate regulations established by law. In our case the transport system lacks, where railway rates are concerned, the security of legal regulation."[50]

On February 7, 1879, he officially presented the case for a regulatory statute to the Bundesrat in the form of a "presidential bill." Despite some efforts at reform since 1876, this lengthy document declared, the existing freight rate structure, which listed 583 different standard rates and 1,370 exceptional rates, did not meet the needs of German shippers for an equitable, comprehensive, and comprehensible rate system. This was especially true where small businesses were concerned. A manufacturer in Cologne, for example, whose goods were shipped in all directions, might pay as many as thirty-six different rates. "Railways are public, monopolistic thoroughfares [licensed] by the state and can only be used by railway entrepreneurs. By granting railway companies the right to expropriate, to exercise police functions, to issue stocks and bonds, etc., the state has abandoned part of its sovereign rights. Sovereign rights are not granted in the interest of the railway owner, but in that of the common good. From this it follows that the exercise of these sovereign rights cannot be in the interest of the railway owner but only in that of the commonweal. This means that the conduct of the railway business may not be left to the arbitrary decisions of railway companies but must be regulated according to the needs of the people and of public commerce. . . . The facts are in any case that specially designed rates give a direct advantage to

[50] Bismarck to Bavarian Foreign Minister von Pfretzschner, Jan. 2, 1879. Poschinger, ed., *Volkswirth*, I, 178–179; GW, XIV, 898. Bismarck to Hofmann, Friedenthal, and Maybach, Jan. 3, 1879. AWB, I, 299–301. Bismarck *Votum* to cabinet, Feb. 7, 1879. AWB, I, 303–306. For the public discussion on the issue of state ownership of all railways see M. Alberty, *Der Übergang zum Staatsbahnsystem in Preussen* (Jena, 1911), pp. 11ff., 91–109, 142–237.

individual industries, promote local production, even give birth to new industries. In this same way the prices of certain wares in certain localities can be kept down. We cannot yield to the desire of individual railway companies to regulate and control in every direction—something like an all-pervading providence—the production and consumption of a nineteenth-century society with its manifoldly complicated factors and conditions. They must not be permitted anywhere in the country to build up individual industries by artificial means such as exceptional freight rates and at the same time to depress or even suppress industries in areas that would otherwise naturally prosper." Differential rates benefited the larger cities and were responsible for an unhealthy concentration of industry and commerce in a few great centers that was both "economically and politically" objectionable.[51]

During the first six months of 1879 the issue of protective tariffs dominated German politics and the public press. Yet Bismarck, in a letter of mid-April to Bavarian supporters, classified it as a secondary issue. "More important than tariffs are the freight rates, which give [to foreign producers] import premiums that not infrequently amount to four to five times the 50 pfennig duty. If we succeed in abolishing this injustice, I expect a greater benefit than can be obtained by doubling or even quadrupling the customs duties now proposed. But, on the basis of prior experience, I have little hope of winning the cooperation of the railway ministers of the larger federal states toward this end and of getting them to agree to a common program."[52] This pessimism was justified. Although Bismarck, in an unusual appearance, presided over the Bundesrat's initial deliberation over the rate regulation bill, the opposition of all medium and some small states was so strong that he finally let the bill die (June 27, 1879) rather than injure the federal principle by overpowering the minority.[53]

Meanwhile, Bismarck and Maybach were moving at full steam to make Prussia the "dominating railway power" in Germany.[54] In November 1879 Maybach presented and defended a government bill in the Chamber of Deputies for the purchase of four major lines. Public ownership, he freely admitted, would harm the bourse by reducing significantly the number of securities traded on the market. "I regard it as a service to limit the activity of the stock market in this connection. I believe that the bourse acts like a poisonous tree [Giftbaum] that casts its pernicious shadow on the life of the nation. For the government to sever the tree's roots and prune back its branches is meritorious." Maybach's metaphor produced indignation in the financial community

---

[51] Bismarck to Bundesrat, Feb. 7, 1879. Poschinger, ed., Volkswirth, I, 185–201.

[52] Bismarck to Baron von Thüngen, Apr. 16, 1879. Poschinger, ed., Volkswirth, I, 215.

[53] Poschinger, ed., Bismarck und der Bundesrat, IV, 92–108. A second bill giving general regulatory power to the Imperial Railway Office expired in similar fashion. Ibid., IV, 108–111. See also Leyen, Eisenbahnpolitik, pp. 80–94.

[54] AWB, I, 232, 311, 314–315.

but no rebuke from Bismarck.[55] In fact, the chancellor threatened to resign (his euphemism for a dissolution of the chamber) if the bill were delayed or defeated.[56] From estate owners and big industrialists—who stood to gain from cheaper and more efficient transport—came strong support for nationalization. Among the speakers favoring it were Friedrich Hammacher and Louis Baare, speaking in behalf of Ruhr industrialists (*Verein für gemeinschaftliche Interessen von Rheinland und Westfalen*). On December 12, 1879, conservatives, free conservatives, and national liberals passed the bill over the opposition of progressives, who deplored the consequence for free enterprise, and centrists, Poles, and Guelphs, who were opposed to greater centralism and "omnipotence of the state." The national liberal railway magnate Victor von Unruh opposed the bill, as did some other Ruhr industrialists. But not all railway entrepreneurs and investors were opposed; the depression had been cruel to railway company profits, and some rejoiced that the state might compensate them well for surrendering depressed railway shares.[57]

The acquisitions of 1879, quickly followed by three others in February 1880, settled the controversy over whether Prussia was to have a publicly owned railway monopoly. In 1878 Prussia had 4,800 kilometers of state-owned railways, in 1888, 22,420 kilometers. During that decade the Prussian state railways produced surpluses of 666,000,000 marks, over the disposal of which the Landtag had only partial control.[58] Simultaneously, there was a revival of interest in canal construction, which Bismarck also promoted and Maybach carried out.[59] The greatest achievement was the Baltic–North Sea canal across Holstein, made possible by the conquest of 1864 and completed in 1895.[60] Maybach was one of the few public officials whose talents and energies Bismarck recognized.[61] Yet, the prince was eager that posterity should know to whom it really owed these achievements in public transport. Maybach, he declared, "was merely the sword in my hand."[62]

Federalism frustrated Bismarck's plans for a German national rail system (the only imperial railway was that of Alsace-Lorraine purchased with the French war indemnity) and even for an Imperial Railway Office equipped with

[55] *SBHA* (1879–1880), I, 109; Anlagen, I, Nos. 5 and 60. See also Jungnickel, *Maybach*, pp. 74–85.

[56] Bismarck to Tiedemann, Nov. 22, 1879. *GW*, VIc, 164–165.

[57] *SBHA* (1879–1880), I, 95–171, 497–600; *HW*, II, 277.

[58] *AWB*, I, 322–323. See also Alberty, *Staatsbahnsystem*, tab. 2.

[59] *AWB*, II, 59–60.

[60] Otto Becker, "Bismarcks Kampf für den Nordostseekanal," *Historische Zeitschrift*, 167 (1943), pp. 83–97.

[61] On Jan. 1, 1881, Bismarck sent the minister a rare letter of congratulations for his "brilliant" success in "surmounting the difficulties" placed in his path by Camphausen, the Ministry of Finance, and House of Lords. *GW*, XIV, 923; see also pp. 921, 936, 945, 949, and Tiedemann, *Sechs Jahre*, p. 385.

[62] Bismarck to Poschinger, May 6, 1889. *GW*, VIII, 658.

effective regulatory authority; yet the Prussian state "railway power" permitted him to attain most of the objectives he sought. Hegemonial size enabled it to dominate the public and private railways of the lesser states in the north and to make its influence felt on railway policy in the south as well. While greatly increasing the economic and social power of the Bismarck government,[63] railway socialism conferred benefits on private enterprise and the general welfare. It ended secret rebates to favored customers and permitted a more rational, stable, and equitable rate structure. Although special and differential freight rates remained, they were used now for "mercantilistic" purposes, including the protection of domestic and particularly agrarian producers against foreign competition. In that capacity they supplemented protective tariffs. One major objective, however, was not achieved. It was not feasible to adjust freight rates in order to retard the growth of large cities. Not even a state-owned railway system could afford the cost of becoming the instrument of an antiurban social policy.[64]

Bismarck's Motives for Protectionism

Once again it is evident how accurately Bismarck spoke when he said, "it was not my way to be single-minded in political action."[65] In a broad-scale "tax reform" composed of protective tariffs, new fiscal tariffs, and new excise taxes he found a common solution to many problems. It offered him the chance: (1) to solve the immediate fiscal crises on three levels—the Reich, state, and local governments; (2) to abolish state assessments and consolidate the Reich financially against both parliament and the states; (3) to compensate for differential freight rates favoring foreign producers in the German market; (4) to replace by successive steps direct taxes on real property and personal income with indirect taxes on consumer goods; (5) to provide class and classified income tax relief for low income groups; (6) to combat the depression and the spread of socialism by increasing the prosperity of German business, providing more jobs and more income for workers; (7) to provide another common bond for big business and big agriculture, the new wealth and the old;

[63] By 1897 the Prussian railways employed 402,119 officials and 65,634 technical personnel. Walther Lotz, *Die Verkehrsentwicklung in Deutschland, 1800–1900* (Leipzig, 1920), p. 33, fn. 2. For comparative statistics on the size of state and privately owned railway systems see *Statistisches Handbuch für das deutsche Reich*, I, 291–299.

[64] Alberty, *Staatsbahnsystem*, pp. 281–344; Lotz, *Verkehrsentwicklung*, pp. 44–45, 56–57, 67. On the definitions of differential, special, and normal tariffs see pp. 53, 64. Bismarck continued to follow developments in the area of freight rates with keen interest, especially where the transport of timber and grain was concerned. AWB, I, 338–340; II, 33–39; GW, VIc, 242–243. An interesting example was his letter to Maybach, Apr. 19, 1881, in which he pointed out that reductions in freight rates had increased the sale of coal but reduced the sale of firewood and damaged the interests of the state forests and private forest owners. GW, VIc, 211–212.

[65] GW, IX, 50.

(8) to drive another wedge into the National Liberal party and, by splitting it apart, make possible a lasting progovernment alliance of moderate liberals, moderate conservatives, and ultraconservatives; (9) to lead Germany away from the politics of doctrine to those of material self-interest, which he regarded as a healthier basis for political life; and (10) to provide another national issue with which to seek the moral integration of a divided people.

These many objectives were not of equal weight. "We must throw a sop to tariff protectionists; they are our surest allies in the matter of tax reform," Bismarck told Tiedemann in April 1878.[66] His basic aim, in other words, was not protectionism but realization of the fiscal-political program he had first outlined to the Reichstag in November 1875. The appointment of four new ministers to the Prussian cabinet in the spring of 1878 (particularly the replacements of Camphausen by Hobrecht and Achenbach by Maybach) gave Bismarck the tighter grip on the Prussian cabinet that he needed for a fresh assault on this fundamental problem. When the new cabinet met on April 5, Bismarck's enhanced position vis-à-vis his ministerial colleagues was clearly evident. The chancellor stated his intentions and issued his orders; judging from the minutes, there was no discussion. He declared that "for some years" the government's economic policy had not been fully in accord with his own views. Bad health and "other considerations" had prevented him from effecting a change. Now he charged Hofmann, Maybach, and Hobrecht with the task of preparing an "economic reform program" that would produce sufficient new income from indirect taxes and tariffs, to permit either a reduction of direct taxes or their transfer to local governments. Whether the reform should be "prepared" by reinstalling the iron tariffs he left for later decision.[67]

In a message to Hobrecht, Bismarck spelled out in detail the "first stage" of his general plan "to shift from the false path of direct taxes onto the smooth track of indirect taxes." By raising 86,000,000 marks in new imperial revenue he wished to abolish state assessments (70,000,000 marks) and distribute the remaining 16,000,000 marks among the states. With its remitted assessment (42,000,000 marks) Prussia could abolish its class tax; with its share (10,000,000 marks) of the remaining surplus, it could abolish the five lowest brackets of the classified income tax. Henceforth the state should not tax incomes under 6,000 marks. The beneficiaries would be the working class and lower middle class. Delinquent taxpayers in the latter category, Bismarck believed, felt the threat of tax execution most, for they could descend the social scale, while the simple worker with an income between 420 and 1,000 marks could descend no further. At a later stage additional funds from the Reich would enable the state to relieve the financial distress of the larger cities either

[66] Tiedemann, *Sechs Jahre*, pp. 254–255.
[67] DZA Merseburg, Rep. 90a, B, III, 2b, Nr. 6, Vol. 90.

by more revenue sharing or by assigning to them the land and building taxes and the remaining brackets of the classified income tax.

Such a far-reaching plan could be achieved neither overnight nor by any single route laid out in advance. The possibility of failure in the Reichstag should be no deterrent. "Politics is long-lived and requires plans whose fulfillment will take generations." As chancellor he would seize every opportunity to advocate the necessary measures, depending on reason to triumph over party politics and rhetoric. "Educated people without a trade, without possessions, uninvolved in commerce or industry, who live only off salaries, honoraria, and coupons will in the course of years either have to yield to the domination of the economically productive part of the population or surrender their places in parliament. . . . Large, basic reforms have by their nature the capacity to attract not only those who hope to gain from them a mitigation of their current burdens but also all politicians who participate constructively in the affairs of state. But also the number of egoistic interests grows the more we present the voting public with healthy economic interests and withdraw from the political pedantry of our parliamentary debates." The "parliamentary system" might mean "ruin" in the end, but there was no substitute for it without resorting to "experiments" of whose absurdity history was a witness. "What I can still do with my own feeble strength to hinder that our new institutions are not shipwrecked by the impractical idealism of political children and doctrinaire intelligentsia and, finally, by the personal conceit of parliamentary speakers who head the caucuses—with a consequent loss of freedom and nationality, a relapse into particularism, and oscillations between anarchy and pure force—*that* I will seek to do at least as long as I live. If I find no support in this effort, I can at least observe the fall of our new grandeur more cold-bloodedly than can those who are busy bringing it about."[68]

During April–June 1878, Hofmann, Hobrecht, and Maybach produced a massive tax bill providing for higher imperial taxes and duties on tobacco (regarded as by far the best vehicle for new income), but also on beet sugar, spirits, coffee, tea, petroleum, illuminating gas, wine, and tropical fruit.[69] In the same meeting (June 6) at which he officially informed the cabinet of the deputization of the crown prince and approaching dissolution of the Reichstag, Bismarck pressed the ministers to finish their deliberations on the bill and present it to the Bundesrat "within a week." His intention was now to produce 120,000,000 marks in new money for the Prussian treasury, permitting the "nearly complete" abandonment by the state of direct taxation.[70] But the ministers did not move so fast, and in early July Hofmann summoned a meet-

[68] To Hobrecht, May 25, 1878. GW, VIc, 110–112.
[69] DZA Potsdam, Reichskanzlei, 2081, pp. 3–96, 103–160, 167.
[70] DZA Merseburg, Rep. 90a, B, III, 2b, Nr. 6, Vol. 90.

ing of the finance ministers of the German states to discuss the Prussian proposal before presentation to the Bundesrat.[71] At Heidelberg on August 5–8 it
was quickly evident that Prussia's fiscal problems were shared by all other
German states. The Prussian delegation, headed by Hofmann, secured general agreement on the proposed tax bill. The announced purpose was to liquidate state assessments, relieve state and local budgets, and avoid imposition
of higher direct taxation.[72] No mention was made, either in the Prussian bill
or in the reported results of the Heidelberg congress, of the tariff problem and
the necessity of reintroducing the iron tariff.

In their draft bill and in the discussions at Heidelberg, Hofmann and associates avoided the issue of restoring the iron tariffs for reasons that historians
have hitherto not suspected. Statistics assembled by the Imperial Statistical
Office disproved its necessity! On June 9, Hofmann was compelled to report
to Bismarck that, judging from the statistics, "the abolition of the duties on
pig iron in [October] 1873 has not resulted in an increase in imports." On the
contrary, the statistics showed a decline in foreign imports from 14,882,411
Zentner in 1873 to 11,009,333 Zentner in 1874. In 1875 imports increased
to 12,512,898 Zentner followed by a renewed decline to 11,677,155 Zentner
in 1877. German exports of pig iron, however, had continued to mount from
3,087,366 in 1873 to 7,278,678 Zentner in 1877. Domestic consumption of
iron, moreover, appeared unaffected by the tariff reductions. From a peak of
144 lbs. per person reached in 1873, it had continuously declined to 80 lbs.
per person in 1877, "regardless of price." German producers, moreover, had
dramatically improved their share of the domestic market in pig iron and fab-
ricated iron products during the same period, despite the liquidation of tariffs.
Their production seen as a percentage of domestic consumption had risen
steadily from a low of 76 percent in 1873 to 114 percent in 1877. "In view of
the foregoing, the conclusion has to be drawn that the statistical material
assembled thus far, even despite the incompleteness of the production statistics for 1877, would not suffice to substantiate the need for reinstatement of
the iron tariffs. . . . If your serene highness is agreed, a discussion of this
matter in the cabinet would hardly be advisable." It was better to await the
outcome of the inquiry into industrial conditions ordered by the Bundesrat.
In the margin of the report Bismarck scratched a laconic "Ja."[73]

According to Tiedemann, Bismarck was engaged during these months in a
serious study of economic and fiscal problems. His textbooks were not the
works of the political economists but the reports of Rhenish-Westphalian
chambers of commerce, import and export statistics, and the pamphlets of the

---

[71] Hofmann to Tiedemann, July 3, 1878. *Ibid.*, pp. 197–200.

[72] Hofmann to Bismarck, Aug. 15, 1878. *Ibid.*, pp. 219–248. *AWB*, I, 280–281; GW, VIc,
115–116.

[73] Hofmann to Bismarck, June 9, 1878. *DZA* Potsdam, Reichskanzlei, 1614, pp. 35–38. Also
Hofmann to Maybach, June 17, 1878. *Ibid.*, p. 39.

Central Federation of German Industrialists.[74] In addition, he secured detailed advice from various individuals: Wilhelm von Kardorff, leader of the free conservatives; Ministerial Counselor Georg von Mayr, whose lengthy memorandum of April 2 on taxes and tariffs and on revenue sharing between the Reich, states, and local governments seems to have provided the basis for the program Bismarck expounded in the cabinet meeting of April 5; Baron Varnbüler, Württemberg's delegate to the Bundesrat, who supplied him on April 18 with a detailed memorandum on tax and tariff policy;[75] Count Guido Henckel von Donnersmarck, Silesian estate owner and big industrialist, from whom he received two memoranda and with whom he appears to have conferred in April and June 1878;[76] and Tiedemann himself, an ardent protectionist, who had already supplied Bismarck in August 1876 with two memoranda on the necessity of keeping the iron tariffs and who, as head of Bismarck's personal secretariat (*Chef der Reichskanzlei*), was in constant contact with the chancellor wherever he was at the moment.[77]

Bismarck found these sources more persuasive than the statistics Hofmann sent him on June 9. "The more Bismarck delved into the details of individual branches of industry, the clearer he came to understand the general emergency," so Tiedemann reported years later. "His thoughts centered on one basic question—where to insert the lever to obtain relief. After a few weeks he found the answer. The new system of our political economy stood in broad outline before his eyes. The formula on which it was built was basically very simple and yet surprising to a high degree. It was the protection of *all* productive labor. Previously the most zealous advocates of tariff reform demanded only the protection of industry. No one had thought of including agriculture. But the prince recognized, with his clear vision, the common interests of both."[78] What the prince recognized was clearly not an economic reality, which his own statistics refuted, but a political opportunity. By extending his "fiscal reform" to include protectionism not only for industry but also for agriculture, he had the chance to mobilize in its behalf the most powerful interest groups in German economic and social life. Protective tariffs, furthermore, were for Bismarck finance tariffs. Here he foresaw a new source of revenue for the Reich that could replace his plan for a tobacco monopoly (whose acceptance by the Reichstag at this time appeared unlikely) as a

---

[74] Christoph von Tiedemann, *Persönliche Erinnerungen an den Fürsten Bismarck* (Leipzig, 1898), pp. 37–38.

[75] DZA Potsdam, Reichskanzlei, 2080, pp. 70–100, 109–152.

[76] Henckel-Donnersmarck to Bismarck, Mar. 29, 1878. DZA Potsdam, Reichskanzlei, 2080, pp. 52–69. Henckel-Donnersmarck to Bismarck, June 16, 1878. DZA Potsdam, Reichskanzlei, 2081, pp. 161–166.

[77] Tiedemann, "Einleitung," undated. DZA Potsdam, Reichskanzlei, 2080, pp. 101–108; Tiedemann, *Sechs Jahre*, pp. 68–89.

[78] Tiedemann, *Persönliche Erinnerungen*, pp. 37–38.

source of revenue with which to carry forward his general plan for tax reform in Prussia.

When the newly elected Reichstag assembled in the fall, the antisocialist law was obviously not to be its only fruit. On October 17, 1878, a coalition of 204 deputies—a majority in the chamber—issued a declaration favoring both industrial and agrarian protectionism. The coalition dubbed itself the "Free Economic Association of the Reichstag" and was chaired by Baron Friedrich von Varnbüler, a Württemberg statesman and long-time advocate of tariff protectionism. Included in it were 87 centrists, 36 conservatives, 39 free conservatives, and 27 liberals—a remarkable combination.[79] Bismarck was now ready to move. On October 25 he informed Varnbüler of his intent to revise the entire tariff system.[80] Three days later he dispatched to the German governments the first statement of his program and its rationale.[81] On November 12 he formally proposed that the Bundesrat create a Tariff Commission to prepare the new legislation.[82] On December 15 he outlined to the commission his views on the scope of the projected revision. When published on December 25, this "Christmas present" produced a sensation. For the first time the wide ramifications of the government's tariff revision became known to the public and the affected interests.[83]

The message of December 15 shows that the fiscal-political motive was still foremost in Bismarck's thought. "My primary interest is financial reform: reduction of the burden of direct taxes through an increase in the Reich's income from indirect taxes."[84] His basic arguments for this reform were those advanced earlier—but with added nuances and changes in emphasis. Indirect taxes were less oppressive than direct ones, which undermined the lower middle class (income to 6,000 marks). The purpose was not to increase the total income of the state, but to shift the tax burden and make it less visible. Germany lagged behind other major European states in exploiting customs revenue. To protect individual industries smacked of privilege and aroused the resentment of the unprotected. What he proposed was protection for German production "in its entirety." To place it on a somewhat more favorable basis than foreign production was an act of "justified national egoism."[85]

The burden of new tariffs would be borne not by German consumers, he insisted, but by foreign producers who would absorb the tax rather than withdraw from the German market. Only a "small minority" of the German population would not benefit—those who consumed but did not produce, that is,

[79] SEG (1878), pp. 167–168; Lambi, Free Trade and Protection, pp. 207–208.
[80] GW, XIV, 896.
[81] AWB, I, 287–290.
[82] AWB, I, 290–294, and Poschinger, ed., Volkswirth, I, 168–170.
[83] Poschinger, ed., Volkswirth, I, 107–177; Lambi, Free Trade and Protection, p. 178.
[84] Poschinger, ed., Volkswirth, I, 171.
[85] AWB, I, 288–290.

persons on fixed incomes derived from annuities, salaries, and fees, a category
that included most lawmakers and state officials. But even they would benefit
in the end from the greater prosperity of the producing classes. He questioned
the assumption that higher tariffs would result in higher prices, asserting that
the abolition of urban milling and slaughter taxes in 1873 had not resulted in
cheaper bread and meat. Other factors affected consumer prices more than
tariffs; for example, differential railway rates had the effect of "import premiums" for foreign producers. "I am also convinced, therefore, that a revision
of railway freight rates must necessarily go hand in hand with the revision of
customs tariffs. The individual states and private railways cannot keep forever
the right to compete at will with the legislative power of the Reich, to neutralize arbitrarily the commercial policy of the allied governments and the
Reichstag, and subject the nation's economic life to the oscillations that necessarily result from higher and changing import premiums for individual
items."[86]

[86] Poschinger, ed., *Volkswirth*, I, 176. In a letter to Maybach on Nov. 21, 1878, Bismarck
reiterated his view that abolition of "import premiums" in the form of differential freight rates
promised "greater success" in protecting domestic industry than the "small protection" to be
afforded by the new ad valorem duties on all incoming goods, which he, Hobrecht, Stolberg, and
Friedenthal regarded as a "finance tariff." GW, VIc, 126.

Triumph of Protectionism

Forging the Tariff Bill

O N NOVEMBER 6, 1878, Bismarck gave his only daughter, Marie, in marriage to Count Kuno zu Rantzau, secretary of legation in the German foreign office, at a ceremony in the salon of the chancellery. The Kaiser used the occasion to present the chancellor with the Grand Cross of the Order of the Red Eagle, embellished with crown, scepter, and sword—the symbols of Prussia's power—in recognition of his achievements at the Congress of Berlin and in securing passage of the antisocialist law.[1] Six days later the chancellor left Berlin for another period of recuperation at Friedrichsruh. He hoped to return by December 5 to witness Wilhelm's triumphal reentry into Berlin, celebrating the monarch's recovery and resumption of power. But on December 3 he had to request four to six more weeks "in work-free isolation and forest air" in order to arm himself for the coming battle for fiscal reform in the Reichstag. His condition, he explained, was worse than it had been in September at the end of his Gastein cure—undermined more by ministerial squabbles than by difficulties with parliament or by his exertions during the congress. "If I cannot finally have at least a few weeks of complete rest, I must give up my position quite apart from whether I want to."[2]

Bismarck remained at Friedrichsruh until February 5, 1879, but his rest was hardly "absolute." Judging from the number of documents he dictated and visitors he received (ambassadors, ministers, Reichstag deputies), he was a busy man. In January Lucius found him "reasonably well" and deep in the study of customs and tariff questions. "It is astounding with what energy he is working his way into this, for him, almost unknown material. He is very serious about his projects and may underestimate the difficulties in his way. He attributes a lot to lack of goodwill on the part of his coworkers that actually lies in the difficulty of the subject itself. He threatens resignation or another dissolution."[3] Tiedemann, who shuttled back and forth between Berlin and Friedrichsruh, bearing threats and instructions, had a similar impression. "The prince is in a very belligerent mood, believes that a lot of dynamite will

---

[1] Horst Kohl, ed., *Fürst Bismarck: Regesten zu einer wissenschaflichen Biographie des ersten Reichskanzlers* (Leipzig, 1891), II, 170–171, and *Anhang zu den Gedanken und Erinnerungen von Otto Fürst von Bismarck* (Stuttgart, 1901), I, 280–284.

[2] GW, VIc, 128.

[3] Freiherr Lucius von Ballhausen, *Bismarck-Erinnerungen* (Stuttgart, 1920), pp. 149–150.

have to be used during the year. Dissolution of the Reichstag, perhaps also dissolution of the cabinet. If his ideas about tax and tariff policy encounter opposition from Prussian ministers, he will return to Berlin, summon a cabinet meeting, and raise the cabinet question. If the ministers do not go along with him, he will request that they look for other posts and will form a new cabinet even if he has to fill the vacant posts with candidates from the ranks of junior officials [*Assessoren*]. The Kaiser agrees with him."[4]

During the first half of 1879 Bismarck, although heavily engaged in political activity, had no complaints about his health as far as the record shows.[5] Nothing appears to have altered his good disposition—neither the sprained arm and thumb suffered in a fall from steps two days after his return to Berlin nor the severe cold in late February that prevented him from attending the funeral of his old friend and ally Field Marshal Roon.[6] Political frictions of the kind that often disturbed Bismarck's equipoise were not lacking—difficulties with Varnbüler over the tariff bill; the Reichstag's resistance to the government's attempt to restrict parliamentary freedom of speech (*Maulkorbgesetz*); the unwillingness of any Reichstag caucus to permit imprisonment of two social democratic deputies, Friedrich Fritzsche and Wilhelm Hasselmann, while parliament was in session. But none appears to have fundamentally affected his nervous system. Guests at his parliamentary dinner on February 15 found him "notably fresh." No "trace" was to be seen of his "well-known nervousness."[7] In early May Bennigsen judged him "very well and cheerful, full of enterprise."[8] After three years of groping, Bismarck had found the weapon with which to flail his foes. As in 1870, the smell of an approaching victory sent adrenaline coursing through his veins. The chance to manipulate the cabinet, Bundesrat, Reichstag, and political parties by mobilizing economic interest groups in behalf of his objectives repressed his hypochondria and galvanized his energies. Once more he had a firm grip on the wires that made the puppets dance.

While the Prussian cabinet had accepted the tax and tariff program approved at Heidelberg, opinions were divided on protectionism. Hobrecht's liberalism led him to oppose it; yet the finance minister lacked both firmness and, by his confession, a grasp of the technical side of public finance. More serious was the opposition of Minister of Agriculture Friedenthal—the Sile-

---

[4] Christoph von Tiedemann, *Sechs Jahre Chef der Reichskanzlei unter dem Fürsten Bismarck* (2d ed., Leipzig, 1910), pp. 360–361. How serious he was about dissolving parliament again can be seen in Lucius, *Bismarck-Erinnerungen*, pp. 149, 152.

[5] On Jan. 15, Bismarck wrote to the Kaiser that his condition was "slowly improving." Kohl, ed., *Anhang*, I, 286–287.

[6] Lucius, *Bismarck-Erinnerungen*, pp. 150–152; BP, I, 157.

[7] BP, I, 153.

[8] Rudolf von Bennigsen to his wife, May 2, 1879. Hermann Oncken, *Rudolf von Bennigsen* (Stuttgart, 1910), II, 402.

sian estate owner, whom Bismarck had so recently praised as the only cabinet member besides himself versed in practical affairs. Among the state governments views were also mixed. Saxony and Brunswick favored the Bismarck program, while Baden, Oldenburg, and the Hanseatic cities opposed it. Other governments wavered between these poles; ministers of the critical states of Württemberg and Bavaria, for example, were divided and the outcome uncertain.[9]

The general confusion mirrored the mixed reactions of the affected interests toward Bismarck's program of universal protection. Merchants who subsisted on the export-import trade (the Hanseatic cities) and on the transit trade (Königsberg, Danzig, Stettin) were naturally unshakable in their loyalty to the principles of free trade. Industrialists (iron, steel, machines), who had long been eager to wall out foreign competitors, were shocked to learn that their own arguments could be used in behalf of farmers and estate owners. Their aim was higher prices, not higher costs. If the worker paid more for a loaf of bread, his income would ultimately have to rise. What came in the front door might well go out the back. Agrarian producers, on the other hand, were not happy over the prospect of higher prices for the manufactured articles they purchased. Those landlords still committed to free trade had to be convinced that the danger of massive imports from the United States and elsewhere was real and that their future lay in domination of the domestic market. Manufacturers dependent upon imported raw materials (for example, Bavarian breweries processing Austrian barley) faced the prospect of higher costs. Every producer, whether industrial or agrarian, who had markets abroad was apprehensive that foreign governments would retaliate. Bismarck's argument that foreigners would bear most of the burden of protectionist duties was enticing, but not universally convincing.[10]

Bismarck's tactics were the familiar ones of seduction, division, public pressure, and the threat of other options. His tariff program, he declared, was like a Christmas table laden with gifts for everyone, including toy rattles for the children.[11] To the many citizens and organizations that wrote him to deplore the state of the economy, he began to send personal replies, insisting on the injustice of direct taxation, on the need to protect agriculture as well as industry, and on the virtues of shifting the fiscal burden to foreign producers

---

[9] Ivo Lambi, *Free Trade and Protection in Germany 1868–1879*. *Vierteljahrschrift für Sozial- und Wirtschaftsgeschichte*, 44 (Wiesbaden, 1963), pp. 181–184.

[10] For the social and economic forces involved in the struggle over protectionism and free trade see Lambi, *Free Trade and Protection*; Karl W. Hardach, *Die Bedeutung wirtschaftlicher Faktoren bei der Wiedereinführung der Eisen- und Getreidezölle in Deutschland 1879. Schriften zur Wirtschafts- und Sozialgeschichte*, vol. 7 (Berlin, 1967); Max Nitzsche, *Die handelspolitische Reaktion in Deutschland. Münchener volkswirtschaftliche Studien*, vol. 72 (Stuttgart, 1905); and Helmut Böhme, *Deutschlands Weg zur Grossmacht: Studien zum Verhältnis von Wirtschaft und Staat während der Reichsgründungszeit* (Cologne, 1966), pp. 421ff.

[11] At a parliamentary dinner on Feb. 15, 1879. *BP*, I, 149–150.

and of taking away the "import premiums" they enjoyed through differential freight rates. These *Bauernbriefe*, as they came to be called, were released to the press and received wide publicity.[12] In dealing with Prussian ministers and federal states the prince resolutely insisted on the indivisibility of his program. Protection for industry, he warned Varnbüler and company, depended on protection for agriculture. If denied the latter, he would "try it again with the free traders."[13] He was equally firm with those who, like Hobrecht, wished to separate the finance tariffs, on whose necessity there was general agreement, from the protective tariffs, on which opinions varied. To keep the latter legislation under his control he presented it as a "presidential bill," the device developed by Delbrück that Bismarck had earlier castigated.[14]

The bill was developed by the Tariff Commission, and Bismarck's first task was to manipulate the deliberations of that body to produce the desired result. Of the fifteen members, three were appointed by the chancellor, three by Prussia, two by Bavaria, and one each by Württemberg, Saxony, Mecklenburg, Hesse, Baden, Weimar, and by the Hanseatic cities collectively. Bismarck's choices as imperial delegates were Tiedemann, his personal adjutant, Emil von Burchard, head of the Imperial Treasury, and as chairman (a brilliant choice as events were to prove) Varnbüler, the most prominent spokesman for industrial protectionists in the Reichstag. While the commission sat, Bismarck was in frequent contact with Tiedemann and Varnbüler.[15] To dominate the body, they required two votes in addition to those of the Reich and Prussia. Since the majority favored protective duties for industry, Bismarck's tactic was to force consideration of the agrarian tariffs first. The message was clear: the states would have to swallow the latter to get the former. The chancellor advocated a single duty of 10 marks per ton on all imported grains, but Varnbüler insisted on 5 marks for rye and corn, and Bismarck had to yield in order to gain Württemberg's vote. When agrarian Mecklenburg deserted the free-trading ranks, a majority of eight was secured for the 5 mark rate. The proposed duty on pig iron was 10 marks per ton, the amount desired by the Association of German Iron and Steel Industrialists, but 4 marks higher than that recommended by the Central Federation of German Industrialists. Bavaria, Saxony, Hesse, and Baden held out for 6 marks, but Weimar and again

[12] For examples of these letters see *GW*, XIV, 899–903, and Heinrich von Poschinger, ed., *Bismarck als Volkswirth* (Berlin, 1889–1890), I, 181–184, 207–208, 211; and Georg Freye, "Motive und Taktik der Zollpolitik Bismarcks" (unpublished dissertation, Hamburg, 1926), pp. 176ff. Many more are to be found in the archives. *GW*, VIc, 129–130.

[13] Tiedemann, *Sechs Jahre*, pp. 361, 363–364; Lucius, *Bismarck-Erinnerungen*, pp. 151–152.

[14] Bismarck to Hofmann, Mar. 7, 1879. DZA Potsdam, Reichskanzlei, 2081a, pp. 136–137. *GW*, VIc, 129–133, 216–227. To Wilhelm he complained that his ministerial colleagues helped little in drafting the bill. Kohl, ed., *Anhang*, I, 287.

[15] DZA Potsdam, Reichskanzleramt, 1614, 1615, 1618.

Württemberg provided the necessary eight votes for the majority. These were the critical issues; other duties were accepted with less difficulty.[16]

Another Bismarck tactic was speed. The protectionist movement had provided momentum; now the moment had come to act before the free traders could organize and ally with those who supported protection for some products but not for others. Working under forced draft, the Tariff Commission, which had assembled on January 3, completed the presidential bill on March 26. For weeks Bismarck had again been stoking the steamroller in order to flatten all obstacles in the Bundesrat. He warned the state governments of the dangers of socialism, of the need for monarchical solidarity, and of the need to combat radicalism by swift action to overcome the depression.[17] By the time the Bundesrat received the bill, groused the Hamburg delegate, nothing was left to do but vote. The chancellor himself presided over the crucial sessions, and on April 4 when the discussion ended, only Oldenburg and the Hanseatic cities voted in the negative. The only significant amendment was one Bismarck proposed—the so-called "retaliatory paragraph" authorizing the Bundesrat to double the duties against foreign states that discriminated against German products. Among the measures forced upon the Bundesrat that day was a resolution requiring that the bill go "to the Reichstag as soon as possible." But during the very hour of its passage the Reichstag deputies, knowing that the tariff bill was on its way, voted to recess for a month.[18] The steamroller ground to a halt.

The Liberals React

The protection of agriculture was Bismarck's child. It is true that the protectionist movement had made progress among German landowners in recent years. The Association of Tax and Economic Reformers, the economic counterpart of the new German Conservative party, was founded on a free-trade program in 1876, but shifted to low finance tariffs in 1877 and to protectionism in 1878–1879. The association was composed of about 700 landowners, many of whom were among the 250 "owners of larger estates" that composed the Congress of German Landowners, which on February 24, 1879, also embraced the protectionist cause.[19] Both organizations, earlier staunchly anti-industrialist, entered hesitantly into an alliance with the Central Federation of German Industrialists to support the Bismarck program. The agreement

---

[16] Lambi, *Free Trade and Protection*, pp. 180–188. On Varnbüler's difficulties with Bismarck on the agrarian duties see Rudolf Vierhaus, ed., *Das Tagebuch der Baronin Spitzemberg* (Göttingen, 1961), p. 177.

[17] Lambi, *Free Trade and Protection*, p. 180.

[18] Lambi, *Free Trade and Protection*, p. 189; Heinrich von Poschinger, ed., *Fürst Bismarck und der Bundesrat, 1867–1890* (Stuttgart, 1897–1901), IV, 55–57.

[19] Bismarck may have had some influence on this decision. *BP*, I, 156.

was one of principle, not detail, for each pressure group had an interest in holding down the duties demanded by the other. In 1878–1879 the bond between big agriculture and big business was by no means firm. Without Bismarck's sponsorship it might not have endured.

German agriculture, furthermore, did not speak with a single voice. In late January 1879 the German Council on Agriculture, elected in 1877 by regional associations throughout the country, voted for fiscal and against protective tariffs.[20] Among east-Elbian landowners there was still a strong commitment to free trade, for many continued to profit from exports. In the transit ports of the Baltic the hard wheat grown on Russian plains had to be mixed with German soft wheat before shipment to the flour mills of western and southern Europe. By the 1870s, moreover, some farmers of the eastern region were raising livestock for the slaughterhouses of Berlin and other cities and required cheap feed. Early in 1879 the diets of the provinces of East and West Prussia rejected protectionism, as did the farmers' associations of Brandenburg, Königsberg, and Silesia. Meadows predominated over grain fields in northwestern Germany, and the cattle breeders and dairy farmers of that region were interested in exports and in low-priced feed. Hence the parliaments of the federal states Lippe and Oldenburg also rejected protectionism. Only in the industrial regions of Upper Silesia, Saxony, and Rhineland-Westphalia, where rural and urban prosperity were closely linked, was there solid support for both agrarian and industrial protectionism. In Baden and Württemberg, where industrialization was less pronounced and small subsistence and livestock farms were common, opinions were contradictory and ambivalent. The same was true in Bavaria, where farms varied widely in size and product.[21]

Where parliament was concerned the vital question was how the National Liberal party would react. "What do you say to the newest Bismarck?" Miquel inquired of Bennigsen in late December 1878. "This chess move is intended to bring landowners and industry under one hat and probably will. The situation is for us extremely difficult, and I am very uncertain whether the liberal middle class, disunited as it is, will be equal to the task."[22] Six weeks later

[20] The views of the council may no longer have been representative of German agriculture. See Lambi, *Free Trade and Protection*, p. 148, and Hardach, *Bedeutung wirtschaftlicher Faktoren*, pp. 125–126.

[21] Lambi, *Free Trade and Protection*, pp. 137–149; Hardach, *Bedeutung wirtschaftlicher Faktoren*, pp. 81–138, 158–164. Hardach has corrected the traditional view that in 1877–1879 east German landowners as a whole turned protectionist (when faced with competition from America and eastern Europe) by showing that the interests of most were still export oriented and that their views reflected their interests. Yet he may have overstated his case. How without statistical verification he can assert that the "majority" of German farmers had "a very small interest in a duty on grain" (p. 125) is hard to see. Hardach's basic finding—that Bismarck was decisive in mobilizing the protectionist movement and that he did so for fiscal and political purposes—does not differ much from that of Lambi. See Lambi, *Free Trade and Protection*, pp. 169ff.

[22] *HW*, II, 227.

Miquel, who as mayor of Osnabrück in Hanover was in a good position to observe, reported the new alliance as an accomplished fact. "Here industrialists and agrarians have gained the upper hand completely. Throughout the west as well, as I hear from every side."[23] Those on the left wing of the party also felt the shock waves from Bismarck's action. "The Bismarck system," Forckenbeck wrote to Stauffenberg, "is developing with fearsome speed just as I always feared. Universal military conscription, unlimited and excessive indirect taxes, a disciplined and degraded Reichstag, and a public opinion ruined and made powerless by the struggle between all material interests— that is certainly the politics of popular impotence, the end of any possible development toward constitutional freedom, and at the same time a terrible danger for the entire Reich and the new imperial monarchy. Is the National Liberal party a suitable instrument to combat such dangers with its present politics, its present program and its present composition? Will we not be led deeper and deeper into the quagmire? Has pure opposition not become a duty?"[24]

When the Reichstag convened in mid-February 1879, the national liberals abruptly rejected overtures from the two conservative parties and succeeded in reelecting Forckenbeck as president and Stauffenberg as first vice-president.[25] They combined with progressives and centrists, moreover, to reject the government's bid to arrest the two social democratic deputies, Fritzsche and Hasselmann, who had dared to take their seats in defiance of a decree banning socialist agitators from Berlin. In early March, moreover, the same combination handed the government another sharp defeat by voting down a presidential bill that would have empowered the Reichstag to censure radical deputies who "misused" the tribune to express their views. Under this "muzzle act," as it was dubbed, the chamber could have expelled recalcitrant deputies, excised speeches from the stenographic record, and forbidden their publication in the public press.[26] Bismarck found this respect for civil and parliamentary rights "irritating" and his disparaging remarks about judges who were more interested in protecting criminals than in protecting society provoked a nasty exchange with Lasker, himself a judge, that even Lucius found harmful for the conduct of parliamentary business.[27]

That the National Liberal party was not now, if indeed it ever had been, a "suitable instrument" for systematic opposition was quickly evident when it confronted the tariff issue. At the end of March the caucus divided, according to Julius Hölder, into three groups: thirty-two protectionists, forty-two free

---

[23] *HW*, II, 232–233.

[24] Forckenbeck to Stauffenberg, Jan. 19, 1879. *HW*, II, 230.

[25] Oncken, *Bennigsen*, II, 401. The second vice-presidency went to the free conservative Robert Lucius after the refusal of Hohnenlohe-Langenburg.

[26] *SBR* (1879), I, 17, 23–39, 248–318.

[27] Lucius, *Bismarck-Erinnerungen*, pp. 153–154; *BR*, VIII, 400–404.

traders, and about twenty-eight who hoped for some kind of compromise. "This is truly a chess game. The question is who will force the others out. Bennigsen must soon decide."[28] By early May Bennigsen estimated that the middle group had grown to fifty-two, while twenty-eight still clung to protectionism and twenty-two to free trade. For Bennigsen to have sought harmony through the expulsion of either group would have been out of character. As usual his aim was to avoid political suicide for the party by finding some basis for agreement with Bismarck that the majority at least could accept. The compromise he fashioned consisted of a moderately protective general tariff, finance tariffs sufficient to balance state budgets, increases in the tobacco tax, later consideration of a beer tax, and devices to preserve the Reichstag's power over the purse even after liquidation of the state assessments. Through such arrangements he hoped to hold down the dissidents to no more than twenty-five deputies, perhaps fewer. If the number were larger, he realized, the national liberals have nothing to bargain with. Instead of forcing expulsion of the free traders, he negotiated with them, to the neglect—and disgust—of Hölder and the protectionists.[29]

By adjourning the Reichstag for an unusually long Easter vacation (April 3–28, 1879), Forckenbeck hoped to gain time for a free-trade counteroffensive which he, Benda, Rickert, Bamberger, and Lasker had plotted on New Year's Eve.[30] Because of his status as an aristocrat (third generation), president of the Reichstag, once president of the Prussian Chamber of Deputies, lord mayor earlier of Breslau and now of Berlin, Forckenbeck had long been regarded as the best candidate for leadership in any attempt to reunite the liberal movement. In the past, he had avoided the kind of parliamentary duels that had made Lasker both famous and notorious and had carefully nurtured a good relationship with both the Kaiser and crown prince. Yet in late 1875, when Lasker and others had wanted to seek "emancipation from Bismarck" and to "develop the constitution,"[31] he had demurred. Now three years later, under circumstances far less advantageous, he finally tried to seize the initiative. He would "rather sink" than "swim with a reactionary current," he told Stauffenberg.[32]

In January Forckenbeck had considered his position at the head of Berlin's city government a handicap for such an action, but now he exploited it. At his instigation the Berlin City Council petitioned the Reichstag (April 6) to reject tariffs on foodstuffs that would lower the living standard of urban dwell-

---

[28] Dieter Langewiesche, ed., *Das Tagebuch Julius Hölders, 1877–1880* (Stuttgart, 1977), p. 169.

[29] Oncken, *Bennigsen*, II, 404–405; *SBR* (1879), II, 1026–1037.

[30] *HW*, II, 230–231. Although generally expected to defend free trade in the Reichstag, Lasker, it was decided, should "remain out of play" insofar as public agitation was concerned.

[31] See pp. 330–332.

[32] *HW*, II, 231.

ers; twenty-three coastal cities joined the protest. Seventy-two cities responded to his call for a "general convention of German cities." But by the time their 117 delegates assembled in Berlin (May 17), the cause was already lost. Few delegates came from the western and southern cities, where protectionism flourished, and even Breslau resisted the invitation of its former mayor. At a banquet in the Zoological Garden, nevertheless, Forckenbeck astonished 150 guests (including many left-liberal deputies) with his oratory. The time had come, he declared after many toasts, for "the German burgher class" to throw its weight into the scales, to develop "a great liberal party" that would defend the interests of all classes (*Stände*), both urban and rural. But the "anti-corn law league" which Forckenbeck, Löwe, Richter, and others envisioned in the alcoholic ambience at the Zoo was stillborn and for good reason. That great, monolithic German middle class (*Bürgertum*), inspired by the classical ideals of economic and political freedom, waiting to be summoned to "energetic action" in behalf of a common program, simply did not exist. Like the "collective will of the nation" and the "genuine German national sentiment," of which Forckenbeck also orated, it was a myth upon which liberal politicians, writers, and professors had fed for decades. Three days later a sobered Forckenbeck, hopelessly compromised, resigned the presidency of the Reichstag. Stauffenberg followed by resigning the vice-presidency.[33] The protective tariff had produced its first sacrifices.

The Center Party Reacts

That Bismarck was not dependent upon the National Liberal party as a whole to secure passage of his protectionist program had been evident since October 1878, when eighty-seven centrists signed the protectionist declaration of the Free Economic Association of the Reichstag. Centrist programs had never committed the party to economic liberalism, and centrist deputies represented regions of the country (south and west) where protectionist sentiment ran high among both farmers and businessmen. But obviously the Center party expected to exact a price for its support of the government's tariff program. Despite the pope's condemnation of Hödel's deed, the party had collaborated in some electoral districts (for example, Mainz and Essen) with social democrats in the July election,[34] and it had voted against the antisocialist

[33] Martin Philippson, *Max von Forckenbeck: Ein Lebensbild* (Leipzig, 1898), pp. 313–321; SEG (1879), pp. 164–168; BP, I, 177. At the end of Dec. 1879 Crown Prince Friedrich Wilhelm told Forckenbeck that on reading this speech he had "rejoiced" over the prospect of a great united liberal party representing the entire German burgher class. But Forckenbeck offered him little information that was "consoling." Ernst Feder, ed., *Bismarcks grosses Spiel: Die geheimen Tagebücher Ludwig Bambergers* (Frankfurt, 1933), pp. 321–322.

[34] Erich Förster, *Adalbert Falk: Sein Leben und Wirken als preussischer Kultusminister* (Gotha, 1927), pp. 541, 543–544, 604; GW, VIc, 120–121. Franckenstein denied there had been any pact. Tiedemann, *Sechs Jahre*, p. 334.

statute in 1878. During the winter session of the Prussian Landtag Ludwig Windthorst, knowing that there was no chance of success, attempted to save the remaining Catholic teaching orders from the dissolution scheduled under the May laws and sought reinstatement of paragraphs 15, 16, and 18 in the Prussian constitution. In January 1879 the Center picked up some support from ultraconservatives by denouncing Falk's secularization of the schools as responsible for the increasing moral degeneration of society.[35] In reply to these assaults, Falk yielded not an inch of the government's position on the Kulturkampf, with the warm approval of Bismarck and the Kaiser.[36] As long as Falk remained in office and the Kulturkampf appeared unabated, liberals could assume they were still necessary to Bismarck at least on this front, despite the signs of his disaffection on others. Evidently for this reason Bennigsen presumed that he still had some leverage on Bismarck.

Falk, however, was already in jeopardy. For months during 1878 he had been at odds with Wilhelm over Protestant church affairs. The Kaiser was deeply disturbed over the dominance that liberal churchmen (the "falsifiers of our doctrines") had achieved in the governance of the Evangelical church. In May the minister tendered his resignation rather than accept two reactionary court preachers whom the king wished to see appointed to the church's highest body (*Oberkirchenrat*). During Wilhelm's incapacitation the matter remained in abeyance. In December, when it had to be faced, Bismarck finally persuaded Falk to yield to the old monarch's whim on the grounds that the issue was secondary compared to the Kulturkampf.[37] Throughout 1878 Bismarck sought repeatedly to reassure Falk of his own constancy in the Kulturkampf. After talks with Masella in August, he summoned the minister to Bad Kissingen to report that no settlement, certainly no surrender was in prospect. Similarly he kept Falk informed during the following months about his responses to the continued overtures of Leo XIII and the new Vatican state secretary, Cardinal Nina.[38] These messages came through many channels and, to the alarm of both Falk and Bismarck, had some effect at court. The pope was eager to ease old tensions with governments everywhere in Europe and, since his efforts were widely reported in the press, both the Kaiser and crown prince feared that Prussia, by not responding, would gain an image of unreasoning intransigence.[39]

Bismarck reacted to these overtures with restraint, his responses dilatory.[40] He was not convinced that the Vatican had much to offer in return for the

---

[35] Förster, *Falk*, pp. 547–592, 594.

[36] Kohl, ed., *Anhang*, II, 513–518; GW, VIc, 126–129.

[37] On the background and course of this crisis see Förster, *Falk*, pp. 352–502.

[38] Erich Schmidt-Volkmar, *Der Kulturkampf in Deutschland, 1871–1890* (Göttingen, 1962), p. 241; GW, VIc, 109–110, 115; VIII, 268.

[39] GW, VIc, 133–134; Förster, *Falk*, pp. 543–545.

[40] Schmidt-Volkmar, *Kulturkampf*, pp. 236–248.

concessions it hoped to exact, and he was no longer so sure that the Vatican could control the conduct of the Center.[41] But at the same time he anticipated that the continuing exchange of notes between the Vatican and Berlin and the stories about improved relations that appeared in the newspapers would produce an uncertainty in the minds of centrists and liberals that would make them more tractable in their relationships with the government. Both had to face the prospect that an agreement between Berlin and the Vatican might undercut the position they had taken in the Kulturkampf.[42] Although his distrust continued, Bismarck had now come to accept the Center as a permanent, perhaps necessary, part of the political scene. Its dissolution, he wrote King Ludwig of Bavaria in February 1879, would contribute little to the strength of the government, for most of its fragments would merely gravitate into other camps.[43] To return to an earlier metaphor, Bismarck had decided to open up the entire chessboard for his coming gambits in domestic politics.

Two days after his return to Berlin on February 5, 1879, Bismarck was "pleasantly surprised" to receive through Lucius an overture from Windthorst, who spoke of giving precedence to political over religious considerations and of his Guelph loyalty as a sentiment that did not influence his attitude on the tariff issue.[44] Shortly afterward, Bismarck granted an interview to Baron Georg von und zu Franckenstein, a prominent Bavarian and centrist leader. Denying that he was a "*Kulturkämpfer* by passion," Bismarck blamed the outbreak of the struggle on the confessional nature of the Center and especially on the need "to save the German language and to spread German sentiment [*Gesinnung*]" in Posen and Upper Silesia. Claiming that he was not a centralist, he spoke of Prussia as being too large and powerful in Germany; several large states would be preferable. Germany and Austria united, perhaps through a constitutional relationship, but not a customs union, would be the best guarantee of European peace. While he could not yield to the Vatican's demands for abolition of the May laws and reinstatement of the excised paragraphs in the constitution, he was "no friend of civil marriage" and had signed the bill only because Roon, Camphausen, and Falk threatened to resign.[45]

On March 31, 1879, the chancellor, during an hour-long private talk with Windthorst, speeded the rapprochement by granting an annual pension to

---

[41] GW, VIc, 115, 133–134, 144–146; VIII, 268–269; XIV, 894. When Cardinal Franchi, whom Bismarck credited with a conciliatory attitude toward Germany, died suddenly on Aug. 1, Bismarck believed the report that he had been poisoned. The pope, he asserted, now talked peace but refused concessions to attain it either because he feared the same fate or because of the new influence of Franchi's opponents in the Vatican. Bismarck to Wilhelm I, Jan. 15, 1879. GW, VIc, 134–135; BP, I, 152.

[42] Bismarck to Falk, Aug. 8, 1878. Förster, *Falk*, p. 533.

[43] GW, VIc, 146. Förster, *Falk*, pp. 604–605.

[44] Lucius, *Bismarck-Erinnerungen*, pp. 150–151.

[45] GW, VIII, 295–298; BP, II, 314ff.

the widowed Queen Marie of Hanover. In discussing a possible settlement of the Kulturkampf, he offered to resume diplomatic relations with the Vatican if the pope would grant the *Anzeigepflicht,* that is, the church's duty to notify the state of nominations for and appointments to ecclesiastical offices and the state's right to veto the same. Windthorst had to reply (probably with some bitterness) that he was uninformed concerning the talks going on between Rome and Berlin. But he doubted that the papacy would ever yield the veto power to the state. Whether the chancellor brought up the subject of the tariff bill is doubtful.[46] He had no need to buy votes from centrists with major concessions in the Kulturkampf, since they had already declared for protectionism. On the eve of the tariff debate (May 2), the Reichstag caucus confirmed its decision to vote for protective tariffs, but also announced its intention to keep a "free hand" where finance tariffs and the tobacco tax were concerned. The centrists' purpose was to preserve the state assessments as a bulwark of federalism.[47] On the following evening Windthorst created a sensation by appearing at Bismarck's soirée for the first time since 1869. Formally dressed in tails, a medal gleaming on his chest, the half-blind little man was warmly received by his host who guided him to a seat where they talked at length, while the deputies gaped. Nor did the deputy from Meppen react when his host accidentally drenched him with beer, bringing a distressed Johanna to his rescue with a napkin. Afterward, a grinning Windthorst warded off all questions about what transpired in the conversation with the comment: "*Extra centrum nulla salus.*"[48]

As the great tariff debate began, Bismarck's chances of success and the options he would face were already taking shape. Protectionism for industry appeared to be assured, that for agriculture less certain, at least not at the higher rates Bismarck desired. By linking industrial to agrarian protectionism, however, he had made both difficult to oppose. The finance tariffs and new taxes, however, were another matter. Here he still faced the obstacle that had ruined von der Heydt in 1868—the reluctance of a goodly segment of the Reichstag, albeit for differing reasons, to surrender the power unexpectedly gained from the annual state assessments. But now at least Bismarck had options. He could either come to terms with the national liberals by granting new guarantees for the Reichstag's power over the purse or settle with the

[46] *BP,* I, 172; II, 327; Margaret Lavinia Anderson, *Windthorst: A Political Biography* (Oxford, 1981), pp. 219–221. The request for this interview came from Windthorst. Windthorst to Bismarck, Mar. 31, 1879. DZA Potsdam, Reichskanzlei, 1400, p. 113.

[47] *SEG* (1879), pp. 112–113, 131–132. See also Windthorst's speech on May 8, 1879. *SBR* (1879), II, 1069.

[48] *BP,* I, 170–171. Earlier in the evening the deputies had been surprised by the appearance for the first time of Alsatian "Protesters." Among other centrists attending was Schröder-Lippstadt, of whose radicalism Bismarck had so bitterly complained in earlier years.

BISMARCK PRESENTS LUDWIG VON WINDTHORST TO JOHANNA AT THE PARLIAMENTARY SOIRÉE ON MAY 3, 1879. A CONTEMPORARY WOODCUT. (BILDARCHIV PREUSSISCHER KULTURBESITZ.)

Center by preserving the state assessments. The first course meant the establishment of new, the latter the preservation of old law.

Passage of the Tariff Act

The Reichstag deliberations on the tariff bills lasted more than two months (May 2–July 15, 1879). They were marked by lengthy and often stormy debates, agitated discussions in the tariff committee, unprecedented lobbying by the affected interests, competitive logrolling among the deputies, heated party caucuses, and many private negotiations between Bismarck and party leaders, particularly with Bennigsen and Windthorst. The press followed the affair with impassioned concern. Assemblies and mass meetings were frequent; petitions poured into Berlin from many quarters. The chancellor, who in recent years had often appeared to be on the verge of physical collapse and forced retirement, was the eye of the storm, the center around which swirled the winds of special interests and the debris of shattered ideals and threatened careers. Never, not even in 1866–1867 and 1870–1871, had he shown greater energy and skill in the manipulation of German public opinion. Again he demonstrated, in the words of a liberal, that he was "one of the greatest rulers of the masses in our time."[49]

On May 2 Bismarck launched the first reading of the tariff bill by summarizing the points he had made publicly and privately during preceding months. His primary case was again fiscal—the need to "consolidate the Reich" by establishing its financial independence, to solve the financial crisis by raising new money, and to reduce the burden of direct taxation on real estate and income. On the protectionist issue he stressed that Germany had become the dumping ground for the surplus products of other countries (France, Russia, America), which were raising tariff walls against German goods. The products he talked about most were those dearest to his heart and purse—grain and timber. In denouncing direct taxation he waxed most eloquent in describing the fate of the farmer: "No industry in the entire country is taxed so high as agriculture." "The work and production of the Fatherland" had to be protected against those abroad (particularly Russians) who "prospered from German gold." The issue should be above politics and factionalism, for it concerned the "welfare of the German people."[50] Bennigsen recognized that the speech, aimed primarily at gentry landlords and their wavering representatives, was a "demagogic masterpiece."[51]

In the debates and literature of the period the protectionist case was presented in nationalistic as well as materialistic terms. At Easter the semiofficial *Norddeutsche Allgemeine Zeitung*, for example, wrote of the need for "economic armament." Germans, it declared, had spent their "precious blood" to expel foreigners and "regain" their national unity. "Henceforth, the new German state will no longer be sacrificed economically any more than politically

---

[49] The quotation is credited to the Württemberg liberal Julius Hölder and is probably authentic, although unverifiable. Heinrich von Poschinger attributed it to Hölder's diary and dated it Mar. 15, 1879. *BP*, II, 338. But the entry cannot be found in the manuscript of the diary. The source was probably a letter now lost. See the editorial comments by Dieter Langewiesche, ed., in *Tagebuch Hölders*, pp. 38–39. Hölder's diary gives eloquent testimony of the awe and fear with which Bismarck was regarded by German politicians during the critical weeks of the tariff debate. *Ibid.*, pp. 178, 180.

[50] *BR*, VIII, 3–11; *SBR* (1879), II, 927ff. See also *GW*, VIc, 136–137, and *BP*, I, 164. Concerning Bismarck's interest in the timber tariff see *ibid.*, I, p. 175.

[51] Oncken, *Bennigsen*, II, p. 402.

to a foreign domination that, among other things, has increasingly impoverished the German Reich from year to year in commerce, agriculture, and
industry and subjected it to the danger of losing in another way the political
independence so dearly purchased."[52] To a country whose national unity, so
recently gained, was still a self-conscious and insecure possession, whose social order was threatened by economic catastrophe and socialist subversion,
and whose population had witnessed a series of menacing international crises
during 1875–1878, the invasion of foreign merchandise seemed as real a
threat as the invasion of foreign troops. The "protection of national labor"
became the favorite battle cry of the protectionist horde and of Bismarck, now
its commander-in-chief.[53] Protectionism assumed the character of a patriotic
cause rather than of favoritism to special interests.

In the Reichstag debates Bismarck's arguments were buttressed by a steady
succession of protectionist speakers, not only from the government itself
(Hofmann, Tiedemann, Burchard), but also from the affected interests: Wilhelm von Kardorff, owner of Silesian noble estates, an industrialist involved
in many enterprises (iron, banking, railways), and a founder of the Free Conservative party and of the Central Federation of German Industrialists; Karl
Stumm, iron and coal magnate ("King Stumm" of the Saar basin), active in
local and national associations of industrialists; Baron von Varnbüler, once a
Viennese industrialist, former minister-president of Württemberg, and owner
of Swabian latifundia; August Rentzsch, secretary-general of the Association
of German Iron and Steel Industrialists; Wilhelm Löwe, physician and former
progressive, brother-in-law of Louis Baare, general director of the *Bochumer
Verein*, one of the largest iron and coal cartels in the Ruhr; Louis Berger, south
German (Horchheim) factory owner; Friedrich Hammacher, Ruhr mine
owner, involved in railways and banking, a founder and chairman of the Association for Mining Interests at Dortmund; Robert von Ludwig, Baron Julius
von Mirbach-Sorquitten, Baron Wilhelm von Minnegerode, Count Udo zu
Stolberg-Wernigerode—all owners of noble estates in eastern Prussia and Silesia; and, incongruously, Alexander Mosle, a Bremen merchant, who voted
for "German national pride" against the "semitic spirit" of laissez-faire and
internationalism.[54]

---

[52] SEG (1879), pp. 120–121; *Norddeutsche Allgemeine Zeitung*, Apr. 13, 1879, Vol. 18, No.
134.

[53] For an example of this attitude see the speech by Baron Varnbüler, May 6, 1879. SBR
(1879), II, 1021. For a discussion of the motives for the spread of tariff protectionism throughout
Europe see Max Nitzsche, *Die handelspolitische Reaktion in Deutschland. Münchener volkswirtschaftliche Studien*, vol. 72 (Stuttgart, 1905), pp. 3ff. Nitzsche argued that the spread of protectionism
was the natural consequence of the wars fought during 1854–1871, the European-wide depression
of the 1870s, and the growth of national chauvinism.

[54] For brief biographies of important protectionist speakers in the tariff debates see Böhme,
Deutschlands Weg, pp. 313–320, 364. On Mosle's conversion see SBR (1879), II, 1071–1072; BP,

The defense of free trade was mostly in the hands of career state officials (Rudolf Delbrück, Eduard Lasker), journalists and publishers (Eugen Richter, Heinrich Rickert, Leopold Sonnemann), a professor and scientist (Rudolf Virchow), a big-city mayor (Max von Forckenbeck), and a lawyer-publicist (Karl Braun). There were a few notable exceptions: Ludwig Bamberger, radical emigré of 1848, banker in Rotterdam and Paris until his repatriation in 1866, international journalist and commentator on economic affairs; Wilhelm Oechelhäuser, director of the *Deutsche Kontinental-Gasgesellschaft* in Dessau; Baron Franz Schenk von Stauffenberg, Franconian estate owner with a law degree; Kurt von Saucken-Tarputschen, owner of a noble estate in East Prussia and one of the diminishing group of Junkers who had formed the original core of the Progressive party. They represented those liberals who, unshaken by the depression of the 1870s, remained committed to the principle of laissez-faire as the necessary complement to political liberalism or who represented export industries, commercial centers (especially maritime cities), and big cities whose welfare depended more on the exchange than upon the production of goods and on low food prices for the urban masses.[55]

Between these extremes of fully committed protectionists and free traders stood the middle groups of conservatives and national liberals. The former were not fully convinced that protectionism would benefit agriculture and were alarmed over its effect on the transit trade in grain in eastern Prussia. The latter favored protection for heavy industry, but not for agriculture, feared the consequences of the new revenues for the budgetary powers of parliament, and desperately hoped that Bennigsen's maneuverings in the chancellery and Reichstag would produce a way out of the morass that would rescue the powers of parliament and keep the party, at least its majority, together and intact with the government.

At the outset of the Reichstag debates the advocates of free trade were aware that the protectionist flood could not be diked.[56] Operating from a strong base in the Center, Conservative, and Free Conservative parties, the protectionists were obviously in full control of the chamber. On May 9 they outvoted the free traders by referring the tariff bill to a committee dominated by protectionists.[57] Another crucial test of strength came on May 16 when, during the second reading of the bill, the chamber rejected (192 to 125) a motion to reduce the proposed tariff on iron, which then passed in its original form by an overwhelming majority of 218 to 88. In the minority were the progressives, a few conservatives, about half of the national liberals, the social democrats, Guelphs, and Poles.[58]

II, 33off., 344–345; Langewiesche, ed., *Tagebuch Hölders*, p. 178; Poschinger, ed., *Bismarck als Volkswirth*, I, 212, 216–217.

[55] For brief biographies of important speakers for free trade see *HW*, II, 457ff.

[56] See Bamberger's confession of defeat in the debate of May 3, 1879. *SBR* (1879), II, 951.

[57] *SBR* (1879), II, 1114, 1203.

[58] *SBR* (1879), II, 1269–1274; *SEG* (1879), p. 164.

Certainty of defeat did not deter the Manchesterites from presenting the case against protectionism at length, if only for the benefit of voters in the next election. The leadoff speaker was Delbrück, who, much to Bismarck's contempt, limited himself to criticizing the technical inadequacies of the bill drafted by his former colleagues. Others dealt with the big issues, mixing tactical arguments with genuine concern over the social and political consequences of high tariffs. A brief summary of their views will suffice. Being interventionist, the tariff program was socialistic; Germany, the land of the middle, could not become a "closed commercial state" such as Fichte had envisioned. The financial difficulties of industry and agriculture were of their own making. It was an illusion to believe that every segment of society would benefit from duties intended to protect big industry and big agriculture, an "unnatural alliance." To substitute indirect for direct taxes was to shift the fiscal burden from the upper to the lower classes, stimulating class conflict and socialist agitation. Urban dwellers in general, particularly the low income groups, would suffer from the increased cost of food and other necessities. Handicraft workers and home industries would be injured by the higher cost of imported raw materials and semimanufactured items. Grain tariffs would not benefit the small farmer specializing in vegetables, potatoes, and dairy products, nor would timber tariffs benefit the forester and woodcutter. Agrarian tariffs were an "apple of discord" tossed into the assembly and country. The demand for protectionism had arisen among the industrialists who took it to Bismarck, who in turn had insinuated it into agrarian circles. That landowners and farmers had not spontaneously called for protection showed that it was alien to their interests.[59] To Richter, Bismarck was a "magician" who pulled everything imaginable out of his hat (not the least of which was a commitment to raise the salaries of government employees). The chancellor, he charged, was concerned with power, not tariffs. "For money is power, and with money the question of power is decided." Without economic freedom there could be no political freedom and vice versa.[60]

Again the discussion was marred by a bitter exchange between Lasker and Bismarck. In attacking the grain tariff, Lasker disputed the prince's claim that estate owners were more highly taxed than the rest of the population, charging him with ignorance of pertinent Prussian statutes. The plan to abolish direct taxes he castigated as the "fiscal politics of property." Even his friends deplored Lasker's tone, but Bismarck was more than willing to answer in kind. Absent during the speech, he replied on the basis of notes taken by an aide. "I can say to Mr. Lasker just as easily that he supports the fiscal politics of the propertyless; he belongs to those who form the majority in the passage of our laws, those of whom the Bible says: They do not sow, they do not harvest, they do not weave, they do not spin—and yet they are clothed. I will not say

[59] SBR (1879), II, 932ff.
[60] SBR (1879), II, 982, 986–987.

how, but they are nevertheless clothed." He defended himself against the charge of "unreliability," a word that Lasker had not used. When Forckenbeck, who presided, tried to interrupt with a light ring of his bell, the chancellor seethed with anger. He denied the right of the chair to call him to order.[61] Lucius feared that Bismarck, by his "irritability and vehemence," would destroy the delicate political web that had been spun; it was as though he deliberately sought to provoke a dissolution and another election, with the intention of producing an even greater rout of his foes than had the socialist issue of 1878.[62]

The free traders failed in their attempt to split the agrarian-industrial front, despite the misgivings of many landowners over the effect of the iron tariff on farm implements and of many manufacturers over the effect of the grain tariffs on the cost of labor. Far from warring against each other, the protectionist interests joined in ever greater collusion. "Appetite comes with eating," says the proverb. For not protesting the duty on pig iron (10 marks), the manufacturers of cast iron products received compensation in the form of higher duties on their own wares. This included agricultural implements, but the agrarians accepted it; in return, they were permitted to double the proposed duty on rye from 5 to 10 marks. That the latter figure was in accord with Bismarck's wishes had been publicly known since mid-April, when he had published a letter to a Bavarian landowner, Baron von Thüngen, expressing his dissatisfaction with the low rate set in the Bundesrat. On July 11 a uniform duty of 10 marks per ton on wheat, rye, oats, and legumes was set by vote of 186 to 160.[63]

Having disposed of free trade, Bismarck stalked the wild boar of finance. What was to be done with the new money provided by the tariff act, an increased tax on tobacco granted in July,[64] and an anticipated tax on beer? This raised again (as in 1868–1869) the thorny issues of the budgetary power of parliament and of the financial independence of the Reich from the states. On May 6, 1879, Bennigsen had outlined the possibilities for compromise with which he hoped to snare both Bismarck and the left-liberals. There were several ways, he declared, to preserve and even improve the powers of parliament: "We can choose a number of taxes and tariffs [later those on

---

[61] May 8, 1879. SBR (1879), II, 1050–1064, 1070–1071; Eugen Richter, Im alten Reichstag: Erinnerungen (Berlin, 1894), II, 118–119; Richard W. Dill, Der Parlamentarier Eduard Lasker und die parlamentarische Stilentwicklung der Jahre 1867–1884 (Erlangen, 1956), pp. 175–178.

[62] Lucius, Bismarck-Erinnerungen, pp. 158–159.

[63] SBR (1879), III, pp. 2280–2304. Lambi, Free Trade and Protection, pp. 220–221. For Bismarck's exchange of letters with Thüngen, see BR, VIII, 52–55; GW, XIV, 902.

[64] Bismarck's push for a government monopoly of the sale of tobacco—one of the issues upon which the Bennigsen candidature formally shattered—had led in June 1878 to the establishment of a Committee of Inquiry to gather statistics on tobacco manufacture and trade. GW, VIc, 102; AWB, I, 275–277. A year later Bismarck ignored the results of this investigation, which were unfavorable to his purposes, insisting on and getting higher taxes on tobacco—a step toward the ultimate goal of a monopoly. Bismarck to Hofmann, Jan. 1, 1879. GW, VIc, 130–131.

coffee and salt were chosen] and subject them in the budget to annual renewal; we can select a number of taxes and tariffs and remit them to the
individual states, while leaving the state assessments intact; or we can combine both of these measures in suitable form."[65] Three days later Windthorst
outlined the Center's counterproposal: establishment of a definite sum (later
set at 105,000,000 marks in an amendment offered by another centrist leader,
Baron von Franckenstein) to be allocated to the Reich, the surplus to be
shared by the states on the basis of population; extraordinary needs of the
Reich were to be covered by continued state assessments set by the Reichstag.[66]

Bismarck had two choices, neither of which gave him everything he
wanted. Bennigsen's terms were consistent with what the prince had so often
declared was his primary objective: the financial independence and consolidation of the Reich. Except on the issue of the state assessments, the liberals
had since 1867 been his most consistent supporters of the general cause of
consolidation, in contrast to the Center which had defended particularism in
the guise of federalism. On the issue of the grain tariffs, moreover, the right
wing of the National Liberal party had shown itself amenable. While his aim
was still that of splitting the right wing off "from the semites" on the left, he
did not wish to drive the moderates "into a corner."[67] To do so might weaken
his strategy of alternative choice by forcing them into permanent opposition,
leaving him dependent upon those "ultramontanes, with whom," he still believed "a permanent understanding is completely impossible."[68] Whose offer
should he accept?

By contrast to the national liberals, the Center was a solid phalanx which,
under the leadership of Windthorst and Franckenstein, made a considerable
effort to come to terms with the chancellor and the two conservative parties.
At Bismarck's demand the "clausula Franckenstein," as it was to be called,
was amended to increase the Reich's allocation to 130,000,000 marks. Furthermore, the Center abandoned its opposition to high duties on coffee and
petroleum and accepted the bill increasing the tax on tobacco.[69] By May 22
the prince had tentatively decided in favor of the Center's proposition, a decision that was hardened one month later when Bennigsen conceded that he
could not deliver enough national liberal votes to produce a majority; thirty
to forty members of the caucus, he reported, would vote against the entire
bill.[70]

[65] SBR (1879), II, 1036–1037.

[66] SBR (1879), II, 1066–1070.

[67] To Lucius, late June 1879. Lucius, Bismarck-Erinnerungen, pp. 163–164.

[68] Moritz Busch, Tagebuchblätter (Leipzig, 1899), II, 557.

[69] Lambi, Free Trade and Protection, p. 223; Lucius, Bismarck-Erinnerungen, p. 167.

[70] Oncken, Bennigsen, II, 410–412; Lucius, Bismarck-Erinnerungen, pp. 162–164; GW, VIII,
313.

After more than a decade of intent and five years of conscious planning and maneuvering Bismarck gave up his attempt to make the Reich financially independent of the state governments. Not only that, he struck a bargain with the party he had once denounced as a "mobilization against the state" and prepared the way for future collaboration with it on other issues. "The best," he often said, "is the enemy of the better." Of the options open to him, the Franckenstein clause was, he decided, less damaging than the budgetary guarantees demanded by the liberals. Teaching the national liberals a lesson, moreover, would speed the purge of liberal ideologues from their ranks and make the remaining rump party of moderates more pliable in the future. Driving them into a corner on the tariff issue, he calculated, would not permanently estrange those for whom opposition was normally a discomfort and embarrassment. Henceforth he could "lean on one crutch or the other or on both."[71]

On July 9, the chancellor gave to the Reichstag and the nation his version of the deterioration in his relationship to the National Liberal party. His decision for the Franckenstein clause, he declared, had been reached only after discovering that the national liberals had chosen a course that he could not travel—one as destructive to the Reich as socialist subversion. For more than a year he had been aware that their goodwill had cooled. They wanted "things I could not grant." They wanted to govern, to increase to a bucketful the "drop of democratic oil" with which the Kaiser was anointed. In the future they must conduct themselves with "greater modesty." Only by supporting the government could they expect to influence it. Instead they had left him "deserted and isolated," had attacked and vilified him in the press in an "unprecedented and mendacious way." As earlier in the case of the conservatives, he was compelled to seek his goals by "other routes." Never had Bismarck made more brutally clear the terms on which he was willing to do business with the parties of the Reichstag.[72]

Among the national liberals there was "utter consternation."[73] Three resignations from the Prussian cabinet heightened the effect. On June 27 Finance Minister Hobrecht—opposed to protectionism, unwilling to compromise himself further with his liberal colleagues, and painfully conscious of his own unsuitability for high public office—had resigned, followed on June 30 by Minister of Agriculture Friedenthal and Kultusminister Falk.[74] Obviously the "liberal era" had ended. Bennigsen and his associates had to decide whether to join the progressives in opposing not only the Franckenstein clause, but also, in view of its certain passage, the entire tariff bill. On July 9,

---

[71] The "crutch" metaphor came from a progressive newspaper. BP, I, 179–180.

[72] BR, VIII, 137–155.

[73] Lucius, Bismarck-Erinnerungen, p. 164; BP, II, 352–353.

[74] SEG (1879), pp. 191–192. On Hobrecht's motives for resigning see Tiedemann, Sechs Jahre, pp. 244, 248.

211 deputies (conservatives, free conservatives, centrists) voted for, and 122 deputies (national liberals, progressives, Poles, Guelphs, and Social Democrats) against the Franckenstein amendment. The final vote on the entire statute on July 12 was 217 for and 117 against.[75] Voting with the majority that day were twenty national liberal deputies, of whom fifteen resigned from the party caucus.[76] It was, Treitschke explained, a "fateful political error" to be labeled as an "opposition party."[77]

The Protective Tariff Act of 1879 left a lasting mark on German parliamentary history. We shall see that, while dividing the National Liberal party, it did not achieve for Bismarck the parliamentary situation he sought—a more flexible party structure with alternative majorities for the government's program. What it did was to bring together a new combination of interest groups (heavy industry, big banking, and big agriculture) to buttress the Prussian-German establishment (Hohenzollern dynasty, Prussian-German bureaucracy, Prussian officer corps, Protestant church, east-Elbian gentry, crowned heads and high aristocracy of the German lesser states). It constituted another of those major steps by which that establishment had, since 1806, steadily accommodated itself to the changing economic and social environment that we now call "the process of modernization." During Bismarck's years in power it was probably as important a contribution to that end as was the renewal of the German Zollverein in 1865 and the capture of the national idea in 1866–1871.

Yet the cost was considerable, for the general scramble of the interest groups unleashed by the Bismarck proposal for protectionism stripped away what remained of the illusion in Germany that politics was a matter of ideals, of lofty aims based upon universal principles imbedded in the nature of man, society, and history. As Richter predicted,[78] it damaged the image of the "old Prussian officialdom" famed for its professionalism, selflessness, and dedication to the general interest. A generation bred in the thought and tradition of German idealism learned again the truth that Hegel had taught, although his metaphysics had obscured the lesson: namely, that men are moved by their passions and interests. But they also learned the error of Hegel's assumption that governments are above the warring interests of civil society. Instead, it was now apparent that they were closely linked to the economic and social élites that dominated the struggle. Not even now, more than a century later, have German historians ceased to lament the loss of innocence suffered in the rape of 1879.

[75] SBR (1879), III, pp. 2215, 2364; RGB (1879), 207–258.
[76] Hermann Block, Die parlamentarische Krise der nationalliberalen Partei, 1879–1880 (Münster, 1930), p. 52.
[77] SEG (1879), p. 211.
[78] May 5, 1879. SBR (1879), II, 981.

CHAPTER SEVENTEEN

Negotiation of the Dual Alliance

ONTROLLING ministers and officials was not Bismarck's only problem in late 1879. His greatest struggle was not with them but with the Kaiser on a critical matter of foreign policy. Within a year Wilhelm had fully recovered from the shotgun wounds inflicted by Nobiling, despite his advanced age. Wilhelm's physician believed, so Bismarck asserted, that the Kaiser had actually benefited, physically and mentally, from "Nobiling's phlebotomy." "The old blood has been drawn off, and he looks much better now than earlier."[1] At any rate the eighty-two-year-old monarch was sufficiently repaired to give the chancellor the hardest, most difficult contest of their seventeen-year relationship. For six weeks the Kaiser strove, tooth and nail, to prevent the negotiation and signing of what has since become known as the Dual Alliance, the first "permanent" alliance of European international politics. That Bismarck won in the end was owed to the presumption of his indispensability in foreign affairs, shared not only by himself and his associates but by the Kaiser as well. The struggle was costly, nevertheless, for it brought the prince after a period of relative health to the verge of nervous and physical collapse.

Tilt toward Austria

Historians have never ceased to search for the beginning point of that fateful alienation between Germany and Russia that ultimately resulted in the French-Russian Dual Entente of 1894. The problem is not easy, any more than is that of the later estrangement between Germany and Britain that persuaded London to join Paris and Petersburg in the Triple Entente of 1907.[2]

---

[1] Moritz Busch, *Tagebuchblätter* (Leipzig, 1899), III, 88.

[2] Publications that bear on these problems are: Andreas Hillgruber, *Bismarcks Aussenpolitik* (Freiburg, 1972); Horst Müller-Link, *Industrialisierung und Aussenpolitik: Preussen-Deutschland und das Zarenreich von 1860 bis 1890, Kritische Studien zur Geschichtswissenschaft*, vol. 24 (Göttingen, 1977); Dietrich Geyer, *Der russische Imperialismus: Studien über den Zusammenhang von innerer und auswärtiger Politik 1860–1914. Kritische Studien zur Geschichtswissenschaft*, vol. 27 (Göttingen, 1977). George F. Kennan, *The Decline of Bismarck's European Order: Franco-Russian Relations, 1875–1890* (Princeton, 1979); Paul Kennedy, *The Rise of the Anglo-German Antagonism, 1860–1914* (London, 1980); Thomas A. Kohut, "Kaiser Wilhelm II and his Parents: An Inquiry into the Psychological Roots of German Policy towards England before the First World War," in John C. G. Röhl and Nicolaus Sombart, eds., *Kaiser Wilhelm II: New Interpretations*

To determine the time and circumstances of both is to trace the development of those rival alliances that fought the First World War with such fateful consequences for the future of Germany, Europe, and the world. The answer seems to be that Germany and Russia parted company gradually over decades by a series of stages, none of which had to be conclusive. The earliest stages are undoubtedly to be found in the events of 1875–1879, from the war-in-sight crisis through the Balkan war and Congress of Berlin to the signing of the German-Austrian alliance of 1879.

As observed earlier, the war-in-sight crisis need have had no lasting consequences.[3] Bismarck's irritation with Gorchakov was purely personal; it was neither shared by their respective monarchs nor grounded in conflicting interests between their two countries. Gorchakov's age and Bismarck's bad health seemed to guarantee that both would soon be out of power, replaced by younger men with other views and aims. That the war-in-sight crisis appears significant for the problem of estrangement is owed entirely to the chance that the eastern crisis came so close behind it. "I have two powerful dogs by their collars," Bismarck said of Austria and Russia in the early weeks of the crisis. "I am holding them apart: first, to keep them from tearing each other to pieces; second, to keep them from coming to an understanding at our expense. I believe I am performing a service not only to each of them, but also to Germany and Europe."[4] As the crisis progressed he feared for Germany the fate of most peacemakers, that of being bitten by one dog or both. If unable to restrain both, the best course was to tighten the leash on the most controllable. While Andrássy was in power, that appeared to be Austria.

In May 1875 Andrássy had wisely kept his distance from the British-Russian démarche at Berlin. When he learned of Gorchakov's intention to admonish Bismarck, he is said to have done a handstand on his desk in delight, exclaiming, "Bismarck will never forgive that!"[5] In the fall of 1876 Austria, as well as Russia, had posed that "indiscreet" question that forced Bismarck to formulate his options prematurely. The Russian inquiry irritated him but not the Austrian, because it came first, was without apparent cause, and was conveyed in a most undiplomatic manner.[6] But there was a more fundamental reason—Bismarck had already begun to think of Austria as the more valued

---

(Cambridge, Eng., 1982), pp. 63–90; and Judith M. Hughes, *Emotion and High Politics: Personal Relations at the Summit in Late Nineteenth-Century Britain and Germany* (Berkeley, 1983).

[3] See pp. 262–278, 434. George Kennan believes, however, that the exploitation of this episode in the newspaper press was seminal in the growth of popular hostility toward Germany in France and Russia, which culminated in the Dual Entente of 1894. Kennan, *Decline*, pp. 11–23.

[4] To Karl Braun, Sept. 1875. GW, VIII, 55–56.

[5] Nicholas Der Bagdasarian, *The Austro-German Rapprochement, 1870–1879* (Cranbury, N.J., 1976), pp. 180–183; Eduard von Wertheimer, *Graf Julius Andrássy: Sein Leben und Seine Zeit* (Vienna, 1910–1913), II, 243.

[6] See pp. 423–425 (fn.).

ally. In explaining to the Kaiser and foreign office his response to Russia, he wrote that Germany should assist Russia wherever such assistance was consonant with German interests, but not at the cost of a "deep and lasting disturbance in our relationship to that ally of ours that has been until now the most useful and that may in the future be the most important and, in its inner circumstances, relatively the most reliable."[7] In February 1878, as Austria faced the possibility of a violent confrontation with Russia, Bismarck again informed Vienna that Germany would remain neutral in such a war. Yet he confessed to Károlyi that Germany, although unable to tolerate a Russian occupation of Moravia, would not take a similarly adverse view of an equivalent Austrian conquest in Russia. In the "later phase" of a war between Russia and Austria, "therefore," Austrian-German relations "might take a turn for the better."[8] When Andrássy proposed on February 28, 1878, at the height of the crisis with Russia, that Austria and Germany form a defensive alliance (with which England might associate), Bismarck declined, but more on grounds of prematurity than preference.[9]

During 1876–1878 Bismarck began to tilt German foreign policy, ever so cautiously, toward Austria. Of the many factors influencing that decision—Austria's strategic geopolitical position in the middle of Europe, her cultural bonds and earlier political links with Germany, German Austrophilism and Russophobia, and the contrasting internal pressures on foreign policy in both countries—the last appears to have been much on his mind at this time. In these years, the statesmen of both countries were compelled by domestic interests to assume postures in foreign relations they would have preferred to avoid. Panslav agitation in Russia had forced Gorchakov and Tsar Alexander into an aggressive action against Turkey, while Austro-German and Hungarian opposition to the incorporation of more Slavs into the empire had kept Andrássy from annexing Bosnia and Herzegovina outright. To force a pigeon down the Austrian throat was far easier than to compel the Russians to disgorge one.

Even as he sent the first faint signal to Austria of his intention to be more protective of Austria's than Russia's position and power in Europe, Bismarck began to suggest ideas concerning the character of Germany's future relationship to Austria. According to Baron von Münch's report to Andrássy of his interview with Bismarck at Varzin in October 1876, the German chancellor held out the prospect of a future "organic alliance sanctioned by the votes of the representative assemblies" of the two governments.[10] A few months later

---

[7] GP, II, 88–89.

[8] Bagdasarian, *Rapprochement*, pp. 217–218.

[9] *Ibid.*, pp. 220–224.

[10] Baron von Münch to Andrássy, Oct. 8, 1876. Quoted in Bagdasarian, *Rapprochement*, p. 200.

he spoke in a similar vein to the Württemberg minister Baron von Mittnacht. "The peaceloving powers in central Europe are dependent upon each other to ward off disturbances to the peace from the west as well as the east. Germany can perhaps attain an organic union with Austria, if not in the form of the empire of seventy millions that was earlier so often discussed."[11] Sometime during 1877 Bismarck amplified these hints in a remarkable interview with Karl Braun that deserves extensive quotation as the fullest statement of what the prince had in mind at this time. "Austria-Hungary is a unique mosaic of different races, religions, and peoples." If not firmly joined, the pieces of that mosaic might strike each other and fall apart. If fixed to a solid wall or floor, they could not fall into disarray, and, furthermore, changes could be made in the composition. "In the former case every internal difference leads to a crisis abroad. But in the latter case domestic issues will find resolution in peace and quiet without exploding externally."

He told Braun—a Nassau lawyer, journalist, and leading member (national liberal) of the Reichstag—that the first task was to determine "what we do not want. We do not wish to reconstitute the German Bundestag [of 1815–1866]. . . . Nor do we want again, as in the time of the blessed Herr von Bruck, to chase after the phantom of customs unification. . . . A customs union is impossible between two states whose monetary, production, and consumption relationships are so different as are those of the German Reich and the Austro-Hungarian monarchy. . . . Finally, we do not want a merely temporary ad hoc union, perhaps for the purpose of a conquest, as at the time of the Schleswig-Holstein crisis. Such a union is without lasting interest and can, as we have seen, suddenly turn upside down at any time. Useful to both parties would be a lasting organic connection," but not one that would produce "either fusion or confusion," either economic and financial community or mutual interference in each other's internal affairs. "Instead the connection should exclude in the strictest and most definite way possible all of [these possibilities] through an agreement that would mutually guarantee the present possessions of both sides and obligate both to maintain the peace of central Europe, offensively and defensively, with the help of permanent institutions. Such a union would not exclude, but rather provide for a series of agreements for uniform arrangements in the areas of jurisprudence, legislation, and administration—as well as in economic and social-political matters—a cooperation that could undoubtedly be most beneficial for two commonwealths that are so well suited to complement one another."[12]

---

[11] Apr. 11, 1877. GW, VIII, 206.

[12] GW, VIII, 237–239; also BP, II, 251. Braun had just returned from a tour of the Danube monarchy where he investigated popular attitudes toward Germany. As a free trader, Braun wanted to report to Bismarck about the economic and commercial differences that made impracticable a customs union between Germany and Austria. Bismarck used the opportunity to put

Many months before the Congress of Berlin and nearly three years before he actively promoted the alliance with Austria, Bismarck had already formed his general conception of that alliance. In Austria's internal difficulties he saw not only potential dangers for European peace but also possible advantages for German foreign policy. The Habsburg Empire's internal weaknesses would make it dependent upon Germany and subordinate to Berlin's leadership in foreign affairs. At the time he spoke to Münch, Mittnacht, and Braun Bismarck was groping for a new economic policy, largely for internal reasons, but had not yet arrived at protectionism. That Germany was still committed to free trade and Austria to protectionism presented no barrier to their future "organic connection," as he conceived it. Nor did his subsequent conversion to protectionism in 1878–1879 alter his vision of the future political relationship between the two countries, despite the expected adverse effect of the new tariffs upon Austrian, as well as Russian and American, exports to Germany.[13] Where major decisions were concerned, economic and political interests traveled on separate and not necessarily parallel tracks in Bismarck's thoughts. Their union was an "ideal goal," but not a realistic necessity.[14]

---

forward his own developing views about the economic and political relationship between the two countries. In what month of 1877 the interview took place is unknown. Clearly, however, Bismarck did not begin in 1879 to think of an "organic union" with Austria as some have believed. See, for example, William L. Langer, *European Alliances and Alignments* (2d ed., New York, 1956), p. 174. The idea had an earlier origin.

[13] See his remarks to Austro-Hungarian Ambassador Count Emmerich Széchényi, Jan. 26–29, 1879, at Friedrichsruh. GW, VIII, 293–295. In February 1879 Bismarck told the Bavarian Reichstag deputy, Baron Georg von und zu Franckenstein, "Even a constitutional relationship between Austria and Germany is conceivable, but certainly not a common customs." BP, II, 317. There appears to be no substance to the assertions of Helmut Böhme that Bismarck took seriously the plan for a European customs union proposed to him in Sept. 1878 by a French economist and editor, G. de Molinari, and that he gave serious attention to a central European version of the idea in the summer of 1879. See his *Deutschlands Weg zur Grossmacht: Studien zum Verhältnis von Wirtschaft und Staat während der Reichsgründungszeit, 1848–1881* (Cologne, 1966), pp. 525–529, 587–601, and the critique by Bruce Waller, *Bismarck at the Crossroads: The Reorientation of German Foreign Policy after the Congress of Berlin, 1878–1880* (London, 1974), pp. 196–197. The signing of the Dual Alliance did not lead to better commercial relations between Germany and Austria. The treaty of 1868, which left Austria's tariffs high in comparison with Germany's, expired at the end of 1877. Despite extensive negotiations on a new treaty during 1877, no agreement could be reached. As a stopgap the two powers extended the treaty of 1868 (with some modifications) annually until 1881, when it lapsed. During the negotiations for the Dual Alliance Bismarck held out the prospect of major tariff concessions, but afterward they did not materialize. In the relationship between Austria and Germany, politics clearly took precedence over economics. Waller, *Bismarck at the Crossroads*, pp. 197–198, and A. von Matlekovits, *Die Zollpolitik der österreichisch-ungarischen Monarchie und des deutschen Reiches seit 1868* (Leipzig, 1891), pp. 30–60, 70–104, 830–833.

[14] See Bismarck's statement to a Hungarian correspondent, Mar. 5, 1880. GW, XIV, 914. In 1863 Bismarck maintained in Vienna that the dual powers should not permit conflicting commercial and industrial interests to interfere with their common aspirations "in the *purely political*

Where economic and political interests did not coincide, the latter took precedence.

The "Two-Chancellors War"

Although the prospect of an alliance with Austria was already evolving in his mind, Bismarck made no attempt to negotiate with Vienna for more than a year after the Congress of Berlin. Several considerations may have influenced this delay: he had not yet fully made up his mind to follow the course he contemplated; he lacked as yet a provocation adequate to overcome the Kaiser's inevitable resistance to a break with Russia; and he needed time to execute his customary tactic, time in which first to seek an accommodation with Russia, if only to prove to himself and others its impossibility.

The war scare of 1875 and the Balkan crisis of 1875–1878 had exposed weaknesses in the relationships Germany had established with Russia and Austria in 1872–1873. The extended and deepening economic crisis in world capitalism probably contributed to this alienation by creating a climate of anxiety whose political effects are often assumed but are difficult to trace. In January 1877 Moltke, concerned about Russian troop concentrations in Galicia, wrote to Bismarck of his fears that, as the economic crisis worsened, Russia's "leading circles" would be all the more inclined "to seek a violent way out of the calamity."[15] To what degree this mood actually contributed to the steam behind the Panslavist movement and the willingness of the government to respond to its pressure is difficult to assess.[16] But certainly the continuing economic crisis exacerbated European international relations in general by mobilizing protectionist movements with xenophobic tendencies.

Although every major European country except Britain soon yielded to these pressures, the first severe jolt occurred when Russia, whose Finance Minister Michael Reutern, hard put to finance the coming war against Turkey, decreed that duties on imported goods be paid henceforth in gold specie rather than in paper currency of the same face value. This change was tantamount to a 30 to 50 percent increase in Russian tariffs, and ironically it be-

---

field." Bismarck to Werther, Apr. 9, 1863. Helmut Böhme, ed., *Die Reichsgründung* (Munich, 1967), pp. 132–133. For other similar utterances see p. 246 (fn. 2).

[15] Quoted in Wolfgang Windelband, *Bismarck und die europäischen Grossmächte 1879–1885* (2d ed., Essen, 1942), p. 45.

[16] The motivation of Russian foreign policy in the Balkan affair is unlikely to be determined from purely German archival and secondary sources as in Müller-Link, *Industrialisierung und Aussenpolitik*, pp. 19–102, 122. For a broader-based assessment see Geyer, *Der russische Imperialismus*, pp. 55–76. Throughout 1876 many Russians in high positions, including the tsar and Minister of Finance Michael Reutern, dreaded war against Turkey precisely because it would compromise the country's economy, public finance, and recent reforms. See Wilhelm von Schweinitz, ed., *Denkwürdigkeiten des Botschafters General von Schweinitz* (Berlin, 1927), I, 317–318, and Sergé Goriainov, *Le Bosphore et les Dardanelles* (Paris, 1910), pp. 321–322.

came effective on the precise day, January 1, 1877, when the last protective duties fell in Germany. Naturally this coincidence was doubly irritating to German manufacturers, who had hoped that Russia would grant reciprocity by lowering its barriers against German goods. Although the primary purpose of the gold decree was fiscal, Reutern was conscious of its protectionist benefits for Russian manufactures.[17] While the Russian "gold tariff" accelerated the demand for German "retaliatory tariffs" and in general reinforced the protectionist movement in Germany, no direct evidence has yet been produced to show that it had a significant effect upon Bismarck's reconstruction of Germany's foreign relations in 1877–1879.[18]

Unquestionably economic, social, and nationalistic pressures activated by the depression did tend to cleave apart the three partners in the Three Emperors League. But those adverse effects were to be seen on the relations between *all* European powers. The decisions, moreover, on whether to yield to those pressures and on what constituted the true "interest of state" lay with the individuals who sat in the seats of power and influence in the palaces and chancelleries. No one was more aware of this than Bismarck. We have seen how eager he was during the Balkan crisis to keep the pro-German Andrássy in power at the Ballhausplatz. His concern over the influences that might prevail in Vienna if Andrássy should be ousted was one of the factors that led Bismarck to consider an "organic alliance" with Austria so binding that it would endure whoever might succeed the Hungarian as chancellor. By the same token the presence of the doddering Gorchakov at the foreign ministry in Petersburg meant to Bismarck that Russian foreign policy would be rudderless and hence subject to winds and currents that were difficult to calculate and likely to be inimical to German interests. For that reason he attempted in the months that followed the congress to unseat "the childish and senile"[19] chancellor and boost Count Peter Shuvalov into the saddle. Shuvalov had won his spurs in the Russian government as chief of the third section, the secret police. As ambassador to Britain, he had been a persistent supporter of Russia's continued participation in the Three Emperors League. Bismarck hoped that, if elevated to the chancellorship, he would consolidate Russia's relations with Austria and Germany and put the lid on the steaming pot of social and political unrest in Russia.[20]

During the Congress of Berlin Gorchakov took care to distance himself

---

[17] Sigrid Kumpf-Korfes, Bismarcks *"Draht nach Russland"*: *Zum Problem der sozial-ökonomischen Hintergründe der russisch-deutschen Entfremdung im Zeitraum von 1878 bis 1891* (Berlin-East, 1968), pp. 8–15.

[18] In asserting the contrary, Müller-Link cites not Bismarck but earlier passages in his own text. *Industrialisierung und Aussenpolitik*, p. 122 (fns. 11 and 12).

[19] Manfred Müller, *Die Bedeutung des Berliner Kongresses für die deutsch-russischen Beziehungen* (Leipzig, 1927), p. 87.

[20] GP, II, 307–310; GW, VIII, 212, and Müller, *Bedeutung des Berliner Kongresses*, pp. 9–92.

from Shuvalov's bargaining in order better to deny all responsibility for an unpopular peace on his return to Petersburg. After the final session he hurried home, while Shuvalov lingered to enjoy the fleshpots of the German capital. By the time the ambassador reached Petersburg he found "the rotten old scoundrel" Gorchakov had "infamously and wickedly slandered" him at the imperial palace. Alexander, who in 1877 had hesitated to yield to the Panslav agitation, but then yielded to it, now feared its wrath. But he had also come to identify with its unreasonable expectations and to fear for the government's authority if they were unrealized. He raged that the congress had been "a European coalition against Russia under the leadership of Prince Bismarck" for Austria's benefit. And yet this often quoted remark was but a momentary outburst. The tsar was inconsistent in his judgments and usually open to the opinions of those around him, who did not speak with a single voice.[21] In August 1878 Gorchakov left Russia on a recuperative leave in western Europe that lasted many months. During his absence Shuvalov's star seemed to ascend.

After the signing of the Treaty of Berlin the chief concern of European diplomacy was its execution. The most critical decisions had been reached in so short a time only by leaving the details to be worked out by commissions. The details were by no means trivial, presenting in some instances the possibility of serious conflicts between the great powers. Bismarck's course was to support the inclination of Austria and Russia to make common cause in the commissions against efforts by the Porte, or by its former subjects, to obstruct the treaty's execution. Where the Austrian position was unclear or unknown, the German delegates initially supported Russian interests in the commissions. For a few weeks Europe experienced something like a revival of the Three Emperors League.[22] Shuvalov's policy appeared to be triumphant, and from London Münster reported to Berlin that the ambassador acted almost as though he were already Russian foreign minister.[23]

As the Balkan disputes reached what seemed to be a "critical phase" in mid-October 1878, however, Bismarck became wary. He feared that the collaboration between Germany's two partners might become too close and might alienate the British, whose trust he had so recently won. Hence he ordered German representatives to keep a low profile in the deliberations of

[21] Bagdasarian, *Rapprochement*, pp. 254–255; W. N. Medlicott, *The Congress of Berlin and After* (2d ed., London, 1963), pp. 154–155; *GP*, III, 3–6; Bernhard von Bülow, *Denkwürdigkeiten* (Berlin, 1930), IV, 450–452. On the conflicting currents of opinion in Russia and their effect on state policy see Kennan, *Decline*, pp. 27ff., and Geyer, *Der russische Imperialismus*, p. 68. Anton von Werner's official portrait of the congress, not finished until 1881, confirmed in an uncanny way Gorchakov's version of events at the congress. It shows Shuvalov (front and center) energetically shaking hands with Bismarck, as Andrássy looks on, while Gorchakov sits heavily in a chair at the end of the conference table yards away. See p. 441.

[22] Müller, *Bedeutung des Berliner Kongresses*, pp. 61–63, 74–81.

[23] Waller, *Bismarck at the Crossroads*, p. 83.

the commissions. They should support Russia and Austria, where those powers were in agreement, but not to the point of conflict with England. Russian requests for German backing must be referred secretly to Berlin for decision. German representatives must avoid any active, mediatory role, lest Germany become a target for those dissatisfied with the outcome. Germany could not afford to endanger its relations with other powers over issues that did not affect its interests.[24] When Crown Prince Friedrich Wilhelm urged a more active role for Germany in suppressing native unrest in Bulgaria, Bismarck sent him copies of the policy memoranda of 1876–1877 (including the "Kissingen dictation") and explained again that lasting peace in the eastern question was not in Germany's interest for, if "neighboring powers, all of whom hate us," had their hands free, they would naturally (given Germany's central geographical position) seek and find common ground against her. Austria could experience "a change of government and system" that would bring to power with surprising quickness anti-German, ultramontane elements that would seek rapprochement and alliance with France.[25]

Bismarck's "see-saw" tactics in the effort to balance Russia against Britain and his wish to keep the Balkan conflict from expiring severely limited the possibility of reviving the Three Emperors League. But it also ran counter to his simultaneous attempt to elevate Shuvalov to the Russian chancellorship. Immediately after the congress adjourned in July Bismarck granted an interview to Henry Blowitz, correspondent of the London *Times*, in which, among other pleasantries, he is reputed to have said, "But for the affair of 1875, he [Gorchakov] would not be where he is and would not have undergone the political defeat he has just experienced." In the German press Bismarck also spread the word that at the congress the half-senile Russian chancellor had been a "calamity for Russia and her friends; not even the best intentions of the latter would suffice to make up for the consequences of his foolishness." By the time Blowitz's report was published (September 7) Bismarck had grown more cautious. Publicly he disavowed, privately he admitted its accuracy. In the following weeks he directed the foreign office press bureau to launch articles in the nongovernmental press lauding Shuvalov's statesmanship; on September 22 the official *Norddeutsche Allgemeine Zeitung* carried such an article authored by Bismarck himself.[26] In the following months he returned to the attack both in the press and in dispatches to Schweinitz, whose contents—complaining of Gorchakov's flirtations with France and praising Shuvalov's support of the Three Emperors League—were intended for the Russian foreign office. In March he took the extraordinary step of sending General Bernhard von Werder, German military attaché at Petersburg, to the tsar with

[24] Bülow to Hatzfeldt, Oct. 12 and 14, 1878. Müller, *Bedeutung des Berliner Kongresses*, pp. 79–81.

[25] *Ibid.*, pp. 82–83; for the Kissingen dictation see p. 432.

[26] Waller, *Bismarck at the Crossroads*, pp. 76–84.

the warning that German-Russian relations could not improve as long as Gorchakov was in charge of Russian foreign policy.[27]

Bismarck's tactics against Gorchakov were similar to those he had recently used to rid himself of Prussian ministers and imperial officials. By these means he had unhorsed Harry von Arnim in 1874–1875, Delbrück in 1876, and Camphausen and Achenbach in 1878. Yet those same tactics had failed against Friedrich Eulenburg and General von Stosch. (Nor did his press vendettas against Empress Augusta and officials of the imperial household achieve results.) In domestic affairs Bismarck had the advantage that Wilhelm, upon whose will the careers of ministers and officials depended, had long since come to look upon the prince as indispensable. But this was hardly true of a foreign monarch like Alexander II, to whom Bismarck's crude attempt to determine who would be Russian chancellor must have appeared intolerable.

By December 1879 it became evident that Gorchakov had been counted out prematurely. Stopping at Berlin on the way to Petersburg, the Russian chancellor appeared somewhat restored—enough at least to launch a counterattack. At a diplomatic reception he openly criticized Austrian policy in the presence of Károlyi and complained that no European power, Germany included, had fulfilled its obligations to Russia. In an audience with the Kaiser he again took credit for preserving peace in 1875.[28] Back in the Russian capital, he clung to the office he had held since 1855, and Alexander would not dismiss him, even though the chancellor obviously could no longer carry out his duties. Following the Congress of Berlin the Russian press had tended to blame Austria and England for what was generally regarded as a catastrophic peace. After Gorchakov's return the current changed, and Bismarck and Germany became the objects of journalistic recrimination—with appropriate responses from Germany. Germany's drift toward protectionism in agriculture was another irritant.[29]

In Gorchakov's view Russia had been foully betrayed by her two allies, and, since France had turned republican, Russia had no recourse but to rely henceforth upon itself alone.[30] On February 4, 1879, came the revelation that Austria and Germany had abrogated article 5 of the Treaty of Prague (1866), which had provided for a plebiscite in northern Schleswig. To the Russians this "odieux escamotage" proved that the broker at Berlin had not been so

[27] Windelband, *Bismarck und die europäischen Grossmächte*, pp. 53–54.

[28] Waller, *Bismarck at the Crossroads*, pp. 50, 82.

[29] Irene Grüning, *Die russische öffentliche Meinung und ihre Stellung zu den Grossmächten, 1878–1894* (Berlin, 1929), pp. 52–68. See Windelband's modification of the Grüning thesis in *Bismarck und die europäischen Grossmächte*, pp. 51–54 and fn. 42.

[30] Schweinitz, ed., *Denkwürdigkeiten*, II, 38; B. H. Sumner, *Russia and the Balkans, 1870–1880* (Oxford, 1937), pp. 556–557; Moritz Busch, *Bismarck: Some Secret Pages of His History* (New York, 1898), II, 391–396.

honest after all; secretly he too had exacted his price for humiliating Russia.[31] Almost simultaneously the German government overreacted to news of a plague on the lower Volga by closing the Russian-German border, a measure so excessive that even Schweinitz thought it motivated more by political "chicanery" than medical necessity.[32] As anger against Germany mounted in Russia, Shuvalov's cause declined. In December 1878 he had already begun to consider resignation, and in May 1879 he took an indefinite leave, from which he never returned to active service. The coup de grâce that Bismarck aimed at Gorchakov felled Shuvalov instead.

What led Bismarck to commit what seems to have been an egregious error in judgment? To assume that personal malice was primary in the action against Gorchakov is to misunderstand Bismarck's modus operandi.[33] As has been repeatedly shown, his tactical instinct required that, before launching a major change in policy, he test the viability of the alternative course. To that end, for example, he had recently sought to bind the National Liberal party to the government before delivering the blows that weakened it at the polls and ultimately divided it. Before seeking the "organic alliance" with Austria, he had to ascertain whether the life of the Three Emperors League might be extended by securing the appointment as Russian chancellor of a person sympathetic to its perpetuation. If not, a more drastic route had to be taken: a closer union between Germany and Austria that would guarantee Germany against isolation in Europe and hopefully assure that Russia, to avoid isolation, would come to terms with Berlin and Vienna, whoever was Russian chancellor.

Alexander's Blunder, Bismarck's Opportunity

As shown, Bismarck returned to Berlin in February 1879 in generally good physical and nervous condition, buoyed no doubt by political progress in domestic affairs and the prospect of success in getting the tariff bill through

---

[31] DDF, II, 437–439. A secret treaty abrogating Article 5 of the Treaty of Prague had been signed on Apr. 13, 1878, but was now postdated to Oct. 11, 1878, in the hope of avoiding the "malicious" charge that Austria had "bought" German support against Russia. The treaty of Apr. 13 came about because Austria was eager to be rid of an obligation in which it had no further interest, while Bismarck wanted to be rid of a neuralgic point in German foreign relations. In seeking its publication, Bismarck expected to undercut Guelph agitation for execution of the plebiscite that arose on the occasion of the betrothal of Princess Thyra of Denmark to the Duke of Cumberland (pretender to the throne of Hanover after the death of his father, the exiled King Georg V, on June 12, 1878). Bismarck had offered to support the duke's claim to the duchy of Brunswick and to restore the Guelph Fund, if he would renounce the Hanoverian crown, recognize the German Reich, and signify his submission by visiting Berlin. The duke refused. See particularly Bagdasarian, Rapprochement, pp. 267–270.

[32] Schweinitz, ed., Denkwürdigkeiten, II, 40ff., 70.

[33] Waller, Bismarck at the Crossroads, pp. 246–248.

Reichstag and Bundesrat. Hence it is not surprising to find him contemplating again the plan for alliance with Austria, first mentioned in late 1876 but dormant now for more than two years. Even as he carried out the action against Gorchakov, he began to prepare the contrary option. Because Russia could no longer be relied on, he told Schweinitz in April 1879, Germany could not antagonize the other powers, particularly England and Austria. "On the contrary, we must strive for a closer understanding with Austria that will lead to an organic relationship that cannot be dissolved without approval by the parliamentary bodies [of both countries]." The reasons Bismarck gave for this change in strategy were: Gorchakov's "continuing coquetry" with France; the "endless" military expansionism of Minister of War Count Dmitry Milyutin; the stationing of avant-garde cavalry units on the German border; and the unbridled language of the Moscow and Petersburg presses.[34] But his most important motive has to be sought not in the danger of Russian aggression—which he certainly exaggerated—but in the dynamics of European power politics. The virtual collapse of the Three Emperors League had left not only Russia but also Austria free to seek other allies. That Austria too might eventually escape the German orbit was not inconceivable. If Germany was to be one of three in an unstable system of five great powers, it must have at least one firm ally; history and geography made Austria the best candidate. Such a powerful combination could be a magnet with which to attract at least one additional partner, perhaps even two. The identity of British and Austrian interests, shown by their recent collaboration at the Congress of Berlin, made Britain the logical third partner.

But such a triple alliance would leave open the possibility that the two excluded powers, Russia and France, would turn to each other for support—a combination that Bismarck had feared since the 1850s. To be sure, the support given Russia by France in the Balkan imbroglio had not measured up to Gorchakov's expectations, and the conquest by republicans of the French cabinet and presidency (May 1877 to January 1879) had widened still further the gap between Paris and Petersburg.[35] If shut out by a British-Austrian-German combination, the excluded powers were, nevertheless, likely to court each other. No more than in the days of the Three Emperors League, however, was Bismarck willing to abandon the fourth power to the embrace of the fifth. To be one of three was good, but one of four was better. Following the defeat of the monarchist factions in France, Bismarck assiduously cultivated better relations with successive republican cabinets.[36]

Bismarck would probably have initiated diplomatic steps toward the new

[34] Schweinitz, ed., *Denkwürdigkeiten*, II, 60.

[35] André Dreux, *Dernières années de l'ambassade en Allemagne de M. de Gontaut-Biron, 1874–1877* (Paris, 1907), pp. 203ff.

[36] *DDF*, II, 432ff. See also Pearl B. Mitchell, *The Bismarckian Policy of Conciliation with France, 1875–1885* (Philadelphia, 1935), pp. 6ff.

relationship with Austria in early 1879 but for the opposition of the Kaiser. To Wilhelm the developing rift with Russia was agonizing; he had no desire to widen it by entering a far-reaching agreement with Austria. Throughout his long life the relationship with Russia, reinforced by kinship ties between Romanov and Hohenzollern, had been the firmest and most enduring pillar of Prussian and German foreign policy. In view of Wilhelm's attachment to this "sacred legacy," Bismarck's plan lay dormant until August 1879, when the Russians themselves forced the issue. They complained to the German foreign office that German delegates on the commissions established to implement the Treaty of Berlin were voting consistently with Austria against Russia. From Kissingen Bismarck ordered his subordinates to respond that assisting Russia had proven to be for Germany a thankless task; as a consequence Berlin must nurture her relationships with other powers.[37] There followed one of those bitter skirmishes in the newspapers of both countries that had become all too familiar.[38]

Now Alexander II committed a blunder that Bismarck was quick to exploit. Since the Balkan war the tsar had become increasingly irritated by what he believed to be Germany's failure to reciprocate Russia's benevolent neutrality during the wars of 1866 and 1870–1871. On August 6–7, 1879, he told Schweinitz bluntly that Germany must change its conduct, if it wished to continue its long-standing relationship with Russia. Otherwise "this will end in a very serious way."[39] Soon afterward, the tsar dispatched a personal letter to his uncle, the Kaiser, sharply rebuking Bismarck's hostile policy toward Russia, which he attributed to the chancellor's personal quarrel with Gorchakov. "The consequences may be disastrous for our two countries." Bismarck attributed Alexander's threatening attitude to the influence of Milyutin (Gorchakov was on vacation), whom he accused of hating all Germans, but also to Alexander's "obvious" desire to fortify his shaky internal position "through warlike action abroad." He counselled a firm, unyielding response, but Wilhelm insisted on a moderate and even reassuring one.[40]

Schweinitz's report on Alexander's remarks arrived in Berlin shortly before news from Vienna of the impending resignation of Andrássy as chancellor of the Dual Monarchy. Although Andrássy had been ill, Bismarck suspected that the Hungarian was actually being forced out of office by those (including the Archduke Albrecht) opposed to his pro-German and anti-Russian course in foreign affairs. Another disturbing event in Austria was the appointment as Austrian prime minister of Count Eduard Taaffe, who believed in the necessity of appeasing the Czechs and other Slavic minorities, a policy which,

[37] GP, III, 7–9, also 12–14.
[38] Grüning, Öffentliche Meinung, pp. 66–68.
[39] GP, III, 9–12; Schweinitz, ed., Denkwürdigkeiten, II, 64–67.
[40] GP, III, 14–22.

if extended to foreign affairs, logically meant rapprochement with Russia.[41] On August 13, Bismarck asked Andrássy for a meeting, a request that became all the more urgent following receipt a few days later of the tsar's letter to the Kaiser. Again Bismarck was troubled by the vision of a resurrected "Kaunitz coalition"—the combination of great powers that had nearly defeated Frederick the Great.[42] Or did he feign such a nightmare in order to justify a course he had already decided to take? At any rate the two chancellors met at Bad Gastein, August 27–28, 1879. At this conference Andrássy, who had long advocated a coalition with Germany, agreed to remain in office long enough to conclude a "defensive alliance" to ward off "any attack by Russia either alone or in concert with other powers against either of the German powers." Kaiser Franz Joseph readily accepted the concept, for he and Andrássy were of one mind on the necessary course. But Kaiser Wilhelm was shocked; such alliances, he declared, were "contrary to his principles."[43]

On August 31, Bismarck dispatched from Gastein the first in a series of memoranda to the Kaiser, explaining why an alliance with Austria was justified in the light of the European situation and the relationships of the great powers. He began by denouncing Gorchakov's persistent flirtations with Germany's enemies. Alexander's recent threats showed that Germany had lost its last remaining friend in the Russian capital. In autocratic Russia the tsar could send the army poised on the Vistula over the German border merely by signing an order, no explanations required. Germany could not depend any more on the goodwill of the tsar to ward off such a disaster, but only on a defensive alliance with Austria, for which he had striven since 1866. Russia could hardly object to the resurrection of an old defensive alliance, to which Russia itself had had close ties after the Congress of Vienna and which had served for half a century as the bulwark of peace in Europe. On the contrary, it would be tempted to become again the third partner in the coalition. Without the certainty of Germany's support against an incalculable Russia, moreover, Austria might seek it in France. If allied to Germany, on the other hand, Austria would find support in Britain. A triple alliance between Germany, Austria, and Britain would be powerful enough to restrain Russia from an attack on either of the central European great powers and prevent France from allying with Russia.[44]

[41] Bagdasarian, *Rapprochement*, pp. 286–288, 296–297; GP, III, 39–40; Wertheimer, *Andrássy*, III, 203–224, and F. R. Bridge, *From Sadowa to Sarajevo: The Foreign Policy of Austria-Hungary, 1866–1914* (London, 1972), pp. 98–101.

[42] GP, III, 23 (fn.), 31, 108.

[43] GP, III, 23, 36; Horst Kohl, ed., *Anhang zu den Gedanken und Erinnerungen von Otto Fürst von Bismarck* (Stuttgart, 1901), II, 522–527; Wertheimer, *Andrássy*, III, 225–310. Additional documentation on the conflict between Kaiser and chancellor has been published by Windelband, *Bismarck und die europäischen Grossmächte*, pp. 66–85.

[44] GP, III, 26–36, also 39–47, 52–59.

By the time Bismarck's plaidoyer reached Berlin (September 2), Alexander had grasped his error and begun the attempt to rectify it. He invited Wilhelm by telegraph to join him at Alexandrovo in Russian Poland, where the Russian army was engaged in routine military maneuvers. From Gastein Bismarck vainly advised against the visit. But the Kaiser was determined to see for himself whether things had gone "as far" with the tsar as they seemed to have.[45] At Alexandrovo on September 3–4, Alexander denied that his letter of August 15, which he alone had written, was intended as a threat. He had merely wanted to warn of the harmful effects of Germany's anti-Russian votes on the Balkan commissions and the newspaper skirmish that followed. Wilhelm, who was fond of his nephew, wanted to be reassured, and was. Before leaving Alexandrovo he even conferred a high decoration on Milyutin, well known for his anti-German views. To ally with Austria against Russia, Wilhelm wrote to Bismarck, would be a dishonorable act that he would never commit; instead he would prefer to abdicate. He forbade Bismarck to visit Andrássy in Vienna. But then, after receiving the chancellor's remonstrance, he reversed himself, insisting only that Russia must not be mentioned in the treaty as a potential foe.[46] Not even on this point was he to get his way.

In his memoirs Bismarck expressed his gratification that in 1879 an Austro-German alliance was popular with almost all factions in German public life, including conservatives, national liberals, and Catholics. On his journey across Austria to Vienna he was applauded by excited thousands at the railway stations, embarrassingly so at Linz where he closed the curtains of his railway car, lest Austrian authorities should think he was deliberately fostering public favor. In Vienna his progress from the railway station to his hotel aroused demonstrations in the streets so continuous that he had to tip his hat the entire way. Today, he meditated, it was scarcely possible for a "great government" to commit its strength to support a friendly power, if that commitment were not backed by the people. But at the same time, he averred that the reasons for allying with Austria were so compelling that he would have concluded the alliance even without popular support.[47]

At Vienna on September 23–24 Bismarck was compelled to accept most of Andrássy's terms. The Hungarian rejected the far-reaching plan for an "organic union" ratified by the parliaments of both countries. For it he substituted a secret treaty lasting five years. But he also insisted on a declaration that, if either power was attacked by Russia, the other would come to the aid of the attacked with all its forces. If either were attacked by any power other than Russia, its ally would maintain benevolent neutrality, unless Russia supported the attacker, in which case the casus foederis would apply. Austria, in

---

[45] GP, III, 24–25, 36.
[46] GP, III, 36–39, 47–51, 62–67; Hans Rothfels, ed., *Bismarck-Briefe* (Göttingen, 1955), pp. 397–398; Kohl, ed., *Anhang*, II, 528–529.
[47] GW, XV, 402–408.

other words, would not commit itself to fight with Germany against France for the defense of Alsace-Lorraine unless Russia joined France in the attack. When he saw that Andrássy was adamant on this point, Bismarck feigned an ultimatum. Rising suddenly from his chair, he leaned close to the Hungarian and said menacingly, "Either accept my proposal or else . . ." Andrássy remained silent, and Bismarck finished the sentence with a laugh, "Otherwise I will have to accept yours."[48]

We are well informed about the dispute between chancellor and Kaiser because it occurred at long distance. While Bismarck was at Gastein and Vienna, Wilhelm was in Berlin, Alexandrovo, and East Prussia. By the time the chancellor reached Berlin, the Kaiser was at Baden-Baden. The separation complicated the debate, but it also enabled Bismarck to marshal his arguments in long dictations, which Wilhelm, being unable to interrupt, would have to read to the end.[49] "As models of political writing, and as specimens of close and cogent reasoning these reports and memoranda," wrote William L. Langer, "are without equals in the literature of modern diplomacy."[50] They are also fine examples of Bismarck's talent for persuasion, the capacity to orient his discourse—without obvious injustice to the facts—to fit the thoughts,

COUNT JULIUS ANDRÁSSY IN 1878. (DIETRICH SCHÄFER, *BISMARCK: EIN BILD SEINES LEBENS UND WIRKENS*, VERLAG VON REIMAR HOBBING IN BERLIN, 1917.)

[48] Wertheimer, *Andrássy*, III, 284; *GP*, III, 68–104.
[49] Kohl, ed., *Anhang*, II, 524–527.
[50] Langer, *Alliances and Alignments*, p. 180.

KAISER FRANZ JOSEPH I, ABOUT 1880. (ARCHIV FÜR KUNST UND GESCHICHTE, BERLIN.)

prejudices, and predilections of the recipient. Wilhelm's counterarguments were also lengthy and skillful for a person his age. The treaty, he declared, was aimed at Russia, and that was both unnecessary and a "perfidious" betrayal of a long friendship. While Germany promised assistance to Austria against a Russian assault, Austria was not similarly obligated to help Germany against France. Hence the obligations were unequal. France was the real foe, not Russia, which should be invited to rejoin Austria and Germany in a revived Three Emperors League.[51]

Bismarck could not dent Wilhelm's confidence in the reliability of Russian foreign policy and the identity of German and Russian interests. Hence he enlisted the support of Crown Prince Friedrich Wilhelm, General Moltke, Prince Hohenlohe (German ambassador to France), ministers of the lesser states, and at the critical moment the entire Prussian cabinet. The final threat that enabled him to align these forces behind his cause was that of resignation. If compelled to follow a foreign policy contrary to his judgment and conscience, he would decline the responsibility and depart—along with the entire cabinet.[52] Since the Congress of Berlin at least, no one was inclined any longer to dispute Bismarck's mastery of foreign affairs. In the end this was true also of the Kaiser, who on October 4 bowed to the prince's ultimatum. "Bismarck," he sighed, "is more necessary than I am." Two days later the treaty was signed in Vienna and on October 17 ratifications were exchanged.[53]

An Option for Austria?

Did Bismarck exercise an option for Austria over Russia in 1879? The question of Bismarck's intentions is important, for, to many historians, the Dual Alliance of that year was the first stone in the construction of that fatal system of conflicting alliances whose rivalry produced the First World War.[54] Undoubtedly he did establish Austria as the closer ally, the partner with whom Germany was henceforth to be the most firmly associated. But the Bismarck

[51] GP, III, 36–38, 47–51, 62–67, 73–74.

[52] GP, III, 46, 84, 91–92, 105–117; Heinrich von Poschinger, ed., Bismarck-Portefeuille (Stuttgart, 1899), II, 194; GW, XIV, 905–908; GW, VIII, 323–334; Freiherr Lucius von Ballhausen, Bismarck-Erinnerungen (Stuttgart, 1920), pp. 173–177; Busch, Secret Pages, II, 222–224; Hajo Holborn, ed., Aufzeichnungen und Erinnerungen aus dem Leben des Botschafters Joseph Maria von Radowitz (Stuttgart, 1925), II, 99–105. On Hohenlohe see Helmuth Rogge, Holstein und Hohenlohe (Stuttgart, 1957), pp. 98–101.

[53] GP, III, 117; Schweinitz, ed., Denkwürdigkeiten, II, 79.

[54] Historians have given varied answers to this question. For a few examples see: Waller, Bismarck at the Crossroads, p. 199; A.J.P. Taylor, The Struggle for Mastery in Europe, 1848–1918 (Oxford, 1954), pp. 264–265; Windelband, Bismarck und die europäischen Grossmächte, p. 87; Eduard Heller, Das deutsch-österreichisch-ungarische Bündnis in Bismarcks Aussenpolitik (Berlin, 1925), pp. 1–2, 55–58.

system called for two allies, not one. Hence the critical question is the identity of the third partner. In the dispute with Wilhelm during August and September Bismarck maintained that a defensive alliance with Austria, even one specifically aimed at Russia, did not preclude good relations with the tsarist regime. Wilhelm suspected and Bismarck denied that the purpose was to isolate Russia by building a coalition between Germany, Austria, Britain, and even France.

Both assumptions were correct. In Bismarck's calculations everything depended upon the dynamics of Russian policy. If Russia continued to demand of Germany actions incompatible with German interests, Bismarck would use the connection with Austria as a bridge to Britain. The three powers would share the objective of frustrating Russian aggression. The conciliatory course of the Waddington government toward Germany left open the possibility that even France might be attached to the combination. If, on the other hand, fear of isolation and revolution should moderate Russian policy toward Germany and Austria, Bismarck was not averse to the idea of reconstituting the Three Emperors League, but only as a supplement to, not a replacement for, the Dual Alliance.[55]

These calculations explain actions Bismarck took in late 1879 that have puzzled historians. On September 14—ten days after Wilhelm's visit at Alexandrovo and seven days before Bismarck's trip to Vienna—the chancellor dispatched to Count Münster, German ambassador in London, copies of the critical documents recording the tsar's "direct threats and far-reaching demands" (without reference to subsequent denials) and directing the ambassador to inquire of Disraeli what the British attitude would be if Germany, "out of friendship with Austria and England," came into conflict with Russia by rejecting demands that did not directly affect German interests.[56] To execute his instructions, Münster, who was on vacation in Germany, had to go to London, where he found no ministers present. On finally reaching Disraeli at Hughenden on September 26, Münster, a pronounced Anglophile, engaged in an extensive and wide-ranging discussion that may have exceeded his instructions. According to Disraeli's account, the German ambassador declared that Russia was preparing to attack Austria and that Germany, to preserve the peace, wished an "alliance between Germany, Austria, and Great Britain."

Münster sent to Berlin a far different account of the conversation. After listening to "a few words" from Münster concerning the "purpose of his coming," the prime minister had taken command of the interview and declared that he too was deeply concerned over the political situation in Europe; he had noted "with satisfaction" that Russia, blinded by an irrational "Slavoph-

---

[55] GP, III, 26–36, 39–42, 52–59, 78–83, 91–99.
[56] GP, IV, 3–6.

ilism," had alienated her old allies and apparently abandoned the Three Emperors League. Britain needed allies and must abandon the old tradition of nonintervention begun by the Cobdenites. "The most natural allies for England are Germany and Austria. *He would enter with pleasure into an alliance with Germany.*" The main problem was France and the possibility of a Russian-French alliance. If Germany should "help" England (and Austria) in the eastern question and in doing so come into conflict with Russia, "we will in that case keep France quiet [Bismarck: 'nothing else?']; you may depend upon us."[57]

At Hughenden Münster discussed both more and less than his instructions required. Worst of all, he did not press Disraeli for a full answer to the specific question Bismarck had asked. On October 8, nevertheless, Bismarck ordered the ambassador not to pursue the matter. In view of his previous overtures to Britain, why did the chancellor make this surprising decision? From Salisbury's later remarks to Münster it is evident that the British government, had it been asked the right question, would have responded favorably.[58] But the question was not repeated, for by the time Münster's dispatch had arrived Alexander II, aware of the German-Austrian negotiations and fearful of isolation, had changed course. On September 26 Peter Saburov, newly appointed as Russian ambassador to Constantinople, arrived in Berlin bearing friendly words from Petersburg. Bismarck and Saburov had already exchanged views in frank conversations at Kissingen in July and August, and the ambassador had succeeded in influencing the tsar and others at the Russian capital of the necessity of improved relations with Germany. From Bismarck he now heard that the purpose of Germany's accord with Austria was to prevent the latter from allying with England and France against Russia. Now that a ditch had been dug between Austria and the western powers, it would be possible to reestablish the Three Emperors League! In Russia, Saburov told him, "the peace party is now on top; they wish an honorable understanding." Afterward Bismarck exulted, "Now I have the best receipt for my Vienna policy. I knew that the Russians would come to us, once we nailed down the Austrians."[59]

In the weeks and months that followed the signing of the Dual Alliance Bismarck had exerted himself to reassure the other great powers of its harmlessness—how well he had learned his lesson from the debacle of 1875! In every direction he described the accord with Austria (the exact terms of

[57] The reports of this discussion by Münster and Disraeli differ markedly. Münster's report is in GP, IV, 7–10, that of Disraeli in W. F. Monypenny and G. E. Buckle, *The Life of Benjamin Disraeli* (London, 1968), IV, 1358–1361. For contrasting views of this episode in German-British relations see Langer, *Alliances and Alignments*, pp. 185–191; Hans Rothfels, *Bismarcks englische Bündnispolitik* (Berlin, 1924), pp. 44–52; and Arnold Oskar Meyer, *Bismarcks Friedenspolitik* (Munich, 1930), pp. 23–29. The brief analysis in GP, IV, 7 (fn.) still seems most probable.

[58] GP, IV, 10–14.

[59] Radowitz, *Aufzeichnungen und Erinnerungen*, II, 198–202.

which remained secret on Andrássy's insistence) as nonthreatening, supportive of European stability, and in the interest of other powers.[60] Langer has correctly described the prince's actions in this period as one of the finest examples of the diplomatist's art. "Here was one of those rare statesmen who could view a given situation from all conceivable angles and adjust his own actions to meet a large variety of contingencies." To Andrássy he emphasized one side of the problem; to the Kaiser, another. To the Russians he said that his goal was restoration of the Three Emperors League, a "triangular rampart" that would maintain both peace and conservative principles. In London and Paris he stressed the necessity of erecting a dam against Panslavism and nihilism and spoke of the value of an Anglo-French entente, which would deter its partners from dangerous adventures. "It will not do to accept any one of Bismarck's statements as the true exposition of his policy. What he aimed at was rather a system of checks and balances." What concerned him was primarily the continent and the issues that affected it. "But throughout he aimed at holding the balance between West and East and at upholding the commanding position of Germany by playing off the one against the other."[61]

[60] *DDF*, II, 574–592; Windelband, *Bismarck und die europäischen Grossmächte*, pp. 93ff.

[61] Langer, *Alliances and Alignments*, pp. 195–196. For a contrasting, adverse judgment of Bismarck's political tactics in this period see Waller, *Bismarck at the Crossroads*, pp. 249–256, and W. N. Medlicott, *Bismarck, Gladstone, and the Concert of Europe* (London, 1956), pp. 319–337, and *Bismarck and Modern Germany* (Mystic, Conn., 1965), pp. 119–146.

+:+

CHAPTER EIGHTEEN

End of the Liberal Era

Ministerial Crisis of 1879

N HIS final speech to the Reichstag defending the tariff bill (July 9, 1879), Bismarck revealed his mood at the end of the legislative session. "Since becoming a minister, I have belonged to no party; nor could I have belonged to any. I have been successively hated by all parties and loved by few. The roles have continually changed." Never had he avenged the hatred and malevolence he had met. His only goal had been to unify Germany, to fortify the union, and to secure the cooperation of all forces willing to maintain it. But his expectations of assistance had been repeatedly disappointed. Instead he had been attacked in the press and parliament in a distasteful and repulsive manner.[1] At this moment of apparent triumph Bismarck played the role of a resentful Messiah, continually deserted and betrayed by his disciples.

This speech was delivered about two weeks after the resignations of Prussian Ministers Hobrecht, Falk, and Friedenthal. The news of Hobrecht's defection on June 27 sent Bismarck striding back and forth, his face contorted with anger. When Falk and Friedenthal followed suit a day later, he smelled a plot. The nearly simultaneous departure of the cabinet's three "liberal ministers" was, he assumed, the tip of a "wide-spread intrigue," extending from the parliamentary opposition (Forckenbeck) to the cabinet and court (particularly Crown Princess Victoria). By precipitating a "ministerial strike" during the final debate on the tariff bill, the conspirators intended a "deadly embarrassment." To show that he was unshaken, Bismarck filled the vacant posts with unaccustomed haste.[2] As minister of agriculture he chose Robert Lucius (Ballhausen), owner of a knight's estate and a free conservative leader; as minister of cultural affairs, Robert von Puttkamer, Pomeranian Junker, conservative deputy, and governor of the province of Silesia; as minister of finance, Karl Bitter, under state secretary in the Ministry of Interior.

Simultaneously Bismarck completed the reorganization of the imperial gov-

---

[1] *BR*, VIII, 145ff.

[2] Christoph von Tiedemann, *Sechs Jahre Chef der Reichskanzlei unter dem Fürsten Bismarck* (2d ed., Leipzig, 1910), pp. 242–249; Freiherr Lucius von Ballhausen, *Bismarck-Erinnerungen* (Stuttgart, 1920), pp. 164–169. The departure of the liberal ministers may have been expedited by the Kaiser's order of Mar. 16, 1879, admonishing all imperial and Prussian officials who had dealings with the Reichstag to reject immediately and emphatically any effort to increase the powers of that body. By its recent actions, he declared, the Reichstag majority had demonstrated its ambition to strike for parliamentary government. *DZA* Potsdam, Reichskanzlei, 656, pp. 1–1a.

ernment that he had planned in 1875. Since Delbrück's dismissal he had steadily reallocated the power and functions of the Imperial Chancellor's Office (*Reichskanzleramt*), ending with abolition of the office itself. In place of a single executive body, the Reich now possessed eight agencies, headed by state secretaries acting under the chancellor's authority: Foreign Office, Imperial Admiralty, Imperial Railway Office, Imperial Post Office, Imperial Office of Justice, Imperial Treasury, and Imperial Office of the Interior.[3] The chancellor's need for a personal secretariat was supplied by an Imperial Chancellery (*Reichskanzlei*), whose initial chief was Tiedemann. The "tractable" Hofmann accepted a demotion from "president of the Imperial Chancellor's Office" to "state secretary of the Imperial Office of the Interior." Whatever pain this caused him was eased by his appointment as Prussian minister of commerce, an office left vacant by Maybach's appointment as minister of public works.[4]

Bismarck had created the "imperial ministries" he had once promised, but not an "imperial cabinet." The state secretaries were not collegial ministers on the Prussian model, but the subordinates and, under the deputation act of 1878, the deputies of the chancellor, who remained the only responsible minister of the empire. During 1879 Bismarck summoned these officials to three "conferences" (apparently the formal term *Sitzungen* appropriate to cabinet meetings was avoided). At the first conference he stressed that imperial agencies must be sharply separated from their Prussian counterparts. The Prussian minister of foreign affairs was the only constitutional channel for the transaction of business between Prussia and the Reich, for he alone could instruct the Prussian vote in the Bundesrat and communicate with other German governments. For this reason that position was held by the Reich chancellor. "Presidential bills" dealing with imperial affairs, including the budget, were to be drafted by imperial agencies alone and communicated to the Prussian ministries only for information.[5] No more did he talk of placing Prussian ministers at the head of imperial agencies, and within a year he concluded that the "personal union" under Hofmann of the Imperial Office of the Interior and the Prussian Ministry of Commerce was a mistake.[6]

Although his path had again changed, Bismarck's destination was still the same—to gain a firm personal grip on the imperial executive and to dominate the Prussian cabinet. The degree of his success is apparent in the changed character of the meetings of the Prussian cabinet that he attended. After 1879 the minutes of these sessions generally open with an extended statement by the minister-president, in which he informed his colleagues what bills were

[3] See pp. 372–375, 388–390.

[4] Rudolf Morsey, *Die oberste Reichsverwaltung unter Bismarck, 1867–1890* (Münster, 1957), pp. 84–104, 219–224.

[5] Hans Goldschmidt, *Das Reich und Preussen im Kampf um die Führung von Bismarck bis 1918* (Berlin, 1931), pp. 250–258; Morsey, *Reichsverwaltung*, p. 102.

[6] Cabinet meeting of Aug. 28, 1880. DZA Merseburg, Rep. 90a, B, III, 2b, Nr. 6, Vol. 92.

to be drafted and what policies to be pursued. The ensuing discussions in the protocols seem more for clarification than decision-making. The impression evoked is that of a schoolmaster dictating to pupils.[7] Bismarck had reached the peak of his executive authority after a long and tedious climb marked by many hesitations and changes of route.

The changes of 1879 also liquidated the last vestiges of the "liberal era." The very titles of the position Delbrück had held and of the agency he established were erased. The imperial government was purged, furthermore, of its last important defender of laissez-faire economics. Otto Michaelis, who had assisted Delbrück after 1867 in shaping imperial economic policies, was transferred from his post as director of the financial department of the chancellor's office to the harmless position of chief administrator of the disabled veterans' fund (*Reichsinvalidenfond*). To head the Imperial Treasury Bismarck chose Adolf Scholz, a career civil servant who had once served a term as conservative deputy in the Prussian Chamber of Deputies. As Scholz's principal subordinate (*Direktor*), he selected Emil von Burchard who, as Prussian delegate to the Bundesrat, had recently been effective in steering the protective tariff bill through the Reichstag. In securing these appointments from the Kaiser, Bismarck referred specifically to the candidates' political qualifications. This was a landmark in the history of the Prussian-German bureaucracy. "Here became visible the beginning in the higher civil service of the transition from bureaucratic expert to political exponent."[8]

The ministerial crisis of 1879 reveals again the difficulty of public service under Bismarck. For a year Hobrecht had swallowed his convictions; privately opposed to tariff protectionism, he had defended the chancellor's policy in the Reichstag. The former mayor of Breslau and Berlin now retired to private life, confessing that he was "unsuited for public service." After months on the verge, Falk resigned primarily out of protest against Wilhelm's conservative course in the affairs of the Protestant church. Bismarck still valued Falk as a threat to the papacy but was unable to persuade him to remain. Friedenthal, whom Bismarck had praised in the preceding year, was now out of favor. The prince denounced him to Wilhelm as ambitious ("his wife perhaps even more so") to become chancellor; this "clever Jew" (at a soirée Bismarck is reputed to have called him a "semitic *Hosensch*") was the shrewdest of five or six "future ministers" waiting to take office under Crown Prince Friedrich Wilhelm. To this end, according to Bismarck, Friedenthal had cultivated liberals as far to the left as Lasker, and his Catholic wife had exploited her religion to attract centrists.[9]

Bismarck found it necessary to explain to his sovereign why so many ministers came and went. Sooner or later, he declared, they discovered that it

---

[7] Good examples are the protocols of Apr. 4, 1879, and Aug. 28, 1880. *Ibid.*, Vols. 91 and 92.

[8] Morsey, *Reichsverwaltung*, pp. 197–203.

[9] Lucius, *Bismarck-Erinnerungen*, p. 168. "Hosensch" is an abbreviation of "Hosenscheisser," an expression of loathing and contempt.

was easier to appease rather than oppose parliament. Even the conservative Friedrich Eulenburg was guilty of this weakness. As the only official responsible for the entire government, the chancellor had constantly to intervene to halt the drift toward parliamentary government. That only rich men could afford office (Wilhelm: "? ?") complicated the task of finding ministers capable of upholding the rights of the crown. The effort to locate suitable candidates, Bismarck asserted, had cost him the illness he had suffered in early 1878 at Friedrichsruh.[10] Bismarck thought of himself as the only effective bulwark against constitutional change in the governmental system he had devised for Germany. He demanded that ministers and officials who served him be mere extensions of himself, capable of grasping his purposes and executing his will, but incapable of independent action and higher ambition.

The "Stroke" of 1880

Bismarck's dispute with Wilhelm over the Dual Alliance was hard on the nerves and health of both, but Bismarck was the one who did the complaining. As he prepared to leave Kissingen on August 19, 1879, he wrote to his daughter that, although the month's cure had been successful, a surge of work at the end had caused a "nervous relapse," which he hoped to make good at Gastein.[11] But at the Austrian spa he had "more to do than in the most difficult times at Berlin." Prevented by his wounded hand from writing more than a few lines at a time, he dictated up to forty pages a day to Herbert.[12] Worse than the work load, however, was the psychological effect of the Kaiser's opposition. "My nerves were most affected by [Wilhelm's] prohibition against my going to Vienna," he wrote privately to Bülow on August 31. That the Kaiser held him "on the leash to this extent" affronted his sense of "personal independence." "Cure and friction" combined had left him "nervous and embittered."[13] To Radowitz he wrote, "I have not recovered from the consequences for my health of similar frictions that occurred at Nikolsburg and Versailles; today my strength is so diminished that I cannot think of attempting to continue to do business under such circumstances." In seventeen years of service he had done his duty, he declared, and now the Kaiser would have to find a younger chancellor. His official resignation, he announced, could be expected within eight to ten days—"if the situation has not changed by then"![14] Again he demanded that people cease making him sick by opposing

[10] Bismarck to Kaiser, July 3 and 5, 1879. GW, VIc, 152–157.

[11] GW, XIV, 903–904.

[12] Herbert Bismarck to Tiedemann, Sept. 9, 1879. DZA Potsdam, Reichskanzlei, 2082, p. 31; GW, VIII, 331, 351; Moritz Busch, *Tagebuchblätter* (Leipzig, 1899), II, 560.

[13] Wolfgang Windelband, *Bismarck und die europäischen Grossmächte, 1879–1885* (2d. ed., Essen, 1942), p. 73.

[14] GP, III, 61.

him. The state of his nerves had long since become a weapon with which to flail his antagonists.

Nervous exhaustion and neuralgia compelled Bismarck to spend a few more days at Gastein even after Wilhelm finally authorized the trip to Vienna. After conferring with Andrássy, he returned to Berlin on September 25 for the final showdown with the Kaiser—their worst confrontation ever in Wilhelm's opinion. From there he dispatched to the Kaiser a series of messages, mostly telegrams, that became increasingly tart and scarcely in accord with his role as the monarch's "vassal." On receiving word from Baden-Baden that one of his telegrams had cost the Kaiser a sleepless night and jangled nerves, Bismarck wired back sarcastically that he and his aide Bülow had "for weeks known nothing but sleepless nights." When the Kaiser finally yielded on October 8, the chancellor asked immediately for permission to take another leave in the country.[15] On the following day he departed for Varzin, where he promptly fell ill—worn out, he said, by six weeks of "uninterrupted daily struggles with the Kaiser." For two months he went from bed to sofa and back again, unable, as he told Andrássy, to regain the strength he had expended "in the service of my master and country." "My stomach—that loyal but much abused servant—has refused further service," he wrote to his son-in-law, "because I have used up elsewhere the gall to which it has a right."[16] The joke had substance. At Varzin on December 13, 1879, Lucius reported that the prince "has had a severe attack of gall bladder disease accompanied by acute pains (perhaps a gallstone). He has been very sick and his cardiac sound was so weak that Dr. Struck became quite anxious. But the recent passage of the railway act made him half well again. I found him in his pajamas busy with a huge bowl of stew (bouillon, rice, and pigeons) and eating with good appetite." Next day, however, Lucius speculated that the prince's problem was a "liver ailment" and, given his constitution, a sudden collapse was quite possible.[17] From Herbert, Tiedemann heard that the chancellor was plagued by neuralgia and by Pomerania's snowy "rheumatism climate," which affected his nerves. Whether a matter presented to him would produce boredom or anger was impossible to predict; usually, the latter.[18]

For more than three months during the winter of 1879–1880, the German chancellor could perform no more than minimal duty. Not until January 27,

[15] GP, III, 74, 77, 83, 120–121; Hajo Holborn, ed., *Aufzeichnungen und Erinnerungen aus dem Leben des Botschafters Joseph Maria von Radowitz* (Stuttgart, 1925), II, 106–107.

[16] GW, XIV, 912.

[17] Lucius, *Bismarck-Erinnerungen*, pp. 179, 181; Norman Rich and M. H. Fisher, *The Holstein Papers: The Memoirs, Diaries and Correspondence of Friedrich von Holstein, 1837–1909* (4 vols., Cambridge, Eng., 1955–1963), III, 48; Helmuth Rogge, ed., *Holstein and Hohenlohe: Neue Beiträge zu Friedrich von Holsteins Tätigkeit als Mitarbeiter Bismarcks und als Ratgeber Hohenlohes* (Stuttgart, 1957), pp. 102–104.

[18] Tiedemann, *Sechs Jahre*, pp. 384–385, 389, 391–392.

1880, was he fit to travel to Berlin. Two weeks later Lucius reported that the prince had returned "eager for work, interfering in every branch of government, irritable and not easy to handle." His effort to protect landowners threatened to impede passage of an agricultural bill on which Lucius had worked for months. To Busch and Baroness Spitzemberg the chancellor complained in March of tiring easily, being unable to walk or stand for long periods without suffering neuralgia. Another visitor, Booth, noted four glasses full of pills on the prince's table, but found him looking well, although denying it. Anyone who had been a violin string for eighteen years, Bismarck said, was unusable. "Someday I will vanish like a cloud."[19] That this last thought was not casual became clear on March 30, 1880, when Bismarck by his own diagnosis suffered a stroke.

At dinner that evening he consumed six hardboiled eggs spread with butter, "endless quantities of iced May wine," and a bottle of port after which, his face flushed, he complained of feeling ill. He left the room, evidently to vomit, and returned pale and stammering "like a drunken person." His cheek muscles and the back of his head felt paralysed. After a sleepless night of vomiting, the prince's speech was still impaired. Struck diagnosed the ailment as stomach influenza temporarily affecting the facial muscles. But Bismarck, "more obstinate than ever," upbraided the doctor and, ignoring his advice, ate a heavy meal of chicken soup, meat, and vegetables, then went for a walk in the rain. Johanna summoned Ernst von Leyden, university professor and prominent internist, who confirmed Struck's finding. But Bismarck persisted in the belief that his affliction was a stroke, blaming it on the difficulties of government service. Not until a third physician—Oskar Schanzenbach, who spoke "more firmly and categorically"—had confirmed the diagnosis did Bismarck accept it. "Whether I die now or in five years is a matter of indifference," the patient stammered. "For you, yes," a guest replied, "but not for us and the fatherland." "Who knows?" said Bismarck, "perhaps it would be better."[20]

Legislative Victories, 1879–1880

Bismarck's extended illnesses, absence from Berlin during the winter, and incapacitation during the spring kept him from participating in important po-

[19] Lucius, *Bismarck-Erinnerungen*, p. 182; Rich and Fisher, *Holstein Papers*, III, 48; Busch, *Tagebuchblätter*, II, 564–565; GW, VIII, 351; Rudolf Vierhaus, ed., *Das Tagebuch der Baronin Spitzemberg* (Göttingen, 1960), p. 182.

[20] GW, VIII, 357–358; Tiedemann, *Sechs Jahre*, pp. 393–394. Years later Leyden remembered the diagnosis somewhat differently. The chancellor, he said, had an "overloaded stomach." Wilhelm Treue, *Mit den Augen ihrer Leibärzte* (Düsseldorf, 1955), pp. 297, 393–394. Schanzenbach, who had treated Bismarck earlier at Bad Gastein, had to be summoned from Munich for the consultation. Radowitz, *Aufzeichnungen*, II, 122–123.

litical and legislative affairs. During August–September 1879 occurred the campaign for election of the Prussian Chamber of Deputies that ended at the polls on October 7. The legislative session of the Landtag began on October 28, 1879, and ended on July 3, 1880, being interrupted by the Reichstag session from February 12 to June 15, 1880. The Bundesrat convened on September 15, 1879, and adjourned on June 30, 1880, an unusually long and at times agitated session. Although important bills were pending in all of these bodies, the German chancellor and Prussian minister-president appeared only once in the Reichstag (May 8, 1880), twice in the Bundesrat (June 8 and 14, 1880), and not at all in the Landtag.

The Prussian election of October 7, 1879, was the first test of the political consequences of the protective tariff. At Bismarck's direction the government press began in August to brand the election of deputies "like Forckenbeck, Stauffenberg, Lasker, and Richter as synonymous with free trade, economic misery, and high direct taxes."[21] Richter and his associates launched their campaign with the slogan, "Bismarck must go," concentrating on the "misguided" economic policy of the government—with catastrophic results.[22] Again voters gave the chancellor what he seemed to want. The coalition that had passed the Franckenstein clause scored an overwhelming victory, the conservatives rising from 34 to 104, free conservatives from 34 to 54, centrists from 88 to 96, and Poles from 15 to 19 seats, while the national liberals sank from 175 to 101, the progressives from 67 to 35 seats.[23] Among those missing from the newly elected chamber were many left-liberals, including Lasker, for whom no seat could be found in the runoff election. Even Richter was defeated in his home district, Hagen, but managed in the runoff to gain a seat in Berlin. Particularly damaging were the losses suffered by liberals in rural areas; the progressives lost 13 of 23 seats they held in East Prussia, long a progressive stronghold. Richter was confident that the setback was temporary.[24] But Prussian liberals never recovered from the defeat of 1879. The three-class system, coupled with no reapportionment, kept them a minority in the lower chamber, which became, like the House of Lords, a bastion of conservative and agrarian power.

Before the assembly met, the Conservative party, which since 1872 had been divided into two caucuses (the "old" and "new" conservatives) reunited, giving the party the capacity to form a majority either with the Center and

---

[21] Herbert Bismarck to Lucius, July 31, 1879. Lucius, *Bismarck-Erinnerungen*, pp. 541–542. Herbert Bismarck to Rantzau, July 27, 1879. Walter Bussmann, ed., *Staatssekretär Graf Herbert von Bismarck* (Göttingen, 1964), pp. 89–91. The chancellor even urged the suppression of the famed humor magazine *Kladderadatsch* for stirring up class hatred.

[22] Felix Rachfahl, "Eugen Richter und der Linksliberalismus im neuen Reiche," *Zeitschrift für Politik*, 5 (1912), p. 305.

[23] The liberals' defeat was not unexpected. *HW*, II, 275–276.

[24] *SBHA* (1879–1880), I, 920.

its Polish allies or with free conservatives and national liberals.[25] Bismarck
was disturbed by this fusion. In every "winged party," he wrote, leadership
tends to migrate to the extremes. The ultraconservatives were "not usable
allies or would not remain so," while the continued presence of "Laskerites"
in the National Liberal party gave to "nihilists" and "republicans" (that is,
Poles, progressives, and "progressives masked as national liberals") the
chance to sway the chamber on crucial issues. As dangerous as these extrem-
ists, or nearly so, was the Center party, whose loyalty to the government
could not be bought by any concessions in the Kulturkampf. "The government will not be able to manage for long with a majority dependent for its
existence on the goodwill of the Center."[26] From Varzin Bismarck intrigued
for an alternative majority, one more amenable to his program. The free conservatives, he wrote to Lucius, could become the "decisive element" in the
chamber by forming the nucleus of a coalition of moderates drawn from the
Conservative and National Liberal parties. To this end he persuaded Bennigsen to reverse his decision to retire from politics and even promoted the Hanoverian's candidacy for the presidency of the chamber. But the Conservative
party joined with the Center to defeat Bennigsen and to elect its own slate of
candidates. The combination that Bismarck himself had encouraged by accepting the Franckenstein clause appeared to dominate the Chamber of Deputies—much to his alarm.[27]

The prince ordered his associates to avoid opting for any combination of
parties; otherwise the government would be dependent upon the favored coalition, whose leaders, be they liberals or conservatives, would try to govern.[28] What he aimed for was the converse, namely dependence of the major
parties on the government. His object was to keep them always hungering,
but never totally starved for influence, willing to be in the minority on some
issues in the hope of escaping it on others. During the coming legislative
session he needed the support of national liberals on a number of important
bills that the Center was sure to oppose. But he also needed to preserve the
option of continuing the Kulturkampf as a means of softening resistance by
the Catholic church to his own terms for its liquidation. Bismarck's overtures
to Bennigsen and his suggestion that moderate liberals and conservatives cooperate brought sighs of relief from the former. "This combination would be,"
one of them wrote, "the strongest dam against a reaction in school and

[25] Hans Herzfeld, *Johannes von Miquel* (Detmold, 1938), I, 450; Eugen Richter, *Im alten Reichstag: Erinnerungen* (Berlin, 1894–1896), II, 143.
[26] Herbert Bismarck to Lucius, Oct. 26 and Nov. 10, 1879; Bismarck to Lucius, Nov. 5, 1879.
Lucius, *Bismarck-Erinnerungen*, pp. 542–544; Tiedemann, *Sechs Jahre*, p. 364.
[27] Herbert Bismarck to Lucius, Oct. 26, 1879. Lucius, *Bismarck-Erinnerungen*, p. 545; Tiedemann, *Sechs Jahre*, p. 364; Hermann Oncken, *Rudolf von Bennigsen* (Stuttgart, 1910), II, 421–
424; HW, II, 276–277.
[28] Herbert Bismarck to Lucius, Oct. 26, 1879. Lucius, *Bismarck-Erinnerungen*, pp. 542–543.

church, that is, against the reaction that we all really fear."[29] This mood helped produce the majority in the Chamber of Deputies that, in December 1879, passed Maybach's bill for public ownership of four major railway lines;[30] in June 1880, four bills for administrative reform;[31] and, in July 1880, the first "utilization statute" (to be discussed in the next section).

In the Reichstag national liberals also joined with the conservative parties in passing two crucial bills: renewals of the iron budget of 1874 and antisocialist act of 1878. The government's military bill was submitted to the Reichstag in February 1880 well in advance of the expiration date (December 31, 1881) of the *Septennat* of 1874. It called for increases in the size of the armed forces corresponding to the growth in population, participation by the first segment of the reserve in peacetime maneuvers, and an increase in military appropriations of about 25 percent. Recent international crises, the apparent alienation of Russia, the possibility of a two-front war, and the strengthening of French and Russian armies made a persuasive case for passage, which Bismarck heightened by launching a scare story in the newspaper press.[32] To the progressives and to Lasker and his associates, however, the vital issue was the government's demand that parliament relinquish for seven more years its right to review annually the military budget. They had bitter memories of the manipulations by which Bismarck had produced a majority for the *Septennat* of 1874. Yet liberals were hardly in a position to regain in 1880 ground lost in 1874 at the height of their parliamentary strength. Speaking for the "overwhelming majority" of his political friends, Bennigsen abdicated all judgment in military and foreign affairs; it was foolish for deputies to assume that they understand these matters better than the experts—Bismarck, Moltke, and Kameke. He praised Bismarck for concluding an alliance with Austria-Hungary against "strong resistance in important circles" and to the applause of "all Germany." Defeat of the bill depended upon the number of "Laskerites" willing to join a motley opposition of centrists, progressives, social democrats, Poles, Guelphs, and Alsace-Lorrainers. But the defectors were only four—Lasker, Stauffenberg, Bamberger, and Forckenbeck[33]—and the statute passed, 186 to 128. The "Laskerites" were generals without troops.

The government's bill for renewal of the antisocialist act until 1884 was also introduced well in advance of the expiration date (March 31, 1881). Like the *Septennat*, it enjoyed smooth passage through the Bundesrat in February

---

[29] Ludwig von Cuny to Johannes Miquel, Oct. 9, 1879. *HW*, II, 276–277; also Miquel to Robert von Benda, Oct. 16, 1879. *HW*, II, 276–277, Oncken, *Bennigsen*, II, 421–425.

[30] See pp. 460–461.

[31] *SBHA* (1879–1880), III, 2003–2005, 2033–2035, 2153–2156.

[32] Friedrich Curtius, ed., *Memoirs of Prince Chlodwig of Hohenlohe-Schillingsfuerst* (New York, 1906), II, 267.

[33] *SBR* (1880), I, 170–219, 579–637; II, 687–739; *RGB* (1880), pp. 103–107; Oncken, *Bennigsen*, II, 427–428.

1880. In the Reichstag the two conservative parties and most national liberals hoped for passage without much debate. Among the latter only Lasker, who had voted for the statute of 1878 with great misgivings, denounced the "exceptional law" and the abuses committed by the governments in executing it. Progressives (especially Hänel) prolonged the discussion by charging again that the statute violated civil rights, diminished popular confidence in the empire as a *Rechtsstaat*, and was ineffective in halting the progress of socialism. Naturally the social democrats, heartened by recent successes in by-elections, exploited the debate to propagate views on social reform that they could no longer express in newspapers and public meetings. The Center, which in 1878 had voted solidly against the statute, split over the issue; a conservative wing headed by the Bavarian Count Georg von Hertling supported the government, while the majority, whose spokesman was Windthorst, remained in opposition. The conservative wing enjoyed the prospect of being in harmony with Bismarck and had lost the fear that centrists as well as socialists might be victims of the statute's proscription of subversive activity. Windthorst, on the other hand, rebuked the governments for exceeding the limits of the 1878 statute in their pursuit of socialist agitators. His followers stressed that they were not opposed to the bill on grounds of principle but of impracticality. On May 4, 1880, the statute passed overwhelmingly, 191 to 94; fourteen centrists voted with the majority.[34]

Legislative Defeats, 1880

While significant, these victories were overshadowed by legislative defeats in both Reichstag and Landtag. Yet another assault by the government upon the Reichstag's power over the budget came to naught. To Bismarck the necessity of drafting and defending yearly budgets had become "unbearable"—"an unceasing, restless activity that exhausts all concerned and uses up parliament itself."[35] He proposed to amend the constitution to provide for biennial rather than annual budgets and for Reichstag elections every fourth rather than every third year. This extension would have made it possible to summon Reichstag and Landtag into session in alternate years. Richter speculated that the bill was a mere decoy put up for the national liberals to shoot down in order to feel better about accepting the *Septennat*.[36] However that may be, the bill

---

[34] *SBR* (1880), I, 289–311; II, 755–819, 1146–1176; *RGB* (1880), p. 117; Wolfgang Pack, *Das parlamentarische Ringen um das Sozialistengesetz Bismarcks, 1878–1890* (Düsseldorf, 1961), pp. 119–129.

[35] Cabinet meeting, Apr. 4, 1879. *DZA* Merseburg, Rep. 90a, B, III, 2b, Nr. 6, Vol. 91. Minister of Justice Friedenthal proposed an interval of eight years between elections, to which Bismarck replied that, while he had nothing against that idea "in principle," he thought it "more expedient" to let the extension of the legislative period appear as a logical "consequence" of the extension of the budget period.

[36] Richter, *Im alten Reichstag*, II, 147–148.

itself has to be taken seriously—another sign of the chancellor's growing determination to depreciate the importance of both parliaments. For many years he insisted that the government must discharge its responsibility by presenting bills it regarded as necessary whether or not passage was likely. That the Reichstag simply tabled the bill in question did not surprise him. By contrast, its rejection of the "Samoa bill" was an unexpected and stinging defeat.

In recent decades German companies, led by Godeffroy and Sons of Hamburg, had gained a near monopoly of trade with the Polynesian islands centering on Samoa, whose importance to German exports was expected to grow following completion of the Panama Canal. Although the trade was profitable, Godeffroy became insolvent in 1879 owing to unwise investments in German mining operations; an English creditor, the banking house of Baring, was eager to foreclose and assume the assets. With Bismarck's encouragement a consortium of German bankers headed by Bleichröder and Hansemann, with participation by the Prussian *Seehandlung*, formed a corporation to take over the Godeffroy enterprise, but they demanded that the Reich guarantee dividends of at least 4.5 percent to investors. This arrangement was not uncommon, having been used in Prussia and other states for the encouragement of railway construction. Bismarck concluded that preservation and expansion of the German commercial position in the South Pacific was a vital "national interest," a view, urged upon him by Bleichröder and by Bernhard von Bülow, that was soon widely trumpeted in the official press.[37] In the Reichstag and liberal press the free traders—Bamberger in the forefront—denounced the "swindle," denying that the rescue of Godeffroy by the taxpayers was a matter of national patriotism. At the end of April 1880 the bill was defeated, 128 to 112, the Center joining the progressives and 21 national liberals in the majority.[38]

Even more humiliating for Bismarck was the fate of the tax reform program that had become since 1875 his principal objective in domestic affairs. Under the Franckenstein clause incorporated in the tariff act of 1879, Prussia was to receive millions of marks in customs and tobacco tax revenues annually from the Reich. Yet this did not suffice to provide the tax relief for low income groups and property owners that Bismarck had planned when he proposed in 1878 that Germany shift "from the false path of direct taxes onto the smooth track of indirect taxes."[39] New and higher imperial taxes were necessary if the states were to receive the revenues from the Reich needed to execute the

---

[37] Bismarck to Scholz, Jan. 1, 1880. Heinrich von Poschinger, ed., *Fürst Bismarck als Volkswirth* (Berlin, 1890), I, 269–272. On the general problem of Godeffroy and the Samoan question see Hans Ulrich Wehler, *Bismarck und der Imperialismus* (Cologne, 1969), pp. 215–223, and Paul M. Kennedy, *The Samoan Tangle, A Study in Anglo-German-American Relations, 1878–1900* (New York, 1974), pp. 1–25.

[38] SBR (1880), II, 857–897, 945–962.

[39] See pp. 463–464.

proposed tax relief. To entice the Reichstag to grant those taxes, Bismarck and his associates proposed to demonstrate in advance how the funds they would produce were to be expended by the Prussian Landtag. The pleasure of reducing old taxes was to ease the pain of imposing new ones. In July 1880 the Landtag passed a "utilization statute" (*Verwendungsgesetz*) providing for liquidation of the four lowest brackets of the class tax, fusion of the upper brackets with the income tax, and allocation of one-half of all real estate tax revenues to local governments (*Kommunalverbände*).[40]

Even without the Prussian request for money with which to fund this reform, the German Reichstag would have had a major fiscal problem in 1880–1881. Increased expenditures for the Reich, particularly for the army, led to a prospective deficit of 44,900,000 marks, despite increased revenues expected from customs under the tariff act of 1879. Without new indirect taxes the imperial government must either borrow money or increase assessments on the states. The government introduced three revenue bills, calling for increases in the brewing tax (a request that had failed in 1879), in the stamp tax (a measure that went beyond the bill defeated in 1878 by including business receipts and bank checks), and a new "defense tax" (*Wehrsteuer*), to be paid by those not drafted into the armed services.[41] While passing the budget bill for 1880–1881 expeditiously, the Reichstag took no action on the brewing and stamp taxes; the defense tax died in the Bundesrat. Having swallowed the *Septennat* again, the liberal and centrist deputies were in no mood to make further sacrifices in parliamentary budget power. But they also had solid backing from brewers, bankers, and businessmen whose interests were affected.[42] Rumors of another government bill inaugurating a tobacco monopoly generated a coalition of progressives, national liberals, and centrists, which on April 28 affirmed its understanding that the government had permanently surrendered this goal in bargaining for the tariff act of 1879.[43]

The failure of the chancellor's tax program in the Reich left the Prussian utilization statute high and dry. Without revenue sharing by the Reich, Prus-

[40] SBHA (1879–1880), II, 1868–1870; *Anlagen*, I, Nos. 17, 18, 19; IV, No. 279; GS (1880), pp. 287–289.

[41] Bitter to Bismarck, Mar. 27, 1880, and Bismarck *Votum* of June 15, 1880. DZA Potsdam, Reichskanzlei, 2082, pp. 137–141, 155–156. Other possible taxes were considered within the government, including a tax on newspaper advertisements, which Bismarck rejected because of the storm it would produce in the press. "A great number of widely distributed newspapers live off of advertisements," he said, "and let themselves be influenced in ways contrary to the true general welfare." GW, VIII, 343. See also AWB, I, 324–325.

[42] SBR (1880), I, 349–364; II, 962–972, 1005–1024, 1444ff.; SEG (1880), pp. 113–115, 117–119.

[43] SBR (1880), II, 973–997; SEG (1880), p. 125. The rumors were not without foundation. GW, VIII, 343.

sia, whose income from direct taxes was shrinking owing to the depression, could not offer tax relief to low income groups and local governments.[44] The conduct of the Center party in allying with left-liberals to bring about defeat of the tax program in the Reichstag justified Bismarck's prognosis of the preceding fall. His manipulations had not succeeded in creating the deferential Reichstag majority of moderates that he wanted, and his strategy of creating alternating majorities by playing the centrists and national liberals off against one another had enjoyed but limited success. Nor had he succeeded in exploiting the Prussian Landtag's desire for financial relief to extract concessions from the Reichstag.

Disciplining the Bundesrat

The most startling event of the legislative year 1879–1880 was not the revolt of the Reichstag and Chamber of Deputies, but that of the lesser states in the Bundesrat. Since 1867 German dynasties and governments had largely accepted Prussian leadership. As Bismarck had planned, the Reichstag was an effective counterweight to the upper chamber of the imperial government. The states had reason to fear for their existence as long as the chancellor emphasized the unitary side of the constitutional balance and collaborated with the national liberals against "particularism." They sought safety in cooperation with Bismarck, apprehensive that opposition would drive him even further into the arms of the parties favoring centralization, an anxiety that Bismarck readily exploited. But now the wind had changed; Bismarck's break with the liberals emboldened the states to become more active in protecting their interests. As shown, their opposition frustrated the chancellor's plan for a nationalized railway system and even for an Imperial Railway Office equipped with effective powers to regulate freight rates.

While Bismarck swallowed this result, it may have influenced his decision in early 1880 to tighten his control over the Bundesrat and the federal states. To that end he launched a two-pronged offensive: one aimed at his underlings, the other at the ministers of the federal states. In March Hofmann was again sharply reminded that under the constitution only the Prussian minister of foreign affairs (that is, Bismarck) could instruct Prussian delegates to the Bundesrat; without his prior knowledge and approval no Prussian bills could be presented to that chamber; as the chancellor's deputy, furthermore, Hofmann had no authority to act except in conformity with Bismarck's policies.[45] At a dinner for Bundesrat delegates on March 15, the prince explained that

---

[44] Bismarck to Bitter, May 4, 1880. DZA Potsdam, Reichskanzlei, 2082, pp. 98–104. See also Wilhelm Gerloff, *Die Finanz- und Zollpolitik des deutschen Reiches* (Jena, 1913), pp. 172ff.

[45] Goldschmidt, *Reich und Preussen*, pp. 271–273.

the Bundesrat was intended to be the "*Aeropag* of the German nation," where Germany's leading statesmen assembled to deliberate on national affairs. Instead cabinet ministers had remained away, sending lesser officials as deputies. As a consequence vital decisions were made in Bundesrat committees under the influence of Prussian privy counselors "with their bureaucratic traits." As a remedy he proposed yearly conferences lasting two to three weeks, during which the ministers would take their seats in the Bundesrat to deliberate upon significant legislative bills, leaving minor ones to their deputies in later sessions. "His purpose in this is to strengthen the federal element, to heighten the prestige of the Bundesrat in Germany, and to work against unitary movements."[46]

Scarcely two weeks after this démarche, an episode occurred in the Bundesrat that sharply revealed Bismarck's actual vision of it as a deliberative body. On April 3, a few days after the prince's "stroke," Paul Fischer, a high official in the Imperial Post Office, appeared in the Bundesrat to support a Württemberg proposal to exempt receipts issued by the postal system from the proposed stamp tax. Since Hofmann and Bitter had defended the tax, to which the chancellor himself attached so much importance, the delegates were treated with a rare case of open conflict within the government. There were "mocking smiles," some said laughter, and the chamber proceeded by a narrow majority to adopt the Württemberg amendment.[47] When told of this scene, Bismarck "boiled over." Since Heinrich Stephan, chief of the postal service, was unavailable, he peremptorily summoned the next in command, an unsuspecting official who arrived proudly for his first face-to-face interview with the German chancellor, only to come stumbling out a moment later, visibly shaken, to fetch the hapless Fischer. To the latter Bismarck said a "few pleasant things" such as, "When I signed your appointment recently, I wondered at your youth; but you are much younger than your years." The stammer was gone.

Next morning, Tiedemann found the prince, after a sleepless night, *Gotha Almanac* in hand, calculating that the thirty delegates forming the Bundesrat majority on the postal receipt issue represented 7,500,000 people; the minority of twenty-eight, 33,000,000. This, he fulminated, was "absolutely contrary to the spirit of the imperial constitution." He could not defend in the Reichstag decisions of the Bundesrat with which he disagreed.[48] At top speed

[46] Spitzemberg to Mittnacht, Mar. 15, 1880. Goldschmidt, *Reich und Preussen*, pp. 274–275. See also GW, VIII, 352–353, and Heinrich von Poschinger, ed., *Fürst Bismarck und der Bundesrat, 1867–1890* (Stuttgart, 1896–1901), IV, 161–162.

[47] Poschinger, ed., *Bismarck und der Bundesrat*, IV, 130–135, 262–265.

[48] Tiedemann, *Sechs Jahre*, pp. 394–396; Rogge, *Holstein und Hohenlohe*, p. 142. The "Fischer affair" generated a correspondence between Bismarck, Hofmann, Bitter, Scholz, and Stephan that reveals again the general haziness of governmental relationships under the system Bismarck

he dictated a despatch to the Kaiser requesting release from office. As arranged, Wilhelm replied by suggesting that the chancellor propose changes in Bundesrat procedures that would prevent a recurrence of such a situation.[49] In newspaper articles written by Tiedemann and Busch, Prussian officials were publicly rebuked for the "lack of discipline" that had developed during the chancellor's absences from Berlin; a case was made for shifting power from Bundesrat committees to that body's plenum.[50]

In Bismarck's dealings with legislative bodies, "resignation" had become a euphemism for ultimatum. To the Reichstag it meant that the chamber must either capitulate or be dissolved and face new elections. To the Bundesrat it meant that the states must either capitulate or accept the dissolution and reconstruction of the Reich. If the "spirit" of the treaties of 1867 and 1871 were violated, Prussia would withdraw from the federal union on the grounds that its governmental machinery had become unworkable; the national union must then be reconstituted at the cost of either the representative principle (the Reichstag) or the federal principle (the Bundesrat). What Bismarck threatened was a *Staatsstreich*, a warning that became all too familiar in the decade ahead. This was the message that Bismarck broadcast in veiled form in the official press and, more bluntly, in his private messages to the state governments.[51] It had the desired effect. Hastening to Berlin, the ministers

---

had devised. Prussian and imperial officials had the legal right to participate in Bundesrat deliberations only as Prussian delegates to that body or as deputies of delegates, both of which required royal appointment. But the rule had been laxly observed in the daily transaction of legislative business. Fischer's mistake was not in testifying in the Bundesrat without such an appointment, but in testifying the wrong way. As Prussian minister of finance, Bitter had tried, by his own testimony, to persuade Fischer not to testify against the proposed tax. Stephan defended his subordinate on the grounds that the imperial post office had received no advance notice of the stamp tax bill, although its interests were affected. Nevertheless, he disavowed Fischer's actions as unauthorized (Bismarck: "Zuchtlos!"). Disciplinary proceedings brought Fischer a formal reprimand. Bismarck used the occasion to lecture his officials, the state governments, and the public about constitutional relationships. But Hofmann, who as presiding officer had permitted Fischer to speak in the Bundesrat, was the chief victim. The episode reinforced Bismarck's growing determination to be rid of him. DZA Potsdam, Reichskanzlei, 1967 (*Die Vorgänge in der Bundesrathssitzung vom 3ten April 1880*), pp. 5–139.

[49] Exchange of letters, Bismarck and Wilhelm, Apr. 6–7, 1880, GW, VIc, 175–176; Horst Kohl, ed., *Anhang zu den Gedanken und Erinnerungen von Otto Fürst von Bismarck* (Stuttgart, 1901), I, 298; DZA Potsdam, Reichskanzlei, 1967, pp. 32–33.

[50] Tiedemann, *Sechs Jahre*, p. 401; Busch, *Tagebuchblätter*, II, 581ff.

[51] Goldschmidt, *Reich und Preussen*, pp. 73–76, 276–277; Poschinger, ed., *Bismarck und der Bundesrat*, IV, 229–231; GW, VIc, 175; Freiherr Hermann von Mittnacht, *Erinnerungen an Bismarck* (Stuttgart, 1904–1905), I, 71. The Baroness von Spitzemberg, wife of the Württemberg delegate to the Bundesrat and close friend of the Bismarcks, was shocked by the chancellor's "most remarkable terrorizing of the Bundesrat" over her husband's protests. She judged that his "inapproachability and increasing heavy-handedness" had cost Bismarck a lot of popularity. Spitzemberg, *Tagebuch*, pp. 183–184.

THE TIRED CHANCELLOR. AN AUSTRIAN VIEW OF BISMARCK'S CONDUCT IN PARLIAMENT. *BERG'S KIKERIKI*, VIENNA, MAY 1880.

of the lesser states took their seats in the Bundesrat, reversed the earlier de-cision on the stamp tax, and accepted the new procedures that in the future required their presence in Berlin for passage of the most important bills. In return they were served a "peace dinner" at the chancellery, where they found their host in "the rosiest mood."[52]

[52] Tiedemann, *Sechs Jahre*, pp. 403–407.

In the past Prussia had on occasion been outvoted in the Bundesrat, and yet the chancellor had never before reacted so strongly.[53] By demonstrating the lengths to which he was willing to go to reverse an unfavorable vote, he gained in effect a suspensive veto over the chamber's decisions.[54] Yet he assured the states simultaneously that he was a defender of their interests and of federalism in general. The federal states, he declared, provided a much stronger barrier to "the advance of republicanism, which is evident in the Reichstag and in Europe as a whole, than would be possible in a unitary state, where only a single government, not a majority of governments, would stand opposed to the Reichstag."[55] While this sentiment was probably sincere, Bismarck's effort to gain a firmer grip upon the Bundesrat had the same consequence as his previous efforts to heighten his influence over the Reichstag and Chamber of Deputies. He elevated his own power at the cost of the system of institutional checks and balances he had created in the Reich constitution. The effect of his narcissistic compulsion upon German federalism can be seen in a passage from Lucius's diary, which summarizes a conversation the minister had on April 20, 1880, with King Johann of Saxony, who had just returned from a visit with the German chancellor. Although still pleasant, Johann reported, Bismarck had aged and was prone to anger. "When the king uttered a differing opinion, Bismarck changed his expression, and the king immediately yielded. It is Bismarck's misfortune, the king declared, that he cannot listen to a contrary opinion and immediately conjectures ulterior motives. This is what happened in the vote on the stamp tax bill, when no one knew that the matter was important to him. Everyone does his will, the Kaiser first of all."[56]

The Coercion of Bremen and Hamburg

The same authoritarian tendency can be seen in Bismarck's campaign of 1880 to force Bremen and Hamburg into the Zollverein. Article 34 of the imperial constitution provided that the two ports at the mouths of the Weser and Elbe Rivers "with such of their own territory and with such adjacent regions as may be necessary for this purpose, shall remain free ports outside the common customs frontier, until they ask to be included within it." Earlier both had surrendered some "adjacent regions," but retained the outports of Bremerha-

---

[53] Poschinger, ed., *Bismarck und der Bundesrat*, IV, 266.

[54] *Ibid.*, IV, 267. In the opinion of Karl Oldenburg, the Mecklenburg delegate, the new procedure reduced the Bundesrat to a mere "voting machine." Goldschmidt, *Reich und Preussen*, p. 72 (fn.).

[55] Stichling, in April 1880. Poschinger, ed., *Bismarck und der Bundesrat*, IV, 165. Also to King Ludwig of Bavaria, June 1, 1880. DZA Potsdam, Reichskanzlei, 656, pp. 2–6.

[56] Lucius, *Bismarck-Erinnerungen*, pp. 183–184.

ven and Cuxhaven and, in Hamburg's case, the Prussian town of Altona.[57] During the drive for a protective tariff in May 1879 Bismarck prodded both cities to initiate their inclusion in the Zollverein. Neither complied. Instead they increased from 3 to 5 marks per head the sum paid annually to the Reich in lieu of tariffs.[58] On April 19, 1880, the Bundesrat received from Prussia, without prior warning to Hamburg, a bill incorporating Altona and part of adjacent St. Pauli into the customs union. Since both were practically inseparable geographically and commercially from Hamburg, this was actually an attempt to force the latter and, by precedent, Bremen as well into the Zollverein.[59]

On April 28 Hamburg countered by challenging the constitutionality of the incorporation of St. Pauli, which had become one of its suburbs. But Prussian delegates to the Bundesrat took the position that the issue was economic, not constitutional. The Bavarian delegate, Gideon von Rudhart, stalled for time by declaring that he must await instructions from his government, but volunteered the opinion that the fate of St. Pauli was indeed a constitutional matter. Next day, on arriving with his wife at Bismarck's parliamentary soirée, he was verbally assaulted by his host in full hearing of the other guests. The envoy, who had a reputation for integrity, joviality, and ineffectuality, was castigated for opposing the "well-known intentions" of Germany's chancellor and of participating in a "conspiracy" of ultramontanes, Hamburg Jews, and progressives. The Bavarian summoned his carriage, left the party, never returned to the Bundesrat, and was soon reassigned by his government.[60]

On May 5 Bismarck himself appeared—a rare occasion—to chair the Bundesrat's tariff committee. Never, he declared, would he grant that the Hamburg issue had a constitutional dimension. The exclusion of the two Hanseatic cities from the Zollverein had always been regarded as temporary; their free ports could be limited to dock and warehouse areas on the waterfront. "As I see the matter, a situation could arise out of this for Prussia like the one that existed in the Bundesrat in June 1866." Nevertheless, he agreed to bypass the constitutional issue by letting a committee of experts determine the most feasible line for the new customs frontier. Except for Hamburg, the state governments leaped at this solution. The experts settled the matter by leaving the whole of St. Pauli within the Hamburg free zone.[61]

---

[57] When the North German Confederation was founded in 1867, Lauenburg, the two duchies of Mecklenburg, and the Hanseatic cities of Lübeck, Bremen, and Hamburg were still outside the customs union. By 1871 all but the last two had joined, although Lübeck retained some entrepôt privileges. W. O. Henderson, The Zollverein (London, 1968), pp. 301, 310–312, 330.

[58] Henderson, Zollverein, p. 332.

[59] Poschinger, ed., Volkswirth, I, 276–280; Poschinger, ed., Bismarck und der Bundesrat, IV, 215ff.; AWB, I, 328–332.

[60] Poschinger, ed., Bismarck und der Bundesrat, III, 404–409; IV, 226; BP, I, 186ff.

[61] Poschinger, ed., Bismarck und der Bundesrat, IV, 226–229. In contrast to Rudhart, who was left nearly speechless by Bismarck's assault, the delegates Versmann (Hamburg), Schmidtkonz,

Obviously bigger issues were at stake for Bismarck than merely the fate of Altona and St. Pauli. Although the bill of April 19 claimed that Altona had suffered from the connection with Hamburg, this was not the opinion of its merchants and city government.[62] In the end it proved to be infeasible to separate even Altona from Hamburg by a customs frontier; the Bundesrat ordinance of May 22, 1880, that authorized its inclusion was never executed.[63] The attack on Bremen and Hamburg had a more political and nationalistic than economic and fiscal purpose. Bismarck wanted to liquidate this "foreign bridgehead on German soil."[64] That the two ports lay outside the tariff wall he had erected around fortress Germany was as difficult for him to accept as was the presence of non-Germanized (in his sense of the term) Poles, Danes, and Frenchmen within the imperial borders. But the chancellor was also bent on imposing his will on the medium and small states by shock tactics of the kind that shook Rudhart. In a dispatch of May 6 to Prussian envoys at the German courts, which was published in order to emphasize its gravity, he declared that as chancellor his duty was to counter particularistic sympathies of the German states as well as the centralistic inclinations of the Reichstag. Any attempt by the states to outvote Prussia on a constitutional issue would re-create circumstances similar to those in the Bundesrat between 1848 and 1866.[65] The message was clear: if crossed on a fundamental issue, Prussia would withdraw from the treaties of federation signed in 1866 and 1870, and German unity would be jeopardized.

The struggle in the Bundesrat had repercussions in the Reichstag. In reply to an interpellation on May 1, Adolf Scholz, state secretary of the Imperial Treasury, speaking for Bismarck, flatly denied that the Reichstag had any voice in the matter. But Richter, Lasker, and Windthorst all rejected this position; Richter charged the government with having violated the constitution.[66] Through a leaked document (a letter from Bismarck to Bitter) the deputies had learned that the chancellor intended to unlimber yet another weapon against the Hanseatic cities—a Bundesrat ordinance incorporating into the Zollverein the entire estuary of the Elbe, stretching one hundred kilometers from Hamburg to the sea. Duties were henceforth to be collected at Cuxhaven or Glückstadt, where ships entered the estuary, rather than at Hamburg or at small ports on the Elbe, where goods were landed. This pro-

and Hermann (Bavaria) stood up to Bismarck's bullying in this session—particularly Hermann, who at the end was rewarded by a handshake from the chancellor.

[62] SEG (1880), pp. 179–180, 207–208. Although industrial interests in Bremen favored entry into the Zollverein, the commercial interests dominating the town were opposed. Ibid., pp. 243–244. On the division of sentiment in Hamburg see ibid., pp. 260–262.

[63] Henderson, Zollverein, p. 333.

[64] Poschinger, ed., Bismarck und der Bundesrat, IV, 215. For other evidence of Bismarck's national motivation see GW, VIII, 370–371, and VIc, 189–190.

[65] Poschinger, ed., Bismarck und der Bundesrat, IV, 229–231; GW, VIc, 179–182; Goldschmidt, Reich und Preussen, pp. 276–277.

[66] SBR (1880), pp. 1071–1086; Richter, Im alten Reichstag, II, 158–160.

posal posed an even greater threat to the entrepôt trade of Germany's greatest seaport.[67] Ordinarily a Bundesrat ordinance was not subject to debate in the Reichstag. But Rudolf Delbrück, now a Reichstag deputy, found a way. In the draft of an Austro-German Elbe navigation treaty he detected a clause that was intended to pave the way for incorporation of the estuary under international law. Since it dealt with commerce, the treaty could be discussed in the Reichstag, and opposition deputies seized the chance to open up the Hamburg-Bremen issue.[68]

This debate was the occasion for Bismarck's only appearance in the Reichstag during the entire session. The chancellor scolded the deputies for intervening in matters beyond their constitutional competence. Liberals had lost their enthusiasm for German unity and were making common cause with particularism. Those who had once glowed for the "national idea" now went "arm in arm" with centrists and others inimical to the Reich. The hostile attitude of the Center over the last six months, he declared, had destroyed his trust in negotiations with the curia. Their conduct was always a barometer of Rome's intentions. Had those who joined the centrists in opposition to the government considered the consequences of their actions for the constitution? It was a dangerous game to encourage lesser states to outvote Prussia in the Bundesrat. For thirty years he had struggled for German unity, during eighteen of which he had accumulated hatreds like every minister long in power. Only the wishes of the Kaiser kept him at his post. If compelled to resign, he would advise the Kaiser to seek his replacement from candidates acceptable to centrists and conservatives. To him it was a matter of indifference if his successor went to Canossa.[69]

Bismarck had no compelling reason to address the Reichstag on the navigation treaty, which went into effect without that body's approval, or on the incorporation of the Elbe estuary, which the Bundesrat had the power to effect and did so on May 22, 1880. Nor did he need Reichstag support in forcing Hamburg and Bremen into the Zollverein. Under continual pressure from the chancellery, Hamburg capitulated in 1881, Bremen in 1884.[70] Bismarck's

---

[67] AWB, I, 325–328; Poschinger, ed., Volkswirth, I, 287. The theft and revelation of a government document, specifically a letter from the chancellor to the Prussian finance minister, was a rare episode in the Bismarck era. Bismarck's private reaction is unrecorded; publicly he reacted coolly. Through the Norddeutsche Allgemeine Zeitung he declared that his position on the Zollverein issue was well known. A chancellor who failed to complete the national unification of Germany "by all constitutional means" would be guilty of neglecting his duty and should be dismissed. If he had known that the opposition placed so much value on finding out that he was doing his duty, he would have written ten such letters for them. SEG (1880), p. 205; Norddeutsche Allgemeine Zeitung, Vol. 19, No. 243, July 25, 1880.

[68] SBR (1880), II, 1139–1141, 1264ff.

[69] BR, VIII, 170–192. See also GW, VIc, 189–190.

[70] As Bismarck had promised, Hamburg retained a free port area of about four square miles. The imperial treasury bore half of the cost of its construction, which was completed in 1888. Bremen received a similar privilege. Henderson, Zollverein, pp. 334–335.

speech of May 8 was an act of personal defiance and contempt. Threats and reproaches flew like angry sparks from a grinding wheel. German patriots he threatened with the loss of national unity, particularists with a reduction in federalism, ultramontanes with renewal of the Kulturkampf, liberals with its abandonment by a reactionary government. Only the conservatives, who had consistently backed his legislation in Reichstag and Landtag, escaped his wrath. Again he depicted himself as an object of universal ingratitude, as a statesman isolated and misunderstood, standing for the common rather than partisan interest, bearing his heavy burden despite illness and fatigue. "I am tired," he said, "dead tired."[71]

Enabling Act and Secession

During the last six months of 1879 serious efforts were made to negotiate an end to the Kulturkampf. By his appointments to the curia Leo XIII surrounded himself with churchmen who wanted a settlement, while the new *Kultusminister* in Berlin, Puttkamer, a staunch Lutheran conservative, was eager to abandon the course followed by Falk. During October–November delegations led by Papal Nuncio Cardinal Jacobini and German Ambassador Prince Heinrich VII Reuss negotiated in Vienna. Bismarck remained skeptical of the outcome, unconvinced that either party could meet the demands of the other, and doubtful that the Center party, whatever the concessions made to it in religious matters, could be harnessed to the government wagon. When the Center opposed the railway purchase act and other government measures in December 1879, he ordered Puttkamer and Reuss to let the negotiations stagnate without explanation. They had served at least to let him smoke out the wants and demands of the papacy.[72]

In late February 1880, Leo sought to revive the negotiation by holding out the prospect of a partial concession in the matter of the *Anzeigepflicht* (that is, the church's obligation to notify the government of nominations for and appointments to ecclesiastical offices), which Bismarck had declared to be the

---

[71] *BR*, VIII, 190.

[72] Erich Schmidt-Volkmar, *Der Kulturkampf in Deutschland 1871–1890* (Göttingen, 1962), pp. 224–259; Christoph Weber, *Kirchliche Politik zwischen Rom, Berlin und Trier 1876–1888: Die Beilegung des preussischen Kulturkampfes. Veröffentlichungen der Kommission für Zeitgeschichte bei der katholischen Akademie in Bayern*, ser. B, vol. 7 (Mainz, 1970), pp. 27–31; *GW*, VIc, 162–164, 171–173; XV, 335; Tiedemann, *Sechs Jahre*, pp. 387–388. If he was to temper Catholic demands while discontinuing the Kulturkampf, Bismarck had to preserve the capacity to renew it. Hence he sought to keep Falk in office, deplored the excessive weakening of the National Liberal party, and sought to keep Bennigsen politically active. His enthusiastic allies in the struggle were to help him liquidate it on favorable terms. Oncken, *Bennigsen*, II, 430. Yet when Falk was gone, Bismarck exploited his successor's conservatism to signal his own good faith in negotiations with the papacy. The first sign of Puttkamer's new course was a decision not to convert on schedule a Protestant into a nondenominational school at Elbing, a step that alarmed liberals but not Bismarck. Lucius, *Bismarck-Erinnerungen*, pp. 180–181.

chief obstacle to a repeal of the May laws.[73] Through Jacobini the pope let it
be known, furthermore, that more concessions were in prospect, once the
Vatican had gained satisfaction on other matters such as reinstatement of
bishops.[74] In a cabinet meeting Puttkamer, seconded by Friedberg, argued
hotly for a favorable response. But Bismarck attributed to the pope's overture
only a "theoretical importance." The offered concession applied only to lesser
clergy, did not clearly yield to the state the right to veto candidates, and could
easily be revoked. Instead of repealing any of the May laws, Bismarck insisted
that the government secure from the Landtag an enabling act giving it discretionary power in their enforcement. "One must have authority to close an
eye, as long as peace is maintained by the other side."[75] On April 12, he
publicly announced the government's intention to seek this authority; simultaneously he proposed to resume diplomatic relations with the Holy See.[76] He
wanted to outdo the pope in the game of good faith by shifting the negotiations to Rome, while gaining through the enabling act a flexible position that
would permit him to ease the government's relations with Catholics, offering
immediate rewards for good behavior on the part of the Center party, yet
preserving the option of reviving the Kulturkampf if he deemed it necessary.[77]

These successive developments created consternation in many quarters.
On hearing that the pope had softened on the requirement for notification,
Windthorst exclaimed, "Shot! Shot in front of the enemy. Shot in the
back!"[78] The government's announced plan for an enabling act also embarrassed the Center, already rent by differences between compromisers and intransigents over the antisocialist act. That the public was left in the dark
concerning the contents of the bill for a full month added to the confusion.
In messages to Rome, articles planted in the press, and a Reichstag speech of
May 8, 1880, Bismarck exploited the situation by contrasting the peace policy
of the papacy with obstructionism by centrists who collaborated with progressives, free traders, socialists, Guelphs, Poles, and other "enemies of the
Reich."[79] In communications to Windthorst and other centrist deputies (Paul
Majunke and Franz Moufang) the Vatican instructed the Center to continue

[73] Leo XIII to Archbishop Melchers of Cologne, Feb. 24, 1880. Rudolf Lill, ed., *Vatikanische
Akten zur Geschichte des deutschen Kulturkampfes* (Tübingen, 1970), I, 353–355; SEG (1880), pp.
73–74.

[74] Lill, ed., *Vatikanische Akten*, I, 375–376.

[75] Cabinet meeting of Mar. 17, 1880. DZA Merseburg, Rep. 90a, B, III, 2b, Nr. 6, Vol. 92;
Lucius, *Bismarck-Erinnerungen*, p. 183; Lill, ed., *Vatikanische Akten*, I, 372.

[76] GW, VIc, 173–174.

[77] Johannes Heckel, "Die Beilegung des Kulturkampfes in Preussen," *Zeitschrift der Savigny-
Stiftung für Rechtsgeschichte*, Kanon. Abt. 19 (1930), pp. 215–353.

[78] Schmidt-Volkmar, *Kulturkampf*, p. 260. Windthorst departed for his home in Hanover determined to give up politics but was persuaded to return.

[79] GW, VIc, 176–179, 185–187; Busch, *Tagebuchblätter*, II, 576ff., 587ff.; BR, VIII, 183–191.
Finally Bismarck went so far as to publish dispatches giving the details of the Vienna negotiations. *Das Staatsarchiv*, vol. 38 (1881), 287ff.; SEG (1880), pp. 164–175.

agitating for repeal of the May laws, keep a free hand in purely political questions, and reserve judgment on the enabling act until its actual provisions were revealed. But Leo also left no doubt that the party was to have no role in any negotiations to end the Kulturkampf; that role was reserved for sovereign heads of state.[80]

The Center was not the only party upset by the enabling act. Even right-wing liberals were incensed by the government's request for authority of unlimited duration to permit pastors to extend their services to neighboring vacant parishes, the recall of government administrators from vacant dioceses, resumption of financial support by the state, and replacement of state administrators by vicars chosen by cathedral chapters. Bennigsen declared that only the curia could rejoice at such proposals.[81] Yet the pope promptly condemned the bill as insufficient.[82] In the Chamber of Deputies a struggle developed between centrists, who sought to convert the bill into a full repeal of the May laws, and liberals, who endeavored to reduce the discretionary power it granted. Although he tried to influence Bennigsen in private talks, Bismarck refused to reveal what he would accept in the way of amendments, complicating the search for a compromise. Ultimately Bennigsen, who in disgust was again considering retirement from politics, brought together a coalition of conservatives, free conservatives, and right-wing national liberals that passed the bill by a majority of four (June 28, 1880), but only after vital paragraphs, including that which allowed the reinstatement of bishops, had been excised.[83] The result was a mutilated statute, which Bismarck, nevertheless, permitted to be enacted into law. "The session ended," wrote Lucius, "in general discord."[84]

---

[80] Schmidt-Volkmar, Kulturkampf, pp. 263–264; Karl Bachem, Vorgeschichte, Geschichte und Politik der deutschen Zentrumspartei (9 vols., Cologne, 1928), IV, 20–21; Rudolf Lill, Die Wende im Kulturkampf: Leo XIII., Bismarck und die Zentrumspartei, 1878–1880 (Tübingen, 1973), pp. 254–282. Windthorst never sought a personal meeting with the pope and was disturbed when he learned that Majunke had been summoned to Rome. Schmidt-Volkmar finds this "politically and psychologically" difficult to explain. Kulturkampf, p. 264. Obviously Windthorst wished to keep some distance between his party and the Vatican, lest the papacy interfere in its political operations. For the record of his contacts with the papacy in this period see Lill, ed., Vatikanische Akten, pp. 352–353, 368–370, 373, 405–408, 411–412, 418ff.

[81] Oncken, Bennigsen, II, 430–431; Tiedemann, Sechs Jahre, p. 409; GW, VIII, 369–370. Falk too opposed the bill, leading Bismarck to publish a letter from him showing that his resignation in 1879 had not arisen from a dispute with the chancellor over church policy. GW, XIV, 916–917.

[82] Lill, ed., Vatikanische Akten, I, 426–427; Bachem, Zentrumspartei, IV, 27.

[83] SBHA (1879–1880), pp. 2043ff., 2163ff., 2377–2450; GS (1880), pp. 285–286.

[84] Lucius, Bismarck-Erinnerungen, pp. 185–187; Oncken, Bennigsen, II, 432–434; GW, VIII, 369–370. On June 6 the Kölnische Zeitung published a purported interview between the chancellor and a "highly placed diplomat," in which Bismarck again threatened resignation, dissolution of the chamber, and, in veiled language, changes in parliamentary institutions; he decried the "Byzantine servilism" of political leaders toward the will of the masses. SEG (1880), pp. 181–182.

That Bismarck appeared to be in a good mood as he listened to Bennigsen's complaints may have been due to the latter's confession that the issue of the enabling act was the final wedge that would split apart the National Liberal party—a Bismarck objective since 1875.[85] Yet the crack between moderates and democrats was not of Bismarck's making; nor was the final cleavage his direct responsibility. The division was as old as the liberal movement itself and had already produced one separation—in 1866. That of 1880 was the consequence of differing responses by the National Liberal party's factions to challenges posed by Bismarck's change of front in domestic politics since 1875. And those responses were themselves conditioned by the development of the German economy, expansion of the German upper *Mittelstand* and growth and divergence of the interest groups composing it.[86]

Bennigsen's talent for compromise was all that had kept the cleavage of 1880 from occurring earlier. Through successive crises he had managed to hold the party together and avoid a lasting break with the Bismarck government. Increasingly, however, his compromises had become less a matter of finding the true "diagonal of forces" than of rationalized subjection to the will of the chancellor. In men like Lasker, Forckenbeck, Bamberger, and Stauffenberg the compromises produced repeated crises of conscience that ultimately became intolerable. Again and again, they sacrificed in the expectation—which deteriorated to a hope—that what was surrendered today could eventually be regained tomorrow, if not under Wilhelm and Bismarck, then certainly under their successors. But Wilhelm survived Nobiling's buckshot, and Bismarck, despite bad health and long absences, remained politically dangerous.

The heated caucuses over the tariff act of 1879 were the most divisive that the National Liberal party had yet known. That they ended with the defection of a right-wing group and not the left-wing faction headed by Lasker was owed only to Bismarck's bargain with the Center party. Passage of the Franckenstein clause compelled moderates and democrats to find common cause in opposition to the entire statute. Stunned by overwhelming defeat at the polls in October, the national liberal caucus in the Prussian Chamber of Deputies held on to its unity during the winter session of 1879–1880. Heinrich Rickert, a relative newcomer, who replaced Lasker as leader of the left wing, avoided forcing the issue.[87] When the Reichstag caucus reconvened in late February

[85] Lucius, *Bismarck-Erinnerungen*, pp. 186, 191. According to Tiedemann, Bismarck teased Bennigsen once more with the prospect of entry into the Prussian cabinet. Tiedemann, *Sechs Jahre*, p. 408.

[86] For a description of the factions that composed the National Liberal party see Hermann Block, *Die parlamentarische Krisis der Nationalliberalen Partei, 1879–1880* (Münster, 1930), pp. 28ff.

[87] Bennigsen avoided forcing the issue by demanding party solidarity on the railway purchase act, allowing Rickert and his left-wing associates to vote against the bill. See Rickert to Stauffenberg, Jan. 4, 1880. HW, II, 286. Twenty national liberals voted against the bill, among them ten of the thirteen who later joined the Secession. Block, *Parlamentarische Krisis*, pp. 64–65.

BISMARCK AT THE WHEEL. THE LIBERAL SPOKE TO THE CENTRIST AND CONSERVATIVE SPOKES: "DON'T
GET COCKY. WHEN THE WIND SHIFTS, I WILL BE ON TOP AGAIN." WILHELM SCHOLZ IN
KLADDERADATSCH, 1879.

1880, however, Bennigsen came face to face again with Lasker, Bamberger,
Stauffenberg, and Forckenbeck, none of whom sat any longer in the Prussian
chamber. His clash with Forckenbeck over the party's position on the military
bill was especially bitter, the disagreement so deep that all four leaders of the
left ceased to attend caucus meetings.[88]

[88] Block, *Parlamentarische Krisis*, pp. 61–73.

Even under these circumstances the national liberals were not entirely toothless. In the Chamber of Deputies Bennigsen continued to fashion his compromises, amending the railway purchase act to establish some legislative control over surpluses that a state-owned system might generate and incorporating liberal features in government bills for reform of the Prussian administration. In the Reichstag many national liberals joined the opposition on the Samoa, Hamburg, Elbe, tobacco monopoly, stamp tax, and other issues that made the government's legislative program for 1880 relatively fruitless. To "Laskerites" the really great issues were renewals of the *Septennat* and the antisocialist act, two compromises of earlier years that imposed painful sacrifices in parliamentary power and popular liberties. To Bennigsen and the moderates, however, those statutes were bulwarks against foreign attack and internal subversion that were now more necessary than ever. Abroad the alienation of Russia in the wake of the eastern crisis and Congress of Berlin raised the specter of a two-front war; at home the continued progress of the socialist movement, evident in recent victories in Reichstag by-elections, meant that the state must retain not only the statutory instrument for legal suppression, but also the military force with which to meet a revolutionary outbreak.

Politicians of both wings sensed a conservative current in the population. From Bavaria Stauffenberg reported general political apathy; no one seemed to have an opinion, unless personal interests were involved. This environment made it easier for moderate liberals to contemplate allying with the conservative parties in support of the government on critical issues. Another motive lay in the dynamics of the parliamentary situation. Not to ally with the conservative parties was to allow for the possibility that conservatives would ally with the Center. Out of that combination could come a "reaction in school and church," which to Johannes Miquel, after Bennigsen the most important leader of the moderates, was of greater concern than political reaction. To Miquel alliance with the conservative parties under these circumstances was a matter of *Realpolitik*; to Lasker "political realism" meant the final effacement of liberal idealism.[89]

By mid-March 1880 the four leaders of the left wing—Forckenbeck, Bamberger, Stauffenberg, and Lasker—were actively discussing resignation from the party. For the time being, however, only Lasker took this decisive step (March 15), no longer able to reconcile the politics of compromise with the demands of conscience. What the protective tariff, *Septennat*, and antisocialist statutes had begun was completed by the enabling act. Bennigsen and Miquel were well aware of the probable consequences for party unity if the mod-

---

[89] Exchange of letters between Lasker, Miquel, Robert von Benda, and Stauffenberg, Oct.–Dec. 1879. *HW*, II, 280–291. Lasker to his constituents, March 1880. *HW*, II, 309. See also Rickert's speech at Danzig, Aug. 19, 1880. *SEG* (1880), pp. 210–211.

erates, in their anxiety to appease Bismarck, should deliver into the chancellor's hands the power to demolish state supremacy over the Catholic church, which liberals had labored so hard to erect. The compromise that Bennigsen finally struck sacrificed the so-called "bishops' paragraph"—for Puttkamer the "nucleus of the bill"—but did make possible the appointment of substitute clerics (*Kapitularvikare*) to administer vacant dioceses by allowing the government to dispense with the oath of loyalty to the May laws. But this concession was too much for half of Bennigsen's colleagues. Forty-three national liberals voted for and forty-five against the bill in its final form.[90]

During July 1880, Forckenbeck, Stauffenberg, Bamberger, and Rickert agreed to join Lasker's exodus. Their aim was to become the nucleus of the great liberal party for which Forckenbeck had vainly called in his city convention address of 1879. Lasker and Rickert wanted to build from the ground up, establishing an organization of "moderate and firm elements" that would carry their cause to the voters. But the signers of the declaration published on August 30—a declaration that stressed the interdependence of economic and political freedom, the preservation of constitutional rights, tax equity for the lower classes, and state control over church and school—were all parliamentary deputies (sixteen from the Reichstag and ten from the Prussian Landtag). The name that they chose—"The Liberal Union"—expressed their hopes. But the public dubbed them "The Secession," a title more in keeping with their prospects.[91]

[90] Block, *Parlamentarische Krisis*, pp. 73–92; Stanley Zucker, *Ludwig Bamberger: German Liberal Politician and Social Critic, 1823–1899* (Pittsburgh, 1975), pp. 157–159. See the letters exchanged between Forckenbeck, Lasker, Bamberger, and Stauffenberg. HW, II, 295, 299–312.

[91] Block, *Parlamentarische Krisis*, pp. 93–99; Thomas Nipperdey, *Die Organisation der deutschen Parteien vor 1918* (Düsseldorf, 1961), pp. 182–183; HW, II, 318–351. For the program of the Liberal Union see Felix Salomon, *Die deutschen Parteiprogramme* (Leipzig, 1907), II, 29–30, and HW, II, 355–357.